A HISTORY OF
BRITAIN

A HISTORY OF BRITAIN

THE FATE OF EMPIRE
1776–2000

SIMON SCHAMA

miramax books

Frontispiece: *State Portrait of Queen Victoria* by Franz Xavier Winterhalter, 1859.

This book is published to accompany the television series
A History of Britain first broadcast on BBC2 in 2000
Executive producer: Martin Davidson. Series producers: Janet Lee and Liz Hartford
Producers: Clare Beavan, Ian Bremner, Martina Hall,
Mike Ibeji, Jamie Muir, Tim Kirby, Paul Tilzey
Series developed by Janice Hadlow

First published in 2002
Copyright © Simon Schama 2002

ISBN 0-7868-6899-6

Printed in the United States of America

For information address:
Hyperion, 77 West 66th Street,
New York, New York, 10023-6298

CONTENTS

*And out you come at last with the sun behind you into the eastern sea.
You speed up and tear the oily water louder and faster, sirroo, sirroo—swish—sirroo,
and the hills of Kent — over which I once fled from the Christian teachings of
Nicodemus Frapp — fall away on the right hand and Essex on the left. They fall
away and vanish into blue haze; and the tall slow ships behind the tugs, scarce
moving ships and wallowing sturdy tugs are all wrought of wet gold as one goes
frothing by. They stand out bound on strange missions of life and death, to the killing
of men in unfamiliar lands. And now behind us is blue mystery and the phantom
flash of unseen lights, and presently even these are gone and I and my destroyer
tear out to the unknown across a great grey space. We tear into the great spaces
of the future and the turbines fall to talking in unfamiliar tongues. Out to the
open we go, to windy freedom and trackless ways. Light after light goes down.
England and the Kingdom, Britain and the Empire, the old prides and the
old devotions, glide abeam, astern, sink down upon the horizon, pass — pass.
The river passes — London passes, England passes …*

H.G. WELLS, *Tono-Bungay* (1908)

*… the country houses will be turned into holiday camps, the Eton and Harrow
match will be forgotten, but England will still be England, an everlasting animal
stretching into the future and the past and, like all living things, having the power
to change out of recognition and yet remain the same …*

GEORGE ORWELL, *England Your England* (1941)

In memoriam
Roy Porter (1946–2002)

PREFACE

Readers in search of an exhaustive account of the careers of Sir Robert Peel or Reginald Maudling should put this book down right now. For, with this last volume of *A History of Britain*, it will be more than ever obvious that the cautionary indefinite article in the title is truly warranted, both in terms of the frankly interpretative reading of modern British history offered, and in the necessarily subjective judgements I have made about which themes to explore in most detail. As with the BBC2 television programmes, I have opted to concentrate on a smaller number of stories and arguments, but to treat them in detail rather than give equally cursory attention to everything bearing on the transformation of Britain into an industrial empire. As with the two previous volumes, this book gives space to many themes which could not be accommodated within the iron narrative discipline of the television hour. But even this does not mean there is any pretence at all to comprehensiveness. No one will be in any danger of confusing *The Fate of Empire* with a text book.

The last half of the 20th century is deliberately treated with essay-like breadth and looseness – partly, at least, because I have trouble treating any period contemporary with my own life as history at all (an illusion, no doubt, of the passing of years). As the title of this volume suggests, however, I have tried to do something not always ventured in histories of 19th- and 20th-century Britain: to bring together imperial and domestic history, trying at all times to look at the importance that India, in particular, had for Britain's expansive prosperity and power, and at the responsibility that the Raj had for India's and Ireland's plight.

New York, 2002

CHAPTER

1

While Britain was losing an empire it was finding itself. As redcoats were facing angry crowds and hostile militiamen in Massachusetts, Thomas Pennant, a Flintshire gentleman and naturalist, set off on his travels in rough Albion in search of that almost extinct species: the authentic natural-born Briton. Amidst the upland crags and chilly tarns of Merionedd, he thought he had discovered them: Britain's very own home-grown noble savages, the descendants of the earliest tribes, whose simplicity had survived, somehow, the onslaught of modern 'civilization.' At Llyn Irdinn he walked round two circles of standing stones, which he believed were undoubtedly the remains of 'druidical antiquities.' Nearby, he discovered the human equivalent, at the house of Evan Llwd, where Pennant was treated to hospitality 'in the style of an antient Briton' with 'potent beer to wash down the Coch yr Wdre or hung goat and the cheese compounded of the milk of cow and sheep. He likewise showed us the antient family cup made of a bull's scrotum in which large libation had been made in days of yore... Here they have lived for generations without bettering or lessening their income, without noisy fame, but without any of its embittering attendants.'

The harsh, rain-soaked countryside was full of such old British marvels, human and topographical. At Penllyn lake Pennant found the hut of the nonagenarian Margaret Uch Evans, although its locally famous resident was off somewhere, perhaps shooting foxes. This was a bitter disappointment for Margaret, he had heard, was a Welsh Diana, a Celtic Amazon: a prodigious huntress and fisher who, even in her 90s, 'rowed stoutly, was queen of the lake, fiddled excellently and knew all the old music, did not neglect the mechanic arts for she was a very good joiner.' She was also blacksmith, shoemaker, boat-builder, harp-maker, and well into her 70s had been 'the best wrestler in the country.'

Pennant became the specialist in documenting the remnants of ancient, outlandish, unpolished Britain: the wildcat and the ptarmigan; the mysterious,

FORCES OF NATURE:
THE ROAD TO
REVOLUTION?

View of Honister Pass, the Lake District.

lichen-flecked megalith and the poor, tough people who lived among them. A few years after his 'excursion' into north Wales – and a year before James Boswell and Dr Johnson – he sailed through the Hebrides, taking with him Moses Griffith, his Welsh manservant and illustrator. There he beheld scenes that filled him, alternately, with melancholy and elation. The island people, like the shepherds of the Merionedd hills, were primitives, often dwelling in windowless hovels and surviving on oatmeal, milk and a little fish. Tens of thousands of them had been forced off their little farms in the 1760s and 1770s to make way for profitable herds of Blackface and Cheviot sheep. In desperation, many had made the Atlantic crossing as emigrants to the New World. Yet there were also little epiphanies: the sight of the herring boats at Barrisdale, 'a busy haunt of men and ships in this wild and romantic tract'; or the view from the top of Beinn-an-oir, the Golden Mountain, one of the (disconcert-ingly, three) Paps of Jura, which laid out for Pennant's exhilarated inspection the scattered pieces of outland Britain – the highland peaks all the way to Ben Lomond in the northeast; the isles of Colonsay and Oronsay in the western ocean; and, to the south, Islay and the distant hills of Antrim in northern Ireland.

The result of all this clambering and trotting and sketching and jotting made Thomas Pennant the first great tour guide of a Britain still waiting to be fully explored by the domestic tourist. Five editions of his *A Tour in Scotland* (1772) appeared before 1790. But he was not the only author making a modest fame and fortune from the rediscovery, the redefinition, of the nation. In 1778, while His Majesty's forces were evacuating Philadelphia, and after Pennant's description of Wales had been published, it was joined by the one of the first guides to the Lake District, written by Thomas West, a Scottish Jesuit living in Ulverston. West, like Pennant, was a scholar, much travelled through Europe. Tired of dragging bored milords through the beggar-infested Forum on their obligatory Grand Tour, he had returned and developed a second career, taking parties of intrepid and interested gentlemen and ladies through the lakes, cliffs and dales. Whether in person or through his guidebook, West would steer tourists to a successsion of visual stations, perfect for drinking in the British sublime.

The message that both Pennant and West had to deliver was simple, but revo-lutionary: come home. The British had wandered too much, too promiscuously, too greedily, from Mysore to Naples. In forcing their native scenery to resemble Italy, tricked out with temples and statues and God knows what – or, just as bad, engi-neering it to resemble foreign paintings, so that they could stroll from the picture gallery to the picnic and not notice the difference – they had somehow lost touch with what made Britain Britain: its own unprettified landscape. By some miracle it had remained unspoiled in the remoter places of the islands, places thought too far, too ugly and too rude for polite excursions. But now the new turnpike roads had cut travel time to Chester or Edinburgh by half, so that the adventurous traveller could be whisked to the verge of sublime Britain – after which, it is true, simpler, rougher modes of transport such as the pony or the small ferryboat might have to suffice. And it was an unpleasant fact that exposure to the sublime meant being rained on a lot and being blown about by winds.

But it would all be worth it, Pennant and West implied, because a trip to the true Britain was not just a holiday; it was a tutorial in the recovery of national virtue. The British needed roughness because they had wallowed too long in vicious soft-ness. Inspecting all those Roman ruins, they had doomed themselves to follow the notorious example of that empire's decay. Long before they had lost America, the Jeremiahs said, Britons had lost themselves. Old British virtues had surrendered to modern British vices. Liberty had been perverted by patronage; justice blinded by the unforgiving glare of money; country innocence contaminated by city fashion. The 'Ancient Constitution' that had kept the British free had degenerated into what its critics called 'Old Corruption' or, more bestially, 'The Thing.' The triumphalists of empire had supposed that commercial robustness and Protestant plainness would immunize Britain from the usual laws of imperial decadence. But trade had become a euphemism for the crude gouging of revenue, enforced by British redcoats, or for the brutal traffic in African bodies. And God and history had inflicted their punish-ment at Saratoga and Yorktown.

The antidote to rot was horror. 'Horrid' was – along with 'bristling,' 'shaggy' and 'precipitous' – one of the terms of choice in the promotional literature of Romantic British travel. At Falcon-Crag in Lakeland, West promised, 'an immense rock hangs over your head and upwards, a forest of broken pointed rocks, in a semi-circular sweep towering inward, form[ing] the most horrid amphitheatre that ever eye beheld in the wild forms of convulsed nature.' At the Falls of Clyde, an obliga-tory stop on the itinerary of the British sublime, according to another gentleman travel writer, Thomas Newte, 'the great body of water, rushing with horrid fury seems to threaten destruction to the solid rocks that enrage it by their resistance. It boils up from the caverns which itself has formed as if it were vomited out of the lower region.' But these frightening experiences were not just perversely organized as holidays in hell; they were a spa for the sensations. The agitation of the senses was meant to shock the visitor out of the jaded appetite and torpor that was eating away the national fibre. The crystal waters of Cumbria, Cymru and Caledonia would be the cure for the diseases, moral as well as metabolical, of empire. In the uplands, away

Top: *Sheelins in Jura and a Distant View of the Paps* by Moses Griffith, from *A Tour in Scotland* (1772)
by Thomas Pennant.
Above: *Dolbadarn Castle and Llanberris Lake* by Paul Sandby, *c.* 1770.

from the noxious filth and polluted air of the metropolis, Britons would be able to breathe again. They would start a new life.

Everything was to be stood on its head. The forces of 'progress' – Romans, Plantagenets – were now to be thought of as the bringers of greed and brutish power. Contemplating the archaeology of defeat brought the traveller into communion with lost worlds of old British virtue, an antiquity that might actually serve as a template for the future. The stone circles and Iron Age terraces that bore the footprints of a Britain flattened by the Romans; the shattered Welsh forts blitzed by Edward I; the ruined abbeys dispossessed by Thomas Cromwell and then burned by Oliver Cromwell – all became invested with tragic eloquence. As early as 1740 the antiquarian William Stukeley's *Stonehenge: A Temple Restor'd to the British Druids* had argued that far from being the bloodthirsty barbarians described by Caesar, the Druids had actually been the descendants of one of the lost tribes of Israel, transplanted to Britain to create a new Promised Land, and had survived as the priestly guardians of an ancient and sophisticated culture. Their Celtic tongue was not just the original British language but the fountainhead of all non-Latin European languages.

Suddenly, being British was not the same as being English. Dolbadarn Castle, in the north Welsh fastness of Gwynedd, where Owain Goch, the son of the last independent Welsh prince, Llewellyn ab Gruffydd, took on the juggernaut army of Edward I, became a place of pilgrimage. Initially those who found their way there were Welsh antiquarians like Pennant, eager to reclaim their patrimony as the 'original Britons,' but soon enough Romantic English sympathizers followed. The shattered piles of masonry silhouetted against the dark sky were seen (and painted) as incomparably more 'feeling' than the brutally intact Plantagenet castles like Conwy and Harlech, called 'the magnificent badges of our subjection' by Pennant. Carrying their copies of Thomas Gray's epic poem, 'The Bard' (1757), reciting the last curses hurled at the oncoming king by the last blind poet to survive the Plantagenet extermination, Snowdonian thrill-seekers would peer into the ravines and shudder as they imagined the bard hurling himself headlong in a gesture of suicidal defiance. If they were very lucky they might be invited by the likes of Sir Watkin Williams Wynn to an Eisteddfod, one of the gatherings at his country seat of Wynnstay in Denbighshire, featuring choirs and old, preferably blind, harpists like John Parry who would sing the tunes and lyrics of his forebears. From the mid-1750s a group of London Welsh calling themselves the Cymmrodorion met in taverns, and between rounds of strong ale, committed themselves to rescuing those epics and ballads from oblivion by writing them down and publishing them.

Wherever they looked, the Romantic enthusiasts of rough Britain believed, there were lessons to be learned that confounded the equation of cultivation with nobility. It was in the places furthest from corrupting fashion, in the heart of Britain's oldest landscapes – the landscapes which gave 'Capability' Brown nightmares – that truly modern marvels were to be beheld. In 1746 a builder called William Edwards had attempted to throw a single 140-foot stone bridge across the river Taff. After two collapses, by 1755 he had succeeded – no one quite knew how – and the bridge was still standing. By the late 1760s and 1770s, the Pontypridd was being compared in prose and verse eulogies to the Rialto in Venice as a 'monument of the strong, natural past and bold attempts of Antient Britain.'

William Edwards was an exemplar of this old-new Britain: a survivor from a rude world, but also a native *genius*. For now, that word was being used in both its ancient and modern sense, to mean someone who was rooted in a particular place *and* someone who was sublimely inspired. It followed, then, that a voyage of British discovery would have to happen as close as possible to the landscape that had protected and sheltered the true nature of Britain. And to do that Britons would first have to get off their high horse. It was only by direct contact with the earth of Britain that romantic tourists could expect to register, through their boots and in their bones, the deep, organic meaning of native allegiance. To be a patriot meant being a pedestrian.

Of course, the fashionable landscaped park had encouraged the estate-owner and his family to take a stroll along the rambling path, beside a serpentine pond or towards an Italianate pavilion, with the prospect of arriving at a poetic meditation, courtesy of Horace, Ovid or Pope. But the new walking was not just physically strenuous but morally, even politically, self-conscious. Picking up a stick, exiting the park, was a statement. In 1783 when John 'Walking' Stewart, the most prodigious of all the Romantic trampers, left India   where, in a 20-year career, he had served successively as East India Company writer, soldier and a minister of native princes – he was bidding farewell to empire in more than the territorial sense. He seems to have become a kind of Indo-Scottish *saddhu*, a holy walker, making his way through the sub-continent, across the Arabian desert and finally home via France and Spain. Before he set off again for Vienna and then the United States and Canada, 'Walking' Stewart became a minor celebrity – a fixture at Romantic suppers, and pointed out in St James's Park. The writer Thomas De Quincey, who knew him, was also in no doubt of the levelling implications of walking. When he calculated (a little dubiously) that William Wordsworth must have walked 185,000 miles, the figure was meant to advertise the poet's moral credentials – his down-to-earth understanding of ordinary people and places. At the height of the revolutionary crisis in France in 1793, during the reign of Terror, John Thelwall, the son of an impoverished silk mercer, who had become a radical lecturer and orator, would publish his eccentric verse and prose narrative of a walk around London and Kent, entitled *The Peripatetic* (1793) – a foot-sore glimpse of the lowly and the mighty.

Not everyone was ready for the sight of 'men of taste' taking to the roads. The first guide expressly written for the 'rambler' in the Lakes, complete with information on footpaths, and carrying the revolutionary implication that the landscape across which they tracked was a common patrimony (and not just the resort of beggars and footpads), would not appear until 1792. Some 10 years earlier, when the German pastor Karl Moritz walked through southern England and the Midlands, he was constantly greeted with suspicion and disbelief. His host at Richmond 'could not sufficiently express his surprise' at Moritz's determination to walk to Oxford 'and still further' and when, on a June day, he became tired and sat down in the shade of a hedgerow to read his Milton, 'those who rode, or drove, past me, stared at me with astonishment, and made many significant gestures, as if they thought my head deranged.' The landlord of the Mitre at Oxford and his family made sure he had the clean linen that befitted a gentleman, but were bemused by his determination to walk. Had he not arrived in polite company, they admitted, he would never have been allowed across the threshold since 'any person undertaking so long a journey on foot, is sure to be looked upon…as either a beggar, or a vagabond, or…a rogue.'

Moritz presented himself as an innocent foreigner in a country evidently mad for speed, its citizens hurtling along the turnpike roads in carriages and on horses. Yet he also knew that walking made him, if not a democrat, then someone who openly and perversely rejoiced in his indifference to rank. It brought him into direct contact with the salt of the earth: a female chimney sweep and a philosophical saddler who recited Homer: the academy of the road. And it showed off the pedestrian as a new kind of man, a Man of Feeling. In that same year, 1782, he would finally have been able to get his hands on the work that rapidly became the Bible of thoughtful pedestrians, the *Confessions* (1782) of the French political philosopher Jean-Jacques Rousseau, and, as an appendix, the *Reveries of the Solitary Walker,* 10 disquisitions each in the form of a walk.

For Rousseau, a walk had always been away from, as much as towards, something. The *Confessions* – made available to the public through the good offices of an English friend and devotee, Brooke Boothby – recorded his first decisive illumination as he walked from Paris to Vincennes to see his then friend, the writer and philosopher Denis Diderot. Somewhere along that road it dawned on Rousseau, as he walked away from the city, that the entire values of the polite world were upside down. He had been taught to assume that progress consisted of a journey from nature to civilization, when that transformation had, in fact, been a terrible fall. Nature decreed equality; culture manufactured inequality. So liberty and happiness consisted not in replacing nature by culture, but in precisely the reverse. Towns, which imposed an obligation to conduct one's life according to the dictates of fashion, commerce and wit, were a web of vicious hypocrites and predators. Towns enslaved; the countryside – provided it too had not been infected with urban evils – liberated. Towns contaminated and sickened their inhabitants; the country cleansed and invigorated them. Rather than education assuming its mission to be the taming of children's natural instincts within the pen of cultivated arts and manners it ought to do precisely the opposite – preserving, for as long as possible, the innocence, art-lessness, frankness and simplicity of those instincts. No books, then, before 12 at least; instead, romps in the fields, stories beneath the trees and lots of nature walks.

All of which made Rousseau's brief, dizzy stay in London, in the winter of 1766, disconcerting to guest and host alike. He had come to England, on the warm invitation of the Scottish philosopher David Hume, because he had run out of asylums and because he had been reliably informed that the country was the sanctuary of liberty. In absolutist, Catholic France his writings had been burned by the public hangman. In his Calvinist native city of Geneva he had not fared much better, falling foul of the local oligarchy when he had rashly and publicly sided with challenges to their monopoly of power. For a brief period he had found an idyllic refuge, together with his mistress, Thérèse Levasseur, on the islet of St Pierre, near Bienne, where he went for botanizing walks or rowed a little boat. His last shelter was the estate of an English-naturalized Swiss, Rodolphe Vautravers, but the long arm of authority, in the shape of the Bishop of Berne's proscription for irreligion, caught up with him. Finally, he accepted Hume's invitation and travelled with him across the Channel.

It was not a pleasure trip. Rousseau arrived at Dover seasick, wet, tearful and cold. In London, where Hume attempted to introduce him to like-minded friends including the actor David Garrick, Prospective Men and Women of Feeling lined up to offer gushing admiration, tearfully sympathetic consolation, discreet applause. But although he came out of his shell enough to drink in the appreciation, and began to appear in his pseudo-'Armenian' peasant's costume of fur cap and tunic, it took no time at all before Rousseau's unique gift for alienating his well-wishers surfaced. When David Hume attempted to recommend him to George III for a royal pension, it was perversely interpreted by Rousseau as a conspiracy. It probably didn't help when, to pre-empt Rousseau's excuse that babysitting his dog, Sultan, prevented

Top: *Jean-Jacques Rousseau* by Allan Ramsay, 1766.
Above: *Sir Brooke Boothby* by Joseph Wright of Derby, 1781.

him from going to the theatre in Drury Lane to meet the king, Hume locked the dog on the inside of the apartment, and, with Rousseau on the outside, insisted on taking him to the show. What Hume thought was a good-natured attempt to bring Rousseau a harmless degree of benign public attention was perceived by its intended beneficiary as a plot to subject him to 'enslavement' and ridicule. Rousseau even believed that Hume was the author of a hoax invitation from Frederick the Great urging him to come to Prussia. (The writer was actually Horace Walpole.) An ugly public row ensued. Hume himself began to realize, depressingly, that his guest was perhaps a little mad.

Escape to the country, in Rousseau's fevered mind, became virtually a matter of life or death. A house was found for him – where else? – in Wales. But there were delays in getting it ready, which of course further heated the philosopher's already seething suspicions about his hosts. Instead, he accepted the offer of a philanthropist, Richard Davenport, to vacate his country house at Wootton in Staffordshire, on the Derbyshire border and thus close to some of the loveliest scenery in England. Rousseau walked through Dovedale in his strange 'Armenian' costume where locals later remembered 'owd Ross Hall coming and going in his comical cap and ploddy gown and gathering his yerbs.' Occasionally, too, he would let himself be taken to Calwich Abbey where he met a group of local admirers and disciples, including Brooke Boothby, who were already committed to remaking themselves as Men and Women of Feeling (a novel by Henry Mackenzie, entitled *The Man of Feeling*, would be the best-seller of 1771).

Needless to say, it was not long before paranoia once again got the upper hand. With scant understanding of English, much less the kind spoken by the local ser-vants, Rousseau became convinced they were saying wicked things about Thérèse and were putting cinders in their food. By the spring of 1767 he was back in France. But his cult of sensibility had put down deep roots among the sobbing and sighing classes of provincial England. Just 10 years later, the craziness had been forgotten and Rousseau's sojourn was remembered with the kind of veneration accorded to an apostolic mission. Something like a Derbyshire Enlightenment had come into being in which radical politics kept company with the cultivation of Feeling. A botanical society had been founded in the little cathedral town of Lichfield by Brooke Boothby and the polymath Erasmus Darwin, both of them luminaries of the circle centring on Anna Seward, the poet and essayist who held a salon at her residence in the Bishop's Palace. Unlike Rousseau himself, moreover, the Lichfield circle had no difficulty in reconciling the exhilaration of science with the cult of Nature. In Derby-shire they seemed to have the best of both, with the Peaks offering the breathtaking upland walks and deep caverns, as well as supplying the coal and iron to be mined from beneath the hills. The county's reputation as a place of exhilaration and mystery was such that in 1779 a play was staged at Drury Lane called, without a trace of embarrassment, *The Wonders of Derbyshire*. It featured 21 sets painted by the scenic artist Philippe de Loutherbourg, depicting waterfalls, Marn and Matlock Tors, the Castleton caverns (both inside and out) and a 'Genius of the Peaks' who rose, mechanically, from 'haunts profound' to bestow his bounty on the locals.

Likewise the most successful Derbyshire artist, Joseph Wright, was equally at home painting the cliffs and gorges of the Peaks around Matlock or Richard Arkwright's mill at Cromford as if it were a romantically lit palace. It was Wright who supplied the definitive image of an English country gentleman, Brooke Boothby, made over into a Man of Feeling, not, as in a Gainsborough portrait, the imperious master of a landed estate, but folded into the greenery in the pensive, heavy-lidded attitude of a Jacobean poet. Boothby's dress is a studied advertisement for the new informality: the double-breasted frock coat and short waistcoat, left unbuttoned the better to expose the transparent sincerity of his heart; a silk cravat replaced by simple muslin. And where an earlier generation of gentlemen might have demonstrated their virtue by holding a copy of the Bible or volumes of the classics, Boothby holds the gospel of *his* generation with the single word 'Rousseau' just legible on the spine. Painted in 1781, the picture is not just a portrait but an advertisement of Boothby's role as the St Peter of the cult. For the book is surely *Rousseau, Juge de Jean-Jacques*, the confessionary autobiographical dialogue on which Rousseau had worked while he stayed in England. Five years earlier, in 1776, Boothby had travelled to Paris and received the manuscript from the great man's own hands. Two years later Rousseau was dead, and the park at Ermenonville (inspired by Rousseau's ideas and where the philosopher spent his final days) was turned into a place of pilgrimage and memory for his cult. No wonder Boothby burned to spread the word.

The self-appointed task of all these disciples of the church of sensibility was not just to transform *themselves*, through pensive walks, into new Britons sympathetic to the sufferings of their fellows and ingenious in devising ways to relieve them. They were also resolved, through literature, education, philanthropy and their own personal example, to raise an entirely new generation reclaimed from the cruelty and corruption of fashionable society. In the midst of modern Albion, they would re-create the kind of ancient British innocence they had seen hanging on (although reduced to poverty-stricken subsistence) in the remote rocky north and west. In fact, what seemed to the cultivated man of the town to be the most miserable aspect of those societies – their weather-beaten coarseness – was precisely the kind of life that had

Above: *Landscape in the Lake District* by Philippe de Loutherbourg, *c.* 1780.
Opposite: *Thomas Day* by Joseph Wright of Derby, 1770.

to be instilled into coming generations if Britain were to be saved from degeneracy. The goal – however impossibly paradoxical on the face of it – was to preserve the instinctive freedom, playfulness and sincerity of the natural child into adulthood. The child, as Wordsworth would put it, would be 'father to the man.' If they succeeded, they would make the first generation of truly free compatriots: natural-born *and raised* Britons.

This, at any rate, was the task that another of the Lichfield Rousseau-ites, Thomas Day, set himself. His mission would be as a father-teacher to a purer generation of Britons, who would respect nature – all of it, for Day had become an ecologist *avant la lettre,* who believed in the inter-connectedness of all created life and was therefore a vegetarian and an ardent foe of the then popular sports of cock-fighting and bull-baiting. Animals, he believed, just as much as humans, could be conditioned by kindness towards a life of gentle happiness. Would he want to treat all creatures with the same consideration, asked a sardonic lawyer friend, even spiders? Would he not want to kill *them?* 'No,' answered Day, 'I don't know that I have a right. Suppose that a superior being said to a companion – "Kill that lawyer." How should you like it? And a lawyer is more noxious to most people than a spider.'

Day set about making the perfect family for himself when, in 1769, he hand-picked, rather as if choosing puppies from a litter, two young girls as candidates for eventual wife and mother. His commitment was to raise them in line with Rousseau's principles, then to marry whichever turned out to be most suitable, and to provide the wherewithal for the other to be apprenticed. A 12-year-old blonde was taken from Shrewsbury orphanage and renamed Sabrina; a brunette from the London Foundling Hospital and given the name of the virtuous wife of Roman antiquity, Lucretia (overlooking that heroine's suicidal end). Not surprisingly to anyone except Thomas Day, the experiment did not turn out as planned. Whisked off to France to avoid the scandal of a grown man playing dubious godfather to two girls, Lucretia and Sabrina fought like hellcats with each other and with their mentor, even while he nursed them through smallpox and saved them from drowning in a boating accident on the Rhône. Brought back to England, Lucretia, condemned by her adoptive father as 'invincibly stupid,' was apprenticed, as Day had promised, to a milliner, while Sabrina was taken to Lichfield where she suffered Day's often inhuman experiments – hot wax was poured on her arm to test her pain threshold, and guns loaded with blanks were fired near her head. Only when Day finally despaired of ever being able to turn her into his dream spouse did he pack her off to boarding school, an escape for which she was deeply grateful. She ended up married to a barrister.

Day, who awarded Jean-Jacques the title of 'the first of humankind,' believed he knew exactly how Jean-Jacques felt, for he too had suffered from the spite of the fashionable. His origins were, like those of his spiritual mentor, undistinguished – he was the son of a well-to-do customs collector. But his heart had been smitten in 1770 by the daughter of an army major, on whom he had struggled to make any kind of impression. To improve his chances, Day had taken himself off to France for a drastic makeover: dancing masters, fencing teachers, tailors, fine wigs, even subjecting himself to the torture of a painful mechanical contraption designed to straighten out knock-knees. It was all to no avail. The object of all these efforts at personal enhancement took one look at the new Day and laughed even harder than she had at the old Day. Stung by his rejection, Day turned his back on the Quality. What did they know of sincerity, of the burning, beating heart? He eventually found an heiress to marry but salved his social conscience by inflicting a Jean-Jacques regime on her: no servants and no harpsichord, for he deemed it wicked to wallow in such luxuries 'while the poor want bread.'

None of these follies and disasters inhibited Thomas Day from imparting his wisdom about childhood in a three-volume novel, *The History of Sandford and Merton* (1783), which, as an extended parable of 'natural instruction' was almost as important in Britain as Rousseau's *Emile*. The book recounted the clash between the spoiled bully Tommy Merton and the quieter epitome of rustic virtue, Harry Sandford, who cries when he realizes he has inflicted pain on a cockchafer. Now deservedly forgotten except in university seminars on the sentimental novel, *Sandford and Merton* was a huge publishing success in its day. Reprinted 45 times after the initial appearance of the first volume in 1783, it was *the* book young parents read when they wanted to savour the victory of natural over unnatural childhood. As for Day himself, his peculiar life ended abruptly in September 1789 in his 42nd year, during an experiment to test his pet theories about taming horses with gentleness rather than breaking them. An unbroken colt he was riding failed to respond to the tender touch, and threw Day on his head.

The problem with Day's experiment, some of his friends might have told him, was that virtuous conditioning could only go so far. Perhaps the damage to Sabrina's and Lucretia's natures had already been done by the time that Day got to them, beginning with the contamination of their mother's milk. For it was another of Rousseau's axioms that virtue began at the nursing nipple, from which moral as well as physical sustenance was imparted. Nothing was more harmful to the prospects of raising true children of nature than the habitual practice of farming babies out to wet-nurses who had no interest in their charges except that of commerce. Not

Above: The tomb of Jean-Jacques Rousseau, Ermenonville, France, *c.* 1778.
Opposite: *Mrs Susanna Hoare and Child* by Sir Joshua Reynolds, 1763–4.

surprisingly, babies from more ordinary families packed off to country women died in thousands. But if fashionable mothers could afford to see their infants better cared for, they had no means of knowing what kind of sustenance was being fed along with the breast milk. Who knew how many innocents had been poisoned and corrupted out of their true nature, from their nurseling months, by women whose milk was already tainted with drunkenness and sexual disease? Breast-feeding began to play a conspicious role in sentimental novels, especially those where both men and women could be redeemed by recognizing the simple power of natural instinct. Men for whom the tantalizing glimpse of nipple was an invitation to lechery could be converted by watching the act of nursing. Women who had flaunted their decolletage, like the wicked wife in Samuel Richardson's novel *Sir Charles Grandison*, could advertise their conversion to virtue by making a spectacle of the same act. 'Never was a man in greater Rapture!…' the wife narrates: 'He threw himself at my feet, clasping me and the little varlet together in his arms. "Brute!" said I, "will you smother my Harriet?…" "Dear-est, dear-est, dear-est Lady G… Never, never, never saw I so delightful a sight!"'

Assuming newborns had been given the healthiest possible start to their lives through the gift of their mother's milk, the next task of parents of sensibility was to ensure that natural instincts were not prematurely crushed by too heavy a dose of either parental discipline or rote learning. In the older morality books animal spirit was by definition a sign of unchristian diabolical beastliness, Satan frolicking in his favourite playground: the soft and receptive bodies of the young. The first duty of parents wanting to save the souls of their offspring was to thrash this devilry, if necessary literally, out of their bodies. But if the connection between animals and humans were now regarded by the likes of Thomas Day as benevolent and not malevolent, and the resemblance to puppyish or kittenish animal play the sign, not of innate wickedness but of innocence, then it was important to preserve and nurture playfulness as the gentlest route to learning, even if the consequences might sometimes seem, to an older generation, shockingly anti-social.

A generation of frantically attentive and slap-shy parents was the result. Erasmus Darwin urged parents to follow his example and 'never contradict children but to leave them their own master,' and was notorious for doing just that (with his own children). Even so flinty a father as Henry Fox, Lord Holland, paymaster-general in Whig governments, capitulated (after hearing endless Rousseau sermons from his wife, Lady Caroline Lennox) to the cult of play. The Foxes were a byword for indulging, not to say grovelling before, the sensibilities of their children. When his son, the future Whig leader Charles James, hurled a brand-new watch to the floor, his helpless papa merely managed a pained smile and muttered, 'If you must, I suppose you must.' On that topic of perennial inter-generational conflict, the length of hair, Fox virtually petitioned his older boy, Stephen: 'You gave me hopes that if I desired it you would cut it... I will dear Stephen be *obliged* if you will.'

Although there were plenty of books which still insisted on the strictly enforced moral policing of the young, rather than simply laying down the law to them, a new literature expressly written to be read *by* as well as *to* the young, and vividly illustrated, aimed to show through exemplary and cautionary stories what would befall those who took the right or wrong path. John Newbery, the entrepreneurial genius of children's books who published the tale of Dame Margery (otherwise known as Goody) Two-Shoes in this genre, also specialized in the sixpenny illustrated books that emphasized playful and practical learning. His bestseller, the first popular science book for children, *Tom Telescope* (1761), was the ancestor of all the 'do your own experiment' books, and aimed to make all kinds of knowledge, historical, geographical and mechanical, exciting as well as 'useful.'

One of Newbery's army of illustrators was someone who had himself, without any benefit of exposure to Rousseau, experienced precisely the kind of natural schooling supposed to make virtuous British patriots. Born in 1753 at Cherryburn House in the parish of Oringham in Northumberland, Thomas Bewick was the son of a farmer who also worked a colliery on his land. His family was, then, solid north country yeomanry, neither very rich nor very poor, but in any event many leagues away from the Derbyshire gentry who panted after Rousseau. Even so, he remembered in the lovely memoir written in the 1820s for his daughter, Bewick was spoiled rotten by his aunt Hannah who 'made me a great "pet". I was not to be "snubbed" (as it was called), do what I would; and, in consequence of my being thus suffered to have my own way, I was often scalded and burned.' At Mickley School, close by the colliery at Mickley Bank, Thomas was entrusted to the none too tender mercies of a local schoolmaster who, to judge by his enthusiasm with the switch, evidently had little time for the New Schooling. His punishment of choice was 'hugging' in which the little offender was mounted on the back of a 'stout boy' – rather like a mating frog – with his bottom bared for the flogging. When subjected to the ordeal, Thomas' reaction was to bite his mount in the neck, and when grabbed by the master, 'I rebelled, and broke his shins with my iron-hooped clogs, and ran off.'

Instead of being made to suffer for his revolt, Bewick compounded matters by playing truant 'every day, and amused myself making dams and swimming boats, in a small burn,' joining his 'more obedient school-fellows' on their way home. The school of nature, then, became his real tutor – much like the childhood of William

Wordsworth 20 years later on the other side of the Pennines. Even when Bewick was eventually obliged to learn fractions, decimals and Latin, he escaped from the dreary chores by filling every surface he could find – slates, books, and then, when he ran out of space, the flagstones of the floor at home, gravestones and even the floor of the church porch – with chalk drawings. His eye feasted greedily on images wherever he could find them, especially inn signs where the birds and beasts of Britain – bulls, horses, salmon – were gaudily displayed. To anyone with half an eye, it was obvious that Thomas had a precocious gift and – after he had chalked his way through every floor in the village – a friend finally supplied him with pen, ink, blackberry juice, a camel-hair brush and colours. His career as the first and greatest of all Britain's naturalist–illustrators, the British Audubon with a difference, had already begun. He painted scenes of the local woods and moors, and the beasts and birds that inhabited them, and got paid, though not very much, for hunting scenes – every hound 'faithfully delineated' on the walls of his neighbours' houses.

Two moments from his childhood years stood out in Bewick's memory as converting him from a rough and ready likely lad of the north into someone already feeling the pangs of sympathy for the rest of God's creation. The first was when he happened to catch a hare that was being coursed, and although he wrote that it had never crossed his mind for a minute that there was anything wrong or cruel about hunting, when he stood there with the warm, palpitating animal in his arms, and when 'the poor, terrified creature screamed out so piteously – like a child … I would have given anything to have saved its life.' Told to hand it over by a farmer, he did so – only to see the hare have one of its legs broken for fun and then made to set off again, limping, in order for the dogs to have theirs; 'from that day forward, I have ever wished that this poor, persecuted, innocent creature might escape with its life.' Bewick was too much a son of the British countryside to be against all hunting, especially where he considered the animals had a fair chance of giving the dogs and men a run for their money – badgers, for example, could fight back ferociously. But he hated gratuitous cruelty. When he knocked a bullfinch off its perch with a rock he took the bird in his hand, where it 'looked me piteously in the face; and, as I thought, could it have spoken, it would have asked me why I had taken away its life,' and suffered another terrible pang of conscience, turning the dead bird over and over as he looked at its feathers. 'This was the last bird I killed,' he wrote, although he added, perhaps referring to all the stuffed birds he would use as models for his spectacular illustrations, many 'indeed, have been killed since on my account.'

Bewick was emphatically not a sentimentalist. He inspected the habits and habitats of the animal kingdom, and especially the combative, bustling universe of insects.

Two centuries before the American sociobiologist Edmund O. Wilson, Bewick had already noticed that the colony of ants on Boat Hill, near Eltringham, formed a coherent social community 'as busily crowded as any among men leading to or from a great fair' and were so well organized that, when disturbed by a stick, they would quickly regroup and continue their business.

The social curiosity and compassion that, all through his long life, would remain one of Bewick's strongest qualities also drew him, when he was still young, towards ordinary people who had their own common, often awesomely encyclopedic knowledge of the world and its ways. One of them was an old pitman from the Bewicks' mine who had once rescued a fellow worker from a colliery accident; sitting on a stone bench, he showed Thomas the constellations in the sky. Another neighbour, Anthony Liddell, was remembered by Bewick as the 'village Hampden,' the epitome of the no-nonsense free man of the village. He had memorized the works of the first-century Jewish historian Josephus and a lot of other history besides, and dressed as if he were some sort of feral person in old buckskin breeches and a doublet 'of the skin of some animal.' Liddell was articulate, stubborn and hot-tempered when it came to the subject of liberty and property, especially birds and fish, which, he insisted, God had provided for everyone, giving him the right to poach as freely as he wanted; for him, 'gaol had no terrors for he lived better there than he did at home.' But it was another of his father's pitmen, Johnny Chapman, who 'thought it no hardship' to work standing up to his waist in freezing cold, filthy water, who stayed in Bewick's mind as something like the ideal working-class stoical hero. He lived on milk, bread, potatoes and oatmeal; rambled, when he felt like it, in the open country or went off to Newcastle for some ale; and paid for his lodging by singing and telling jokes and stories in his broad Geordie dialect. When he got sick and old, Chapman, the innocent, was turned away from one parish after another as each attempted to offload its responsibility for poor relief. Living hand to mouth from odd jobs, 'he was found dead on the road between Morpeth and Newcastle.'

These, along with his open-air Northumbrian playground, were the scenes that lodged in Bewick's mind when he recollected his childhood; and which in their gritty, black, sharply defined detail were translated into the extraordinary wood-engraved vignettes that punctuate the beginnings and ends of his bird and animal books. Between the plover and the waxwing, and in the guise of little morality tales, he smuggled in a portrait of an entire rural world – one a long way removed from the prettified illusions of ploughmen, shepherds and woodsmen who populated the Gainsboroughs on the walls of Palladian country houses. Bewick's country people do not pose in fetchingly ragged pastoral dress, nor are their babes in arms all

Wood engravings by Thomas Bewick from his *History of British Birds* (1804), showing the life of ordinary people. By the riverside, a young beggar hangs himself (top). In a garret, a blind old crofter eats gruel (centre left). Watched by a hungry dog, a crippled soldier gnaws at a bone (centre right). By the stony roadside, a man breaks rocks (bottom).

apple-cheeked and dimpled. At the end of the Preface to Volume I of the *History of British Birds* (1804) a smartly dressed country gentleman, armed with a gun, points adamantly down the road to an old wanderer huddling against a stone wall for some shelter from the Northumbrian wind. The gentleman is not giving helpful directions. Between the black grouse and the red grouse a circle of men huddle strangely together, their backs to the beholder. They are watching cocks tear each other to pieces. Between the spoonbill and the crane, an old soldier with a wooden leg gnaws at a bone, watched by an equally hungry dog. Above him, just visible, is a grand country house. Bewick's country people break rocks by the side of the road; slurp gruel in a wretched garret; or hang themselves by the wayside. They are documents of a new kind of British politics: the politics of what contemporaries called 'social affection' and we would call sympathy: the assumption expressed in the novelist Laurence Sterne's sermon on philanthropy (based on the Good Samaritan) that 'there is something in our nature which engages us to take part in every accident to which man is subject.' Bewick carried *his* sympathy for the many 'accidents' befalling the poor of 18th-century Britain wherever he went. When, for example, he walked through the Highlands, unlike more sentimental tourists he saw immediately that the sweeping vistas and empty uplands that so delighted Romantic ramblers were actually the result of the mass clearance of crofters: the conversion of a country which had once supported families to a country supporting sheep.

Although there is nothing in the canon of illustrated natural history quite like Bewick's vignettes (Thomas Pennant's zoology, for example, was scrupulously confined to animal and bird classification), every so often an image of shocking clarity registers an exception to the visual platitudes of Happy Britannia: the country gentleman and family posed on a walk, or resting before their richly improved property. In 1769, for example, a retired officer with a restless moral conscience, Philip Thicknesse, wrote a horrifying account, accompanied with an equally horrifying print, of *Four Persons Found Starved to Death, at Datchworth*. Such things were not supposed to happen in Hertfordshire, in what were called the Home Circuits surrounding the capital.

But there were probably as many wretched people like the Datchworth victims in the south (especially the impoverished southwest of England) than in Bewick's Northumbria. For it was in southern England that the social results of 'rural improvement' – for good as well as for ill – were most dramatically apparent, especially in the lean years of the 1760s, when a succession of wheat harvest failures sent prices soaring and unleashed food riots in the towns and cities all the way from London to Derbyshire. The oat-eating northern counties were for the moment,

A View of the Poor House of Datchworth in Herts. addressd. to the Overseers of England, detail of an engraving from *Four Persons Found Starved to Death, at Datchworth* (1769) by Philip Thicknesse.

in less distress. To the boosters of a rapidly modernizing countryside economy, like Arthur Young, whose *Six Weeks Tour through the Southern Counties of England and Wales* was published in 1769, after some of the worst harvests of the century, there was absolutely nothing to apologize for: 'Move your eyes whichever side you will and you will behold nothing but great riches and yet greater resources.' England's *truly* Glorious Revolution (he often used the word) had been achieved not with speeches and acts of parliament (unless they happened to be enclosures) but with turnips, seed drills and sainfoin. Manure moved him to rapture, to the point where he made a verb out of the noun 'dung.' Much as he appreciated the 'extensive views' engineered by the Marquis of Rockingham at his 2000-acre estate in Yorkshire, the very highest compliment he could bestow was to declare it 'amply dunged.' Drooling with excitement at 'one compost of which manure mixed with dung ... was in so complete a state of corruption that it cut like butter and must undoubtedly be the richest manure in the world.' Let idle Romantics ruminate on the Druids as they crossed Salisbury Plain. All Young could think about was the criminal waste of so much good unenclosed land that might be fenced, divided and ploughed into profit.

To Young, sentimental hand-wringing about enclosures only betrayed ignorance of the basic facts of rural history and economy. Enclosures – taking the common land, or what was left of the open fields, previously worked cooperatively or in divided strips – were a necessary condition of realizing the full productivity of farmland. And those strips and fields that the poets pined for had been incapable of supporting a peasantry that lacked the capital and – how Young bitterly regretted this – the knowledge to understand even the rudiments of modern farming: proper manuring, letting land lie fallow between crops, the use of seed drills and the like. Besides, although the process had admittedly speeded up in the 1760s, enclosures had been going on for centuries. Moreover, the tool employed to launch the new wave of enclosures, the private act of parliament, required the consent of four-fifths of landowners in any parish.

But not, the critics pointed out, with the consent of, or even consultation with the hundreds of thousands of smallholders and copyholders who had clung to little lots and patches of land on which they could eke out a living so long as they also had access to common grazing land for their animals. Now they were reduced to wage labourers. Young insisted that the booming market actually generated more, not less, work for the rural poor; that in their new circumstances they were much better off than when they had been attempting to make a living from inherently unviable scraps of land. Many of them did find work in local, rural manufactures, shopkeeping, or newly-learned work like shoemaking. But newcomers to these trades would be competing with the already established, and some were reduced to finding casual, seasonal labour as ditch-diggers. Young complained bitterly that in Yorkshire such men earning as much as three or four shillings a day 'scarce ever work above three days a week but drink out the rest' and that the price of their labour was pushing up wages so much that 'labourers in winter [are] so saucy that they are forced to be almost bribed to thresh.'

It was not, in any case, enclosures that most distressed and angered the critics of Improvement. That dubious honour went to what was called 'engrossment': the replacement of many tenants by few, often the result of the incursion of 'new' commercial money into the high-price, high-rent land market. The economies of scale were said by Young and others to be another necessary condition for making the kind of investment that would bring about improved crop yields and better livestock, and thus enable the burgeoning population of Britain's cities to be fed. And they were probably right. But the casualty of the estate manager's relentless drive towards maximizing rents and profits was, so those same critics insisted, not just the countless numbers who now swelled the migrations to the towns – of America as well as Britain – but the collapse of an older, communally based way of life. In one of the great best-sellers of the 1760s (six editions in 10 years) Frances Brooke's *The History of Lady Julia Mandeville,* a 'Lord T' is upbraided for:

> pursuing a plan, which has drawn on him the curse of thousands, and made his estate a scene of desolation: his farms are in the hands of a few men, to whom the sons of the old tenants are either forced to be servants, or to leave the country to get their bread elsewhere. The village, large and once populous, is reduced to about eight families; a dreary silence reigns over their deserted fields; the farm houses, once the seats of cheerful smiling industry, now useless, are falling in ruins around him; his tenants are merchants and engrossers, proud, lazy, luxurious, insolent, and spurning the hand which feeds them.

The complaints and laments were, of course, unrealistically nostalgic for a bucolic utopia of caring parsons, avuncular squires and humane magistrates that had never existed except as an imaginary counter-example to the iron laws of country property. But the wishful quality of this fantasy rural past did not prevent those who wept for its passing in verse and prose from rising to the most extraordinary eloquence in their protest, and from exercising an almost hypnotic influence on a generation yearning to respond to the call for social affection. The most powerful of all those verse polemics came from the prolific pen of Oliver Goldsmith, born in County

Longford, Ireland, much travelled, often ruinously hard up, but finally in the 1760s arrived at metropolitan fame and fortune, and admitted to the select company of the Literary Club, along with Sir Joshua Reynolds, Dr Johnson and James Boswell. Goldsmith's earlier poem 'The Traveller' had already put in a poetic nutshell his retort to those who justified what was being done in the country by the fact that it was all perfectly legal and above board:

> Each wanton judge new penal statutes draw
> Laws grind the poor and rich men rule the law.

In 1769, a year before Thicknesse produced his shocking image of starvation in Hertfordshire, Goldsmith published his long poem *The Deserted Village*, one of the greatest of all verse laments for the death of a dream hamlet – 'sweet Auburn.'

> loveliest of the lawn,
> Thy sports are fled and all thy charms withdrawn;
> Amidst thy bowers, the tyrant's hand is seen,
> And desolation saddens all thy green:
> One only master grasps the whole domain,
> And half a tillage stints thy smiling plain.

Goldsmith's couplets wander around the scenery of the dream, stopping at all the places and people that had made it a community. He visits the 'village preacher's modest mansion':

> The long-remember'd beggar was his guest,
> Whose beard descending swept his aged breast;
> The ruined spendthrift, now no longer proud,
> Claimed kindred there and had his claims allowed;
> The broken soldier, kindly bade to stay...

the schoolmaster and, not least, the inn where 'nut-brown draughts' were served, but which was much more than just an alehouse:

> Thither no more the peasant shall repair
> To sweet oblivion of his daily care;
> No more the farmer's news, the barber's tale,

THE

DESERTED VILLAGE,

A

P O E M.

BY DR. GOLDSMITH

The sad historian of the pensive plain.

L O N D O N:
Printed for W. GRIFFIN, at Garrick's Head, in Catharine-street, Strand.
M DCC LXX.

Frontispiece to *The Deserted Village* (1770) by Oliver Goldsmith, engraved by Isaac Taylor.

No more the woodman's ballad shall prevail,
No more the smith his dusky brow shall clear,
Relax his ponderous strength and lean to hear;
The host himself no longer shall be found
Careful to see the mantling bliss go round;
Nor the coy maid, half willing to be pressed,
Shall kiss the cup to pass it to the rest.

Departing from his forlorn tour of the ghost world of 'Auburn,' Goldsmith then turns to face the contemporary, commercial England that has engineered this desolation:

Ye friends to truth, ye statesmen, who survey
The rich man's joys increase, the poor's decay,
'Tis yours to judge, how wide the limits stand
Between a *splendid* and a *happy* land.
Proud swells the tide with loads of freighted ore,
And shouting Folly hails them from her shore;

…the man of wealth and pride
Takes up a space that many poor supplied;
Space for his lake, his park's extended bounds,
Space for his horses, equipage and hounds;
The robe that wraps his limbs in silken sloth
Has robbed the neighbouring fields of half their growth.

Justified or not, there is no question that Goldsmith's rhymed accusation had an immense influence on late 18th-century public opinion. It affected moralizing critics like Bewick and nostalgic Tories like Dr Johnson, both of whom mistrusted the concentration of economic and political power in the hands of the landowning oligarchs of England. The country came out of the fiery years of food riots, troop mobilizations and hangings with its institutions intact but with its faith in the paternalism and even the moral legitimacy of the aristocracy, the judiciary, shaken. Only King George III himself, the first farmer of the country and manifestly a walking embodiment of the touted virtues of simplicity, honesty and sincerity, escaped the increasingly vocal criticism. The 1770s and 1780s saw the launching of any number of social crusades mobilized by determined, articulate pamphlet-writers, petitioners and sanctimonious trouble-makers. They took aim at particular evils, invariably and significantly described as 'unnatural': prison sentences for unmarried mothers (often made pregnant by debauched young and not-so-young gentlemen); the state of the prisons to which they, as well as debtors and common criminals, were sent; the indiscriminate application of the death penalty for trivial felonies. The plight of children – so often at the core of all the heart-tugging causes of the Romantic generation – was guaranteed to inspire pathos and fury from the growing constituency of social virtue, whether they were poor newborn infants given the virtual death sentence of being dispatched to one of the London wet nurses in the slums of St Giles's or St Clement Danes; African children torn from their families and villages, and herded on to the slave ships; or the 'climbing boys' sent up filthy, soot-caked chimneys to contract cancer of the scrotum and respiratory diseases before being got rid of at 12 or 14 as too big to do the job.

Common to all these crusades was their intense religious fervour. Most of the evangelists who burned to correct the evils of their age believed that the established Church had become too rich, too complacent, too aristocratic, to fulfil its Christian pastoral mission, and was part of the problem rather than an instrument for solving it. In response, the 1770s and 1780s saw the most extraordinary spiritual rebirth in Britain since the 17th century; a great flowering of dissenting faiths and Churches in which the Bible was read (as it had been by the radical sects of Oliver Cromwell's Commonwealth) as a proclamation of the doctrine of common humanity, and the gospel of compassion for the poor and downtrodden.

Not all of those Nonconformist Churches were necessarily radical. After all, true evangelicals, with their emphasis on mystical revelation, required surrender to its power. And John Wesley, the founder of Methodism, detested Unitarians and their rejection of the divinity of Christ, calling it 'poison.' But the intensity of his tirades was a backhanded compliment to the attraction of what could for the first time be called, without uttering an oxymoron, 'rational Christianity.' It was, in fact, hard to find a Unitarian preacher in the 1770s and 1780s who was *not* also a sharp critic of the social and political status quo. For men such as Joseph Priestley (better known to posterity as a scientist, one of the discoverers of oxygen) and the Welsh Dr Richard Price, Jesus was no longer to be thought of as the son of God but as the first of the reformers, an all round good egg and socially concerned citizen who, more than any other, had preached the indissoluble bonds of obligation tying the more fortunate to those less so.

'Am I not a Man and a Brother?' read the inscription on the famous anti-slavery ceramic medallion produced by Josiah Wedgwood's factory at Etruria in

Staffordshire. And the new Churches of brotherhood under Christ preached their spiritualized civics using every means at their command: hymns; anthems; charismatic meetings at which the spirit of righteousness burst from their lungs; series of lectures; pamphlets and petitions to parliament; and, not least, the powerful medium of images, designed by artists who included William Blake and printed on every available surface – drinking goblets as well as paper. Each cause had its own particular story of infamy, repeated over and over as a rallying cry. The scandal of the slave ship *Zong*, when over 100 sick Africans were thrown overboard so that the master could collect on insurance, was used time and again to mobilize indignation against the so-called triangular trade – cheap manufactured goods from Britain to West Africa, that cargo then exchanged for slaves to the West Indies, in turn replaced by sugar and rum for the third leg back to Britain. The fresh converts thus recruited came from almost every class of society: reform-minded aristocrats as well as preachers, country gentlemen, lawyers, physicians and tradesmen – the same kind of broad church of the righteous, in fact, that had made the revolution of the 1640s. But this time it also conspicuously included men from the world of science and industry; very often they were the second generation of famous names, like Thomas Wedgwood, who felt they had to earn or even atone for their good fortune, and who wanted to distinguish it from money made from the trade in black humans. And among the congregations of the indignant were now counted completely new constituencies: well-read women, both genteel and middle class, and even domestic servants who were said to sit in the back rows of Dr Richard Price's meeting house on Newington Green in London.

That parliament needed reform was obvious. The electorate was actually 3 per cent smaller than it had been before the Civil War; there were rotten boroughs, like Old Sarum with an electorate of seven, which still returned a member. 'Placemen' bought their seats on the understanding that they would vote with the government; and the newly populous towns were grossly under-represented. But was the unreformed parliament beyond redemption? The first and most intensely felt complaint was the narrowness with which the Act of Toleration enacted in 1689 had been construed. The Dissenters wanted more than just to be allowed to worship; they wanted full civil equality – the abolition of the Test Acts, which denied them access to public office. (The Tory view was that Toleration had only been granted in the first place on condition that that was all that would be given.) But the reformers were forced to concede that there were occasions when 'Old Corruption' could be moved to act on their urgent appeals, especially when the issue was moral rather than political. In response to the campaign for climbing boys (which inspired Blake's poem

'The Chimney Sweeper,' 1789), an act was passed in 1788 prohibiting the employment of children under the age of eight and sending them up a lit chimney. It also stipulated that they should be washed at least once a week. But the Act was largely unenforced, and for those people who were most concerned about the fate of the poor, it was not nearly enough. Attempts to reform poor relief based on the system adopted by the Berkshire parish of Speenhamland, which, in an effort to keep paupers from the workhouse, linked a wage supplement, funded from the parish rates, to the price of bread, depended entirely on the goodwill of local communities. To the critics, this was just sending the problem back to the consideration of those most likely to ignore it.

When Thomas Bewick began work as an engraver's apprentice in Newcastle, he smoked pipes and drank ale with well-read, articulate young men who had no hesitation in sounding off about the wicked indifference of the high and mighty. The most radical of all was the diminutive, pugnacious school-teacher Thomas Spence, whom Bewick described as 'one of the warmest philanthropists in the world. The happiness of mankind seemed with him to absorb every other consideration. He was of a cheerful disposition, warm in his attachment to his friends, and in his patriotism to his country; but he was violent against people whom he considered of an opposite character.' In the spirit of the Diggers of the 1650s, Spence had become convinced that all modern ills emanated from the original evil of ownership of land. He declaimed his communism at a debating society (one of thousands formed all around the provinces in this period, including some in London, expressly for women) that held its sessions in Spence's schoolroom on the Broad Garth. Although he evidently warmed to Spence's enthusiasm and to his 'sincere and honest' concern for the unfortunate, Bewick believed his ideas dangerously utopian, fit for some 'uninhabited country' but shockingly wrong in presuming to 'take from people what is their own.' On one day the argument got over-heated and the two moved from angry words to cudgels. 'He did not know that I was a proficient in cudgel playing, and I soon found that he was very defective. After I had blackened the insides of his thighs and arms, he became quite outrageous and acted very unfairly, which obliged me to give him a severe beating.'

But while property for Bewick remained very definitely sacred, there was much else about the self-satisfaction of the ruling order that angered him. For those meeting and debating the present and several ills of the country at Swarley's Club in the Black Boy in Newcastle, or listening to the reverends John Horne Tooke, Richard Price or Joseph Priestley denounce 'Old Corruption,' it was less the facts of the unreformed parliament that stuck in their craw than the fantastic and self-serving

Top: Abolitionist medallion, designed by Josiah Wedgwood, *c.* 1787, depicting a shackled slave and inscribed with the words, 'Am I not a Man and a Brother.'
Above: *A Negro Hung Alive by the Ribs to the Gallows* (left) and *Flagellation of a Female Samboe Slave* (right), engraved by William Blake, 1792, from *A Narrative, of a Five Years' Expedition Against the Revolted Negroes of Surinam* (1796) by John Gabriel Stedman.

mythology by which this state of affairs was defended. Much as the modern fantasy of the well-ordered, benevolent country estate, with all its tenants and labourers toiling and tilling in the land of plenty, hid the ugly realities of rural poverty, so the endless recitation of how very fortunate Britons were to be living in the free-est, most wisely managed, just and prosperous of all states came to grate on the nerves of the manifestly unfortunate and unrepresented.

The window-dressing of power came in two versions: Tory and Whig. The Tory version categorically laid down as a divinely ordained truism that the 'people' had no claim whatsoever to determine the ordering of their government; and that their natural and proper state was obedience and submission to a benevolent monarch, the Church and a parliament elected by those who, through their property and interest, had a right to be included in the electorate. The Whig version was that the Glorious Revolution of 1688 had been all that would ever be needed to secure the 'ancient constitution' against the threat of monarchical tyranny, and that the 'Revolution Settlement,' with its enactment of toleration and its guarantee of parliaments (elected only every seven years), was enough of a shield for the liberties of the free-born Englishman.

But the centenary of that revolution – approaching in 1788 – was an unavoidable occasion for looking long and hard at both those justifications of the status quo. Such a critical re-examination was made to seem more urgent by the failure of William Pitt the Younger, first in 1782 as a 22-year-old MP and then in 1785 as a 25-year-old prime minister, to secure even a modest measure of parliamentary self-reform; and by Pitt's active opposition, in 1788–9, to the repeal of the Test Act. Across the Atlantic, Tom Paine's *Common Sense* (1775) had already taken an axe to most of the status-quo assumptions by asserting the right, in fact the duty, of the Americans to resist in terms of a defence of natural rights (for the taxed to be represented and free from forced billeting of British soldiers). The American lesson had, of course, not gone unheeded on this side of the Atlantic, especially by those who had always been critics of the war recently fought there. In the 1780s, proselytizing organizations like the Society for the Promotion of Constitutional Information and the Westminster Association, who numbered among their members not just preachers, professionals and artisans but also the radical fringe of the Whigs (the 3rd Duke of Richmond, the 3rd Duke of Grafton and the playwright–politician Richard Brinsley Sheridan, who met at Holland House, home of their silver-tongued leader, that child of a permissive Rousseau-ite nursery, Charles James Fox), began to flirt with a potentially democratic justification of government, one that began with the right of the people to choose or change their own rulers. That right, moreover, was said to be rooted not just in nature but in history. According to that view all governments had originated with the unforced, voluntary agreement of the people to assign their authority to representatives (be they kings or parliaments) for the express purpose of protecting their freedom and security. This agreement had always been understood as a mutual contract. The people would give their allegiance only so long as the government to which they had provisionally entrusted the protection of their rights respected them. Should those same authorities be judged guilty of violating rather than upholding those natural rights, the sovereign people were at perfect liberty to remove them.

This was heady stuff: part regurgitation of old 'Commonwealthmen' doctrines left over from the radicals of the 17th century; part American republicanism with a dash of Rousseau added for extra force. But it was the essence of what a succession of speakers – James Burgh, Priestley, Price, Horne Tooke, Major John Cartwright – had to say to the discontented of the 1780s. That such opinions were far from being restricted to a tiny minority of agitators out of touch with the mainstream is borne out by the astounding sales of their often indigestibly severe opinions. Richard Price, for example, sold 60,000 copies (the kind of figure surpassed only by Tom Paine) of his daunting *Observations on the Nature of Civil Liberty* (1776). The fact that many of these opinions had been aired before, not least by John Milton, was far from being a sign of weakness (as some modern historians have assumed) but actually the secret of its appeal. For the late 18th century was becoming obsessed with the British past, especially the 'Gothick' Middle Ages – not just its political history, but its architecture, dress, furniture and armour, all of which saw compendious and beautifully illustrated histories published. So when Alfred the Great, the wise, the strong, the good, was trotted out yet again (by the anti-slavery campaigner Granville Sharp, for example) as the paragon of a popular monarch who worked in benevolent mutual collaboration with that mother of all parliaments, the Anglo-Saxon Witenagemot, history was taken not as some obscure and arcane irrelevance but as the model of what truly native British government was supposed to look like. The sealing of Magna Carta, another mythical moment when 'the people' had, through their barons and burgesses, exercised their right to call a despot to account, was also celebrated as an episode pregnant with significance for the present and future. It was just at this time, moreover, that the militant vegetarian–antiquarian–tramper Joseph Ritson's researches into Robin Hood were recasting that legendary character as a romantic popular hero (with wood engravings by Thomas Bewick).

Since the 16th century, the '88s' had always been critical years for Britain and for the fate of the monarchy; each generation adopted the epic of the last '88' as a touchstone for the next. The supporters of William III in 1688 claimed to be the heirs of Elizabeth's resistance to Catholic tyranny in 1588, the year of the Armada. In 1688, the Catholic James II had taken leave of his throne; in 1788 George III (whom some critics had accused of aiming at a 'Stuart' absolutism) had taken leave of his senses. By the time he was restored to them, in 1789, the fate of monarchy had been transformed by the stupefying events taking place in France. And those who were celebrating the centenary of the Glorious Revolution naturally embraced this latest revolution as the logical consummation of what had happened 100 years before. Providence, they thought, worked to a meaningful calendar.

On the face of it, the position of the two kings on opposite sides of the Channel in 1789 could not have been more different. While Louis XVI was being dictated to by the National Assembly and suspected (rightly) of planning a military coup to regain his absolute authority, George III was recovering his grip both on his sanity and on the nation. At the same time that Louis was obliged to leave Versailles for Paris to put the best face on his predicament and pretend, at least, to fold himself in the tricolour of the Revolution, George went on a tour of the West Country to recuperate. Everywhere he went he was regaled with booming choruses of 'God Save the King'; at Weymouth, indeed, he was surprised, while taking the waters, by a small but evidently loyal band concealed in the next bathing machine.

But none of these noisy demonstrations of loyalty deterred the true believers in a great British alteration from thinking that, if the walls of the Bastille could be stormed by the people of Paris, a day of reckoning with Old Corruption was not far off. In 1785 Joseph Priestley earned himself the nickname of 'Gunpowder Joe' by comparing the work of the radicals to 'laying gunpowder, grain by grain under the old building of error and superstition which a single spark may hereafter inflame so as to produce an instantaneous explosion.' When the Bastille fell, they hoped that its spark might carry right across the Channel. Glasses were hoisted at Swarley's Tavern; in the Bishop's Palace at Lichfield; in aristocratic Holland House. Charles James Fox celebrated it as 'much the greatest event that has ever happened in the history of the world and how much the best.' Although it was awkward to have the French, jeered at for generations by Whigs and Tories alike as the hopeless lackeys of despotism, complete what had begun in 1688 as a British revolution, it was after all the Americans who had already made the point that the 'true' spirit of Liberty, although born in Britain, had evidently migrated elsewhere. The fact that it had now returned across the Atlantic with the French general Lafayette, who had fought so ardently for the Americans, was only proof that the irresistible urge for popular self-government was the indivisible natural right of all mankind.

Yet the unfortunate Frenchness of the event did, for all their higher feelings,

King George III by Sir William Beechey, *c.* 1800.

make the 'new Whigs' (the most radical of the party, committed to broadening the franchise, to secret ballots, to pay for MPs and the like) defensive. In 1789 they felt obliged to argue that cheering on the French revolution was not incompatible with true patriotism, but rather a sign of its good health. That was the message of Dr Richard Price's sermon on 'The Love of Our Country,' preached, significantly, on 4 November 1789, almost to the day the 101st anniversary of William III's landing at Torbay, to the Society for Commemorating the Revolution at the Unitarian meeting house in Old Jewry, London. 'Country' properly considered, Price argued, was not just 'the soil or the spot of earth on which we happen to have been born; not the forests and fields, but that community of which we are members; or that body of companions and friends and kindred who are associated with us under the same constitution of government, protected by the same laws, and bound together by the same civil polity.' In other words, it is our politics and not our topography that gives us our true national allegiance. All the rest is just selfish bluster. And the politics of the great and glorious French Revolution, he said, were unmistakably connected with our own; were indeed the completion of what we had begun. Had not the meaning of 1688 been that the people had the right to resist tyrannical rule, get rid of the unlawful ruler and restore to themselves their undoubted right to self-government? And was that not precisely what the French were now doing? Their lesson was timely, for in Britain the representation of the people had become a bad joke; a 'shadow' freedom, the reality of which was corrupt oligarchy and a ministerial government that worked its will through paid yes-men in parliament.

If the fall of the Bastille and the transformation of the monarchy in France from an absolute to a popular monarchy was shocking, surely the shock was healthy; good for the constitution, like a cool dip at Weymouth or an excursion in the Lakeland drizzle. Price bridled at the craven 'servility' of the congratulations offered to George III on the recovery of his wits, 'more like a herd crawling at the feet of a master, than like enlightened and manly citizens rejoicing with a beloved sovereign, but at the same time conscious that he derives all his consequence from themselves.' They, in other words, were the true sovereign, and if he had been in the position of addressing the king, Price said, he would have spoken up thus:

> I rejoice, Sir, in your recovery. I thank God for his goodness to you. I honour you not only as my King, but as almost the only lawful King in the world, because the only one who owes his crown to the choice of his people. May you enjoy all possible happiness. May God shew you the folly of those effusions of adulation which you are now receiving, and guard you against their effects. May

you be led to such a just sense of the nature of your situation, and endowed with such wisdom, as shall render your restoration to the government of these kingdoms a blessing to it, and engage you to consider yourself as more properly the *Servant* than the *Sovereign* of your people.

This was already daring enough. But at the end of his remarks Price abandoned all pretence of deference and unleashed a thunderclap of apocalyptic revolutionary prophecy: 'Tremble all ye oppressors of the world! Take warning all ye supporters of slavish governments, and slavish hierarchies!…You cannot now hold the world in darkness. Struggle no longer against increasing light and liberality. Restore to mankind their rights, and consent to the correction of abuses, before they and you are destroyed together.'

It was the two central assumptions of Price's remarks – that the French Revolution was the continuation of the British (an assumption epitomized by one of the celebratory toasts, 'To the Parliament of Britain – may it become a National Assembly') and that the monarchy of Britain was, or ought to be, not an hereditary succession but accountable to the sovereign *people* – that provoked the Irish writer, orator and MP (for a pocket borough) Edmund Burke to write his devastating and vitriolic *Reflections on the Revolution in France* (1790). As much as anything else, it was Price's timing that so appalled Burke. He had greeted the French spring with cautious optimism, which by the autumn had turned to horrified disbelief. Everything that had happened after 14 July – the lynchings; the château burnings; the careless abandon with which the nobility liquidated their own privileges; and above all the expropriation of Church property to fund the national debt – struck him as a perverted act of national self-dismemberment. Most preposterous of all for Burke was the fiction that Louis XVI was an enthusiastic sponsor of all this demolition when he was, in fact, just the prisoner of the wrecking-gang. In November 1789 – precisely when Price had seen fit to lecture George III on his duty to consider himself the 'servant of the people' – the true state of Louis XVI's position had been exposed in the most brutal way. A march of Parisians to Versailles, led by the market women demanding bread, had degenerated into an attack on the palace as the marchers penetrated the private apartments of the royal family. Before it was over two Swiss guards were dead – although neither was, as Burke wrote, a sentry – and the king and queen, after making a nervous appearance on the palace balcony at Lafayette's urging, were ignominiously taken back to Paris in a coach. Preceded by heads stuck on pikes, the royal couple did their best to put a brave face on their captivity and pretend to be 'united' with the people. 'This king … and this queen, and their infant children (who once would have

Above: *Edmund Burke*, studio of Sir Joshua Reynolds, 1771.
Opposite top: *Dr Richard Price*, engraved by anon, *c.* 1780.
Opposite below: *Demolition of the Bastille* by Hubert Robert, *c.* 1790.

been the pride and hope of a great and generous people),' wrote Burke, laying on the sensation with a trowel, 'were then forced to abandon the sanctuary of the most splendid palace in the world, which they left swimming in blood, polluted by massacre, and strewed with scattered limbs and mutilated carcasses.'

How was it possible that Dr Price – who bore the butt of Burke's acid sarcasm – should celebrate such events as though from them flowed the milk of human benevolence? And how was it that he could have the audacity to claim kinship between the Glorious Revolution of 1688 and what for Burke were the utterly inglorious deeds of a century later? Only by utterly falsifying what that first, altogether British revolution had been about in the first place.

It was only in defiance of historical truth, he said, that Price could claim it had been licensed by the people's right to choose their own form of government and hire or fire kings at their pleasure, or as they judged those monarchs protected the 'natural rights' of individual liberty. That had been the view of the men not of 1688 but of 1648 – of Milton and the king-killing generation. William III had been invited to England, not as the people's choice, much less to make a fresh government from any sort of abstract principles, but to defend a form of law, Church and government that had always been there; the 'ancient constitution' violated by James II. It had thus been the most conservative of revolutions; hence its bloodlessness, hence its glory. And above all, Burke insisted, the 'ancient constitution' had the authority of countless generations – from Magna Carta, perhaps even Anglo-Saxon England – as its weight; pinning it to the earth of Britain rather than letting it be borne dangerously aloft by the hot-air balloon speculations of political philosophers like Rousseau. Governments could not simply be dreamed up from imagined first principles. Such 'geometric' or 'arithmetical' constructions were, by definition, lifeless. 'The very idea of the fabrication of a new government,' Burke wrote, '…is enough to fill us with disgust and horror.' Governments, legitimate governments at any rate, drew their authority from the immemorial experience of their practical use. That, at any rate, was Britain's native way of doing things. 'This idea of a liberal descent inspires us with a sense of habitual native dignity.' So the 'spot of earth on which we happen to have been born' made light of by Price was, in fact, of the utmost importance in giving us a sense of our community. 'In England we have not yet been completely embowelled of our natural entrails; we still feel within us, and we cherish and cultivate, those inbred sentiments which are the faithful guardians, the active monitors of our duty.' Our territorial ancestry, complete with what Burke – heavily in love with heraldry – called 'armorial bearings,' *was* our birthright, our political constitution. We damaged it at our peril.

As the prophets of international peace and understanding sang hymns to the coming universal communion of humanity, Burke thundered back, in effect: Nature! I'll tell you about *Nature*. You imagine it's all the same, daisychains and hands across the seas and songs of fraternity. But what *you're* talking about is the brotherhood of intellectuals who sip from the same little cups of chocolate, chatter away the same clichés and dream the same puerile dreams. But *nature*, my friends, is lived, not thought. Nature is familiarity, a feeling for place. Nature is a patriot.

The 'people' whom the demagogues so freely apostrophized had been revealed in France to be ignorant, credulous and bloodthirsty. Democracy was mobocracy. 'The occupation of a hairdresser or of a working tallow-chandler cannot,' Burke insisted, 'be a matter of honor to any person … Such descriptions of men ought not to suffer oppression from the state; but the state suffers oppression if such as they … are permitted to rule.' But they didn't know what they were doing. The unforgivable responsibility for giving them the illusion of their own importance and power lay with those who should have known better: class traitors, gentlemen or clergymen who toyed with democracy like a pastime and were rich enough to evade its lethal consequences, who fantasized about exchanging their allotted role in the political order for mere 'citizenship.' In England it was the dukes and earls – Richmond, Grafton, Shelburne and, regrettably, his old friend Charles James Fox – who, by lending their voice to the destruction of their own nobility, were recklessly cutting the golden chain that tied one generation to the next, the past to the future. They imagined they could, like Lafayette, ride the tiger of the mobs to power and glory. But they would be the first to be devoured.

Burke's *Reflections* was, by the standards of the day, a commercial success as well as a polemical *tour de force*, selling 17,000 in the first three months (at a time when a generous print run for a novel would be about 1500 copies). It was seen by some of the radical Whigs as an act of apostasy from someone who had the reputation (not quite accurate) of having been a friend to the Americans. (Burke had, in fact, sought Anglo-American reconciliation, but once the conflict began was a British loyalist.) But what distressed Price (who died in 1791, his voice hopelessly drowned out by the thunder of Burke's rhetoric) was its parochialism: the insistence that the British political inheritance *was* unique; that at their birth Britons had received not 'natural rights' but a distinctly native inheritance, quite irreconcilable with universally applicable liberties. Nature, Burke seemed to be saying, could never be cosmopolitan.

In the humiliation of Marie Antoinette fleeing 'almost naked…to seek refuge at the feet of [the] king' Burke had seen and lamented the death of chivalry in France. Reverse chivalry – when a woman might spring to the defence of a violently abused man – would never have occurred to him. Such an occurrence he would certainly have characterized as 'unnatural.' But that is precisely what did happen. Barely a month after the appearance of Burke's *Reflections*, Mary Wollstonecraft, who had met Price when she opened a school in Newington Green, a stone's throw from his chapel, published her counter-attack, *A Vindication of the Rights of Men* (1790). She had obviously been stung to see Price the subject of Burke's withering scorn. He had been her first real mentor when she had returned to London from Yorkshire, a self-taught bluestocking nobody, and had encouraged and befriended her as he had many other women writers, such as the children's author (also a radical) Anna Letitia Barbauld.

Mary had needed all the help she could get, for she had led a gypsy life, constantly fretting about her siblings and never earning quite enough money from her reviews and essays. Her father, the son of a Spitalfields silk weaver, had tried a bit of this and a bit of that – farming in Essex, provincial swagger in Yorkshire – and had failed at each venture. Mary had perforce been mother hen to her sisters, even when one of them walked out on her husband for reasons unexplained but easily guessed. She had, of course, soaked herself in the tepid pool of Jean-Jacques Rousseau's sentimental education and had got all warm and sticky with dreams of emotional purity and immortal friendship. But one of Rousseau's truisms about nature – the nature of the sexes – struck her as monstrous. It was the philosopher's assumption, set out in his novel, *Emile*, that girls had to be raised for one supreme purpose – to be a comfort and helpmate to their spouse and the mother (a nursing mother, naturally) to his children. Providence had ordained the sexes to be so unbridgeably different that any women who got it into their heads to be like, to act like, men were by definition biological and moral monsters, robbing their families of the quality that made an abode a home, *tendresse*.

Mary had seen her own mother's sad attempts to lavish such tenderness on her prodigal, drunken husband, and she thought it over-rated. Partly inspired by the example of the growing number of women who seemed to live from their pen, she wrote a little treatise on the education of daughters, arguing, in spite of *Emile*, that girls had the potential to be every bit as educated as boys. And she sent it to the man who seemed to be the hub of all the free spirits and radical writers in London, perhaps in England: Joseph Johnson.

Johnson, a short, neatly wigged, Liverpudlian bachelor, held court above his business at 72 St Paul's Churchyard, for centuries the favourite haunt of London's book publishers. To radical London he was the Johnson who really mattered – not just publisher of the *Analytical Review* (between 1788 and 1799) but patron and good

Top: *Mr. Joseph Johnson* engraved by William Sharpe, after Moses Haughton, *c.* 1770.

Above: *Wha' Wants Me, I Am Ready & Willing to Offer My Services to Any Nation or People ... Desirous of Liberty & Equality*, cartoon by Isaac Cruikshank, 1792, satirizing Tom Paine and his radical best-seller *Rights of Man* (1791–2).

uncle to his 'ragged regiment' of disciples. He was someone who could find a review to assign, a job to fill (for Mary he found a position as governess in Ireland, but with mixed results), a short-term loan or even (again, for Mary) a roof. She ate with him several times a week and was a regular at Johnson's famous Sunday dinners where the honest 'patriot' fare (a lot of boiled cod and peas) was spiced by interesting company: visionary artists like William Blake and Henry Fuseli; veteran stalwarts of the Society for the Promotion of Constitutional Information like the Reverend John Horne Tooke and Major John Cartwright; celebrity democrats like the black-eyed, red-faced Tom Paine; and, invariably, a group of articulate, unblushing, intelligent women like Barbauld and the actress Sarah Siddons. Accounts of Mary's appearances at Johnson's dinners describe an ungainly, strong-minded, immensely animated woman, her long curly hair powdered when it wasn't crowned with a beaver hat in the style of Benjamin Franklin or Rousseau. Self-consciously careless with her dress, she was a tremendous interrupter. The social philosopher William Godwin, who came to listen to Paine, found himself irritated by Mary talking incessantly over him.

The mix of stormy passion and tenacious argument, heart and head working like a right and left punch, which was already Mary Wollstonecraft's trademark, would have made her especially indignant at Burke's savage onslaught on the great and good Dr Price. But it was much more extraordinary that she should make the move from indignation to publication. Although her *Vindication of the Rights of Men* has been overshadowed by the more famous *Vindication of the Rights of Woman* (1792), published two years later, as well as by Paine's blockbuster *Rights of Man* (1791–2), Mary's intervention was not just the earliest counter-attack on Burke but one of the cleverest. Instead of doing what would have been expected (not least by Burke) of a woman and writing in a primly sanctimonious manner, Mary used Burke's own weapon of venomous irony to attack his credentials as the guardian of traditional institutions. If he were so deeply exercised about the sanctity of hereditary kingship, she wondered out loud, was it not rather peculiar that when King George had gone mad Mr Burke had been in such indecent haste to replace him (with the Prince Regent, Burke's patron's patron)? 'You were so eager to taste the sweets of power, that you could not wait till time had determined, whether a dreadful delirium would settle into a confirmed madness; but, prying into the secrets of Omnipotence, you thundered out that God had *hurled him from his throne…*' Was not that the very same dissolution of the bonds of loyalty that Burke had found so shocking in the French? The goal was to make Burke look not just wrongheaded but ridiculous, mocking his pet obsessions; his comical gallantry towards Marie Antoinette ('not an animal of the highest order'); his infatuation with the escutcheoned past; the myopia (more fun with Burke's famous eye-glasses, even though Mary used them herself) in not seeing that the 'perfect Liberty' was only perfect for those who had the property to enjoy it. More seriously, if the sanctity of the 'ancient constitution' were never to be tampered with, were we not then doomed to 'remain forever in frozen inactivity because a thaw that nourishes the soil spreads a temporary inundation?'

Mary was the sniper; Tom Paine the heavy artillery. In the early days of the French Revolution Paine had assumed that Burke, as an old 'friend of Liberty,' would be sympathetic, and had actually sent him a cordial letter from Paris. The *Reflections* disabused him. Gripped by anger and urgency, in just three months Paine produced 40,000 words of Part I of *Rights of Man* (1791), his demolition job on the 'bleak house of despotism.' Much of it had been said before, by John Milton, Algernon Sidney and, indeed, by Paine himself: the rights of men, including their natural equality as well as individual liberty, are God-given at birth and, since they precede all forms of government, cannot be surrendered to those governments. On the contrary, governments were instituted to protect those rights, and are obeyed on the condition of such protection. But Paine added an extra note of sardonic ridicule at the mere idea of hereditary governments – aristocracies as well as monarchies. To entertain such a notion, much less defer to it, was no less absurd than believing in, say, inherited lines of mathematicians.

More important than what Paine said, however, was the way in which he said it. His own origins as a maker of stays and corsets in Norfolk, where he had grown up on a bare hill known as 'The Wilderness' facing the local gallows and had been taken to Quaker meeting houses, meant that Paine was not among those whom Burke wrote off as radical playboys with more money than morals or sense. Before his burst of fame in America, Paine had known what it had meant to be poor, itinerant, almost entirely self-educated. His real schooling had taken place amidst the bawling arguments of pipe-smoking tavern politicians. The rough-house clamour of American politics had added another string to his crude but powerful bow. And closeness to the language of the inns and the streets served him well in the combat with Burke since he understood, with an almost 20th-century shrewdness, that a battle of ideas was also necessarily a battle of language. Burke had deliberately chosen the most high-pitched vocabulary, alternating between Gothic histrionics when describing (at second hand) lurid scenes of mayhem in France and lordly grandiloquence when lecturing the 'swinish multitude' on their richly merited exclusion from public affairs. Paine called those set-piece performances 'very well calculated for theatrical representation, where facts are manufactured for the sake of show.'

In calculated contrast, as if to make Burke's worst nightmare – the political education of ordinary people – come true, Paine chose to write with aggressive simplicity: 'As it is my design to make those that can scarcely read understand … I shall therefore avoid every literary ornament and put it in a language as plain as the alphabet.' Many polite readers who picked up *Rights of Man* were shocked less by the predictable twitting of the monarchy and the aristocratic establishment than by the coarseness of his language. As if anticipating the crinkling of noses and the fluttering of fans, Paine virtually belched his ideas in their faces.

The swinish multitude ate it up. Joseph Johnson had agreed to publish it in time for George Washington's birthday on 22 February (the general duly got a copy and thanked Paine). But on the appointed day Johnson, whose shop had already published attacks on Burke, including that of Mary Wollstonecraft, got an uncharacteristic attack of nerves. Paine was forced to shop around for another publisher, and when he found one hired a horse and cart to take the unbound sheets to the new premises. Johnson might well have regretted his panic, for *Rights of Man* sold out briskly and a second printing was needed three days after the first. By May there had been six editions and 50,000 sales of a book that, at three shillings, was not inexpensive. Even with foreign sales (for many copies undoubtedly went to Boston, Amsterdam, Paris and Dublin), this made Paine's work the most colossal best-seller of the 18th century, knocking Burke's readership into insignificance. Part II, with its even more radical 'welfare state' agenda (which divided the reformers), redistributing national income through progressive taxation to fund government obligations towards children, the aged, the infirm and the poor, did even better, selling, according to Paine, between 400,000 and 500,000 copies in the first 10 years. Even allowing for an element of exaggeration the figures make nonsense of the claims of some modern historians that radical opinions at this time were confined to a small and unrepresentative minority. At a meeting of the suddenly revived Society for the Promotion of Constitutional Information, a vote of thanks was passed to Paine in the sung form of a new version of the national anthem:

> God save the Rights of Man
> Let despots if they can
> Them overthrow…

By the summer of 1791, with Louis XVI and Marie Antoinette caught at Varennes while trying to flee France, brought back in disgrace to Paris and held prisoner in their own palace of the Tuileries, two sets of self-designated British patriots were at each other's throats. In May, in the House of Commons, the erstwhile friends and allies Edmund Burke and Charles James Fox had had a bitter and irreparable falling-out. Goaded by Pitt, Fox remained defiant that the new French constitution and the Declaration of the Rights of Man and Citizen were 'the most stupendous edifice of liberty' that the world had ever seen. And in private he accused Burke of being no more than Pitt's hired mouth, an accomplice to the dirty war of tarring him with the brush of being a republican. In the Commons on 6 May, a speech by Burke was a signal from Fox's ardent young band of radicals, whom Burke called 'the little dogs,' to howl and hiss. Burke publicly aired his anger that 'a personal attack had been made upon him from a quarter he never could have expected, after a friendship and intimacy of more than 22 years.' Rehearsing other disputes that had divided them, but had neither compromised their closeness nor split the Whigs, Burke was about to say that this particular argument over the French Revolution was fatal to both. Fox interjected: 'There is no loss of friendship.' 'I regret to say there is,' responded Burke. 'I have done my duty though I have lost my friend.' Fox rose, became tearfully incoherent, but finally spoke unrepentantly of the disappearance of 'horrid despotism' in France. Burke responded again that he hoped no one would trade away the British constitution for a 'wild and visionary system'.

This courtly if emotional exchange disguised the polarization taking place, fast and furiously, in the provincial towns of England and even more ominously in Scotland. Certainly, London was also a storm-centre of both radical and loyalist politics. But the 'new Britain' – Manchester, Sheffield, Belfast, Birmingham and Glasgow, as well as older towns transformed by commerce and industry such as Derby, Nottingham and Bewick's Newcastle – was experiencing a real baptism of fire. It was in those places that meeting house 'rational religion,' debating clubs, the printing and publishing trades and radical newspapers were all tied together. In Sheffield the bookshop owner John Gales, also the editor of the *Sheffield Register*, was the prime mover of the city's Constitutional Society, which rapidly acquired over 2000 members. The question of just how radical these organizations were to be often put a strain on their solidarity. Some wanted to follow the more 'Friends of the People,' Fox-ite, constitutional line of pressing for parliamentary reform, perhaps even manhood suffrage as a 'birthright of freeborn Britons'; others quickly became intoxicated with millenarian visions of the coming just society as outlined in the gospel according to Tom Paine.

Amazingly, 14 July – the anniversary of the fall of the Bastille – replaced 4–5 November – the anniversary of both the Gunpowder Plot and the Glorious Revolution – as a critical day in British politics. On that same day in 1791 a huge crowd in Belfast – both Protestant and Catholic – cheered the dawn of liberty, especially for Ireland, while another crowd in Birmingham was trashing the precious library and laboratory of Joseph Priestley in the name of Church and King. The 'spark' had indeed caught for 'Gunpowder Joe,' but it had lit a fire under the wrong people. By the spring of 1794 Priestley had emigrated to America, settling in Northumberland, Pennsylvania, where he founded a cooperative community that at last corresponded, somewhat, to his social idealism.

Britain, on the other hand, seemed further off than ever from being converted into an Elysium of peace and freedom. Any 'Friend of the People' hoping to work some sort of miraculous constitutional change from within would have been sadly disenchanted when, on 6 May 1793, Charles Grey's measure of parliamentary reform (more equal representation and more frequent elections) was defeated by 282 votes to 41. That was about the size of the Fox-ite 'New Whig' remnant in parliament. So when, in May, a royal proclamation was issued outlawing seditious assemblies, the government expected and got Whig support; Fox voted against but the Duke of Portland, and of course Burke, were in favour. However, since the parliamentary road seemed, for the moment, to be a dead end, Paine's more revolutionary politics became more, not less, appealing. In January 1792, the shoemaker Thomas Hardy established the London Corresponding Society (the 'mother of mischief' according to Burke), with John Thelwall as its major theorist and spokesman; it was an overtly democratic Paine-ite organization pressing for manhood suffrage and annual parliaments. To the government, fretting about national as well as social disintegration, it suddenly seemed sinister that Hardy was a Scot – all the more so when, in December, Edinburgh was the chosen meeting place for a 'Convention' of Scottish 'Friends of the People.' Since the bloody change from a monarchy to a republic in France had produced a 'Convention' the very term (despite a quite different tradition of usage in Britain) seemed to presage a similar upheaval. The Edinburgh Convention numbered 160 delegates from 80 sister societies in no fewer than 35 towns. Government spies reported that there were Irishmen at the Edinburgh Convention – and for that matter Scots in Belfast and Dublin. When one of the conveners, the lawyer Thomas Muir, spoke of liberating 'enslaved England,' the jump from Jacobite to Jacobin suddenly did not seem so fantastic. Part of the savagery of the government's counter-attack – arresting its leaders, trying them for sedition and sentencing them to 14 years' Australian transportation – was undoubtedly due to the fear that the Anglo-Scottish union was about to be subverted or that an attempt to replace parliament with a 'British Convention' might begin in some sort of northern democratic heartland stretching from Nottingham to Dundee.

Agents also noticed that the corresponding societies were packed with rowdy, violently verbose types: a new generation of uppity weavers, godly nailmakers, republican tailors and, most ominously for those who felt the hairs rise on the nape of their neck when they read of the revolutionary horrors in Paris, Sheffield cutlers. Raids occasionally produced the odd cache of pikes or axes, which only fed the hysteria. In the Commons Burke poured on the paranoia, comparing something that he called the Revolutional and the Unitarian Societies to insects that might grow into huge spiders building webs to catch and devour all who stood in their way. Less phantasmagorically, William Pitt warned that if the opinions of Tom Paine were allowed to spread unchecked among the common people 'we should have bloody revolution.'

With the connivance of the government, pre-emptive action was taken. The militia was called out in 10 counties, but they looked the other way when the target of the mob was the radicals. Presses were smashed; literature deemed 'seditious' taken and burned. Cartoonists like the genius James Gillray were hired to show, as graphically as possible, what would happen should a revolution happen in Britain. John Reeves, a sometime Chief Justice of Newfoundland now returned to Britain, was so disturbed by the brazenness of the clubs that in November 1792 he founded his own Association for Preserving Liberty and Property Against Levellers and Republicans 'to support the Laws, to suppress seditious Publications and to defend our Persons and Property.' As well as arming loyalists, the Association promoted the publication of tracts specifically to disabuse credulous working men of the views of Paine. Once war with the French had broken out in February 1793 a whole new seam of neurosis about the consequences of a French republican invasion could be richly mined. One of the tracts featured a patriotic master taking the time and effort to explain to his gullible apprentice just how wicked and dangerous Paine's opinions were. 'Right Master,' replies his journeyman, overcome with gratitude. 'I thank you for explaining all this and instead of going to the Liberty Club I will begin my work for I should not like to see the Frenchmen lie with my wife or take the bread out of my children's mouths.' The evangelical Hannah More, whose reputation had been built on improving literature for children, now took it on herself to supply timely patriotic definitions for all ages. Her *Village Politics* (1793) has 'Jack Anvil' explain to 'Tom Hod' that a democrat was 'one who likes to be governed by a thousand tyrants and yet can't bear a king.' The *Rights of Man* prescribed 'battle, murder and sudden death' and a 'new patriot' was 'someone who loves every country better than their own and France best of all.'

If, despite all the intimidation and danger, you were a committed 'Friend of the People' in the stormy years of 1792–3 what were your options? If you were prudent,

Above: *Rioters Burning Dr. Priestley's House* by J. Eckstein, 1791.
Opposite: *The Republican Attack*, satirical cartoon of the French Revolution by James Gillray, *c.* 1790.

and mistrustful of the excesses of Paine-ite revolutionary enthusiasm, you might make Thomas Bewick's choice and decide to button your lip, hunker down and hope that at some time, preferably in the not too distant future, British common sense, public decency and justice *would* prevail. In the meantime he would content himself with reading the local radical newspaper, *The Oeconomist* (distributed in London by, of course, Joseph Johnson); or relish the ferociously satirical attacks on Pitt in, say, his old friend Thomas Spence's *Pigs' Meat, or Lessons from the Swinish Multitude* (1793–5); get on with his birds and beasts, and smuggle, for those who wanted to look carefully between the illustrations, images of brutality, misery, daring and death. Or, from the relative safety of a Hepplewhite chair in your club, you might cheer on the dwindling band of 'New Whigs' in parliament – Fox, Sheridan, Charles Grey and Shelburne – who persisted in opposition to measures infringing the freedom of press or suspending habeas corpus and who refused to recant their benevolent views about the French Revolution. Or, if you were very brave, very angry or very drunk on revolutionary optimism you might take the plunge and join one of those artisans' clubs where you could drink rounds to the health of Paine, the imminent realization of a British republic and the death of despots. Given the ubiquitousness of government spies, you would be putting yourself in jeopardy, even for unguarded toasts. When John Thelwall, now the prime orator of the London Corresponding Society, swiped the froth off a head of beer and remarked (according to a spy), 'This is the way I would serve up kings,' the joke would come back to haunt him in the Old Bailey.

There was another option, of course: leaving Britain altogether. You could cross the Channel to inhale some of that heady air of liberty, equality and – especially – fraternity, and work for the day when you might return in the vanguard of the forces of freedom. The French seemed to be treating British radicals as brothers and sisters. Tom Paine had been made an honorary citizen. To go to the fountainhead of freedom and to drink deeply would be more than a gesture of political tourism. It was the promise of a new life.

Try as they might, however, not everyone could make the leap. At some point in the summer or autumn of 1792 John Thelwall took a little time off from lecturing on the cause of freedom and justice (to bigger and bigger crowds) to walk through Kent. In the guise of his literary *alter ego*, the Peripatetic Sylvanus Theophrastus, he arrives at the White Cliffs of Dover and looks out at the 'foaming billows' separating him from the land of liberty. The place for him is the essence of British sublimity, but there is so much to look at that he cannot decide whether the beach or the clifftop provides the more breathtaking view. He wants it all and scrambles up and down 'above a dozen times.' But then he gets too ambitious and tries to climb a near perpendicular rock 'with no better hold than a spray of elder, or a fragile tuft of thyme.' Three-quarters of the way there, the Peripatetic is well and truly stuck: no way up; no way down. Which describes allegorically, of course, Thelwall's political predicament. The Cicero of the corresponding societies, arch-republican demagogue to the authorities, he has no way up, no way down. So he perches 'though my heart beat an audible alarm … with all the calmness I was master of, beneath the hanging precipice, and contemplated the beautiful serenity of the spangled sea.' He turns 'a longing eye towards the distant cliffs of France; and could not but regret the impossibility of exchanging my present situation for the more honourable … danger of defending with the sword of justice, the gallant struggles of that brave people in the cause of their new-born Liberty.'

He can't do it. Ultimately he knows he is, in his way, a British patriot. His feet have to be on its ground. So somehow 'I contrived to let myself down, from precipice to precipice, till I arrived at last in safety on the beach, together with a fleck of chalk, and a sprig of thyme … Trophies purchased with more innocence … than all the sanguinary honours of the plunderers and destroyers of the world: the Alexanders and the Caesars, the Edwards and the Henrys, by whom the peace of mankind has been so repeatedly disturbed.' Poor Thelwall – who would end up trying to be a farmer in the Black Mountains of Wales at Llyswen before turning to elocution teaching in London – would always be on the verge of happiness.

A man struggles to survive in a swollen river. Wood engraving by Thomas Bewick, from *History of British Birds* (1804).

In the spring of 1792, and of his life, William Wordsworth had none of John Thelwall's paralysing anxieties. Going to France was 'pleasant exercise of hope and joy!'

> For mighty were the auxiliars which then stood
> Upon our side, us who were strong in love!
> Bliss was it in that dawn to be alive,
> But to be young was very Heaven!

That, at any rate, was the way he remembered it 12 years later even when he was feeling a lot less charitable towards the French Revolution. The chronicle of his journey in and out of revolution forms part of *The Prelude*, the greatest autobiographical poem in English (or perhaps any other European language); the first section of which was written in 1798–9, exactly at the point when Wordsworth was undergoing a deep change of heart.

The momentous theme of *The Prelude* is the struggle to hang on – through memory – to the instinctive life of childhood, even while being pulled inexorably towards an adult sense of individual self-consciousness. Immersion in nature is the great ally in this war against the inevitable erosion of innocence by time and social experience. Nature is freedom; the business of the world a prison. The mature Wordsworth becomes a child of nature again through the act of intense recollection. What he describes is a Cumbrian childhood spent escaping from, fighting against, what we would now call 'socialization': against the rote-learning, fact-packed lessons at his school in Hawkshead. Instead, nature was his tutor and his playground:

> Oh, many a time have I, a five years' child,
> In a small mill-race severed from his stream,

FORCES OF NATURE:
THE ROAD HOME

England: Richmond Hill, on the Prince Regent's Birthday (detail) by J.M.W. Turner, 1819.

> Made one long bathing of a summer's day;
> Basked in the sun, and plunged and basked again
> Alternate, all a summer's day…
> or when rock and hill,
> The woods, and distant Skiddaw's lofty height,
> Were bronzed with deepest radiance, stood alone
> Beneath the sky, as if I had been born
> On Indian plains, and from my mother's hut
> Had run abroad in wantonness, to sport
> A naked savage, in the thunder shower.

At St John's College, Cambridge, Wordsworth was in no hurry to oblige his father's expectation that he enter the Church or the law. Nor was he particularly enthralled with learning:

> Of College labours, of the Lecturer's room
> All studded round, as thick as chairs could stand
> … Let others that know more speak as they know.
> Such glory was but little sought by me.

Restive, anxious, dimly aware that something big was waiting for him, in the summer of 1790 he decided to go with a friend, Robert Jones, on a walking tour of the Alps – in that generation very much a statement of moral and political temper. The two undergraduates landed in Calais – surely not by accident – on 13 July, the eve of the first anniversary of the fall of the Bastille, and witnessed, first-hand, the ecstatic festival of flowers and freedom. On their journey south and east through France, they

> found benevolence and blessedness
> Spread like a fragrance everywhere, when spring
> Hath left no corner of the land untouched.

At one point along their journey they found themselves swallowed up in a throng of celebrating villagers, 'vapoured in the unruliness of joy,' who gave them supper and got them to dance in a circle:

> All hearts were open, every tongue was loud
> With amity and glee; we bore a name

Honoured in France, the name of Englishmen,
And hospitably did they give us hail,
As their forerunners in a glorious course.

Two years later, after his second journey to France, the dewy innocence might have
gone, but not the political idealism. Still fending off family concern about his profession, Wordsworth had gone to London, where he met Joseph Johnson and the
St Paul's Churchyard circle during the height of the Burke–Paine furor. He saw
Burke himself in the Commons:

Stand like an oak whose stag-horn branches start
Out of its leafy brow, the more to awe
The younger brethren of the grove …
Declares the vital power of social ties
Endeared by Custom; and with high disdain,
Exploding upstart Theory, insists
Upon the allegiance to which men are born.

But the retrospective eulogy of Burke as the personification of English nature – the
gnarled and knotty oak defying the worst the revolutionary storm can hurl at him
– is very much the recollection of the older Romantic conservative. Given the
Paine-ite attacks on established authority that Wordsworth was still to write, it seems
very unlikely that at this time he would have felt quite so warmly.

Much later, too, Wordsworth insisted that his second journey to France, in
1791–2, had been just a study-trip to learn the language. But this is where memory
turns disingenuous. At that very moment, France was facing a desperate war
launched by the Emperor of Austria (Marie Antoinette's brother) and the King
of Prussia expressly to uphold the rights of monarchy and to liberate Louis XVI
from the grip of those who had usurped it in the name of the people. It would have
been rather like maintaining that a journey to Russia in 1920 was purely a matter
of studying Pushkin. And Wordsworth did admit to a friend, albeit in rueful sorrow,
that 'I went over to Paris at the time of the Revolution – in 92 or 93 – and was
pretty hot in it.' Hot for revolution he certainly must have been, since all his
contacts in France were fire-breathing expatriate militants like Robert Watt,
Tom Wedgwood and the novelist and poet Helen Maria Williams, to whom, much
smitten, Wordsworth had written a lyrically soppy poem on the spectacle of her
in tears.

Which is not to say that he might not have had, from the beginning of his stay, some reservations. The beautiful account of his mixed feelings while roaming Paris:

> I stared and listened, with a stranger's ears,
> To Hawkers and Haranguers, hubbub wild!
> And hissing Factionists with ardent eyes,
> In knots, or pairs, or single …

has the undoubted ring of truth.

> Where silent zephyrs sported with the dust
> Of the Bastille, I sate in the open sun,
> And from the rubbish gathered up a stone,
> And pocketed the relic, in the guise
> Of an enthusiast; yet in honest truth,
> I looked for something that I could not find,
> Affecting more emotion than I felt.

Failing to find his friends in Orléans, as they had arranged, Wordsworth made his way down the Loire to Blois, now turned into a garrison town in the expectation that war, both foreign and civil, was not far away. But the war that broke out was in Wordsworth's own heart and mind. Although he 'became a patriot, and my heart was all/Given to the people' in Blois, his allegiances were torn by the fiercest emotions he had yet experienced, of both love and friendship. His love affair was the purest Rousseau melodrama, forbidden passion between tutor and pupil, but this time with the sex roles of *La Nouvelle Héloïse* reversed. His teacher was Annette Vallon, daughter of a fervently Catholic family who took the lonely young English poet under their wing, gave him all the affection he craved and tried to convert him to their hatred of the revolution. But the friendship that Wordsworth made with a young army officer from the Périgord, Michel Beaupuis, pulled him in precisely the opposite direction. Beaupuis struck Wordsworth as the model of selfless patriotism precisely because he had relinquished his aristocratic pedigree and rank to become a true citizen of the new France of equals, a soldier for liberty.

Beaupuis might also have struck Wordsworth as a kindred spirit because he too was moved, less by high-minded philosophical speculation than by the sight of physical distress. At home in the Lake District he had encountered woebegone old

William Wordsworth, pastel by Henry Edridge, 1805.

soldiers whose rags and tatters moved him inexpressibly, and, walking the streets of London, Wordsworth had been moved by a blind beggar

> who, with upright face,
> Stood, propped against a wall, upon his chest
> Wearing a written paper to explain
> His story, whence he came, and who he was.

In Blois, too, right on cue, nature showed up to teach a lesson when Beaupuis and he chanced

> One day to meet a hunger-bitten girl
> Who crept along fitting her languid gait
> Unto a heifer's motion, by a cord
> Tied to her arm, and picking thus from the lane
> Its sustenance, while the girl with pallid hands
> Was busy knitting ...

' 'Tis against that which we are fighting,' said Beaupuis, and Wordsworth agreed

> That a benignant spirit was abroad
> Which might not be withstood, that poverty
> Abject as this would in a little time
> Be found no more ...
> That legalised exclusion, empty pomp
> Abolished, sensual state and cruel power,
> Whether by edict of the one or few,
> And finally, as sum and crown of all,
> Should see the people having a strong hand
> In framing their own laws, whence better days
> To all mankind.

The dream of a harmonious marriage between liberty and equality turned out, of course, to be a lot harder than shouting the slogan. As the war sliced deeper into France, paranoia replaced euphoria and a republic replaced the monarchy, bloodily, on 10 August 1792, when Parisians stormed the Tuileries, butchered the Swiss guards and imprisoned the king. It was incumbent on anyone harbouring reservations about the Republic, or who had been born into privilege, to demonstrate that they were purer than the pure. Beaupuis predictably went off to die a citizen-soldier's death, one of hundreds of thousands of young men who were to sacrifice themselves for ideals that were being violated daily on the streets of Paris. Wordsworth mourned his fallen republican friend, but in the meantime he had put himself in danger by fathering a baby royalist. Born in December, the girl was given the name of Caroline and registered in Paris as the daughter of a Citoyen Williame Wordwort. He now had a painful decision to make. With war between Britain and the Republic very much on the cards (it was declared in February 1793) he could either stay and care for his mistress and infant daughter, especially now that they were more, not less, likely to need protection from the prying eyes of suspicious authorities; or, like some of the British expatriates, including Watt, who were already beginning to feel the chill, have second thoughts and worry about being cut off from their home, he could take the packet for Dover. Wordsworth chose the latter course, still procrastinating, telling himself he was going to London to raise money for both of his divided allegiances – the British revolutionary cause and his counter-revolutionary lover and their child. But it would be 10 years before he would see Annette and Caroline again.

As he departed, other staunch Friends of Liberty, many of them fellow-diners from 72 St Paul's Churchyard, were still arriving. The publication of the second, even more radical, part of *Rights of Man* in February 1792 had made Tom Paine public enemy number one in the charged atmosphere of bullish Britain. On 21 May he was summoned to answer a charge of seditious libel; but it seems likely that the government eventually became convinced that he would do less damage on the other side of the Channel than as a courtroom martyr, and gave him ample opportunities to escape. In the capital of what, since August, had become the French Republic, One and Indivisible, Paine was given a hero's welcome, made an honorary citizen, elected deputy for Calais to the National Convention and, although he spoke virtually no French, a key member of its constitutional committee. A fraternal 'British Club' (or, more grandly, 'The Association of the Friends of the Rights of Man Meeting in Paris') gathered at White's Hotel in the Passage des Petits-Pères, near the Palais-Royal, and its members, together with assorted American and Irish republicans, busied themselves drafting addresses to the Convention expressing the yearning of the People of Britain for their own liberation from the yoke of despotism and aristocracy. Among their number were the painter George Romney; the young businessman and essayist Thomas Christie; the Scottish poet and former soldier John Oswald, who drilled volunteers for the liberation of Britain; the democrat–aristocrat Lord Edward Fitzgerald, another former soldier, who was planning the same for

Ireland; Helen Maria Williams and her lover, the wealthy businessman John Hurford Stone; and Tom Paine himself. Joining them, about a week after Wordsworth's departure, was Mary Wollstonecraft.

Much had changed for her since her guerrilla attack on the pretensions of Edmund Burke. The surprising fierceness of her criticism had inevitably given her the reputation of an 'amazon' among both friends and enemies. Horace Walpole had been less appreciative, calling her a 'hyena in petticoats.' Tom Paine and Joseph Johnson, however, saw that they had found a gifted and exceptionally tough polemicist; someone who was not going to run away from trouble, even in difficult and dangerous times. It may have been Paine, who was spending time in Paris even before his flight from the law, who suggested she write something on what women should ask of the dawning age of liberty and equality. Paine was close to the social and political philosopher the ex-Marquis de Condorcet, who was one of the very few writers in France to extend his progressive vision of social and political democracy to women.

Whatever or whoever spurred her to it, Mary leaped at the chance to air her own views on the subject. Six weeks of hell-for-leather writing produced *A Vindication of the Rights of Woman*. Perhaps she should have taken six months. But, chaotically organized, digressive and repetitive though the book is, none of those faults obscures or compromises its trenchant bravery, nor the fundamental correctness of its historical analysis of the relations between the sexes. Many of its insights – the conditioning of girls to correspond to male stereotypes of the doll-playing, dress-loving miniature coquette; the surrender of independence of mind and body for the slavery of idolization; the assumption that their anatomy disqualified them from serious thought – have since become commonplaces of the feminist critique of a male-ordered world. But when Mary Wollstonecraft set them out they were still profoundly shocking, even to those who thought themselves on the side of Progress and Liberty.

What may have been especially disconcerting was her choice of arch-villains, namely the sainted Jean-Jacques Rousseau, whom Mary believed (not without reason) had done most damage by restating the traditional *canard* of the unbridgeable, biologically determined difference between the sexes as a modern point of view. It was Rousseau, whose 'ridiculous stories' were 'below contempt' and obviously based on no first-hand knowledge whatsoever, who had perpetuated the fable that all girls were good for was cooking, primping, idle prattle, and who had insisted that their entire education should be shaped around their destiny as wives and mothers. It was Rousseau who had argued that, the more like men they were persuaded to become, the less power they would have over them. 'This is the very point I aim at,'

Mary Godwin (née Wollstonecraft) by John Opie, *c.* 1797.

she wrote. 'I do not wish them to have power over men; but over themselves.' No wonder Rousseau had taken for his companion the 'fool' Thérèse, so 'conveniently humble.' Not being able to raise her to the status of a rational being, he had been determined to lower the rest of the sex to her level. Instead of dooming women to the imprisoning platitudes of their 'delicacy,' Mary declared, they should be given identical educational opportunities; indeed, boys and girls should share the same schools right through their youth so that they could become easily familiar with each other's common humanity and reasoning faculties, and not be segregated either from each other or from their parental home. (Mary detested the idea of boarding schools.)

Rousseau had also been at fault for fetishizing the transports of romantic love, which encouraged marriages to be made (when they were not mere property transactions) with expectations that were doomed to be disappointed since 'Love, considered as an animal appetite, cannot long feed on itself without expiring.' Hard on the heels of that inevitable disenchantment came betrayal, debauchery and bitterness. How much better to educate girls with enough strength of mind that they could become not just an adult doll but a true partner, a *friend*, and with that friendship withstand the inevitable decay of desire. Friendship was, after all, 'the most sublime of all affections, because it is founded on principle, and cemented by time… Were women more rationally educated, could they take a more comprehensive view of things, they would be contented to love but once in their lives, and after marriage calmly let passion subside into friendship – into that tender intimacy, which is the best refuge from care.'

But while Mary was writing these things she was also becoming seriously infatuated with one of Johnson's regulars: the middle-aged, eccentrically voluble Swiss artist Henry Fuseli. Weird and wonderful best describe Fuseli, whose work encompassed neo-classical histories; startling pre-Freudian 'Nightmares' of ash-pale virgins draped over yielding beds, upon whose loins squatted goblin-like succubi; Shakespearean phantasmagoria (Macbeth's witches and Bottom's new head); and, not least, a steady output of pornographic prints and drawings, featuring impractically phallic coiffures – for women. The model for many of these fantasies was Sophia Rawlins, whom Fuseli, hitherto a confirmed bachelor, had married in 1788. The peculiarity, not to mention the compulsiveness, of his erotic obsessions, often notoriously revelled in out loud, ought to have excluded Fuseli as a partner for Mary Wollstonecraft since *A Vindication* singles out sexual desire as the root of corruption in the relations between men and women; the source of romantic self-delusion; the destroyer of reason and friendship. But perhaps Mary saw Fuseli more as a detached analyst than as an accomplice of desire. At any rate, whether from desperation or from principle she flirted with him, offering herself as an intimate companion, a soulmate, rather than as a lover. Fuseli seems to have been disconcerted by her persistence, but in the summer of 1792 the odd foursome of Johnson (very definitely no womanizer), Mary, Fuseli and Sophia planned a six-week trip to France. By the time they got to Dover, Paris was in the grip of the fighting that ended the monarchy. The news was of bloody chaos. The party turned back and, dejected by this anti-climax, Mary became impulsive, knocking on Sophia's door to announce to the understandably astonished young wife that the three of them must establish a house-hold together: 'As I am above deceit, it is right to say that this proposal arises from the sincere affection, which I have for your husband, for I find that I cannot live without the satisfaction of seeing and conversing with him daily.' She had no claims on him as a husband – those she would generously cede to Sophia – but mentally they had to be together. Sophia's horrified reaction was to slam the door after forbidding Mary ever to cross the threshold again.

Baffled, wounded and miserable, Mary Wollstonecraft decided to make the trip to France by herself. Although she made light of the risks, describing it as a romantic adventure ('I am still a Spinster on the wing. At Paris, indeed, I might take a husband for the time being, and get divorced when my truant heart longed again to nestle with its old friends'), she knew that even in ordinary times this would have been a brave, not to say foolhardy, journey. But these were extraordinary times. By early December 1792, when Mary finally crossed the Channel, the Revolution was enter-ing its beleaguered and paranoid phase. It had escaped a Prussian occupation of Paris only by the skin of its teeth and the mobilization, thanks to the furious rhetoric of one of the Jacobin leaders, Georges Danton, of the entire Republic's human and material resources. In the knife-edge climate of elation and terror, today's heroes could be tomorrow's traitors; those who showed themselves most demonstrative in their loyalty to the Republic might find their professions of revolutionary ardour taken as a smokescreen for espionage. The position of the foreign communities in Paris was becoming especially precarious. Unless they showed themselves passionate enthusiasts for the war of national defence and liberation, more republican than the republicans, they were vulnerable to charges of being a 'fifth column.' It was this jumpy atmosphere that Wordsworth had decided to escape and in which Mary now found herself. The White's Hotel gang all helped to soften the shock. But Mary struggled with spoken French, discovering, like so many, that the thoughtful transla-tions she had made in England had been no preparation for making one's way through the streets of Paris. She lodged with Aline Fillietaz, the newly married daughter of a schoolmistress acquaintance from London. The Fillietaz house was on the rue Melée in the Marais, which put it not only in the heart of one of the most militant revolutionary districts of the city, seething with clubs and pikes, but also directly along a main route from revolutionary prisons to one of the places of execution.

So, whether she wanted it or not, Mary had a ringside view of the drama of mass death and retribution. A few weeks after her arrival she saw Louis XVI being taken to his trial and, astonished at the dignity of his composure, confessed to Joseph Johnson that 'I can scarcely tell you why, but an association of ideas made the tears flow insensibly from my eyes.' But the letter shook with trepidation.

> Nay, do not smile, but pity me; for, once or twice, lifting my eyes from the paper, I have seen eyes glare through a glass-door opposite my chair, and bloody hands shook at me. Not the distant sound of a footstep can I hear ... I wish I had even kept the cat with me! – I want to see something alive; death in so many frightful shapes has taken hold of my fancy. – I am going to bed – and for the first time in my life, I cannot put out the candle.

This was not the revolution, nor the life, Mary had expected. By the spring of 1793, Britain and France were at war with each other. French military reverses in the Netherlands and the defection of generals prompted the inevitable accusations of betrayals from within. The apparatus of summary 'revolutionary' justice was established. The fatal rhythm of denunciations, arrests and beheadings began. And it was precisely those republican politicians with whom the White's Hotel crowd had the closest relations – Condorcet and the moderate group known as the Girondins, many of whom had voted against condemning Louis XVI to death – who were now identified by the Jacobin revolutionary government as false patriots, enemies in fact to the *patrie*. By extension the British – whether they liked it or not, natives of an enemy country – were now, starting with Tom Paine, deeply suspect.

The most famous vote cast against the execution of the king was indeed Paine's, and many of those who wanted clemency actually invoked Paine as an example since, as he had said himself, his republican credentials were impeccable. Nonetheless Paine – who expressed the wish that the French Republic would abolish the death penalty altogether, perhaps the summit of his unrealistic optimism – argued eloquently that Louis 'considered as an individual' (rather than an institution) 'was beneath the notice' of the Republic; and that the Revolution owed compassion to its enemies as much as to its friends. To the Jacobins this was so outrageous an

Top: *Death of Louis Capet, 21 January 1793*, engraving of the execution of Louis XVI by Faucher-Gudin, *c.* 1793.
Above: *William Pitt Addressing the House of Commons on the French Declaration of War, 1793*, by Karl Anton Hickel, *c.* 1793. Pitt, standing on the right of the Speaker, addresses the Commons from the government side. Facing him on the opposition front bench are Charles Fox (in the black hat), sitting alongside Lord Thomas Erskine (with raised hand) and Richard Sheridan (in the buff jacket).

apostasy that their most militant spokesman, Jean-Paul Marat, shouted that the inter-
preter must be mistranslating Paine's words. When they were indeed confirmed, he
declared that since Paine was 'a Quaker' and thus opposed to the death penalty on
principle (his parentage was indeed Quaker), he ought not to be allowed to vote.

Paine voted anyway, but after the revolutionary government and the apparatus
of the Terror was established in the summer of 1793, Paine found himself in the
unusual position of being demonized as an enemy of the state in both monarchist
Britain and republican France! The British Club had broken up shortly after the
king's trial, but once its French patrons and friends had been purged from the
National Convention, imprisoned, put on trial and executed, it seemed only a matter
of time before the Britons would share their fate. One of Paine's fellow-lodgers,
William Johnson, became so unhinged at the prospect that he attempted to commit
suicide on the staircase of their hotel, stabbing himself in the chest and rolling operatically down the steps. After the British navy took Toulon in late August, occupying the naval base and town, any kind of association with Britain was a deadly
liability. Paine was arrested, along with Helen Maria Williams and some other
members of the club, and incarcerated in the Luxembourg, once a royal palace. He
missed his date with the guillotine only by a fantastic stroke of luck. Cell doors were
marked to indicate the intended victims of the next day's executions. His were by
accident left open. In haste the mark was made on the inside and, when the doors
were later slammed shut, became invisible. Or so Paine's version of the story goes.

Just as bad for Mary, the *bête noire* of *A Vindication* – Jean-Jacques himself – was
everywhere. The image of the patron saint of the Republic of Virtue appeared on
placards, on drinking glasses and on patriotic pamphlets. The women's clubs that had
agitated for their inclusion in the franchise and for legal rights were shut down by
the Jacobins and their leaders arrested or beaten up on the streets if they opened
their mouths. The duties of women to the Fatherland were exactly as Rousseau had
prescribed: indoctrination in the arts of 'tenderness'; a solace for citizen–soldiers,
breast-feeders for the *enfants de la patrie*.

Mary had no choice but to play by the rules of the enemy; to find some sort
of refuge from fear and insecurity. It materialized in the good-looking shape of the
American revolutionary soldier and author, Gilbert Imlay. Imlay was now in the
business of selling revolutionary happiness, or more specifically the real estate on
which happiness could be planted in farming settlements and small towns. His
Topographical Description of the Western Territory of North America (1792) was, like Imlay
himself, an attractive thing of many parts: travelogue, land survey and commercial
promotional literature. He certainly understood the power of romance and something

drew him towards the alternately exuberant and insecure Mary Wollstonecraft. A love affair began, which quickly turned serious. As 'Mrs Imlay,' Mary's status as an American citizeness protected her from the hostility and suspicion directed at the British, subjects of a king with whom the Republic was at war. By June she was settled in a cottage at Neuilly on the western outskirts of the city, tending a garden and cooing over the *soupers à deux* she was sharing with Imlay. The author of *A Vindication*, who had made such a powerful case against the delusory and destructive nature of romantic passion, was now in the rhapsodic throes of it. Sensing, already in August, Imlay's reservations about being smothered in so much emotional intensity, she wrote to him with the note of imploring desperation that she had despised in sentimental novels: 'Yes I will be good, that I may deserve to be happy; and whilst you love me, I cannot again fall into the miserable state, which rendered life a burden almost too heavy to be borne.' Mary Wollstonecraft had become a dependent.

By January 1794 she was pregnant, and became anxious and weepy whenever Imlay disappeared on business trips. The more clinging she became, the more regularly he disappeared, leaving her overwhelmed by despondency at the ebbing of 'tenderness.' Only the prospect of the baby pulled her out of this morbid brooding. Determined to go through a modern pregnancy, she made sure she had regular exercise and and when her girl, named Fanny, was born in May, Mary horrified the midwife by getting up from her bed the next day, refusing the purification ritual of covering herself in ashes, and resuming, almost immediately, her routine of country walks. Needless to say, she nursed Fanny herself – even though, as she wrote frankly to Ruth Barlow, her 'inundations of milk' were sometimes inconvenient. But Imlay was away a lot, and when he wasn't he fell sick. And the little life added to hers had given Mary a fresh aversion to the tide of death running through France. 'My blood runs cold and I sicken at the thought of a Revolution which costs so much blood and bitter tears.'

With the fall of Robespierre and his execution in reaction to the Jacobin Terror, there was a little more breathing room. Tom Paine and the rest emerged from prison, permanently changed by their ordeal. Now that travel around the country was easier, Imlay took advantage of it to see to his shipping business in Normandy. Swooping up and down between love-sick euphoria and suicidal gloom, Mary followed him to Le Havre with the baby only to find him crossing the Channel repeatedly. Trying to calm her, Imlay wrote from London that that she should perhaps come home. Despite writing that 'England is a country which has not merely lost all charms for me, but for which I feel a repugnance' she made the crossing, only to have her worst fears confirmed. Imlay would not turn himself into a husband and father, not least because he had a new love interest. Mary took an overdose of laudanum. Although shocked by the attempted suicide, Imlay was not shocked enough to want to resume their old life. Instead, he came up with the perverse plan of distracting her by sending her off to Norway on business to track down a missing shipment of silver.

Of all the roles she chose to assume in her wandering life, Mary Wollstonecraft, commercial investigator, was the oddest. But off she went with little Fanny and a maid as her only companions, making her way through Sweden and Norway, trying, and not surprisingly failing, to track down her feckless partner's cargo of bullion. In an inn built of logs, painted red and yellow and overlooking the dark sea, Mary, who had been so brutally manhandled by politics and passion, did at last find something akin to a state of grace in nature. She swam, sat on the rocks in the windy northern sunlight and jotted in a journal. In the 'Letters' she planned to publish as a meditation on the times, she wrote that the Norwegian fishermen were indeed the children of nature she had been searching for: instinctively, artlessly free, without the need of ranting philosophy to instruct them in their liberation.

The restoration of her sanity, however, was only temporary. Returning to London, she discovered that Imlay's reluctance to set up house did not extend to establishing a ménage with an actress, his new mistress. One night in October 1795 she went out in a torrential rainstorm, meaning to drown herself. Battersea Bridge, chosen for the jump, proved somehow disconcertingly public, so she paid a boatman to row her up-river to Putney. She walked up and down for half an hour to make sure her dress was saturated enough to sink her, then paid her halfpenny toll to get on the bridge, climbed on to the railing and jumped. 'Let my wrongs sleep with me!' she had written in the suicide note addressed to Imlay. 'When you receive this, my burning head will be cold … I shall plunge into the Thames where there is the least chance of my being snatched from the death I seek.'

But she hadn't reckoned with the ubiquitousness of modern philanthropy. The Royal Humane Society had been set up, subsidized by public money, specifically to reward boatmen who pulled would-be suicides from the river. The Thames was full of rowers just waiting for a jumper. Mary was duly rescued and taken to the Duke's Head tavern in Fulham to recover. Mortified and wretched, she lost no time proposing to Imlay that they live together in a *ménage à trois*, so that at least their daughter would know her father. For a moment Imlay wondered, and brought Mary to see their house before (in all likelihood) the actress put her foot down.

Mary Wollstonecraft was 37 and seemed to have lost everything except her child: her faith in the liberating humanity of revolution; in a marriage based on friendship rather than passion; in the possibility of a truly independent woman's life. As for the benevolence of nature, it must have seemed a cruel joke. A letter to Fuseli asking for her letters back became a cry of pain: 'I am alone. The injustice, without alluding to hopes blasted in the bud, which I have endured, wounding my bosom, have set my thoughts adrift into an ocean of painful conjectures. I ask impatiently what – and where is truth? I have been treated brutally; but I daily labour to remember that I still have the duty of a mother to fulfil.'

Her friends, especially the long-suffering Johnson, who published Mary's *Letters Written During a Short Residence in Sweden, Norway and Denmark* (1794–5), did what they could to help. But then they had other things on their minds than the personal fate of Mary Wollstonecraft. The same week that she jumped into the Thames saw a huge demonstration of at least 100,000 people against Pitt, the war with the French and 'famine.' Britain seemed closer than it had ever been to revolution.

Through the spring of 1794 the British government had been bringing prosecutions against those whom it deemed to be the writers, publishers and purveyors of seditious literature. Its object was to employ the usefully vague medieval charge of 'compassing the death of the king' to make into an act of outright treason publications and discussions on the concept of a republic or even on manhood suffrage (for how would *that* be accomplished, one prosecutor argued, without the overthrow of the lawful constitution?). Testimony given by a government witness (later discredited as a drunk and a perjurer) that Thomas Walker, the Manchester radical, had been heard to say 'Damn the King' was the kind of thing taken seriously as evidence. In almost all the cases the accused were defended by Thomas Erskine, one of the genuine champions of British freedom, whose name deserves to be better known. Erskine put his fortune and reputation on the line to insist on the principle that utterance or publication alone (without any evidence of a conspiracy to commit 'tumult' much less regicide) could not be incriminating, and especially not retroactively after the government established ever broader categories of sedition and treason. In May 1794 Thomas Hardy, John Thelwall, John Horne Tooke and 11 other members of the London Corresponding Society were arrested. The right of habeas corpus (no imprisonment without trial) was suspended the same month, and by late in the year 2000 people were being held without due process. A mass meeting at Chalk Farm just north of London declared that Britain had 'lost its liberties.'

Thelwall, Hardy, Horne Tooke and the rest – perhaps in keeping with the medievalism of the charges – were incarcerated in the Tower of London. Traumatized by Hardy's imprisonment, fearful that he would pay with his life for the 'treason,' his wife miscarried and died. Thelwall was kept in solitary confinement for five months before being taken to the 'dead hole' of Newgate, which, deprived of almost all light and air, was even worse. On 25 October the prisoners were formally arraigned for 'conspiring to overthrow the government and perpetrate the king's death.' Three days later the first trial, that of Thomas Hardy, opened. Jostling crowds surrounded the Old Bailey. They weren't there to cheer on the prosecution. For nine hours the Attorney-General, Sir John Scott, laboured to stitch together shreds of circumstantial evidence into a treasonable conspiracy to depose and kill the king. 'Nine hours!' shouted the fat ex-Lord Chancellor Thurlow when he heard. 'Then there is no treason, by God!' And the government's case did indeed rest almost entirely on analogies with France in respect, for example, of what had been meant by a 'Convention.'

At the end of the week's proceedings Erskine responded for the defence with a mere seven-hour speech. Echoing a pamphlet published by William Godwin, he insisted that whatever had been said (by Hardy, for example – and he had said a lot) had to be proved to be an actual plot to kill the king in person, not just complaints about parliament or even the monarchy as an institution, since that had still been protected as free political debate. By such unconscionably elastic definitions of treason Hardy was being tried for his life on account of activities that were undoubtedly peaceful and lawful. 'I hope,' said Erskine, brilliantly throwing back at the prosecutors the imputation of disloyalty, 'never to hear it repeated in any court of justice that peacefully to convene the people on the subject of their own privileges, can lead to the destruction of the king; they are the king's worst enemies who use such language.' At the end of his heroic oration he croaked to the jury: 'I am sinking under fatigue and weakness,' and then indeed sank. Appreciative of great theatre, the jury applauded. Hardy was acquitted and spoke to the roaring crowds outside: 'My fellow countrymen, I return you my thanks.' The crowd untethered the horses from the carriages of the accused and pulled them down the Strand, past the Palace of Westminster and along Pall Mall. When the subsequent trial of Horne Tooke opened on 17 November and that of Thelwall on 1 December, the verdicts seemed hardly in doubt before they got under way, although Horne Tooke played it safe and pleaded – disloyally but not incorrectly – that he had been a moderate compared to other indicted firebrands. Thelwall had prepared not so much a defence as a manifesto of British Rights of Nature and was about to give it his oratorical all until Erskine buttoned his lip. Miffed at the loss of an opportunity to address posterity he published it in 1796.

The bitter winter of 1794–5 only made Pitt's government more feverishly defensive. The war was going badly. French armies occupied first the Austrian

Netherlands; then the Rhineland and finally the Dutch Republic, where an old ally, the Stadholder William V, was deposed in favour of a new revolutionary Batavian Republic. Harvests were disastrous, sending the price of wheat rocketing by 75 per cent. At the same time an export slump caused lay-offs in the textile industry. In London, the population responded with violent action. The steam-powered Great Albion Flour Mill was attacked by rioters. In the summer mass meetings were held at St George's Field. On 28 October 1795 another – said by the London Corresponding Society to be to 200,000 strong, although others put it at between 40,000 and 100,000 – assembled in a field by the Copenhagen House tavern in Islington to hear the 22-year-old Irishman John Binns attack the war and denounce the Pitt government. The chant was 'Peace! Bread! No Pitt! Down with George.'

On the following day the coach taking George III to open parliament was mobbed in the Mall by an angry crowd, some of them holding bread loaves wrapped in black crepe and shouting, 'No war, no famine!' In Parliament Street the coach was pelted with mud and stones, smashing its windows. At some point on the journey a projectile made a small hole that the king thought had been caused by a bullet. When he reached the House of Lords he is said to have stammered, 'My Lords, I … I … I have been shot at.' His route back to St James's Palace was no friendlier, with more missiles and broken windows. The state coach was abandoned and torn to pieces when spotted in Pall Mall; one of the royal grooms fell under its wheels, breaking his thighs and dying of the injuries. When the king tried to reach Buckingham House in a private coach, he was recognized (no one else, after all, looked like George III). The coach ground to a halt in the mêlée, and it was said that someone opened a door and attempted to drag the king from it. Only the appearance of the Horse Guards riding to the rescue saved the situation from becoming even uglier. The threat to lay hands on the king was taken especially seriously, since the previous year there had been a 'pop-gun plot' (probably a fiction invented by spies) to fire a poisoned dart at him from a custom-designed air-gun. Stories were also rife of other plots for a revolutionary coup, to take place simultaneously in London, Dublin and Edinburgh, in which the magistracy and judges would be locked up, aristocrats put under house arrest and parliament liquidated.

The mobbing of the royal coach was, of course, a godsend to Pitt's government, so much so that suspicious radicals speculated Pitt and the Home Secretary, the Duke of Portland, might have orchestrated it themselves (although their coaches were roughly treated as well). Riding the tidal wave of loyal addresses of indignation and loyalist passion, in December Pitt introduced two bills for the protection and policing

Top: *William Godwin* by James Northcote, 1802.
Above: *Thomas Holcroft and William Godwin at the Treason Trials of 1794*, pencil drawing by Thomas Lawrence, 1794.

of the realm. The first made meetings of more than 50 people illegal. If an assembly refused to disperse when ordered, those present could be charged with a capital crime. The second enlarged the scope of sedition still more broadly to encompass any advocacy of changes to the government, other than by acts of parliament. In other words: no pamphlets, no petitions, no meetings, no reform. Wordsworth, who on returning to England had published in 1793, in the form of a letter to the Bishop of Llandaff, a ferociously Paine-ite assault on the hereditary principle, would now have to keep his peace. Up in Newcastle Thomas Bewick – no Paine-ite revolutionary democrat – gritted his teeth. Later he remembered this as a scoundrelly time when 'Knaves and their abettors appeared to predominate in the land; and they carried their subserviency to such a length that I think, if Mr Pitt had proposed to make a law to transport all men who had pug noses, and to hang all men above 60 years of age, these persons … would have advocated it as a brilliant thought and a wise measure.'

Not surprisingly, the combination of propaganda, gang intimidation, genuinely patriotic volunteer militias, censorship, political spying and summary arrests succeeded in stopping the momentum of democratic agitation. Critics and reformers like William Godwin who had come to the aid of the accused in the treason trials now withdrew from direct political action, and tried to reflect on social utopias away from the furor. In any case, Godwin had come to mistrust any proposals that made the state the agency of betterment. His *Enquiry Concerning Political Justice* (1793) was the perfect tract for the disillusioned, since it argued that the only obligation for reasoning individuals was the realization of their own freedom and happiness. Any institutions that got in the way needed removing; so no religion, no system of government, no criminal law (it was, Godwin believed, hypocritical for societies to punish crimes it had generated itself), no systematic education, no accumulation of property beyond what was required to satisfy individual needs, and especially no marriage, an institution that held couples hostage to their transient passions.

That last sentiment was perhaps the only opinion that he held in common with Mary Wollstonecraft. He remembered her, not particularly warmly, as the person who wouldn't shut up when he had wanted to listen to Tom Paine at one of the Johnson dinners. But when Godwin read the Scandinavian letters he declared that 'If ever there was a book calculated to make a man in love with its author, this appears to me to be the book.' Love and Mr Godwin, short, earnest, pedantic, almost inhumanly cerebral, had not kept close company. Yet women – actresses, writers whom he called 'the Fairs,' some of them hot with romance – set their cap at him.

But it was Mary who melted his chilly soul. And he in turn made her a more reflective, quieter person. After all the miseries she had inflicted on herself through the years of torment with Imlay, Godwin's mixture of coolness and clumsiness seemed positively winning. She relaxed in the growing certainty of his feeling, and the woman who had gone on record as mistrustful of sex now took shameless pleasure in initiating Godwin, reassuring his anxieties: 'If the felicity of last night has had the same effect on your health as on my countenance, you have no cause to lament your failure of *resolution*: for I have seldom seen so much live fire running about my features as this morning when recollections – very dear, called forth the blush of pleasure, as I adjusted my hair.'

Mary became pregnant. In March 1797 William Godwin, the sworn enemy of marriage and churches, got married to 'Mrs Imlay' (her first union being considered merely a republican civic convenience and thus not binding) at St Pancras Church. Mary was satisfied that she had not 'clogged my soul by promising obedience,' and the two of them let it be known that they would not continuously cohabit, but continue to respect each other's independence and see others of the opposite sex, sharing lodgings some of the time but keeping their own respective places. It was bravely said. But as Mary's belly grew, Godwin found himself unaccountably enjoying the small pleasures of domesticity and companionship. Theirs was growing into exactly the kind of intimate conjugal friendship that Mary – without ever having experienced anything like it – had prescribed as the formula for enduring married happiness.

Which is what made the end so unbearably sad. When the time came for her labour, on 30 August, she called a local midwife. But after the baby, another girl (the future author of *Frankenstein*), was born, the placenta failed to descend down the birth canal, threatening sepsis. A physician, hurriedly summoned from Westminster Hospital did what he could, but the placenta ruptured in fragments as Mary lay haemorrhaging in agony.

Eventually the bleeding stopped. Mary was strong enough to tell Godwin that she would never have survived had she not been determined to continue sharing her life with him. The next day she felt much better and was happy to have her old, best mentor, Joseph Johnson, visit. The following day she seemed better still and Godwin thought it was safe enough for him to take a walk. When he got back he found her convulsed with shivering fits and obviously running a high fever. She never got better. A week later, on 10 September 1797, Mary Wollstonecraft died of septicaemia.

She was 38. Godwin, the supreme rationalist, was distraught. He wrote to a friend, 'My wife is now dead ... I firmly believe that there does not exist her equal in the world. I know from experience we were formed to make each other happy. I have not the least expectation that I can now ever know happiness again.' It was the best and most unlikely epitaph: that she had been the bearer of happiness to the man who had declared war on marriage. Through Mary, the thinker had learned to feel. Through Godwin, the creature of feeling had recovered her power of thought. Wollstonecraft is properly remembered as the founder of modern feminism; for making a statement, still powerful in its clarity, that the whole nature of women was not to be confused with their biology. But nature, biology, had killed her.

On 17 October 1797, the Austrian Empire gritted its teeth and made its peace at the Italian town of Campo Formio with a 28-year-old Corsican called Bonaparte, whom no one (in Vienna at any rate) had heard of a few years before. Napoleon did so without waiting for permission from his civilian masters in the Directory. But since much of Italy, including some of the greatest cities and richest territories, now passed either into French control or under its influence, the Directors were hardly likely to repudiate their military prodigy. The ending of the war with Austria now allowed France to redeploy a large number of troops to a different theatre and its one remaining enemy. Within a month more than 100,000 of them were camped between Rouen – William the Conqueror's old capital – and the Channel coast. The point of the massive troop concentration was not lost on Pitt's government. Suddenly the world seemed a more dangerous place.

Since the war with the French Republic had begun in 1793 it had been an axiom in Westminster that, sooner or later, the revolutionary origins of that state would prove its military ruin; that an army built from rabble would, after an initial burst of self-deluded energy, collapse in on itself. The Terror's habit of guillotining its own generals, should they be careless enough to lose the odd battle, only confirmed this diagnois. But with Bonaparte's Italian campaign, so shocking in its speed and completeness, and with the French tightening their grip on a whole swathe of continental territory from the Netherlands down through the Rhineland, threatening even the Swiss cantons, it seemed that this bandit state had done the unthinkable and actually created a formidable fighting machine. Its troops did not run away. It seemed to manufacture more and more guns; and it obviously knew how to transform conquest into workable military assets, taking money, horses, wagons and conscripts as it rolled along. James Gillray might be starting to draw caricatures literally belittling this Bonaparte as a scrawny scarecrow wearing plumed hats a size too big. But William Pitt and his intelligent, inexhaustible secretary of war, the Scot Henry Dundas, knew he was no joke. Tom Paine, for one, believed he would be the long-awaited Liberator of Britain; urging him to prepare a fleet of 1000 gunboats,

Top: *A Stoppage to a Stride over the Globe*, 1803, lithograph, the English School, caricaturing Napoleon's dramatic advance across Europe.
Above: *The Plum Pudding in Danger*, 1805, lithograph by James Gillray, satirizing the greedy designs of Napoleon and William Pitt, who carve up the globe between them.
Opposite: The French Revolutionary and Napoleonic Wars between England and France, 1793–1815.

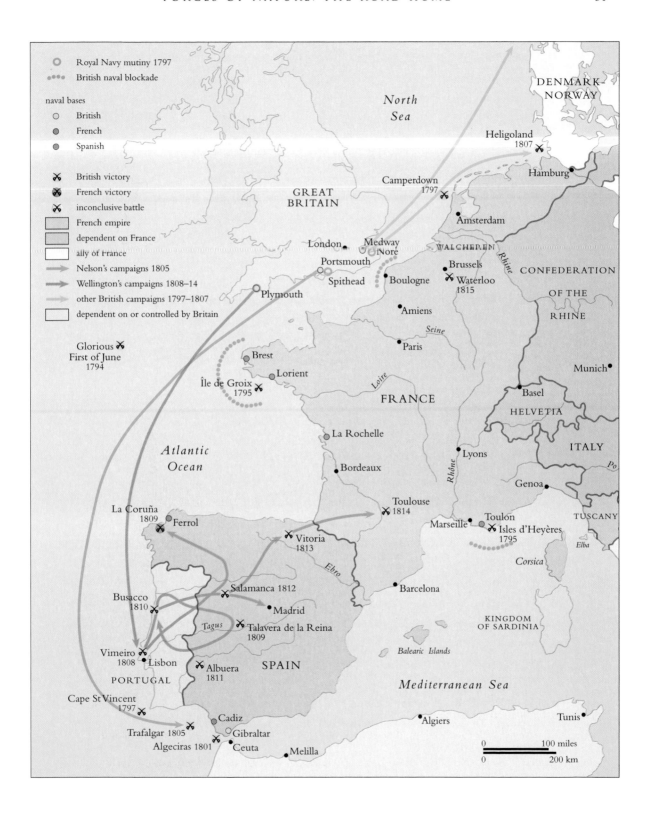

Royal Navy mutiny 1797

British naval blockade

naval bases
- British
- French
- Spanish

British victory

French victory

inconclusive battle

French empire

dependent on France

ally of France

Nelson's campaigns 1805

Wellington's campaigns 1808–14

other British campaigns 1797–1807

dependent on or controlled by Britain

North Sea

DENMARK-NORWAY

Heligoland 1807

Hamburg

GREAT BRITAIN

Camperdown 1797

Amsterdam

London

Medway Nore

WALCHEREN

Brussels

Rhine

CONFEDERATION

Portsmouth

Spithead

Boulogne

Waterloo 1815

OF THE

Plymouth

Amiens

RHINE

Seine

Paris

Glorious First of June 1794

Brest

Munich

Lorient

Île de Groix 1795

Loire

FRANCE

Basel

HELVETIA

La Rochelle

ITALY

Atlantic Ocean

Bordeaux

Rhône

Lyons

Po

Genoa

TUSCANY

La Coruña 1809

Ferrol

Toulouse 1814

Toulon

Marseille

Isles d'Heyères 1795

Elba

Vitoria 1813

Corsica

Ebro

Salamanca 1812

Barcelona

Busacco 1810

Madrid

KINGDOM OF SARDINIA

Tagus

Talavera de la Reina 1809

Vimeiro 1808

Lisbon

Albuera 1811

SPAIN

Balearic Islands

Mediterranean Sea

PORTUGAL

Cape St Vincent 1797

Cadiz

Algiers

Tunis

Trafalgar 1805

Gibraltar

Algeciras 1801

Ceuta

Melilla

0   100 miles

0   200 km

he did his best to persuade the future Emperor that in the event of an invasion there would be a huge uprising, for 'the mass of the people are friends to liberty.' Initially, at any rate, Bonaparte was impressed enough with Paine to appoint him leader of a provisional English Revolutionary Government to travel with the invasion fleet when the order was given to sail. But the order never came, Bonaparte turning his attention instead to Egypt.

The prospect of Paine's return was not, however, high on the list of the British government's concerns. Even before the magnitude of Bonaparte's victories in Italy had sunk in, something happened in the spring of 1797 that did indeed seem to turn the world upside down: mutiny in the Royal Navy. The base at Spithead in the Solent, off Portsmouth, had been the first to go; then the Nore in the Thames Estuary. At one point the mutineers managed to blockade the Thames itself. Their demands were pay and the cashiering of some officers, not any kind of radical agenda. But the commonplace was that a third of the navy's 114,000 manpower was Irish, and since Ireland had apparently become a breeding ground for revolutionaries and known agents of the French, the mutinies suddenly took on the aspect of a conspiracy. In fact, the 'Irish third' was a myth. Irish sailors – often the victims of impressment – numbered no more than 15,000. But even this was enough to scare the Lords of the Admiralty, who had had a frighteningly narrow escape the previous December. A fleet of 43 French ships and 15,000 troops, commanded by the general thought to be the most dangerous of all, Louis-Lazare Hoche, and the Irish republican Theobald Wolfe Tone, had been prevented by foul weather from making a landing at Bantry Bay on the southwest tip of County Cork.

Ireland was, as always, the swinging back door to Britain. Had Hoche managed to land his troops, they would have had an immediate numerical superiority over the defending British garrison of at least six to one. For a country known to be so vulnerable it was, as Wolfe Tone had correctly pointed out to the Directors in Paris, complacently defended. There were perhaps only about 13,000 regular British troops stationed there, who in wartime might be reinforced by another 60,000 militia. And even these estimates of the defence were based on the loyal turn-out of the Volunteer movement during the American war; since then, especially in the last few years, the political situation in Ireland had drastically changed.

If it had changed for the worse, moreover, it was largely the fault of Pitt's own mishandling of the situation; his refusal to act on his own intelligent instincts. Since the creation of an Irish parliament in 1782, an articulate, energetic political class – both Catholic and Protestant – had been able to air its grievances against the narrow ascendancy of the Protestant oligarchy who ruled from Dublin Castle. The American lesson of the risks of imposing taxation without representation seemed even more pertinent in Belfast than in Boston. A meaningful degree of political devolution and electoral reform – not least the enfranchisement of the Catholic majority – was urged. But for all the flamboyant rhetoric of the lawyer Henry Grattan, the leader of this movement, there was no thought of a revolutionary break-away. A freer Ireland was supposed to be a more, not a less, loyal Ireland – and the hope was that George III would in fact be less, not more, of an absentee. When the French Revolution broke out, Pitt's first thought was that the natural conservatism of Irish Catholics could be used to tie the Irish reform movement closer to Britain and make sure they did not enter some sort of unholy alliance with the non-conformist Dissenter radicals, especially in Belfast. The Dissenters' sympathy for the Revolution was only too clear, not least from their jubilant celebration of the anniversary of the fall of the Bastille. But the precondition of a rapprochement between the Catholics and the British government was, obviously, their emancipation, or at the very least the relief of their legal and civic disabilities, limiting their rights to vote and hold political office.

It was in the mid-1790s, then, that a scenario to be repeated time and again over the next two centuries miserably played itself out. The prospect of a British government selling out the Protestant ascendancy threatened a backlash to the point of a complete breakdown of the Dublin Castle system of government. And the leaders of the ascendancy were able to use the generalized social panic spread by the Revolution – and apparently confirmed in the violent acts of armed militias, such as the Catholic 'Defenders' and the Protestant Peep o' Day Boys, in Irish country towns and villages – to persuade Pitt that this was no time to be toying with liberalism. In 1795 a new Whig viceroy of Ireland, Earl Fitzwilliam, came to the point rather more abruptly than Pitt cared for, peremptorily dismissing a number of high officers of the Castle and making known his plans for a sweeping emancipation of the Catholics that would give them equal rights with Protestants. He was recalled after only seven weeks in office.

The removal of Fitzwilliam – however clumsy his tactics – was a true turning point in the swift downhill ride of Irish politics towards sectarian misery, terror and war. For it finally disabused the 'United Irishmen' – an organization formed in 1791 with many Protestant as well as Catholic members – of any remaining optimism that fundamental justice and reform would be gained from continued collaboration with the British government. Increasingly, as wartime conditions began to pinch, the question of precisely what quarrel Ireland had with *France* became voiced. Young Irish republicans like Lord Edward Fitzgerald (the cousin of Charles James Fox) and

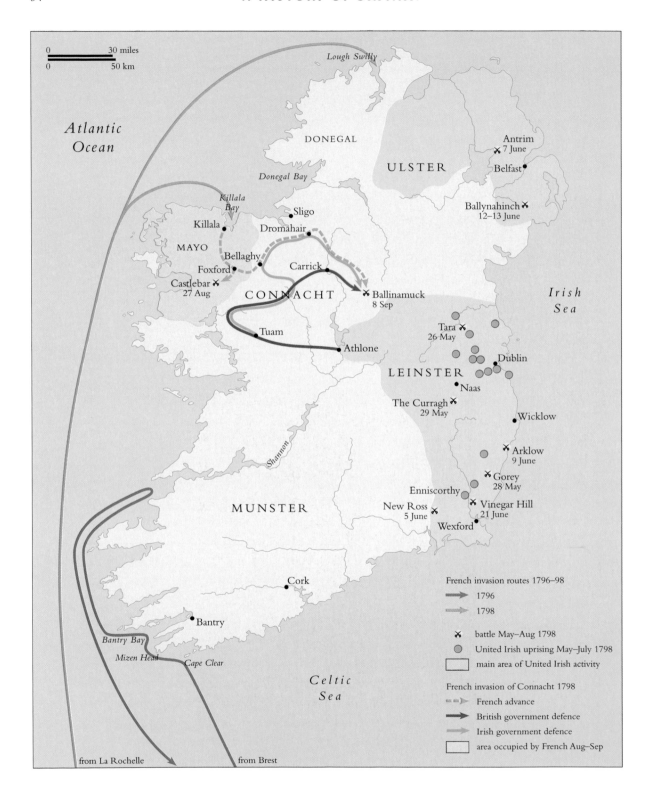

0   30 miles
0   50 km

*Atlantic
Ocean*

Lough Swilly

DONEGAL

ULSTER

Antrim
✗ 7 June

Belfast ●

Donegal Bay

Ballynahinch ✗
12–13 June

*Killala
Bay*

● Sligo

Killala ●   Dromahair ●

MAYO   Bellaghy ●

Foxford ●   Carrick ●

Castlebar ✗
27 Aug   CONNACHT   ✗ Ballinamuck
8 Sep

*Irish
Sea*

Tara ✗
26 May

Tuam ●

● Athlone

Dublin ●

LEINSTER

Naas ●

The Curragh ✗
29 May

Wicklow ●

Shannon

✗ Arklow
9 June

✗ Gorey
28 May

Enniscorthy ●
New Ross ✗
5 June

✗ Vinegar Hill
21 June

Wexford ●

MUNSTER

Cork ●

French invasion routes 1796–98
→ 1796
→ 1798

✗ battle May–Aug 1798
● United Irish uprising May–July 1798
▢ main area of United Irish activity

French invasion of Connacht 1798
⇢ French advance
→ British government defence
→ Irish government defence
▢ area occupied by French Aug–Sep

Bantry ●

Bantry Bay

Mizen Head   *Cape Clear*

*Celtic
Sea*

from La Rochelle   from Brest

Top: *Queen's Own Royal Dublin Militia Going into Action at Vinegar Hill, the Light Company Advancing and Firing Covering the Band*, engraving, 1798.
Above: *Theobald Wolfe Tone*, in French uniform, engraved by T. W. Huffam, *c.* 1785.
Opposite: The Irish Rebellion, 1798.

Arthur O'Connor had been in Paris invoking a connection between the two causes that went back to 1689, attempting to persuade the French government to extend its 'liberation' strategy of revolutionary assistance to their own country. But the conversion of Wolfe Tone, the Protestant secretary of the Catholic Committee, from a mainstream constitutional reformer into a full-fledged republican nationalist, prepared to wear the uniform of a French general, was symptomatic of the line Irish politicians were now prepared to cross to realize their dream of national self-government. Once, not so long ago, Tone had hoped to work *with* the British government to move towards autonomy. But after that government broke up the United Irishmen (forcing its members into Britain itself, to make contact with Scots and English revolutionary radicals), and following Fitzwilliam's removal, Tone's public utterances defined the enemy oppressor and conqueror as 'England.'

A deteriorating military situation in Europe and a consciousness of their limited resources in Ireland meant that Dublin Castle could not afford to dispense with the help of Protestant militia – like the Orange Order, founded in 1795 – to counter Defenderism, and thus instantly aggravated the situation. By the beginning of 1798, then, the tragic spectacle of modern Irish history was already on view: rival, armed sectarian irregulars committing mutual atrocities against the backdrop of an embattled Britain fighting to close its own back door against invasion.

While the French army was encamped on the Normandy coast, Irish agents had been sent to England and Scotland to sound out the possibility of a domestic uprising in the event of an invasion. They returned deeply pessimistic, but much more optimistic about a rebellion in Ireland itself. For months, the familiar game of 'after you' was played out, reminiscent of the disastrous strategy used by the Scottish Jacobites during the first half of the century: the French waited for signs of insurrection, while the United Irishmen waited for news of a French expedition. Finally, in the spring of 1798, the Irish acted first, attacking Dublin Castle and bringing out much of the southeast in revolt. However, Ulster in the north, the key to success, remained ominously quiet. The customary atrocities were committed by both sides and at Vinegar Hill on 21 June the Irish were brutally routed by British troops, giving the new viceroy, the now aged but still vigorous Cornwallis, his last, bloodiest success in a career devoted to cleaning up the messes made by the British Empire.

French help did come, but it was too late and landed at Killala on the shore of County Mayo in the west, as far away as it was possible to be from the decisive southeastern theatre of conflict in Leinster and Munster. But the western province of Connacht *was* poor, angry and overwhelmingly Catholic. It had strong Defender support in the villages and country towns and an impromptu army, led by schoolteachers, farmers and priests, and armed with pitchforks and pikes. Connacht rallied to the French. Before the British and the yeomanry could regroup the insurgents had some success, at Castlebar; but before long their supplies of men and munitions dwindled and capitulation was inevitable. To cap the disaster, a small fleet with Tone on board, which had barely made it past the British blockade at Brest, was caught off the coast of Donegal. Tried and found guilty of treason, Tone committed suicide in prison before he could be hanged.

A bald summary of the military ebb and flow of the events of what became known as 'the year of the French' does not, however, properly record the magnitude of the misery of 1798. At least 30,000 Irish were slaughtered; an economically and politically dynamic world turned into a charnel house of invasion, repression and sectarian massacres – although, once the immediate military threat had passed, the government sensibly commuted many of the sentences passed on rebels. More decisively, hopes of Irish freedom were replaced by the fact, in 1801, of Irish absorption into Britain: the completion of the last cross on the Union Jack. The parliament at Dublin (retrospectively considered the root of the problem) was abolished and Irish members would now sit at Westminster. But this move was anything but a quid pro quo. The number of Irish boroughs, and so the number of representatives in parliament, was steeply reduced and the Irish debt (unlike the Scottish equivalent a century earlier) remained separate – and a serious taxable burden on the people of Ireland. Henry Grattan, who had lived through all this, was only telling the truth when he declared that the union was 'not an identification of people, as it excludes the Catholic from the parliament and the state … it is … not an identification of the two nations; it is merely a merger of the parliament of the one nation in that of the other; one nation, namely England, retains her full proportion; Ireland strikes off two thirds … by that act of absorption the feeling of one nation is not identified but alienated.'

But 1798 was not just 'the year of the French'; it was the year of the British too. For when the French landed in Ireland, some of those who had believed most fiercely in the imminent brotherhood of man decided, philosophically, to come home. A large number of the 'Friends of Peace' had argued that 'Pitt's war' was a thinly disguised instrument of oppression, giving pretexts for attacking free speech and closing down the avenues of protest while making the monied richer and the labouring people poorer. (Joseph Johnson probably still felt that way when he and J. S. Jordan, Paine's publisher, were indicted for publishing attacks on the loyalist Bishop of Llandaff.) Many, however, were coming to have almost as dim a view of Bonaparte and the France of the Directory, which seemed, to those who had been there and those who had heard, just as much a tyranny imposed by the propertied classes. Perhaps, too, with a powerful 'Army of England' arrayed across the Channel, they were beginning to concede the power of Burke's axiom in the *Reflections* that there was something unnatural about cosmopolitanism; that the impartial distribution of affection only testified to the shallowness of those sentiments. Nature, he had said, was particular, local. 'To be attached to the subdivision, to love the little platoon we belong to in society, is the first principle, the germ, as it were, of public affections. It is the first link in the series by which we proceed toward a love to our country and to mankind.' In other words, there was no humanitarianism except through patriotism.

At any rate, this was certainly the emotion budding in the warm breast and mighty brain of the 26-year-old Samuel Taylor Coleridge. In the spring of 1798 a quarto edition of three of his long(ish) poems announced, simultaneously, his disillusionment with France and his concern about the fate of Britain. The fact that the publisher of the poems was Joseph Johnson is itself eloquent about the shifting direction of the apostles of nature. Like so many of his generation Coleridge had fervently believed – at Cambridge University and afterwards – that the cause of the French Revolution, the cause of Jean-Jacques Rousseau, opened a new age in which mankind would live according to the rules of nature. The first of the poems, 'Fears in Solitude,' written during the height of the invasion panic – before Napoleon took his expedition off to Egypt instead, to attack Britain's Indian empire from the rear – is an extraordinary work of conflicted anguish and ecstasy. Coleridge grieves for the normalization of the continuing war:

> We send our mandates for the certain death
> Of thousands and ten thousands! Boys and girls,
> And women, that would groan to see a child
> Pull off an insect's leg, all read of war,
> The best amusement for our morning meal!

But he has also come to accept that, given the nature of the enemy, there may be no alternative and his verses swell into a patriotic threnody:

> O native Britain! O my Mother Isle!
> How shouldst thou prove aught else but dear and holy
> To me, who from thy lakes and mountain-hills,
> Thy clouds, thy quiet dales, thy rocks and seas,

> Have drunk in all my intellectual life,
> All sweet sensations, all ennobling thoughts …
> … O divine
> And beauteous island! thou hast been my sole
> And most magnificent temple …

The embrace of homeland is followed by the repudiation of the hypocrite aggressor. The second stanza of 'France: An Ode' recalls in sorrow the euphoria of 1789:

> When France in wrath her giant-limbs upreared,
> And with that oath which smote air, earth, and sea,
> Stamped her strong foot and said she would be free,
> Bear witness for me, how I hoped and feared!

At school at Christ's Hospital the 16-year-old Coleridge had indeed written an ode celebrating the fall of the Bastille, and it was to be 10 years before any sort of recantation crept in. At Jesus College, Cambridge, he had continued to be a notorious trouble-maker, one of the rowdiest supporters of the Unitarian Reverend William Frend when the university brought proceedings to remove him from his fellowship for his attacks on the Church and his 'seditious' opinions. Although his prodigal ways had driven Coleridge to enlist briefly (and under an assumed name) as a trooper in the 15th Dragoons, his political and social idealism (as much as a cripplingly embarrassing case of saddle sores) got him out of uniform again, certified by the discharging officer as 'insane'. (Coleridge was always a superb actor.) En route to the mandatory summer walking tour for democrats, where he followed the Pennant tour of the Brito-Celtic sublime, at Oxford Coleridge met the equally ardent young student, Richard Southey. Together the two idealists planned to establish in America a social utopia, a 'Pantisocracy,' in which (to the delight, perhaps, of Mary Wollstonecraft if she could but have known it) men would do the house cleaning. The nearest Coleridge got to the banks of the Susquehanna river, though, was Bristol, where for 10 months in 1795–6, during which he met William Wordsworth, he gave public lectures and edited his paper, *The Watchman*. Throughout this period Coleridge remained a coruscating critic of Pitt and his government, referring to the prime minister as 'the fiend' and to his speeches as 'Mystery concealing Meanness as clouds envelope a dunghill.' He attended a dinner in honour of Charles James Fox, went to see the trials of Horne Tooke and Thelwall, and became a friend of the latter, the 'Peripatetic,' even while scowling at his atheism. Above all, the ex-trooper's lectures and articles were full of hatred for the war itself, as a misery inflicted by the rich and powerful on the poor and helpless who paid for it with their taxes and their blood.

In 1798 Coleridge's tune changed dramatically. *The Watchman* had, predictably, folded, leading its editor to comment that 'I have snapped my squeaking baby-trumpet of sedition and have hung up its fragments in the chamber of Penitences.' The extinguishing by the French of the independent Confederation of Swiss Cantons had made it unmistakably clear that the threat was not from a liberator but from a common-or-garden military aggressor. Switzerland, moreover, was not just another anachronism to be knocked over. To the Romantics who, like Wordsworth in 1790, had hiked all the way there (after celebrating Bastille Day in France) it was the temple of liberty and the place, *par excellence*, where the fortress of nature had preserved a people in simplicity, innocence and freedom. Rousseau himself had been born in the shadow of Mont Blanc; William Tell had been reinvented (along with Robin Hood in Britain) as one of the classic heroes of defiance against tyranny; the oath sworn on the Rütli meadow, binding the cantons against their Austrian over-lords, had been immortalized by Henry Fuseli. To violate its sanctity, as the French had done, was to unmask themselves as squalid oppressors, all the more detestable for mantling themselves still in the tricolour and pontificating hypocritically about the Rights of Man. Appalled at the betrayal, Coleridge let fly his curse:

> O France, that mockest Heaven, adulterous, blind,
> And patriot only in pernicious toils!
> Are these thy boasts, Champion of human kind?
> … To insult the shrine of Liberty with spoils
> From freemen torn; to tempt and to betray?

Disillusionment with France did not make Coleridge a reactionary. His dilemma now was how to sustain his 'social affection' for the downtrodden beyond the pos-turing and polemics, the sound and the fury, that had turned ordinary people into cannon fodder. The answer came to him in the third of the three poems in the Johnson-published quarto, 'Frost at Midnight,' where he looks at his infant son and imagines him far and free from city din:

> But thou, my babe! shalt wander like a breeze
> By lakes and sandy shores, beneath the crags
> Of ancient mountain, and beneath the clouds.

Nature would be both consolation and instruction, but its head tutor now would be not Rousseau but God. Looked at with the honesty and seriousness it deserved, nature did have the power to transform each and every life – but not in the sense of drafting a political agenda. Constitutions and revolutions now seemed absurdly beside the point compared with the illumination to be had from the embrace of the natural and the simple. A vote would never make one happy. A snowdrop in February, the arc of a lark's flight, the babble of a crawling babe just might.

Needless to say, these insights did not come to Coleridge in the bustling commercial port of Bristol. He had taken a cottage at Nether Stowey in north Somerset where, on a previous trip, he had met someone whom he thought of as the epitome of the honest, natural man, the tanner and enthusiastic democrat Thomas Poole. Poole had found Coleridge the house, but, more important, it put him within walking distance (given that Coleridge thought nothing of walking 40 miles) of Wordsworth, who was living with his sister Dorothy at Racedown in Dorset. In the years since his return from France, Wordsworth, encouraged by his sister, had also moved away from the shallow apostrophizing of 'mankind' and towards an active sympathy with the plight of particular individuals, often the outcasts of society: crippled veterans, itinerant beggars, ragged waifs and orphans, destitute labourers. In 1795 Dorothy described the 'peasants' of the southwest as 'miserably poor; their cottages are shapeless structures (I may almost say) of wood and clay; indeed they are not at all beyond what might be expected in savage life.' During the second half of 1797 and the spring of 1798, after Wordsworth had moved closer to Coleridge, taking a rather grander house at Alfoxden, the two planned something unprecedented. They proposed to compile a collaborative anthology of their work, which would use the plain speech of the labourers and cottagers of the West Country people, and be utterly free of the ornamental fantasies of the pastoral tradition. The 'Lyrical Ballads' would not be pretty. They would look at the broken bodies and ruined hovels with a clear eye and an open heart. Often they would sound impolite, and their meter might tread as heavily as a hob-nailed boot on a parlour floor. But to be true to the sovereign force of nature meant, above all, not treating it as a bookish idea, much less a political slogan; it meant living with it as a physical reality. *That* would be their revolution.

Some of their greatest and certainly their most intensely compassionate work resulted from this collaboration. Following the plodding round 'The Old Cumberland Beggar' from house to house, Wordsworth adopted precisely that body of men whom the powerful had judged most expendable of all.

Above: Samuel Taylor Coleridge's study at Coleridge Cottage, Nether Stowey, Somerset.
Opposite: *Samuel Taylor Coleridge*, pencil drawing by Robert Hancock, 1796.

> But deem not this man useless – Statesman! ye
> Who are so restless in your wisdom, ye
> Who have a broom still ready in your hands
> To rid the world of nuisances …

Why? Because the beggar, through his visits, knitted together in a common act of sympathy a mere aggregate of men and women and fashioned them into a true community, a village. And he also brings together the past with the present:

> While from door to door,
> This old man creeps, the villagers in him
> Behold a record which together binds
> Past deeds and offices of charity
> Else unremembered …
> … Among the farms and solitary huts,
> Hamlets and thinly-scattered villages,
> Where'er the aged Beggar takes his rounds,
> The mild necessity of use compels
> To acts of love …

Although he may not have owned up to it yet, Wordsworth's growing preference for individual acts of charity over collective acts of policy; his budding Christian sense of the importance of individual, face-to-face encounters, often deep in the country; and his dawning realization of the unforced strength of tradition, all put him much closer to Burke than Paine. But to some of the locals, who were bemused by the poets hob-nobbing with their inferiors (especially since Coleridge decided to express his social sympathy by wearing the clothes of the Somerset country people), these eccentricities started to seem dangerously peculiar. It was rumoured that the gentlemen spoke French. Perhaps some sort of plot was being hatched in the Quantocks in the year of national peril? The appearance of John Thelwall, who – naturally – had *walked* the 150 miles from London, only confirmed their suspicions. After his acquittal for treason, undeterred by the spies who stuck to him like leeches, Thelwall had become the star lecturer on the provincial radical circuit, in 1796 alone giving 22 lectures in places as far apart as Derby and Norwich. When it became obvious that Thelwall was the reason that the Quantocks poets were attracting talk he decided to move on, taking the spies with him. He believed that, despite fierce arguments with Wordsworth and Coleridge over atheism, he and they were essentially of a like mind; it was a view, alas, not reciprocated.

Among the pilgrims who came to Nether Stowey and Alfoxden, none was more awe-struck than the 19-year-old William Hazlitt. To Wordsworth and Coleridge, Hazlitt – painfully shy and slightly peculiar – was a puppyish oddity, an amusement. Nothing in his manner suggested that this gauche, pop-eyed aspiring painter and son of an Irish Unitarian minister in Shropshire would become the greatest essayist in the English language. Hazlitt, who in January 1798 had walked 10 miles in the frozen mire to Shrewsbury to hear Coleridge deliver one of his stupendous Unitarian sermons, was by his own overwrought account 'dumb, inarticulate, helpless, like a worm by the wayside, crushed, bleeding, lifeless.' From the minute Coleridge opened his mouth, his voice rising 'like a steam of rich distilled perfumes,' Hazlitt was a goner; the big man with the long, dark, flopping hair and full lips put him in mind of St John crying in the wilderness, 'whose food was locusts and wild honey.'

Later that week the great man actually came to visit Hazlitt's father on Church business. William, as usual, sat staring at the floor, tongue-tied except when blurting out speeches on some topic on which he happened to feel passionately and supposed (not wrongly) that Coleridge felt the same – Burke, Mary Wollstonecraft, William Godwin. On the table was a haunch of Welsh mutton and a dish of turnips. Flooded with happiness at talking to, and being talked at by, Coleridge, Hazlitt savoured each mouthful as if he had never tasted food before. Then, in a daze of veneration, after being invited to Nether Stowey in the spring, he followed the poet six miles down the road (passing the Romantic qualification of having good walking legs).

In Somerset, Hazlitt was taken to Wordsworth's manor house and met Dorothy; slept in a blue-hung bed there opposite portraits of George I and George II, and saw William return from Bristol and 'make havoc' with half a Cheshire cheese. He got to take morning walks with the poets and listened to them recite drafts of their verses with, he said (tantalizingly), 'a decided chaunt'; Coleridge was always more theatrical, Wordsworth more quietly lyrical. On one of those walks, just before Coleridge left for Germany to study philosophy and go wandering in the Harz mountains, they took another long saunter along the path above the seashore, then 'loitered on the "ribbed sea-sands"' and examined odd species of seaweed; it was there, finally, that Hazlitt thought he understood what they meant by living naturally. A fisherman told them there had been a drowning the day before and that he and his mates had tried to save the boy at the risk of their own lives. 'He said,' wrote Hazlitt later, 'he did not know how it was that they ventured, but, "Sir, we have a nature towards one another."'

'One another!' *This* was 'social affection' in action, and what Hazlitt thought he saw in the poets' shared households in Somerset was an unforced community based on mutual sympathy: unaffected family life; easy conversation with the people of the villages; the rediscovery of unspoiled humanity far from the fads and frenzies of metropolitan fashion.

When, in 1802, Hazlitt wanted to see the poets again he had to go north, for both of them had resettled in the Lake District: Wordsworth was living with his sister and brother John in a little cottage at Grasmere, and Coleridge in the much grander Greta Hall nearby. But something had cooled along with the climate of their countryside. Nature now seemed, not to connect them with the daily world beyond their immediate company, but rather to detach them from it. The words 'solitude' and 'solitary' started recurring, especially in Wordsworth's poems; and when he introduced figures, hewn almost from the rocky landscape, they were seen as desolate apparitions silhouetted against the bare hills. To Hazlitt, the only serious connection of 'the gang' seemed to be with each other. Grasmere had become a little commune of family and friends, reading to each other, taking possession of the countryside by carving their names into rocks and trees; sharing meals. If they still thought of themselves as poet–philosophers, what they preached, Hazlitt found, was not any sort of public reformation (much less revolution) but rather the recasting of individual lives by re-establishing the simplicity and intensity of the connection to nature experienced in childhood. Coleridge's idea of a great change was to turn the Lake District yellow by surreptitiously sowing laburnum seeds in the woods.

This intense self-absorption irked Hazlitt, now 25 and a struggling artist who kept himself alive by hack journalism. He knew perfectly well that, for all the ostentatious simplicity of their lives in the Lakes, the poets could not have afforded it without the help of gentleman patrons like Sir George Beaumont. So when Coleridge ruled out Hazlitt as a travelling companion for his friend Tom Wedgwood (the ex-British Club member from Paris), describing him as intellectually brilliant but personally '99 in 100 singularly repulsive – : brow-hanging, shoe-contemplative, strange … he is jealous, gloomy, and of an irritable Pride – addicted to women,' and when Wedgwood maliciously repeated this to the horrified and hurt Hazlitt, the disenchantment was total. He was the essayist, after all, who would write the definitive piece on 'The Pleasures of Hating,' and in the years ahead he seldom missed an opportunity to sink his sharp little teeth into Coleridge's ailing, opium-addled reputation. It was personal but it was also political. Hazlitt never forgave Wordsworth or Coleridge their apostasy; the indecent eagerness with which they echoed Edmund Burke when he made Nature not a revolutionary, but a patriot.

William Hazlitt, chalk by William Bewick, 1825.

In 1802 the signing of the Peace of Amiens briefly opened the sea lanes to safe passage in and out of France. Tom Paine, who had never really recovered from the typhus he had contracted in jail, but who was suffering even more from a clinical aversion to Napoleon ('the very butcher of Liberty and the greatest monster that Nature ever spewed') had finally given up on France as the haven of freedom and social justice. He sailed from Le Havre to the United States where, after predictably quarrelling with George Washington and John Adams, the country's first two presidents, he moved to the 300-acre farm in New Rochelle, New York, presented to him by the grateful state in 1784. He lived there almost until the end of his days, amidst a few hogs and cows. Pilgrims who came to visit him (and there were many) were disconcerted by his return to a state of nature, so relentlessly frugal that he dried out his used tea leaves after a pot to recycle them for further use. Poverty finally forced him to sell the farm, and he died in New York City in 1809, near penniless.

Not everyone shared his horror of the state of despotism that France had become. William Hazlitt, for example, had become enthralled by the Napoleonic epic and would, in fact, never free himself of it, later writing a biography that is perhaps the dullest of all his works. In 1802 he somehow scraped up enough money to go to Paris, where he stood in the Louvre, agog at the masterpieces, while conveniently overlooking the fact that the First Consul had accumulated the contents of the museum by plundering the churches and galleries of Europe. In the Salon Carré he saw Charles James Fox – touring Europe during the brief period of peace – now grown fat and grey but still Hazlitt's indomitable hero for refusing to truckle to Pitt's wartime security state.

And much as he despised Bonapartist France, Wordsworth too made the summer packet boat crossing along with his sister Dorothy. He had no intention of recapturing his youthful passions, but rather proposed to put a seal on them. He had decided to marry and, before he could do so with an easy conscience, needed to set eyes once more on Annette and his daughter Caroline; perhaps assure himself that they would not stand in his way. For her part Annette had practical reasons for seeing her old lover. She needed to be certain that, once he was married, he would continue to pay the modest maintenance he had been sending for Caroline's upbringing. And since, in Napoleon's misogynist state, mothers of illegitimate children had no rights over their offspring, she also needed to feel certain that Wordsworth would not try to take their child from her. The reassurances were duly given. The poet, who found he could not give much else, bestowed on mother and child a volume of his verses. They went their separate ways.

Both Coleridge and Wordsworth were now fast turning into all-out propagandists for John Bull. When the truce with France broke down in May 1803, and an invasion seemed even more likely than in 1798, Coleridge wrote in back-to-the-wall proto-Churchillian mode, revelling in insularity, in the concept of Britain as the last refuge against European tyranny: 'Englishmen must think of themselves and act for themselves … let France bribe or puzzle all Europe into a confederation against us. I will not fear for my country … the words of Isaiah will be truly prophetic. "They trod the winepress alone and of the nations there was none with them."'

In these Boneyphobic years it was Coleridge, not Hazlitt, who was in tune with the vast majority of Britons. The threat was not, after all, imaginary. In 1803–4 there were at least 100,000 French and allied troops camped at Boulogne, and 2300 vessels (most of them, admittedly, small) waiting for the order to sail. When Napoleon put the Bayeux Tapestry on display for the first time the point was not lost, neither on the massed ranks of the Army of England nor on the defenders 20 miles across the narrow straits. By the end of 1804, Britain was also at war with Spain.

William Pitt, however, had not survived 10 years of brutal, global war only to go down with an arrow in his eye. Recognizing the scale of what he was up against on his return to office in May 1804, he and the new First Lord of the Admiralty, Henry Dundas, mobilized national resources on a scale and with a thoroughness not seen even in his father's heyday as a war leader 50 years before. More impressively, they did it for the most part without coercion, unlike the Prussians or the Russians. (Although more than once impressment officers, tipped off that he was lecturing, had tried to seize the irrepressible Thelwall, who took to carrying a loaded pistol and on one occasion pressed it to the temples of the assailant who tried to take him.) While the loyalism of the early years of the war had been exhibited mostly by the gentry and patriot middle classes, who delivered men-at-arms to the government reserve, the extraordinary numbers who volunteered to fight against the Napoleonic threat of invasion did so in a much more spontaneous manner. It is a phenomenon that recent histories call, without anachronism, 'national defence patriotism.' Sometimes the authorities' worst problem was avoiding the chaos of being inundated with manpower, virtually all of it untrained and much of it undisciplined. A Defence of the Realm Act ordered lists to be compiled of every able-bodied male between 17 and 55, so that a home guard could be formed and called on in the event of an invasion. In 1804, at the height of the scare, more than 400,000 came forward – around half of those asked. Many of the keenest came not, as the government had predicted, from the countryside but from the southern ports (most immediately in the front line) and the industrial towns of the Midlands and the north which, just a decade earlier, had been written off as hotbeds of disloyalty and sedition. By late 1804, the country had been transformed into 'Fortress Britannia.' Out of a population of 15 million, 3¾ million men were of an age to bear arms. And over 800,000 – one in five – were in fact part of the national defence; 386,000 as volunteers, of whom 266,000 were in the army and 120,000 in the navy.

The Scottish contribution to this massive mobilization was huge. Highland contingents – to the satisfaction of Dundas, a Lowlander Scot, who, since he had a holiday house on Loch Earn, rather fancied himself an honorary Highlander – were conspicuous. It was, after all, an alternative to emigration, and during this war the Black Watch, the Gordon Highlanders and the Cameron Highlanders all achieved mythic status. Much was made of the fact that the first blessed martyrs of the land war – Sir Ralph Abercromby, killed in Egypt in 1801, and Sir John Moore, killed in Spain in 1809 – were Scots. Although Scottish soldiers had served in America and India, it was in *this* war, above all, that Scotland's sense of itself was enhanced, rather than diminished, by being British.

The king, of course, was the symbolic focus of all this genuine patriotic feeling. When George III reviewed 27,000 volunteers in Hyde Park in October 1803 a crowd of a half a million watched the spectacular parade. Bad memories of the mobbed coach in October 1795 must have seemed a very long way away. He was able, now, to enjoy public appearances again and between 1797 and 1800 even attended 55 theatre performances to drink in the applause of the audience. It was in these years and for this king that 'God Save the King' (rather than 'God Save the Rights of Man') became, definitively, the national anthem. Burke's loyalism, defined by him as a popular sentiment, appeared, at this moment anyway, to have been vindicated; the territorial imperative of defending hearth and home established as the most natural instinct of all.

It was exactly at this moment that the mythology of Merrie England, of the sceptred isle, was born, complete with especially passionate revivals of the appropriate Shakespeare histories. *Anything* historical found an enthusiastic following, a market, as now, perhaps for the first time, the past became a pastime, but a serious pastime – a way to discover Britishness. The romance of Britain had begun as radical geography and had come of age as patriotic history. Books for children sprouted illustrations and scenes that told little Johnny and Jane Bulls their island story. King John at Runnymede, Queen Elizabeth at Tilbury, Bonnie Prince Charlie at Glenfinnan, all sprang off the page. They reappeared in Madame Tussaud's new wax-work museum, and in popular paintings by illustrator–artists like Thomas Stothard.

King George III at a Review (detail) by Sir William Beechey, *c.* 1897–8.

Meeting the craving to make contact with the ancestors, books on historical costume, furniture, sports, weapons and armour all appeared. And after the great authority on medieval arms and armour, Samuel Rush Meyrick, was invited by George IV to reorganize the collection at Windsor Castle so that phantom knights could be stood beneath the big histories painted by Benjamin West, an entire generation of country gentlemen went to their barns and attics to clean the rust off ancient swords and helms and reassembled them in their newly Gothicized 'Great Hall.'

As well as the chronicle of their own war, history had become patriotic entertainment. And the biggest boon to the business was its most fantastic showman, Horatio Nelson. He may have been not much over 5 feet tall, with only one arm, blind in one eye, prematurely grey hair and no teeth, but in every way that counted Nelson was larger than life. As a naval commander he was a genius, and no one was more convinced of that than Nelson himself. He came along at precisely the moment when the Romantic cult of genius was itself being born. Conventionally, the pantheon of God-kissed talent was reserved for the great artists – Shakespeare, Milton, Michelangelo. But Nelson's astounding career and his own equally prodigious talent for self-promotion made it possible for a military man to be treated this way too. From the start, the impresarios of patriotic entertainment made him their star. The victory at the battle of the Nile in 1798 had, after all, everything calculated to pull in the crowds – Mameluke warriors, camels, crocodiles and the French going down *en masse* to Davy Jones's locker. Henry Aston Barker set box-office records with his 360-degree panoramic 'Battle of the Nile.' But for William Turner, ex-coachmaker and painter, even huge pictures in the round didn't do justice to the epic. Off Fleet Street Turner built a water theatre called the Naumachia, after the Roman flooded arenas. Queues formed round the block to get into Turner's 1½-hour Nelson spectacular, complete with ear-splitting cannon and smoke machines. (The other Turner would inspect what was left of the *Victory*, along with his fellow artist Philippe de Loutherbourg, whose unerring instinct for public taste had taken him from Derbyshire wonders to naval battle pieces, so that he could achieve in 1808 his astonishing *coup de théâtre, The Battle of Trafalgar, as Seen from the Mizen Starboard Shrouds of the* Victory.)

But it was hard to upstage the little man himself. Everything about him, even (or especially) his passion for Emma Hamilton, was a gift to the cult of celebrity. Although Pitt and the king and the stuffed shirts at the Admiralty cringed at his refusal to disguise his relationship with the much-painted woman who was, after all, the wife of the British ambassador to Naples, Nelson's reputation for naughtiness did nothing to harm his popularity; quite possibly the reverse. He was already the glamorous, charismatic outsider, and all his well-known vices of vanity, recklessness and arrogance were sold, not least by him, as part and parcel of the heroic bravura. Nelson played on his cult like a harp. He dressed to kill and be killed, jangling with decorations, whether on parade or the poopdeck, so it was no surprise when all that glittering hardware did, in fact, make him the perfect target for the French mizenmast sharpshooters, one of whom hit his target at the battle of Trafalgar on 21 October 1805. Nelson had known that the battle would be decisive for the preservation, not just of British maritime dominance, but the very independence of the island. Had Napoleon been able to unite the French and Spanish fleets in a single armada, he might well have been able to launch an invasion. The Grande Armée was still camped on the Channel coast. So his heroic death guaranteed life to Great Britain.

Like James Wolfe a generation before, Nelson virtually designed his own apotheosis – his translation to the immortals. The huge ceremony in January 1806 completely overshadowed William Pitt's funeral the following month and, for that matter, was on a scale that outdid royal ceremony. Like Winston Churchill's funeral a century and a half later, everything was finely designed to tap into deep patriotic emotion. The body, preserved in alcohol, was unloaded from the shattered hulk of the *Victory* at Greenwich, then borne to a lying-in-state, where the hero's coffin could be viewed by ordinary sailors and the people whose love he had cultivated and genuinely cared for. Black barges carried the bier downstream, like Arthur to Avalon, to a four-hour service at St Paul's Cathedral, where royals were allowed by their own anachronistic protocol to attend only in their capacity as private individuals. But unlike Churchill, this was where Nelson stayed in the black marble sarcophagus originally meant for Cardinal Wolsey, buried right beneath the centre of the dome.

Politically, as his enthusiastically vindictive role in propping up the autocratic Bourbons of Naples made clear (a commitment backed up by torture of political prisoners and a carnival of hangings, all under Nelson's direction), the vice-admiral was a dyed-in-the-wool reactionary. But he still belonged to the streets and the taverns, to the ordinary seamen and dockers, and had got their blood up and pulse racing in a way none of the epauletted grand dukes could ever manage.

It was a time hungry for heroes, for as much as Britain loved him, the king was old and increasingly mad. The Prince of Wales was a fat, often drunken lecher; his brothers, like the Duke of York – who had been the sole official representative at Nelson's funeral – just as dissolute. No one was surprised, only appalled, when it was revealed that, to please his mistress, the courtesan Mary Ann Clarke, the duke had been awarding military promotions to anyone on her 'A' list. Scandals like this put a

Above: *The Battle of Trafalgar, as Seen from the Mizen Starboard Shrouds of the* Victory by J.M.W. Turner, 1806–8.
Opposite: *Horatio Nelson, Viscount Nelson* by Sir William Beechey, 1800.

face on that ancient radical bugbear 'Old Corruption' and gave an opportunity, even in the midst of war, for the critics to find their voice again. In 1807, the same London crowds who had turned out in hundreds of thousands to pay their last respects to Nelson now cheered the patrician Sir Francis Burdett, as well as an even more unlikely hero, the naval commander Thomas Cochrane – ex-privateer, notorious eloper, jailed (and then escaped) for stock-exchange fraud. This pair were the new radical candidates for the two Westminster seats, one of which had, until his death in 1806, been held by Charles James Fox.

Dissent – political and religious – had not, in fact, gone away. It was just busy with moral causes untainted by the accusation of flirting with the enemy. In 1807 a huge petitioning campaign, driven by a Nonconformist army, mobilized not in barracks but in chapels and meeting houses, had succeeded in making the slave trade illegal in the British Empire, though not in freeing slaves in British colonies. A year later Burdett and Cochrane swept away the official Whig candidates on a programme of impeccably patriotic revivalism. Give us back the True Britain, they said, the Free Britain, the Britain that had been stolen by the dukes and the dandies. Give us our birthright: annual parliaments, a secret ballot, manhood suffrage! Figures from the recent past, like Major Cartwright, resurfaced from a silence imposed by intimidation, their voices louder than ever. With them on their banners were figures from the not-so-recent past – Robin Hood and the Civil War parliamentarian John Hampden, rediscovered as the heroes of an alternative history: the people's history.

When this new army of Christian soldiers and Magna Carta warriors marched to win what they insisted were the 'natural rights' of blacks and Britons, they seemed unstoppable. By contrast, the performance of the armies commanded by the dukes kept on stopping. The nursery rhyme about the 'Grand Old Duke of York' refers to one of his many wartime fiascos, the latest occurring on the Dutch island of Walcheren in 1809 when an enormous expedition of 40,000 troops, supposedly laying down a beachhead on Napoleonic Europe, was cut down by fever and had to be ignominiously evacuated. In its first few years the campaign against the French in Portugal and Spain, known as the Peninsular War, seemed, equally, to specialize in gallant defeats and pyrrhic victories. Frederick Ponsonby wrote to his mother, Lady Bessborough, after the British won the battle of Talavera with droll disenchantment: 'We had the pleasing amusement of charging five solid squares with a ditch in front. After losing 180 [troopers] and 222 horses we found it was not so agreeable and that Frenchmen don't always run away when they see British cavalry, so off we set and my horse never went so fast in his life.' One of Wordsworth's most stinging poems was written in despair at the 'Convention of Cintra,' when it seemed that Britain had abandoned the Spanish resistance. None of this bad news, of course, prevented the Prince of Wales from throwing a party at his grand London residence, Carlton House, featuring a 200-foot-long table into which had been carved an artificial canal for wine, its banks lined with silver and gold, and the wine driven by miniature pumping machines; a small-scale industrial revolution engineered to amuse the Quality. Only Arthur Wellesley, the Duke of Wellington, would draw huge and enthusiastic crowds, bonfires and marching bands whenever he scored a victory.

But in 1810, there was no inkling of a Waterloo around the corner, except in India and the Caribbean. Napoleon, in fact, seemed largely unbeatable. The Spanish guerrillas deserved admiration, but the French controlled all the great cities of the peninsula from Madrid to Seville. One by one his adversaries had made their peace. The Habsburg Emperor of Austria, Francis I, had even married his daughter to the man once reviled as the Corsican ogre. King Frederick William of Prussia and Tsar Alexander of Russia had both made treaties. Unchallenged on most of the continent, but thwarted in his invasion plans and frustrated by the Royal Navy from making any serious inroads on the empire, Napoleon attacked Britain in a campaign designed to cripple the island economy. Sealing off continental Europe against its exports he created the embryo of a common market on the other side of the Channel. It very nearly worked. European industry, protected by the blockade and driven by the technical innovations of French technology (in chemistry and engineering for example), surged. In Britain, with export demand on the floor, a deep slump set in. Handloom weavers, who had been heavily in demand as factory-spun cotton yarn surged in output, were now the first victims of the sharp downturn of trade. Unemployment and food prices soared at the same time.

In 1811 and 1812, well-organized gangs calling themselves the soldiers of 'General Ludd's Army' after their originator, a worker named Ned Ludd, smashed hand-powered machines in the Midlands and factory machines in Lancashire. The Luddites, who signed themselves 'Enoch,' did their work with sledge-hammers. Letters were sent to employers, especially those notorious for cutting wages, that General Ludd's soldiers were coming their way. Legislation was enacted making machine-breaking a capital crime, but it persisted almost as long as the economic crisis.

In 1812 a ruined businessman, driven to distraction, shot and killed the prime minister, Spencer Perceval, at point-blank range in the ante-chamber of the House of Commons. To the horror of the governing classes, the assassin was noisily toasted in the inns of London, Birmingham and Manchester. So when, at last, in 1813 news arrived of Wellington's spectacular victories in Spain and of the destruction of

Overleaf: *French Cuirassiers Charging the Highlanders at The Battle of Waterloo on 18 June 1815* by Felix Philippoteaux, 1874.

Napoleon's Grande Armée in the Russian snows, no one with any sense took much comfort from the happy, drunken, patriotic uproar. Some 12,000 regular troops – more than Wellington had to use against the French – were stationed at home to deal with the marches, riots and machine-wrecking that had become a regular feature of British life. After Wellington's decisive defeat of Napoleon at Waterloo in 1815, when a quarter of a million demobilized soldiers were thrown on to an already depressed labour market, the situation became even more serious. The one ray of light amidst the gathering economic gloom ought to have been lower food prices, now that the blockade and the artificially high demand of the war had gone. But in response to complaints from landowners that their incomes would collapse, a Corn Law had been passed, letting in foreign grain only when home prices hit a designated ceiling. The effect, as intended, was to keep British farmers' profits artificially high. So bread remained punishingly dear at a time when the Quality looked as though it were embarking on an orgy of house-building, each construction more extravagant than the last. Brighton Pavilion, the Prince Regent's Indo-Sino-Moorish funhouse, was being rebuilt, sporting iron columns and a gaslit ballroom, at the same time as 45,000 paupers, many of them bearing scars from the battlefields of India, America and Europe, were hammering on the doors of Spitalfields poorhouse.

For some of the angriest, most articulate radicals, these shocking contrasts were an insupportable obscenity. Thomas Bewick's old sparring partner, Thomas Spence, had taken to making much, symbolically, of his slight stature, casting himself as Jack and calling his latest publication *The Giant Killer*. Shortly before his death in 1814, he did some revolutionary sums, calculating that since the estimated rental value of the houses and estates of England and Wales was £40 million and stock another £19 million, and since the population of the country was 10½ million, each taxpayer was shelling out about £6 annually to support 'the drones in luxury and pomp.'

Even Spence's fury, however, pales beside the wrath of William Hazlitt. He had finally given up his dreams to be a painter and was scraping along as a writer, in almost any genre, for any newspaper that would pay him. He served an apprenticeship in the new job of parliamentary reporter, but also reviewed theatre performances, art exhibitions, even boxing matches, and in so doing transformed each of the journalistic media he tried. But his vocation in these bitter years was to attack the class he felt had turned Britain into a sink of corruption and unnatural social cruelty. What especially made his blood boil was to be told that the misfortunes of the poor were only to be expected in the shift from a wartime to a peacetime economy; just a structural dislocation – nothing, really, to get agitated about. Hazlitt, responding in a series of vitriolic essays in the *Examiner*, begged to differ: 'Have not the government and the rich had their way in everything? Have they not gratified their ambition, their pride, their obstinacy, their ruinous extravagance? Have they not squandered the resources of the country as they pleased?' And what had his old heroes – Wordsworth and Coleridge – to say about any of this? Nothing. They had become, to Hazlitt's horror and disgust, Tories.

In 1816 he defined for his readers, in an unforgettably savage portrait of a country in pain, the character of a 'Modern Tory.' He was, wrote Hazlitt (*inter alia*):

> a blind idolater of old times and long established customs … A Tory never objects to increasing the power of the Crown, or abridging the liberties of the people, or even calls in question the justice or wisdom of any of the measures of government. A Tory considers sinecure places and pensions as sacred and inviolable, to reduce, or abolish which, would be unjust and dangerous … accuses those who differ with him on political subjects of being Jacobins, Revolutionists, and enemies to their country. A Tory highly values a long pedigree and ancient families, and despises low-born persons (the newly created nobility excepted), adores coronets, stars, garters, ribbons, crosses and titles of all sorts. A Tory … deems martial law the best remedy for discontent … considers corporal punishment as necessary, mild, and salutary, notwithstanding soldiers and sailors frequently commit suicide to escape from it … sees no hardship in a person's being confined for thirty years in the Fleet Prison, on an allowance of sixpence a day, for contempt of the Court of Chancery … A Tory … is averse to instructing the poor, lest they should be enabled to think and reason … and reads no poetry but birthday odes and verses in celebration of the battle of Waterloo. A Tory … lavishes immense sums on triumphal columns … while the brave men who achieved the victories are pining in want. A Tory asserts that the present sufferings of the country … are merely temporary and trifling, though the gaols are filled with insolvent debtors, and criminals driven to theft by urgent want, the Gazette filled with bankruptcies, agriculture declining, commerce and manufactories nearly at a stand, while thousands are emigrating to foreign countries, whole parishes deserted, the burthen of the poor rates intolerable, and yet insufficient to maintain the increasing number of the poor, and hundreds of once respectable house-holders reduced to the sad necessity of soliciting admission into the receptacles for paupers and vagabonds …

Much of what he said was inaccurate and unjust, since the Whigs were hardly less, indeed perhaps more, narrowly aristocratic, and there were certainly many Tories –

Coleridge and Wordsworth, for example – who were deeply moved by the plight of the poor, but their solution was to rekindle a sense of social and moral responsibility in the governing classes, not to challenge their legitimacy. In 1808 Wordsworth organized an appeal for the children of two smallholders who had died in a terrible blizzard, and took in one of the daughters himself at his home at Dove Cottage. But it was exactly this personal, traditional charity that Hazlitt judged so patronizing and sentimental. When Coleridge proposed to deliver what he called (reverting to the old Unitarian days, when Hazlitt had sat wonder-struck by his eloquence) a 'Lay Sermon' on the ills of the time, even before he had seen it he exploded at its presumptuousness. Reading it would not have abated his anger. Hazlitt took exception to men who had once advertised themselves as the mouthpieces of the common people now consenting to the gagging of those who wished to combine in their own defence; or who were prosecuted for expressing discontent, like his own friend Leigh Hunt, who was jailed for describing the Prince Regent as 'this "Adonis in loveliness" … a corpulent man of 50! … a violator of his word, a libertine …'

Wordsworth, whom Hazlitt still revered as a great poet, was perhaps the most culpable of all, for he had accepted a post from his local magnate, the Earl of Lonsdale. While Hazlitt was scribbling furiously away in John Milton's old lodgings at 19 York Street, Westminster, a holy place of the British republican tradition, Wordsworth was living in his new home at Rydal Mount supported by the earl and by his sinecure as Distributor of Stamps for Westmoreland. It was even known that the old country tramper, the friend of beggars and poor veterans, had got himself up in knee breeches and silk stockings to go and dine in London with his noble superior, the Commissioner of Stamps. Hazlitt's reaction was acid: 'Cannot Mr Wordsworth contrive to trump up a sonnet or an ode to that pretty little pastoral patriotic knick-knack, the thumbscrew … On my conscience he ought to write something on that subject or he ought never to write another line but his stamp receipts. Let him stick to his excise and promotion. The world has had enough of his simplicity in poetry and politics.'

Undeterred, in 1818 Wordsworth campaigned in the *Kendal Chronicle* for the earl's sons when the radical Henry Brougham had the unmitigated gall to contest one of the two county seats of Westmoreland, both of which had been safely in the family's gift for generations. Lonsdale and his family, the Lowthers, were everything that Hazlitt hated. They owned hundreds of thousands of acres of north-country land, an estate so big that it was said the earl could walk across the Pennines from the Cumbrian to the Northumbrian coast without ever leaving it. They owned coal mines, and in the middle of the worst slump in living memory the earl was building a vast Gothic Revival castle, Lowther Park, with fantastic turrets and timbered halls – his very own dream palace of Merrie England, Walter Scott-style.

Hazlitt was not alone in his contempt for this synthetic version of tradition, which pretended to embody the old paternalistic virtues while acting out its fantasies through cupidity and brutality. Thomas Bewick was now an elderly gentleman, the successful author and illustrator of *History of British Birds* (1804) and *A General History of Quadrupeds* (1790). Although still full of creative energy, his eyes had been so badly damaged by the fine work of his wood engravings that he needed help from his son and pupils to execute, in 1818, his long-cherished project of an illustrated *Aesop's Fables* (1813). He continued to insist he was no Frenchified revolutionary. Unlike Hazlitt (who had gone on a grief-stricken four-day bender at the news of the battle of Waterloo) he was no admirer of Napoleon. But Bewick was astonishingly forthright about 'the immense destruction of human beings, and the waste of treasure, which followed and supported this superlatively wicked war.' And now it was over, he thought Britain had become a plunder-land for an unholy marriage of old titles and new money, 'The shipping interest wallowed in riches; the gentry whirled about in aristocratic pomposity.' For Bewick, theirs was a system of power sustained, above all, by lies about the true nature of the countryside with which they affected to be intimate, but from which they were actually cut off behind the elegant gates of their Palladian or Gothick mansions. Bewick was displeased, for example, to be told that his engravings of cattle and sheep commissioned for landowners should resemble, not what he had drawn from sight, but paintings of them (done by other artists, who were happy to flatter for a fee) shown to him in advance: ' … my journey, as far as concerned these fat cattle makers, ended in nothing. I objected to put lumps of fat here and there where I could not see it … Many of the animals were, during this rage for fat cattle, fed up to as great a weight and bulk as it was possible for feeding to make them; but this was not enough; they were to be figured monstrously fat before the owners of them could be pleased.'

The very opposite of this deceit was pictured in Bewick's own *Quadrupeds*: the bulls of Chillingham, a herd of wild cattle preserved in woodlands owned by the Earl of Tankerville but prized and cherished by Bewick's close friend, the engraver and agriculturalist John Bailey, who lived at Chillingham. The cattle, with their dazzling white coats and black muzzles, were said to be the survivors of an ancient, undomesticated breed that had wandered the woods of Britain before the Romans had arrived. For Bewick and Bailey, these creatures were the *real* John Bulls of Britain: untameable, unpolluted by cross-breeding, unsuitable for fancy farm shows. In order to make his drawings without them either disappearing back into the woods or,

Opposite: *Thomas Bewick*, engraved by F. Bacon after James Ramsay, *c.* 1810.
Top: *The Wild Bull of the Ancient Caledonian Breed, Now in the Park at Chillingham-Castle, Northumberland*, from *A General History of Quadrupeds* (1790), wood engraving by Thomas Bewick, 1789.
Above: One of the surviving bulls of the original Chillingham herd.

more alarmingly, charging him, Bewick had to wait patiently in cover by night and then approach at dawn, crawling on his hands and knees, in an attitude that, his own account makes clear, was as much one of respect, wonder and happiness as of prudence. The result, an image of massive power, is the great, perhaps the greatest, icon of British natural history, and one loaded with moral, national and historical sentiment as well as purely zoological fascination.

Rural authenticity in an age of lies mattered deeply to such as Bewick. And he responded, like tens of thousands of others, to someone who seemed to exude it: the two-legged, bellowing bull called William Cobbett. Cobbett was pure country, although his appeal went straight to town. Born in 1762, he had grown up working on his father's farm at Farnham in Surrey, moving to London at the age of 19, where he worked as an attorney's clerk. But his real apprenticeship and his education had been served, along with countless other ploughboys, in the king's army in New Brunswick. He had then spent some years in Philadelphia teaching and writing before returning to England in 1800 with a reputation already made for pithy, popular journalism, couched in the language of country people. Astoundingly, he met with Pitt and William Windham, his spymaster, who were interested in subsidizing a pro-government daily paper that Cobbett called *The Porcupine*, which would shoot its quills at the Friends of Peace and anyone suspected of disloyalty. For three years at least Cobbett dutifully banged the patriotic drum, urging the government to give the people inspirational popular histories with role models like Drake and Marlborough, and promoting (to the horror of evangelicals) as martial training violent sports like 'single stick,' in which men with one arm tied behind their backs whacked each other with cudgels until 'one inch of blood issues from the skull of an opponent.'

Around 1803–4, when the country was going through its patriotic paroxysm, Cobbett went through an almost Pauline moment of conversion. His Damascus road was a village called Horton Heath. It was one of the few still to have an unenclosed common, and he noted that the villagers used the green to accommodate, cooperatively, 100 beehives, 60 pigs, 15 cows and 800 poultry. Notwithstanding Arthur Young's truisms that such commons were an uneconomic waste, Cobbett believed that, on the contrary, they served the *village* economy very well indeed. Then he began to make some calculations in earnest. A report published in 1803 admitted that there were around 1 million paupers in England and Wales; the vast majority, of course, in the countryside. One in seven in Wiltshire was a pauper, receiving Poor-Law relief; one in four in Sussex. Cobbett relayed this horrifying news to his readers in his new, furious voice: 'Yes in England! English men, women and children. More than a million of them; one eighth part of our whole population!' Oliver Goldsmith, written off as a hopeless sentimentalist, had been right!

What was more, Cobbett felt deeply that, while the platitude was to crow about how rich Britain was, the condition of the common people of rural Britain must have been getting progressively worse over the past half century. Misery, on this scale he thought, was *modern*! He blamed the *nouveaux riches*; the capitalists; the money men who had bewitched the traditional squires and landlords from their old roast beef and plum pudding paternalism and let their labourers fend for themselves on the market. They were the 'bullfrogs' who gobbled down at a gulp the small tenants. 'Since the pianofortes and the parlour bells and the carpets came into the farmhouse, the lot of the labourers has been growing worse and worse.'

Cobbett's *Weekly Political Register*, in which these evils were enumerated, was an extraordinary, almost revolutionary, broadsheet. It used not just aggressively earthy language but the kind of village-pump and alehouse talk calculated to be read out loud. And its main feature, as Hazlitt justly observed, was William Cobbett: 'I asked how he got on. He said very badly. I asked him what was the cause of it. He said hard times. "What times," said he, "was there ever a finer summer, a finer harvest … ? Ah," said he, "they make it bad for poor people for all that." ' Throughout his long journalistic career, Cobbett also remained an active farmer and benevolent landlord, housing bachelor labourers in one of his own houses, paying his adult male farm workers on average 15 shillings a week or what he claimed was 20 times the going market rate – and still making a profit.

Living as close to the people as he did, Cobbett took violent exception to the kind of language used to characterize ordinary people – 'the peasantry' or Burke's 'swinish multitude.' Cobbett felt that such an epithet actually maligned hogs, with whom he warmly identified ('when I make my hog's lodging place for winter I look well at it and consider whether, in a pinch I could … make shift to lodge in it myself'). The problem with the conditions endured by labourers he saw at Cricklade in Gloucestershire was that their dwellings fell *below* pigsty standards 'and their food not nearly equal to that of pigs.'

Since parliament seemed deaf to this misery, Cobbett signed on for the usual radical platform: the purge of 'Old Corruption'; the sweeping away of placemen and sinecures and rotten boroughs; but also and always, social justice for the poor. His aim, as he saw it, was not to accelerate social disintegration but its opposite: the rebuilding of the ties of social sympathy that he thought had once – not so very long ago – connected farmers with smallholders and labourers. It was his genius to bring the distress of the country and town together. He knew, of course, that they could

The Life of William Cobbett – Written by Himself (1809), etching by James Gillray illustrating Cobbett's rural childhood.

and would understand each other, if for no other reason than that the industrial towns of Lancashire, Yorkshire and the Midlands were crammed with first-generation migrants from Arthur Young's capital-intensive, labour-extensive, commercialized countryside. Both were now suffering. Weavers and knitters had no work; hedgers, farm-hands, ditch-diggers and shepherds were now hired for shorter periods and in the winter sometimes not at all.

Not surprisingly, Cobbett's landscape does not look anything like Wordsworth's idyll of God-sheltered Lakeland. It is, instead, usually filthy, diseased, on the edge of starvation, at its worst reminiscent of shocked evangelical reports of destitution and poverty in India, with squatters and beggars huddled by the road. And he saw that in what were sometimes assumed (wrongly) to be the poorer regions – the north and northwest – the labourers were actually better off. In the great engine of agrarian prosperity, on the other hand – the grain belt of the Home Counties and East Anglia, where land had been most heavily exploited to maximize profit – the condition of the labourers was worst; he predicted, accurately, that it would be there, if anywhere, that a new peasants' revolt would catch fire.

The red-faced, loud-mouthed, piggy Cobbett rode and rode through the counties, poking into barnyards and poorhouses, picking on the bailiffs and absentee landlords who had the most infamous records, and reporting everything in his newspaper. Despite its editor being harassed by the government, who were understandably livid at his betrayal, as they saw it, and despite his doing time in Newgate for an article (not actually published) attacking flogging in the army, Cobbett's *Weekly Political Register* sold, at its height in 1817, 60,000 copies a week, overwhelmingly more than any other publication. He was certainly no saint. A vicious anti-semite, he also hated blacks and, until he saw that abolitionism was popular in his working-class constituency, insisted that the 'greasy Negro' in the Caribbean had a far better time of it than the British working class. But there is no doubt that no one since Tom Paine had quite got to the ordinary people of Britain in the way that Cobbett did and turned them into political animals.

There is also no doubt, however, that the new crusade for the restoration of 'natural rights' and old liberties was sent on its way by another surge of religious enthusiasm amongst the middle-class and working people of the country. Some of it was fuelled by disgust at well-publicized scandals in the heart of the ruling order.

When the notorious 'Impure' Harriette Wilson published her instantly best-selling memoirs in 1825, it emerged that her long list of aristocratic clients included the Duke of Wellington (who shared her with the Duke of Argyll) and the Marquis of Worcester. His amusement was to dress her up in a replica of his uniform as an

Above: *The Massacre of Peterloo* (detail), a line drawing, 1819.
Opposite: *William Cobbett*, attributed to George Cooke, 1831.

officer of the 10th Hussars and accompany her out riding in that get-up (the only way, she claimed, to get him out of bed). Along with the predictable strain of moral outrage at the shamelessness of the new Sodom, there was also a distinct tinge of millenarian urgency. A great change *was* coming, and the regiments of the righteous would be its advance guard. The Unitarian meeting house and the evangelical chapel and schoolroom were often the places where petitions were drafted and marches and assemblies organized. Their demands included both political and moral reform: an end to the monopoly of the Church of England and to slavery, as well as to the worm-eaten parliament. On the fringe of this mass enthusiasm, and hoping to tap its anger, were men who were genuine revolutionaries, like Bewick's old print-shop sparring partner the millenarian communist Thomas Spence. Slightly less extreme were journalists like Thomas Jonathan Wooler, the editor of *The Black Dwarf*, always in and out of prison for inciting the overthrow of the government. Spies were once again sent to infiltrate the most dangerous cells but this time as *agents provocateurs*, engineering conspiracies that would allow the authorities to make arrests and break the organization.

In November 1817, two deaths occurred which seemed to symbolize the polarization of the country. The only genuinely popular member of the royal family other than the king, Princess Charlotte Augusta, the beautiful and apparently liberal-minded daughter of the Prince Regent, died and the country fell into a paroxysm of grief, uncannily anticipating the mourning for a 20th-century princess to whom the same qualities would be attributed. Augusta was said to be the princess who *understood* the lives of ordinary people; who, given the age and decrepitude of her father and uncles, might well be in the line of succession and who, at any rate, might have produced an entire dynasty of compassionate, intelligent monarchs. At almost the same time, three radicals who in the spring of 1817 had been duped by one of the most energetic of the government secret agents, William Oliver, to lead a 'rising' of a few hundred stocking knitters and weavers at Pentridge in Nottinghamshire were convicted of sedition and sentenced to be hanged and – in the modern 19th century – quartered, though in the end they were just hanged until dead.

The rising had from the beginning been a trap set by the home secretary, Lord Sidmouth, to smoke out artisan revolutionaries before they could do damage. Wordsworth and Coleridge bought the government's line, and defended the politicians for stamping on the spirit of insurrection before it grew into a godless Jacobinical hydra. But along with the horrified Hazlitt, a younger generation of their admirers – including the poets John Keats and Percy Bysshe Shelley – recoiled and wrote angry verses denouncing the apostasy.

With the knowledge that the government was waiting for a pretext to use its muscle, the organizers of reform meetings took great care not to oblige them. So when, in the summer of 1819 while Cobbett was away in America, a mass meeting was called at St Peter's Fields on the outskirts of Manchester, the organizers – the Manchester Patriotic Union Society – took every precaution to ensure that the assembly would be peaceful. No opportunity would be given to the forces of 'order' to represent the meeting as a bestial, Jacobin mob bent on pillaging property and tearing down Christian civilization. 'It was deemed expedient,' wrote the weaver Samuel Bamford in his account of what quickly became known as the Massacre of Peterloo, 'that this meeting should be as morally effective as possible, and that it should exhibit a spectacle such as had never before been witnessed in England.'

The crowd of some 50,000–60,000, gathered from all over the northern counties, duly appeared on 16 August in an orderly procession beneath banners for 'Universal Suffrage,' some of them singing Primitive Methodist anthems, more like a revival meeting than a revolution. But the local magistrates were not interested in awarding marks for good behaviour. They were out to break the meeting. Among the speakers were the white top-hatted 'Orator' Henry Hunt and Samuel Bamford. Orders were given to the Manchester and Salford Yeomanry – merchants, manufacturers, publicans and shopkeepers – to arrest Hunt, which was done in short order: they roughed him up and pulled his trademark white hat over his head. But in cutting a way through the crowd, the yeomanry trampled a small girl who happened to be in the way of their mounts and killed her. At that point they found themselves surrounded by furious demonstrators, hemming in the horses and showering them with abuse. The yeomanry began to panic; regular cavalry – hussars – were sent in to try and extricate them. They did so with sabres unsheathed, slicing a path through the tight-packed people. A desperate rush to escape the troops ensued. Eleven people were killed; 421 seriously wounded, 162 with sabre cuts. At least 100 of the hurt were women and small children.

Bamford described the mêlée with poetic economy:

The cavalry were in confusion: they evidently could not, with all the weight of man and horse, penetrate that compact mass of human beings; and their sabres were plied to hew away through naked held-up hands, and defenceless heads; and then chopped limbs, and wound-gaping skulls were seen; and groans and cries were mingled with the din of that horrid confusion. 'Ah! ah! for shame! for shame!' was shouted. Then, 'Break! break! they are killing them in front, and they cannot get away … For a moment the crowd held back as in a pause;

then was a rush, heavy and resistless as a head-long sea; and a sound like low thunder, with screams, prayers, and imprecations, from the crowd-moiled … and sabre-doomed, who could not escape.

Lord Sidmouth congratulated the Manchester magistrates on their firmness. William Wordsworth appears to have felt much the same way. Others were nauseated by what had taken place, comparing it with the worst atrocities inflicted by European absolute despots on their populations. There was something evil about Peterloo, which for many mocked the pretension of the government to be upholding British traditions against innovation. Peterloo was not, the critics believed, a British event. Shelley was in Italy but that didn't prevent him from writing a savage anti-government poem, 'The Mask of Anarchy' ('I met Murder on the way/He had a mask like Castlereagh'), which marked his divorce from the older generation of poets.

In the shocked aftermath of Peterloo the radicals themselves divided into those like 'Orator' Hunt, cheered on the streets of London by 300,000 people as he was taken to his appeal hearing, who felt it was important to persist with lawful, constitutional change, and other less patient types who had been driven over the edge. Arthur Thistlewood, for example, a down-at-heel gentleman radical who had planned the Cato Street conspiracy (to assassinate the Cabinet and attack the Tower of London, the Bank of England and parliament), was the perfect subject for a show trial followed by execution and government repression. By the end of 1820 most of the leaders of the democratic movement – Sir Francis Burdett, 'Orator' Hunt and Thomas Wooler – were in prison. Since 1819, when the Six Acts were passed, magistrates had the right to search houses for seditious literature or arms and to ban meetings of more than 50 persons, and a new stamp duty of sixpence put most popular publications safely beyond the reach of literate working men and women.

This was the moment when William Cobbett reappeared from America, bearing (until he dumped them in Liverpool) the bones of Tom Paine. Cobbett had obviously inherited Paine's mantle as the People's Friend. As a crowd-puller and the man who could articulate anger the people's way, he was desperately needed. But something odd had happened to William Cobbett. Instead of mobilizing against the repressive Six Acts, he decided to mobilize his loyal following against tea. Roasted wheat or American maize, he told them over and over, is much better for you. Instead of attacking the infamy of Peterloo, he attacked the infamy of potatoes. Instead of honouring the memory of Paine, he went on at numbing length about his new currency policies and the 'Jew dogs' who had turned London into the 'Jew

Wen.' A pity, he thought, that England couldn't return to the sensible policy of Edward I and make them wear badges.

With the tribunes of the people out of harm's way or, like Cobbett, self-destructed, and with a measurable improvement in the economy, the government could congratulate itself that a British revolution had indeed been nipped in the bud. But theirs was an unmerited and unwise complacency. The shoots of anger had been clipped, but the roots of anger ran deep. Bewick, for one, had not been pacified. The last straw for him was the cynicism with which Wellington and Castlereagh, the foreign secretary, had allowed Britain to be hitched to the heavy wagon of pan-European policing, orchestrated by the Austrian Foreign Minister, Klemens von Metternich, at the Congress of Vienna in 1815. To do the bidding of foreign despots while remaining obstinately deaf to the cries of Britons was, for Bewick, a dangerous as well as a morally reprehensible policy. Waxing prophetic, he warned that the oligarchs and aristocrats and bishops had

> sinned themselves out of all shame. This phalanx have kept their ground, and will do so, till, it is to be feared, violence from an enraged people breaks them up or perhaps, till the growing opinions against such a crooked order of conducting the affairs of this great nation becomes quite apparent to an immense majority, whose frowns may have the power of bringing the agents of government to pause upon the brink of the precipice on which they stand, and to provide in time, the wise and honest measures, to avert the coming storm.

Bewick was writing in the 1820s, a few years before his death in 1828, and the sustained note of moral urgency he strikes was typical of the decade, notwithstanding its deceptively quiet politics. They were the years when, from the west of Ireland to Bewick's Newcastle, town halls, chapels, assembly rooms and taverns were filled to overflowing with earnest crowds, often addressed by evangelical preachers. The targets now were not so obviously political as religious and social. In Ireland they included the delivery of the promise, made by Fitzwilliam 20 years earlier, to remove the ban on Catholics taking public office and standing for parliament, the great aim of the Catholic Associations led by the charismatic Kerry lawyer and landlord Daniel O'Connell. It was a movement with which Dissenting, Nonconformist religion in England and Scotland now made common cause, since they sensed that their adversaries were indeed the same. In the industrial towns a new, largely middle-class campaign for parliamentary reform, launched in Birmingham by the banker Thomas Atwood, tapped into the atmosphere of moral crusade. In 1824, a cause that might have been dear to Bewick's heart was consummated when the Society for the Protection of Cruelty to Animals (Royal, when Queen Victoria became its patron) was established. By parliamentary statute, it became an offence to inflict gross cruelty on cattle being driven to Smithfield. But the same act also outlawed the traditional pastimes of bull-baiting and November bull-running – one of the staples of popular village life, especially in the Midlands. When a bull-run was held at Stamford in Lincolnshire, despite the new law, it took a company of dragoons and police to enforce the suppression.

The army of righteousness was very much on the march, and their most successful crusade was the abolition of slavery. Originally a Quaker speciality, the abolitionist cause had swollen into a great evangelical campaign that crossed party and confessional lines. Although it had to contend with some crude working-class racism it had strong popular support in Yorkshire and Lancashire, and it was at Oldham in 1832 that Cobbett finally announced his own conversion to the cause. The abolitionist George Thompson, who risked his life lecturing against slavery in the United States, claimed to have spoken to 700,000 in Liverpool alone.

All these campaigns were revolutionary in ways that neither Tom Paine nor Mary Wollstonecraft could have imagined. They gave rise to the first professionally organized popular pressure groups. To defeat the Protestant landlords' chosen incumbents in Ireland, O'Connell used paid agents, carefully compiled voters' lists, and organized travel for those who needed it to get to the polls. The abolitionists were prepared, if necessary, to organize a systematic boycott throughout the country of West Indian sugar, which, given the enormous numbers involved in the campaign and the existence, since the Napoleonic wars, of commercially farmed sugar beet, might well have inflicted huge economic damage on West Indian slave owners. And they all brought the old instrument of the petition into the age of mass mobilization. Hundreds of thousands of signatures would be gathered, sewn into one immensely elongated sheet designed specifically for the spectacular effect, and delivered to the floor of the House of Commons by a supporting MP. If the organizers had done their job properly, the petitions would be so weighty that they would need four or even eight members to carry them into the chamber. In the first three years of the 1830s, 4000 such petitions were brought to parliament. The best research now suggests that fully one in five adult males had signed their name on an abolitionist petition in 1787, 1814 or 1833. Even more astonishingly, the petition of the women of Britain bore 187,000 names and needed four members to lug it on to the floor of the House in a scene that would have made Mary Wollstonecraft happy had she been alive to witness it.

In the hands of the new social church, politics became a theatre of virtue; one in which the assumption of authority by old, tight-hosed lechers at court and parliament seemed increasingly grotesque. The traditional symbols of power – coats of arms and battlemented manors – now gave way to the travelling exhibition, organized by men such as the great abolitionists, the MP William Wilberforce and the writer Thomas Clarkson, who displayed whips and chains, models of slave ships and the commodities used in the trade of humans. Instead of an image of the king, Clarkson's famous print of the sardine-can slave ship with hundreds of bodies crammed between decks, or Blake's horrifying prints of the sadistic treatment meted out to rebel slaves were seen everywhere in Britain, in public places and private houses alike.

By the end of the decade party divisions seemed less important than moral boundaries separating the righteous from the heedless. Abolitionism finally brought together in the same big tent William Hazlitt and William Wordsworth; the privileged inside the system and the vocal outside it. And the campaigns were capable of bringing about changes of heart in men who had sworn they would never tamper with the best of all constitutions. As prime minister, the Duke of Wellington felt that he had no choice but to assent to Catholic emancipation as the price of buying off O'Connell's formidable Catholic Association. And the Whigs, who for many years were no keener than the Tories on parliamentary reform, were now faced with the possibility of their own redundancy should they not find some way to harness the steam-driven energy of moral radicalism to their own old coach and four.

The summer of 1830 unexpectedly gave them their chance but it also confronted them with an end to procrastination. The countryside – the same countryside that plodded gently along in Constable's landscapes; the country that was still celebrated as the solid heartland of Old England, the imperturbable realm of squire and parson – went up in smoke, exactly (suspiciously, some thought) as Cobbett had predicted. He made no secret, in fact, of his sympathy: 'Never, let what will happen, will these people lie down and starve quietly.' The winter had been very bad. As usual, the consequences were high prices, labourers unemployed or put on short hire, and starvation wages. But this time the 'army' of 'Captain Swing' made itself felt, burning hayricks and smashing threshing machines. Swing cut a huge swathe through southern England, as far west as Dorset and as far east as East Anglia and Lincolnshire. Pitched battles between yeomanry and rebels broke out in Hampshire, Cobbett's home county, Kent and east Sussex, close to where he had addressed a crowd of 500 at Battle – a coincidence that put him on trial in 1831, with the predictable acquittal. Nearly 2000 Swing prisoners were put on trial and 19 were executed, but more than 200 other death sentences were commuted to Australian transportation.

The great argument for pre-emptive reform came from France, where another revolution in July 1830 had removed the Bourbon king Charles X and replaced him with Louis-Philippe, the son of the Duke of Orléans who had sat in the first Revolution's Convention as 'Philippe Egalité.' The power of historical memory was sobering and unhesitatingly used by Whig historians and orators like the young Thomas Babington Macaulay. Only timely reform, they argued would prevent a *modern* revolution from happening in Britain. But the Tory prime minister, the Duke of Wellington, who had accepted Catholic emancipation, put up the barricades. 'The state of representation,' he said, 'was the best available' and he 'would never introduce and always resist parliamentary reform.' As it became known that King William IV felt much the same way, the monarch's popularity evaporated.

But the consensus that repression without reform would calm the country was collapsing within the political elite. It was now an argument about the wisest means of collective self-preservation. By November 1830 Wellington was gone, and the first Whig administration since before the Revolution of 1789 took office on condition that a measure of parliamentary reform would be introduced. The new prime minister, Charles Grey, Charles James Fox's protégé, had first attempted a Reform Bill almost 40 years before. This, at last, would be the endlessly delayed vindication of that '40 years' war.' Since this Whig government was at least as aristocratic as the Tories (Grey himself was an earl), few were prepared for the thunderbolt that struck when the details of reform were unveiled in the Commons in March 1831. Macaulay described with pardonable over-excitement the state of shock on the Tory front bench: '… the jaw of Peel fell, and the face of Twiss was as the face of a damned soul and Herries looked like Judas.' They could be forgiven their consternation. Some 140 boroughs with fewer than 4000 residents were to lose either one or two members (60 being wiped out altogether), who were to be redistributed to the new towns of industrial Britain and to London.

Between the time that this first bill went down to defeat in the Lords and its reintroduction, the more apocalyptic warnings of the Whigs seemed about to be fulfilled. Riots broke out in Derbyshire, Nottingham and Bristol, where the Bishop's Palace was burned to the ground. In the coal and iron country of south Wales (where there had already been a serious strike in 1816), hunger fused with political anger when a crowd at Merthyr Tydfil attacked a courtroom, liberated pro-reform prisoners and took over the town. A detachment of cavalry from Swansea was ambushed and hundreds of troops had to be sent from Monmouth before some sort of order was restored.

Against this background of gathering chaos and violence, a new election was called. The campaign was, for once, taken to almost every town in the country, big and small, with very clear principles dividing the contending parties. The result was a Whig majority big enough to demand from a mortified William IV the instant creation of 50 new peers, enough to carry the measure through the Upper House, where it had been twice rejected. The Reform Bill became law in June 1832. Most historians have insisted on its deep social conservatism: the preservation, not the destruction, of the aristocratic flavour and dominance of land. And that was, in fact, the intention of the Whigs. 'No-one,' as Macaulay wrote, 'wished to turn the Lords out of their House except here and there a crazy radical whom the boys on the street point at as he walks along.' On the contrary, by betting on anti-revolutionary instincts of the £10 household suffrage (granting the vote only to men holding property worth £10), the Whig grandees like Lord John Russell, Earl Grey and Viscount Durham believed that it was *more* likely to preserve the stabilizing power of the aristocracy from the threat of all-out 'American' democracy. Their aim was to split a potentially much more dangerous alliance between middle-class moralizing activists and truly radical, universal-suffrage democrats.

The strategy worked. The reform made half a million Britons new voters and created a new House of Commons, one that had room for Daniel O'Connell, 'Orator' Henry Hunt, Thomas Atwood and William Cobbett – the last, somewhat improbably, the member for industrial Oldham. This was a parliament in which a vague air of common-sensical liberalism had indeed stopped revolution in its tracks (although there would still be countryside riots, the worst in Kent in 1838). And yet the changes did matter. When Cobbett threw one of his 'Chopstick Festivals' for 7000 labourers to celebrate the Reform Act, supplying 70lb of ham and wagonloads of mutton, beef and veal, he knew he was seeing the bloodless death of 'Old Corruption'; the sweeping away of 'potwallopers,' placemen and pocket boroughs.

Conversely, there was a reason why King William IV was so beside himself with rage that he could not bring himself to sign the act, leaving it to royal commissioners. In 1829, with the passing of the Catholic Emancipation Act, the monopoly of the Church of England had gone. Now the independence of the House of Lords had been irreversibly compromised by the threatened instant creation of a politically pliant majority. And with the recognition of the campaigning success of Thomas Atwood's Birmingham Political Union, so soon after O'Connell in Ireland, the way was open (although it would not be immediately taken) for the machinery of modern party politics, using all the techniques of mobilization pioneered by the

abolitionists and the emancipators – hustings, mass petitions, newspaper campaigns
– to contest power in Britain.

A year later, in 1833, the reformed but still undemocratic Commons made
Britain the first nation to outlaw slavery in all its colonies, at a time, notwithstanding recent historical writing, when the demand for slave-products was increasing and
not diminishing. It had been destroyed, overwhelmingly, by the force of moral argument; by the final victory of the view that argued for a common human nature.
Which is not to say that when the Houses of Parliament burned down in 1834 the
fire could be taken as some sort of providential announcement of a new age of moral
miracles. The victories had still been only partial. Catholics now had access to office
but in Ireland had lost the 40-shilling freehold vote. It was replaced, as in the counties
of mainland Britain, by the suffrage bar – of the £10 annual household rental –
which effectively excluded the vast majority of those who had lined up behind
Paine, Cobbett and Hunt. True manhood suffrage would have to wait until 1918.
Even in the Caribbean, slave-holding plantation owners had to be compensated for
their losses; and initially a system of transitional 'apprenticeship' created a twilight
world between servitude and genuine freedom.

Nothing had quite worked out as any of the forces of nature had imagined. The
British had not walked their way to democracy and social justice. The ramblers and
peripatetics had, in fact, been overtaken by a high-speed, steam-driven, economic
revolution which they were powerless to arrest, much less reverse. And yet, industrial Britain – the most extraordinary transformation in the history of Europe – had
happened, so far without bloody revolution. An age which had begun with fast roads
had been replaced by another with unimaginably faster railway trains. Some of them,
to Wordsworth's dismay, were violating the sanctuary of the Lakes; belching smoke,
making a demonic noise and bringing working people virtually to his doorstep.
There were walkers all right, hordes of them, carrying with them Thomas West's and
his own guide, in a hurry to mark off the obligatory stops on the route. He had
himself become a tourist site.

This wasn't what he wanted at all. Like Rousseau, Wordsworth believed that the
British countryside ought to be the antidote to, not the accomplice of, modernity.
But the opposites had somehow come together, got *inside* each other; country
people wanting town things; town people yearning for a piece of the countryside.
And they got it. The most industrial society in the world was also the most attached
to its village memories. Within every early Victorian town were green spaces and
places: miniaturized corners of the country, created as a palliative or memento of
what had been lost. The railway companies gave their workers allotments beside the

The Opening of the Birkenhead Park, engraving from the *Illustrated London News*, 1847.

tracks where they could grow vegetables and flowers or keep a pig and some chickens, an echo of the strips and common land they had lost in the enclosures. It was not Cobbett's imagined Merrie England of village greens, small ale and roast beef, but people were still better off for having the allotment than they would have been without. For the first time, too, thanks to pioneers of green spaces like John Claudius Loudon, a 'park' meant not the private estate of an aristocrat but a public place where there were no barriers of class or property; designed, as in the park at Birkenhead, opened to the public in 1847, with rambles and cricket pitches, ponds and meadows; the kind of place where ordinary Britons could come and give their children something of nature's pleasures. Such places were not, I suppose, sublime. But neither were they at all ridiculous.

3

Somewhere – beyond the 24-ton lump of coal; the 80-blade Sportsman's Knife; the mechanical oyster opener billed as 'The Ostracide'; beyond the Gutta Percha Company's steamship furniture (convertible into a buoyant liferaft in case of mishap); beyond the tea party of stuffed stoats – were the glass beehives, designed by John Milton 'Inventor of London.' The little queen, in her pink watered-silk gown and tiara, stopped in front of the exhibit and peered in at the teeming occupants. What struck her most was their virtuous indifference to public inspection. There was honey to be made and they got on with making it. 'Her Majesty and Prince Albert frequently bestowed their notice on the wonderful operations of the gifted little insects whose undeviating attention to their own concerns in the midst of all the various distractions of sound and sight that surrounded them afforded an admirable lesson.' It was a lesson that did not need labouring. There would be times when Victoria would feel the indecency of visibility. Ten years on, robbed of the long, protecting shadow of her husband, she would pull the curtains; douse the gaslight; bury herself in blackness.

But not on this sparkling May Day 1851; 'the *greatest* day in our history, the most beautiful and imposing,' she wrote to her uncle, King Leopold of the Belgians. On this day, inside the Crystal Palace, Victoria was perfectly content to be the queen of the humming hive. She could return the stares of 30,000 season-ticket holders and feel nothing but a welling of sacred exhilaration. A misty drizzle had been falling as the queen and Albert rode up Rotten Row (a corruption of *Route du roi* – the Royal Way). But as if deferring to the majesty of the occasion (as Victoria noted), it had given way to the pearly sunshine of a Hyde Park spring. Passing through the Coalbrookdale iron gates and walking into the Palace, heralded by a blaze of trumpets, the space a mass of palm fronds and heaped flowers, Victoria was momentarily blinded by the radiance as 300,000 panes of glass, each exactly 49 inches by 10, flooded the space with intense light. It was, *assuredly*, the light of the Lord, who had, like her, recognized the goodness of her husband's great work. Now, as he stood by

THE QUEEN
AND THE HIVE

The First of May, 1851 by Franz Xaver Winterhalter, 1873.

her side, together with Vicky (the Princess Royal), in her Nottinghamshire lace and white satin with wild roses in her hair, and little Bertie, dashing in his Highland kilt, they were all washed by the effulgence. With the perfume of the eau-de-Cologne falling from the 20-foot crystal fountain, and her ears full of the euphony of a 600-voice choir and of the five organs strategically placed to exploit the building's shuddery resonance, Victoria felt borne aloft into a state of sublime transcendence. She was not alone. The usually hard-bitten reporter of the *Daily News* waxed spiritual when he heard a sound akin to 'the noise of many waters heard in some apocalyptic vision, making the hearts of the hearers vibrate like the glass of the edifice that inclosed them.'

The prophetic visions swimming in the head of the Prince Consort – harmony; peace; unity within and between nations (sentiments exhaustively enumerated in a long speech, while his starstruck queen gazed adoringly on) – did not, on this particular May Day, seem unrealistically sanctimonious. The Great Exhibition *was* in its way a sort of miracle. Although the Crystal Palace was the largest enclosed space on earth (more than ⅓ mile long), it had been built from scratch in Hyde Park in just over six months (the principal construction taking just 17 weeks). Once Fox and Henderson, the glass and iron manufacturers, had received the basic design it took them a week to prepare full estimates, and the architect had taken just eight days from his original conception to draft a full set of working drawings.

Despite initial apathy, even resistance, in parliament and carping in the press, Prince Albert's enthusiasm finally inspired philanthropy, which was quick on its toes when it came and as sure of its mission as the designers and builders. Funding for the exhibition had been launched by some £70,000 of private subscription, after which guaranteed money had flowed in. But then the entire occasion confounded conventional expectations. The welcoming grace of the prefabricated and infinitely extendable building made nonsense of the romantic cant about the infernal grimness of industrial society. The rigidity of iron had been bent into lacy, feminine curves. Painted in the hues of medieval heraldry – yellow, red and blue – the interior, which had a Gothic revival 'medieval court' as well an array of piston-driven heavy machinery, seemed to announce the happy marriage of past and future. Although manufactures were supposed to be the death of artisanal craft, the Palace showcased both engineering and the best that artisans could produce. Every one of those panes had in fact been hand-blown. Together the iron and the glass wove a filigree web that, instead of blocking out open space, seemed to contain it as if in a delicate membrane. (There was in fact some not unjustified anxiety about whether the Crystal Palace would be leak-proof and wind-resistant.)

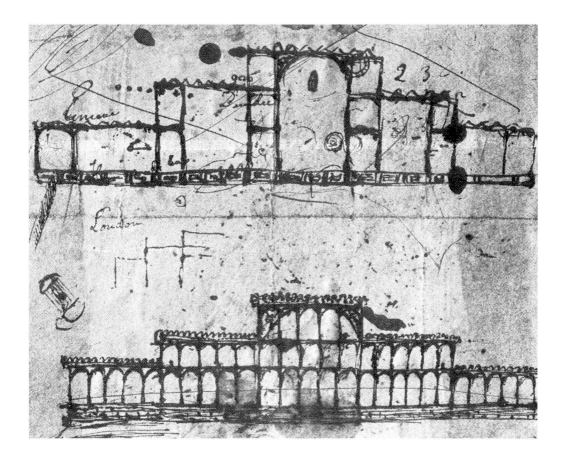

Joseph Paxton's sketch for the Crystal Palace made on a sheet of blotting paper in the Boardroom of the Midland

The fiercest critics of the machine age also routinely cast it as the enemy of nature. The true Merrie England, they said, was the village green, the cosy cottage and the benevolent squire. But when the members of the royal commission that had been set up to organize the exhibition, with Prince Albert at its head, picked May Day as opening day they knew what they were doing.

Their chosen architect, who had not submitted designs for the original competition, was the young, but well-connected landscape designer Joseph Paxton whose own career – as both greenhouse designer and board member of the Midland Railway – exemplified the easy fit between horticulture and industrialism. (He had doodled the first sketch of the building in a bored moment at a railway board meeting.) So when the proposed siting in Hyde Park was attacked, especially by Colonel Charles Sibthorp, MP for Lincoln and a truculent enemy of all things modern, as a 'tubercle' on the lungs of London, Paxton rose to the challenge. He

raised and bent the framing ribs of the 'transept' to form a semicircular roof enclosing the two ancient 90-foot elms whose impending destruction Sibthorp had made
the test case of the 'humbug' exhibition's expensive vandalism. Instead of being casualties of the show, the elms were now its green presiding guardians, offering extra
shade (along with the fabric awnings) to anyone sweating in the glassy humidity, and
a promise that the industrial future need not sound the death knell for the British
landscape.

If nature and industry, the bees and the glass hive, could be reconciled, so could
other perennial antagonists: science and religion; aristocracy and enterprise; technology and the Christian tradition. The membership of the royal commission over
which Prince Albert presided had been thoughtfully composed so as to include all
possible cultural constituencies other than protectionists. There were entrepreneurial
aristocrats like Francis Egerton, the Earl of Ellesmere, and the Duke of Buccleuch
and Queensberry; free-trade politicians like William Gladstone and Richard
Cobden; a Gothic Revival architect, Charles Barry, who had designed the new
Palace of Westminster; and a self-made developer, Sir William Cubitt. There was
room both for the founding force of the National Gallery, Charles Lock Eastlake,
and for the President of the Geological Society, Sir Charles Lyell, whose own work
had thrown serious doubt on the literal truth of the Book of Genesis. The driving
spirit of the show, who had persuaded Albert to lend his patronage, was the extraordinary Henry Cole, who had been the editor of the *Journal of Design and Manufactures*
between 1849 and 1852, and had produced the first commercial Christmas cards and
the first sets of children's building blocks. Cole may have started with the idea that
the exhibition would be a showcase for the best of British design (he himself had
created a famous all-white Minton tea service); but by the time it was finished, he
and Prince Albert shared a more messianic vision. The Great Exhibition would not
be just a grand national and international bazaar; it would be a template for the
peaceful future. Carried away by his personal mission, and encouraged by Cobden,
Albert had already thought – out loud during an extraordinary speech at a banquet
in York for the Lord Mayor of London on 25 October 1850 – that the post-
exhibition world would be an indivisible human community of growers, makers,
and, not least, happy shoppers. In such a world, war between states would become
an anachronistic absurdity, replaced by the peaceful competition of commerce.
Shows like the Great Exhibition would be the alternative to the military parades of
martinet autocracies.

Machinery, which had been depicted by the fearful and the ignorant as a
Moloch, delivering humanity into its maw and spitting them out again as labour

Opening of the Great Exhibition, 1 May 1851 by Eugène Louis Lami, 1851.

units of the profit calculus, without regard for the communities, the families and the individual lives it had devoured, would now be seen as socially and morally benevolent. At this precise moment, when the word 'Victorian' entered the English language, another word, 'industry,' did a semantic somersault, conveying henceforth not the expenditure, but the saving of physical labour. Together the two spelled a third of the age's favourite doctrine: progress. The big machines themselves, brightly burnished and hissing odourless steam, mesmerized the crowds, who stood for hours watching them from behind crimson ropes. Broad-gauge locomotives like the Great Western's green giant *The Lord of the Isles,* capable of generating 1000 horse-power, were ogled as friendly Titans, not least because the railways had been crucial in accomplishing the professed objective of the exhibition: to bring Britons, divided by both class and geography, together. Of the 6 million-plus visitors who came to see the Exhibition during the six months it was open, from May to October, at least three-quarters of a million came by railway train. Transport on this scale had hitherto been achieved only at times of military mobilization, by armies on the march and civilians fleeing from their advance. But the greatest mass movement of population to this point in all of British history was entirely peaceful; the triumph, not of state power, but of curiosity and commerce. Excursions, including lodging, were organized by Thomas Cook, and visitors from relatively humble backgrounds, the 'respectable working class,' could take advantage of a special cut-price admission. Hundreds of thousands did.

There had been other industrial exhibitions. Embarrassingly, it had been Napoleonic France that had invented the genre. But this was the first time that an entire nation was redefined by a trade show. Let tinpot tyrants parade their hussars and their field cannon. The workshop of the world would boast Nasmyth's steam hammer. 'These, England's triumphs are,' wrote Thackeray in his May Day Ode to the Exhibition in 1850, 'the trophies of a bloodless war.'

So the Great Exhibition was meant to dispel virtually all the social and political nightmares of mid-19th-century Britain, replacing isolation by commercial connection. But would the *classes* of Britain itself be quite so harmoniously reconciled? The poetic pieties were doubtless all very nice, thought the octogenarian Duke of Wellington, still the commander of the London garrison, but they were no substitute for guns and cavalry to keep the dangerous rabble at bay. Wellington believed that 15,000 troops at a minimum were needed, along with an overpowering display of police, to safeguard the metropolis. He was still haunted by the narrow escape of spring and summer 1848, when London had been the scene of mass Chartist demonstrations for political equality, threatening to spread the revolutionary contagion that had overthrown governments from Paris to Rome and Vienna. But three years later there were no bloody barricades; only the patient queue for the turnstiles.

The prospect of masses of the great unwashed freely mingling with the quality in what was already, at 2 million, the most populous city the world had ever seen worried guardians of order like Wellington. Never mind the piety of spreading peace among nations, the active encouragement of foreigners to visit London for the Exhibition seemed criminally irresponsible. Bearded revolutionaries (their full whiskers thought to be an unmistakable sign of political deviance) would be stalking the streets of Kensington in the guise of innocent tourists. Surveillance and containment would stretch to breaking point. Prince Albert was only half joking when he wrote that

> The opponents of the Exhibition work with might and main to throw all the old women into a panic and to drive myself crazy. The strangers, they give out, are certain to commence a thorough revolution here, murder Victoria and myself, and to proclaim the Red Republic in England; the plague is certain to ensue from the confluence of such vast multitudes and to swallow up those for whom the increased price of everything has not already swept away. For all this I am held responsible.

But both Albert and Paxton stood their ground. Because of the attempts that had been made on her life (four in the 1840s) it was assumed that the queen would be given a private tour of the exhibition by the prince on opening day before the public was let in. But as far as Albert was concerned, if the exhibition was to be a demonstration of the unique virtues of the constitutional monarchy it was essential that the queen be seen in the midst of her loyal subjects. Against the objection that ill-intentioned parties might insinuate themselves among the ranks of the respectable, the bolder Albertian view prevailed. Dignitaries dominated the proceedings on 1 May, which included a blessing pronounced by the Archbishop of Canterbury that gave the terms 'nave' and 'transept' used for the building an odour of authentic sanctity. But Victoria made a point of walking round the displays – including Mr Milton's glass beehive – and she would come back with the family 13 times before it closed.

Paxton's views about the populism of the event were even more audacious. His proposal to make admission free after the end of May was greeted with incredulous horror. But his insistence (shared by Cole and Prince Albert) that the Great Exhibition was the best possible display of the British 'third way,' neither republican nor autocratic, extended to arguing that bringing working people into the Palace would soften, not sharpen, their sense of separateness from the ruling classes. It would show them the cushily upholstered future waiting for the thrifty and industrious – the worker bees of the Workshop of the World. Soothed by the spectacle, they would be transformed from agitators into consumers. The result was that a compromise was struck. After 26 May, admission would be set at one shilling from Tuesdays to Thursdays, with even cheaper season tickets for women. On the first 'shilling day' 37,000 people came to the Palace. Subsequently the number averaged between 45,000 and 65,000 a day. No revolutionary hordes materialized. In fact, over the six months of the exhibition's life not a single act of vandalism was reported. By October 1851, between 90,000 and 100,000 were coming every day. As *The Times* rightly reported, 'the People have now become the Exhibition.'

The first great British show of the 19th century was defined, above all, as a family outing – starting with the royal family. There is no doubt that, had the Great Exhibition not been her husband's pet project, it would have been considerably less likely to have aroused so much of Victoria's enthusiasm. But she believed it to have been emphatically his creation (poor Henry Cole would never emerge from the long shadow of that myth) and 1 May 1851 was, for Victoria, primarily the product of Albert's persevering benevolence. She responded, too, to the prince's strong conviction that the exhibition should be a vision of domestic Britain, strengthened, rather than stressed, by its industrial transformation. The overstuffed displays of home fabrics and furniture, dinner plates and nursery toys, pianos and cast-iron garden seats all seemed to translate the picture of Britain's economic power into a middle-class idyll. The royal family's personal memento of the occasion was not the ceremonial views so much as the artist Franz Xaver Winterhalter's family group called *The First of May* (1851), depicting the scene when the old Duke of Wellington, on his own 82nd birthday, came to bring a present to his godson, the one-year-old Prince Arthur, on his. In the background of this modern Adoration of the Magus holy sunbeams bathe the Crystal Palace.

It went without saying that this sunlit bourgeois future would also warm the chillier prospects of the British working class. Or so Prince Albert hoped. Encouraged by Thomas Bazley, the Manchester businessman who prided himself on the benevolent treatment of his workers – and who seems to have invented Friday paydays – the Prince Consort set himself to think how the exhibition could give some momentum to redesigning the domestic lives of working people for better health and comfort. As President of the Society for Improving the Dwellings of the Working Classes, he commissioned Henry Roberts to build a gabled, two-storey,

THE POUND AND THE SHILLING.

"Whoever Thought of Meeting You Here?"

Top: *The Pound and the Shilling*, a topical cartoon from *Punch*, 1851, illustrating the mixed crowds at the Great Exhibition, attracted by the cut-price shilling tickets.

Above: A model house for working-class families, Kennington Park, London. Commissioned by Prince Albert, it was originally created in the grounds of the Hyde Park Barracks for the Great Exhibition, 1851.

four-unit model apartment house for working families. Built from hollow bricks to reduce the price, these dwellings incorporated tall windows for maximum light and a central staircase for better ventilation, and could be extended through modular replication, either horizontally or vertically. The show houses were erected in Hyde Park beside the exhibition and, after it was over, dismantled and rebuilt on Kennington Common (significantly the site of the Chartist demonstrations) where they still stand, albeit in woebegone condition.

Decades later, in the 1880s, emerging, just a peek, from her widow's shrouds, Victoria too would also interest herself in the housing of the poor. Shocked by published reports on the slums of London, and doubtless moved by a conviction that it was what Albert the Good would have wanted, she wrote to Gladstone's government urging them to turn their attention to the problem, and her benevolent nagging resulted in a royal commission. The issue was important to the queen because she subscribed to the contemporary liberal commonplace that if industrial Britain had proved uniquely stable in a world of war and revolution, it was due not just to the political, but also to the social, constitution with which the country was blessed. That constitution rested on the moral bedrock of family life of which the queen was the chief exemplar, as wife, then bereft widow and, always, mother. She was, in fact, the first British sovereign–mother; although often, in her 64-year reign, the paradox gave her no joy – she fretted that her duty to be a good woman 'amiable and domestic' was at odds with both her character and her duty to reign, especially in an empire where so much emphasis was placed on the ideal of Christian manliness.

But then Victoria believed that this dilemma was, to some extent or other, also the lot of her sex. She felt that all over Britain there must have been countless good daughters, wives and mothers, torn between their obligation to be the 'angel at the hearth' (in the poet Coventry Patmore's famously sentimental poem 'The Angel in the House,' 1854) and the unforgiving necessities of daily life: children to be nursed; work to be done; tables to be laid; prayers to be said. And the mother–queen flattered herself, even when she was immured at Windsor or Osborne or wrapped up in the bracing world of Highland 'Balmorality,' that she understood the condition of Britain's women; the burden of their duty and the weight of their fortitude.

But did she?

In the autumn of 1832 the 13-year-old Princess Victoria, *en route* to Wales, had her first glimpse of industrial Britain. The visits to a cotton mill at Belper and a school at Bangor, where she laid the foundation stone, were carefully orchestrated to disarm the hostility of the 'labouring classes' and symbolize the union between the future sovereign and the ordinary people. Who could hate a rosebud? But somewhere

near Birmingham, Victoria's coach rolled through coal country and she saw something deeply un-English: black grass. She wrote in her journal:

> The men, women, children, country and houses are all black. But I can not by
> any description give an idea of its strange and extraordinary appearance. The
> country is very desolate every where; there are coals about and the grass is quite
> blasted and black. I just now see an extraordinary building flaming with fire.
> The country continues black, engines, flaming coals, in abundance every
> where, smoking and burning coal heaps, intermingled with wretched huts and
> little ragged children.

The naivety of this wide-eyed picture of a British inferno is hardly surprising. The
whole purpose of Victoria's upbringing to this point had been isolation. After her
father, the Duke of Kent, the fourth son of George III, had died on 23 January 1820,
eight months after her birth on 24 May 1819, she was brought up almost entirely in
the company of women: a small, stuffy world dominated by her mother the duchess
(in whose room she slept) and her governess Baroness Lehzen, and riddled with
petty court and family intrigues. At Kensington Palace, Victoria was to be fenced off
from squalor and wickedness, otherwise known as King George IV and his successor
King William IV, her uncles. In an age in which Evangelical fervour had taken hold,
not just of the middle classes but of a significant part of the aristocracy too, the
purity and piety of the heiress presumptive were touted as a desperately needed
correction for a monarchy badly compromised by scandal. The queen–saviour was
intended to have been George IV's daughter, Princess Charlotte Augusta, whose
virtue and liberal intelligence were supposed to give the raddled monarchy a fresh
start. But, to genuine and unforced national grief, she had died in childbirth. Her
widower (who was also Victoria's mother's brother and thus her uncle twice over),
Leopold of Saxe-Coburg-Gotha, later king of the Belgians, obviously saw the little
princess as Charlotte's natural successor; he passed on advice books, and began to
tutor her as he would have done his wife, 'Our times are hard for royalty,' he wrote
to her when she was just 13, 'never was there a period when the existence of real
qualities in persons of high station has been more imperiously called for.'

It was the truth. When George III had died in 1820, his passing had been
marked by genuine sorrow for an endearingly simple man. Although in later years
he was blind and behaved as if mad, he was always thought to have understood the
hardships of the humble as well as, if not better than, the pomp of the mighty. But
when George IV was lowered into the vault at St George's Chapel, Windsor, in 1830

Top: *Princess Victoria*, self-portrait, aged eight, 1827.
Above: Hand-coloured map of Europe by Princess Victoria, *c.* 1830.

(by undertakers who were drunk), while his successor, his brother King William, made a scene of himself by chatting noisily throughout the funeral service, it was a demise conspicuous for its lack of regret, much less grief. Massively bloated and terminally debauched, George IV and his excesses had seemed to moral critics like Hazlitt and Cobbett especially offensive at a time when so many, in both the countryside and industrial towns, were in dire want. When, at the time of his coronation, he had had the doors of Westminster Abbey locked against his wife, the estranged Queen Caroline, and then had her tried for adulterous treason, violent rioters had shouted support for her cause.

William IV's contribution to the monarchy's public standing was not much more auspicious. In contrast to his elder brother, the famous bluff simplicity of the sailor king – he had served for decades in the Royal Navy – went down well. But the new king squandered much of that popularity by his entrenched and publicly declared opposition to parliamentary reform. It did not, moreover, go unnoticed that, while he had no surviving legitimate children, he had no fewer than 15 illegitimate ones – a record for the British monarchy. Perhaps it was because she was scandalized by the king's insistence on keeping company with his current mistress, the actress Mrs Jordan, that the Duchess of Kent went out of her way to forbid Victoria his company (although the girl seems to have been personally quite fond of her uncle). The duchess was certainly concerned to keep the priceless political capital of Victoria's moral, as well as physical, virginity intact. But she also bitterly resented what she thought the king's niggardly refusal to grant her what she thought her proper share of the civil list.

Necessity, however, can be the mother of politics. And, much as the duchess hated it, a virtue was made of the frugality imposed by financial stringency, so severe at one point that mother, daughter and governess had to move out of Kensington Palace to more ordinary, even suburban, residences at Ramsgate and Sidmouth. Compared with the distasteful luxury of the court, the Kent household could be made to seem a model of austere self-denial. Victoria's childhood suppers, she recalled, were very simple (up to a point) – bread and milk from a little silver basin. Wherever she was, Victoria was subjected to the full Evangelical regime of constant prayers and self-inspection for the blemish of the day. She inherited the forbidding guidance manual written for Princess Charlotte by the arch-evangelical Hannah More, *Hints Towards Forming the Character of a Young Princess* (1805). And she kept (or was made to keep) a Behaviour Book, in which all these failings, as well as a strict accounting of how she had spent her time, were mercilessly recorded. One much-underlined, self-chastising entry, that for 21 August 1832, reads, 'Very very very TERRIBLY naughty!'

It may have been that the duchess and Baroness Lehzen schooled the girl in Christian correctness and domestic propriety only too well. For as she grew, and became more solemnly conscious of the destiny awaiting her, Victoria also became deeply unsettled by what seemed to be her mother's craven dependence on the Irish adventurer Sir John Conroy, ostensibly her household secretary but, even to a young girl, quite evidently something more. Although she still slept in the duchess's bed-chamber, she was beginning to keep her own company and commune with the past. 'I am very fond of making tables of the Kings and Queens,' she wrote to Leopold, ' … and I have lately finished one of the English Sovereigns and their Consorts as, of course, the history of my own country, is one of my first duties.' Anne Boleyn was 'extremely beautiful, but inconsiderate'; Elizabeth I 'a great Queen but a *bad* woman.'

And as her trim figure filled out, so Victoria became awkwardly aware that she was the most desirable catch in Europe. Like any mother trawling for a suitable match, the duchess threw banquets and balls to show her off, the invitation list prominently featuring eligible bachelor princes – Dutch, Portuguese and German. As a Saxe-Coburg-Gotha himself, Leopold of the Belgians was keen to promote the cause of the princes of his own family, Ernest and Albert; but a first encounter with the latter at Victoria's 17th birthday ball was not promising. Although undeniably good looking in a grave, erect kind of way, Albert seemed silent and prim, and turned so ashen white during the dancing that he needed to leave in haste lest, it was thought, he should faint. Victoria was also growing more curious about the public world beyond the court and society; she read the newspapers, and became initiated into the rituals of royal philanthropy that would become one of the mainstays of the modern monarchy. In 1836 she visited an asylum for 'vagrant girls' and, closer to home, all but adopted a distressed gypsy family, the 'Coopers,' whom she had discovered camping near the gates of her childhood home, Claremont House, but whose family virtue in adversity she pronounced so exemplary as to make it clear that these gypsies, at any rate, were good English Christians. 'Their conjugal, filial and paternal affection is *very great* as also their kindness and attention to their sick, old and infirm.'

As she moved out a little into the wider world, Victoria became more reluctant to do her mother's bidding so meekly. She was becoming painfully aware that the duchess and the adhesive Conroy were shamelessly exploiting her prospects in order to feather their own nests. Should she become queen while still a minor, they could establish a kind of regency. But when William IV died, on the night of 20 June 1837, Victoria had already turned 18. The duchess was put on notice what this would mean when one of the first acts of the new queen was to move her bed out of her mother's room and insist on dining alone. She was, henceforth, to be very much her own mistress.

William IV's extended decline into fatal sickness (punctuated by startling revivals of good cheer when he would summon ministers to dine, stipulating that they each consume two bottles of wine) had given Victoria ample time to contemplate her impending translation. She faced her situation with striking self-possession. To Leopold she wrote, with a winning combination of modesty and courage, 'I look forward to the event, which, it seems, is likely to occur soon, with calmness and quietness; I am not alarmed at it, and yet, I do not suppose myself equal to all; I trust, however, that with *good will*, honesty and courage, I shall not, at all *events fail*.' The astonishing tone of clear purpose continued on the famous night itself, when she was woken (first by her mother) to find the Lord Chamberlain and the Archbishop of Canterbury sinking to their creaking knees: 'Since it has pleased Providence to place me in this station, I shall do my utmost to fulfil my duty toward my country; I am very young and perhaps in many, though not in all things inexperienced, but I am sure that very few have more real good will and desire to do what is fit and right than I have.'

Breakfast was taken with the prime minister, William Lamb, Baron Melbourne, in whom Victoria was lucky enough to find a supremely skilled and almost tearfully dedicated guardian; the next in succession, after her uncle Leopold, in her line of surrogate fathers. From their first meeting the relationship was one of mutual devotion, which bordered, almost, on compulsive love. The age difference was not a barrier; it was, in fact, the permitting condition of the reciprocal adoration. Lord Melbourne was a Whig grandee who had lived the kind of life from which Victoria might have been expected to recoil. But as far as she was concerned he had been more sinned against than sinning, and this was not entirely untrue. When his wife Caroline had been jilted by her lover, Lord Byron, Melbourne's instinct was to care for her as best he could. When he was named in a divorce suit by Lady Caroline Norton's husband, he accepted the role even though it seems more likely the relationship had been platonic. A year before he met Victoria his only son, Augustus, had died. So he came to the queen with an allure of battered gallantry, more than ready for his avuncular role.

Romanticized in the newspapers as 'England's Rose,' Victoria needed a tutor who could help develop a public persona, gently build her confidence and launch her on the vast and terrifying stage of British history. Rose she may have looked, with that pink complexion, those round cheeks and blue eyes; but Melbourne understood very quickly that she also came with her fair complement of thorns. In the 4-foot-11 doll, he already saw the formidable woman – impetuous and head-strong. So he never made the mistake of talking down to Victoria, or of treating her as a child in need of basic schooling. Instead, he spoke to her as someone sophisticated enough to appreciate his shrewd political information and his droll, elliptical humour; even his waggish take on English history. (Henry VIII? 'Those women bothered him so.') Victoria's journal entries describing their meetings are full of complicit laughter.

Those meetings were a constant feature of the young queen's life. Reporting on politics – the state of the economy and international affairs; playing chess with Victoria; accompanying her riding; dining with her (seated always on her left); poring together over the royal collection of prints and drawings – Melbourne spent on average four or five hours with her each day. She watched the faded peacock preen himself and strut, in a tottery sort of way, for her benefit; lean over at dinner to impart a sly titbit of intelligence; or just tuck in ('He has eaten three chops and a grouse – for breakfast!'). And she carefully noted down his pearls of wisdom even when they scarcely amounted to dazzling insight ('People who talk much of railways and bridges are generally Liberals'). Their intimacy was not without costs – the occasional jeering shout of 'Lady Melbourne' came the queen's way at Ascot. But such costs were more than compensated for by the benefits. Victoria now had a pseudo-father who was not always disappearing back to Belgium and, with Melbourne's encouragement, she decisively liberated herself from the tentacles of the unfortunate duchess and Conroy. Two months after her accession, in September 1837, the Queen inspected her Guardsmen and Lancers in Windsor Great Park and carried the event off with extraordinary dash and confidence. Her account is strikingly reminiscent of that 'great' queen but 'bad woman' Elizabeth I. 'I cantered up to the Lines with all the gentlemen and rode along them. Leopold [the horse, not the king] behaved most beautifully, so quietly, the Bands really playing in his face. I then cantered back to my first position and there remained while the Troops marched by in slow and quick time … The whole went off beautifully and I felt for the first time like a man, as if I could fight myself at the head of troops.'

She needed to be sure-footed: the economy had taken a sharp turn for the worse, and radical movements, such as Chartism, were beginning to attract a serious following, so not everyone was in thrall to the spell of the Rose of England. But at least Victoria was not an active liability, and among the propertied classes won relieved respect from unforced acts of kindness and a disarming frankness that was half ingenuous, half knowing. She was also becoming quickly convinced of the

Princess Victoria by Henry Collen, 1836.

soundness of her own judgement. When she knighted the Jewish Moses Montefiore in 1837 over a fit of raised eyebrows at court, she wrote that he was 'an excellent man … I was very glad to do what I think quite right, as it should be.'

As for spectacle, Victoria sensed – again, perhaps, guided by Melbourne – how important it was to the survival of the monarchy. George IV had been determined to stage a coronation of stupendous lavishness, complete with pseudo-medieval banquets in Westminster Hall (and in Scotland at Holyroodhouse) at which the King's Challenger would enter in chain mail ostensibly to do combat with anyone who presumed to question the succession. But the more elaborately got up he was – and George IV was an apparition in ostrich plumes – the more grotesque he appeared. It seemed right that, when the chain-mailed Challenger cantered over to kiss his sovereign's hand, he fell off his horse. William IV had no time or taste for such flummery. But Victoria's accession was a heaven-sent opportunity for the impresarios of monarchy, with a canny sense of publicity, to present a tableau – almost a modern masque – of the rebirth of Britannia's innocence and virtue. Images of sweet nature abounded. Victoria's train was carried by eight ladies dressed in white satin with wreaths of silver ears of corn in front, and wreaths of pink roses (by now the talisman of the new reign) behind. And despite having to bear the considerable weight of robes and regalia, Victoria carried off the occasion with satisfying aplomb. When the 87-year-old Baron John Rolle tripped as he attempted to mount the steps before the throne to do homage, the queen's instinct was to rise and go down to help him, an act of consideration that was widely noticed. When it came to Melbourne's turn, she noticed tears welling in his eyes. Her even more spectacular wedding ceremony a few years later would further capture the popular imagination.

Her strong-minded piety, although an undoubted asset, could sometimes threaten to become a headache for the worldly wise prime minister. She disliked Baron John Lyndhurst, she told him, because he was a bad man. 'Do you dislike all bad men?' he asked roguishly. 'For that comprises a large number.' And although she indulged, even enjoyed, Melbourne's raffish past she was quick to make censorious judgements. Toleration for human frailty was the one quality he failed to impart. So when the shape of her mother's unmarried lady-in-waiting Lady Flora Hastings started to become suspiciously round, Victoria assumed it was a pregnancy and demanded that she be punished (another echo of the Virgin Queen) for her immorality by being removed from court. A medical inspection to which the unfortunate young woman was subjected judged that her condition was a liver tumour, not a pregnancy. Initially the queen refused to believe she was actually ill, provoking some criticism at court for her lack of sympathy; but once she was persuaded by Melbourne of the truth she steeled herself – also at his firm suggestion – to go and see the dying woman. Victoria held her hand, and on departure cried, 'Poor Lady Flora.'

When Melbourne's administration fell, to be replaced by a Tory government under Sir Robert Peel, Victoria took the change as a personal affront. She tearfully stormed over the removal of her friend and mentor, expressed her disgust at the uncouth chilly manners of Peel (a mere manufacturer, after all), and adamantly refused to abide by the convention that her ladies of the bedchamber change with the altered government. Although Melbourne did his tactful best to explain that the queen really had no choice, Victoria refused to understand that this was a constitutional, not a personal, matter. The precondition of the monarchy's survival was its distance from political partisanship. She herself might see her ladies as her own attendants, but the fact was that they had been Whig appointees and retaining them meant – as far as the incoming government was concerned – tolerating a fifth column in the Palace. Eventually Victoria conceded, but only with a fuming sense of indignity.

By the time Melbourne was departing in 1839, plans were advanced to find Victoria someone else to lean on: a consort. It had been King Leopold, in cahoots with her old governess Lehzen and Baron Christian von Stockmar of Saxe-Coburg, who, in the summer of 1839, had suggested she might like to think again about her cousin Albert. She initially took strong exception to being cajoled, even by the two men she trusted most – Melbourne and Leopold ('the whole subject was an odious one and one I hated to decide about'); but eventually she relented. When Albert arrived in England, in October, Victoria was immediately startled by the 'beauty' of his person, especially on the dance floor where a few years before he had cut such a pallid figure. She was overcome by the 'exquisite neck'; 'such a pretty mouth with delicate moustaches and a beautiful figure, broad shoulders and fine waist; my heart is quite going – it is quite a pleasure to look at Albert when he galops and valses.' When allied to his moral seriousness, his evident intelligence and unimpeachable virtue, the 'angelic' good looks prompted her to make up her mind – fast. To the amused delight of the cartoonists, it was obvious that it had been the queen who had proposed. 'At about half past twelve I sent for Albert; he came to the Closet where I was alone and after a few minutes I said to him that I thought he must be aware of why I wished him to come here and that it would make me too happy if he would consent to what I wished (to marry me); we embraced each other over and over again.'

Expeditious was the word. Victoria supplied the ring, asked Albert for a lock of his hair, wallowed in the long kissing sessions, and decreed that two or three days was quite enough for the honeymoon. 'You forget, my dearest love that I am the

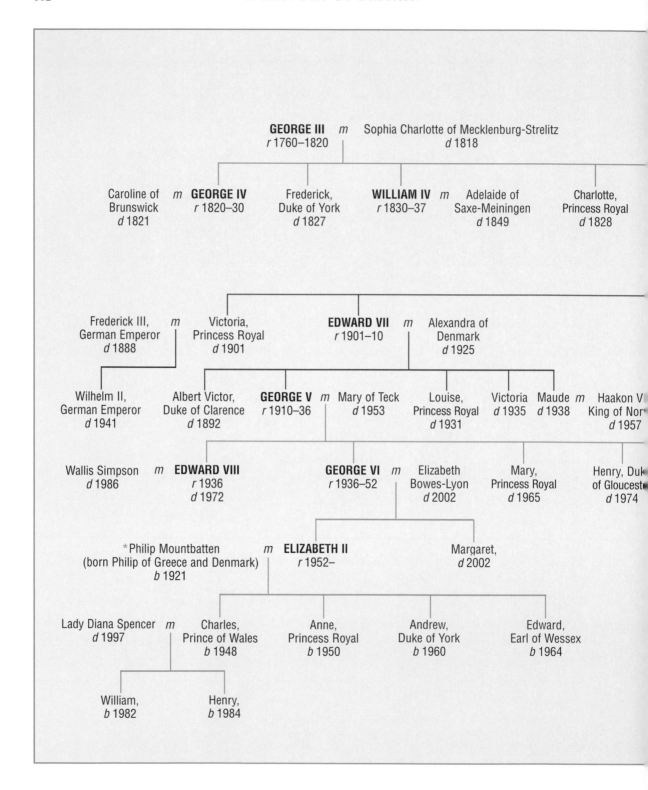

GEORGE III *m* Sophia Charlotte of Mecklenburg-Strelitz
r 1760–1820   *d* 1818

Caroline of *m* GEORGE IV   Frederick,   WILLIAM IV *m* Adelaide of   Charlotte,
Brunswick   *r* 1820–30   Duke of York   *r* 1830–37   Saxe-Meiningen   Princess Royal
d 1821   *d* 1827   *d* 1849   *d* 1828

Frederick III, *m* Victoria,   EDWARD VII *m* Alexandra of
German Emperor   Princess Royal   *r* 1901–10   Denmark
d 1888   *d* 1901   *d* 1925

Wilhelm II,   Albert Victor,   GEORGE V *m* Mary of Teck   Louise,   Victoria   Maude *m* Haakon V
German Emperor   Duke of Clarence   *r* 1910–36   *d* 1953   Princess Royal   *d* 1935   *d* 1938   King of Nor
d 1941   *d* 1892   *d* 1931   *d* 1957

Wallis Simpson *m* EDWARD VIII   GEORGE VI *m* Elizabeth   Mary,   Henry, Duk
d 1986   *r* 1936   *r* 1936–52   Bowes-Lyon   Princess Royal   of Glouceste
                   d 1972   *d* 2002   *d* 1965   *d* 1974

*Philip Mountbatten *m* ELIZABETH II   Margaret,
(born Philip of Greece and Denmark)   *r* 1952–   *d* 2002
b 1921

Lady Diana Spencer *m* Charles,   Anne,   Andrew,   Edward,
d 1997   Prince of Wales   Princess Royal   Duke of York   Earl of Wessex
                      b 1948   *b* 1950   *b* 1960   *b* 1964

William,   Henry,
b 1982   *b* 1984

THE ROYAL HOUSES OF HANOVER,
SAXE-COBURG-GOTHA AND WINDSOR

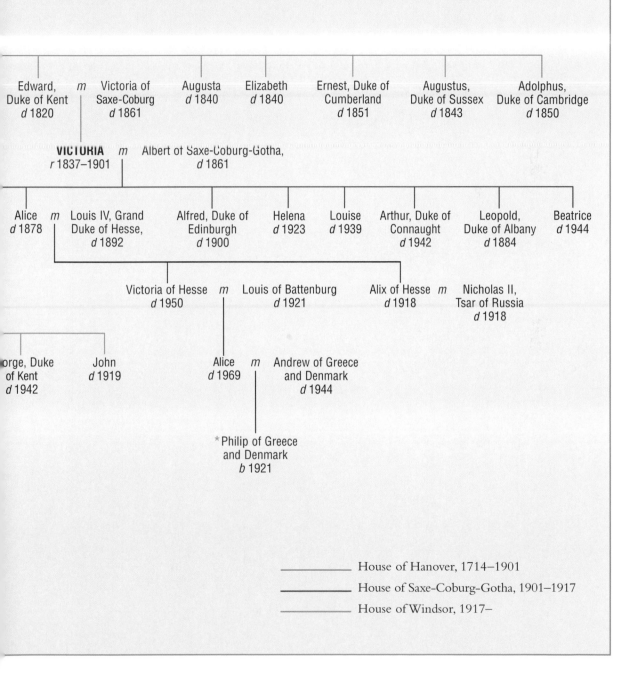

Edward, Duke of Kent *d* 1820 — *m* — Victoria of Saxe-Coburg *d* 1861 — Augusta *d* 1840 — Elizabeth *d* 1840 — Ernest, Duke of Cumberland *d* 1851 — Augustus, Duke of Sussex *d* 1843 — Adolphus, Duke of Cambridge *d* 1850

VICTORIA *r* 1837–1901 — *m* — Albert of Saxe-Coburg-Gotha, *d* 1861

Alice *d* 1878 — *m* — Louis IV, Grand Duke of Hesse, *d* 1892 — Alfred, Duke of Edinburgh *d* 1900 — Helena *d* 1923 — Louise *d* 1939 — Arthur, Duke of Connaught *d* 1942 — Leopold, Duke of Albany *d* 1884 — Beatrice *d* 1944

Victoria of Hesse *d* 1950 — *m* — Louis of Battenburg *d* 1921 — Alix of Hesse *d* 1918 — *m* — Nicholas II, Tsar of Russia *d* 1918

orge, Duke of Kent *d* 1942 — John *d* 1919 — Alice *d* 1969 — *m* — Andrew of Greece and Denmark *d* 1944

*Philip of Greece and Denmark *b* 1921

————— House of Hanover, 1714–1901

————— House of Saxe-Coburg-Gotha, 1901–1917

————— House of Windsor, 1917–

Albert, will you marry me? A playful cartoon of the royal pair's popular betrothal, 1839.

sovereign and that business will stop and wait for nothing.' A more serious shock was the discovery that the queen would lay down the law as to who would be his personal secretary. While she would fight like a tigress (especially with Peel) to resist Albert's allowance under the civil list from being whittled down as the Radicals in parliament wanted, it was depressingly apparent to him from the start that his function was supposed to be decorative, supportive and generative, possibly in that order. He was her 'angel in the house'! But if Victoria tested their affection by her adamant assumption that her husband could have no part in matters of state, condemning Albert to a state of uselessness that he found humiliating and un-Christian, there were also times, early in the marriage, when she simply melted away in the amazed bliss of conjugal love. After their first night together, she wrote:

> When day dawned, for we did not sleep much and I beheld that beautiful angelic face by my side, it was more than I can express! He does look so beautiful in his shirt only with his beautiful throat seen …
>
> … Already the second day since our marriage; his love and gentleness is beyond everything and to kiss that dear soft cheek, to press my lips to his is heavenly bliss. I feel a purer, more unearthly feeling than I ever did. Oh! Was ever woman so blessed as I am …
>
> … My dearest Albert put on my stockings for me. I went in and saw him shave; a great delight for me …

Albert and Victoria's passion for each other was, of course, a strictly private affair (only later revealed to us through her diaries, edited by her daughter Princess Beatrice). But very soon – and with an equal degree of innocence and calculation – it became a public asset for the monarchy, especially as the economic climate deteriorated. At first sight, the Plantagenet Ball of 12 May 1842 – at which Albert and Victoria appeared as the legendary happy royal couple, Edward III and Philippa of Hainault, with medieval dress and décor designed by the medieval antiquarian James Planché – looks like the most unconscionable extravagance, not to say appalling tactlessness, in a year of acute economic distress. While the queen's jewelled and brocaded stomacher was revealed as having cost £60,000, industrialists in Lancashire and Yorkshire, exploiting their power at a time of high unemployment, caused by mechanization, were imposing wage cuts of as much as 25 per cent. They were met by a wave of strikes. Teams of workers pulled plugs from the steam engines, so as to cut power to the factory floor. No wonder that Friedrich Engels, the future translator and collaborator of Karl Marx but now working for the family cotton firm in Manchester, assumed Britain

Above: *Queen Victoria Riding Out* by Sir Francis Grant, *c*. 1840.
Opposite: *Queen Victoria and Prince Albert at the Bal Costumé of 12 May 1842* by Sir Edwin Landseer, 1842.

would be the theatre of the first great class war between capital and proletariat. That same year there were two assassination attempts on the queen.

But the organizers of the ball were not suicidally obtuse. Since the proceeds would go to relieve the plight of distressed silk weavers in Spitalfields, they billed the event as an example of heartfelt royal philanthropy, Victoria's sympathy with the poor and unemployed. Thanks to the ball, the apologia ran, the Spitalfields weavers got some piecework and their charities received an inflow of funds. The weepy story – once known to all schoolchildren – of Queen Philippa interceding with her warrior husband in the Middle Ages to spare the lives of the burghers of Calais was now given a modern gloss as a philanthropic melodrama of the 19th century: a tender-hearted monarch moved by the plight not of hostages but of unemployed artisans. 'We have no doubt,' declared the *Illustrated London News*, somewhat optimistically, 'that many thousands are this day grateful for the temporary aid which this right royal entertainment has been the means of affording them.'

Not everyone was persuaded, however, especially when it was revealed that half the proceeds from the ball were going to meet the expenses of the occasion. One newspaper printed lists of workers said to have starved to death in May 1842, and alongside it the expenses of the Plantagenet Ball. A minister preached a sermon warning that 'when Charity took to dancing it ceased to be charity and became wanton.' And for the seer of Ecclefechan, Craigenputtock and Chelsea, Thomas Carlyle, it was a monstrous case of medieval dilettantism, all the more offensive because medievalism was not, in his view, something to be toyed with as a fashion. It was the ideology of resistance to the despotism of the machine age.

In *Past and Present*, written in 1843, a year after the Plantagenet Ball, Carlyle reiterated his argument that the sacred relics of medieval Christian England were not just material for dressing up and dancing, much less bucolic reveries of 'Merrie England.' They were a reproach to the inhumane soullessness of an age in which everything was determined by material calculation; in which the engineers of felicity greased the cogs of power and profit, and people got trapped between the flywheels. Travelling through East Anglia (where the young Victoria too had made a tour, wrinkling her nose at the sub-human specimens she found amidst the turnips and the brussels sprouts) while beginning research on his hero Oliver Cromwell, Carlyle visited the ruins of the great Cistercian monastery at Bury St Edmunds. The overpowering sense of another world, removed from the present not just by the passage of centuries but by a universe of morality, was what drove him to write *Past and Present*; part tract, part historical novel, it evoked the actual chronicle of the monk Jocelin of Brakelond. On the same trip Carlyle had visited the poorhouse at

St Ives and had waxed wrathful at the inhumanity of systems that kept men either idle or, under the New Poor Law, in places designed to be like prison.

So Carlyle had the Plantagenet Ball squarely in his sights when he wrote, feelingly, of old Bury that

> these grim old walls are not a dilettantism and a dubiety; they are an earnest fact. It was a most real and serious purpose they were built for! Yes, another world it was, when these black ruins, white in their new mortar and fresh chiselling first saw the sun as walls long ago. Gauge not, with thy dilettante compasses, with that placid dilettante simper, the Heaven's Watchtower of our Fathers …
>
> Their architecture, beltries, land-carucates? Yes, – and that is but a small item of the matter. Does it never give thee pause, this other strange item of it, that men then had a *soul* – not by hearsay alone and as a figure of speech; but as a truth they practically *knew* and practically went upon! Verily it was another world then … Another world truly and this present poor distressed world might get some profit by looking wisely into it, instead of foolishly.

That world was dead and gone now, for sure. But Carlyle wanted to rescue its moral force, its lesson for the present, from the antiquarians and the fake medievalists; somehow to reinstate its spiritual power amidst a culture otherwise capitulated to godless machinery. He had grown up in southwest Scotland, one of the most intensely Calvinist corners of the country, listening to perfervid preachers call down the wrath of Providence on the vain and the profligate. To the summer thunder of their eloquence Carlyle had added German metaphysical philosophy, especially its musings on the historical Spirit of the Times, the *Zeitgeist*. Together they gave him his voice. And it was the voice of a modern Moses, exhorting the worshippers of the new Golden Calf to fall on their faces in front of the revealed light of truth before they were consumed in wicked self-destruction. In 1829, while still perching on his 'Hawk's Crag' at Craigenputtock, Carlyle had burst on the polite rationalist pages of the *Edinburgh Review* with a tirade against the tyranny of the machine and its destruction of the work of the hand. It was, in effect, a counter-blast to the jubilant mechanical triumphalism of the Brunels, the Cubitts and the Stephensons; and to the ethos that would produce the Great Exhibition.

> Nothing is now done directly or by hand; all is by rule and calculated contrivance. For the simplest operation, some helps and accompaniments, some

Above: Thomas Carlyle in his attic study, Cheyne Walk, Chelsea, engraving, 1840.
Opposite: *Contrasted Residences for the Poor*, from *Contrasts* (1836) by A.W.N. Pugin, comparing the Victorian model (top) and medieval (below).

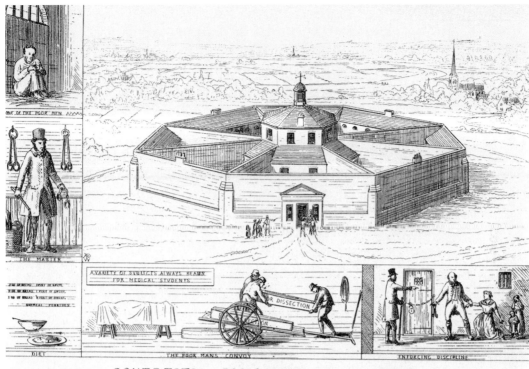

ONE OF THE POOR MEN

THE MASTER

DIET

A VARIETY OF SUBJECTS ALWAYS READY FOR MEDICAL STUDENTS

FOR DISSECTION

THE POOR MANS CONVOY

ENFORCING DISCIPLINE

CONTRASTED RESIDENCES FOR THE POOR

ANTIENT POOR HOYSE.

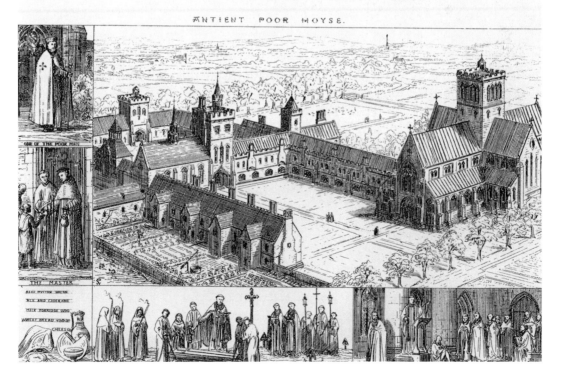

ONE OF THE POOR MEN

THE MASTER

cunning abbreviating process is in readiness . . . On every hand the living artisan is driven from his workshop to make room for a speedier, inanimate one. The shuttle drops from the fingers and falls into iron fingers that ply it faster. The sailor furls his sail and lays down his oar, and bids a strong unwearied servant, on vaporous wings [steamships] bear him through the waters. Men have crossed oceans by steam; the Birmingham Fire-King has visited the fabulous East. . . . There is no end to machinery. . . . We have machines and mechanic furtherances; for mincing our cabbages; for casting us into magnetic sleep. We remove mountains and make seas our smooth highway. Nothing can resist us. We war with rude Nature, and by our resistless engines, come off always victorious and loaded with spoils.

Machinery, for Carlyle and those increasing numbers who thought like him, was, moreover, not just moving metal parts. It was a state of mind: the utilitarian mentality that believed in a finely calibrated science of happiness. The scientists would detect a social or economic misfortune, an aberration from the mean of human felicity; then they would statistically measure its magnitude, devise the necessary correction, draft a report, lobby parliament to make it law and create the necessary administrative machinery (the word could not be avoided) to see it implemented and inspected for efficiency. 'Has any man or society of men,' wrote Carlyle in *Signs of the Times* (1882) in a pitilessly exact anatomy of the procedures of modern social benevolence, 'a truth to speak, but must first call a public meeting, appoint committees, issue prospectuses, eat a public dinner, in a word construct or borrow machinery, wherewith to speak it and to do it.'

It would be easy to write off Carlyle as a prophet crying in the wilderness, were it not for the fact that so much of his attack on materialism, on the government of the world through material satisfaction and the calculus of outward appearance, found an extraordinary response inside the Victorian world, ostensibly so frantic in the pursuit of speed, goods and power. To catalogue the very greatest, the most richly eloquent voices of the Victorian world – Charles Dickens, John Ruskin and, later, Matthew Arnold – is to enumerate the apostolic succession of Thomas Carlyle's preaching. And it was a gospel – voiced against the degradation of the division of labour, the reduction of humans to automata; against the stultifying captivity of mindlessly repeated tasks, all so that some manufacturer could reduce unit costs – that endured. Perhaps not enough people read John Ruskin today. But no one reads Samuel Smiles's runaway success, *Self-Help* (1859), and his paeans to the heroic age of the industrial engineers.

Whatever else might be said about the Victorians, it is impossible to accuse them (unlike later empires of material self-congratulation) of complacency. The more Carlyle berated them for preferring the physical over the spiritual, easy comfort over difficult beauty, social engineering over individual redemption, the practical over the profound, the more they lapped up the punishment and took it to heart. Whether they took the tongue-lashing in their stride, bowed their heads in a gesture of regret on Sundays and then got on with making more money is another matter. But at least their favoured architectural style – Gothic Revival – made a gesture towards this 'lost' world of medieval virtue, grace and hand-fashioned integrity that Carlyle and Ruskin lamented.

That the look of Victorian Britain went directly against the grain of its gung-ho lunge for profit was due to an extraordinary degree to the intense, proselytizing genius of Augustus Welby Northmore Pugin, the greatest of all the Gothic Revivalists. The son of a French immigrant stage-set designer and part-time architect, Pugin was a prodigy who, at the age of 15, had been summoned by George IV to design furniture for his Gothic Revival apartments. He shared Ruskin's rhetorical demand, voiced later, that when we look at a building and wish to judge its true value we should ask not how much or how little it cost to make or buy, but a quite different question: was the worker happy when he built it? Pugin devoutly believed that when the builders and craftsmen of the 14th century – in his book the last great age of English architecture – created their churches and guild halls, flooded them with the colour of tapestries and stained glass, sent buttresses flying and spires soaring, there was an instinctive communion between maker and user, bonded by shared Christian purpose. Those buildings, even the few that survived, were statements of a coherent community, not the expression of fatuous social grandeur seen in an aristocratic country house or a plutocratic mansion.

Contrasts (1836), with its systematic line-up of invidious comparisons between then and now – the beauty and coherence of the medieval town at the flowering of English Perpendicular against the chaotic mess of bastard Greek, bastard Roman and even bastard Egyptian town halls, cemeteries, workhouses and prisons – was Pugin's devastating visual correlate to Carlyle's *Past and Present*. Unlike Carlyle, however, Pugin did not despair that the lost Christian age was irrecoverable. He believed that some of the spirit, at least, survived in Britain, waiting to be given a new lease of life against the dead hand of classicism – the gaunt child of soulless geometry. Providence might always supply an opportunity for the work of revival. Just such an occasion delivered itself in 1834 when parliament burned down and a debate ensued about whether it should be rebuilt in the Gothic or neo-classical styles. The winner of the

Top: *Perspective View of the New Houses of Parliament* by Charles Barry, *c.* 1840.
Above: The House of Lords, Westminster, London, interior designed by A. W. N. Pugin, *c.* 1845.
Opposite: St Giles Parish Church, Cheadle, Staffordshire, designed by Pugin, 1846.

Engraved frontispiece to *The True Principles of Pointed or Christian Architecture* (1841) by A.W.N. Pugin, who appears in the guise of a medieval master mason.

competition, Sir Charles Barry, had made drawings that amounted to an almost fantastic vision of a Gothic medieval palace; not, in truth, a structure that owed its precedent to anything truly medieval, but a decorated 'module' of pointed Gothic, extended indefinitely along the Thames as far as money and the needs of government dictated. It was a far cry, in fact, from Pugin's beautifully crafted fit between form and function.

But the arguments rehearsed to justify a Gothic Revival parliament must undoubtedly have appealed to the romantic historian in Pugin. For they were all about acknowledging that the distinctive characteristic of the 'ancient' British constitution — its liberty and the rule of common law — was a medieval inheritance. The pediments and columns, the dominant squatness of classicism, were thus made to seem, somehow, not only 'foreign' but also the expression of authority, in a way in which the pinnacles and pointed arches of Gothic building were not. Classicism was top down; Gothic was bottom up. Classical architecture was the visible declaration of hierarchy, built by slaves, in Ruskin's view; Gothic was about the community of craft, designed by free men. Inside a classical legislature, rulers would lay down the law; inside a Gothic parliament, they would make it accountable to the people. Such a building would not only be a dignified convenience for the law-makers; it would, by connecting them intuitively, with the world that had produced Magna Carta, also ensure that they would legislate in a spirit of freedom, justice and virtue.

This was indeed a work in which Pugin could rejoice, should he ever get the chance to participate in it. In 1836, at the age of 24, the same year that he published *Contrasts*, he joined Barry in the crucial role of designing much of the interior of the House of Lords and a good deal of the fabric of Big Ben. There, his spiritual intoxication with colour, with the happy richness of ornament, was allowed full expression in the encaustic tiles, wallpaper, hangings, woodwork and furniture he designed and whose creation he supervised. And, already alert to the dangers of pastiche, Pugin avoided merely replicating medieval design in the rendering of flowers, for example. Instead he aimed at stylized, flattened, brilliantly coloured forms that created almost mesmerizing patterns; a true evocation of the essence of what he thought was medieval decoration, rather than a dumbly literal repetition of it.

What Pugin wanted for secular building, he wanted even more urgently for Britain's churches. In 1819 a commission, responding to the evangelical tenor of the times and a burgeoning urban population, had recognized the crying need for a systematic rebuilding programme after decades of stagnation. But Pugin and other Gothic Revivalists were determined that new churches were not going to be constructed in the relentless Palladian idiom that they believed had sucked the spirit out of the houses of God in a vain, essentially secular preoccupation with light and proportion. Pugin wanted to dim the lights, the better to flood churches with stained-glass illuminations in which the worshipper could again feel himself in proper communion with the Saviour, a quality lost since the Reformation. And that, of course, was precisely the problem. Pugin's crusade to restore ornament was not theologically innocent. It was immediately and correctly seen as a campaign to drag Protestant faith, with its aversion to papist 'baubles,' back to the idolatries it had left behind in the 16th century. And Pugin confirmed these suspicions when he himself converted to Catholicism in 1834.

The apostasy should have killed off his budding career. It certainly cramped it, but he was too obviously gifted to be left by the wayside. Brazening it out, Pugin went to live in Salisbury to be close as possible to the cathedral – glorified, of course, in the great, shimmering canvases of Constable – which more than any other embodied his vision of the pure and perfect Christian past. Later still he moved to Ramsgate, where Victoria had spent some of her childhood. Here he worked for high-minded, well-to-do Anglo-Catholic and Roman Catholic patrons, and continued to publish his manifestos against the debasement of contemporary taste. On the frontispiece of *The True Principles of Pointed or Christian Architecture* (1841), Pugin himself appears in the guise of a late medieval Christian builder, surrounded by altar-pieces, lecterns and finely wrought crucifixes, wielding that ancient instrument the compass to craft his design. His last hurrah, before dying at the brutally early age of 40, was the creation of the Medieval Court for the Great Exhibition; an ensemble of some of the most perfect work produced by his own shop and his favoured crafts-men, brought right within enemy-occupied territory. But all the newspaper reports make it clear that, while the Medieval Court was treated with reverence and respect, the crowds were distinctly thin compared to the throngs who hurried past to gawk at the locomotives and the steam hammers.

Pugin did not despair, however, of making some impression on industrial Britain. At Cheadle in Staffordshire, a community of miners and textile workers, he was commissioned by the Roman Catholic Earl of Shrewsbury to restore and redecorate the parish church of St Giles. The result was arguably his greatest mas-terpiece and the only building, he said, about which he had no regrets: a glowing vault of intense, radiant colour.

Yet not many miles away in Manchester, Pugin's heaven-on-earth had been replaced, decisively, by what Sir Charles Napier described as 'the entrance to hell realised!' Napier was more used to fighting on the northwest frontier of India than on the northwest frontier of England, but had been commissioned in 1839 to keep order in what had come to be seen as an endemically violent and criminal city. Here, instead of heaven-reaching spires there was a mass of chimneys. Together they made the entire city one vast 'chimney of the world, rich rascals, poor rogues, drunken ragamuffins and prostitutes form the moral soot made into paste by rain … and the only view is a long chimney: what a place!' A succession of reports (beginning with Sir James Phillips Kay-Shuttleworth's *The Moral and Physical Conditions of the Working Classes Employed in the Cotton Manufacture in Manchester* (1832), had exhaustively documented Manchester's reputation as the 'shock city' of the industrial century, the very worst and the very best crammed into the 'Cottonopolis' of 150,000 souls. If the population of Britain had been multiplying at its fastest rate ever in the first decades of the 19th century, nowhere had this expansion been more spectacular (or terrifying) than in Manchester, where its numbers grew 600 per cent in less than 60 years, the vast majority by immigration from the countryside.

Not surprisingly, dwelling conditions were horrific. A government *Report on the Sanitary Conditions of the Labouring Population of Great Britain* published in the year of the costume ball, 1842, when between a quarter and a third of Manchester's male population was unemployed and when, according to a Salford newspaper, 'haggard and half-clothed men and women are stalking through the streets, begging for bread,' described a typical lodging house in the city:

> Six or eight beds … contained in a single room … it seems to be the invariable practice to cram as many beds into each room as it can possibly be made to hold … the scene which these places present at night is one of the most lamentable description; the crowded state of the beds filled promiscuously with men, women and children, the floor covered over with the filthy and ragged clothes they have just put off and with their various bundles and packages containing all the property they possess, mark the depraved and blunted state of their feelings … the suffocating stench and heat of the atmosphere are almost intolerable.

One result of this overcrowding and primitive sanitation was the lightning spread of infectious diseases like typhus, typhoid and cholera. Statistically, the average life expectancy, the report stated, for 'mechanics and labourers' in 1842 was 17 years. (For 'professional persons' in Manchester, it was 38.)

A long-term optimist might have supposed that the era of change ushered in by the Reform Act of 1832 would also have been more sensitive to the hardships of cotton spinners and handloom weavers – the latter beginning to feel the pinch as power looms replaced artisanal labour. If so, a bitter disappointment was in store, for arguably the 'new' political class empowered by the Act in fact took a tougher view of the plight of the unemployed. Kay-Shuttleworth's report on Manchester, issued the same year, may have documented poverty but also made much of the 'moral degeneracy' of those who wallowed in dirt (especially, of course, the population of 'little Ireland'). The New Poor Law enacted by the Whig government in 1834 was designed expressly to deter these habitually slothful types, as they were perceived, from sponging off the rates by making the regime inside the workhouse so close to that of a prison that no one remotely capable of gaining any kind of legitimate work would submit themselves to it. Inmates of the 'Bastilles' (as they were popularly known) were brutally shorn, so that they were instantly recognizable on the 'outside,' and dressed in uniform drab. Husbands were strictly separated from wives and both from their children – the most heartbreaking aspect of the institutions. In a society supposed to value the family as the school of social morality, it was the first casualty of misfortune. But of course, most of the Poor Law Guardians solemnly believed that that misfortune had been earned through some sort of moral failing. Weakness of backbone, then, had landed the reprobate in the workhouse. It would do him or her no favour to make the place flow with the milk of human kindness.

Likewise the Manchester oligarchs – cotton masters and bankers like the Gregs, Heywoods and Potters – who ran the city, who had cleared out its centre to build their swaggering neo-classical warehouses, made no bones about the fact that their first, in fact their supreme obligation was to the profitability of their business. It was from this, and only from this, that the welfare of the workers could be augmented. If the vagaries of the business cycle (like the collapse of foreign demand in the first five years of Victoria's reign) required wage cuts or lay-offs so that the firm might survive, who ever said capitalism was a funfair or a hand-out? If they thought the situation was dire now, let them see how much worse it could be if mills were to go under because of the 'blackmail' of high wages and demands for shorter hours! As far as the bosses were concerned, trade unions were nothing more than conspiratorial extortionists and saboteurs who would rather see legitimate business concerns fail than relinquish control over the gullible. Besides, they said, if the price of bread was too high it was undoubtedly the fault of the wicked Corn Laws, established to protect the 'landed interest' from the proper workings of the free market, which otherwise would have imported cheaper foreign grain. If the mill hands wanted to do something constructive about the earning power of their wages, they could do nothing better than join the great middle-class crusade of the Anti-Corn Law campaign, whose temple was the Manchester Free Trade Hall.

A few leaders of the working people of industrial Britain believed in self-improvement through education, temperance and religion, and for a while flirted with the possibility of some sort of broad middle- and working-class alliance. More of those leaders, however, remained deeply suspicious, believing that the abolition of the Corn Laws and the arrival of cheaper grain, flour and bread would just be a pretext for employers to lower wages further. Only if the mass of working men (women were only rarely an issue, despite the fact that they were very active in the movement, especially in Scotland and Lancashire) were granted the vote, only if a true democracy were created, could they be sure that 'reforms' would not be the means of even greater exploitation by the masters. James Bronterre O'Brien, the editor of the *Poor Man's Guardian*, put the matter succinctly: 'Knaves tell you that it is because you have no property that you are unrepresented. I tell you, on the contrary, it is because you are unrepresented that you have no property.' The answer was a Magna Carta for the modern age: a People's Charter, demanding universal manhood suffrage, no property qualifications for the vote, equal representation (each vote to count equally), annual parliaments, paid MPs and the secret ballot. Many of these issues, of course, had featured in the old radical gospel of the days of Major Cartwright, William Cobbett and 'Orator' Hunt, who were all now dead. But it was precisely the 'traditionalism' of the grievances that made them seem, in the eyes of activists who came together in torchlight meetings and processions in 1838 and the millions who signed the monster Chartist petitions in 1839, 1842 and 1848, their indisputably legitimate birthright as free-born Britons.

Inevitably the petitions, solemnly brought to parliament in hackney cabs or decorated farm wagons, and dragged on to the floor of the Commons, met with a dusty, not to say derisory, response. As economic conditions in the Midlands and north worsened, these repeated snubs divided the Chartists into those for whom only peaceful means of pressing their case were acceptable and those like John Frost, a draper from Newport in south Wales, and George Harney, a journalist from London, for whom the rejections were a provocation to armed insurrection. Reginald Richardson, a Salford radical who had given up his trade as a carpenter to become an Anti-Poor Law campaigner, then a Chartist journalist (and whose wife distributed its tracts and pamphlets from their print shop), now concluded that 'there was no hope for the people of England but in hanging a sabre or some other offensive weapon' over his mantelpiece. Even so, the 'physical force' Chartists often liked to invoke the canon of British law – Sir William Blackstone – in justifying the right of resistance to 'tyrants.' According to the frightened local authorities, in April 1839 the London Chartist Henry Vincent told a crowd in Newport that 'when the time for resistance arrives, let your cry be, "To your tents, O Israel" and then with one heart, one voice and one blow, perish the privileged orders! Death to the aristocracy! Up with the people and the government they have established.' This turned out to be more than just incendiary hot air. In the autumn, while Albert and Victoria were billing and cooing, south Wales saw a dramatic armed uprising as small armies of thousands of Chartists marched on Newport and Ebbw Vale. At Newport on 3 November a battle took place between the Chartists and the authorities, resulting in at least 15 dead and at least 50 seriously wounded. It was the largest loss of life inflicted by a British government on its own people at any time in the 19th or 20th century.

The risings, which took place in Yorkshire as well as Wales, were crushed, but the resistance was certainly not over. As long as the brutal slump continued, so did the nocturnal meetings and processions on moors in Lancashire and Yorkshire; the 'conventions' of delegates from Chartist associations throughout the country; and, above all, the waves of local and regional strikes. A mass petition was mobilized to commute the death sentence passed on the rising's leader, John Frost. Crowds sang the variation of the national anthem they had once used for Tom Paine:

God Save our Patriot Frost
Let not his cause be lost
God save John Frost.

And, prudently, preferring removal to martyrdom, the authorities commuted Frost's sentence to transportation to Australia. But governments, whether Whig or Tory, now began to see the Chartists as a vanguard of armed worker revolution. Richardson was one of many who were arrested, and spent nine months in prison (during which time he still managed to smuggle out newspaper articles) for 'incitement to tumult and insurrection and to use force to procure resistance to the law of the land.'

By 1842 the Chartists had an effective and charismatic leader in the lawyer Feargus O'Connor, nephew of the old United Irishman Arthur O'Connor, who was still alive but exiled in France. Inheriting Cobbett's parliamentary seat in Oldham, O'Connor founded the *Northern Star* (named after his uncle Arthur's Belfast broadsheet) as an Anti-Poor Law paper but turned it into the major organ of Chartist politics, edited by the fire-breathing socialist George Harney. O'Connor's task in holding the moderate and militant wings of the movement together was difficult and perhaps ultimately impossible, for he needed to steer a prudent course between alienating 'moral force' Chartists, scared off by the stockpiling of arms, and abandoning the strikers of 1842 who had responded to factory owners wage cuts with the 'plug' strikes. But O'Connor managed to convert what had essentially been an uncoordinated scattering of regional insurrections into something like the shape of a modern political pressure-group campaign, with local units organized by, and answering to, a national coordinating office. The new strategy, partly borrowed from the phenomenally successful middle-class, Bible-quoting Anti-Corn Law campaign, worked well enough to produce a second monster petition in 1842 with over three million names on it. Needless to say, it was rejected out of hand once more on the floor of the Commons.

After 1842, with economic conditions improving, some of the steam went out of the Chartist campaign. But when the trade cycle took another dip in 1847-8 neither the grievances, nor the bitter memories of rejection had gone away. The most powerful account of the stinging humiliation felt by a Manchester Chartist appeared in a novel, *Mary Barton*, written by the bravest woman writer of the early Victorian age, Elizabeth Gaskell. Her tragic hero, the widower John Barton, struggling and failing to make a living for himself and his daughter Mary, politicized by unemployment, destitution and despair, goes to London with the Chartist petition of 1842. The marchers, in their clogs and ragged clothes, move slowly through streets choked with fashionable traffic; they are prodded and beaten by truncheon-wielding policemen who, he tells his daughter and friends when he gets back, inform him,

> 'It's our business to keep you from molesting the ladies and gentlemen going to Her Majesty's Drawing Room.'
> 'And why are WE to be molested?' asked I, 'going decently about our business which is life and death to us and many a little one clemming [starving] at home in Lancashire. Which business is of most consequence i' the sight of God, think yo, ourn or them gran ladies and gentlemen as yo think so much on?' But I might as well ha held my peace for he only laughed.

When asked about the scene in parliament itself, John Barton is too angry to say anything at all except something deeply ominous, for himself and, so it seemed in 1848, the year *Mary Barton* appeared, for Britain.

> It's not to be forgotten or forgiven either, by me or by many another, but I canna tell of our down-casting just as a piece of London news. As long as I live our rejection that day will bide in my heart and as long *as I live I shall curse them as cruelly refused to hear us.*

Both Carlyle and Charles Dickens were admirers of Mrs Gaskell and *Mary Barton*. For although there had been 'social realist' novels before, there had been nothing quite like this one. Disraeli's *Sibyl* had purported to set the 'two nations' problem before the country, but told its story mostly through the eyes and mouths of the 'millocracy.' Although Elizabeth Gaskell was firmly middle class, as the wife of a Unitarian minister in Manchester, she had followed him into the most unsavoury and distressing areas of the city and its hovel-dotted outskirts, to places like Miles Platting, where children played in dark, filthy alleys with rats for their company. Nothing escapes her steely attentiveness: the gin palaces, the open sewers, even the sad little patches of wild flowers hanging on to scraps of dirt amidst the smoke and grime. For the first time, too, in the pages of *Mary Barton* the polite middle-class reader in Herne Hill or Bath could hear the voice of working-class Manchester, even its songs like 'The Oldham Weaver':

> Oi'm a poor cotton weyver, as moiny a one knoowas
> Oi've nowt for 't yeat and oi've worn eawt my cloos
> Yo'ad hardy gi tuppence for aw as oi've on
> My clogs are both brosten and stuckings oi've none
> Yo'd think it wur hard
> To be browt into th'world
> To be clemmed an do th'best as you con.

'Clemmed' – starved – is the word that strikes like a hammer blow over and over again in *Mary Barton*. It is both reproach and battle cry: 'Theyn screwed us down to the lowest peg in order to makie their great big fortunes and build their great big houses and we, why we're just clemming many and many of us. Can you say there's naught wrong in this?' When John Barton visits a fellow-worker lying sick in a tenement cellar, where 'the smell was so fetid as almost to knock a man down,' his eyes gradually become accustomed to the darkness and he makes out 'three or four little children rolling on the damp, nay wet, brick floor through which the stagnant filthy moisture of the street oozed.' The father tells the children to hold their noise as a 'chap' has got some bread for them. In the dimness, Barton feels the hunk of bread torn from him and gone in an instant.

Not surprisingly, Elizabeth Gaskell found herself cold-shouldered by the Manchester cotton barons and bankers, who thought she had given a grossly unjust account of their relations with their hands and had caricatured their own lifestyle without saying anything about their philanthropy and civic activism. They did, in

Elizabeth Cleghorn Gaskell by George Richmond, 1851.

fact, have a point. But the writer courageously stuck to her guns. There was something more important at stake than her own social popularity. 'My poor "Mary Barton" is stirring up all sorts of angry feelings against me in Manchester,' she wrote to her cousin Edward, 'but those best acquainted with the way of thinking and feeling among the poor acknowledge its truth; which is the acknowledgement I most desire because evils once recognized are half way towards their remedy.'

The Manchester cotton barons may have felt that 1848, the year of revolutions in Europe (there was already a republic in France by February), was the most tactless moment imaginable for a Unitarian minister's wife to unburden herself of her social conscience. But it was just *because* Britain seemed to be on the threshold of another crisis that Elizabeth Gaskell felt duty-bound to tell the truth about the immense distance separating the fortunate and unfortunate classes. Only if she were able to make those who had the vote and a share of Britain's power and property fully aware of the anger, as well as the distress, of the millions who had neither might she be able to forestall a second civil war.

In the complacent light of hindsight, 1848 figures as the great anti-climax of the campaign for political and social democracy in Britain. The sense of a bogus panic was made much of in the sunny smugness of the Crystal Palace years, as if 'British Revolution' were itself an oxymoron. But that is certainly not how it appeared at the time, either to the foot soldiers of the People's Charter or to those who were determined to prevent them taking control of the capital. George Harney had no doubt at all about what was coming: 'From the hill tops of Lancashire, the voices of hundreds of thousands have ascended to Heaven the oath of Union and the rallying cry of conflict … Englishmen have sworn to have THE CHARTER and REPEAL [of the New Poor Law] or … "Vive la République." '

Feargus O'Connor, who, after being arrested, had come back to parliament as MP for Nottingham, held back the 'physical force' wing of Chartism only by promising a final attempt at moral persuasion. A Chartist Convention would meet in London at the beginning of April and present the latest monster petition – five million names, it was said, on a document so immense that it would have to be taken to parliament in great bales, loaded on to a farm wagon pulled by four big dray horses. Supporters, including a sizeable contingent of Irish nationalist 'confederates,' would descend on the capital from the Midlands and the north, Wales and even Scotland; would meet in morning assemblies at Russell Square, Bethnal Green, Clerkenwell Green and Stepney Green; and move south in converging processions towards the Thames bridges, and thence to their mass meeting place at Kennington Common. After speeches had been made, the petition was then to be brought to Westminster. Whether the crowds would follow it and make their presence felt, if not irresistible, was, of course, the crucial question. Was this to be the final act of a peaceable demonstration, or the first of a revolution? A 'Charter,' after all, as they were all well aware, had been the beginning of the end of the Bourbon monarchy in France in 1830. And now there had been another revolution there   this time, it seemed, one in which middle-class radicals, artisans and workers had all been united. With the traditional party of order, the Tories, broken by Peel's repeal of the Corn Laws two years earlier, O'Connor must have thought he had the best chance yet of gaining at the very least some concessions.

On an unseasonably warm spring morning, Monday, 10 April, the Chartist crowds gathered at their four London rallying points. The atmosphere was festive, rather than threatening. The Bloomsbury crowd (who picked up the enormous bales of paper) were beribboned and rosetted in green, red and white; the Bethnal Green marchers in pink and white; and the East Enders carried white flags. The spectators who looked at the marchers, and at the carts and cabs bearing Chartist slogans –

Top: The Great Chartist Meeting on Kennington Common, 10 April 1848, contemporary daguerreotype photograph.
Above: View of the south front of Chartist Cottage, Great Dodford, Worcestershire, one of the surviving cottages erected by the Chartist Land Company, *c.* 1845.

'Live and Let Live'; 'Liberty is Worth Living and Dying For' — and who saw a boat-load of military pensioners, shipped in from Woolwich, join the parade over the bridges, seemed quiet or gently encouraging. This was despite the authorities' advance demonology that bloodthirsty British Jacobins were out on the streets.

Taking no chances, Lord John Russell's government certainly prepared as if they were expecting not just a rebellion, but an enemy invasion. With governments tumbling like skittles the previous month, there was a serious scare that French, Italian and German republicans, sworn to revolutionary internationalism, would take advantage of London's crowds to spread their subversive creed. Riding the panic, a Removal of Aliens Act was hastily sent through parliament, requiring foreigners to register with the authorities and alerting patriots to those with suspiciously insurrectionary facial hair.

And if there were a ghost of a chance that danger was approaching across the Channel, who better to repel it than the Duke of Wellington? With his Hyde Park mansion, Apsley House, boarded up, the white-haired old warrior, still quite trim if a little creaky at the joints, assumed command of his last army — now to be mobi-lized against the British working class, who were rumoured to have five cannon of their own! Some 85,000 men were sworn in as special constables to supplement the 4000 Peelers of Sir Robert Peel's Metropolitan Police and 8000 regular troops. Government offices were barricaded with crate-loads of official papers and copies of *Hansard*. Guns and cannon were posted at critical sites: the Bank of England and the Tower of London. The Stock Exchange volunteered some 300 of its own employees as 'specials' to defend the bastion of capitalism. Defensive stations, complete with light artillery, were set up on the Mall to prevent access to Buckingham Palace. (The royal family had in any case, on the advice of the government, taken themselves off to the Isle of Wight to avoid anything disagreeable.) Orders went out to allow controlled access over the bridges to Kennington — but, if necessary, to bar the route back.

One ex-radical, John Cam Hobhouse, then an anxious government minister working at the India Office in the ghostly centre of the capital, mostly deserted except for green-ribboned demonstrators, was worried about being separated from his family at such a critical moment. The front door of his London house had been 'chalked' by the Chartists, identifying him as a declared Enemy of the People. 'I sat down to office business not expecting, but thinking it by no means improbable, that I should hear discharges of musketry or cannon from the other side of the river. Indeed the slamming of doors made me start twice.'

He need not have been quite so anxious. Given this overwhelming display of force, O'Connor had the same decision to make that faced all the leaders of

European marches and demonstrations in the springtime of 1848: whether to force the issue by attacking the soldiers head-on and hoping for defections, or to opt for a tactical stand-off or even retreat. And here, perhaps as he knew, the geography of rebellion was not on the Chartists' side. In Paris, Berlin, Budapest, Prague and Vienna the foot soldiers of liberty were local artisans and workers who barricaded themselves in their quarters, hoisted the flags of revolution and defied government troops to come and get them. They could legitimately appear to be defending hearth and home. But Londoners *en masse* were not so unified in hatred of the government, still less of their rose-queen. It was the rank-and-file Chartists from the provinces, some with Irish, Scottish or Welsh leaders, who had been cast as the occupying army. Besides, O'Connor looked at the logistical odds should he choose to force a bloody confrontation and realized that his Chartists could never win. At Kennington, speaking through Repeaters standing on platforms dispersed through the huge crowd, surrounded by his Irish praetorian guard gathered beneath a huge green flag decorated with the harp, O'Connor announced that his orders were not to provoke any kind of incident with the soldiers and police, however greatly the demonstrators were goaded. A pretext for slaughter was just what the authorities wanted. The trouble was that he himself, and certainly Harney, had raised the stakes very high. Some of the banners hanging from the petition wagon had rashly proclaimed that there would be 'No Surrender' or 'No Way Back.' Predictably, then, some of the younger men were not in the mood to hear the voice of the turtle dove. There were shouts and scuffles. On Blackfriars Bridge on the way back, faced with a solid wall of truncheon-wielding police, there was heaving and stone-throwing, charges and counter-charges. Arrests were made, and then the prisoners were rescued by the crowds. Heads bled along with disappointed hearts.

But O'Connor really had no choice. The bloody days of June in Paris, when the provisional government of the Second French Republic turned its guns on the workers' barricades, would show just how resolute the 'forces of order' could be when faced with ongoing popular strikes and insurrection. What good would a similarly futile and tragic scenario have done the cause of popular democracy in Britain? A glance at the photograph of the meeting at Kennington speaks volumes about the Chartist tradition handed down from the 17th and 18th centuries: it shows a disciplined, Sunday-best dressed 'respectable' protest by workers always anxious to give the lie to their demonization as a drunken, semi-criminal rabble.

After the immediate threat was over, not everyone was cackling with glee at the fake names said to have padded the numbers on the petition – all those 'Mr Punches' and 'Queen Victorias.' Those *canards* – faithfully repeated in the textbooks I grew up with, which treated a 19th-century revolution in Britain as though it were a biological impossibility – formed part of the self-congratulatory mythology of the governing class. At the time, opinion was often much more sober and uncertain. The *London Illustrated News* – certainly happy that 'the mountain has laboured: the mouse has been born' – still admonished those who had belittled the petition in parliament, or greeted it 'amidst great laughter,' stating that it ill became those who derived 'their only real power from the people' to ridicule a document which, if 'a hundredth or even a five hundredth part of the signatures are bona fide … is a petition which the Legislature of England ought to receive with seriousness.'

The jitteriness with which he had handled 10 April spelled, indisputably, the end of Feargus O'Connor as a credible political leader of a mass movement. But it was certainly not the end of Chartism as a militant working-class crusade. Some of its stalwarts became early trade union leaders; others, like the fictional, traumatized John Barton, turned to desperate acts of terrorism. Just three months after Kennington, all the sniggering went suddenly silent when 50,000 demonstrators showed up at the newly built Trafalgar Square. On Whit Monday, at Bonners' Fields, London, another huge crowd appeared carrying tricolour republican flags and calling for 'More Pigs, Less Parsons' and 'England Free or a Desert' before colliding with a solid wall of police. Fitful rebellion still rumbled on in Lancashire, Cheshire and Yorkshire. The 'Wat Tyler of Bradford,' Isaac Jefferson, organized more skirmishes, went on the run, was arrested (although his wrists were too big to be handcuffed), was sprung from captivity and managed to keep thousands of soldiers busy before the town finally calmed down at the end of the year.

If democratic agitation was not going to put bread on the table, perhaps quieter, less confrontational means might do better. A single cottage at Great Dodford in Worcestershire is all that survives of one of those peaceful schemes of working-class self-improvement, the Chartist Land Company. The company had been established by O'Connor in 1845 in fulfilment of a dream inherited from the 17th-century communes and more recently from Irish reformers. Its aim was to take back to the rural world from which they or their forebears had come those workers – often handloom weavers or stocking frame knitters made redundant by the new power machinery – who had been stranded in the slums of industrial Britain. (The vast majority of factory workers were still, in fact, first-generation immigrants from the countryside.) Those able to put down a little money would be given a plot of a few acres on which food could be grown and a few animals kept: this was the resurrection of the strips and back lots they had lost to enclosure and engrossment.

The Land Company was a classically British combination of dreamy utopianism and solid business sense. It tapped into the already active instincts of working men – and especially working women – to save. Enough money was raised to buy property including the land at Great Dodford. Subscribers were sold shares corresponding to their investment, and the first settlers chosen by lottery; then, when lotteries were made illegal, by auction or by the placing of direct deposits.

'Do or die' was the motto of the newcomers at Great Dodford, and their work was certainly no picnic. Boulder-strewn land had to be cleared, roads and paths laid out, hedges planted, all with no certain outcome. But some of the settlers did make a go of it. Ann Wood, for example, was an Edinburgh charlady who had had enough Scottish thrift to save £150, a sum impressive enough to give her the pick of the lots at Great Dodford. After settling at number 36, along with her two daughters, Ann did well enough to lead a long life in the village, dying at 86.

The conspicuous presence of women in the Chartist Land Company village may be another indicator that, once the worst of the hard times were over, working families might be prepared to settle for a home rather than a revolution; a world in which the Great Exhibition, rather than Marx's *Communist Manifesto* (1848), pointed the way to the future. And although it is true that the propertied, political classes, having survived Chartism, would be in no mood to introduce a fuller democracy for another generation, it would be a patronizing mistake to write off the will to build domestic security as some sort of defeatist placebo. Arguably it was precisely the quieter, constructive strategies of the 1850s and early 1860s – cooperatives; friendly societies; peaceful unionism; the profile of a self-improving, responsible, labouring and lodging class – that made it possible for both Tories and Liberals to embrace household male suffrage in the second Reform Act of 1867, without fearing (although some inevitably did) that they were instigating a revolution by the back door.

The family may have been the great mid-Victorian fetish. But the boom economy of the decade and a half between 1848 and the 'Cotton Famine' of the mid-1860s did make it possible to stitch back together some of the fabric of domestic life that had been so badly ripped up in the first phase of the 19th-century Industrial Revolution. The militants of the 'hungry forties' had been, typically, surplus-to-requirement craftsmen and artisans, especially cotton spinners and handloom weavers, who had been put out of work while women and children (the 'tenters' of the mills, hired for menial but dangerous work like crawling under moving machinery to clean cotton fluff) formed a disproportionately large part of the factory labour force. Elizabeth Gaskell's portrait in *Mary Barton* of despondent, demoralized and finally desperate men looking for some way to express their fury was based on a good deal of social truth. In 1851, for instance, 255,000 men and 272,000 women struggled for a living in cotton mills. But the 1850s did, in fact, make good on many of the promises made by the manufacturers and money men of Manchester, Salford, Bradford and Halifax. Rising export-led demand for manufactured cloth generated nearly full employment. The real value of wages rose. Savings were possible. And for the first time men became integrated in large numbers into the manufacturing labour force. Working the new steam-driven mules, they were given, as foremen, the right to hire and organize both men and women (and sometimes children), thus reinstating, in ways incalculably important for the restoration of morale, some of their lost domestic self-respect. Weaving — the last of the textile sectors to become mechanized — now developed its own technology, which could be manned by a male, as well as a female, labour force. In some other industries — especially coal mining — it was, on the other hand, the legislated removal of women and children from work in the pit (where sweltering conditions dictated virtual or actual nakedness as well as brutal physical labour) that, although taxing the domestic economy, actually restored to mining community homes a semblance of matriarchal domestic order.

The prosperous years of the mid-century made for a less confrontational labour force. Women powerloom weavers in Lancashire and Clydeside formed their own unions. But they seldom needed to strike. In the 1860s legal trade unions became more like welfare associations and less like training camps for the class war. Union leaders themselves stressed that the strike would be the weapon of last resort. Dealing with a less confrontational labour force in turn allowed employers to rethink their paternalism. Where once, in return for compliance with wage cuts, they had offered what they claimed were benefits, like the provision of food, now they made room for unions, friendly societies and cooperatives to organize, collaboratively, more of their own independent culture. The 1850s were the decade when works brass bands appeared, sometimes with an initial investment by the owner; when annual works outings to the country, the seaside and the Crystal Palace, re-erected at Sydenham, south London, after the Great Exhibition closed, were organized. Of course, many of those occasions were custom-designed to show off the benevolence of the new industrial squirearchy: the summer tea party at the turreted rose-brick, Gothic Revival mansion on the hill where the full complement of servants (many of them from the same families as the factory hands) would be serving cakes and lemonade; the cricket match between owners (the sons just down from one of the 'new' public schools, such as Marlborough and Tonbridge) and the 'men.'

Reginald Richardson, ex–physical force Salford Chartist and gaolbird, was himself one of those working men who, in the less abrasively confrontational climate

One of the earliest works bands, the Cyfartha Brass Band of Merthyr Tydfil, South Wales, formed in 1838, photograph 1905.

of the mid-Victorian boom, reserved his campaign energies for quite different battles. In the mid–1850s he took on the 'slink' trade, accused of slaughtering diseased cattle and 'dressing' them so they could be passed off as food. He campaigned for public rights of way on ancient footpaths in the countryside between Cheadle and Altrincham. In 1854 he waxed lyrical in the *Salford Evening Weekly*, while lamenting industrial pollution: 'How many thousands yet living remember the beautiful walk from Oldham Lane and down the Adelphi across Bank Mill Yard and along the southern side of the river, with its fine green bank shelving down to the pure stream overshadowed by tall poplars. . . . Along the river bank to Springfield . . . every inch of this has been absorbed – to use a mild term – by the rapacity of those who have built works along the river side.' The old warrior for working men's democracy had become – in advance of the invention of the term – an ecologist. The British revolution had been put out to grass.

Photographing Queen Victoria, the results make clear, was seldom an opportunity for a sunny grin. But then smiling seemed beside the point for most 19th-century photographers and their subjects. They were after grander things; in the case of the royal family, a fine balance between majesty and familiarity. Being summoned to take photographs of Albert, Victoria and the children must have been daunting for Roger Fenton and John Edwin Mayall; but also perhaps exhilarating. Who else got to tell a sovereign to sit perfectly still, even in the most respectful style of address? Lady Day, about whom little is known, went to Osborne House on the Isle of Wight in the summer of 1859 and managed to capture just the slight degree of informality that the prince and the queen had allowed themselves: a country bonnet and an easy lean against a creamy wall. It helped, of course, that the royals were such enthusiasts of the new art. A darkroom had been built and stocked at Windsor. Whenever painters came to do a portrait in oils, the first thing Victoria did was to press on them a photograph as a way of indicating her expectations. This put them on the spot. Were they really supposed to record, with the camera's unblinking faithfulness to the truth, the podgy cheeks, the rather alarming eyes and the excessively compact royal form?

Plainly, the queen was not vain. But the queen was also not stupid. She and Albert knew precisely what they were doing when they commissioned photographs. The thousands of prints made between the late 1850s and the end of the reign transformed the relationship between crown and people more thoroughly than anything since the Civil War. Lady Day's photographs of the Osborne summer were engraved for public circulation; but 14 of the plates from a series made a year later by Mayall were specifically chosen for publication as cartes-de-visite. Invented by the French photographer André Disdéri, these were multiple (usually eight) exposures that could be taken from a single plate, and were originally meant, as their name implied, as trade or artistic advertisements to be exchanged between photographers

WIVES, DAUGHTERS, WIDOWS

Osborne House, Isle of Wight, the royal family's summer retreat from 1845.

themselves, either amateur or professional. In Britain, however, they were circulated – so the authority on royal photographs, Helmut Gernsheim, claims – in hundreds of thousands. Escaping from the rarefied circles of photography into the public domain of the middle class, the cards were prized, collected and traded as cherished objects. Family albums, specially designed with windows into which cartes-de-visites could be slipped without the need for gum, meant that for the first time the image of the royal family could appear on the drawing-room tables of the British middle classes.

That image, carefully designed by Albert and Victoria themselves, was itself an extraordinary departure from tradition. 'They say no Sovereign was ever more loved than I am (I am bold enough to say),' the queen had written to her uncle, King Leopold, in 1858 in a rush of pardonable self-congratulation. And she had no doubt why. It was 'because of our domestic home; the good example it sets.' So none of the Mayall, Day or Fenton photographs of the royal couple showed Albert and Victoria in anything remotely approaching a ceremonial role, or in military finery, swagged with the tiers of medals and ropes of epaulettes favoured by European auto-crats. It would have been unthinkable, of course, for Victoria to have donned a uniform, and Albert had specifically declined the Duke of Wellington's proposal, in 1850, that he should serve as commander-in-chief of the army. So the prince filled his frock coat as majestically and martially as he could, while little Victoria, plumping out to the pudding shape that would be her enduring image, ballooned in satin crinoline. It was the rituals of the bourgeois calendar that were most on show – the holidays in the Highlands and on the Isle of Wight; the stroll with the dogs in the park; carol-singing around the Christmas tree; Albert playing Mendelssohn at the organ; Victoria adoringly cross-stitching. There was even a white-haired, bonneted granny to round out the scene since a chastened Duchess of Kent, far removed from her dynastic adventurism, had been welcomed back into the family fold. Never mind that the holiday homes were palatial; the park was Windsor and mostly off limits to the public; and that none of these activities was exactly comparable to the annual round of a Tunbridge Wells solicitor, much less a Solihull grocer; the artfully conveyed impression was of a reassuringly solid, unpretentious and, above all, Christian–patriotic way of life. Reciprocal visits in 1855 of the Emperor Napoleon III and the Empress Eugénie to Britain, and of Victoria and Albert to Paris, only rein-forced the image of the queen as wholesomely innocent of glamour (although not of gaiety). Sniggering criticism of her fashion sense, or lack of it, was provoked not so much by dowdiness as by unfortunate gaudiness; typical (it was insinuated in Paris) of the bourgeoise trying a little too hard to be cheerful. The black and white collotypes of the 1850s do little to suggest the brilliant stripes and checks loved by Victoria, along with parasols of clashing colours. Parrot green was apparently a favourite.

Especially when compared to modern royal photography, the albums from 1859, 1860 and 1861 seem startlingly candid in registering the strains and ambiguities of a relationship that had somehow to preserve the authority of a husband over a wife, while conceding the inferiority of the consort to the queen. Albert stands patriarchally lofty – but not so lofty as he would have been had the queen herself not been standing on steps concealed beneath the hooped crinoline. Victoria appears just as she must have been: weary of being a baby factory for dynastic posterity ('Vicky,' the first of nine surviving, was born in 1840, 'Baby' Beatrice, the last, in 1857).

Serial pregnancies had taken their toll on the dewy-eyed romance with which Victoria had begun her marriage. When her eldest child, Vicky – who had been married at 18 to the Crown Prince of Prussia, 10 years her senior – became pregnant for the first time, making her a grandmother in her early 30s, she wrote gushingly of the Expected Event. The queen, however, responded with tactless earthiness: 'What you say of the pride of giving life to an immortal soul is very fine, dear, but I own I cannot enter into that; I think much more of our being like a cow or a dog at such moments; when our poor nature becomes so very animal and unecstatic.' Inevitably, some of the royal children fell ill, sometimes dangerously. Fierce arguments erupted between Victoria and Albert as to which of the doctors to trust. It was then that the conflict between the dual role of the couple – on the one hand husband and wife, on the other sovereign and consort – became most aggravated. When Vicky was desperately sick, an unusually distraught Albert told Victoria that 'Dr Clark has mismanaged the child and poisoned her with calomel and you have starved her. I shall have nothing more to do with it! Take the child away and do as you like and if she dies you will have it on your conscience.' The queen shot back, operatically, 'You can *murder* the child if YOU want to!' No wonder that Albert thought, 'Victoria is too hasty and passionate for me to be able often to speak of my difficulties. She will fly into a rage and overwhelms me with reproaches of suspiciousness, want of trust, ambition, envy. '

But even these temporary estrangements were testimony to the fact that Albert and Victoria were both intensely engaged in the welfare of their family. Albert constructed an elaborate and exhaustive educational programme for the children and, although there were tutors to carry it out, supervised the instruction down to the last detail. When, to his growing anxiety and exasperation, Bertie, the Prince of Wales, showed no sign of applying himself to his lessons (quite the reverse, in fact),

Opposite: Victoria and Albert (top), with their nine children. From left to right: Edward, Victoria and Alice (second row); Alfred, Helena and Louise (third row); Arthur, Leopold and Beatrice (last row), 1854–80. Above: Victoria's grandchildren, Alix (left), Wilhelm (right); and standing (centre), Victoria's daughter-in-law, Alexandra, with her five children (clockwise): George (seated), Louise and Albert (standing), Maude (holding Alexandra's hand) and Victoria (kneeling), 1864–1900. Left: Victoria with her great-grandchildren (clockwise): Albert (cross-legged), Mary, Edward and baby Henry, 1900.

Albert bore down on him with relentless interrogations in an attempt to discover whether it was intellectual or moral failing that was the problem. Equally, however, there were times when both the queen and the prince allowed themselves the luxury of cosiness. Victoria's journal recorded many such moments of bedroom happiness: 'Albert brought in dearest little Pussy [Vicky] in such a smart white merino dress trimmed with blue which Mamma had given her and a pretty cap, and placed her on my bed, seating himself next to her and she was very dear and good. And as my precious invaluable Albert sat there and our little Love between us I felt quite moved with happiness and gratitude to God.'

The bliss might not have been perfectly symmetrical. For many years in the late 1840s and 1850s, Albert chafed at the limitations placed on his part in public business. It did not help that they had been self-imposed, apparently willingly. Albert's German background in Coburg explains a lot about his mixed constitutional feelings. The smaller German states in the mid-19th century were on the cusp of making important decisions about how best to avoid the fate of the red republicanism that Karl Marx had confidently predicted for them (as well as for Britain). Would liberalism or authoritarianism be the best preventive against revolution? Albert was not so obtuse as to imagine Britain would even flirt with the latter possibility. In fact, after a period of innocence he had rather fallen in love with English (as distinct from British) constitutional history, swotting up on Sir William Blackstone's *Commentaries on the Laws of England* (1723–80) and, over-optimistic about Victoria's own eagerness to be enlightened about her monarchy, reading aloud to her passages from Henry Hallam's *The Constitution from the Accession of Henry VII to the Death of George II* (1827). But Albert's own mentor, Baron von Stockmar, had warned him that Britain was in danger of establishing, by political *fait accompli*, a mere 'ministerial government' in which the monarchy did no more than rubber stamp the decisions of parliament and the political parties. And to begin with – until put right by Sir Robert Peel's careful but firm guidance – Albert shared Victoria's uneducated instinct that the crown should reserve the possibility at least of withholding confirmation of ministerial appointments or policies of which it disapproved. What Stockmar wanted was that the sovereign be akin to a 'permanent Prime Minister' – above the fray of party – and therefore somehow entitled to the trust and respect of both politicians and the people.

It was to Albert's credit that he rapidly understood this to be an impossibly over-ambitious plan. Instead, the sketch of his duties written in 1843, and revised and extended in 1850 when he turned down the Duke of Wellington's invitation to command the army, described a subtler role. He would, he said, 'sink his own

Queen Victoria and the Prince Consort in the gardens of Osborne House, Isle of Wight, photograph by Miss Day, July 1859.

individual existence into that of his wife . . . assume no separate responsibility before the public but make his position entirely a part of hers.' This sounds like an act of almost perverse (and uncharacteristic) self-effacement – until, that is, one reads on in the Consort's job description and discovers that Albert also commanded himself to 'continually and anxiously watch every part of the public business, in order to be able to advise and assist her at any moment. . . . As the natural head of her family, superintendent of the royal household' (in which he had rapidly made swingeing cuts – no more wine allowance for the 'Red Chamber' at Windsor); 'manager of her private affairs, sole *confidential* adviser in politics, and her only assistant in her communications with the officers of the Government, he is, besides, the husband of the Queen, the tutor of the royal children, the private Secretary of the Sovereign and her permanent minister.'

The most extraordinary thing about this list was not its exhaustiveness, but its conversion of domestic authority into a substantive political equivalent. This was not the passive companionship exercised by the last 'Prince Consort,' George of Denmark, husband to Queen Anne in the early 18th century, still less the nervously tentative presence of King Philip of Spain, the husband of Mary Tudor in the mid-16th. Albert was to be ubiquitous, watchful, omniscient; always there at the back of the chair, behind the desk; available for consultation even when not asked. What he had drafted was in some ways a throwback to the ancient privileges of the Groom of the Stool – the person, who, closest to the body of the monarch, made himself the indispensable medium through which politicians sought, and were granted, access to the sovereign. Whenever ministers were in the presence of the queen, so was Albert.

Exerting his authority by appearing not to, being a presence by confining himself to being a husband, father and secretary, was all very nice in theory but often tricky in practice. While it put little strain on the constitution, paradoxically it put a lot of strain on the royal union. Early in the marriage he had complained that he was 'husband not master of my own house'; and he continued to fret that his necessarily inferior political standing somehow undermined his patriarchal role in the family, however ardently Victoria protested to the contrary. Neither of them would have disagreed with Carlyle's repetition of the truism that it was 'an eternal axiom [and] the law of nature that man should bear rule in the home and not the woman.' The queen, was, in fact, painfully conscious of the anomaly by which her public presence was supposed to convey, simultaneously, both wifely decorum and regal superiority. She was a conscientious and opinionated reader of state papers; but, as Albert came to have more outlets for his driven sense of civic responsibility, so Victoria came to feel that perhaps he had more of an appetite for this work than she did herself. Sometimes, especially in the chaotic years after the fall of Peel in 1846, with governments coming and going, she felt at sea politically. During these years Victoria leaned heavily on Albert's views, changing her opinion of Peel himself. Originally she had detested him as the common manufacturer who had usurped the rightful place of dearest Lord M; but, when seen through Albert's eyes, he turned into a figure of tragic rectitude. The terrier-like Lord John Russell had to be endured. Lord Henry Temple, Viscount Palmerston, whom they gigglingly nicknamed 'Pilgerstein' (from the German for 'palmer' or 'pilgrim'), with his dyed whiskers, languid manners and cynical jingoism, they could barely tolerate and wrote off as a suspicious adventurer – a staggering underestimate of the foreign secretary's dangerous talent. It was all very wearying. 'I love peace and quiet,' Victoria wrote in her journal, 'in fact I hate politics and turmoil. . . . Albert grows daily fonder of politics and business and is so wonderfully fit for both – such perspicacity and courage – and I grow daily to dislike them both more and more. We women are not made for governing – and if we are good women, we must dislike these masculine occupations; but there are times which force one to take an interest in them.'

The place where the ideal of a family partnership came closest to realization was Osborne House. It was there, as at Balmoral in Aberdeenshire at the other end of the island, that the day would be divided into a governing morning and a family afternoon. And it was there that Victoria made the all-important symbolic gesture of providing Albert with his own desk, placed beside hers, so that incoming ministers would see the two of them, side by side, and get the message that this was indeed the Saxe-Coburg-Gotha monarchy. Albert had bought the 1000-acre estate on the Isle of Wight in 1845, on the advice of Peel, as a retreat for the queen; a resort where the cares of state could be balanced by the pleasures of family life. The prince claimed that the pine woods gently sloping down to the bay reminded him of the coast near Naples (as well as the forests near his birthplace at Rosenau), an impression made only a little less improbable by the brightly painted Italianate house with its yellow and white towers and formal gardens and fountains, whose every detail he either designed or supervised. By the time Albert had finished with the house it had cost a cool £200,000, an immense fortune by the standards of the mid-19th century; the 'retreat' had become, in effect, an alternative place of government, with ministers and dispatch boxes, to the queen's chagrin, constantly arriving. But the working routine of Osborne (and Balmoral) did indeed work: a walk before breakfast; newspapers with or after breakfast, followed by spirited discussion; the queen inspecting papers that Albert had already screened and prepared (in his capacity as private secretary) for her signature; *joint* meetings, if necessary, with ministers. And after luncheon, further informal discussion of the implications of the morning's business.

But afternoons were also the time when the family romance could be most fully indulged with picnics, fishing trips and pony rides. In Scotland there would be deer stalking; heavily unannounced 'visits' to local crofters; reels and flings in the evening, with the queen got up in the freshly invented Balmoral red and grey tartan. In both places Albert set his mind to all kinds of Improving Projects, which would provide, at the same time, physical exercise, moral instruction and even a little harmless play for the children. The *pièce de résistance* was the Swiss Cottage at Osborne, with its own kitchen garden, built in the park by the prince acting as foreman to his four eldest children – Vicky, Bertie, Affie and Alice – who provided the labour. It featured furniture and even working cooking stoves, all scaled down to child size, so that they could play house.

The idea was that the royal children should inherit from their parents the idyll of the happy family. (Predictably the boys, and most notoriously Bertie, the Prince of Wales, who felt most put upon by their father, spurned the role as soon as they were of an age to escape.) But although she never stopped believing she had been uniquely blessed in her husband and (between tantrums) confiding professions of her love to her diary, Victoria was also capable of statements of startling disenchantment, especially when her daughters were contemplating their own dynastic marriages. Marriages were all very nice, she let it be known, assuming they were *happy* marriages. But many were anything but happy, and then a heaven could indeed turn into a hell. Single people were, she thought, much better off than partners who were doomed to inflict unrelenting daily misery on each other. Moreover, the chances of happiness were much slimmer than poor naïve girls, groomed for the altar, were made to believe by their ambitious parents. Keenly feeling the burdens of continuous childbirth, she declared, 'All marriage is a lottery, the happiness is always an exchange – though it may be a poor one. Still, the poor woman is bodily and morally the husband's slave – that always sticks in my throat.'

Victoria, of course, was no feminist, but at times like this she certainly sounded like one. The chances are that she knew about a number of notorious court cases highlighting the plight of unhappily married wives. The best known had been that of Lord Melbourne's intimate friend Caroline Norton, whose brutal husband, George, had then deserted her, denying her custody or even access to their children and leaving her without any means of support. The reason was that, as Blackstone had laid down (and therefore Victoria and Albert, both assiduous Blackstone students, knew), 'by marriage, the husband and wife are one person in law, that is the very being or existence of the woman is suspended during the marriage, or at least is incorporated … into that of the husband under whose wing, protection and cover she performs anything.' In practice, this meant that, until reforms in the last quarter of the century, married women were incapable of owning property or of being party to any kind of contract, much less suing for divorce. It meant that Elizabeth Gaskell, for example, was not entitled to any of the earnings from her own novels, but had to satisfy herself with an allowance from her husband. Vindictively, George Norton had used his conjugal power to prevent Caroline from receiving any income after they were separated. The publicity given to the case had resulted in an act of parliament in 1839 that gave abandoned mothers custody of children under seven – but not thereafter.

Since Victoria was always inclined to give Lord M the benefit of the doubt, it is likely that she accepted his insistence, when Norton named him as co-respondent in the divorce, that his relationship with Caroline had been perfectly above board; so she would have been able to see Caroline as a victim, and her battle for custody and support as heroic as it genuinely was. But, 20 years on, could the queen conceivably have been reading the *Englishwoman's Journal*, published by the Victoria Press from 1860, which contained articles forcefully arguing the right of married women to their own property and, exactly like the queen, routinely compared bad marriages either to a lottery or to slavery? Perhaps Victoria had noticed or read Barbara Leigh Smith's *Brief Summary in Plain Language of the Most Important Laws Concerning Women* (1854), and even sympathized with its mission of educating young women in what to expect from marriage.

The possibility of Victoria's familiarity with early feminist writing is not quite as staggering as it might seem. The founder of the Victoria Press (which employed women compositors) was the remarkable Emily Faithfull, of whom the queen thought well enough to appoint her as her own Printer and Publisher in Ordinary in 1862 – not a position she would have given to someone who had incurred her disapproval. As a friend and colleague of Barbara Leigh Smith, Faithfull was a member of the Langham Place Circle – writers, social activists and critics who, at 19 Langham Place, just off London's Regent Street, spurred by Jessie Boucherett's Society for Promoting the Employment of Women, had established a register (in fact an employment agency) for women seeking work as teachers and governesses. The aim was to extend the list to the enormous category of domestic service, as had been done in Bristol. There, a similar office sent out inspectors to ensure that places of employment were physically and morally sound, and that working conditions and

Top: Queen Victoria's sitting room at Osborne House, Isle of Wight, with the original writing desks at which Victoria and Albert worked side by side, photograph by Jabez Hughes, 1876.
Above: *Swiss Cottage, Osborne House*, watercolour by William Leighton Leitch, *c.*1875.

pay were decent. The Langham Place Circle's office included a reading room where women could peruse newspapers (including the *Englishwoman's Journal*) while they were looking at job opportunities, sign petitions for the campaign for married women's property, and read essays by Barbara Leigh Smith, Isa Craig and Bessie Rayner Parkes, editor of the *Englishwoman's Review* from 1858. These writers argued for the importance of women's work, and believed that it should extend to watch-making, journalism, medicine, prison and workhouse inspection and custodial work, the arts and, of course, teaching in schools and colleges set up for girls.

These women were, admittedly, an exceptional, but middle-class vanguard. They had little in common with the Edinburgh Maidservants' Union, which in 1825 had had the temerity to threaten a strike. On the contrary, they depended on the 1.3 million women domestic servants to give them the freedom to agitate. Barbara Leigh Smith was a cousin of Florence Nightingale and the illegitimate daughter of the Radical Unitarian MP for Norwich, Benjamin Smith, who had deliberately refused to marry her mother, and who had settled an annual income on his golden-haired daughter precisely so that she might lead an independent life. But the 26,000 signatures that she and her colleagues secured for a petition to urge a Married Women's Property Bill on parliament in 1855 is evidence enough that the Langhamites were neither tiny in number nor insignificant. Among those who actively joined the cause were some of the best-known and most widely read and admired of all Victorian women writers – Elizabeth Gaskell, of course; but also Elizabeth Barrett Browning, Mary Ann Evans a.k.a. George Eliot, Harriet Martineau and Harriet Taylor. It is ironic that Taylor's part in the Victorian battle for women's rights (itself undeservedly less well known than the later militant suffragettes) is often best remembered as the recruitment of her husband, John Stuart Mill, the 'saint of rationalism' and the greatest pillar of mid-Victorian liberalism, to the feminist cause. Mill himself was at pains, especially in his *Autobiography* (1873), to insist that it was Taylor who had educated him in the outrageous anomalies of women's position in marriage, in the labour force and in political society; who had been his true partner in works like *Principles of Political Economy* (1848), where the absence of women as a subject for the discussions of social science was first explicitly addressed; and that the work for which he would be best remembered, *On Liberty* (1859), formally dedicated to his wife, was the result of their joint authorship.

Some of the urgency and passion that Mill (whose prose, as he endearingly knew, seldom smoulders with either) evinces here was due precisely to his dismay at Harriet's part in all this, being reduced to that of Supporting Wife. The ideal helpmeet as sketched in John Ruskin's *Sesame and Lilies* (1865) was permitted to cultivate only the kind of knowledge already acquired by her husband, and was expected to act as permanently indentured proof-reader, inkwell-filler and – when the reviews came in – up-cheerer. That, insisted Mill, had not been the case with him and Harriet at all. Theirs had been a meeting of minds long before a mating of bodies. Mill may have been stronger in the technical science of ideas, especially economic theories, but Taylor had understood and passed on two sorts of knowledge in which he was decidedly the weaker party – grand metaphysical ideas as well as practical human applications (the spiritual and the social). All that he, Mill, was left with was the 'intermediate' realm, which in his *Autobiography* he implied, disingenuously, any old pedant could master as best he could. The psychological subtext of this elaborately formal apologia was in fact powerful, even sensational. For what John Stuart Mill really meant was that when he had met Harriet, he found someone who emancipated *him* – from thralldom to his father.

It was 1830; he was 24. She was a year younger, married, with three children to John Taylor, a City trader in medical drugs, whose Scottish family was well known to the originally Scottish Mills. Harriet had already published poems, book reviews and essays. Mill was working as a clerk in the Examiners' Office of the East India Company, drafting dispatches to be sent out to the company's legal and fiscal councillors. His father, who also worked for the Company, had found him the job. But then James Mill had done everything he possibly could to make John Stuart, the eldest of nine children, in his own image. Mill senior had committed himself, as thoroughly as he knew how, to furthering the utilitarian creed of his friend and mentor Jeremy Bentham, which was to increase the 'greatest happiness of the greatest number' of mankind. Beginning with the presumption that man was a bundle of sense-receptors, responding to either pleasure or pain, the enlightened legislator would aim to maximize the former and minimize the latter. For the first time the ills, material and moral, that plagued humanity were to be systematically and scientifically analyzed: their magnitude measured, the causes diagnosed and the remedies prescribed. A report would be issued and recommendations made for legislation; a salaried inspectorate would be recruited to see to its execution and enforcement. Hitherto, empires had been run by power. The British Empire would be run by knowledge. James Mill had become a candidate for the position in the Examiners' Office after publishing an immense, not to say unreadably exhaustive, *History of British India* (1817).

John Stuart Mill was just 11 when his father's *magnum opus* was laid before the world. But his training to be one of the propagators of felicity had begun much earlier. Since a child's mind was a sheet of smooth, soft wax, perfectly empty but perfectly receptive, the impress of instruction could not be made too early. Three was just about the right age, James decided, to begin teaching his son Greek. Initiation was Aesop's *Fables* (in the original), swiftly followed by Plato, Herodotus (all of it) and Xenophon. Arithmetic was a lot less fun, but by eight there was always Latin, Nathaniel Hooke's *The Roman History from the Building of Rome to the Commonwealth* (1738–71) and John Millar's *An Historical View of the English Government from the Settlement of the Saxons to the Accession of the House of Stewart* (1787) for light relief. The Mills lived in the favourite suburb of radical Improvers and feminists, Dr Price's Stoke Newington Green. And it was while striding around the Green and on longer walks into what was still countryside that Mill senior drilled his 10-year-old in differential calculus, Roman agrarian laws and the analysis of Greek rhetoric. When his father was appointed to his post with the East India Company, it was John Stuart's turn to teach his younger siblings. In his spare time between reading the proofs of his father's *The History of British India* and being put through political economy and logic, he managed to smuggle in a little literature – mostly Shakespeare. At 14 he was allowed a trip to the Château Pompignon near Toulouse; but when he returned, his father's relentlessly intensive instruction continued.

James Mill had been breathtakingly successful in turning John Stuart into a thinking machine crammed full of every conceivable kind of knowledge, his powers of calculation and computation perfectly calibrated. But he had also made a creature already cowed by the burden of his assigned mission to Know Everything That Mattered; fearful of his unyieldingly stern father; racked by a terror of his own inadequacy. But at least, he supposed, he had been given the foundation of wisdom and the vocation of virtue. That supposition was profoundly shaken by a series of attacks made in the middle and late 1820s on Jeremy Bentham and James Mill by some of the brightest and sharpest essayists writing in the *Reviews*, not least Thomas Carlyle and (in a different spirit) the young Thomas Babington Macaulay. Carlyle attacked utilitarianism for assuming that human beings and the cultures into which they were gathered were akin to machines that might be retooled as and when they showed signs of malfunction. Only the victims of a higher naivety could remain impervious to the manifest truth that it was spirit, not base matter, that made the difference between the happiness and the misery of societies. Macaulay attacked utilitarianism for its refusal to concede that there might be a direct conflict between the imposition of scientifically optimized reforms and the protection of liberty.

The rest of Mill's life was to be spent working out exactly those conflicts – between freedom and amelioration, but also between the competing claims of logic and feeling. So when his father's Unitarian minister, William Johnson Fox, brought

Top: *Harriet Taylor Mill*, by anon. *c.* 1834.
Opposite: Barbara Leigh Smith, later known as Barbara Bodichon, *c.* 1860.

Mr and Mrs Taylor to the Mills' house, and Mill drank in the huge eyes, the swan neck and the confident, eloquent speech, he knew instinctively that he had found an altogether new kind of instruction. Within a short time he learned that Harriet, who had been married very young, was now bitterly unhappy. Her husband had committed no cruelty. By the standards of the day he might even have been judged a good spouse. It was simply that, measured by the exalted sense of what a properly companionate marriage might be, she saw the depths of their incompatibility; his imperviousness to everything she most cherished: art, poetry, philosophy. Tied to him, she would be no more than a dutiful helpmeet. John Stuart Mill, on the other hand, plainly admired her for precisely the qualities of spirit and independent thought that had made her feel her marriage was a prison. Within a few more weeks they were writing to each other as 'dearest.' In the summer of 1833 Mill wrote, 'O my own love, whatever it may or may not be to you, you need never regret for a moment what has already brought such increase of happiness and can in no possible way increase evil. . . . I am taking as much care of your robin [her bird] as if it were your own sweet self.'

Although, over the next 20 years of a tortured romance, Harriet Taylor and John Stuart Mill would spend as much time as they could in each other's company and achieve an extraordinary intimacy, it seems certain that Mill was telling the truth in his *Autobiography* when he insisted that no boundaries of physical propriety had ever been breached. Sexual consummation would only happen once they were married. But their predicament certainly made the two of them turn their attention to the obstacles in the way of divorce in Victorian Britain.

Given that, legally (as another of the Langham Place feminists, Frances Power Cobbe, put it), married women were in the same category as 'criminals, idiots and minors,' they were disqualified from suing for divorce, although they themselves could be divorced by their husbands for adultery. A Divorce and Matrimonial Causes Bill was passed in parliament in 1857, but it was not what it seemed. Enacted specifically to pre-empt a measure that would have given married women property rights, this piece of legislation perpetuated, rather than corrected, the inequities between the sexes. Husbands could divorce their wives for adultery, but wives could only return the favour if that adultery took the form of rape, sodomy, bestiality or some indeterminate act of cruelty. And, needless to say, so long as injured wives still had no title to their own property or income, the heavy costs involved in bringing a suit all but precluded it ever being brought. The notion that a divorce action might be brought (as Harriet would have done) for mere incompatibility remained the most fantastic prospect.

By the time the Divorce Act was passed, Harriet and John Stuart Mill had been married for six years. During most of the 20 years that preceded it Harriet had lived apart from Taylor, who, after Mill and his wife had gone off to Paris together for six months, was sufficiently humiliated to ask for a separation. But the peculiar arrangement somehow persisted. Mill would call on the Taylors (reunited for a while) for dinner, whereupon the husband would obligingly make himself scarce at his club. John and Harriet seemed armoured by the certainty of their love against the discomfort and distaste they provoked even in people whom they had thought of as friends, like the Carlyles. When one night John Stuart abruptly drove up in the company of Mrs Taylor, Carlyle professed himself relieved to discover that a distraught Mill was confessing that a maidservant at his house had burned the entire first draft of Carlyle's *French Revolution*. Bad as that was, Carlyle thought, it was actually better than the expected announcement – that Taylor and Mill had run off together! (Jane Welsh Carlyle, who never liked Harriet, persisted in suspecting that somehow she had been responsible for the destruction of the manuscript.)

All these vexations were endured for the sake of an ideal union founded on mutual respect and love. The clarity and steadfastness of the conviction led the couple to submit the conventions of Victorian marriage to unsparing criticism, much of which was incorporated in *The Subjection of Women*, published by Mill in 1869. The entire institution, they argued, was gift-wrapped in a tissue of falsehood and hypocrisy. Young girls were indoctrinated with the fallacy that 'marriage was the true profession of women,' and that it would be an abode of perfect contentment thereafter. By a conspiracy of silence and expediency, the sacrificial victims of the arrangement were kept in ignorance, not just of the physical but also of the social reality of what really lay in store for them as wives. Marriage among the propertied classes was overwhelmingly a business transaction, rationally calculated to accumulate wealth, status and power. Bargains of mutual profit were made between the contracting parties. A family of high rank but depleted fortune would be allied to one that was its complementary opposite. The driving force, always, was hard interest, not soft sentiment. While marriage was ostensibly ordained for the containment of lust, the practical circumstances in which many unions were entered into more or less guaranteed the opposite, once the partners who had been brought together by the spurious claims of romance became inevitably disillusioned. The women then found themselves corrupted and ensnared in a diabolical bargain. They kept their fashionable clothes, their fine carriage, their servants, their children and their social position (and even, if they were very discreet, their lover); their husbands got to keep their mistresses. It was, Mill and Harriet supposed, a sort of cohabitation, but 'if this be all that human life has for women, it is little enough, and any woman who feels herself capable of great happiness and whose aspirations have not been artificially checked will claim to be set free from this, to seek more.'

It was only John Taylor's death, in 1849, that set Harriet free. The couple married two years later at Melcombe Regis register office, a month before the opening of the Great Exhibition, ostracized by Mill's family and many of their old friends. Before they tied the knot, Mill insisted on signing a formal renunciation of the conventional legal rights of the Victorian husband. It is, perhaps, the most high-minded pre-nuptial declaration ever made:

> Being about, if I am so happy, as to obtain her consent, to enter into the marriage relations with the only woman I have ever known with whom I would have entered into that state, and the whole marriage relation as constituted by law being such as she and I entirely disapprove … I, having no means of legally disinvesting myself of those odious powers (as I most assuredly would do if an engagement to that effect could be made legally binding on me) feel it my duty to put on record a formal protest against the existing law of marriage … And in the event of marriage between Mrs Taylor and me I declare it to be my will and intention and the condition of any engagement between us that she retains in all respects whatever, the same absolute freedom of action and freedom of disposal of herself and of all that does or may at any time belong to her, as if no marriage had taken place and I absolutely disclaim and repudiate all pretension to have acquired any rights whatsoever by virtue of such a marriage.

Their domestic happiness was short-lived. Both of them were suffering from what developed into fatal tuberculosis. As Harriet's more advanced condition grew worse, they separated for months at a time while she tried to slow the progression of the disease by stays at Swiss sanatoria, or in the warmer, drier air of Provence. Conscious that he himself had a limited time, Mill busied himself with what he called 'the sacred duty' of transcribing Harriet's thoughts on the equality of the sexes. The doctors, who were not altogether candid with them about the galloping deterioration of Harriet's condition in particular, insisted on separate rest cures, even though the separation was agony for Mill. Trapped inside a railway carriage in France, his route back to Harriet and England blocked by impassable snow, Mill brooded poignantly on their shared plight, and on the sense of warmth and security 'given by the consciousness of being loved [and] by being near the one by whom one is … loved the best … I have experience at present of both these things for I feel as if no really dangerous illness could actually happen to me when I have her to care for me … yet I feel by coming away from her I have parted with a kind of talisman and was more open to the attacks of the enemy than when I was with her.'

Harriet died in November 1858 at Avignon, *en route* to the Mediterranean. Mill bought a house close to her grave and lived there for much of the rest of his life, while he finished the treatise *On Liberty* that immortalized him as the strongest pillar of Victorian liberal thought, and that he dedicated to his wife. Although he faithfully reproduced Harriet's opinions, he did not wholeheartedly agree with all of them. Whilst he made no bones about the right of women to seek and gain 'useful' work outside the home, he was not at all convinced that doing so would necessarily make them happier. But if that were their choice, or their necessity – and the census of 1851 showed that fully half the six million adult women of Britain were in fact employed – then, it went without saying, Mill believed, that they should have equal pay for equal work. To those, like psychiatric researcher Dr Henry Maudsley, who argued that their 'biology' (a euphemism for the menstrual cycle) precluded them from working for as much as eight days a month, Mill responded bluntly: 'What is now called the "nature of women" is an eminently artificial thing. . . . I believe that their disabilities are only clung to, to maintain their subordination in domestic life because the generality of the male sex cannot yet tolerate the idea of living with an equal.'

In 1865 Mill, now a nationally known figure, was approached by a group of Westminster electors and asked if he would stand for parliament. It was a critical moment. Prodded by its radical wing, the leadership of the Liberal party, Lord John Russell and William Gladstone, had decided to embrace a measure of parliamentary reform that, for all its circumspection and caution, would still end up extending the franchise to almost all householders. Mill's voice would be powerful in support not so much in spite of, but because of, the fact that he was actually against universal suffrage and the secret ballot. The crucial qualification, as far as he was concerned, was education (indeed he actually wanted votes weighted to reflect the amount of education, rather than rateable property, possessed by the voter). He was well aware of the eccentricity of his views. 'I was convinced that no numerous or influential portion of any electoral body really wished to be represented by a person of my opinions.' As if that was not enough, he refused to stand as the candidate of any party, to campaign or canvass or spend a single penny on his own behalf.

And there was another issue that he thought would make his election even more improbable. Following an article published by Harriet in 1851 in the *Englishwoman's Journal,* Mill insisted that if household suffrage were granted in the boroughs it must include women as well as men. For although married women could not own houses in their own right, there was nothing to stop single women or widows; and there were, almost certainly, tens of thousands of women who fell into that category. For that matter, 'householder' in 1866 included rate-paying tenants, and that would have multiplied the eligible female franchise even more.

Mill's stepdaughter, Helen Taylor, with whom he shared much of his life after Harriet's death, was determined to keep this flame lit. It was she who encouraged Barbara Leigh Smith (now legally Madame Bodichon, having married a French-Algerian sculptor — from whom, needless to say, she lived apart half the year) to approach Mill about presenting a petition to parliament. Some 1200 women had signed their names, asking for the franchise. Mill was constitutionally shy about stirring up noisy publicity on the streets, but he got the vocal support of the Langhamites whether he wanted it or not. One of their number, Emily Davies (later the founder of Girton College, Cambridge, the first Oxbridge college for women, set up in 1874, some 25 years after the first London colleges, Queen's and Bedford), remembered that during the campaign 'Madame Bodichon hired a carriage, occupied by herself, Isa Craig, Bessie Parkes and myself, with placards upon it, to drive about Westminster. We called it "giving Mr Mill our moral support" but there was some suspicion that we might rather be doing him harm as one of our friends told us he had heard him described as "the man who wants to have girls in Parliament." '

Mill was not, of course, arguing for women members of parliament (although he saw no reason why, one day, that too should not come to pass). But he believed it both absurd and manifestly unjust that half the otherwise qualified suffrage should be barred from exercising their right to vote solely on grounds of their sex. What was already an uphill battle was made more difficult when the Liberals fell from power in August 1866. When, under a Conservative government in February 1867, Disraeli presented his version of the bill, Mill stuck to his guns, if anything even more adamant than the Langham Place campaigners in his demand that women (not just single women) be admitted to the franchise. In March he presented another petition (one of three that arrived in the Commons), bearing over 3000 signatures from Manchester. On 20 May 1867, in an eloquent and moving speech, Mill formally submitted his amendment to the Representation of the People Bill, proposing to substitute the word 'person' for 'man' in the clause dealing with criteria for extending the franchise to householders in the counties (not achieved until 1884). The surprise was not that the amendment went down to defeat, but that Mill actually managed to persuade no fewer than 73 members to vote for it (81 including pairs). His supporters included some eminent Mancunians — the Radical Thomas Bayley Potter and Sir Thomas Bazley, manufacturer and self-styled workers' friend.

In a Manchester by-election in November 1867 (when John Bright's more radical brother Jacob stood on a platform that included women's household suffrage), a widowed shopkeeper, Lily Maxwell, became the first woman to cast a vote in a British election. She was only on the register as the result of a clerical error; but once she was discovered by Jacob Bright and the suffrage campaigner Lydia Becker, they were determined that she should go through with it. Escorted to the poll, she cast her vote to a round of loud applause. An obviously disconcerted pioneer, Lily must none the less have had a great deal of gumption, not to mention sympathy with the aim of the suffragists (who had been campaigning peacefully for the vote since 1866), to play her part in what became an elaborately staged event. A surviving photograph certainly suggests a woman with a good deal of flinty determination. As far as Bright and Becker were concerned, she was a gift to the cause. Like the Chartist Land Company settler Ann Wood, Lily Maxwell was a classic example of gritty Scottish thrift: an ex-domestic servant who had saved enough to become a shopkeeper, and who paid the respectable weekly rent of 6 shillings and 2 pence for her place in Ludlow Street, a mix of artisan and lower middle-class, two-up, two-down brick dwellings. When her case became famous – or, to the conservative press, shocking – Lydia Becker wrote a dignified letter to *The Times* on 3 December 1867, describing her as a model voter of the kind intended to be emancipated by the Reform Act, 'a widow who keeps a small shop in a quiet street in Manchester. She supports herself and pays her own rates and taxes out of her own earnings. She has no man to influence or be influenced by, and she has very decided political principles, which determined her vote for Mr Jacob Bright at the recent election.' As a result of the publicity around Lily Maxwell's vote, Lydia Becker was able to open a register to enrol qualified women householders. By the end of 1868, her list numbered 13,000.

All this appalled Queen Victoria. She may have occasionally voiced her own reservations (at least privately) about the distance between the sentimental dream and the harder realities of marriage. She may even have sympathized with measures designed to restrain physically violent and flagrantly licentious husbands, or to take care of cruelly abandoned wives. But addressing injustices and cruelties was, to her mind, emphatically not a licence for any degree of political emancipation. In October 1867 she had been surprisingly liberal on the need to expand the suffrage to the 'lower classes' since they had become 'so well informed and are so intelligent and earn their bread and riches so deservedly' in contrast to 'the wretched, ignorant high-born beings who live only to kill time.' But any discussion of women's fitness to exercise political rights made her apopleptic. 'It is a subject,' she wrote, referring

Top: *John Stuart Mill*, pastel by E. Goodwyn Lewis, 1869.
Above: Mary Seacole, *c.* 1855.

to herself as usual in the third person, 'which makes the Queen so furious she cannot contain herself.' And again she vituperated against 'this mad wicked folly of "Womens' Rights" with all its attendant horrors on which her poor feeble sex is bent, forgetting every sense of womanly feeling and propriety.'

How did the queen feel about the other great feminist cause: work for middle-class women? She continued to be a dutiful reader of dispatches and papers. But, after marriage and motherhood, she never felt that it was more than a painful chore imposed on her by her constitutional obligations, and (until it started to kill him) that Albert was in every way much better suited to the work. For the most part, too, she subscribed to the middle-class truism that marriage was woman's profession. So it is extremely unlikely that Victoria would have given much thought to another revelation of the census of 1851, that there were (and, according to the demographic statisticians, there seemed always likely to be) around half to three-quarters of a million more women of marriageable age than men. This 'spinster surplus,' thought the Manchester political economist and manufacturer William Rathbone Greg, might be reduced by projects of emigration to the colonies. But that would none the less leave around half a million single women who were to be either condemned to a permanent sense of their own redundancy, or trapped in notoriously underpaid and little-respected jobs such as governesses. In the late 1850s the *Englishwoman's Journal* and its editor, Bessie Rayner Parkes, had taken up the call of middle-class women to be employed, as paid professionals rather than genteel volunteers, in a broader variety of fulfilling professions: teaching in girls' schools and colleges; prison and reformatory work; 'deaconess' visits to the homes of the poor in country and town; and the one profession that had been officially declared a 'noble' field for women: nursing.

Nursing was the one single-woman's profession that the queen felt perfectly fitted with the feminine qualities of tenderness, solace and healing. And the carnage of the Crimean War, of course, had everything to do with this. The genuinely epic history of Florence Nightingale, the single woman *par excellence* who had spurned marriage for the sake of a higher calling; who had brought her band of 38 young women to the hell of the barracks hospital at Scutari; who had taken on the mutton-chop whiskered medical corps and the army bureaucrats to wring from them the barest necessities: bandages, splints, soap; who had made the washtub her personal escutcheon – all this had stirred the nation, not least the queen herself. Many times Victoria had expressed her bitter regret that she was not the right sex to be able to join the soldiers in their heroic privations and combat. She knitted mufflers, socks and mittens; and sent letters to the front, and visited returning soldiers in hospital, so that the troops should know that no one grieved more deeply for their suffering or felt more warmly for their sacrifices. The heavy losses suffered at Balaclava and Inkerman kept her and Albert awake at night. And as the news, reported in October 1854 by one of *The Times*'s war correspondents, Thomas Chenery, of incompetent management and command, and of shortages of basic supplies became more and more appalling, so Victoria's sense of maternal concern grew more acute.

The nurses at Scutari were surrogates for her own presence. When Florence Nightingale returned to Britain after the armistice in 1856, Victoria invited her to Balmoral to hear, first-hand, her account of the ordeal. But there was another heroine of the Crimea whose work was unknown to the queen (until her own step-nephew Captain Count Victor Gleichen told her) but who was the soldiers' own favourite pseudo-mother. In the same year that Nightingale met the queen, a gala banquet and concert, with 11 military bands, was held by guards regiments at the Royal Surrey Gardens to benefit Mary Seacole, who had been declared bankrupt. There was a good reason why the returning soldiers so admired Mary. If you had been sick or wounded and managed to get taken to her 'British Hotel,' you stood a decent chance of surviving. It was not so at Scutari.

But Mary Seacole was the wrong colour to be an officially canonized Victorian heroine. Born Mary Grant, she was the mulatto child of a Scotsman and his Jamaican wife. After marrying one of Nelson's godsons, Edwin Horatio Seacole, she had run an establishment in Jamaica that was part hotel, part convalescent home; during both the cholera epidemic of 1831 and the even more serious yellow-fever outbreak of 1853 she had acquired a reputation for working miracles of recuperation among the critically sick. Her antidotes for dysenteric diseases and the associated dehydration, which almost always proved fatal, were all drawn from the Caribbean botanical pharmacopeia. This origin guaranteed that they would be ridiculed as 'barbarous' potions by the medical establishment and that Mary's application to go to the Crimea to treat the cholera and typhoid victims (which accounted for the vast majority of fatalities) would be dismissed out of hand, not least by Florence Nightingale herself.

Unlike Nightingale, Seacole had no Baron Sidney Herbert at the War Department to argue her case. But, using her own funds, she somehow got herself to the eastern Mediterranean along with two of her most trusted Jamaican cooks. Once there she made, not for the barracks hospital in Turkey where it was clear she was unwelcome, but for the Crimea – the theatre of war itself. About two miles from Balaclava, Mary spent £800 of her own money building – presumably in imitation of her Jamaican establishment – the British Hotel: a combination of supply depot, refectory for soldiers about to go into action, and nursing and recovery station for the sick and wounded. Unlike the Scutari wards, the British Hotel was kept warm and dry. The best thing that could happen to a soldier laid low with cholera or typhoid was to be cared for on the spot, rather than endure the excruciating, sometimes three-week passage across the Black Sea to the deathtrap hospital at Scutari.

There were rats, of course, at the British Hotel too – caught in legions by 'Aunty Seacole's' exterminators at first light. Once they were dealt with, she would begin the morning routine. Coffee and tea by 7 a.m.; then chickens plucked and cooked, hams and tongues (where did she get them?), broth, stewed rhubarb, pies and Welsh rarebits prepared, and the *pièce de résistance* – her patented milkless (and therefore safely transportable) rice pudding. Even without the milk there was something especially maternal about that pudding: comfort food spooned out to soldiers who, amidst all the terrors of war, were allowed to become small boys again, fed by their big mulatto nanny. 'Had you been fortunate enough to have visited the British Hotel upon rice pudding days,' wrote one returning soldier, 'I warrant you would have ridden back to your hut with kind thoughts of Mother's Seacole's endeavours to give you a taste of home.'

Alexis Soyer, the celebrity chef of the Reform Club who in 1855 had come out to provide his own brand of stews for the soldiers (Mary watched him ladle it out with his fleshy, bejewelled hands), approved her fare as wholesome and her courage as heroic. Once the convalescents had been taken care of, she would saddle up two mules and load a wagon with hot and cold food and basic surgical supplies – bandages, blankets, splints, needles, thread and alcohol. She would then set off straight into the thunder of the siege and, guided by a Greek Jew who knew the lines of the trenches and the positions of the camps, would disappear into the smoke, looking for wounded men – sometimes enemy Russians as well as British and French – who needed rescuing along with a mug of tea, a word of consolation and as, she instinctively understood, the touch of a clean handkerchief. Mortars whizzed past the old lady and her mules plodding through the fire. More than once, when she heard shouts of, 'Lie down mother! Lie down,' 'with very undignified and unladylike haste I had to embrace the earth.' She became inured to horror. One soldier whom she found had been shot in his lower jaw. Mary put her finger in his mouth to try to open it enough to get some fluid down, but the teeth clamped down on her finger, cutting through it, and she needed help to prise them open.

Those who did manage to survive the nightmare of sickness and slaughter seldom forgot Mary Seacole. When she came back from the Crimea to London there were no invitations to Balmoral; only a press of creditors. But the fundraising events – at Covent Garden and Her Majesty's Theatre, as well as the Royal Surrey Gardens – saved her from bankruptcy. Alexis Soyer and William Russell both made

Victorian tomb sculpture, typical in scale and grandeur, Kensal Green Cemetry, London, *c.* 1880.

sure her work would be given public recognition. And Queen Victoria's half-nephew, Prince Victor of Hohenlohe-Langenburg, who had served in the war and was an amateur sculptor, made a bust of the woman he knew as 'Mami.' It was probably through him that she eventually became known to Victoria, who in 1857 wrote to Seacole officially recognizing her work. Seacole lived on until 1881, and left an estate worth £2000 – all subscriptions from those whom she had cared for. But her memories were still haunted by the casualties: the frostbitten and the hopelessly mutilated; young men she thought should have been playing cricket, but who died in the mud, their eyes 'half-opened with a quiet smile' or 'arrested in the heat of passion and frozen on their pallid faces, a glare of hatred and defiance that made your warm blood turn cold.'

The Victorians – especially leathery old nurses like Mary Seacole – ought to have been hardened to death. It was all around them: in the typhus-riddled barracks of soldiers; in the cholera-infested slums of the poor; in the sputum-stained handkerchiefs of the tubercular middle classes. The high-minded salons would be reduced to silence by sudden, terrifying fits of uncontrollable coughing while well-dressed guests stood suspended between compassion and terrified self-preservation as the mucus droplets misted the aspidistras.

The omnipresence of death seemed disproportionately chastening to a generation breezy with not entirely undeserved confidence that they had done more than any of their predecessors to master their physical environment. A civilization that had made steam-driven ships float on the oceans, that had thrown great iron spans across broad rivers, and that had shrunk the world by electric telegraph must soon, surely, conquer disease. It was indeed at this moment that advances in lensed microscopy were revealing, for the first time, the existence and culture of pathogens; although not (other than by the use of the scrubbing brush) how their multiplication might be checked.

In this tantalizingly slight gap between knowledge and mastery, mortality entered to mock the Victorian sense of control over life. Perhaps the shock of translation from apparently omnipotent physical presence to the dumb inertia of death – the *grievance* of mortality – explains the extreme peculiarity of their rites of mourning; their determination to make the dead commandingly visible amidst the living. The immense scale and grandeur of Victorian tombs, with their passionate, hyperbolic masonry – so much more flamboyant than anything allowed for the living – are all attempts to postpone oblivion and absence. With every ton of alabaster and porphyry, every weeping cherub and crepe-draped portrait, the lost one seems evermore available, waiting in some recoverable world just around the corner.

No one wanted this more desperately than Queen Victoria, vexed with God for reneging on what she felt sure had been his promise never to have Albert abandon her to the woeful burden of her constitutional toil. 'To see our pure happy, quiet, domestic life which *alone* enabled me to bear my *much* disliked position CUT OFF at forty-two – when I had hoped with such instinctive certainty that God never *would* part us, and would let us grow old together – is too *awful*, too cruel!' Part of her anguish was precisely because the manner of Prince Albert's decline and death seemed to testify to the indispensability of partnership as the only way to make the duties of both family and sovereignty supportable. By doing more than his share – for their family, for the country and for (she would not hesitate to say) humanity – he had worked and worried himself to death. Nor did it help that he had been under-appreciated in Britain. Instead of being granted the 'King Consort' title she had wanted, he had had to make do, in 1857, with 'Prince Consort' (as Wellington and the Tories, fearing foreign, even papal interference had blocked 'King Albert'). Nor, for all the town halls and model factories he had visited, the innumerable hospital foundation stones he had laid, was Albert the Good and Great ever regarded as other than a foreigner; the very seriousness with which he took his duties being further proof of that for the drawling aristocracy, who still, to Victoria's chagrin, seemed to set the tone for Society.

Not all of this was the widow's fantasy. Albert's obsession with the 'Eastern Question' and the Crimean War did seem to age him. Just because he had been suspected in the Russophobic years before the war of being soft on the Tsar, he over-compensated by throwing himself into a madness of statistical investigations, plans, inquiries. His comments on the state of the army (not good); on the need for a proper training camp; on the horrors of military medicine; on the pitfalls of logistics; on the condition of the Ottoman government; on naval issues at the Bosphorus, and so on and so on, fill 50 folio volumes. By the time Victoria arrived at her desk each morning there was a neat tower of pre-sorted, pre-screened papers for her to peruse, approve, sign. After the war was over Albert turned his attention to the complications of the Peace of Paris and relations between the two allies; the implications for Britain's economy of the likely civil war in the United States; not to mention plans for the improvement of native cattle; schemes to use urban sewage for agrarian manure; and his work for the British Association for the Advancement of Science. Always an early riser, Albert now took to getting up in deep darkness to work in the green glow of his desk lamp. Even in more easy times he 'enjoyed himself on schedule,' according to one court commentator, noting that it was at lunch and only at lunch at Balmoral or Osborne that heavy puns were allowed. By the late 1850s, although Albert stalked the deer at Balmoral with unrelenting devotion, even the plodding jokes seemed fewer and further between. More and more time was spent by himself or lost in his own anxieties. They were turning into the royal Jack Spratt and his wife. Albert, ever more sallow and gaunt and on a hair-trigger of anger; Victoria, the perpetual mother, her wrists now disappearing into bracelets of flesh, sitting solidly by his side. He worried for Britain and she worried for him.

Both of them worried for Bertie, the Prince of Wales. Vicky, their eldest, so sweet and so sensible, had gone to the Prussian court as the Crown Princess, at just 17, amidst much unhelpful wailing on the part of her mother that she was sending her 'lamb' to be 'sacrificed' on some Teutonic marriage bed. Albert, too, missed her badly. Her departure threw her eldest brother's chronic inability to conform to his parents' expectations into even sharper relief. 'Bertie's propensity is indescribable laziness,' his father fumed. 'I never in my life met such a thorough and cunning lazy-bones.' Away from the suffocation of the court Bertie was, in fact, a cheerful, open-faced young man who was not quite as allergic to his duties as his father thought. He did not disgrace himself academically at Christ Church, Oxford, and a tour of Canada was an out-and-out personal triumph. A spell at the Irish military camp at the Curragh, however, was less of a success. For there, as everywhere else, there was no getting away from the fact that Bertie liked his pleasures, especially when they came voluptuously corseted. It was the notoriety of his philandering that seemed, to his father and mother, calculated to wound their own publicly promoted sense of the decencies of domestic morality. His irresponsibility threatened to undo all their hard-won achievement in making the British monarchy respectable again.

Plans to marry Bertie to Princess Alexandra of Denmark were accelerated. Alix's ravishing beauty of face and figure, as well as her genuine sweetness of char-acter, would surely be enough to satisfy the Prince's yen for lechery within the marriage bed. But even as the negotiations with the Danish court were under way, late in 1861, Albert and Victoria learned that Bertie was having an affair with a notorious 'actress.' Horrified by this latest act of almost treasonable sabotage, they wrote brutally candid letters to the prince warning him of the wanton self-destruc-tion that this latest dalliance could bring – disease, pregnancy, blackmail, the repub-licanism of the boudoir and the bordello! At the same time, Albert was in the throes of dealing with a diplomatic crisis when Captain Charles Wilkes of the USS *San Jacinto* stopped the British mail steamer *Trent* and removed Confederate agents, in violation of the laws of neutrality during the American Civil War. Palmerston's Whig government, sympathetic to the South, was prepared to take the issue to the very edge of belligerence against Lincoln's government in Washington. Albert was

doing everything he could, constitutionally, to soften that response and avoid another futile war.

In late November the Prince, already 'feeling out of sorts' from a 'chill' caught during a recent visit to Sandhurst, went to see Bertie near Cambridge and read him the riot act. The weather was that of a classic East Anglian Michaelmas, with driving rain and slicing winds. On his return to Windsor, Albert's chill worsened and refused to abate. He had once mused morbidly, when planting a sapling at Osborne, that he would not survive to see it mature. Now, to the acute distress of Victoria, he seemed to be measuring himself for his shroud: 'I am sure if I had a fatal illness, I should give up at once, I should not struggle for life. I have no tenacity of life.' His physician, Dr James Clark, was the same man whose diagnosis and treatment of the children had driven Albert to raging despair many years before. Now Clark disposed of his critic by failing to realize that what the Prince Consort was actually suffering from was typhoid fever. By the time Palmerston-Pilgerstein had managed to summon a different doctor, it was too late.

Albert wandered in and out of clarity and from room to room in Windsor Castle, finally settling down in the Blue Room and not moving. Princess Alice played some hymns from an adjoining chamber. The queen came to read him Sir Walter Scott's *Peveril of the Peak* (1823). The copy survives in the Royal Library, the flyleaf inscribed in Victoria's hand, 'this book read up to the mark on page 81 during his last illness and within three days of its terrible termination.' The relevant paragraph on page 81 reads, incredibly, 'He heard the sound of voices but they ceased to convey any impression to his understanding and within a few minutes he was faster asleep than he had ever been in the whole … of his life.'

Was this truly coincidence? Or had the point she had reached in her reading of Scott's novel been chosen by Victoria as a literary valediction – especially since it describes, in fact, not a death at all but a deep healing slumber? For a moment on the afternoon of 14 December, Albert stirred, seemingly better, began to arrange his hair as if he were about to dress for dinner, and murmured, '*Es ist nichts, kleines Frauchen* (It's nothing, little wife).' Victoria left the bedside for a moment or two. When she came back he was gone, and out from that plump little face there came a howl of unutterable misery.

The sovereign of the greatest empire on earth had been vanquished by the one power against whom there was no defence. She spent so many hours collapsed in great, ragged, half-choking spells of sobbing that her secretaries and ministers thought she would go mad. 'You are right dear child,' the queen wrote to her almost equally distracted eldest daughter, 'I do not wish to feel better … the relief of tears

Opposite: Prince Albert and Queen Victoria in Anglo-Saxon dress by William Theed III, the Royal Mausoleum at Frogmore House, Windsor, 1871.

Queen Victoria and Princess Alice mourning Prince Albert, photograph by Prince Alfred, 1862.

is great and though since last Wednesday I have had no very violent outburst – they come again and again every day and are soothing to the bruised heart and soul.' When she came to visit in 1862, Vicky saw her mother crying herself to sleep with Albert's coat thrown over her, hugging his red dressing gown. 'What a dreadful going to bed,' Victoria had written in her diary. 'What a contrast to that tender lover's love! All alone!'

If Victoria did ever seriously contemplate suicide, duty and memory held it at bay. 'If I live on,' she confided to the diary, 'it is henceforth for our poor fatherless children – for my unhappy country which has lost all in losing him and in doing only what I know and feel he would wish for he is now near me – his spirit will guide and inspire me.' As it turned out, this was an understatement. Denying death the cruel victory of separation, sustaining the illusion of the prince's proximity, became a compulsion. Victoria spent £200,000, the same cost as the whole of Osborne, on the elaborate Italianate mausoleum at Frogmore for their tombs (which also accommodated her mother, the Duchess of Kent, who had died earlier that year) by Carlo Marochetti and the extraordinary statue by William Theed III of the two of them in Anglo-Saxon dress – the costume that defined the union of the Saxe-Coburg dynasty with what lingering historical mythology believed to be the ancient English constitution. But cold marble was not allowed to declare finis. Everything in Victoria's world – other than the widow's black and white cap that she would wear for the rest of her life – was designed to maintain the fantasy of Albert's continued presence, turning court life into one long séance. The Blue Room in which he died was preserved not as a German death-chamber, a *Sterbezimmer*, but exactly and for ever as it was when he was still alive. Should the upholstery wear out, it had to be replaced with its precise replica. Every day, hot water, blade and shaving soap were laid out along with fresh clothes. His other clothes remained untouched except those on which, in her distraction, Victoria insisted on sleeping. Even when she became somewhat more composed, she continued to take his nightshirt to bed along with a plaster cast of his hand. On Albert's side of the bed was a large photograph of the prince and a sprig of evergreen, symbolizing in the Germanic Christian tradition not just immortality but resurrection.

Widowhood became the queen's full-time job. What was left of Victoria's life (and, as it turned out, there was a lot) would be committed to the supreme vocation of perpetuating Albert's memory amongst her under-appreciative subjects. If there must be merriment, it had better not be in her presence, not even during the weddings of Bertie to Alix and of Alice to Prince Louis IV, Grand Duke of Hesse-Darmstadt – both of which seemed to the guests more like funerals, and were

obviously torture for Victoria. At Alice's nuptials she confessed to her journal that 'I say "God bless her" though a dagger is plunged in my bleeding desolate heart when I hear from her that she is "proud and happy" to be Louis's wife.' The only tolerable literature consisted of requiem poems like the Poet Laureate Tennyson's *In Memoriam* (1850). A new edition was dedicated of course to the late Prince. Victoria herself resolved to create a memorial bookshelf, commissioning an anthology of Albert's speeches; a biography of his early life; and another five-volume biography of the complete career and works. Memorial stones went up everywhere. Granite cairns were put up along the Highland trails where Albert had stalked deer, the most imposing bearing the inscription 'Albert the Great and Good, raised by his broken-hearted widow.' Statues were erected in 25 cities of Britain and the empire. Victoria left her seclusion in November 1866 to travel to Wolverhampton to unveil yet another, alighting from the train with 'sinking heart and trembling knees' to the noise of military bands and cheering, flag-waving crowds. The queen was so moved by the occasion that she called for a sword to knight the Lord Mayor, who was momentarily terrified that he was about to be beheaded. An epidemic of civic monuments broke out, to the point where Charles Dickens wrote to a friend in 1864 that 'If you should meet with an inaccessible cave anywhere to which a hermit could retire from the memory of Prince Albert and testimonials to same, pray let me know of it. We have nothing solitary or deep enough in this part of England.'

Other signs of restiveness began to register. A fund was launched to build a memorial hall at Kensington, as close as possible to the site of Albert's triumph, the Great Exhibition, with yet another monumental statue facing it. But only £60,000 was subscribed of the £120,000 needed, leaving the memorial committee no option but to commission the statue alone in Kensington Gardens. Sir George Gilbert Scott's Gothic Revival design was to make the massively enthroned figure of the prince, sculpted by Marochetti, the centrepiece of a shrine, with Albert as the gilded relic in a pinnacled ciborium or reliquary, set above a monumental base unhappily compared by its critics to a giant cruet or sugar sifter. The canopied shrine was flanked by the four colossal greater Christian Virtues. Another four statues personified the moral virtues, and eight bronzes the Arts and Sciences whose qualities he had personified and patronized. At the base were emblems of the Four Continents to which the blessings of the Albertian empire had flowed, and above them was a 200-foot frieze featuring 170 of the geniuses of European civilization, so that Albert would keep company with fellow-immortals such as Aristotle, Dante, Shakespeare, Hogarth and Mozart. As the biographer Lytton Strachey perceptively remarked in *Queen Victoria* (1921), this massive embalming of the sainted prince did some

Opposite: The Albert Memorial, Kensington, 1868–71, commemorates the Prince Consort, who is flanked by the Virtues and Liberal Arts, and surrounded by 170 geniuses of civilization.

disservice to the complicated, open-minded and unquestionably gifted man who had acted, in effect, as the first presidential figure of modern British society.

But for Victoria he had become not the entrepreneur of modern knowledge so much as the Perfect Christian Chevalier. Devotion to His Way of Doing Things bade her rise every morning, punctually at 7.30, then tunnel her way through state papers and dispatches (as He had done). When a prime minister like Lord Derby or Lord John Russell presumed to suggest an end to the official period of mourning, or even that the queen might perhaps consider resuming her constitutional duty to open parliament, Victoria responded with a mixture of self-pity and outrage that anyone could be so heartless as to inflict further stab-wounds on 'a poor weak woman shattered by grief and anxiety.' After a decent interval, Victoria's total disappearance from the public eye began to provoke irreverent comment in the press and to nourish the most sustained British flirtation with republicanism since the Civil War of the 17th century. It was especially serious during the passage of the Reform Bills of 1866 and 1867, when radicalism had its head of wind, and the Tory leader Benjamin Disraeli, in particular, needed the solidity of the monarchy to assuage fears that he was going down a road whose outcome no one could predict. In 1866, despite protesting to the prime minister Lord Russell her abhorrence of being subjected to a spectacle whereby people could witness 'a poor broken-hearted widow, nervous and shrinking, dragged from deep mourning,' Victoria did finally consent to open parliament, but so grudgingly that the occasion probably alienated more of her subjects than it won over. As a condition of her appearance the queen had stipulated no state coach, no procession, no robes and especially no speech from the throne. Instead, the Lord Chancellor read the address while Victoria sat in deep gloom in her widow's cap and mourning black. She was not eager to repeat even this gesture. The next June, when Victoria again failed to open parliament, a famous cartoon appeared in the satirical journal *The Tomahawk*, showing a throne draped by an enormous shroud bearing the legend: 'Where is Britannia?' Earlier, someone had put a satirical poster against the railings of Buckingham Palace announcing: 'These commanding premises ... to be let or sold in consequence of the late occupant's declining business.'

Any attempts to persuade Victoria to emerge from this politically damaging seclusion bounced off the immovable guardianship of the one man whom the queen seemed to be able to lean on in her unrelenting grief: the Balmoral ghillie John Brown. The fact that he had been Albert's personal favourite naturally recommended him to Victoria, for whom he became an indispensable and ubiquitous presence, and to whom she allowed liberties unthinkable in her secretaries, children or ministers. To their horror and embarrassment Brown would address her as 'wummun,' comment

WHERE IS BRITANNIA ?

Where is Britannia?, cartoon from the satirical journal *The Tomahawk*, 1867, parodying Victoria's long seclusion and deep mourning after Prince Albert's death in 1861.

on her dress, tell her what was the best plan for the day and always protect her against the importunate demands of the rest of the world. In return she created the special position of 'Her Majesty's Servant.' Brown organized her daily pony-trap rides and the Scottish dances at Balmoral, and was not always sober when he did so.

It would take the near fatal illness of the Prince of Wales in 1871, combined with another narrow escape from assassination (Brown personally caught the culprit), to shock Victoria out of this deep, self-willed isolation. When Disraeli proposed a day of national thanksgiving for Bertie's recovery, complete with a service in St Paul's Cathedral (not least because the republican movement was at its height), Victoria relented. She was rewarded with huge crowds. In the same year, the completed Albert Memorial was finally unveiled in Kensington Gardens. (A joint-stock company would later build the Royal Albert Hall.) Three years later, in 1874, Disraeli finally managed to give Victoria a renewed sense of her own independent authority with the passing of the Royal Titles Bill that made her Queen–Empress of India.

But as far as the queen herself was concerned, she never swerved from the vow she had taken after Albert's death that '*his* wishes, *his* plans, *his* views about *every*thing are to be my law.' This, indeed, was what she supposed was the right and proper duty of widows, just as during the life of a marriage the whole duty of wives was to dissolve their own wills into that of the domestic household. Widows like Margaret Oliphant, who of necessity turned to popular novel-writing (she published a hundred of them before she died), were objects of pity rather than admiration. For how could a commercial career ever be thought compatible with the ordained role of women to preserve the sanctity of the home from the beastly masculine jungle of the capitalist marketplace? This, at any rate, was the message delivered by the holy trinity of works dedicated to the destiny of womanhood, and all published at the time of Victoria's bereavement: Coventry Patmore's long verse effusion 'The Angel in the House' (1854); Ruskin's 'Of Queen's Gardens,' one of the two lectures delivered in Manchester in 1865, and subsequently published as *Sesame and Lilies*; and not least Mrs Isabella Beeton's *Book of Household Management* (1861). All three were extraordinary best-sellers. *Sesame and Lilies* sold 160,000 in its first edition, not least because it became a standard fixture on prizegiving days at girls' schools, but it was overshadowed by Mrs Beeton's book, which sold two million copies before 1870. None of these books, however, portrayed domestic women in a state of perpetual submission. Ruskin especially was at pains to reject the 'foolish error' that woman was only 'the shadow and attendant image of her lord.' In fact the popularity of these works owed a lot to the delivery of messages that credited women with a great deal of power – and power of a more concrete kind than that attributable to romantic seduction.

Coventry Patmore and Mrs Beeton were the complementary bookends of the cult of hearth and home, the poet lyricizing the transcendent mystery of wifeliness, the *Book of Household Management* providing over 1000 pages of instruction on how the 'shrine' was actually to be kept spotless. If one was a kind of liturgy for the high priestesses of the home, the other was an exhaustive manual for domestic command and control. The very first paragraph of Isabella Beeton's truly astonishing book says it all: 'As with the commander of an army or the leader of any enterprise, so is it with the mistress of a house.' Ruskin's stance was more complicated. As his title implied, his essay–lecture added to the metaphors of priestess and general that of the 'queen.' Her sovereignty was not just a matter of making sure the pillows were

Queen Victoria with the Scottish ghillie, John Brown, holding the reins of her pony in the grounds of Balmoral Castle, Scotland, 1863.

plumped and the roast cooked on time. To her fell the exalted responsibility of protecting society against the corrosions of acquisitive capitalism. The illiberalism of the home was its defence against the vulgar battering ram of the marketplace; the guarantee that inside the front door, at least, values other than those of competitive individualism would prevail – those of a 'Place of Peace, the shelter not only from all injury, but from all terror, doubt and division.'

Ruskin's personal qualifications for making these prescriptions, had they been known, would not have done much for his credibility. His marriage, to Effie Gray, had been an unconsummated fiasco. He had written *Sesame and Lilies* while hypnotically spellbound by his own spotless lily, the adolescent Rose La Touche, to whom he acted as tutor and mentor before deluding himself that she ought to be his wife. Rose fled in horror from the proposal, triggering first in her, and then in the spurned Ruskin, an almost equally violent mental collapse. The crisis had been brought about by Ruskin's apparently reckless change of role from trusted tutor, moral and intellectual guardian to would-be lover and husband. Ruskin failed to see this disaster in the making precisely because, as 'Of Queen's Gardens' made clear, he imagined that through intense reading women would actually be liberated from unattractively vapid servility to their husbands (and from the worthless chatter of fashion) and would instead be converted into their equals. Art, philosophy and morals would be ventilated over the breakfast marmalade.

But unlike some of the more conventional Victorian legislators of domestic virtue, Ruskin did not, in fact, insist that women belonged *only* at home. 'A man has a personal work or duty, which is the expansion of the other, relating to his home and a public work or duty relating to the state. So a woman has a personal work or duty relating to her own home and a public work or duty which is also the expansion of that.' What had he in mind by that? Anything, in fact, that would help *others* out in the world, especially out in the world of the poor, make their own homes: 'what the woman is to be within her gates as the centre of order, the balm of distress and the mirror of beauty; that she is also to be without her gates where order is more difficult, distress more imminent, loveliness more rare.' The commercial success of *Sesame and Lilies* enabled Ruskin to help young women philanthropists and reformers like Octavia Hill to be 'angels *outside* the house' in just this way. Hill was the granddaughter of the social reformer Rowland Hill, and Ruskin had met her when she was just 15. Although she was single and obviously committed to a career other than that of wife and mother (at least until she was 40), Ruskin saw Octavia as a home-maker for others, if not for herself. It was his money that enabled her Charity Organisation Society to buy up its first London tenements and convert them into 'improved' lodgings for working-class families. But Octavia's aim was to remodel the tenants as well as their buildings. When her volunteers came to collect the rent they arrived bearing a stack of forms on which the residents were required to make a report of their weekly conduct. 'Persons of drunken, immoral or idle habits cannot expect to be assisted' [with a charity allowance] unless they can satisfy the committee that they are really trying to reform.' Incorrigible delinquents and recidivists would be removed as morally infectious. For Ruskin, this was a perfect instance of the benevolent exercise of 'queenly' power to make domestic peace where before there had been only dirt and clamour. A den of beasts would be turned into the abode of beauty and faith.

Suppose, however, that a happily married middle-class Victorian woman would actually dare to import into her home some business that more properly belonged to the world? Could that enterprise, especially if it came with the trappings of art, be reconciled with domesticity, or would it inevitably pollute the sanctity of what Ruskin had called 'the vestal temple'? All that Victoria had to do to test the issue would have been to drive her pony trap a few miles down the Freshwater road on the Isle of Wight, past the house of her Poet Laureate, Alfred, Lord Tennyson, to 'Dimbola,' the enlarged pair of cottages that, from 1863, were the studio as well as the residence of the greatest of all the Victorian photo-portraitists, Julia Margaret Cameron.

The case was complicated by the fact that photography in the 1860s was very much divided between genteel amateurs practising their art, and professionals turning out travel views, pictures of literary and military celebrities, police and medical documentation, and, for a more arcane but lucrative market, pornography. The considerable expenses of equipment and processing (not least the chemically reduced silver nitrate needed to sensitize glass plates and gold bullion for toning) confined the hobby to the upper middle class and Victorian gentry, who often worked out of studios and darkrooms in their own houses. The greatest of Cameron's immediate predecessors, Clementina, Lady Hawarden (whose startlingly unconventional and sensually loaded talent was cut brutally short at the age of 42), was herself from an Irish aristocratic family. She used her house at Dundram as one of her first studios, but when she and her husband moved to South Kensington, a stone's throw from the site of the Great Exhibition, she was able to annex part of the apartment for her photography – and use her own daughters, each of them on the verge (or over it) of sexual maturity – as models. In other words, for all her dazzling originality Lady Hawarden presented no problem and no challenge to the authority of the lords of the new art, the award of the Photographic Society. She exhibited – just three times, in 1865–6 at the London print sellers P. & D. Colnaghi's, in 1866–7 at the French

Gallery, London, and in 1867–8 at the German Gallery, London – and was awarded a silver medal for her work and showered with richly merited praise.

Julia Margaret Cameron was an altogether different kettle of fish. Her background was respectably, even reassuringly, colonial. As Julia Pattle she was one of seven children born to a French mother and British-Indian father. The Pattle girls, however, became famous in India as eccentric beauties, who favoured brilliant Indian silks and shawls rather than the decently demure Victorian dress expected of the memsahibs. 'To see one of this sisterhood float into a room with sweeping robes and falling folds,' wrote one of their admirers, 'was almost an event in itelf and not to be forgotten. They did not in the least trouble themselves about public opinion.' In 1838, at the age of 23, Julia made a serious marriage – to Charles Hay Cameron, a classical scholar (Eton and Oxford) who had aspired to be professor of moral philosophy at London University but had been turned down for not being in holy orders. Cameron had gone on to an eminent career as a member of the Governor-General's Council and law commissioner for Ceylon (Sri Lanka), where he had extensive plantations.

In 1848 Charles Cameron suddenly gave all this up and retired with Julia to Britain, where he evidently meant to devote himself again to the Higher Things and write a treatise on the Sublime and the Beautiful. Through the Prinsep family – a dynasty of orientalist scholars in India and painters and poets in London – the Camerons mixed in salon society that included Tennyson and the great astronomer Sir John Herschel. While visiting Tennyson at Freshwater, Julia saw the pair of cottages that, remodelled, became 'Dimbola.' There they established themselves along with their children, and Charles Cameron became, if not exactly a recluse amidst his books, then certainly the retiring philosopher whom Tennyson once glimpsed asleep in his bedroom, 'his beard dipped in moonlight.'

At some point, probably early in 1863 when she was 48 years old, Julia was given a camera – the hefty wooden-box apparatus of the time. She swiftly converted her coalhouse at 'Dimbola' into a darkroom and the henhouse into what she called 'my glass house' – the studio. Most accounts of her career make this departure seem like the enthusiasm of an amateur who needed a hobby to fill in time between the polite rituals of middle-class life on the Isle of Wight and the rounds of Pre-Raphaelite visitors. In fact, it is evident from family papers that from the outset Julia was up to something much more serious, both artistically and commercially. With coffee harvest after coffee harvest failing in Ceylon the Camerons were becoming seriously hard-up. There was no sign of Charles, buried ever more deeply in his library, being willing or able to recover their fortunes. In September 1866 her

Top: Clementina, Lady Hawarden, self-portrait, *c.* 1850.
Above: Julia Margaret Cameron, self-portrait, *c.* 1862.

son-in-law, Charles Norman, asking one of Julia's patrons for a loan of £1000, wrote that 'my father-in-law for the last two months has been utterly penniless so that his debts are increased by butchers' bills.' So whether or not Julia had always meant to be a professional, now she felt bound to succeed for the sake of the family. Clementina Hawarden could afford to sell her work at a fête to benefit the 'Female School of Art'; Julia had to sell hers to benefit herself. But her professionalism was not going to compromise her aesthetic standards. One of her models believed that Mrs Cameron 'had a notion that she was going to revolutionise photography and make money.' Making money cost money. Charles, who evidently worried about his mother-in-law as well as his father-in-law, reported to a creditor that he had 'told my mother for positively the last time that any assistance of this kind can be given her and that her future happiness or discomfort and misery rests entirely with herself.'

But then this was exactly the opportunity Julia Margaret Cameron was looking for – to make her own way. And she had the toughness to persevere. Although some of her Tennysonian images of luminous madonnas and gauzy damozels reinforced, rather than undermined, the more fantastic stereotypes of women as embodiments of the pure and the passionate, there was not much of the angel about Julia herself. Unable to afford assistants, she did all the mucky work of the wet collodion process herself: staining her fingers and dresses with silver-nitrate sensitizer, making sure the glass plates were exposed while still wet, washing and fixing images, and developing the prints. Since she depended on natural light, in the not invariably sunny Freshwater, to obtain the intensely expressive effects of light and shade that characterized both her portraits and her 'poetic' studies, she needed extraordinarily long exposures, sometimes of 10 minutes or more. Not only her own children, and domestic servants who obediently posed, but also the good and great – the artists George Frederic Watts and William Holman Hunt; Carlyle, the astronomer Sir Frederick Herschel and Tennyson – all were bullied into keeping stock-still for unendurable periods of time. Herschel – one of the most distinguished men in Britain – was told to wash his hair so that Julia could fluff it up with her blackened fingers to get just the right look of back-lit electrified genius. As is evident from the famous portraits – some of the most mesmerizing face-images in the history of art – Carlyle did fidget. But the photographer turned this to advantage. His head, she had thought, was a 'rough block of Michelangelo sculpture.' But Carlyle's personality was also notoriously edgy and mercurial. So she gives us a head that is both monumental and energized – the authentic hot tremble of the Carlylean volcano, the burning 'light in the dark lantern.'

Predictably, the extreme manipulation of focus and exposure did not meet with the approval of the eminences of the Photographic Society, who sneered at Julia's 'series of out of focus portraits of celebrities' as tawdry vulgarities in which technical incompetence masqueraded as poetic feeling. ('We must give this lady credit for daring originality,' a typically snide review in the *Photographic Journal* commented, 'but at the expense of all other photographic qualities.') The more popular she became, the nastier they got: 'The Committee much regrets that they cannot concur in the lavish praise which has been bestowed on her productions by the non-photographic press, feeling convinced that she herself will adopt an entirely differ-ent mode of reproduction of her poetic ideas when she has made herself acquainted with the capabilities of the art.' The subtext of this was, of course, that women, with the rare exceptions of noble amateurs such as Clementina Hawarden, had no busi-ness prematurely parading their work without mastering the one quality by which photographic excellence was properly judged: crispness of definition. Crispness, of course, like the heavy lifting and chemically saturated processes of photography, was a matter of self-effacing mechanics; a stiff-upper-lip kind of art, definitely not the flouncy, dreamy, mushy thing that they believed Julia Margaret Cameron executed.

But crispness repelled Julia. She had no interest in making dumbly literal facsimiles of nature. Her aim was to make a poet out of a lensed machine. The great 'heads' that so disconcerted the Photographic Society were meant to take Romanticism's exploration of the external signs of interior emotions (anger, sorrow, elation, ecstatic vision) a step further – to create expressive images of the thinker/artist-as-hero. Although she also bathed children, servants and obedient friends in the more diffused light she needed for her poetic costume dramas, Cameron was capable, on occasions, of deliberately, even cruelly, playing with the self-consciousness of sitters in their allotted roles. Her sublimely beautiful portrait of the 16-year-old actress Ellen Terry (who had gone on the boards at nine) as 'Sadness' is as poignant as it is precisely because her marriage to the much older Watts was evi-dently already falling apart on their honeymoon in Freshwater. At the opposite end of the emotional spectrum are the photographs of Cyllene Wilson, the daughter of a repent-or-be-damned evangelical preacher who had been adopted by the Camerons. To get just the right look of despair on Cyllene's powerful face, Julia was not above locking her in a cupboard for a few hours until the expression came naturally. Perhaps this was, in the end, too much for Cyllene, who ended up running off to sea, marrying an engineer on an Atlantic steamship line and dying in her 30s of yellow fever in Argentina.

Julia was successful but not, it seems, quite successful enough. Held at arm's length by the photographic establishment, she had secured crucial patronage from

Above: Thomas Carlyle, photo-portrait by Julia Margaret Cameron, *c.* 1866.
Opposite: Sir John Herschel, photo-portrait by Julia Margaret Cameron, *c.* 1867.

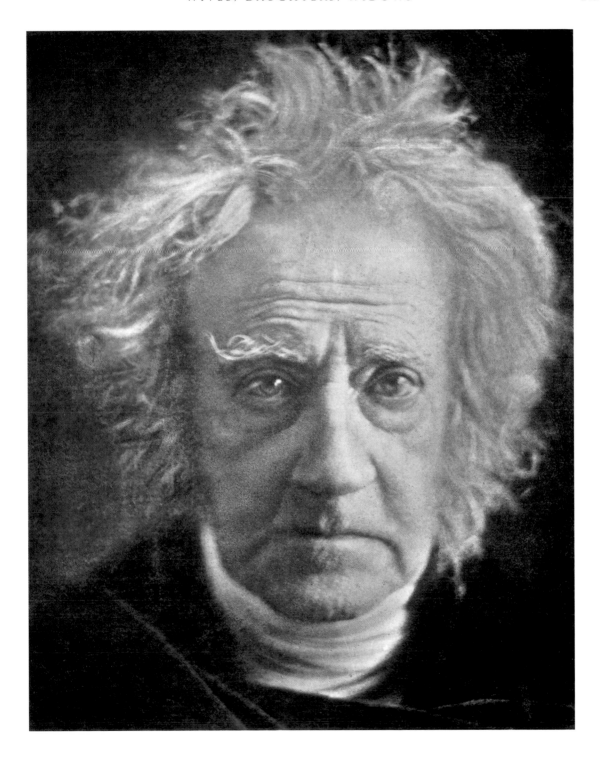

Top: *Sadness* (Ellen Terry), photograph by Julia Margaret Cameron, 1864.
Above: *The Cenci,* photograph by Julia Margaret Cameron, *c.* 1867.

one of her husband's old Etonian friends, the banker Samuel Jones Loyd, Baron Overstone, to whom she assigned some of her most extraordinary albums in return for his investment. She showed and sold at Paul Colnaghi's gallery and entered into a contractual arrangement with the Autotype Company to publish carbon reproductions. To ensure herself against piracy, Julia registered 505 of her photographs under the recent Copyright Act (1869), giving the impression that she meant to profit as much as she could from her originality and popularity. Thanks to the efforts of dealer and publisher, her work became famous. But it never held ruin at bay. In 1875 she and her husband, with their fortunes evaporating, returned to Ceylon, where she died in 1879. Although there was a flourishing Indian-Oriental photo-industry under way, views of temples and tea parties were not Julia Margaret Cameron's line. The images petered out and then stopped altogether. But the power of her accomplishment was already enough to have wiped the sneer from the face of those who condescended to 'lady artists.'

It is almost certain that, through Cameron's photographs to illustrate Tennyson's 'Idylls of the King' (1874–5), a poem associated in the queen's mind with the memory of Albert, Victoria knew of her work and would not have disapproved of a woman photographer. A woman doctor, on the other hand, was a great deal more shocking. The very idea of girls familiarizing themselves with the gross details of human anatomy, much less dissecting corpses in the company of men, was, needless to say, perceived by the queen as a revolting indecency. And those who took the first courageous steps in this direction could only do so while pretending to study for the acceptable work of nursing – paradoxically regarded as less shocking despite nurses' equal familiarity with living anatomy. In the year of Prince Albert's death, 1861, Elizabeth Garrett was – to the consternation of the examiners at the Middlesex Hospital, who had not realized that 'E. Garrett' was a woman – placed first in the teaching hospital's qualifying examinations. The daughter of a rich Suffolk business-man, Garrett had left school at 15. But instead of grooming herself (perhaps through a Ruskinian education in reading and drawing) for the altar and parlour, she had quite other ideas. A speech by Elizabeth Blackwell changed Garrett's life. Blackwell, born in Bristol, had been transplanted to the United States where in 1849, at the age of 28, she had become that country's first accredited woman doctor. After losing the sight of an eye while working at the obstetric hospital of La Maternité in Paris (where women were welcomed, according to her, as 'half-educated supplements' to the male physicians), Blackwell had returned to America, set up a one-room dispensary in 1853 in the New York tenements, and eventually, in 1857, opened the New York Infirmary and College for Women. She was, in short, a living inspiration.

Elizabeth Garrett was determined to do for Britain what Blackwell had done for the United States. Initially horrified by her bone-headed temerity and obstinacy, her rich father was eventually won round – enough, at any rate, to subsidize her ostensible education as a nurse, which included her attendance at medical college lectures. Despite being ostracized by the male students and prevented from full participation in dissections, Elizabeth was undeterred, buying body parts and dissecting them in her bedroom.

Begged to keep quiet about the result of her examination in 1861, Garrett (possibly egged on by a number of articles in the *Englishwoman's Journal* that advocated the creation of a corps of women doctors specializing in female and paediatric medicine), chose instead to publicize it, scandalizing the profession. Her application to matriculate at London University was denied – but only after a divided 10:10 vote in the Senate, with the Chancellor, Lord Granville, voting explicitly against the recommendation of his Liberal party colleague Gladstone, an early admirer of Garrett's. In 1865 she took and passed the examination of the Society of Apothecaries, who, horrified at their oversight, passed a statute retroactively excluding women from the profession. In 1870, after performing two successful surgeries and passing written and oral examinations in French, the University of Paris awarded her their medical degree. But this was by no means the end of the battle for women's medical aspirations. In the year that Garrett achieved her French licence a group of five women, led by Sophia Jex-Blake, were subjected to the physical intimidation of a near riot when they attempted to take the Edinburgh University medical examination. When a path was cut through the jeering crowd to the examination room, a flock of sheep was pushed in after the women. Whether it rankled or not, it was, inevitably, often a supportive marriage that gave these women power. When Elizabeth Garrett became Elizabeth Garrett Anderson, as the result of marrying a steamship owner, she was finally in a position to open her New Hospital for Women.

Her refusal of what had been the accepted confines of proper women's work was becoming less of a rarity by the 1870s, a decade when the Victorian litany of the Great Exhibition – Peace, Prosperity, Free Trade – was starting to sound off-key. The great pillars of commerce had been shaken by a series of bank upheavals and mergers in the late 1860s. In Europe, the Pax Britannica seemed helpless to stop the wars of national aggression by which new nation states and empires were being roughly forged. Irish violence and Balkan massacres were beginning to supply the sensation-hungry popular press with headlines. But something even more explosive had been set off in the libraries and debating circles of the Victorians and that something was Darwin's *Descent of Man* (1871).

In their mothers' and grandmothers' generation, the urgent longing to be, above all, useful – beyond the duties set out by Mrs Beeton – had been filled by Christian works of healing and charity. But although Darwin himself often protested that the implications of his theory were no threat to faith (starting with his own), there was at least an element of disingenuousness in the protest. The fact was that the great sheltering dome of faith – authority based on direct revelation – had been shattered by Darwin's vision of a morally indifferent, self-evolving universe. Once it was read, digested and believed, it was hard, if not impossible, for at least some young women born around the time of the Great Exhibition to surrender themselves to the male-governed kingdom of prayer. In place of the old gospels of Church and Home, they now needed the new gospels of education and work. And since competition, the struggle for survival, seemed to be the truth of the way in which the world worked, why should they themselves flinch from the fray? Against Ruskin's appeal that the 'queens' stand above and against the noisy, frantic shove and bustle of the world, the champions of women's higher education and more ambitious fields for women's work argued that, on the contrary, it was direct experience of the wider world that would make them better wives and mothers, and at the very least better women. The queen needed to get out of the garden and into the urban jungle.

Ruskin, of course, had been a sponsor, not a critic, of women's education. But he had made it very clear that the content of that education was never to extend beyond subjects deemed fit by males; and that its function in the end was to make young women more interesting wives and companions. Better a dinner table at which the Angel of the House could talk about Tennyson or Tintoretto rather than crinolines and curtain lengths. Whilst Emily Davies, a friend and contemporary of Elizabeth Garrett, certainly agreed that marriages would be the better for educated, rather than uneducated, wives, she wanted more out of that education than the training of amusing partners. 'All that we claim,' she wrote when arguing, unsuccessfully, for women to be awarded degrees at the University of London, 'is that the intelligence of women … shall have full and free development.' And for that to happen required not just schooling but higher education. Of those men who insisted that women were somehow biologically unsuited to mathematics or science, Davies inquired how they would know when so many men could be accused of precisely the same failing. What she hated most of all was the acceptance by so many women themselves of the degrading assumption of 'mental blankness.'

Since London University was evidently not going to countenance the award of full degrees to women students at Bedford and Queen's (at least not until 1878), Davies herself, the daughter of an evangelical minister, began in 1866 to raise funds for the creation of a women's college. In 1869, Hitchin College opened its doors to the first six undergraduates, and four years later reopened as Girton College, a few miles north of Cambridge. Fired by her battles to prove that women's intellect was indistinguishable from that of men, Davies insisted on a curriculum identical to that offered by the Cambridge faculties. A fellow-enthusiast, the moral philosopher and economics don Henry Sidgwick (who founded a residence for women students in 1871, which evolved into Newnham College in 1880), disagreed with Davies on what kind of education would best advance the learning and professional skills of women students. Let the ancient disciplines decay in their male seminaries, he thought, while women would be the vanguard of those embracing the new sciences – economics, history, modern philosophy and politics – and be all the better fitted to become full citizens of the world. Davies, however, was not convinced by arguments that only a 'soft' education was suitable for women. If making the point of their intellectual equality meant compulsory examinations in Greek, so be it.

At least as important – and revolutionary in its implications for the fate of women – was the fact that colleges like Girton now provided young women with an alternative home, a community of the like-minded. Among the most precious gifts bestowed on each Girtonian was a scuttle of coal every day, so that she might be as independent as she wished in her own study. Sometimes, however, the elation of the child became (as parents of college-age offspring have known ever since) the transparent unhappiness of a mother or father. As one young Girtonian, Helena Swanwick, later the author of *The Future of the Women's Movement* (1913), wrote:

> When the door of my study was opened and I saw my own fire, my own desk, my own easy chair and reading lamp – nay my own kettle – I was speechless with delight. Imagine my dismay when my mother turned to me with open arms and tears in her eyes saying, "You can come home again with me, Nell, if you like!" It was horrible ... I hardly knew how decently to disguise my real feelings. To have a study of my own and to be told that, if I chose to put 'Engaged' on the door, no-one would so much as knock was in itself so great a privilege as to hinder me from sleep.

Whether it meant the first break with a life of idle grooming for the marriage market, or the makings of a new professional career, college represented freedom, self-discovery, the beginnings of independence. Another Girtonian, Constance Maynard, who recalled that she and her sister had been 'shut up like eagles in a henhouse' at home, now could exult, 'At last, at LAST, we were afloat on a stream that had a real destination, even though we hardly knew what that destination was.' For some of them, that destination might be other schools or colleges so that they might produce further cohorts of ambitious, independently minded young women. Constance Maynard, for instance, went on to found Westfield College, London University. Others – like Elizabeth Garrett's sister the suffrage leader Millicent Garrett Fawcett – might re-create the Mill–Taylor equal intellectual partnership in their marriage. Millicent married the blind political economist and Radical politician Henry Fawcett, Postmaster-General in Gladstone's second government, and, after he died in 1884, instead of shrinking into the shell of the devoted widow embarked on an outspoken career of promoting public causes. But almost 30 per cent of the first generation of Oxbridge women graduates (from the colleges of Somerville, St Hugh's, Newnham and Girton) did not marry at all. And, faced with a barrage of evidence about the immense and increasing distance between rich and poor Britain, many of them decided to abandon not just domesticity, but the whole world of liberal, Victorian middle-class comfort, and take their hard-won independence into the factories and the slums. In 1887 the Women's University Settlement opened its first lodgings in Southwark, where young women from Oxbridge colleges went to live alongside some of the poorest people in London.

Many of the women who came of age in the 1880s looked around and saw that, if you were middle class, there was much to celebrate. By 1882 married women finally got control over their own property. Nine years later, legislation was passed making it unlawful for husbands to lock up their wives for refusing sexual relations and allowing beatings 'so long as the cane was no thicker than his thumb.' By the mid-1880s it was possible for women to vote in some local elections and for school boards, and in 1885 no fewer than 50 of them, including Helen Taylor, Harriet's daughter, were elected to the London School Board. And there were other subtler but no less subversive agencies at work – the latch key, the cheque book and the bicycle – all of which would render obsolete the Patmore fantasy of the hermetically isolated priestess of the domestic shrine.

If, on the other hand, you happened to be a 15-year-old East End girl and needed a pound or two to make the difference between food and famishing, fancy talk about repossessing the integrity of your body would not mean much. Middle-class women reformers had first become involved in the life of street girls in the 1850s. Led by Josephine Butler, they had campaigned more vocally against the double standard of the Contagious Diseases Act (1864), which required brutal physical inspection of prostitutes while doing nothing about diseased male clients. The Act was repealed in 1883, and in the same year the age of consent raised from 13 to 16, thanks to the efforts of the muckraking editor of the *Pall Mall Gazette*, W.T. Stead, who, to prove that his allegations about the trade in virgins were not a figment of his over-heated imagination, went to the East End, bought one for himself, got her story and then turned the girl over to the Salvation Army.

Stead was one of the most eloquent of a generation bent on doing construc-tive damage to the complacency of late Victorian Britain as it moved towards the Queen's Golden Jubilee year of 1887. Instead of the middle classes reading the queen's sequel to her massive best-selling *Leaves from a Journal of Our Life in the High-lands*, with its picture of the royal couple taking tea with adoring crofters, Stead wanted them to wake up to the destitution of outcast London, and read George Sims' *How The Poor Live* (1883). As far as Stead was concerned, the steady drumbeat of imperial self-congratulation, the histrionic wailing and weeping over the martyr-dom of poor General Charles Gordon at Khartoum, and the elaborate fanfares tuning up for the queen were just so many charades masking a society divided between the swells and the slums. His pessimism was contagious. One day, warned the young George Bernard Shaw, sheer force of demographics would force a reckoning: 'Your slaves breed like rabbits, their poverty breeds filth, ugliness, dishonesty, disease, obscenity, drunkenness and murder. In the midst of the riches which they pile up for you their misery rises up and stifles you. You withdraw in disgust to the other end of town and yet they swarm about you still.'

It was, in fact, the apparent correlation between 'breeding' and poverty that moved one of the most daring young women of her generation, Annie Besant, to try to do something about it. In 1877, Besant, the estranged wife of a Lincolnshire clergyman, was tried alongside the atheist republican MP Charles Bradlaugh on a charge of obscenity. Their crime was to have reprinted a treatise, the 'Knowlton Pamphlet,' originally published in 1830, euphemistically called *The Fruits of Philosophy* but actually full of practical advice on contraception. It was all very well, Besant and Bradlaugh believed, for the fashionable classes to have – and increasingly make use of – this knowledge, but until it had become part of working-class life there would be no possibility (especially in the hard times of the 1880s) of their ever being able to budget for survival, much less savings. All the high-minded lecturing that philanthropists such as Octavia Hill inflicted on her tenants in the Dwellings would be pointless hypocrisy unless poor families were given some control over their size. Bradlaugh and Besant went out of their way to make sure they would get prosecuted – and so attract the necessary publicity – by actually delivering copies of the book to the magistrates' clerks at the Guildhall.

Top: Elizabeth Garrett Anderson, photo-portrait by Stanislas Walery, *c.* 1870.
Above: The Girton Fire Brigade, 1887.

During their trial – in which the Solicitor-General himself handled the prosecution – the two shamelessly used the proceedings to proselytize for sex education
and birth control. They were eloquent enough for the judge to declare that he
thought the case absurd. The jury was less enlightened, finding that, although the
book was indeed obscene, the defendants had not meant to corrupt public morals.
The order to desist from publishing was, of course, just what the accused were waiting
for. They duly refused to abide by the judgement. Bradlaugh went to jail, but *The
Fruits of Philosophy*, with its graphic description of pessaries, condoms and sponges,
enjoyed brisk undercover sales for months.

Annie Besant suffered a harsher penalty for her temerity than prison. Her
husband, who already had custody of their son, now brought a suit to remove their
young daughter, Mabel, from her mother on the grounds that consorting with
atheists and purveyors of filth proved beyond a shadow of a doubt that Annie was
unfit to be a parent. The loss of her child threw Annie into a deep depression. What
pulled her out of it was socialism. 'Modern civilisation,' she wrote in 1883, 'is a
whited sepulchre ... with its outer coating of princes and lords, of bankers and
squires and within filled with men's bones, the bones of the poor who built it.'
Two years later she joined the Fabians, who worked for a peaceful and democratic
revolution.

The attraction of socialism to young, altruistically minded women of Annie's
generation was an inadvertent payback for years of being told that their sex was
supposed to be the softer, humane face of capitalism. Even John Stuart Mill had
written of Harriet Taylor's governing impulses as social and humane while his were
theoretical and mechanical. Now women could do something in keeping with this
unasked-for assignment as nurses to the wounded of liberal capitalism – they could
try to change it. This was what moved another young founding Fabian, Beatrice
Potter (later Webb), to leave Octavia Hill's organization of philanthropical snoopers
and go to live among the Lancashire mill girls of Bacup; she ended up editing the
17 volumes of Booth's *Life and Labour of the People in London* (1892-7).

Annie Besant found her workers' cause in the plight of the teenage match girls
who worked for Bryant and May's at their Fairfield Works in the East End. The match
girls had a history of conspicuous public action: they had participated in a mass
demonstration at Victoria Park in 1871 against Gladstone's government's proposal to
impose a tax on matches. The publicity was such that it moved even the queen to
write indignantly to Gladstone that it would punish the poor much more heavily
than the well-off and 'seriously affect the manufacture and sale of matches which is
said to be the sole means of support for a vast number of the poorest people and

LITTLE CHILDREN!' The mass meeting and the march down the Mile End Road were shamelessly exploited by Bryant and May themselves, who had no interest at all in seeing their product penally taxed. When the measure was dropped, the company paid for a victory celebration and the construction of a drinking fountain in Bow Road.

The factory-feudal mobilization of their young workforce, however, backfired against Bryant and May a decade and a half later, when *The Link*, the crusading investigative half-penny weekly founded by Stead and Annie Besant, published an article exposing the conditions under which the match girls worked. Wages were between 4 and 12 shillings a week, at least half of which went on rent for a single room, often shared with brothers and sisters. The girls were subject to a managerial regime of draconian severity. If they were judged to have dirty feet (few could afford shoes) or an untidy bench, fines would be deducted from their already meagre wages. Many of them suffered from the disfiguring condition of 'phossy jaw' caused by the phosphorus fumes they inhaled, at a time when other matchmaking companies had abandoned the chemical. Whilst the company claimed that narrow profit margins made it impossible for them to be more generous, it was paying hefty dividends to its shareholders, a disproportionate number of whom seemed to be Church of England clergymen. For the muckrakers this was pure gold. 'Do you know,' Annie asked rhetorically in *The Link*, piling on both the agony and the irony, 'that girls are used to carry boxes on their heads until the hair is rubbed off and their heads are bald at fifteen years of age? Country clergymen with shares in Bryant and May, draw down on your knee your fifteen year old daughter, pass your hand tenderly over the silky clustering curls, rejoice in the dainty beauty of the thick, shiny tresses.'

To crank up the publicity machine further, Besant stood outside the gates of the Fairfield Works along with her socialist colleague Herbert Burrows, handing out specially printed copies of the article to the match girls. A few days later a delegation of the girls came to their Fleet Street office to tell Besant and Burrows that they had been threatened with dismissal unless they signed a document repudiating the information contained in the article. Instead, they had gone straight to *The Link* with their story. 'You had spoken up,' one of them told Annie. 'We weren't going back on you.' A strike committee was formed to resist the threats of the company. Photographs of the plucky, photogenically salt-of-the-earth girls were taken. In another brilliant and shaming stunt, Besant and Burrows solemnly promised to pay the wages of any girls dismissed for their action. George Bernard Shaw volunteered to be treasurer and cashier of the strike fund. Some 1400 of the girls came out. Hugely embarrassed and economically damaged by both the publicity and the stoppage, Bryant and May eventually settled, and the match girls won a raise in July 1888. Annie Besant was hailed as the champion of London working women and was immediately sought after by many other constituencies in need of a campaign – boot-finishers and the rabbit-fur pullers who worked for the felt trade in even more horrible conditions than the match girls. In 1888 Annie entered the political fray through the same route used by many of her generation of 'platform women': election to a school board, in this case Tower Hamlets. She campaigned from a dog cart festooned with red ribbons. Incredibly, 15,296 votes were cast for her.

Could the queen – just entering her 70s – comprehend, much less sympathize with, any of this? The answer is less straightforward than one might imagine. Her chosen role, now that she was a little more in the public eye again, was that of matriarch, and her motherliness or grandmotherliness extended to utterances and even acts of sympathy for the victims of an increasingly plutocratic Britain. She was much more likely to erupt in rage against the immorality, idleness and general worthlessness of the upper classes than the lower classes and took special exception to those who defamed the working families of Britain by painting a portrait of them soaked in beer and beastliness. She too read *The Bitter Cry of Outcast London* (1883), by the Congregationalist minister Andrew Mearns, and was so shaken by its revelations of the one million East Enders living in horrifyingly overcrowded and insanitary conditions that she pressed Gladstone's government to spend more of its time on the problem of housing for the poor. Her indignant pestering paid off with the setting up of a royal commission.

The last of Victoria's many roles – after English rose, model wife and grief-stricken widow – was that of imperial matriarch. As such, she genuinely felt herself to be mother or grandmother to all her people. But in the ever expanding household of her empire there were more and more orphans; millions kept shivering on its doorstep. And, lest the queen become unduly distressed at the spectacle in the streets, there were always servants who Knew What Was Best – to close the carriage blinds until cheerful, loyal throngs could be guaranteed. It is unlikely, for example, that Victoria would have known that on 19 March 1887, in her Jubilee year, fully 27 per cent of 29,000 working men, when asked about their last job, replied that they were unemployed. A third of those had not worked in over three months. The previous year, in February 1886, she would certainly have noticed that something was unsettled. A mass meeting of unemployed dock and building workers in Trafalgar Square had listened to radical and socialist orators denounce the heartlessness of the rich and the unscrupulousness of capitalists. On their way to Parliament Square, the processing demonstrators were assaulted by missiles thrown from the open windows

Top: Annie Besant, photograph at the time of her trial, 1877.
Above: The Match Girl Strike Committee, 1888.

Top: *Her Majesty the Queen Laughing*, a Jubilee photo-portrait, 21 June 1887.
Above: Homeless people sleeping in open coffins in a London Salvation Army shelter, engraving, 1892.

of Pall Mall clubs where the well-heeled members were jeering. The procession turned into a riot. Gangs looted shops; windows were smashed and carriages overturned.

Victoria gave Gladstone, whom she thought had no idea how to keep order, a piece of her mind: 'The Queen cannot sufficiently express her indignation at the monstrous riot which took place in London the other day and which risked people's lives and was a momentary triumph of socialism and a disgrace to the capital.' She consoled herself with the certainty (not entirely misplaced) that the vast majority of working people in Britain were of an unrevolutionary temper. When she went to Liverpool and Birmingham as a warm-up for the Jubilee celebrations, she saw nothing but adoring crowds cheering themselves hoarse, even though in Birmingham she had been warned that she would be moving among the 'roughest' kind of people. During the summer festivities, tens of thousands of the unemployed who were sleeping in the parks of central London were turfed out and moved on to more remote heaths away from the royal gaze. Some used the open coffins that lay around in undertakers' yards as improvized beds. When she got to Hyde Park all Victoria saw were 30,000 poor schoolchildren, their faces well scrubbed, who each got a meat pie, a piece of cake and an orange to celebrate the great day. 'The children sang "God Save the Queen,"' she wrote, 'somewhat out of tune.'

All the people whom she really cared about expressed their devotion, starting with her own extended family, which had by now expanded to a small army. Exactly 50 years to the day after she had been woken, an 18-year-old in a nightdress, to be told she was queen, she rode in an open carriage from Buckingham Palace to Westminster, wearing not the state robes that she had been implored to don but her usual black and widow's cap. In front of the carriage were 12 Indian officers, and in front of them her posterity: 'My three sons, five sons-in-law, nine grandsons and grandsons-in-law. Then came the carriages containing my three other daughters, three daughters-in-law, granddaughters, one granddaughter-in-law.' The evening before, she had been surrounded by this enormous troop of royals, 'the Princes all in uniform and the Princesses ... all beautifully dressed.' Two days later a deputation from 'The Women of England' presented her with a gift on behalf of millions of their sex. At Eton, as Victoria was *en route* to Windsor Castle, it was the boys' turn. 'There was a beautiful triumphal arch, made to look exactly like part of the old College and boys dressed like Templars stood on top of it. The whole effect was beautiful, lit up by the sun of a summer evening.' On the Isle of Wight, the general good cheer was so heartwarming that a toothy smile broke out between the plump cheeks. Her private secretary's wife, Lady Ponsonby, claimed it happened more often than people

imagined, coming 'very suddenly in the form of a mild radiance over the whole face, a softening, a raising of the lines of the lips, a flash of kindly light beaming from the eyes.'

It would be like this for the rest of her life, through another Jubilee a decade later: the country bathed in summer evening light; the throngs on the street, much flag-waving; brass bands from barracks and collieries; a great Handel–Harty coda on the opening night of the big round Albert Hall, finished at last. But *that* reminded her that there was someone missing from the family photographs. In Westminster Abbey, in June 1887, she felt the sudden pang and wrote that 'I sat alone (OH!) without my beloved husband for whom this would have been such a proud day.' It would be another 14 years before she would be reunited with 'him to whom I and the nation owe so much.' Sir Henry Frederick Ponsonby, her private secretary, said that there was nothing Victoria enjoyed so much as arranging funerals, and her own was no exception. This would be the one occasion when, in anticipation of her reunion, she would doff the widow's black. When she had taken Tennyson into the mausoleum at Frogmore, 'I observed that it was light and bright, which he thought a great point.' So Victoria ordered an all white funeral. The queen was robed in white, her body covered with cheerful sprays of spring flowers like some bedecked virgin bride. Some of them, however, had to be tactfully placed since, along with the locks of hair, rings and many other keepsakes she had ordered to be placed in the coffin with her, there was also, embarrassingly, in her *left* hand, a photograph of John Brown; it was carefully concealed by lilies and freesias.

There was another problem, too, that Victoria had left for the managers of the obsequies. For, when Albert's memorial effigy had been ordered from the sculptor Carlo Marochetti in 1862, Victoria had insisted on hers being made at the same time, and in the likeness of her at exactly the time the prince had been taken from her. (If anything Marochetti followed his orders too well, and made Victoria seem more like she had been when they were first married.) They were supposed to be reunited, at least in marble, at the same age they had been in the glowing prime of their union. The trouble was that this had been so long ago that no one could seem to remember where the Victoria sculpture was. It was finally discovered behind one of the walls of a renovated room in Windsor Castle. The image of a young, medieval princess lies next to her *preux chevalier* as if the clocks had stopped along with the heart of the Prince Consort.

But Albert, above all others, knew that they had not; that progress had indeed been the mainspring of his modern century. By 1900 that progress had extended beyond anything he could have imagined – and not just to science, technology and

Previous pages: Queen Victoria's funeral cortege at Paddington Station, London, 1901.

Lady Constance Lytton, photograph by Lafayette, *c.* 1912.

commerce, but to the lives of Britain's women. Education and politics had begun to give the angels in the house an altogether earthier set of ambitions. And those subtle but powerful revolutionaries, the latch key, the cheque book and the bicycle, would go a long way to realizing them.

Young ladies would never be quite the same. Riding with the body of Queen Victoria from London to Windsor was Lady Lytton, the widow of one of her viceroys of India, the Earl of Lytton. Seven years later her daughter Lady Constance, in prison as a militant suffragette, hunger-striker and compulsive cell-scrubber, would make *her* statement about the future of women in Britain by desecrating the 'temple of purity' so slavishly adored by the fetishists of domestic life. Her idea was to carve the slogan of her movement on her upper body all the way up to her face. She chose a piece of broken enamel from a hatpin as her tool of mutilation, but it took her 20 minutes to carve a great 'V' on her breast before the prison officers caught her in the act. Never mind. 'Con' had made her statement. It was 'V' not for Victoria, but for Votes.

5

The British Empire, Lord Curzon could state without fear of contradiction, was quite simply 'the greatest force for good the world has ever seen.' And he, perhaps, was its purest personification. Curzon was, at any rate, exceptionally, almost unnaturally, white. Someone who saw him in his prime as viceroy of India described him as having 'the complexion of a milkmaid and the stature of Apollo.' (Years later, seeing Tommies bathing in the First World War, Curzon would be astonished how white the skins of the working class could be once scraped of grime and, one supposes, blood.) The viceroy's bearing was conspicuously erect, the ramrod posture only partly the effect of the steel and leather backbrace he had been forced to wear since adolescence. Every day, he composed himself into an expression of stoic indifference to discomfort. It was the perfect pose of paramountcy; the burden that weighed but did not crush.

Puffers of empire, like J. R. Seeley, the Professor of Modern History at Cambridge University, talked often and loudly of Britain's civilizing 'destiny.' But Curzon didn't need lectures. He knew in his aching bones that he had been summoned to rule. To a well-intentioned friend who presumed to suggest he might be a little less unyielding in his views he retorted, 'I was born so, you cannot change me.' Born and raised, it seemed, for the very architecture of the Viceroy's House in Calcutta was a virtual copy of his house in Derbyshire, Kedleston Hall. Curzon had first seen the Calcutta edifice in 1887, 11 years before he became viceroy, and declared it, morally as well as architecturally, home from home. Prophetically, Robert Adam's 18th-century façade at Kedleston had incorporated a solidified version of the Arch of Constantine in Rome. So George Nathaniel Curzon, with his aquiline nose and conqueror's jawline, would have been stirred, early on, like all boys of the British ruling classes steeped in classicism, by visions of imperial triumph. (Emperor Constantine, the boy prodigy would have known, was supposed to have been born in northern Britannia.) Eton, Balliol and All Souls would have done nothing to

THE EMPIRE OF GOOD NTENTIONS: INVESTMENTS

Exterior façade of the Victoria Memorial Monument, Calcutta.

dilute this precocious sense of vocation. Nor would his appointment as private secretary to the most unapologetically imperialist of all the Victorian prime ministers:
Lord Salisbury. Not content with being made under-secretary at the India Office
when he was just 32, at the first possible opportunity Curzon nominated himself for
the viceroyalty and, to decreasing astonishment, got the job. So when the moment
to fulfil all this long-heralded potential arrived and Curzon entered his Calcutta
Kedleston in 1899, with his Irish peerage fresh-minted for the occasion and his
American vicereine, Mary, rich and glamorous, at his side, it must have seemed only
right that he should be greeted by the bust of Augustus Caesar.

Curzon knew all about oriental empires. He had travelled the Silk Road and
had written elegantly three books on Russian imperial ambitions in Central Asia and
Persia. So he also knew that great Asiatic empires were expected to express their
majesty in magnificent monuments. Building such edifices was not just a matter of
vulgar bragging: the Raj owed it to its subjects to give them a sense of the strength
and endurance of the power to which they were fortunate enough to be subjected.
And it went without saying that, at the dawn of the British Empire's fourth century, it
seemed its staying power could be taken for granted, at least for the foreseeable future.
And why should he not think this? The Union Jack flew over a fifth of the globe
and nearly a quarter of its population – some 372 million by the turn of the century.
In June 1897, 50,000 troops from every corner of the empire – Camel Corps and
Gurkhas, Canadian hussars and Jamaicans in white gaiters, the procession led by the
loftiest officer in the army, 6-foot-8 Captain Ames of the Horse Guards – had marched
or trotted through London to celebrate Queen Victoria's Diamond Jubilee. The tabloid
imperialist press (above all, the *Daily Mail*) had been ecstatic; the crowds drunk with
top-nation elation. Up and down the country, on 22 June schoolchildren were given
the day off, herded into parks and, courtesy of the queen, given two buns and an orange.
Mass singing of the national anthem was reinforced by a new 'Imperial March' composed for the Jubilee by Edward Elgar. The queen, now very lame, conceded just
enough to the delirium to decorate her black satin with Cape ostrich feathers.

Even the most swollen-headed imperialist was not such a fool as to need
reminding by the likes of Kipling that all this too, some day, would pass. But that day,
surely, was a long, long way off. On the evening of Curzon's installation in Calcutta
there was a viceregal banquet and ball. George wore a mantle of sky blue silk. 'The
message is carved granite,' he wrote, 'it is hewn in the rock of doom, that our work
is righteous and it shall endure.'

So when the queen passed away in January 1901, Curzon lost no time in
commissioning a great monument to her memory. It would be, he told the committee

responsible for drafting designs, 'a standing record of our wonderful history, a visible monument of Indian glories and an illustration more eloquent than any spoken address or printed page, of the lessons of public patriotism and civic duty.' It would, in fact, be the British Taj Mahal. The Taj was much on Curzon's mind since it had been he who had made it beautiful again. He had cleared out the bazaars in front of it and restored Shah Jehan's exquisite reflecting pools. The Calcutta Victoria Memorial Monument would also have water gardens and it would even be faced with marble drawn from the same Makrana quarries in Rajasthan that had supplied the stone for the Taj. But there the resemblance would stop. The Taj Mahal was often called a poem in stone; the perfect lament of an imperial widower. But Curzon was not interested in architectural sorrow. His building would be more in the way of a proclamation. As befitted the heirs to the Mughals, there would be references to their architecture and subtle allusions to Hindu temple vernacular. But the overwhelming impression that the building would give, expressed in dome and colonnades, would be of an edifice built by the Romans of the modern age; the carriers of a civilization supported by wisdom and engineered for justice and progress. It must have seemed right, then, to entrust much of the building to Vincent Esch, whose reputation had been built as assistant chief engineer to the Bengal and Nagpur Railway.

Ground was broken in 1904. Two years later the most uncompromising, brilliant and adamant of India's viceroys was gone, leaving behind at Government House an ornate £50,000 electric lift (still in working order today) and a government in Bengal that was almost completely broken down by riots, strikes and boycotts. Curzon's lordly plan to partition Bengal and move the capital from Calcutta to the ancient seat of the Mughals in Delhi had raised a hornets' nest of discontent. 'Hundreds of poor ignorant natives are being paid to hold up placards (frequently upside down) with English inscriptions painted upon them in Calcutta' was his patrician dismissal of the mass agitation. But his authority had been broken by it all the same. Arriving as the epitome of benevolent autocracy, the viceroy who worked 14 hours a day, who prided himself on knowing everything from the price of rice in Madras to the number of chickens ordered for a state dinner (always too many!), Curzon left in impotent, exhausted dismay, pursued by shouts of 'Bande mataram!' (Hail motherland!), the first great slogan of the movement for *swaraj* or self-rule. This is how the endgame of the empire would play out: grandeur mocked by chaos. By the time that Curzon's vision of a great new capital city at Delhi had been realized by Herbert Baker and Edwin Lutyens in 1921, and the Victoria Memorial Monument in Calcutta had been completed, the writing was already on the wall for the Raj. The incoming viceroy, Lord Irwin, would be greeted (like his

Above: A starving family in India, *c.* 1900.
Opposite: *Their Excellencies Lord and Lady Curzon with First Day's Bag in Camp near Nekonda, Warangal District, Hyderabad*, photograph by Lala Deen Dayal, 1902.

successors, Lords Minto and Hardinge) with a bomb. He would survive, but illusions of benevolent imperial endurance would not.

Even in 1901, there had been those who had their doubts about whether a British pseudo-Taj was, in fact, the best way for the revenues of India to be spent. In the same year that Curzon announced the grandiose project, the medical journal *The Lancet* – not given to incendiary statements – lamented that during the previous decade the excess deaths (over the usual high rates) in India from famine and disease had been at least 19 million, or, as the journal expressed it, the equivalent of half the population of the United Kingdom. The horrifying famine that had gripped western and central India in 1899–1900 had taken, according to a reliable modern historian, Burton Stein, at least 6.5 million lives (W. Arthur Lewis puts it at more like 10 million). In 1901 alone a quarter of a million, mostly in and around Bombay, had died from bubonic plague. In 1903, during the staging of the durbar that proclaimed Edward VII as Emperor of India, Lalmohan Ghosh, the president of the Indian National Congress, asked rhetorically, 'Do you think that any administration in England, France or the United States would have ventured to waste vast sums of money on an empty pageant when Famine and Pestilence are stalking over the land and the Angel of Death was flapping his wings almost within hearing of the light-hearted revellers?'

By the time Curzon's viceroyalty ended in 1905, 3 million had perished from that epidemic. Cholera had taken an even more savage toll. Even average Indian death rates, which in the 1880s had been at the already shocking level of 41.3 per 1000, had risen, by the time the Memorial Monument was completed, to 48.6 per 1000. So the period when its triumphalists were boasting most noisily of the material and medical benefits that the British had brought to the subcontinent happened also to be the decades when India experienced the most horrific death-toll in its entire modern history. In the regions most stricken by the turn-of-the-century droughts and epidemics, like Orissa, Gujarat, Rajasthan and the United Provinces, they reached over 90 per 1000, or one in 11 of the population. An earlier famine in Orissa in 1865–6 had, according to government sources, killed fully a quarter of the population. And there is, of course, no memorial to those victims. But if you look carefully at the statuary in front of the Victoria Memorial you will find grateful natives being succoured at the breast of the Mother Raj.

What in God's name had happened? The white sahibs and memsahibs who sat at their desks, played out their chukkas, danced and drank in the clubs, lorded it in the courts, gathered the revenues, built the railways and extolled the blessings they had brought were not monsters of hard-hearted callousness. They had – most of them – only the very best of intentions. They shared Curzon's confidence that the British Empire was the greatest the world had ever seen. Its splendour was, its celebrants believed, to be measured not by square miles or millions of subjects, still less by battleships and Gatling guns, but by its incontrovertible altruism. There was indeed money to be made, and the Russian bear to be kept from getting his hairy paws on it. But what was that beside the noble dedication to eradicating poverty, disease and ignorance, which was the truly British imperial mission? Peoples whose worlds had been crippled by those maladies for who knew how long (it was invariably a much shorter time than the British supposed) would be healed. India would one day rise and walk again on its own two feet and be judged (by the British) capable once more of governing itself. On that great day of magnanimous self-liquidation, the 'heaven-born' (as the Indian Civil Service liked to call itself) would depart in peace leaving its erstwhile charges grateful, devoted, peaceful, prosperous and – this was the special bonus for that future modern world – free. Long after it had gone, historians would pronounce the world to have been a better place for the existence of the British Empire.

That, at any rate, was the idea of 'trusteeship': the vision that was habitually recited to justify the immense military, tax and economic juggernaut that described the reality of the late Victorian empire. There is no doubt that those ideals were sincerely held; even as their realization was constantly thwarted and, in the end, indefinitely postponed. There is equally no doubt that it seldom occurred to the governors of the empire (although it certainly did to its adversaries) that their military and economic power had actually caused many, if not most, of the problems they claimed to be in India to correct. The conditions in which British ideas of 'progress' and 'civilization' were introduced were, at the same time, the conditions that doomed them to failure. During Curzon's own viceroyalty, 4 per cent of India's revenues were spent on public works such as irrigation and nearly 35 per cent on the army and police. None of this means, however, that those ideals were, from the beginning, a fig-leaf for economic and military despotism. The liberal promise of shared betterment without bloodshed, of the evolution of self-government through educated citizenship (as pertinent, its champions believed, for the fate of Britain as for the colonies), remains, arguably, one of the nobler wrecks of western optimism. Its submerged ruins still lie deep in the modern consciousness, sending up ripples of pride or guilt to the surface of contemporary British life. At the very least, then, no account of British history, however provisional, can avoid diving into the depths to see through the murk what happened: just how the good ship 'Victoria' ran aground.

The launch, at least, was ebullient. In 1834, Thomas Babington Macaulay, who had been born with the 19th century, was still a historian in the making. The dazzling essayist for the *Edinburgh Review*, social lion of fashionable Whig society in London, precocious parliamentary orator and MP for the newly enfranchised manufacturing borough of Leeds decided that, considering he had just £700 in the bank, he was in need of a decidedly bigger fortune. The place to get one, as any fool knew, was India. Not that he was himself going into business – although, of course, there were many perfectly splendid people in Leeds whose occupation that was. His purpose, rather, was to earn £10,000 a year by bringing Progress to benighted Asia.

In 1833 parliament had finally liquidated the commercial side of the East India Company. What profits were to be made from indigo, sugar, cotton and the only steadily lucrative business of the time, narcotics (opium traded to China in return for tea), would henceforth be harvested by private traders. The 'Company' was now candidly what for many generations it had actually been, a tax-and-war machine, or, as it liked to think of itself, a government. As a member of the 'Board of Control' – the body answerable to parliament and co-governing India with the Company's Court of Directors – it fell to Macaulay to justify the Whig government's policy in the Commons. The prospect, despite Macaulay's reputation as the 'Burke of the age,' was not one that packed the benches. ('Dinner bell' Burke had himself often emptied them, of course.) On 10 July 1833, speaking to a chamber only a third full, Macaulay delivered his vision of British responsibility to India. It was a performance of stirring, Ciceronian eloquence in which, however, ignorance competed with arrogance. But it was, none the less, the manifesto of the liberal empire of good intentions. Even as Macaulay charted the beginning of the enterprise, he looked forward to its gloriously disinterested end:

It may be that the public mind of India may expand under our system till it has outgrown that system; that by good government we may educate our subjects into a capacity for better government; that, having been instructed in European knowledge, they may, in some future age, demand European institutions. Whether such a day will ever come I know not. But never will I attempt to avert or retard it. Whenever it comes, it will be the proudest day in English history. To have found a great people sunk in the lowest depths of slavery and superstition, to have so ruled them as to have made them desirous and capable of all the privileges of citizens, would indeed be a title to glory all our own. The sceptre may pass away from us. Unforeseen accidents may derange our most profound schemes of policy. Victory may be inconstant to our arms. But there

Thomas Babington Macaulay, Baron Macaulay by John Partridge, 1849–53.

are triumphs which are followed by no reverse. There is an empire exempt from all natural causes of decay. Those triumphs are the pacific triumphs of reason over barbarism; that empire is the imperishable empire of our arts and our morals, our literature and our laws.

The long march that England had undertaken from Magna Carta to the 1832 Reform Act (and that would go on until all Britain's people were educated into citizenship) could, and would, God willing, be reproduced in Asia. The British Empire, like that of the Romans, might be in the road-building enterprise but no road would be finer, straighter – or longer – than the road to parliamentary nationhood. Moreover, the economic beauty of this empire would be the fit of its interlocking parts, just like the industrial machinery that Macaulay found so inspiring. Taking the 'indolent' and 'superstitious' Orient and giving it a good shaking-up through British law, education, light taxes and honest administration would supply the stability necessary for the religion of Progress to take hold. Under the protection of such government peace would break out and urban markets would flourish. No longer held to ransom by armed brigands and rapacious, corrupt tax collectors, the 'cultivators' would have some incentive to produce for those markets. And as their income kept pace with rising urban demand, their ability to introduce 'improvements' would make them still more productive. Up and up they would go, manuring their way to prosperity, just like their counterparts in Norfolk. Cash crops would yield surpluses that would be exported, not least to the mother country. In return Britain would send its textiles and its machinery, its plumply studded sofas and its damask drapes to India where they would find a ready market among all these thriving merchants and Turnip Singhs. With greater 'ease' (as the Victorians liked to put it) would come even more demand for cultural goods and services – colleges; newspapers; in the fullness of time, parliaments; even, dare one hope, True Religion. The entire project as Macaulay sketched it in his brightly reasoning imagination – taking 'inert' Asia (another favourite cliché) and injecting it with the dynamism of progress – flooded him with exhilaration. Bradford broadcloth, Sheffield cutlery and Bombay readers of the *Edinburgh Review* were just around the corner, he felt sure.

In February 1834, two weeks before embarking on the four-month voyage to India, his chests packed with the kind of things he judged really indispensable in the tropics – 300 oranges and the complete works of Homer, Horace, Gibbon and Voltaire – Macaulay treated the electors of Leeds to some parting words. Half valediction, half benediction, they offered both a blessing from the Church of Irrevocable Progress and a headmasterly reassurance that this was All for the Best.

Be of good cheer, was the general drift; you are not losing your MP but gaining the world:

> May your manufactures flourish; may your trade be extended; may your riches increase. May the works of your skill and the signs of your prosperity meet me in the furthest regions of the East and give me fresh cause to be proud of the intelligence, the industry and the spirit of my constituency.

Macaulay's conviction that he could Make a Difference was the authentic 'spirit of the age' (a term that had just become popularized, not least by William Hazlitt). Arguably, Britain had never had a generation more determined to do what Viscount Palmerston (the great drum-beater of Britain's global power) called 'world bettering.' But 'Clever Tom' Macaulay had grown up with that impulse in the Clapham household of his evangelical parents, Zachary and Selina Macaulay, who had been ardent campaigners for the abolition of slavery. Between constant prayers and obligatory accounting for their time, he and his brothers and sisters had been inculcated with a driving need for self-justification. However jaunty a materialist Macaulay was to become (to the acute disappointment of his perfervid father), he never quite lost that early anxiety.

For Zachary it might have been worse. Tom might have become a Benthamite, for whom a human being was little more than a walking sense-receptor. Macaulay never did become a utilitarian, although in India he discovered that the utilitarians' schemes of improvement generally ended up being improved by a strong dose of reality. But even when he had attacked the utilitarian philosopher James Mill for reducing men to machines, Macaulay was certainly aware of the attraction of the 'political economists' and 'philosophical radicals' for all those who saw nothing wrong about trying to optimize pleasure and minimize pain. As far as Jeremy Bentham himself was concerned it would have been all very fine if, left to its own devices, the mass of humanity could find its own way to this golden mean. But self-evidently it needed help. And that help had to come from government; from exceptionally knowledgeable, disinterested men prepared to ascertain, scientifically, the causes of whatever particular social evil they were committed to correct. They should be zealous enough to investigate every aspect of the problem; draft their report and thrust it under the noses of whichever power could do something about it; generally make pests of themselves until the remedy became law; and then ensure that it was properly carried out through cadres of professional inspectors. The vision – even if never completely enacted – was a true turning point in British history, signalling the inadequacy of an older, more socially sentimental idea of aristocratic and ecclesiastical benevolence to deal with the modern industrial-imperial world of the 19th century. The squire, the justice of the peace and the parson would be replaced by the professional civil servant, the government's blue-book statistician and the health inspector.

This is not to say that the 'philosophical radicals' wanted to burden society permanently with overbearing and expensive government. Their notion was, rather, to invest in enough initial investigatory zeal and intelligence to have society correct itself. There would be short-term pain, fiscal and social, in return for long-term, cost-efficient gain. But where the most conspicuous exercises in Benthamite social improvement were concerned – the New Poor Law of 1834 in particular – the pain seemed a lot more visible than the gain. Paradoxically, it took money to make the workhouses so horribly penal that even the desperate would not want to surrender themselves to them.

And in times of extreme economic distress like the 1840s in Britain, even the most 'brutilitarian' regime was preferable to starvation. The ebb and flow of the numbers in the workhouses, their critics rightly pointed out, was no index of true social misery; only of those moving in and out of the institutional walls. Very often, moreover, the reforms attracted the maximum of odium with the minimum of relief for the burdens of public administration. Even when, under the auspices of the arch-Benthamite in government, Edwin Chadwick, the utilitarian reformers did something as demonstrably benevolent as attempting to lower mortality rates in the towns and cities of Britain through cleaner water and piped sewage, their work ran into the ingrained suspicion, not to say hatred, of state busybodying that ran through all classes of the population.

That is why the colonies – swarming with chaos, sickness and violence – promised a more fruitful field for Benthamite idealism. In India, there was no tradition of bloody-minded liberty to get in the way of strong but necessary doses of Improvement. On the contrary, so the reformers believed, the crumbling of the Mughal Empire over the 18th and 19th centuries had left a subject population desperate to feel the strong hand of authority. 'Happiness before freedom' or 'firm but impartial despotism' was the working rubric of this generation. Utilitarianism had certainly had an impact on the teaching at Haileybury, the East India Company college established in Britain to educate the new generation of Indian civil administrators (of whom there were still only around 900 in the 1830s). But the people with whom Macaulay, as the fourth legal member of India's Governor-General William Bentinck's council, had to become acquainted were certainly not just tropical transplants of Jeremy Bentham.

Bentham's principles, after all, presupposed universal laws governing human behaviour. But the British governors of India who had come of age in the first two decades of the 19th century had gained an early understanding that the difference between success and failure lay precisely in the degree to which general principles had to be adapted to local peculiarities. The young men who were borne aloft on their *palkhee gharee* litters, sweating in the dusty heat, their heads filled with Marcus Aurelius, the Indian *Rig Veda* and the arithmetic of millet yields, were Britain's first true imperial soldier–scholars, equally at home with the sabre and the theodolite. Many had been young protégés of the exuberant, unapologetically expansionist Marquis of Wellesley. Some of them had graduated from, others had taught at, Wellesley's college of Fort William in Calcutta, which had been established as the barracks of the empire of knowledge, created to reinforce the rule of the sword. Governor-General Richard Wellesley – in so many ways a more complicated figure than his much more famous younger brother, the Duke of Wellington – had not just been a gung-ho generalissimo. To govern the huge territories his armies had gained during the wars against the Indian allies of the French, he believed, would need men broadly and deeply versed in the topography, history, languages and culture of India. And his college was supposed to provide – through Brahmin teachers known as *munshis* – their initial instruction in Sanskrit, Hindustani, Persian (still the language of the Indian courts), Arabic and some of the vernacular tongues.

What got created – for a brief, dazzling generation during the first quarter of the 19th century – was a non-English British Indian government; perhaps the best the British ever made in Asia. Virtually all of its stars were Scots, Irish or Welsh. The most phenomenally knowledgeable and culturally tolerant of them were Scots like Sir Thomas Munro, Sir John Malcolm and Mountstuart Elphinstone, and a little later James Thomason in the northwest provinces. All took to India the lessons of the Scottish enlightenment, especially the budding sociology of Adam Ferguson and John Millar, in which wise public action had to be grounded on deep local understanding. It was, in fact, just because so many of them felt that English government had so misunderstood and so mistreated their own country that as Britons they were determined not to repeat the mistake in Asia. Many of them became authorities on the minutiae of the history, law and agrarian economics of the territories under their rule. To act effectively meant knowing in depth the states and societies with which one was dealing. So Malcolm wrote extensively on the Sikhs, and published *The History of Persia* (1815). Elphinstone, who had fought with the Maratha princes, produced an encyclopedic *Report on the Territories Conquered from the Paishwa* (1821). And those writings were often strikingly free of the stereotypes about 'anarchy' that coloured the work of the later Victorians. Elphinstone's *History of India* (1841) was at pains to portray Mughal rule as a golden age of peaceful relations between Muslims and Hindus.

Local knowledge changed the Scottish soldier-scholars. But it also forced them to face the contradictions of their position. On the one hand, the East India Company had promised that its bloody, disruptive campaigns were the precondition of establishing enough stability for a resurgent India (or at least Bengal, Bombay and Madras) to prosper. But somehow each campaign seemed to generate another. Pushing northwest into the Punjab to pre-empt the expansionism of the new enemy, Imperial Russia, brought them into collision with one of the few truly cohesive states of the region, the Sikh power of Ranjit Singh. Instead of creating a stable frontier the British engineered an unstable one, which in turn guaranteed even more military activity. It never stopped. It was always back to front. The nomadic horse troops of Rajasthan and the Deccan were declared 'bandits' – as indeed many of them were. But they had been turned into criminal predators by the relentless destruction by the British of their state patrons, the Marathas. Every intervention postponed, rather than hastened, the desperately wished-for moment of 'settlement.' In the meantime there were soldiers to be paid – almost a quarter of a million of them by the 1830s, making the East India Company army (overwhelmingly made up of Indian soldiers, the sepoys) by far the biggest military force in Asia and one of the biggest in the world. That, in turn, meant that taxes had to be levied. The further hardship caused by those taxes generated more distress, hardship and anger.

Although local knowledge clouded the sunny optimism of the liberal vision of tutelage, it could at least do something about mitigating hardship. Thomas Munro had discovered that the *zemindar* – the middlemen with whom the government in Bengal had insisted the peasants make their assessment and pay their taxes were, far from being a tradition, more or less unknown in southeast India. James Thomason would believe the same was true for the Punjab. Those useful middlemen had simply interjected themselves with a blank cheque for extortion. Instead a *ryotwari* system, with every peasant settling directly with the officers of the government, was introduced, even though it presupposed a more or less complete land survey of every single holding, including data on the fertility of the soil and weather conditions experienced in the tax year. It was a monumental task (and only conceivable with the help of the same native agents who were the target of the paternalists' criticism). But to do anything else, Munro, Thomason and the knowledge-harvesters argued, would be to betray their 'trusteeship.'

In London, Macaulay is supposed to have dutifully plunged into the tomes, filling up his famously cavernous memory bank with details of salt evaporation in

Gujarat or the niceties of caste. What he learned he almost certainly retained. But his heart was not in his homework. Too much knowledge of India, he thought, ran the risk of bewitching a healthily rational, liberal, progressive mind with the mumbo-jumbo of exotic culture. Although he had been a critic of James Mill he certainly read his influential *History of British India* (1817), and, to those who objected that its author had never actually been to India, Macaulay would have endorsed Mill's opinion that 'whatever is worth seeing or hearing in India can be expressed in writing … a man who is duly qualified may obtain more knowledge of India in one year in his closet in England than he could during the longest life by the use of his eyes and ears in India.' Besides, Macaulay had it on good advice that perfectly decent, sensible fellows went out there only to become infatuated with the erotic abominations of temple sculpture or bogged down, beyond hope of rescue, in senselessly elaborate attempts to codify Hindu law. As if any sound 19th-century administrator with a modicum of common sense could suppose that that was what India needed! What India needed was the crisp reasoning of Europe. Perhaps he would not have gone quite as far as Curzon, who in a characteristic outrage told an audience at Calcutta University that 'truth is a Western concept'; but he would not have demurred either.

Macaulay's prejudices were, to a great extent, shared by the Governor-General, William Bentinck, 'the clipping Dutchman' who had brought a dose of his own personal evangelicalism with him to Calcutta. Bentinck spoke, one visitor thought, like a Pennsylvania Quaker, and he certainly dressed like one in black broadcloth frock coats, in deliberately reproachful contrast to the flashier older generation's fondness for Indian scarves and brocaded waistcoats. When its charter had been renewed in 1813, under evangelical pressure the Company had been made to open territories under its control to the penetration of 'Western' ideas – often a code phrase for the beginning of serious missionary activity. Whilst Bentinck was too prudent to lend his authority to something bound to stir up trouble he was also not shy of identifying 'abominations,' the removal of which might pave the way for the reception of 'enlightenment.' And lest he slide in this determination there was always Charles Trevelyan, his political secretary, to remind him of the call of duty. Trevelyan was the son of the Archdeacon of Taunton and had grown up full of un-coordinated zeal. The East India Company College at Haileybury, where he had been taught by the grimly brilliant economist the Reverend Thomas Malthus (an experience that would have a profound and terrible influence on his later career), had given Trevelyan's civic anxiety direction and purpose. He had arrived in Delhi in 1827 at the age of 20 ardent with the kind of passions only Trevelyan's generation could enthuse over: tariff reform, for example. When, a few years later, he pursued

The extent of the British Empire in 1914.

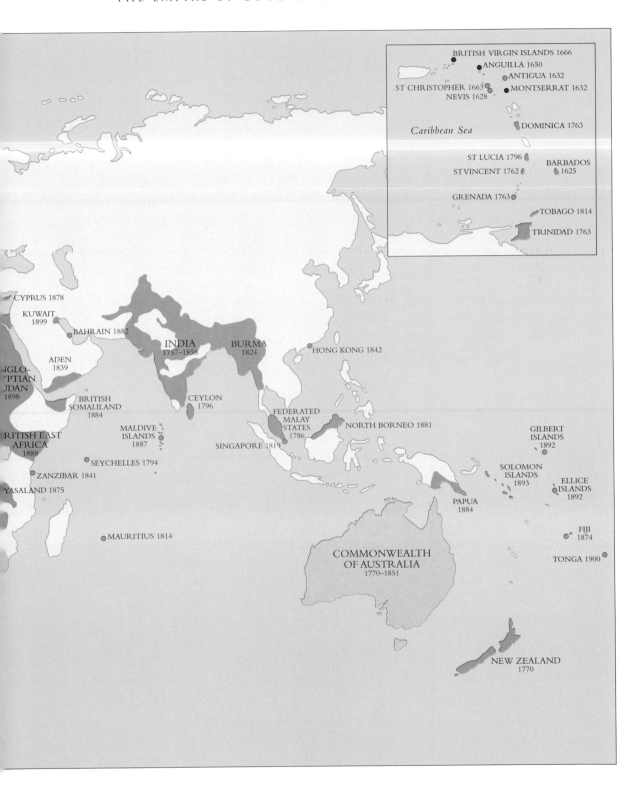

BRITISH VIRGIN ISLANDS 1666
ANGUILLA 1650
ANTIGUA 1632
ST CHRISTOPHER 1663
MONTSERRAT 1632
NEVIS 1628

Caribbean Sea

DOMINICA 1763

ST LUCIA 1796
BARBADOS
ST VINCENT 1762
1625

GRENADA 1763

TOBAGO 1814
TRINIDAD 1763

CYPRUS 1878
KUWAIT 1899
BAHRAIN 1882
INDIA 1757–1858
BURMA 1824
HONG KONG 1842
ADEN 1839
NGLO-
PTIAN
JDAN
1898
BRITISH SOMALILAND 1884
CEYLON 1796
RITISH EAST AFRICA 1888
MALDIVE ISLANDS 1887
FEDERATED MALAY STATES 1786
NORTH BORNEO 1881
GILBERT ISLANDS 1892
SINGAPORE 1819
SEYCHELLES 1794
ZANZIBAR 1841
SOLOMON ISLANDS 1893
ELLICE ISLANDS 1892
YASALAND 1875
PAPUA 1884
MAURITIUS 1814
FIJI 1874
COMMONWEALTH OF AUSTRALIA 1770–1851
TONGA 1900
NEW ZEALAND 1770

Macaulay's sister Hannah, his courtship repartee (according to the admittedly possessive Tom) consisted of 'steam navigation, the education of the natives, the equalization of the sugar duties, the substitution of the Roman for the Arabic alphabet. He is by no means as good a wooer as a financier ... and he never read, I believe, a novel in all his life.' Hannah accepted him all the same.

Trevelyan, then, was a prig; but he was a prig for the empire. Corruption made him smoke with fury. He had been in Delhi only a few months when, at the age of 21, he took it on himself to expose Sir Edward Colebrooke, the chief magistrate and a noted authority of the older generation on Hindu and Muslim law, for accepting gifts. Even if it had occurred to Trevelyan that refusing those gifts would have caused a far greater sense of grievance and anger among those who offered them, he would have been horrified that the Company could possibly lend its authority to such wicked customs. Publicly vilified, Colebrooke (whose threats against the whipper-snapper puritan had made him even steelier) was sent home in disgrace, a broken man. Trevelyan felt the pleasure of vindication, not to mention promotion. He moved to Calcutta as Bentinck's deputy political secretary.

Trevelyan was not a bigot. He had been a thoughtful tutor to the son of the Raja of Bhurtpore and he encouraged young Brahmins who were interested in Western learning to come to him for guidance. He himself (unlike Macaulay) had been a brilliant student of Indian languages, both classical and vernacular. This, however, did not make him a cultural pluralist. The sanction of tradition left him cold. The fact that a disreputable custom had been long practised, he believed, made it in no way less reprehensible. And in the case of *sati* – the ritual cremation of a widow alongside her husband – Trevelyan and Bentinck saw an unqualified abomination. There were others – female infanticide, child betrothals and forced consummations – that were also self-evidently abhorrent. But abolishing *sati* – even though there were no more than perhaps 500 documented cases every year in all of India – became a test case of the application of 'civilized' values to India.

Although a reading of the Westernizers' literature on the subject suggested that this was a campaign they had dreamed up by themselves, it was in fact the *cause célèbre* of Hindu reformers like Rajah Ram Mohan Roy. As early as the 1820s he had attacked *sati* as unauthorized by the sacred Hindu scriptures known as the *Vedanta*, and brought a group of equally learned Hindu reformers to the Governor's House to urge him to abolish the practice. Bentinck certainly made the abolition of *sati* his own mission. In 1829, after heated speeches had been made and volumes of investigations published by parliament, Bentinck decreed that it was banned. Officers were now authorized to intercept widows *en route* to the pyre. Shortly afterwards,

Sir Charles Trevelyan, engraving by D.J. Pound after John Watkins, *c.* 1845.

a statue of the Governor presiding over native women plucked from the flames was set on a pedestal in the park immediately behind where the Victoria Memorial Monument would stand in the next century. Beneath his expression of amiable benevolence, Hindu widows – their features absurdly Westernized to resemble the standard early Victorian epitome of maidens in distress – are rescued from the clutches of sinister turbaned types as they are marched towards the flames.

Although the abolition of *sati* was part of an Eastern campaign to purify Hindu practice and reform what Ram Mohan Roy thought was the illegitimate, usurped authority of Brahmin caste authority, it became a self-congratulatory mantra for Westernizers convinced that their idea of ethics would be an unqualified boon for India. They spoke as though their government were the first truly to know India without their freedom of action being compromised by the knowledge. In fact, they knew a lot less than their predecessors and a lot less than they supposed. *Sati* was taken as an emblem of the cruel obscurantism of Hinduism when in fact Hinduism did not call for it. And it was invariably twinned in the apologias for British supremacy with the phenomenon of *thagi*, the ritual strangling with scarves said to be practised by devotees of the goddess Kali (whose very mention was guaranteed to send a shiver up Victorian spines). *The Confessions of a Thug* (1839), written by Philip Meadows Taylor from information given to him by one of the criminals, became a best-seller as soon as it was published. Queen Victoria was so impatient to read it that she demanded the galley proofs 'as corrected by the author,' and sat up late in bed much excited by its revelations. Major William Sleeman, thug-hunter-in-chief who became an early Victorian hero, cast himself as an imperial mastermind who had been able, with the help of informants, to penetrate the occult language and underworld of the pan-Indian cult conspiracy. When they were on leave in the home counties many sahibs and memsahibs were treated as instant authorities, pestered for samples of the killer scarves or accounts of the juiciest murders. For example, Harriet Tytler, the young wife of an army officer, was sure that, whilst an initiate was required by religious vows to Kali to commit an assigned number of murders a year (usually three), should a bat or owl suddenly appear at the moment he was about to strike this evil omen would cause him to stay his hand. Although not particularly successful at making the trunk roads safer, uncontrolled thugophobia in Britain and India in the 1830s did, however, hugely expand the police power, not to mention the moral self-importance of the government, permitting the authorities to make pre-emptive arrests of persons suspected of belonging to the cult even when there was no evidence of a crime having been committed. Much of the hysteria was an elaborate fantasy laid over the genuine reality of violent lawlessness on the highways, the product of the breakdown of the local Indian authorities that British military power had done much to accelerate. The 'secret language' that Sleeman claimed to have decoded, which was said to bind together the underworld brotherhood of stranglers, was in all likelihood nothing more than local gang slang.

But thugophobia, at its height when Macaulay arrived in Calcutta, certainly played to the British sense that, notwithstanding the overwhelmingly military character of their power, they were a force for peace. As a member of the governor's council (although often so bored by meetings that during them he wrote to his friends back home), Macaulay was responsible for drafting reports on reforms to be made to the penal system – even though, as his enemies later pointed out, he knew virtually nothing about traditional India. As far as he was concerned, however, familiarity with the minutiae of Hindu law would do nothing to shake his conviction that a single, unified penal code, applicable to Indians and British alike, and available in English, not Persian, should be the foundation of any respectable system of justice.

But it was his February 1835 Minute on Education that threw Macaulay head-long into a furious debate about the entire meaning and direction of British rule in India. The ostensible issue was whether it should be English or Indian languages that were subsidized by the company for use in higher education in India. This was, of course, a generation for whom education was the mightiest of all engines of social progress. As far as Macaulay and Charles Trevelyan (who took the cause of English as his personal crusade) were concerned, access to the rational, scientific enlightenment was a universal right. Depriving Indians of the chance to jump aboard the mighty steam locomotive of benign change, just because of some misplaced sensitivity towards their indigenous languages and texts, was not to do them any favours. Macaulay's pithiest remark along these lines, the one for which his name is still infamous in India, was that 'I have never found [anyone] distinguished by their proficiency in the eastern tongues who could deny that a single shelf of a good European library was worth the whole native literature of India and Arabia.' No Ayurvedic medicine or Sanskrit literature for Clever Tom.

Why would one wish to patronize 'medical doctrines which would disgrace an English farrier, astronomy which would move girls in an English boarding school to laughter, history abounding with kings thirty feet high and reigns thirty thousand years long and geography made up of seas of treacle and seas of butter.' (How easily, when it suited him, had the encyclopedic Macaulay memory deleted from recollection the chronologies and the miraculous apparitions of the Old Testament!)

For Macaulay and Trevelyan, the issue was not just a matter of enlightening the 'benighted Asiaticks' for its own sake. On the creation of an English-educated class of Indians depended the entire viability of the imperial enterprise. There were just too many Indian millions and too few bright, decent chaps to civilize them (the chaps were notoriously vulnerable to the broth of infectious diseases cooked up under the southern Asian sun). Besides, there wasn't time to learn all the minutiae of caste and religious practice, let alone in the 18 most common languages of India. Cultural go-betweens were, therefore, a necessity: 'a class of persons Indian in blood and colour but English in taste, opinions, morals and in intellect.' Such men, exposed to Newton as well as Shakespeare, imparting 'useful' as well as refining knowledge, would be the human conduits through whom an immense cultural transformation would flow. The system would be like a monitorial system for the millions, with the top boys instructing those lower down in the form and so on until the work of civilization spread through the length and breadth of India. The consequences of this change would be momentous. It was not just a question of creating Indians who could recite Milton and Blackstone, admirable though that undoubtedly was. Through English, they would be open to 'proper' concepts of justice and develop a healthy aversion to 'barbarous' customs, dress and manners. They would become, in short, the stuff of citizenship, which in turn would make them avid customers for the best that Britain had to offer from the common law to broadcloth. It was not entirely to be ruled out that some of them, one radiant day, would also become Christians.

As far as the reformers were concerned, then, the issue of the medium of instruction was not just some high-minded quibble. It was the Archimedian point on which the future of the empire turned. For with a Westernized population there would be such natural sympathy between rulers and ruled that coercion would be unnecessary; the numbers of the military and the weight of taxation needed to fund them could be reduced. With disposable income beyond the needs of subsistence, the masses would share Britannia's bounty. 'We shall exchange profitable subjects for MORE profitable allies,' Trevelyan had written. Above all, the English language was to be understood as the electricity of change; the jolt that could galvanize Asian 'inertia' into dynamism. It would produce light *and* power.

But this obsession with English-language instruction was dismissed as just another 'visionary absurdity' by the orientalist the Boden Professor of Sanskrit at Oxford, H. H. Wilson, who had spent many years in India and, like his friends and colleagues, understood its languages, law and religion at a depth that neither Trevelyan nor Macaulay remotely approached. All they knew, Wilson and the Company civil servant Henry Thoby Prinsep fulminated, was the world of the Calcutta clubs, insulated from the vast, unyielding reality of Indian village life.

English, the orientalists insisted, would never penetrate anything but the upper-crust commercial and legal classes in the towns and cities whom the British administrators already knew. Instead of creating a group that could diffuse such knowledge downwards, English would merely create a clique detached from the rest of Indian society. Even if Macaulay, Trevelyan and like-minded men should succeed, what they would spawn would be a cultural mongrel group, with a vested interest in telling the sahibs what they thought they wanted or needed to hear.

Besides, in the orientalist view it was not the proper mission of the British to make India some sort of cultural satrap of the West; or even to refashion it in the image of the European enlightenment. Ever since Warren Hastings's governor-generalship in the 1770s and 1780s the Company had accepted that it had a duty to repair and restore India's own institutions, however apparently diverse and contradictory. That was why Hastings himself had learned Persian; why the judge and scholar Sir William Jones and the great Sanskrit authority Henry Colebrooke had eaten up years of their life attempting to clarify and codify Hindu law; why Vedic scholars like Ram Mohan Roy could respond positively to what the West had to offer, since it did not presume to impose its values on them. And by posing the issue as a choice between Indian classical languages and modern English, the orientalists worried that opportunities to teach modern subjects in popular vernaculars such as Hindustani would also go by the board.

A bitter debate ensued in the 1830s, with the heavy artillery of the orientalists, Prinsep and Wilson, appalled at the ignorance and presumption of their aggressively Westernizing adversaries. Some 20 years later, in the 1850s, testifying before the House of Lords, Wilson commented acidly that 'Macaulay knew nothing of the people; he spoke only from what he saw immediately around him, which has been the greatest source of the mistakes committed by the advocates for English exclusively.' But for better or worse, Macaulay's and Trevelyan's way was the way of the future. They told Bentinck – and they were not in fact altogether wrong – that much of the demand for English, rather than traditional, instruction was coming from Indians themselves. The Governor-General duly abolished the government grants to the Islamic Madrassa and the Hindu Sanskrit College set up in Hastings and Wellesley's day, along with Fort William College, which, at the time of its liquidation, was giving excellent instruction in six Indian languages to its British students. All that was left of that programme were the Sanskrit courses at Haileybury, which students in succeeding generations treated as an excruciatingly tedious joke. Although the defeated party, the orientalists, have become a byword for cultural imperialism, the stubborn fact remains that they were the first and only generation

Top: *A Jemadar of Thugs* (left) and *A Noted Thug Leader* (right) by Charles Wade Crump, *c.* 1850.
Above: *The Emporium of Taylor & Co. in Calcutta* by Sir Charles D'Oyly, *c.* 1825–8.

of the British in southern Asia who had both the capacity and sympathetic enthusiasm to understand the culture in which they had planted themselves. When, referring to Macaulay and Trevelyan, Wilson spoke of 'individuals of undoubted talent but of undeniable inexperience … who set themselves up to undo all that was effected by men at least their equals in ability and their betters in experience and who can never be surpassed in an ardent desire to accelerate the moral and religious amelioration of the natives of India' he was not far off the mark.

What struck the orientalists as particularly naïve – or hypocritical – was the argument that through English the millions presently divided by many languages and dialects, religions and castes would be brought together, both with each other and with their rulers. In fact, they prophesied all too accurately that the adoption of English as an official lingua franca would guarantee that the language of government was the language of a ruling caste, whether British or Westernized Indian; a code that would alienate the mass of the people from their rulers, just as had been the case with Mughal court Persian. Instead of turning their backs on the past, as the British kept on promising, they were recycling it with a different accent. Charles Trevelyan actually recruited Indian graduates of the English College at Delhi as interpreters and personal assistants to English agents sent on embassies to neighbouring states. The progress of their conversion into Westernized Indians was monitored by the assiduousness and punctiliousness with which they kept journals of their missions. Before long some of them, like Shahamat Lal, who went with Major Claude Wade to the Punjab in 1837, and then on the catastrophic military expedition to Kabul in 1839, were heard complaining about native 'superstitions' and 'despotisms' in a voice of disgusted ridicule that perfectly echoed that of their colonial masters.

Selective promotion was not, of course, the same as genuine cultural cohabitation. The rhetoric was about engagement; but the reality was separation. The sahibs and memsahibs of the Victorian 1840s and 1850s – the heirs of the Company Raj of Trevelyan and Bentinck – looked back on their orientalist predecessors, depicted in late-18th-century paintings lounging on divans or smoking hookahs, with undisguised distaste. Their closeness to Indian habits, they thought, had made them soft, corrupt, effeminate – there were few worse words in the moral vocabulary of the early Victorians. They had clad themselves in flimsy muslins and gaudy turbans; gone to their cockfights and horse-races; soaked themselves in oriental liquor; ogled the nautch dancers; prowled the brothels. Some of them had even kept Indian mistresses and fathered mixed-race children. Occasional eccentrics had even been known to marry them! But if the British were to be serious about their imperial vocation, all that had to be a thing of the past. Was India not built on hierarchies? Well, then, aloofness was the precondition of authority. It was an issue of moral, as much as physical, sanitation. Of all the diseases that had to be kept at bay, the delusion of 'mixing' was the most serious.

Some concessions, to be sure, had to be made to climate and circumstances. Small children must be entrusted to Indian servants and even wet nurses, with the likelihood that they might, unless vigilantly monitored, be infected with the notorious softness and languor of vaporous Bengal. In its *Child's Wreath of Hymns* the *Calcutta Review* warned that 'a child brought up in this country [presents] a fair prospect of becoming in afterlife a lover of eating and of all other bodily indulgences … yes even little girls are entrusted to native men!' Then there was the food problem. Given that this was still before the age of steamships or the Suez Canal, which speeded up the sea passage from the home country, an amazing amount of British food – jams, potted meats and sauces – was to be found on European tables in India; but there was no avoiding bhindi or black dal, often referred to in the same oleaginous terms as the natives – 'slippery,' 'slimy' and the like.

This was the age when 'bungalow' and 'verandah' entered the English language, and houses were built for the burrah (senior) sahibs that maximized shade and ventilation with high ceilings and cool, dark basements. But except for their single-storey height, the bungalows of the 1840s were not remotely similar to the dwellings of even the wealthier merchants and local patricians of the north Indian towns. Indian houses, the *haveli* or *manzil*, had no lawns laid out like a green rug back and front with a grand carriage driveway to their door. Instead, their walls faced directly on to the street and were pierced by a single gateway. At each of the three other corners of the quadrangle enclosing an open courtyard were the only function-specific rooms – storehouse, kitchen and latrine. The remainder of the rooms were simply divided by gender – *zenana* for the female quarters (used also for the children); *mardana* for the men. Apart from the yard the great common space was a flat roof used for dovecotes, for the drying of clothes and spices, for entertaining friends and neighbours, who reached the roof through connecting passages, and for sleeping on hot nights.

This, to put it mildly, was not the way the white sahibs and memsahibs lived in their bungalows. Their roofs were often pitched; the houses solid pavilions with functionally divided spaces – receiving room, dining room, library or smoking room and bedrooms – all giving on to the verandah, which wrapped around the entire building. Vigilantly guarding access was the critical manservant – the *chokidar* watch-man – who decided who could be let into the grounds, which tradesmen might be permitted on to the verandah and which might penetrate the inner sanctum. There,

they would be greeted by much the same décor as in a country house back home –
if more obviously made of tropical materials like bamboo and teak, and with the
walls decorated with pig-sticking lances rather than ancestral portraits. Still, there
would be the deeply upholstered sofas and settees; big wooden wardrobes and side-
boards full of Wedgwood and Leeds Creamware; and heavy printed curtains – all of
it imported. The most conspicuous concession to India was the punkah fan with its
hanging cloth sails, pulled by the punkah wallah to and fro. Kitchens, with their
unavoidable smells, were isolated from the main house along with resident servants,
who were often spoken of as a comparably pungent but unavoidable nuisance.

An enormous amount of labour went into the creation and cultivation of the
feature that most spoke of as the stamp made by the white sahibs on their conquest:
their gardens. The British took pride in integrating tropical species – like the prickly
aloe, which often served as a daunting hedge – into the design of their bungalow
gardens, but laid them out as if they were in Hampshire, with lawns back and front,
ornamental fishponds, herbaceous borders, pergolas and, of course, roses. When little
Harriet Earle (later the wife of Captain Robert Tytler of the 38th Bengal Native
Infantry) was taken to Barrackpore House, the country residence of the Governor-
General 16 miles from Calcutta, she marvelled at its gardens. The military cantonment
– always set at a distance now from the pullulating heap of the old Indian towns –
was famous for its setting of green freshness. Comparisons were invariably made
with the home counties. The crowning moment of imperial possession ought to
have been the presentation to Governor-General Auckland of the first two strawberries to be successfully grown in Barrackpore gardens, had not Harriet been so
overwhelmed by temptation that she stole them and popped the delicacies into her
greedy little mouth. Just 20 years later, in March 1857, hardly a stone's throw from
the strawberry beds, a very different event would take place on the Barrackpore
parade grounds. A sepoy of the 34th Native Infantry called Mangal Pande, dressed in
regimental jacket above the waist and only his dhoti below, would take a pot-shot at
his British adjutant and his sergeant-major before trying to blow his own head off.
Pande was hanged, and when the rest of the regiment were disbanded as a precaution, they took their caps off and trampled them in the dust.

There had, in fact, been trouble at Barrackpore before, when a mutiny broke
out in 1824. But by the time Macaulay went home in 1838, together with his
brother-in-law Trevelyan, his assumption was that the British position in India was
invincible. After just four years in Calcutta, Macaulay fancied himself an authority
on India, past and present, and quickly burst into print with reflections on the 18th-
century careers of Robert Clive and Warren Hastings. The essays were studded with

Above: Barrackpore House, Calcutta, *c.* 1830.
Opposite: *Emily Eden* by Simon Jacques Rochard, 1835.

predictable stereotypes about the constitutional softness and languor of the 'Bengalees,' living as they did 'in a constant vapor bath'. Presumably Macaulay was not thinking of the languor of the bearers who had carried him on their shoulders in palanquins, or the bargemen who poled cargoes down the river Hooghly, or the peasants who bent themselves double in the indigo fields. But all of them, he thought, more than any people who had ever existed, were 'thoroughly fitted by nature and habit for a foreign yoke'.

Trevelyan, whose experience, linguistic erudition and discernment were several notches above those of his brother-in-law, and who was temperamentally a lot more pessimistic, settled into his next job in London as assistant secretary at the treasury (where he remained for 19 years), thinking much darker thoughts about the fate of the empire. While Macaulay had been all for the introduction of a free press, as an indispensable instrument in the diffusion of 'useful knowledge,' Trevelyan and many others had noticed how quickly the Indian vernacular press in particular had been used to voice grievances rather than expressions of gratitude. 'We are, I fear,' he wrote, 'notwithstanding all our efforts for the good of the people an unpopular domination.'

There was, after all, much to complain about. It was precisely during the years when the Westernizers were bragging about the benefits brought by Britain to India that the Indian economy had become deeply depressed. Once the East India Company lost its monopoly of the indigo trade the major houses supplying it crashed, devastating precisely the most modern sectors of the economy that were supposed to blossom in the liberal dream. Exports – except opium – dwindled, while imports from Britain poured in. Traditional craft industries like Indian printed silks and cottons – the staple that had brought the British to India in the first place – were now all but destroyed by the astonishingly quick and complete penetration of the Indian market by Lancashire-manufactured textiles. Despite the occasional efforts of British entrepreneurs, like Thomas Wardle, who tried to invigorate Indian produc-tion, towns like Allahabad, Surat and Dacca, which had owed their fortunes to the Indian textile industry, stagnated or worse. Entire local infrastructures, based on the thriving 'little courts' of local, semi-independent nawabs which had driven the pros-perity of late Mughal India, collapsed when those states were liquidated by the British policy of 'lapse' – annexation into the Company territories when there were no direct male heirs. The modernizing 'political economists' of the West saw this as the inevitable, and healthy, replacement of anachronisms by the modern reality of the international market. But there was, in fact, nothing inevitable about it. Even if they were not industrially mechanized, local industries and trade had boomed for gener-ations as part of the new, not the old, India. Multitudes of weavers, dyers, printers, jewellers, silversmiths, tailors, furniture makers, cooks, musicians, palace guards, courtesans and shopkeepers were left without patrons; many of them were thrown back into an already stressed countryside.

British visitors in the late 1830s and 1840s who arrived in the port cities of Bombay, Madras or Calcutta, which were better able to insulate themselves from this rolling economic demolition job, seldom saw the true extent of the damage. Until, that is, they took a trip up country. In late 1837 and early 1838, as Macaulay and the Trevelyans were getting ready to go home, largely satisfied that they had done their best by India, Emily Eden from Beckenham, Kent, along with her brother George, now Lord Auckland, Bentinck's successor as Governor-General, embarked on a long journey northwest to the Sikh court of Ranjit Singh. On the Hooghly they travelled in what Emily called 'a simple way': the governor's barge *Sonamukhi* (Golden Face), painted gold, green and white, complete with marble baths, was rowed along the river and followed by a fleet of boats carrying the 400 servants needed to wait on Auckland and his entourage. On land progress was even more stately, by carriage, buggy, tonga, hackery (bullock cart), palkie (native-borne palanquin litter), horse and elephant slowly up the Ganges valley. Stretching behind was a procession of 850 camels, 140 elephants, hundreds more horses, bullocks and wagons, extending a full 10 miles to the rear. Occasionally George – not much of a sportsman, if the truth be told – would take a shot at hare and quail from his lurching howdah, because that was what governors-general were supposed to do. Emily, a gifted artist patronized by Queen Victoria, would sketch and paint and write entries in her journal, which oscillated between trembly exhilaration at the jangling, dazzling, peacock brilliance of India and exhausted nausea at the assault on her senses (a literary motif that would get repeated all the way to E. M. Forster and Paul Scott). On Christmas Day 1837, when she evidently missed the hoarfrost and the plum pudding, Emily wrote to her sister that she was 'particularly *Indianly* low to-day. There is such a horrid mixture of sights and sounds for Christmas. The servants have hung garlands at the doors of our tents, and (which is very wrong) my soul recoiled when they all assembled, and in their patois wished us, I suppose, a happy Christmas. Somehow a detestation of the Hindustani language sounding all round us, came over me in a very inexplicable manner.'

Compassion jostled for attention with disgust. Moving further east through Awadh (Oudh), towards Kanpur (Cawnpore), Emily couldn't help but be exposed to the overwhelming reality of a raging famine. In the camp stables she found a desperately famished baby 'something like an old monkey, but with glazed, stupid eyes, under the care of another little wretch of six years old'. She took the infant under her wing, and, with his mother's consent, fed him milk every day in her tent as if he were a pet. But the horror of the famine, born of a failed monsoon, closed relentlessly in on the huge caravan, together with the hordes of beggars and walking scarecrows who descended on it as it lumbered through the drought-stricken countryside: 'You cannot conceive the horrible sights we see, particularly children; perfect skeletons in many cases, their bones through their skin; without a rag of clothing, and utterly unlike human creatures.' Auckland fed a few hundred every day, but the outriders and local magistrates brought reports of three or five villagers dropping dead daily of starvation. 'We can do no more than give what we do . . . ,' Emily wrote, 'and the sight is much too shocking. The women look as though they had been buried, their *skulls* look so dreadful.' She was a long way from the lawns and flower borders at Barrackpore, 'so fresh and green,' which she herself had re-landscaped and which would be renamed Eden Gardens.

Emily's distress at the spectacle of famine was genuinely heartfelt, but relative. When her pet flying squirrel died after eating a cholera-infected pear in August 1839 Emily became really upset. But then, as she confessed, 'my own belief is that as *people in India* are uncommonly dull, the surplus share of sense is "served out" to the beasts, who are therefore uncommonly clever.' The Westernizers of the 1840s had a mixed reaction to the shocking spectacle of mass starvation in India. The gung-ho improvers like James Thomason in the Punjab, or the new Governor-General Lord Dalhousie, who succeeded Auckland in 1842 after the catastrophic Afghan war in which just one army surgeon from a force of 4000 survived a winter retreat over the Hindu Kush, were strengthened in their belief that the gifts of the West, like new roads, railways and irrigation canals, were the long-term answer. A great Ganges canal was built, expressly to avoid a repetition of the famine of 1837–8. But there were other voices for whom famines were the inevitable, if regrettable, pangs of a difficult transition to the modern world economy. In a country of too many mouths to feed, with plots of land that were too small to be viable producers for the cash market, there were bound to be some casualties of the process of rationalization. In due course their labour would be absorbed by a booming urban sector, just as had happened in industrial Britain. But nothing of this magnitude happened without suffering. What was more, the obstacles to modernization were as much social and cultural as structural. Peasants were accustomed to an easy-going, unambitious seasonal round in which long periods of sloth were punctuated by frantic activity. If they were to be profitable producers they had to be made self-reliant, persevering and, above all, regular in their labour. A cursory glance at an ant-hill would give them the idea.

This, at any rate, was what Charles Trevelyan believed, not just about India but also about Ireland, where the most horrifying of all modern western European famines occurred between 1846 and 1850. During those years Ireland lost a quarter of its population: 1 million died of starvation or famine-related diseases, and another million turned to emigration as their only chance of survival. In the worst-hit regions of the west, like County Mayo, nearly 30 per cent of the population perished. It was Charles Trevelyan at the treasury who had been responsible for direction of relief operations, but who believed, without malice yet without senti-mentality, that the ordeal had been inflicted by Providence to bring Ireland through pain to a better way of life. His bleak conclusion was that it had all been 'the judge-ment of God on an indolent and unself-reliant people, and as God had sent the calamity to teach the Irish a lesson, that calamity must not be too much mitigated: the selfish and indolent must learn their lesson so that a new and improved state of affairs must arise'. *The Times* was even more brutal in its insistence that the famine had been a blessing in disguise. Where no human hand or wit had been capable of getting Ireland out of cycles of poverty and dependence, all knowing Providence had supplied a 'check of nature'. 'Society,' the newspaper announced like a Greek oracle, 'is reconstructed in disaster.'

Although, on the face of it, the cases of India and Ireland seem separated by more than oceans, there is no doubt that they were closely connected in much of the most serious Victorian thinking and writing about the intractable problems of over-population and under-production. Thomas Malthus, of course, had taught at Haileybury, the East India Company college, and Charles Trevelyan had been his star pupil, steeled for life by Malthusian doctrine against the spectacle of famine in either India or Ireland. One of Malthus's disciples, William Thomas Thornton, published his *Over-Population and its Remedies* in 1846, exactly at the moment when the enormity of the Irish disaster was becoming plain, and his proposals for thinning the density of cultivators, partly by voluntary birth control, partly by emigration, had a direct impact on contemporary debates. Anti- or non-Malthusian liberals who directed their fire at British governments for tolerating the practices of absentee landlords, determined to extract the last penny in rent from the maximum number of peasant plots, also made a habit of talking about India and Ireland in the same breath. The philosopher John Stuart Mill, in one of the series of articles he wrote on the Irish land problem between 1846 and 1848, insisted that 'those Englishmen who know something of India are even now those who understand Ireland best.' George Campbell, a district commissioner for provinces in central India, wrote the book on Ireland that, more than any other single source, moved William Gladstone to grasp the nettle of land reform in the 1870s. Reports of poverty and insecurity in County Mayo or County Cork, Campbell wrote, 'might be taken, word for word, as the report of an administrator of an Indian province.'

The difference, Mill thought (with the benefit of his own relative ignorance about the subcontinent), was that those who decreed benevolent reform for India did not have to worry about politics, nor were they inheriting iniquities from the conquests and land settlements of centuries before. A benign, educated administrator, he thought, could decree 'Improvement' for the cultivators of Bihar or Gujarat and it would happen. Indeed, under Dalhousie, Mill thought it was indeed happening, in the shape of the Ganges canal.

It was certainly true that those charged with managing the nightmare of the Irish potato famine – from the two prime ministers, Sir Robert Peel and Lord John Russell, to their presidents of the board of trade and chancellors of the exchequer, and treasury officials like Trevelyan – all had to think hard about the political implications of any move they made. But it was also true that most of the politicians and civil servants were in the grip of a set of moral convictions that allowed them to think that whatever they did would always somehow be over-ridden by the inscrutable will of the great Political Economist in the sky. God willed it, apparently, that, as *The Times* put it, the 'Celts' stop being 'potatophagi.' God willed it that the feckless absentee landlords take responsibility for the evil system they had perpetuated. God willed it that there should be a great exodus and that vast tracts of western Ireland should become depopulated. Or was it heresy to think that these things had been made, or made worse, by the hand of man? One of those heretics was the Tory prime minister Sir Robert Peel, who had to deal with the first phase of the calamity. In February 1846, in a speech to the Commons, trying to persuade them to abandon the Corn Laws that prevented the free import of, among other grains, American corn, Peel concluded by advising the members:

> When you are again exhorting a suffering people to fortitude under their privations, when you are telling them, 'these are the chastenings of an all-wise and merciful Providence, sent for some inscrutable but just and beneficient purpose,' when you are thus addressing your suffering fellow-subjects. May God grant that by your decision of this night, you have laid in store for yourselves the consolation of reflecting that such calamities are, *in truth* [my emphasis], the dispensations of Providence – that they have not been caused, they have not been aggravated by laws of man, restricting in the hour of scarcity the supply of food!

What, then, if anything, could have been done to make the misery less brutal? Could, for example, the scale of the disaster have been predicted? During the second half of the 19th century a whole school of writers published what they took to be famine predictors for another part of the empire that suffered famines – India: a combination of meteorological cycles (still imperfectly understood); price indices as early warnings of shortages; and assessments of depleted grain reserves. And with a great deal of experience behind them, they still got it wrong. So even though there had been failed potato crops in the 1820s and 1830s, nothing in those earlier crises could possibly have prepared governments, central or local, for what was about to happen in 1845. The fungus *Phytophthoera infestans* had attacked American crops, which gave it its grim nickname of 'the American potato cholera.' The disease that appeared first on the underside of the leaves and ended by turning the potatoes to blackish-purplish slimy mush had indeed never been seen in Europe before. Even when it arrived (in Belgium and the Netherlands, as well as Ireland) it was thought – not least by many of the botanical experts called on to pronounce on the blight – to be the symptom, rather than the cause, of the rotted crop; the result of a spell of unusually cold, heavy rain. With only a quarter of the 1845 crop lost, officials in Dublin, anxious not to be alarmist, were calling the shortfall 'a deficiency.' The optimistic assumption was that, with better weather (and there was a long, warm, dry period in the summer of 1846), there would be a return to relatively normal harvests. Misunderstanding of how the blight was transmitted was then compounded by poor advice. In the face of anxiety that there should be enough seed potatoes for the following year, peasant farmers were told (or at least not discouraged from doing so) merely to cut away rotten sections of the tubers and store what was left for planting the following spring. The microscopic spores over-wintered, and when the infected tubers were planted a second season of ruin was guaranteed.

The problem, of course, was that even in good years a very high proportion of the Irish population was living on a razor's edge between survival and starvation. That population had trebled between the middle of the 18th century and 1845, rising from 2.6 million to 8.5 million. Two-thirds lived off the land, the vast majority on holdings too small to count as even modest 'farms.' Ireland had traditionally been a grazing economy and the better-off regions in the north and east still produced and exported dairy goods to Britain. But rising demand from industrializing Britain had turned Ireland into an exporter of grain, especially oats and barley. Farmers who had the capital and the unencumbered land rose to the opportunity. But in the centre and west of the country, where the population rise had been steepest, landlords (often absentee) exploited the imbalance between population and available

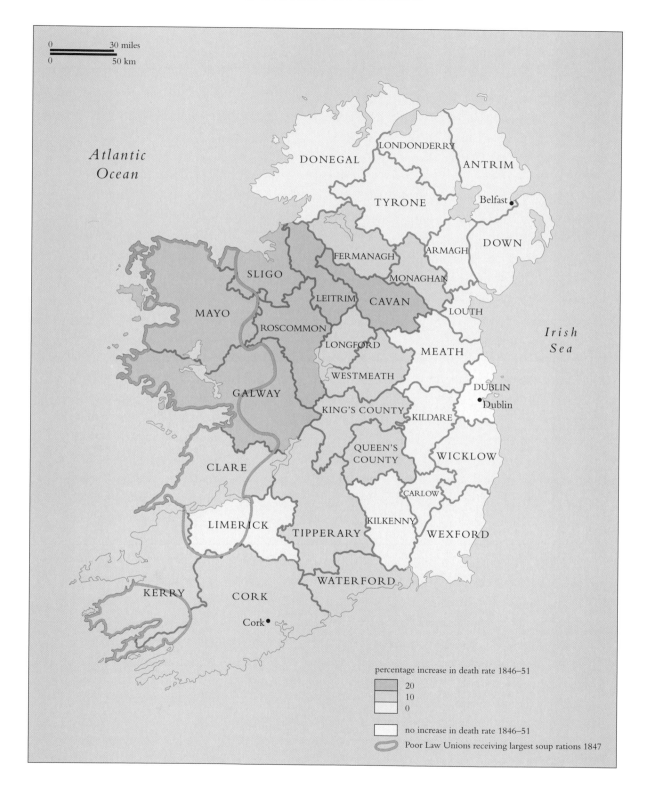

0   30 miles
0   50 km

*Atlantic
Ocean*

*Irish
Sea*

LONDONDERRY

DONEGAL   ANTRIM

TYRONE   Belfast•

DOWN

FERMANAGH   ARMAGH

SLIGO   MONAGHAN

LEITRIM   CAVAN

MAYO   LOUTH

ROSCOMMON

LONGFORD   MEATH

WESTMEATH

GALWAY   DUBLIN

KING'S COUNTY   •Dublin

KILDARE

QUEEN'S
COUNTY   WICKLOW

CLARE

CARLOW

LIMERICK   KILKENNY

TIPPERARY   WEXFORD

KERRY   CORK   WATERFORD

Cork•

percentage increase in death rate 1846–51

20
10
0

no increase in death rate 1846–51

Poor Law Unions receiving largest soup rations 1847

Above: *Sir Robert Peel, 2nd Baronet* by John Linnell, 1838.
Opposite: The Great Famine in Ireland, 1845–9.

land to raise rents and lower wages. By the 1840s, the process of shrinking income and plot size had created a huge semi-pauperized population. There were 135,000 plots of less than an acre; 770,000 of less than 10 acres. The only sure thing was that the crop that promised the best yield from the wet, heavy ground, was potatoes: 10–12 pounds of them were being eaten every day by each Irish man and woman. But that was the beginning and the end of their diet, which if they were lucky was augmented by a little milk for protein, or by fish or kelp if they lived close to the shore.

There were some in Peel's government who, even at the end of 1845, thought they were seeing something like a plague of Egypt at hand. Sir James Graham, the first lord of the admiralty, wrote to the prime minister in October, 'It is awful to observe how the Almighty humbles the pride of nations ... the canker worm and the locust are his armies; he gives the word: a single crop is blighted; and we see a nation prostrate, stretching out its hands for bread.' By December the price of potatoes and other foodstuffs had doubled and Peel, who had been returned to office in 1841 committed to retain the Corn Laws (but who had had a change of heart), now felt that he could not wait to use the Irish crisis to persuade parliament – and especially his own party – to repeal them. Secretly he bought £100,000 worth of American corn and had it ground and distributed at cost to special depots, run by local committees throughout Ireland. His hope was to use the reserve at best to stabilize prices, at worst for immediate relief. As a social by-product, perhaps the experience of cornmeal mush (initially greeted with horrified suspicion by much of the population as 'Peel's brimstone') would also wean the Irish from their addiction to potatoes.

By August 1846, with a second blighted crop, it was glaringly obvious that Ireland was already in the grip of a famine. The Reverend Theobald Mathew, who wrote to Trevelyan imploring more direct free aid, saw the misery with his own eyes: 'On the 27th of last month I passed from Cork to Dublin and this doomed plant bloomed in all the luxuriance of an abundant harvest. Returning on the 3rd instant I beheld with sorrow one wide waste of putrifying vegetation. In many places the wretched people were seated on the fences of their decaying gardens wringing their hands and wailing bitterly [at] the destruction which had left them foodless.'

Against the wishes of his party, but with strong Whig support, Peel had suc-ceeded in pushing through the repeal of the Corn Laws in June 1846, resigning a few days later. Yet the new Whig government, led by Lord John Russell, looked at the multiplying misery dry-eyed. For some years Russell had, in fact, been one of the most severe critics of the ruthlessly exploitative habits of Irish landlords. But that was precisely why he was loath to use state aid from London to bale them out of responsibility for the consequences of their selfishness and greed. If the Almighty was laying a scourge across their back (for the assumption was that Irish property owners would not let their own people starve), who was he to stay His hand? This was the way in which not only Russell but also Sir Charles Wood, his chancellor of the exchequer, thought and spoke. And it was music to the ears of Charles Trevelyan, who all along had suspected Peel of being soft; and had objected, whenever and however he could, to any interference with the 'natural' and commercial operation of the grain market. It was not for the government, Trevelyan believed, to step in and buy up corn. If the price were right – and surely it was – private business would naturally send it to the markets where it was most needed. Manipulating those markets out of a misplaced sense of benevolence was a presumptuous meddling with God's natural economic order. Stopping the *export* of oats, for example, was unthinkable. When the head of the relief commission, Randolph Routh, wrote to Trevelyan, 'I know there is a great and serious objection to any interference with these exports, yet it is a most serious evil,' Trevelyan replied, 'We beg of you not to countenance in any way the idea of prohibiting the exportation. The discouragement and feeling of insecurity to the trade from such a proceeding would prevent its doing even any immediate good. . . . indirect permanent advantages will accrue to Ireland from the scarcity . . . the greatest improvement of all which could take place in Ireland would be to teach the people to depend on themselves for developing the resources of their country.'

Pending this miracle, people were becoming desperate. Russell's response was to continue Peel's programme of outdoor relief, but to make public-works projects a test of character. Pay (averaging ninepence a day) was to be pegged to labour, and the labour was deliberately made so back-breaking that it would not attract shirkers, since, as Harry David Jones, the chairman of the board of public works, reported to Trevelyan, 'I believe everyone considers the government fair game to pluck as much as they can.' There would have to be a lot of digging and breaking of rocks and backs before the pittance would be handed over. On the High Burren in County Clare a brass ring was used to judge whether the rocks had been broken into pieces small enough to warrant the payment of threepence an hour. Never mind that these roads seemed not to go anywhere. 'The labourers work for their wages,' Captain Henry O'Brien wrote from County Clare, 'but seeing clearly that what they are doing is of no clear value, their heart, they say, is not in it.'

Brutally penal as these work gangs were, for the desperate they were the only alternative to starvation. To the dismay of the government in London, the Irish relief authorities felt they could no longer turn away the hordes of women and children

Above: Rocks along the coast of Connemara mark the graves of infants who died during the Great Famine, 1845–9.
Opposite: Lord John Russell, *c.* 1848.

pleading for the work. By December 1846, in an exceptionally harsh winter, 441,000 of them were employed; by the following March, 714,000. In the worst-affected western counties, like Clare, more than 20 per cent of the entire population was being kept alive – though barely – by hard labour. Whether its harshness killed some of them seemed to the book-keepers of calamity just a statistical footnote.

By this time, some of the more ghoulish spectacles were being graphically reported in the English press. The dying and the dead of the Skibbereen workhouse, where, between October 1846 and January 1847, 266 of the inmates perished, became known to all Victorian newspaper readers along with their post mortems. Vegetable refuse and grass were being consumed to stave off starvation. In January, the Dublin paper *The Nation* reprinted a post mortem from the *Mayo Constitution* recording that 'Bridget Joyce and four children died in a small sheep house in a small field at Gleneadagh … it appeared in evidence that the deceased and her family were in the utmost state of destitution and one of the children had nothing to wet the lips of its dying parent but a drop of water and a little snow. The body lay for eight days before a few boards could be procured to make a coffin, in such a state of destitution was the locality. Verdict – death from starvation.'

Small girls were selling their hair to stay alive. Mothers in Donegal walked miles to sell a little wool to be able to buy some meal to feed their family, although women with meal were a prime target for the desperate. Charlock – wild cabbage – became almost a staple, with families flocking to the wet fields where it grew to rip the young leaves out and boil them at home. It wasn't enough. Communal burial pits were filling up; some families concealed deaths so they could continue to receive relief. So many village priests were dying that newborns were often unable to be baptized before they too perished and so were denied a consecrated burial ground. Mothers were seen carrying dead children on their backs to a remote burial site. In Connemara, on the Atlantic shore, it seems to have been the fathers' task to take their dead babies to the edge of the ocean, to the ancient limbo-spaces of water, land and sky, and to dig little graves, marked by a rough stone cut from the cliffs. Circles of 30 and 40 of the wind-scoured, lichen-flecked stones, their jagged grey edges pointing this way and that, stand by the roaring surf, the saddest little mausoleum in all Irish history.

Worried by public reaction, though still convinced it was all a blessing in disguise, Trevelyan cranked up the mighty engine of Victorian philanthropy. A British Association for the Relief of Extreme Distress in Ireland and Scotland (for there was also a serious potato blight in the Highlands) was established in January 1847, with the queen donating the first £1000; when invited to do better by its founder, the courageous Stephen Spring-Rice, she doubled her contribution. Albert gave £500; the great and the good – Barings and Rothschilds, the Bishop of London, the Earl of Dalhousie, Benjamin Disraeli, William Gladstone and even the Ottoman Sultan – chipped in to increase the fund to £470,000 (about £20 million in today's money). Trevelyan, Peel, Wood and Russell all gave generously. The fund helped supply the soup kitchens.

While the milk of Victorian charity was flowing the Whig government's attitude to what could be done to mitigate suffering was, if anything, hardening. The road and harbour works had been so overwhelmed by numbers that the original pretence to provide pay for specific work had all but collapsed, leaving Trevelyan and Sir Charles Wood deeply uneasy about what they were doing. The migration of huge numbers towards the works had also, they thought, depleted country towns of their population. A decision was taken to close the works down. In their place would be the philanthropically funded soup kitchens (where the Quakers had already, and, characteristically, taken the initiative), and the 130 workhouses established by the Irish Poor Law of 1838. There was no reason to suppose, of course, that when the choice was between the penal regime of the workhouses (even with its uniforms, separation of families and prison diet) and starvation, they would not be as overwhelmed by sheer numbers as the relief works. So the Tory MP for Dublin, William Gregory, passed an amendment to the act that restricted workhouse relief to peasants with a quarter of an acre or less. The practical consequences of the Gregory clause ushered in a completely new, and monstrously inhumane, phase of the tragedy. The vast majority of even the poorest peasants had needed more than a quarter of an acre if they were to house their family in just the most primitive stone cabin and supply them with a subsistence diet. Now, with no potatoes and no money, they were faced with the choice of surrendering their acre or two to the landlord to be eligible for workhouse relief, or staying put, starving and probably facing forcible 'ejectment' for failure to pay rent. It was no choice at all.

This was precisely the 'social revolution' that Trevelyan was looking for: the voluntary migration of the poorest smallholders to the ports or the workhouses; or their eviction. In either case it opened the way for the consolidation of a multitude of economically unviable plots into tenant farms that had, as far as he was concerned, a solid economic future. It would hurt, but it would be the birth-pangs of an Irish yeomanry.

In some peculiar way Charles Trevelyan – and the majority of the government such as Wood and Russell, who thought just like him – believed that this huge social upheaval represented some sort of lesson for everyone concerned. The selfish

The Ejectment, engraving from the *Illustrated London News*, 1848.

landlords who had thought that the British treasury would bail them out from years of neglect and exploitation were now told that *they* were going to bear the cost of funding workhouse relief from their own local rates. This was supposed to make them 'self-reliant,' just as a spell in the workhouse, a passage in steerage to New Zealand or a job as a landless labourer working for the new 'yeomanry' was supposed to wean the peasants from illicitly brewed poteen and potatoes. What actually happened, of course, was an almost animal struggle to survive, with the weakest going to the wall quickest. The landlords screamed at the government, to no avail. If they were going to have to bear the cost of the workhouses (they had 100,000 occupants by the end of 1847), they would also make sure that those who had left their plots to go there would not come back. Cabins were broken down; roofs smashed in. Their pathetic ruins still stud the low hills in Clare, Mayo and Galway. At Kilrush in County Clare in 1849, 1200 people, many of them suffering from cholera, saw their dwellings demolished in a fortnight. At Erris in County Mayo the Quaker activist James Hack Tuke saw police, reinforced by soldiers, throw sticks of furniture and kitchen pots out from people's homes:

The tenants make resistance – for these hovels have been built by themselves or their forefathers who have resided in them for generations past – seem inclined to dispute with the bayonets of the police for they know truly that when their hovels are demolished the nearest ditch must be their dwelling and thus exposed, death could not fail to be the lot of some of their wives and little ones. . . . Six or seven hundred persons were here evicted, young and old, mother and babe were alike cast forth without the means of subsistence! A favoured few were allowed to remain on condition they would voluntarily depart. . . . At a dinner party that evening, the landlord, as I was told by one of the party, boasted that this was the first time he had seen the estate or visited the tenants.

The most determined survivors built 'scalpeen' (from the Gaelic *scailp*, for shelter) huts from the smashed ruins of their cottages and squatted there in the debris.

For those who resigned themselves to losing their land, the workhouse, which most Irish had looked on with repugnance, was no sure salvation. However destitute and famished they might seem, should it be proved that the 'breadwinner' was earning even ninepence a day (nowhere near enough to feed a family) mother and children might be refused admission. That might have been a mercy since the workhouses, filled to bursting, were breeding grounds for deadly cholera, typhus and tuberculosis. It was also at workhouses that food – usually soup or 'stirabout' – was supplied as 'outdoor relief.' But those who received it had to travel so far, often in poor health, that they more often got American cornmeal – until, that is, the corn ran out.

There was a point when disaster succeeded disaster so relentlessly that the English and Scots began to get sick of hearing about it. By 1848, and certainly 1849, 'compassion fatigue' had begun to set in. Although the Irish were themselves bearing the great burden of caring for their own destitute and starving, the English press was full of complaints about having to pay for the hopelessness of the Paddies, who were often depicted as semi-simian, wily, incorrigible wastrels – and dangerously revolutionary, seeking money for arms rather than food. A typical cartoon in *Punch* in December 1846 had an Irishman asking an unamused John Bull 'to spare a trifle, yer Honourr, for a poor Irish lad to buy a bit of ... blunderbuss with.'

One last way out of despair remained: emigration. Between 1845 and 1851 nearly a million and a half took it. In 1846 more than 100,000, especially from the western and southwestern counties, departed; in 1847, 200,000; and in 1851, even after the famine had subsided, a quarter of a million departed Ireland for good. At least 300,000 went to Britain itself, congregating either in port cities like Liverpool or in the industrial centres like Birmingham and Manchester where they were most likely to find work, and it seems, from the 1851 census, that many of them – over a third – found work in England as skilled and professional workers. Some landlords, such as Major Denis Mahon of Strokestown in County Roscommon, saw emigration as the solution to the point of laying out £4000 to enable 1000 of his tenants to sail to Canada. Their journey, in steerage, was no holiday cruise, and the vessels were not called 'coffin ships' for nothing: a quarter of Mahon's emigrants died of disease before landing; Mahon was eventually murdered by one of his own tenants in 1847. Aubrey de Vere, the young Irish poet and nephew of Lord Monteagle, one of the government-appointed heads of the Relief Commission, travelled to Canada in steerage so that he could offer direct witness of the privations endured by the Irish emigrants. Sanitation was almost completely absent, he reported; water and beds foul; food 'ill-selected and seldom sufficiently cooked ... the supply of water hardly enough for cooking does not allow washing. In many ships the filthy beds, teeming with all abominations are never required to be brought on deck and aired.' Worse still (at least for the incognito, pious Protestant Irish aristocrat), there were no prayers – nor, since the captain himself made money from selling grog, was there any attempt to restrain drunkenness or 'ruffianly debasement.' Once at their destination, the long quarantine period at stations like Grosse Isle in the St Lawrence, downriver from Quebec, guaranteed precisely what it was supposed to prevent: another wave of mass deaths among the passengers.

Those who survived all these rigours did not, of course, forget, whether they journeyed near or far. The lawyer and journalist John Mitchel, for example, had not been a voluntary emigrant. In May 1848, he had been sentenced to 14 years' transportation to Tasmania for publishing seditious views in his paper the *United Irishman*. Five years later he escaped and made his way to the United States, where he became the most militant and wrathful of the memorialists of the Great Hunger. The famine, he insisted, had been not a work of nature but a work of man – of Englishmen. There had been blight all over Europe (here he was exaggerating – thousands, rather than millions, had died in the Netherlands), but there had been famine only in Ireland: 'The Almighty indeed sent the potato blight, but the English created the famine. . . . A million and a half of men, women and children were carefully, prudently and peacefully slain by the English government. They died of hunger in the midst of abundance which their own hands created.' In Canada, Australia and New Zealand, but especially in the United States, the genuine tragedy of the famine became translated by mythic memory into an Irish Exodus, bitter with plagues, sorrows and uprootings. The fact that the reception of the Irish immigrants in Boston, New York or Poughkeepsie was anything but welcoming; that they continued to suffer alienation and exploitation at the hands of 'native' Yankee elites; and that they were invariably concentrated in the lowest-paid, most physically dangerous jobs only intensified the tightness of their ghetto world and the fierce tribal determination to take 'revenge for Skibbereen.'

One figure among the heedless, heartless English was demonized more than any other for causing untold, unnecessary misery: Charles Trevelyan. Mitchel set the tone by depicting him as the murderer, unwitting or not, of the Irish future: 'I saw Trevelyan's red claw in the vitals of those children … his red tape would draw them to death.' The damning judgement on Trevelyan has been repeated over the generations, most fiercely in Cecil Woodham-Smith's account *The Great Hunger* (1962), which came closest to accusing the English government of perpetrating, almost knowingly, genocide. That was certainly not the case. Neither Charles Trevelyan nor government members who shared his prejudices, his moralizing and his bleak conviction that Ireland would never make the transition to modernity without a heavy dose of social pain took any satisfaction from the agony of the famine. But it is also possible to overdo the aversion to strong emotion – to mistake actual tragedy for melodrama, to throw out all those dead babies (who were, after all, no sentimental fiction) along with the bathwater of nationalist demonology. It is possible, in Trevelyan's and the government's case, to be over-eager to acquit as well as over-eager to prosecute. For if Trevelyan did not actually want to kill and dispossess large numbers of the Irish, neither was he excessively distraught about their disappearance. If he can be acquitted of villainy, he can be convicted of obtuseness; when it combined absurd confidence in the will of God with an ingrained certainty that, short of trauma, the 'indolent' and 'unself-reliant' Irish would never help themselves, that obtuseness did, in fact, have lethal consequences.

And, after all, not everyone in England shared his hands-off attitude to intervention. Sir Robert Peel had been just as much a free trader but had been willing to set the dogma aside in the midst of crisis. His shipments of American corn unquestionably and measurably saved lives in 1846. By the time Trevelyan and Russell realized they needed additional imports, it was too late. Against Trevelyan's smug optimism that in the long run the experience would actually draw Ireland closer to England through reaping the 'natural' benefits of its social transformation, many others drew the opposite conclusion: that a wound had been opened that would ultimately bleed the union to death. A journalist wrote in *The Times* that, whatever happened, generations of Irish would remember that 'In their terrible distress, from that temporary calamity with which they were visited, they were to have no relief

Above and opposite: Interiors at the Foreign and Commonwealth Office, Westminster, London: the Durbar Court (above) and the state staircase (opposite).

unless they gave up their holdings. That law, too, laid down a form for evicting the people, and thus gave the sanction and encouragement of legislation to exterminate them. Calmly and quietly, but very ignorantly – though we cheerfully exonerate the parties from any malevolence; they [the government] … committed a great mistake, a terrible blunder, which in legislation is worse than a crime.'

Trevelyan, of course, was either oblivious to the odium or shrugged it off as inevitable resentment towards his unsentimental economic realism, much like a Victorian headmaster resigned to being remembered with mixed feelings by boys who had been birched in their own best interests. He was knighted for his sterling work in famine relief, and his reputation in England had never been higher. In the 1850s, while his brother-in-law Macaulay was beginning the epic history of England's parliamentary liberty, Charles Trevelyan, even though still only assistant permanent secretary to the treasury, became the personification of its destiny as an imperial government, the most powerful and authoritative of that empire's invisible hands. It was Trevelyan who, with Sir Stafford Northcote, headed a commission of inquiry into the Civil Service. Their report of 1854 opened the service for the first time to competitive examination, transforming British government (though not, of course, overnight) from a grazing ground of aristocratic patronage to a true meritocracy. The test of talent, not family connection or the influence of land and fortune, would produce the proconsuls that the best of empires needed.

And it was Charles Trevelyan who in the 1850s decided that this new, purified government needed to be housed in centralized but spacious new quarters. What he had in mind was not just bigger office space but a virtual city of government. To stave off the objections of pinch-penny chancellors of the exchequer, Trevelyan defended his visionary project on grounds of cost-efficiency: connecting adjacent departments would save on the hackney-cab fares needed to get from one to another. But his real motives were transparently imperial. In 1856 Trevelyan argued that:

> We have a very important national duty to perform … this city is something more than the mother of arts and eloquence; she is a mother of nations; we are peopling two continents … and we are organising, christianising and civilising large portions of two ancient continents, Africa and Asia; and it is not right when the inhabitants of those countries come to the metropolis they should see nothing worthy of its ancient renown. Now I conceive that a plan of the kind I have sketched … would give the honour due to the focus of our liberties, of that regulated freedom which we hope will overspread the world.

Under the rubric of the commission, the foreign secretary alone would have to have five reception rooms *en suite*, capable of taking 1500 visitors at a time; a state dining chamber for 50; plus tea rooms and a commodious library: nothing short, in fact, of a palace of imperial government.

The Crystal Palace had embodied the technological and commercial power of the empire, whilst Barry's and Pugin's Houses of Parliament (nearing completion), in their neo-Gothic grandiloquence, represented the continuity of the 'ancient constitution.' Now an imposing range of offices in Whitehall, deliberately sited close to the Palace of Westminster and with a new foreign office at their heart, would complete the trinity of industry, liberty and wise administration. In a brilliant public-relations move, designed to pre-empt accusations of profligacy, in May 1857 there was staged an exhibition of 218 competing architectural submissions; the 2000 drawings were displayed in, of all places, Westminster Hall, more usually the scene of royal audiences and lyings-in-state.

That same week, on 5 May, a member of the Civil Service in Delhi wrote to his correspondent in London: 'As usual, no news to give you. All quiet and dull. Certainly we are enjoying weather which at this season is wonderful. Morning and evening are deliciously cool. . . . In fact punkah wallahs are hardly come into use.' Six days later the mutilated bodies of the officers of the 54th Native Infantry were thrown into a bullock cart at the Kashmir Gate. Teachers at the local school had been killed in their schoolroom. The editor of the *Delhi Gazette*, along with his wife, mother and children, had died by his proofs, and the manager of the Delhi Bank, Mr Beresford, had been killed at the tills along with his family. The first Asian rebellion against the empire of the Europeans had begun.

6

On 9 May 1857, 85 Indian sepoys of the 3rd Light Cavalry, army of Bengal, were marched on to the parade ground at Meerut, northeast of Delhi, for military degradation. Their offence had been to refuse to drill with Lee-Enfield rifle cartridges that they believed to be greased with beef tallow, pig fat (taboo to Hindus and Muslims respectively) or both. Under a dark sky their uniforms were stripped from them, their boots removed and their ankles shackled. Clanking, they were led off under escort to the military prison to start a 10-year sentence for insubordination. A young cornet, John McNabb, thought the sentence excessively severe: 'It is much worse than death. They will never see their wives and families and one poor old man who has been forty years in the regiment and would have got his pension is now thrown back the *whole* of his service.'

The next day troopers from the 3rd as well as soldiers from the 11th and 20th Native Infantry broke open the gaol to free the prisoners. They set fire to their mud barrack huts, killed 50 of their British officers and civilians, including women, and cut the telegraph wires. By riding hard overnight the mutineers were in Delhi the following morning, 11 May, to declare the restoration of the Mughal Empire. This put the octogenarian 'King of Delhi' Bahadur Shah, the last of the imperial line, in a painful predicament. In all probability he would have much preferred to be left alone to write his elegant Persian court poetry, especially since he never harboured many illusions about the eventual outcome of the restoration. But cornered by the inflammatory force of the rising, and pressed by the devotion, half embarrassing, half touching, of its leaders, Bahadur Shah had no option but to lend his name to its authority. Proclamations were issued calling for the extirpation of the rule of the *feringhi*, the foreigner: 'It has become the bounden duty of all the people, whether women or men, slave girls or slaves to come forward and put the English to death … by firing guns, carbines and pistols … shooting arrows and pelting them with stones, bricks … and all other things which may come into their hands. . . . The

THE EMPIRE OF GOOD INTENTIONS: THE DIVIDEND

Sikh soldiers from Hodson's Horse regiment, photograph by Felice Beato, 1858–9.

sepoys, the nobles, the shopkeepers and all other people of the city, being of one accord, should make a simultaneous attack on them … some should wrestle and through stratagem break the enemy in pieces, some should strike them with cudgels, some slap them, some throw dust in their eyes. . . .'

Even before the rebel sepoys arrived in Delhi, Captain Robert Tytler of the 38th Bengal Native Infantry knew something bad was happening. At dawn on the 11th the order for the hanging of the first leader of the mutiny at Barrackpore was read out to the native troops as a way of making an exemplary point. The demonstration did not go down well. While the order was being read out in clipped military shouts, Robert heard the response coming from the ranks: a writhing snake of a mutter travelling down the rows of men. Fluent in Hindustani (Urdu), he knew exactly what it meant. Later he saw groups of men standing about in the sun and told them to move into the shade. It was, after all, 138°F. 'We like the sun,' they replied, not moving. 'Harriet,' he told his wife a little later, 'my men behaved infamously today. They hissed and they shuffled with their feet while I was reading out the order, showing by their actions their sympathy with the executed sepoy.' Not long afterwards, with her husband running round trying to secure magazines against the worst, popping in and out of the bungalow to make sure his wife was safe, Harriet, eight months pregnant with her third child, 'could see there was something very wrong. Servants running about in a wild way, guns [light field cannon] tearing down the main street as fast as the oxen could be made to go, and Mrs Hutchinson the Judge's wife, without a hat on her head and her hair flowing down loosely on her shoulders, with a child in her arms and the bearer carrying another, walking hastily in an opposite direction to the guns. What could it all mean?' Harriet's French maid, Marie, who must have been in Paris in 1848, knew exactly what it all meant: 'Madame, this is a *revolution*.' Women and children were told to gather at the flagstaff tower. And although Robert had ordered her not to move from their house she obeyed the new orders, saving her family from certain massacre. Inside the tower, sitting and standing on the stairwell were a quiet, frightened group of overdressed Victorian women, children and maidservants, sweating into their crinolines (for it was 100 degrees in the shade). Bad news started to pour in: a colonel of the 54th bayoneted by his own men at the Kashmir Gate, just a few hundred yards away. 'Mama, will these naughty sepoys kill my Papa,' asked her four-year-old boy Frank, 'and will they kill me too?' 'He was a very blue-eyed, fair child,' Harriet later wrote. 'I gazed at his little white throat and said to myself, "My poor child, that little throat will be cut ere long, without any power on my part to save you." It was a dreadful moment, but I pulled myself together and said, "No, darling, don't be frightened.

No one will harm you. Stay close to your mother."' She heard more bad news: the slaughter of many more officers; 40 women and children dragged from a hiding place and butchered; a huge explosion and white cloud drifting over Delhi when the powder magazine went up. Shouts of 'Prithiviraj ki jai' – 'Victory to the sovereign of the world' – could be heard all over the city.

Robert's familiarity with the language of his sepoys probably meant that there was enough sympathy between them for him to persuade some at least to cover his family's escape from Delhi towards the big military station at Umballa, almost 120 miles to the northwest. When he asked them to be honest with him, some of the men came and touched him on the forehead: a good sign. In dangerously bright moonlight they made their way, first by buggy together with another couple, the Gardners (the wife being also eight months pregnant), then, when the wheels came off, by foot. Harriet carried her two children as well as her own very heavy body along the roads and tracks. Looking back at the burning bungalows of the cantonment, Harriet recalled, 'was a sickening sight, knowing all that we valued was lost to us forever, things that no money could ever purchase – a beloved dead child's hair, manuscripts and paintings for a book my husband was going to publish some day; all my own paintings, books, clothes.' When they finally reached Umballa they lived in a bullock cart, watching out for the 9-inch black centipedes that would lodge a leg or two in one's own leg and, even when cut away, would cause blood poisoning. Blood was on everyone's mind. To distract her two-year-old daughter Edith, Harriet pricked holes in her own feet to make them bleed so that the child could 'play nursey' and stanch the bleeding with her handkerchief. When the wounds healed Harriet would open them again for the little girl's amusement. It was on the straw of the bullock cart that her baby boy was born. To commemorate their ordeal the Tytlers saddled him with the name of Stanley Delhi-Force and assumed, since he was a dysenteric infant, that he would not survive to be embarrassed about (or proud of) his middle name. Indeed, Harriet was pessimistic about their own chances of survival, and kept two large bottles of laudanum with her at all times to kill her children and herself if the worst came to the worst. But Stanley Delhi-Force did live. Better yet, he seemed to some of the loyal soldiers an omen. If a baby is born, they told her, it meant there would be reinforcements because he was the first of the troop. The next day reinforcements arrived at Umballa.

One of the first selected targets of the rebels at Delhi, as well as at Meerut, had been the brand-new electric telegraph. The cutting of the lines and the killing of the operators was an apt beginning for the revolt: it represented not just a shrewd tactic but, more emblematically, the rejection of the gifts of the West – its technology, its science, the whole package of its 'civilization' — that Macaulay and Trevelyan had been so sure would bind India and Britain together in close and mutually beneficial imperial connection. The rank 'ingratitude' of the natives — a word repeated often both in India and in Britain — seemed especially iniquitous given that the 1840s and 1850s had witnessed the bestowal of so many blessings on this 'inert' and backward country. Those decades had seen the first railway lines; the introduction of Western medicine; the arrival of the lithographic printing press, adapted for publications in vernacular languages; and an acceleration of the reforming impulse of what the brisk new style of governors-general, especially the young Marquis of Dalhousie, charac-terized as 'decadent' courts and governments, 'sunk in sloth and luxury,' as the standard phrase prefacing an annexation had it. The pretext for such annexations was the 'doctrine of lapse,' by which the absence of a male heir was deemed to end the ruling line. But for as long as anyone could remember, native rulers without male issue had been entitled — and expected — to adopt heirs to take care of the succession. Riding roughshod over that ancient principle seemed yet another violation of the understandings by which local rulers had submitted to British paramountcy in the first place. In Jhansi, a Rajput Marathan state in northeast Rajasthan, the 18-year-old Rani Lakshmi Bhai made a personal protest to Dalhousie when her husband the rajah died childless in 1853, but was contemptuously brushed aside. Four years later, during the uprising that followed the Mutiny, she became one of the most formida-ble of central India's horseback guerrilla leaders.

The alienated native rulers were not fools. They knew that the annexations were more often than not driven by British strategic and financial interests, rather than by any high-minded commitment to 'improved' government. The massive exer-cises in data-gathering, like the Great Trigonometric Survey of India, were intended in the first instance to supply military intelligence. The railways and trunk-road extensions would make not only the penetration of Indian markets but also the deployment of troops easier and faster.

Which is not to say that a new missionary push did not provoke trouble. Under the over-assertive Dalhousie, whose term of office lasted from 1848 to 1856, the new lithographic press was used more aggressively than ever before to publish missionary literature. The suspicion — exaggerated or not — that a new campaign of conversion was under way was not allayed by the British policy of taking Muslim and Hindu children orphaned in the famines of 1838 and bringing them up as Christians. (It was no accident that a civilian unlucky enough to be called Mr Christian would be one of the first to be shot in cold blood, along with his wife, by the rebels at Sitapur.) In December 1858, trying to rally the insurgents against the British, Hazrat Mahal, the Muslim Begum of Awadh (Oudh), listed all the reasons why the revolt had been, first and foremost, a holy war, an Islamic *jihad*. The British had, she said, not only defiled Hindu and Muslim sepoys by making them bite cartridges greased with cow and pig fat; they had also deliberately tried to make Indians lose caste by making them eat with Europeans as a requirement of a particular job. The British had arrogantly destroyed temples and mosques in the pretence that they needed to widen roads; had allowed clergymen to go into the streets, alleys and bazaars to preach Christianity; and had established English schools to take young Hindu and Muslim boys from the path of the faithful.

Proclamations were issued by the Delhi rajah, Feroze Shah, in 1858, justifying the rebellion by warning that the English were going to prohibit traditional physicians from participating at childbirths and to make the attendance of Western doctors compulsory; that no marriages would be legal unless at least witnessed by Christian clergy; and that Muslim and Hindu sacred books would be burned. This long list of outrages was, of course, a fantasy but the relatively new conspicuousness of missionaries and Christian literature, as well as the systematic derision of Ayurvedic medicine, was enough to give them credence. (To the Western campaign of small-pox vaccination, Hindu doctors responded quite rightly that *they* had popularized cowpox swabs among the poor of the villages before Dr Jenner had been born.)

Indian vernacular documents make the *jihadi* backlash quality of the revolt – part of a trans-regional mid-19th-century Islamic Wahabi (Muslim purist) messianic revival that stretched all the way from the western Sudan to northern India – unmistakable. As early as November 1856 the Maulvi (Muslim law teacher), Ahmadullah Shah, a Sufi itinerant preacher called the 'Dauka shah' or 'Maulvi with a drum' because a big drum preceded his palanquin, preached the *jihad* in Lucknow. As the holy man was carried through the streets accompanied by 1000 chanting disciples, some of whom swallowed burning coals, the message of a holy war was carried to a huge crowd. In Faizabad in February 1857, Ahmadullah – the epitome of a Wahabi messianic warrior – was so incendiary that he was arrested and imprisoned. When mutineers freed him on 8 June, his first act was to take a crowd of his armed disciples with him to Lucknow. And Ahmadullah was not alone. Liaqat Ali in Allahabad and Fazal Huq Khairabadi in Delhi were preaching much the same inflammatory message, and another self-proclaimed imam, Qadir Ali Shah, whose following was said to number as many as 11,000, was confident enough to fix a date for the uprising – the 10th and holiest day of the month of Muharram – which, in the Western calendar, was 11 September! The war 'began with religion,' the Begum of Awadh flatly stated – and she should have known – 'and for religion millions have

been killed.' Yet somehow the religious ferment that gripped the Muslim community in particular from the autumn of 1856 to the spring of 1857 seems to have been
completely discounted – or just misunderstood – by the British authorities, for
whom the cartridge-grease issue was the only source of concern.

It was not only religious sensibilities that had been alienated. When educated,
urbanized Indians looked at what were supposed to be the economic benefits of
the British modernizers, they saw things that seemed to be designed more for the
interests of the rulers than for those of the ruled. The beginnings of railway construction in India, for example, made it easier for grain to be *exported* (in years of
dearth as well as plenty) in order to stabilize grain prices in Britain. One of the
triumphs of British 'engineering' in India was the building of the 'Great Hedge,' a
staggering 1500-mile barrier of thorns and acacia designed to prevent Orissa salt
from being smuggled into Bengal to compete with imported salt from Cheshire; any
that did get through was subject to penal tariffs. As many as 13,000 men were
employed by the customs police to enforce this discriminatory practice, even as the
pieties of free trade were being trumpeted in London and Manchester.

And although the showcases of imperial trade at the Great Exhibition of 1851
were meant to promote the idea of mutual advantage, most of those who enjoyed
them were white. It was in Canada, Australia, New Zealand and the southern African
Cape Colony that the liberal vision of exchange between colonial producers and
home manufacturers was beginning to be realized, along with measured doses of
self-government. The 'natives' who were being 'improved' under this arrangement
were not, of course, the indigenous population – unless one counts dispossession and
decimation from disease as improvement; they were the white settlers, whether
ex-convict or free emigrants. Any account of the successful operation of free-trade
colonialism in these countries needs to see the immense dislocation of native
cultures not just as an unfortunate sideshow, but as the precondition of that success.
If securing huge areas of grazing pasture for Australian merino sheep meant moving
on or slaughtering the occasional tribe of Aborigines, so be it. A bloody and
prolonged 'Kaffir' war was fought against the Xhosa to overcome their resistance to
cattle ranges in the Cape. What was it that Palmerston had said about the march of
peace and prosperity going hand in hand?

There were 'peripheries,' too – Ottoman Turkey and Latin America – which
were not part of the formal British Empire but whose governments were persuaded
that modernization was in their national interest. Once they were so persuaded,
capital would flow in from British banking houses such as Baring's and Rothschild's.
Harbours would be built or improved to take the new steam-fired, steel-hulled ships

that would sail to and from the mother country; railways laid down and supplied with rolling stock engineered in the Midlands; warehouses and processing centres constructed; commercial consuls and agents planted in strategic locations to connect producers with shippers, to pressure local authorities to lower customs barriers and to give traders immunity from local courts. Before long ladies' academies, opera houses and racecourses would follow; tea would be taken at five, sherry at seven; and big copper pudding moulds would begin, ominously, to appear in whitewashed kitchens from Smyrna to Montevideo.

With the most unapologetically bullish of ministers, Palmerston, at the Foreign Office, for 15 years between 1830 and 1851, and later at 10 Downing Street, from 1855, the pretence was that by sheer force of commercial ingenuity and energy the world's markets had become Britain's oyster. But the truth was that Palmerston and Lord Grey at the War Office hadn't hesitated in West Africa or lower Burma (where teak forests were being coveted) to use the knife to prise them open and get at the pearls. Unaccountably, for example, the Chinese were defying the logic of the global economy by refusing to open their ports to British trade, or to give British traders the customs-free, extra-territorial legal protection they said they needed to function safely and effectively – even, or especially, when their inventory consisted almost entirely of narcotics. The Scottish house of Jardine and Matheson, for example, whose elders were capable of pounding the Bible in indignation against the cruelty of heathen Chinese justice, footbinding and kowtowing, were also shameless in putting the rhetoric of 'British justice' and 'fair and free trade' to the service of narco-imperialism. If the Ch'ing empire for some reason wanted to close its upstream rivers to the traders who were busy turning millions into opium addicts, then they had to be given a lesson in commercial ethics by the surgical use of gun-boats. That lesson was beaten into them in two wars – in 1839–42, and, together with France, in 1856–61, when the allied armies burned the Summer Palace in Beijing, partly as a convincing demonstration of the price to be paid for spurning the joys of commercial cooperation. The conclusion of the First Opium War was the seizure of Hong Kong and the extortion of treaty ports with their own system of local government and justice, immune from Chinese policing, as if it were the most natural thing in the world. The pretext was always that opium was merely the thin end of the wedge that would open obscurantist 'mandarin' China to the embrace of Western modernity. Addiction today, John Stuart Mill tomorrow. Before they knew it, the hundreds of millions would be wearing broadcloth and eating with Sheffield knives and forks – lucky things. But of course the British and the rest of the Europeans were not arresting, but accelerating, the destruction of imperial China;

Top: *James Ramsay, Ist Marquis of Dalhousie* (detail) by Sir John Watson-Gordon, 1847.
Above: La Martinière school, Lucknow, photograph by Felice Beato, 1858.
Opposite: *The Maharajah Duleep Singh* by Franz Xaver Winterhalter, 1854.

and then, as the century wore on, making the resulting 'anarchy' a pretext for
further military and political intervention. It was as if the doctors who had brought
the disease in the first place were decent enough to show up offering – at a price –
the cure.

And India was the major supplier of the dope. By the year of the Great
Exhibition, opium accounted for fully 40 per cent of Indian exports; and there was
no commodity traded within the British Empire that was, pound for pound,
remotely as lucrative. Just 20 years after Trevelyan and Macaulay had envisaged the
peaceful diffusion of benevolent Western culture throughout India, the reality was a
self-perpetuating military juggernaut that, especially under Dalhousie, just couldn't
stop expanding. There was, of course, always the justification of the 'unstable' frontier,
a fear gingered up by neurotic Russophobia and visions of Cossacks pouring
through the Caucasian khanates of Central Asia, into Afghanistan and down the
Khyber Pass to descend in hordes on the defenceless Indus-Ganges valley. Anxieties
about the vulnerability of buffer regimes and the promise that their incorporation
into British India would make them safer managed to justify, usually retroactively,
what would otherwise have been naked imperialist adventurism on the northwest
frontier, first in Sind (annexed in 1843) and then in the Sikh kingdom in the Punjab
(annexed in 1849).

The case of the Punjab was especially egregious. The death of its formidable
old prince, Ranjit Singh, removed the last native ruler the British were prepared to
trust as a dependable barrier against a Russian-influenced Persia and Afghanistan.
Dalhousie's predecessor, Viscount Hardinge, did the usual thing, installing a conven-
ient puppet maharajah, but when his army rebelled a full-scale military campaign
was launched. Dalhousie subsequently converted a punitive war into one whose
object was the all-out extinction of the Sikh state. After an initial embarrassing
reverse, the huge sledgehammer of the Bengal army was applied with predictable
results. Along with the enormous, mountainous territory of the Punjab that now
passed into direct British control came the legendary treasury at Lahore, whose contents were summarily removed. Dalhousie took personal charge of its most fabulous
prize, the enormous Koh-i-noor diamond, ordering a custom-designed belt to be
made for him to carry the treasure safely to Bombay, from where it would be
shipped to England and presented as a personal tribute to Queen Victoria. With it
went the dethroned surviving boy-prince of Ranjit Singh's family, Duleep Singh, his
dynastic pedigree carefully discredited to pre-empt accusations of British usurpation.
Although Duleep was miffed at discovering the confiscation of 'his' diamond (it had
actually been taken from Persia in an earlier history of war and plunder), he was

allowed custody of it on the understanding that he could make a personal presentation to the queen. This he did and in return became a court pet, painted in turbaned finery by the German portraitist Franz Xaver Winterhalter, promised the life and income of a gentleman and encouraged to convert to Christianity, which he eventually did.

It was not surprising, then, that the gluttonously annexationist Dalhousie should also have cast greedy eyes on Awadh, the broad, rich territory between the Ganges and the Himalayas that since 1819, encouraged by the British, had declared itself to be an independent kingdom. Under its 18th-century Muslim nawabs, originally provincial revenue-collecting governors attached to the Mughal Empire, Awadh, with its fertile valleys and populous towns, had been one of the most prosperous and successful regions of all India. Lucknow, its capital, with a population of around 650,000, had been famous for the lushness of its pleasure gardens, the noise of its peacocks, the sumptuousness of its palaces; for its golden-roofed mosques and minarets, its delicately spiced, voluptuous cuisine, its profusely wrought silverware and jewellery, the strength of its fighting rams, the sensuality of its poets and the frightening empire-building of its courtesans. Earlier generations of more open-minded British travellers and official agents – the Residents – loved it; sometimes, as in the notorious scandal of James Achilles Kirkpatrick, who took an aristocratic Muslim woman as lover and then as wife, a little too much for the company's sense of prudence and propriety. Then there were Awadh's soldiers, who made up almost three-quarters of the manpower of the Bengal army, which by 1850 was 240,000 strong with only 40,000 of these troops British. Patronized by the British as 'manly,' in contrast to the 'soft' and languidly androgynous Bengalis, the Awadhis were regarded – especially on the strength of their conduct in Sind and the Punjab – as the toughest and most dependable of the native regiments. Officially, the Awadhi sepoys were seconded to the company army as part of an agreement with the still ostensibly independent kingdom, which meant that as serving in 'foreign territories' they were entitled to double *batta* or allowance, and, more importantly, when they returned home to Faizabad, Salon, Sitapur or Lucknow they could strut around in their scarlet coats enjoying doubly special status and flaunting their immunity from the usual depredations of Awadhi officialdom.

By Dalhousie's day Lucknow, once one of the most gregarious and socially mixed cities of India, was becoming more divided between its native and Western quarters. But it was still nothing like so sharply segregated as Calcutta, with its 'black town' and white riverside villas with gardens, or as Madras. At Lucknow, the packed old city stretched south from the Gomti river with the *ganj* market bazaar at its centre;

each of its districts marked, as it is to this day, by a specific community of artisans —
silversmiths, millers and bakers, and tanners. The town houses of courtiers and
nobles, the mosques and pleasure gardens were mostly situated at the southern and
western rim of the conurbation. And at the northern edge, separated by a little clear
ground and the beautiful Kaiserbagh garden, was the 34-acre compound of the
Residency, raised on a small plateau. At its heart was the Residency itself, built in
thick, dusty rose brick, with Doric columns, a verandah, a little flag tower and a cool
underground swimming bath. Scattered about the gardens were a church, post office,
treasury, the financial commissioner's house and the Begum Kothi, which had once
been the quarters of the nawab's European wife. The cantonment proper, with its
barracks and bungalows and racecourse, were some miles off, north of the Gomti
and the Faizabad road. Further to the west was the prodigious neo-Baroque pile of
a school known as La Martinière, designed and endowed by the French soldier
of fortune and hot-air ballooning polymath Claude Martin, who had served the
nawabs and then the East India Company. The school was now the epitome of the
Macaulay educational mission, drilling its *pukka* schoolboys in Thucydides, Milton
and musketry.

This division of zones, although clear, still put the centre of British life — the
Residency — very much inside, rather than outside, the city itelf. Historically this was
precisely because the Residents had always claimed an unusual degree of comfort,
living amidst the native community. Under the current Resident, Sir William
Sleeman, in the early 1850s, the familiar, rather easy-going cooperation by which the
British expected to get no trouble from Awadh (and recruit a lot of sepoys) seemed
to be working well enough still to make any drastic alteration unnecessary. With
Whig governments taking flak from liberals like Richard Cobden for promoting
expensive, 'cruel' and needless imperialist adventures, and with wars under way in
southern Africa, China, Burma and the Crimea, the last thing that Britain needed
was to provoke another in India.

But of course Dalhousie — who bequeathed the forthcoming disaster to his
successor, Charles Canning — hardly saw the danger coming. As far as he was concerned, a pseudo-independent Awadh, barely governed at all (in his view) by a joke
nawab, Wajid Ali Shah (whose proudest boast was his success at breeding a pigeon
with one white and one black wing, and who was notorious for spending his days
trying on jewellery, writing poetry and reposing with his courtesan of the week),
was not just a luxury but a danger. Had not the foreign secretary to the Governor's
Council, H.M. Elliot, the posthumous author of *The History of India, As Told by Its Own
Historians* (1867), pointed to the 'evil' of tolerating such iniquitous maladministration?

'We behold,' Elliot had written, 'kings, even of our own creation, sunk in sloth and debauchery.' Time, then, to unmake them. 'The British Government,' Dalhousie wrote, 'would be guilty in the sight of God and Man, if it were any longer to aid in sustaining by its countenance an administration fraught with evil to millions.' Besides, Dalhousie relished the contribution its revenues would make to cutting the £8 million deficit that his military adventurism in the Punjab had incurred. When he heard that the nawab and his ministers were being 'bumptious' he confessed in private that he hoped this was indeed the case, since 'To swallow him before I go would give me satisfaction.' In February 1856, despite a journey to Calcutta by Wajid Ali Shah and his chief ministers to plead personally with the Governor-General, Awadh was duly annexed. Dalhousie wrote, scarcely concealing his pleasure, that as a result of the annexation 'Our gracious Queen has five million more subjects and one point three million pounds more revenue than she had yesterday.'

What might have seemed almost a bureaucratic decision in Bengal set up immediate shock waves in both the towns and countryside of Awadh. Overnight an entire population that had served the court and nobility of the kingdom was, in ways barely discernible to the sahibs, not just demoted but shamed. Spilling back into the countryside, they found another crucial class of influential Awadhis – the *taluqdars*, sometimes also known as rajahs, who were hereditary owners of land-tax jurisdictions, which, as elsewhere in northern India, carried with them a bundle of manorial rights and obligations – summarily dispossessed of many of their villages, lands and titles. The official British idea – already implemented in Sind and the Punjab – was that something as important as the land tax (which paid, of course, for the huge army) should be directly administered and not left to village notables, invariably (and inaccurately) described as 'intermediaries,' to cream off profits and perks while bleeding the peasants dry. These 'intermediaries' were classified, in the bureaucratic mind of British officials, as somehow alien to the villages; whereas in fact their title, status and authority went back many generations into the Mughal past, when Rajput warriors had been assigned districts and villages for their support. In some cases the 'rajahs' were themselves not much more than village farmers and, through clan and caste connections, lived very close to the peasant communities.

The British assumption was that since, in many cases, the amount of revenue they were taking would be less than under the old *taluqdar* system, they would receive the devoted gratitude of the farmers. But the Awadh countryside turned out to be a poor experimental study for the utilitarian measurement of pain and relief. The *taluqdars* and rajahs had always been far more than tax collectors: they were manorial, godfatherly patrons, surrounded by personal militia whom it was still an honour to join. Established in their *kutcha* mud or *pakka* gravel-and-cement trench forts deep in the jungle, with rifles and light field guns, they were very definitely the power in the land. And that power was not, as the superficial British inquiries had it, a one-way exploitation. In return for the taxes they received in money and kind from the peasants, the *taluqdars* oversaw the life of their villages; helped the destitute in times of dearth; smoothed out marriage arrangements and disputes; and patronized local mosques and temples. Sometimes they helped with the harvest themselves. Their summary dispossession was not, then, the removal of an obvious anachronism; it was a culture shock that rippled down all the way to local markets, mosques and villages. It made the intruding company *bahadur* (governor) seem crass, brutal and demonstrably alien. When the smoke cleared from the 1857 rebellion, many British professed their amazement that, instead of remaining loyal or at least neutral, the peasantry in tens of thousands followed their rajahs and *taluqdars* into resistance. But for both sets of Awadhis, Muslim and Hindu, it was the most natural thing in the world.

Many of those *taluqdars* and peasant families, of course, had brothers and sons who were sepoys; and who with the disappearance of Awadh had now lost the status they had enjoyed as 'seconded' men, not to mention their double *batta*. Well before the cartridge-grease debacle, there had been many acts of tactlessness that had put a strain on the loyalty of the army rank and file. High-caste soldiers, for whom travel by sea was a taboo, had been threatened by the loss of their caste when ordered to ship to the Burma front to serve in one of Dalhousie's endless wars. Informed of their objections, but also of the men's willingness to march to Burma, the Governor's response was, 'Oh they are fond of walking, are they? They shall walk to Dacca, then, and die there like dogs.' (And so they did.) Humiliating corporal punishments, especially flogging, stood in stark contrast to the care taken in earlier decades not to inflict acts of public shame on men for whom loss of respect was the most mortifying of all disgraces. In the charged atmosphere that Dalhousie had chosen to ignore – but that the more alert incoming Governor-General, Viscount Canning thought heralded trouble – rumours flew that the *attah*, rations of flour, ground in the company's new mill near Kanpur (Cawnpore), contained pulverized human bones from corpses collected on the banks of the Ganges and was yet another fiendish plot to defile the purity of both Muslims and Hindus. Not all these shocks were fantasies. In Jhansi, the elimination of the independent state was followed by the mass slaughtering of cattle, a direct cause of uprisings near the fortress city of Gwalior.

The issuing of the new Lee-Enfield rifles with greased cartridges that needed the ends to be smartly bitten off before being inserted into the breech was not, of course, a deliberate provocation. It was precisely the casually unintentional nature of the offence that was so typical of the modus operandi of the Dalhousie era. No one in fact seemed to know whether the offending grease was pork fat, beef tallow or a mixture of the two, thereby outraging both Muslims and Hindus. As soon as the blunder was acknowledged, it was corrected by having cartridges lubricated with vegetable oil. But the damage had already been done. (At Meerut on 9 May the cartridges were not in fact greased with animal fat, but since there was no way for the sepoys to be certain they were not prepared to risk defilement; it was a moment that defined the collapse of trust between officers and men.) To their cost, the British tended to discount the kind of information the telegraph was not equipped to pick up: rumours and prophecies. One of them, circulating in the bazaar at Lucknow and Delhi predicted that the Company's rule would last no more than precisely the century from the date of the battle of Plassey – 23 June 1757. Cryptic messages to native regiments in the cantonments were relayed through torn chapattis and lotus flowers.

Within weeks of the outbreaks at Meerut and Delhi, British military power seemed to have collapsed in the Ganges valley. The news that the reign of the English was over carried the spark from the Bengal army to the towns and villages of the northwest provinces, Awadh and northern Rajasthan. At Lucknow the sepoys mutinied on 30 May. At Gonda military station, 80 miles north of the city, Katherine Bartrum, a Bath silversmith's daughter of 23 who was living the bungalow life along with her husband Robert, assistant surgeon in the army, and their 15-month-old son Bobby, began to notice an ominous change in the attitude of their servants. Quite soon the punkah wallahs, gardeners, stewards, cooks, *chokidar* watchmen and ayahs started to disappear, and with them went the world Kate Bartrum had thought would last for the rest of her Indian life: 'I think we have all become fearfully nervous,' she wrote anxiously to her father. 'Every unusual sound makes one start; for who can trust these natives now, when they seem to be thirsting for European blood?... For many nights we had scarcely dared to close our eyes. I kept a sword under my pillow, and dear R. had his pistol loaded ready to start up at the slightest sound, though small would have been our chance of escape had we been attacked. . . .'

As the situation suddenly deteriorated, and news arrived of the mutiny at Lucknow and the carnage at Meerut and Delhi, as well as the unlikelihood of immediate British troop reinforcements, Robert knew that Kate's best chance of survival was getting her and the baby to the relative safety of the defensible Residency compound. At Secrora, 65 miles from Lucknow, they were told there would be a small military detachment to take them and other women and children who were stranded in the country, to the Residency. But they had to get there first. Robert, Katherine and the baby set off together with a Mrs Clark and her husband and small

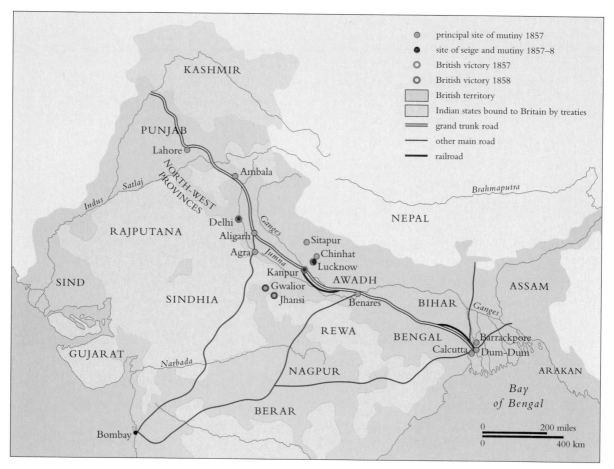

Above: The Indian Mutiny, 1857–8.

Opposite, top left: Robert and Katherine Bartrum, *c.* 1855.

Opposite, top right: Harriet and Robert Tytler, *c.* 1855.

Opposite below: The ruins of the Chutter Manzil Palace, after the siege of Lucknow, photograph by Felice Beato, 1857–8.

child, all on the backs of elephants, but when they got to Secrora the military escort, worried about time, had already left. The men were needed at their regiments, so, after terrible agonizing, the two women, with a small group of loyal sepoys, made their own way, in temperatures of well over 100°F, through what had suddenly become the hostile country of the rajah of Gonda (as it turned out, one of the most militant rebels) to the domes and minarets of the 'Golden City.'

They reached the safety of the Residency on 9 June, but even so it was clear that there would no easy salvation. By the end of the month, 8,000–10,000 sepoys, including 700–800 cavalry, had ringed the Residency defences. Two-pounder rebel batteries were soon in full action, along with 12 other field-gun emplacements, which kept up a steady barrage on the compound. Shallow trenches had been dug immediately behind the guns, in which the gunners could lie and still operate the cannon while being virtually invisible to defending counter-fire. Inside the walls were just 1700 male defenders – 800 British troops, 700 loyal sepoys, with the remainder drawn from the civilian and merchant colony including 50 schoolboy cadets from La Martinière. The chief commissioner of Awadh, the veteran military commander Brigadier-General Sir Henry Lawrence, was already seriously ill and quarrelling with the financial commissioner, Martin Gubbins, about whether to keep or send away (without arms) the sepoys inside the Residency. Gubbins, the pessimist, was for getting rid of them.

On 30 June an attempted counter-attack under Sir Henry's command was ambushed disastrously at Chinhat by rebel troops led by, among others, the fighting Maulvi, Ahmadullah Shah, who, although wounded in the foot, pursued the retreating British. When the badly beaten force returned under heavy fire to the Residency, it was obvious that the ensuing siege was to be grim and lengthy, for it was at least two weeks before relief could be expected. In the event, it took 87 days to arrive. Ahmadullah's shelling of the old Machi Bhawan fort to the west of Residency had forced its evacuation: 118 British troops had been killed; 54 wounded had been brought back to the Residency and lay on litters, given laudanum or alcohol to dull their senses while shattered limbs were amputated. Bandages ran out and had to be improvised from torn clothing. Sir Henry himself died of a shell wound received while inside his quarters.

By 2 July the rebels were in control of the old city. Ahmadullah Shah, the holy prophet, had set up his own headquarters at the bungalow of a *munshi* (Brahmin teacher), was hugely popular with the poor and was challenging the authority of the Begum of Awadh, Hazrat Mahal, who wanted to make her young son the new nawab, accountable only to Bahadur Shah in Delhi. The city itself was close to anarchy.

A nervous member of the old upper-class Lucknow elite described how the streets were run by armed gangs:

> They went round to the doors of the wealthy and gave threats and exacted money … they took halwa and puri and sweets from the shops; they reviled all sorts of people. They took gunpowder and other explosives from the firework makers and paid them inadequately. There was a pile of hay in the garden of the school Kothi to which they set fire and thus produced bonfires which lit the city. They brought Mir Baqar Ali who lived at Pakka Pul and cut him into pieces at the gate of the Bara Imambara with the sword. No-one can say why they committed that sacrilege … they moved about with naked swords in their hands.

From the Residency look-outs, golden Lucknow seemed to be mantled in smoke, din and terror. Conditions inside were rapidly deteriorating. Along with a crowd of the women, Katherine and Bobby were living in the old women's quarter, the Begum Kothi. The summer heat was almost unendurable, and its punctuation by torrential rain made things even worse. The stench from the overflowing latrines triggered vomiting. With hay and water at a premium, bullocks and cavalry horses staggered around the compound mad with thirst before dropping dead. So many rotting carcasses piled up that men had to be detailed to wrench the remnants from the carrion crows and kites and bury them – not least because they were a breeding ground for millions of huge flies. As soon as any food, even the 'black greasy dal' (lentils) that so turned Katherine Bartrum's stomach, was set out it was instantly covered by a seething, buzzing mass. In the earlier stages of the siege, Deprat, a French merchant, had given away his supplies of canned, truffled sausages. The lucky ones at Gubbins's house got sauternes and even champagne as well as tinned salmon, carrots and rice pudding. But that all disappeared. Soon the champagne was reserved for those about to undergo amputations, a whole bottle drunk in a few gulps by the unfortunate patient. Desperate for a smoke, men pawned or traded pieces of clothing or their gold watches for a cigar, and the auctions of clothing and possessions that had belonged to the dead were the scene of hot bidding. Pet dogs were shot to save food.

After a month of this, the mask of Victorian dignity cracked open. The death rate from wounds, cholera, dysenteric diseases and smallpox rose to 10 a day. Drunkenness, usually from bottled beer, was common. There were duels and suicides, and a lot of screaming. No one cared any more what they looked like. Boils and carbuncles appeared on many faces. To the shock of some of the more demure, wives and mothers abandoned their corsets; let their hair down; and went around in

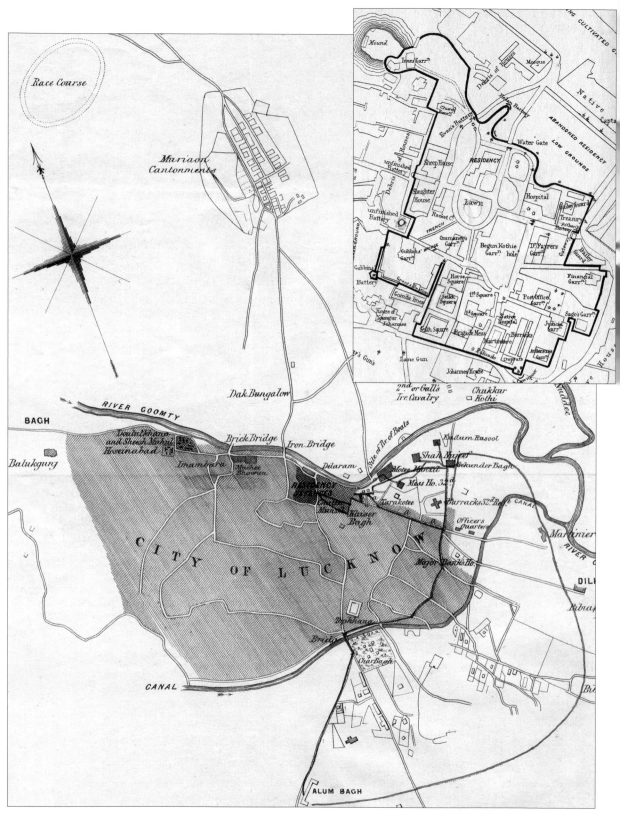

Map of The City of Lucknow, and its Environs by Lieutenant Anderson, Madras Engineers, c. 1858.
Inset: *Plan of the Intrenched Position of the British Garrison at Lucknow* by Lieutenant W. Moorsom, HM 52nd Light Infantry, 1857.

whatever was loose enough and cool enough to stop them becoming unhinged by the heat and terror. Paradoxically, enduring months of these conditions inured the inmates to the incoming shells and bullets. A direct hit, after all, was in the hands of God. A slow death from one of the infectious diseases seemed worse. L. E. Rees, a British merchant from Calcutta who had taken part in the defence of the compound, was probably not just bragging when he claimed that 'Balls graze our very hair, and we continue the conversation without a remark; bullets race over our very hair and we never speak of them. Narrow escapes are so very common that even women and children cease to notice them.' Much more frightening was the possibility that tunnels had been mined under the Residency and that in the dead of night they might find the compound alive with sepoys coming up from below. Mrs Clark, Katherine's travelling companion, had given birth on the day of a sepoy attempt to break into the Residency, and now she and the baby were dying. When she asked Katherine, whose son Bobby was himself sick with cholera, to prepare her things as she was going on a long journey, they were dutifully laid out before she died, the baby following shortly afterwards and her elder child two weeks later.

It was late September before two relatively small relieving forces, one led by the new chief commissioner of Awadh, Sir James Outram, the other by Major-General Sir Henry Havelock, managed to join up and cut and shoot their way through to Lucknow. Havelock was coming via Kanpur, where there had been a terrible massacre of the entire British community. Nana Sahib, the Peshwa (ruler) of the Mahratta and the political and strategic leader of the uprising, along with his field commander Tantia (Daddy) Topi had given a promise of safe conduct to evacuate downriver the besieged British inside Kanpur, only to have them, mostly women and children, shot up and sliced to pieces once they were aboard the boats. Some 200 survivors were taken back to Kanpur, imprisoned and then in their turn killed, the bodies thrown into a well. After Havelock retook Kanpur, the officer left in charge of the town, the ferocious Colonel James Neill, ordered that any sepoys taken prisoner be executed – some of them blown from cannon – and had the well filled in and dedicated as a shrine to the first 'martyrs' of Albion. But the onward advance to Lucknow of Havelock's troops right through the heart of sepoy-held territory cost them many casualties. One of them, as she learned, was Katherine Bartrum's husband, the surgeon Robert, who had been shot through the head on the threshold of the Residency's defences while going to help one of the wounded.

But the great rebellion had been contained. It could only grow or die away and it never succeeded in spreading beyond the heartland of Awadh, the northwest provinces and northern Rajasthan. Although this was itself a huge area – and took the British until the end of 1858 and in some cases well into 1860 to pacify completely – it was decisive for the fortunes of the empire that both eastern Bengal, notably Calcutta at one end and the recently conquered Punjab at the other, remained loyal. The relatively speedy recapture of Delhi in September 1857 was also crucial in persuading undecided peasants and townsmen to stay neutral. And there were some native soldiers who were actually eager to fight the rebels: not just the Gurkhas from Nepal but the Sikhs, who were delighted to return the punishment they had received at the hands of the Awadhi sepoys during the Sikh wars of 1845–6 and 1848–9. Despite the relatively good relations between Hindu and Muslim sepoys (carefully cultivated by Bahadur Shah), some traditional ethnic and regional feuds remained a much stronger force than any kind of embryonic anti-colonial pan-Indian solidarity.

Before he got to Kanpur, James Neill had undertaken a lightning march from Calcutta to pre-empt serious trouble at Benares. Neill's savagery in burning villages and ordering mass executions of those suspected of collaborating with the rebels worked. The terrorized countryside around Benares remained quiet, and the holy city became the forward station for advances on Allahabad and Kanpur. If the telegraph had been the wrong kind of listening device to pick up early signals of discontent (listening to the mullahs, the native postmen and the gossips and fortune-tellers in the markets would have been more to the point), the cables did now make a difference to containing the damage. Governor-General Canning was able to wire the home government about his critical manpower shortage quickly enough for Palmerston to divert a regiment intended for China (where of course it was going to punish the Ch'ing coastguards for insulting the flag) to the Indian theatre.

After the relief of Delhi in September, Bahadur Shah, a pathetic fugitive, was found together with his two sons and grandson by Major William Hodson, a cavalry officer, in the beautiful tomb of his ancestor Hummayyun, 16 miles from the centre. A very unlikely arch-villain, in his incarceration he quickly turned into a pitiable anachronism: stared at, photographed, ridiculed, certainly not forgiven for what had been done in his name.

The euphoria inside the Residency that greeted the arrival of Havelock and Outram was short-lived: the sepoy army closed in around them once more, making it apparent that this had been not so much a relief as a new stage of imprisonment. An attack on the Baillie Gate by the Maulvi came perilously close to success. In November a second relief attempt was made to break the siege, under Sir Colin Campbell, heralded by pipers playing 'The Campbells Are Coming'; he managed to hold an exit route open long enough to evacuate the civilians. After six months of extreme privation the 400 surviving women, children and male civilians, including Katherine and Bobby Bartrum and 1000 sick and wounded soldiers, finally left the compound. Over the winter, however, fresh rebel troops mobilized by *taluqdars* closed in again. Ahmadullah led a series on attacks on the walled defences from December right through to the end of February. It was only when Campbell brought a huge army of 25,000 in March 1858 that the city was finally taken and what was left of the Residency liberated. On 15 June 1858, Ahmadullah Shah was killed in action, then beheaded; his ashes thrown in the river. Even when all the major cities in the Ganges valley had been restored to British rule rebel rajahs held out in their small but heavily armed forts; some of them were never, in fact, subdued. Hit-and-run raids were staged on isolated outposts by mounted partisans belonging to the irregular armies of Raja Beni Madho, who was rumoured to have died in November 1859 fighting the Gurkhas in Nepal along with the orchestrator of the Kanpur massacre, Nana Sahib. The already legendary Rani Lakshmi Bhai of Jhansi, said to have been surprised while resting her horses and drinking sherbet, was shot in the back as she was charging back into action, a sword in each hand, the reins of her pony held in her teeth. She died in a mango grove after giving her gold anklets and pearl necklace, taken from the Maharajah of Gwalior, to her soldiers.

Just before Katherine Bartrum was due to take ship back to England from Calcutta her son, Bobby, became seriously ill: nothing that a four-month sea voyage wouldn't take care of, the doctors assured her. The day before she sailed, Bobby died on board the *Himalaya*. Katherine went home alone, remarried, had three more children and died of tuberculosis in 1866.

As the fighting petered out, the debate about how to treat the rebel provinces, and more generally India altogether, heated up. In Britain, the bloody dramas of Delhi, Kanpur and Lucknow had already been relayed by reporters like William Howard Russell, but then sado-masochistically embellished to feed the publishers' need for sensationalism. For some years it was generally believed that lily-white Victorian women, the 'angels of Albion,' had been raped and sexually mutilated, although there was no evidence whatsoever of such abuse. The Royal Academy show in 1858 included a painting by Sir Joseph Noel Paton called *In Memoriam*, showing a group of the Lucknow heroines and babes in pallid, pink-eyed distress (but otherwise in remarkably good shape) with 'maddened Sepoys hot for blood' about to penetrate their refuge. Some of the critics thought the painting too indelicate for the public gaze; others believed it was a modern icon that merited a memorial chapel to itself. But in response to protest, Paton overpainted the dusky assailants with kilted Highlanders coming to the rescue.

Above: *Jessie's Dream, The Relief of Lucknow* (detail) by Frederick Goodall, 1857. Legend has it that Jessie dreamed she heard the sound of pipers coming to relieve Lucknow.
Opposite top: Interior of the Secundra Bagh courtyard, Lucknow, after the slaughter of 2000 rebels by the 93rd Highlanders and 4th Punjab Regiment, photograph by Felice Beato, 1857.
Opposite below: The execution of the Delhi mutineers, photograph by Felice Beato, *c.* 1858.

Photographers, too, very rapidly got into the act. Robert and Harriet Tytler, both keen photographers, took pictures of some of the scenes around Lucknow with which they illustrated Harriet's account. But the most commercially savvy photographic reporter was the Italian Felice Beato, who, even before it was physically safe, rushed to Delhi, where he took 60 pictures and then went on to Lucknow, where he followed Sir Colin Campbell's assault on the city and took another 60 images — some of them among the most extraordinary albumen silver prints of the 1850s. The sites were chosen for their familiarity to the avid Mutiny-readers both in Calcutta and in Britain: the Kashmir Gate in Delhi; the well of the martyrs at Kanpur; the ruined room at Lucknow in which Sir Henry Lawrence had been fatally wounded; the massively pitted walls of the Lucknow Residency. Most shockingly of all, Beato took elaborate pains to construct a photograph of the courtyard of one of Lucknow's fabled walled pleasure gardens, the Secundra Bagh, where 2000 rebels were slaughtered during Campbell's first attack. To reconstruct the scene Beato disinterred bones to scatter them about the yard, although some seem to have been those of horses and bullocks rather than humans. All these places acted as the Via Dolorosa of the passion play of the Mutiny. Although enormous areas of Indian Lucknow, including many of its old pleasure gardens, palaces and mosques, were brutally razed so that oversized boulevards could be built (not least for easy access by troops), the half-destroyed remnant of the Residency was to be preserved for imperial posterity, the Union Jack flown (until midnight on 14 August 1947) over the shattered, blackened ruins.

All these images stoked the fires of retribution. At the Cambridge Union, Charles Trevelyan's son, George Otto, heard an undergraduate orator brush away suggestions of clemency by proclaiming 'when the rebellion has been crushed out from the Himalayas to the Comorin, when every gibbet is red with blood, when every bayonet creaks beneath its ghastly burden, when the ground in front of every cannon is strewn with rags and flesh and shattered bone, then talk of mercy [may be heard]. This is not the time.' He was roundly applauded by the undergraduates. The first wave of British troops, along with their generals, were prepared to satisfy this demand for revenge, blowing sepoys from cannon and giving no quarter. But given the intensity of the passions, the race hatred against the 'damned niggers' and the genuinely dreadful things that had actually befallen the British in Kanpur, Delhi and Lucknow, it is surprising that more were not dealt with so savagely and sadistically. Much of this was due to Canning's own creditable determination to master the instinct for indiscriminate revenge. He was horrified, for example, when he learned that William Hodson, who commanded a troop of irregular Sikh horsemen, had murdered the two sons and the grandson of Bahadur Shah after they had surrendered

Bahadur Shah, the ex-king of Delhi, in captivity, *c.* 1859.

to him. Although he suffered ridicule in both Calcutta and London as 'Clemency Canning' for ordering local officers to stop arbitrary and summary executions and the burning of villages, he believed this was the pragmatically, as well as morally, correct response. Throughout the trauma he had agonized behind walls of dispatch boxes on what had gone wrong; whether there was some point that might not have been reached, something that might have been attended to, that would have avoided the butchery. Once it had happened, his concern had been to contain the rebellion within the Ganges valley; and this had happened. Now he had no intention of jeopardizing the future stability of the empire by alienating all of India. When he was severe – declaring the whole of Awadh to be forfeited land, for instance – it was only so that he could promise *taluqdars* who made submission in a timely fashion that they would have their lands, titles and districts back again. Punishment was the prelude to reassurance and restoration. As it happened, he had two allies in Prince Albert and Queen Victoria, who wrote to him: 'Lord Canning will easily believe how entirely the Queen shares *his* feelings of sorrow and indignation at the un-Christian spirit shown – alas! to a great extent here by the public towards Indians in general and to sepoys without discrimination!'

The proclamation of 1 November 1858, which ended the existence of the East India Company and put British India under the direct rule of the queen's

Top: Samuel Bourne, photograph by Alfred Cox & Co., *c.* 1880.
Above: The picturesque village of Dunkar, Spiti, photograph by Samuel Bourne, 1866.
Opposite: His Highness, the Maharajah of Pannah, *c.* 1880.

government, with a viceroy, a council and a secretary of state, made a special point of promising to respect the religions and traditions of India. Canning took the proclamation seriously enough to embark on a long progress through the subcontinent, accompanied by a retinue of military magnificence, holding canopied durbar assemblies, distributing the newly created Star of India to local notables and doing everything in his power to make a personal viceregal bond with the rajahs, nizams and maharajahs. More importantly, he restored the right of childless native rulers to adopt heirs, even insisting that the Maharajah of Mysore do so at once.

The Mutiny, then, produced an extraordinary about-face in the official attitude of the British towards the most important colony in the empire. Instead of dreams of Westernization a more frankly conservative principle was now followed, which conceded that India would not and could not be modernized in a generation or two; and that the first obligation of a government was to make sure that its own society and institutions were healthy and above all free from sedition. The change of mind was more than a little schizophrenic. Trevelyan, who returned to India in 1859 to be governor of Madras and immediately get himself into trouble protesting at the attempt by the new central government to impose income tax, had established the principle that positions in the Indian Civil Service would be open to competition without distinction of race. The reality, of course, was that no Indian, however hard he tried to turn himself into the 'brown Englishman' of Macaulay's fantasy, however well he learned his Milton and his Shakespeare, ever got near any of the responsible (as distinct from menial) judicial, police or fiscal appointments for many generations. The universalist assumption of the Enlightenment that all men, given the right education, could become much the same had been replaced by the harder, 'scientific' fact of incommensurable difference; it was put most brutally in the 1890s by one viceroy the Earl of Elgin, who jovially complained what 'a terrible business [it is] this living among inferior races.'

Although the success stories of British India in the second half of the century were mostly urban ones, the prevailing attitude of its rulers, from successive viceroys after Canning (with the significant exception of the liberal Lord Ripon) right down to district collectors, was that cities like Calcutta, Bombay and Madras, with their swarms of clerks, merchants, doctors and over-literate, under-employed intellectuals, had become mongrel places, neither of one culture nor the other. The 'real' India, on the other hand, was out there in the countryside with the water buffalo. Urban India was beginning to run by the clock; a tick-tock India full of all those 'little' men (they were always 'little' in sahib-speak) in steamy, sweaty, monsoon-muddy, busy-busy Bombay and Calcutta with their spectacles, fob watches and umbrellas, always fretting about timetables, the post, the trains and the ferries – and always being late; the clerks with grimy collars; the doctors who knew too much for their own and their patients' good; the yappy 'little' journalists with their self-important third-hand parroted liberal opinions; the jumped-up johnny book-lawyers who made themselves such damned nuisances in the magistrates' court. 'Out there,' 'up country' and 'in the hills' was 'timeless' India (the one thing India has never been, in fact, is timeless). They called it primordial, 'immense' and 'magnificent' – another favourite word used with equal passion for the moustaches of a maharajah or the Himalayas seen from Simla.

The main chance for commercial photographers, like the inexhaustible Samuel Bourne (of the famous Bourne and Shepherd studio), was now not the documentary record of cities smashed by shells but the creation of what they themselves called the 'Indian picturesque' – exactly akin to the English 'discovery' in the late 18th century of noble ethnic remnants in the remote corners of Britain. The topography of this tropical picturesque was just the same as it had been in the Hebrides and the Peak District: dramatic waterfalls and ancient eroded cliffs, with jungly temples taking the place of ruined abbeys and the scenery generally edited to exclude the actual people who lived there – skinny things who failed to live up to the Romantic idealization, but might occasionally be included as indicators of scale. Where once the 'savage' races of India had been seen as target opportunities for the civilizing and Christianizing mission they were now looked on by ethnographers as treasures to be preserved in all their wild and, in the notorious case of the Andaman islanders, naked innocence. Uncovered breasts began to appear in photographs of tribal women in the 1880s. Most spectacular of all were the portrait studies, many of them dramatically executed, of the Indian nobility: boy princes in jewelled turbans; swarthy Rajput warriors; plump and perfumed sybarites swelling luxuriantly against the silk. Many of them sported the insignia of the Star of India, the symbol of the queen's compact to preserve them in all their finery on condition of their absolute loyalty. A generation or two earlier, this was precisely the India that British reformers had declared must be roused from its 'sloth' and 'inertia.' After the energy of the Mutiny a little inertia didn't seem such a bad idea. Let India move at its own tempo: the speed of an elephant's walk. Let *us* do the bustling.

Seen from the cool distance of a century and a half, it is easy to spot an extraordinary self-deception on the part of the sahibs in this turn towards neo-feudal exoticism. The reality of British power in India was coming to depend more, not less, on the world of the great port cities they had created; on the ruthless exploitation of plantation economies in Assam and Burma for teak, mahogany, tea and the always tempting though seldom reliable indigo (with chemical dyes it would fade altogether); on the mesh of connections that brought together Indian entrepreneurs with the British bankers, shippers and insurance men who made the import-export businesses tick along. The 'jumped-up' urban *babus* and *bhadralok* whose pretensions the sahibs found so offensive or comical were precisely the people on whose custom the booming British export business was coming to depend.

But then, that self-deception was exactly of a piece with the way that late Victorian Britain – or some of its most powerful spokesmen – reacted to their own industrial society. The empire that had been designed as an integral piece of the economic design of greater Britain now became culturally something like its opposite just at the moment when that heavy investment was at last beginning to pay off. This disconnection between economic reality and social perception was one of the defining peculiarities of modern Britain. Those who ran the empire, especially the new Indian Raj, were no longer the orientalists and knowledge technicians who had come from Fort William and Haileybury in the first generations. They were now the 'manly' (the most over-used term of the imperial elite) and chivalric products of the Rugby headmaster Dr Thomas Arnold's school of modern altruism: sworn to inflexible justice and military self-sacrifice. Over-intellectualism was despised and suspected, whether among Their Own Sort or (especially) among the subject races. Their ethos was of fatherly, headmasterly sternness.

The politician who – though certainly neither fatherly nor headmasterly himself – did most to perpetuate what was essentially a fantastic, rather than realistic, vision of modern Britain was Benjamin Disraeli. It is often said that Disraeli was a cynic; but if so he was the most formidable kind, one who at least half believes the fantasies he manipulates. Take a look at his Buckinghamshire country house, Hughenden Manor, with its stupendous over-decoration (unerringly like Osborne House); imagine its terraces full of peacocks, and the sense of Disraeli the sorcerer – or 'magician,' as his friends and enemies liked to say – becomes more plausible. One of the worst things his enemy, William Gladstone, thought up to say about Disraeli was to call him 'Asiatic,' by which he meant constitutionally irresponsible, amoral and shamelessly devoted to pleasure, self-indulgence and dandyism. But the real magic of Disraeli's public as well as private personality was to make precisely these human foibles and imperfections the mark, not of the foreigner but of the deep-dyed Englishman. It is easy to overdo the stereotype of his exoticism. After all his father, Isaac, lived the life of a country gentleman with literary pursuits; and one of Benjamin's brothers was a gentleman–farmer. If Disraeli himself was happy in town, he was equally happy strolling through the grounds and gardens of Hughenden, relishing his view of the Chilterns. It was not just as the aristocracy's pet Jew – so clever, so amusing – that he returned the favour by sentimentalizing them. He genuinely believed (against what we now know to be the historical truth) that amidst what he called the 'wreck of nations' England's aristocratic constitution had survived because it had always been permeable to those who sought to live by the 'principle of our society, which is to aspire and excel.'

Was a baptized Jew leading the party of the country gentry and the Church of England less amazing than a baptized Jew who was also a romantic novelist, the author of *Tancred*? But that, of course, was precisely Disraeli's major qualification. As a youthful member of the dissident Tory group known as Young England, and then much later in the preface to the 1870 edition of his novels, Disraeli wrote of the necessity of 'imagination' in British government, a quality he insisted was no less important than 'reason.' 'Imagination' only made sense, though, when defined negatively. It was *against* utilitarianism, the vision of human society as a sense-receptor machine; *against* commercial and industrial materialism; *against* the individualism at the core of free-trade liberalism; *against* the monotonous 'levelling' of egalitarianism; *against* the relentless campaign of moral and civic self-improvement that the High Minds of liberalism were always talking about. Disraeli started nothing; but he tapped into a rich and stubborn vein of sentiment in British life that was shared to a strong extent by Queen Victoria. Instead of all the above, it valued historical memory, the textured sensibility of the past, and wanted to recycle some of it for the future – in the look of Gothic revival churches and in the preservation and embellishment of ceremony and ritual. It idealized country life and the old manorial relations between squire and tenant that were rapidly evaporating before the pressures of world markets; it honoured the craft workshop and the college choir. Disraeli's way had been prepared for him by the romantic rhetoric of Edmund Burke; the massive popularity of the novels of Sir Walter Scott; the nostalgic 'troubadour' history paintings like Paul Delaroche's *Lady Jane Grey*; Pugin's mind-bogglingly profuse interior for the House of Lords; the neo-chivalric canvases of the Pre-Raphaelites; the Christian paternalism of the old Poet Laureate Wordsworth and the Arthurian idylls of the present incumbent, Tennyson. Disraeli was Carlyle with a smile; Charles Dickens with a white silk handkerchief.

It was telling that Disraeli had made his name in the 1840s as MP for Shrewsbury by taking down the cotton-manufacturer prime minister Sir Robert Peel. Peel's assumption was that the Tory party's future hinged on slipstreaming itself behind Britain's laissez-faire internationalist industrialism. The ferocity of Disraeli's attack implied something like the opposite – that the real future of the party lay not in making itself indistinguishable from Whiggishness or liberalism but in keeping faith with precisely the opposite set of values – crown, church, country (to which he would later add empire). Young England's stance was to make the Tory leaders uneasy at being so apologetic about the institutions of which Disraeli insisted they should be boasting; not least the insular interests of Britain itself. Young England was meant to be the kiss of life for Olde England.

What seemed at the beginning to be a stance of quixotic futility turned out to be a strategy of genius; massive social self-denial turned into political paydirt. It was a theory of political action that confounded almost every other theory of 19th-century progress – not just Mill and Macaulay but Marx. Who could have imagined that, as the franchise gradually became extended, the working class whom it embraced would become interested less in political egalitarianism and more in social improvement; that they would want, not political union with their self-designated emancipators among the Liberals but cleaner water, less noisome slums (mistakenly ridiculed by Gladstone as 'the politics of sewage') and ra-ra British imperialism? Disraeli, however, claimed to have known this all along when, as leader of the House of Commons, he pushed through the Second Reform Act in 1867, trumping the Liberals at their own game. The working class, once admitted to the vote, he said, would not be a Trojan horse for revolution but on the contrary were Conservative in the 'purest and loftiest' sense, in that they were 'proud of belonging to a great country and wish to maintain its greatness – that they are proud of belonging to an Imperial country, and are resolved to maintain, if they can, their empire – that they believe on the whole that the greatness and the empire of England are to be attributed to the ancient institutions of the land.'

Cynical or not, there was at least a grain of truth in Disraeli's intuition that when the queen protested at being addressed like a public meeting by Mr Gladstone she was voicing the irritation of millions of her subjects – from farmers to publicans. The Liberal religion, perfectly personified by Gladstone, demanded that Britons should every day do better, try harder and live more purely. But not everyone wanted to prowl the streets looking for fallen women to save; not everyone had it in them to be up and doing every blessed waking hour of the day. How the two giants of Victorian politics spent their own leisure hours says a great deal about the contrast of their personalities. When he allowed himself time off from the dispatch boxes or from translating Homer, Gladstone rolled up his sleeves and chopped down trees at his estate at Hawarden in Flintshire. A collection of his axes still exists in his 'temple of peace' library at Hawarden. Disraeli, on the other hand, rose at a reasonable seven-thirty in the morning, would read the newspapers and do a little government business; then he might stroll along the terrace amidst his peacocks (the perfect Disraelian bird) and peruse a few more documents between daydreams in the library, where 'I like to watch the sunbeams on the bindings of the books.' For Gladstone, the binding was just something that held together what mattered – the contents.

Disraeli's scepticism about the moral imperatives of policy did not in any way make him politically lazy. In the run-up to the election of 1874, in which Gladstone defended the record of his own reformist government, Disraeli took the fight right to the heart of the enemy. His pronouncements about the working class's enthusiasm for the traditions of church, crown and empire, and their preference for social improvement over political equality – in effect the survival charter of modern Toryism – were deliberately made through rousing speeches in the temples of liberalism: the Free Trade Hall in Manchester and the Crystal Palace in London. Buildings that had long been associated with the ethos of an internationalist peace-loving scripture of harmony between peoples, the morality of entrepreneurial striving, were now reconsecrated by Disraeli's rhetoric into bastions of British self-assertion. The election that followed vindicated all of Disraeli's optimism, giving the Conservatives a huge majority of 110 seats in England alone. The government then proceeded to deliver on some, at least, of its promises. The home secretary, Richard Cross, hitherto a complete unknown in government, introduced a batch of reforms that measurably and concretely improved the life of the urban working class – better regulation of food and drugs; cleaner water through legislation on river pollution; the first slum-clearance legislation (on which, however, few local authorities acted); expanded legality for trade-union action.

After the bread, the circus. For Disraeli was equally (if not more) committed to feeding the people's 'imagination' as their bellies; and he knew that the restoration of public spectacle had to start at the top, with the monarchy. His elaborate, daring and shameless wooing of the reclusive queen – begun in earnest when he had become prime minister for the first time in 1868 – was part of a long strategy to secure the future of the monarchy by persuading it to re-emerge from the thick cocoon of grief in which Victoria had wrapped it. The timing, Disraeli thought, was urgent, since republicanism – at the high-water mark of its popularity in the late 1860s and early 1870s – fed on the notorious absenteeism of the monarch. Why bother with a queen who seemed not to want to be bothered by the office herself? But Disraeli's success in charming Victoria out of her seclusion only worked because he was genuinely touched by the increasingly odd, emotionally tormented, obstreperous, stout little matriarch. The gallantry may have been a ploy, but it was turned on with deep and genuine warmth and affection. 'He is very peculiar … but

Above: Benjamin Disraeli, Earl of Beaconsfield, KG, photograph by Jabez Hughes, 1876–8.
Opposite: William Gladstone rests from his tree-felling in the grounds of his country house at Hawarden, *c.* 1890.

very clever and sensible,' Victoria wrote after an early meeting. And before long Disraeli's huge gamble at maintaining an easy-going mixture of chivalric devotion and brazen informality worked wonders, surely because it brought back girlish memories of Lord Melbourne, who had died in 1848. Like Melbourne, Disraeli wrote Victoria lengthy, often whimsical and gossipy letters about the doings (and follies) of politicians. Like Melbourne, he encouraged her to take a strongly (in fact unrealistically) assertive view of her constitutional prerogatives. This last was deeply disingenuous, since Disraeli had strongly disapproved of what he felt had been Prince Albert's ambition to tilt government in Britain towards a court-influenced style of administration, so much so that, according to Lord Stanley, he thought the Prince Consort's death would be the 'start of a new reign.' That he could persuade the queen that he was promoting her dear departed's way of doing things while actually doing the opposite was the mark of his dexterity. And she rewarded Disraeli with extraordinary familiarity. He could sit in her presence, rib her with mild, twinkle-eyed banter. In February 1866, Victoria opened parliament in person for the first time since Albert's death, nearly five years earlier in 1861. But she did so sulkily, grumbling about the chore and flatly refusing to wear ceremonial robes. But with a prime minister she trusted absolutely, Victoria was prepared to expose herself (up to a point) to the public gaze. Just as Disraeli had steered his party towards a new identity for the modern age, so he did with the monarchy, becoming the impresario of its public re-emergence.

Imperial spectacle was a vital element in all this. Although she was grudgingly dutiful as queen, the prospect of becoming empress whetted Victoria's appetite for grandeur. When in 1876, Disraeli, with the help of the Rothschilds, pulled off the huge coup of buying the Khedive of Egypt's shares in the Suez Canal (and with it control of European access to India), he transformed the strategic and economic prospects of the British Raj. But the hidden wiring of that power had to be accompanied by the display of majesty. The same psychology that informed Disraeli's conviction that the mass of the people of Britain wanted to have good done *to* them, rather than be urged to endless exercises in moral self-improvement, fitted well with the paternalistic temper in the post-Mutiny government of India. Canning's successor as viceroy, Lord Elgin, had unblushingly and cynically insisted that 'all orientals are children, amused and gratified by external trappings and ceremonies and titles and ready to put up with the loss of real dignity if only they are permitted to enjoy the semblance of it.'

Ever since Canning's progresses up-country, viceroys had been assiduous in holding local durbars, or audiences, at which they bestowed the 'semblances' of

New Crowns for Old Ones! A popular cartoon, from *Punch* 1876, satirizing Queen Victoria's new imperial title, Empress of India.

Victorian dignity on local Indian princes. The policy was the exact antithesis of Dalhousie's brutal 'lapse' annexationism: the tropical projection of Disraeli-ite neo-feudalism, with the gaekwar of Baroda or the rajah of Jaipur standing in for the bauble-heavy landed aristocracy of Caithness and Cambridgeshire. Under the Mughals, durbars had been a ritual by which local governors made a personal formalized submission to the emperor in return for which they were brought within the embrace of his personal aura – symbolized by the 'exchanging of gifts and bestowal of titles and official appointments.' But the British, with their much more instrumental view of ceremony, turned the durbars into the kind of ritual they understood and were good at: demonstrations of pecking order, with the good boys pushed up the ranking and the bad boys demoted or ignored; together with the award of trinkets – medals, ribbons, insignia. Compared to the personal touch of the Mughal ceremonies, the British version was brassy, garish and remote. But, backed as it was by the unarguable power of the sword (prudently adjusted since the Mutiny

Top: Edward Bulwer-Lytton as viceroy of India, Calcutta, 1877.
Above: *The Delhi Durbar, 1877* by Alexander Caddy, *c.* 1877.

so that the ratio of Indian to British troops was four to one instead of six to one), it worked. The maharajahs lined up to get their gongs.

Although it was out of the question for Victoria herself to attend a durbar, she was quite happy for her children to go to India to spread the regal aura. Alfred (Affie), the Duke of Edinburgh, did the tour in 1869 (tigers, maharajahs, polo, heavily crenellated railway stations). In 1876 it was Bertie, the Prince of Wales's turn, the trip (all of the above plus huge, military brass bands, a custom-made silver howdah for his elephant and parades of loyal turbans) orchestrated to coincide with the announcement of a change in Victoria's style. Henceforth, in addition to being queen she would be the empress of all India – Kaiser-i-Hind. The title had been dreamed up by the Hungarian-born Professor of Oriental Languages at the Punjab University College at Lahore, G. W. Leitner, a believer in the 'Indo-Aryan' linguistic trunk from which European and Asian languages had (alas) separately branched. To the sceptical, 'Kaiser-i-Hind' sounded like the purest operetta, but then, as Disraeli might have proposed, who does *not* adore operetta? Now, at any rate, there was no danger of the queen being embarrassed by protocol that impertinently elevated members of her own extended family above herself just because they happened to style themselves 'Kaiser.' In Edward Bulwer-Lytton, the future 1st Earl of Lytton, moreover, Disraeli imagined he had found the perfect viceroy to summon a durbar of heavily costumed grandeur for the formal proclamation of Victoria's elevation to queen-empress.

Depending on your point of view, the 44-year-old Lytton was an inspired or catastrophic choice. His father, Edward Bulwer-Lytton Senior, had been a massively popular novelist who specialized in the historically exotic such as *The Last Days of Pompeii*, which made him a kindred spirit to Disraeli. Paternal loyalty did not prevent Bulwer-Lytton from accusing his son, whom he must have recognized as an inferior talent, of plagiarism. The younger Lytton wrote bad poetry under the pseudonym 'Owen Meredith' (the queen apparently loved his verses); had been ambassador to Portugal; and had generally led the life of a handsome, self-consciously lofty man of taste, unsure whether he should or should not be in politics and government. Originally he had been no higher on the list of candidates than fourth. But the Lyttons of Knebworth House were Hertfordshire neighbours of the secretary of state for India, Lord Salisbury, and Disraeli's own misplaced confidence in Lytton's 'imaginative' potential may well have jumped him up the ranking. There was no doubt that Lytton was able, on demand, to strike a pose of decorative refinement, although the much photographed aristocratic slouch to the right was probably more the result of his chronic haemorrhoids, or the opium habit he had acquired in order to deal with them, than any studied neo-Roman affectation. Taken aback by the government's invitation, Lytton was not at all sure he wanted the job, not least because of his 'absolute ignorance of every fact and question concerning India.'

On the other hand, perhaps a second-rate poet with a handsome head might be just the right ornamentalist in David Cannadine's sense, to act as master of ceremonies. After his arrival in India in April 1876, most of Lytton's attention was directed towards accomplishing the grandiose durbar of Disraeli's dreams. The site was carefully chosen: not the broad greenswathe of the Maidan at Calcutta, but the high ridge, a mile and a half northwest of Delhi, where the survivors of the Mutiny massacres had retreated and held out for four months; a place that, like the well at Kanpur and the Lucknow Residency, had become a site of obligatory pilgrimage for newcomers to the Raj. Spectacle would now exorcize the memory of slaughter and humiliation. To the task of stunning the child-like orientals into awestruck submission Lytton cheerfully addressed himself. His own notion of paramount rule, echoing Disraeli's own paternalism, was that it should be felt, not through the handful of Civil Service officials, but through India's own native princes and 'gentry' (whoever they were). Neo-feudalism was the right term for this. The omnipotence and magnificence of the Raj would persuade those native princes to deliver their unconditional loyalty, and in turn the millions subject to the rajahs would treat the Raj as an authentically Indian institution. 'Politically speaking,' Lytton wrote in one his typically grandiloquent clichés, '[India] is an inert mass – if it ever moves at all it will move in obedience, not to its British benefactors but to its native chiefs and princes however tyrannical they may be.'

The durbar of 1877, then, was conceived as a kind of penance for Macaulay's sin of having created, through liberal naivety, the Western-educated class of Indian whom Lytton described as 'baboos whom we have educated to write semi-seditious articles in the native Press and who really represent nothing but the social anomaly of their own position.' Instead a 'Statutory Civil Service' would appoint the Other Kind of Indian – young men from princely dynasties who in reality would not have touched Lytton's inferior-grade bureaucracy with a barge-pole. Paradoxically, then, the durbar was presented not as the theatrical fantasy it actually was but as the 'reality' of ancient India, the India of princes and peasants, soldiers and brahmins. Gathered in the 'Indian camp' were its finest specimens – 300 of the flower of the nobility, along with their retainers, each allotted a miniature 'territory' in the encampment, marked by banners (designed by a Calcutta authority on heraldry), richly caparisoned horses and heavily brocaded elephants. The rajahs and maharajahs were differentiated with excruciating attention to pedigree, antiquity and quasi-, semi- or pseudo-independence. (This had already become an institutional orthodoxy in the secretary of state's office in Whitehall, where two sets of doors had been built so that princes of exactly equal rank might be received simultaneously!) Precedence at the 1877 durbar was defined by gun-salute entitlement, which in turn prescribed size of entourage. Thus the 17-gun-salute princes (the true grandees like the Gaekwar of Baroda and the nizam of Hyderabad, for example) were permitted an entourage of 500 retainers, whilst the 11-gun-salute princes only rated entourages of 300. These still added up. The population of the 'Indian camp' alone numbered over 50,000. The 'imperial' camp, in other words white, was 10,000 strong and supplied with its own post, telegraph and police stations. Add to that 14,000 parade soldiers and the total durbar encampment accommodated 84,000 souls: a sizeable town in its own right and one that needed Major General Frederick Roberts, who was about to fight an Afghan war for Lytton, to keep it in order.

Very little of the feudal flummery was remotely authentic. The armorial bearings; the punishingly heavy, 5-foot-square, farcically unwieldy banners; the specially minted decorations were all the production of British heraldic enthusiasms, as peculiar and artificial a synthesis of orientalism and 19th-century Gothic revival as the 'Indo-Saracenic' architectural style, then in fashion, which too was supposed to represent the recovery of a common tradition. And the Punjab – because it was somehow deemed the most 'manly and martial' of the provinces – played a large part in this spurious east–west hybrid. Lockwood Kipling, Rudyard's father, assigned the unenviable task of making decorations for the 220-square-foot viceregal dais, was principal of the Mayo School of Art in Lahore. The Pre-Raphaelite-influenced artist Val Prinsep, son of Macaulay's old orientalist enemy, was commissioned to paint the event but flinched at the abomination (even while taking the job). 'Oh horror! What have I to paint? A kind of thing that outdoes the Crystal Palace in hideosity. … The Viceroy's dais is a kind of scarlet temple, eighty feet high. Never was such a brummagem ornament … the size gives it a vast appearance like a gigantic circus.'

Lytton was less fastidious. A week before the climactic elevation to the dais, he and Lady Lytton processed for three hours, on the silver elephant's howdah made for the Prince of Wales, through Delhi to the Indian camp. This could not have been comfortable for the pile-stricken viceroy. At the stroke of noon on New Year's Day 1877 he made his entry to the march from Wagner's *Tannhäuser*, sounded by trumpeters in medieval livery. Following the national anthem there was a 101-gun salute, so shattering that some of the elephants stampeded and killed a number of spectators. Unperturbed, the celestial viceroy, 80 feet up, spoke in the name of the queen-empress, claiming that Providence had chosen the British to succeed the evidently moribund empire of the Mughals. The Indian Civil Service was thanked for its

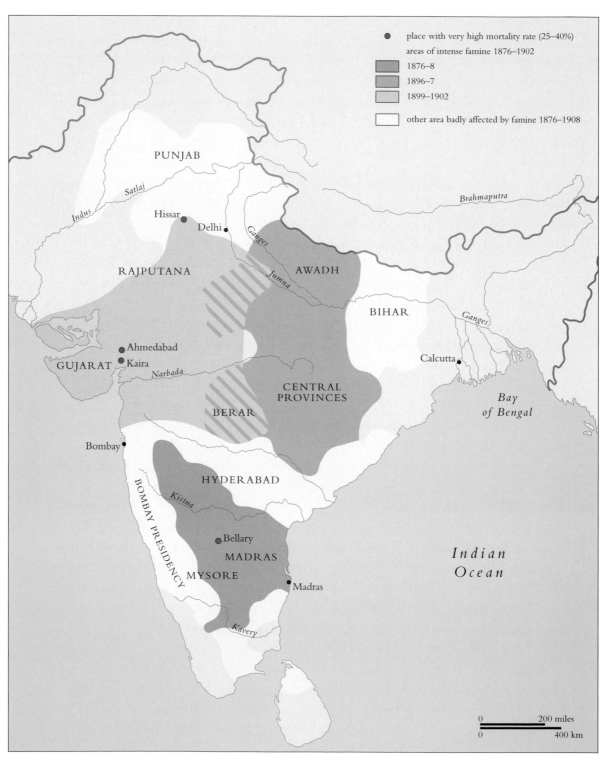

The major famine zones in India, 1876–1908.

'public virtue and self devotion unsurpassed in history;' princes and chiefs were thanked for their loyalty, and – eventually – the people of India were instructed (in no uncertain terms) that 'the permanent interests of this Empire demand the supreme supervision and direction of their administration by English officers.' The only concession to the liberal vision was that natives too might be allowed to share in the administration but that they should know there would have to be a place for the 'natural leaders' – the aristocratic grandees assembled in their tents. Finally, a message from the new empress was read, promising (as usual) to rule through liberty with justice and to promote 'prosperity and advance welfare.'

There was at least one British official, the governor of Madras, Richard Grenville, the Duke of Buckingham and Chandos, who was very uncomfortable to be in Delhi in the first week of 1877. The monsoon had largely failed in southeast India, and famine had already engulfed the region. In the circumstances the governor had asked the viceroy whether he might be excused from attending. But he got short shrift from Lytton, who told him that his presence was mandatory since, in the long run, the 'failure' of the durbar would be more damaging to India than the failure of the monsoon. The duke duly showed up; and in that same week, according to an English journalist, 100,000 were estimated to have died of starvation and cholera in Mysore and Madras.

Although the implicit promise of British rule in India ever since the Mutiny had been the delivery of better times in return for loyalty, each decade was scarred by devastating famine in some region of the country. In 1860, 2 million had died in the Punjab. In 1866 nearly 27 per cent of the population of Orissa, some 800,000, had died; in 1868 a quarter of the population of Ajmere. In 1877–8, during Lytton's administration, the famines have been responsibly calculated to have cost over 7 million lives. One understandably indignant early Indian nationalist reminded the British that, while there had been some hand-wringing over the loss of an eighth of the Irish population during the Hunger of 1845-9, the equivalent of nearly the entire population of Ireland had died in India in 1877–8.

The rulers of the Raj were not indifferent to the calamity. But, as in Ireland, most of them, in obedience to the non-interventionist orthodoxy, had decided it was a 'natural' or 'Providential' event that it was beyond the powers of government to ameliorate. But there were, of course, things that the government could do, even negatively, to help. Its own officials, for example, often recommended a temporary suspension or at least postponement of land taxes. But when this was suggested for Orissa in 1866, the commissioners of the Board of Revenue in Calcutta dismissed the idea. Instead, the advice was uncannily similar to that given to Ireland in 1846–9:

'Don't let the people get downhearted … set the people to help themselves – a somewhat difficult matter in Orissa. But there is nothing like trying.' This was rich, coming from a government that by systematically destroying the production of salt in Orissa – not merely taxed out of existence by discriminatory tariffs but actually prohibited by law – had removed precisely the local income that made it possible for the poor to feed themselves, especially in years when shortages sent prices sky-high. Then, of course, it might have been possible for the government to import grain, at the very least to stabilize or reverse price inflation. This, again, was suggested in 1866 in the case of Burmese rice. Back came the reply in February: 'Your message received … the Government decline to import rice. . . . If the market favours, imported rice will find its way into Pooree without government interference which can only do harm.'

Mindful of the infamous disaster that ensued when there had been a serious threat of famine in Bengal and Bihar, in 1873–4 Sir Richard Temple had purchased rice from Burma and distributed it as free rations to the neediest. But he had been violently attacked by those who, in the Trevelyan-ite vein, had judged this an unconscionable interference with the free market. Lytton was one of them and, sensing Temple's need to make amends for his lapse, sent him as famine delegate south to Madras and Mysore, where both governors were indulging in suspiciously prodigal efforts at public relief and private philanthropy. An Anti-Charitable Contributions Act (something that should modify our assumptions about the ubiquitous philanthropy of the Victorians) was passed expressly to prevent aid coming from Britain and the Indian cities, which was said to be delaying the necessity of 'soft' Indians being made to stand on their own two feet. The regime that Temple put in place, in the face of angry opposition from Buckingham and his Bombay counterpart, Sir Philip Wodehouse, was a more draconian edition of Irish relief in the 1840s. In return for punishing coolie labour – usually breaking rocks for roads (again!) or laying railway tracks – a modest daily allowance of 1.2 lb of rice was given plus a small allowance of dal. This was altogether too lenient for Lytton, who struck millions from the rolls, banned relief for the adult able-bodied, and decreed that none of it could be given to anyone living within 10 miles of the work camps. Desperately malnourished people, therefore, had to walk long distances to be given severe physical labour – and, under Temple's new rules, only 1lb of rice a day and no lentils at all.

The results were predictable. One official described a roadworks in the Bombay Deccan as resembling 'a battlefield, its sides strewn with the dead, the dying and those recently attacked.' Destitute and starving weavers pleaded to be arrested since they had heard (correctly) that gaol was one of the few places where some sort of sustenance was guaranteed. At the same time, grain depots in Madras and Bombay were full of imported rice, heavily guarded by troops and police to prevent thefts or riot. The famished, as horrified journalists like William Digby (who published a two-volume history of the famine) testified, dropped dead in front of the fenced stockpiles. By a bitter irony, by the end of the century it was evident that it was those areas of India that had the most railway mileage and the most commercially developed economies that suffered most brutally in famine years, because of the ease of transporting grain to markets where it could be *hoarded* to maximize the profit from price rises.

In August 1877, with much of south and south-central India turning into a charnel house, the viceroy deigned to descend from the coolness of Simla for a few days to tour the most stricken areas around Madras with Buckingham. Of the relief camps he wrote to Lady Lytton, back at Viceregal Lodge, 'You never saw such "popular picnics" as they are. The people in them do no work of any kind, are bursting with fat … the Duke visits these camps like a Buckingham squire would visit his model farm, taking the deepest interest in the growing fatness of his prize oxen and pigs.' Missionaries, and appalled local officials and reporters, had a different view: cholera victims crawling to cemeteries and lying down between graves with crows and kites hovering above them; huge armies of the desperate trudging out of British India into territories like that of independent Hyderabad, where the nizam was prepared to hand out free rations. 'Recently,' wrote one of the missionaries, 'the corpse of a woman was carried along the road slung to a pole like an animal, with the face partly devoured by dogs. The other day, a famished crazy woman took a dead dog and ate it, near our bungalow.' Such scenes were becoming commonplace in the India of the queen-empress. But they didn't stop the young Cecil Rhodes, then an undergraduate at Oxford, being confident enough to write that same year, with the messianic voice of the new imperialism, that 'the more of the world we occupy, the better it is for the human race.'

Not everyone felt the same way. Florence Nightingale, the most revered woman in Britain after the queen, read the reports of missionaries and journalists like Digby and pronounced them a 'hideous record of human suffering and destruction [such as] the world has never seen before.' But aside from grieving for the millions of dead, what could be done to prevent future miseries on a similar scale? Lytton, who had actually cut back on funding for water storage and who had derided the schemes of those whom he called 'irrigation fanatics,' now made a show of supporting them. He also moved to establish a famine fund, financed of course (as in Ireland) by the disadvantaged country. Lytton's secretary of agriculture, Allan Octavian Hume, son

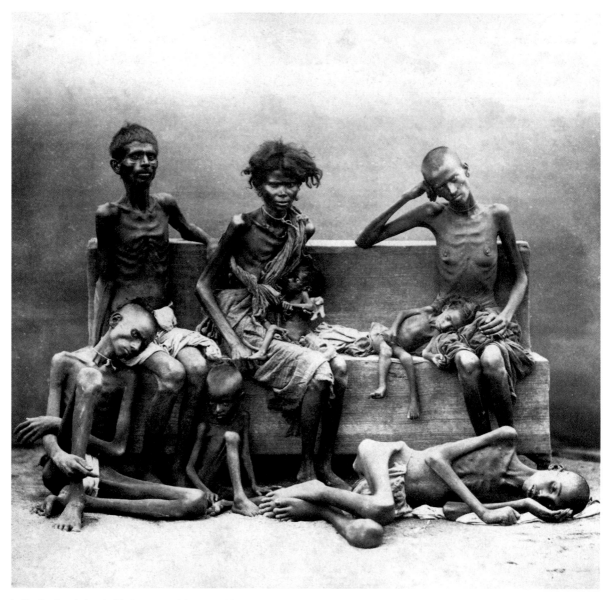

Indian famine victims in Madras, one of the worst-hit areas, 1876–7.

of the Scottish founder of the Radical party, Joseph Hume, argued strongly that a progressive income tax should be levied so that those who could best afford it contributed most to the financing of the relief fund. When the viceroy vetoed the idea, preferring to increase already onerous taxes such as those on salt, Hume resigned, to become one of the most eloquent critics of British economic policy in India and ultimately the founder of the Indian National Congress! In fact an entire cohort of the early supporters and leaders of Congress – some British, some Indian – had washed their hands of the empire of good intentions precisely because famine policy seemed always to have been sacrificed to military power and naked economic self-interest. William Digby, whose history of the famines is one of the most damning, founded the journal *India* to counteract the usual 'India hand' stereotypes about the unfitness of Asians for self-rule. Dadabhai Naoroji, the Bombay Parsi who in 1892 became Britain's first Asian MP (for Finsbury Central) and who was also three times elected president of Congress, set out his bitter disillusionment in the classic *Poverty and Un-British Rule in India* (1901).

The problem, as Naoroji and many others recognized (and as Amartya Sen points out, it indeed remains today in cases of global famine), is one of income, not of gross food supply. The argument was over the means to raise Indian livelihoods to a level at which food would be obtainable even in years of shortage. Defenders of the imperial record insisted that the classical economic system – the markets themselves and their stimulus for India – would eventually do the trick. Critics like Hume and Naoroji pointed to the hypocrisy of a policy that purported to be free trade but was in fact unscrupulously interventionist. Tariffs were nakedly manipulated to favour British imports and disadvantage Indian products; millions of tons of grain were shipped out in 1877–8 to stabilize British home prices, while Indian prices were allowed to soar in Bombay and Madras to levels that guaranteed starvation. Lytton had even enacted a cut in the tariffs on imported British cottons at the precise time when the Gujarati weavers were suffering more than most urban populations in India. And still could be heard the reiteration of the ancient, sanctimonious nostrums: let them stand on their own two feet.

What was in the process of utterly breaking down was the original liberal axiom of reciprocal prosperity. Prosperity at home in Britain seemed to be bought at the expense of the accumulation of wealth in India. Only those in India who collaborated with this institutionalized and legislated economic inequality, such as grain shippers and textile importers, got their due rewards. Three particular circumstances in the 1870s and 1880s made this unlikely to change. First, Britain itself was in an economic downturn and very unlikely to feel charitable towards India at the expense of its own recovery, or to raise not just prices but the spectre of working-class unrest at home. Second, the home economy was feeling the pinch of competition from the United States and European rivals like Germany; exports were shrinking and once again Britain was unlikely to sacrifice its captive imperial markets for the sake of long-term economic maturity. (By the end of the century India was easily the biggest of all Britain's export markets, taking fully 10 per cent of total exports – overwhelmingly cheap manufactured Lancashire cottons, the product that more than any other had destroyed the Indian textile industry.) Of all the facts to refute the 'benevolent development' thesis of British imperialism, this is perhaps the most irrefutably damning. Finally, revenues for investment in infrastructure that would actually benefit Indian peasant producers (rather than import–export merchants) had to compete with what, for viceroys like Lytton, was the supreme and over-riding interest – that of strategic military expansion on the northwest frontier lest the Cossack hordes come pouring through the Khyber Pass. The Indian taxpayer paid the full price for British strategic paranoia.

What was worse, the paranoia often led directly to fiasco (and thus another round of penal taxation). In 1878, Lytton finally succeeded in engineering the Afghan war, for which he had been manoeuvring since the very beginning of his tenure as viceroy. The pretext was the emir's refusal of British 'help' in repelling what Lytton insisted was an immediate Russian military threat – although in fact it was nothing more than the appearance of a Russian diplomatic mission in Kabul. The usual British invasion was followed by the equally time-honoured local uprising and wholesale slaughter of the British mission, which as usual required a second, punitive campaign – in this instance punitive for the British in the losses of both men and money. Pyrrhic victory in Afghanistan was made no more palatable when it transpired that the famine-relief fund so piously established had been pillaged for the campaign.

Disraeli had been against the Afghan strategy from the beginning and had only been persuaded to support it against his better judgement by a new Secretary of State for India and Lytton devotee, Lord Cranbrook. When the news of the expensive disaster came in the prime minister was appalled, but put a brave face on it. In the same year, 1879, another British imperial army was torn to pieces by the Zulu king Cetawayo at Isandhlwana. By the time the damage was contained in South Africa another £5 million had gone down the drain and Britain had – just as it had often done in India – destroyed one of the few viable African nations in the name of bringing peace and security. Perhaps this is what Lord Beaconsfield (as Disraeli became in 1876) meant when he spoke in the Lords of the 'millions bound to us by military sway [a nice euphemism for coercion] because they know they are indebted to it for order and justice.' Increasingly, however, Gladstone felt bound to retort, what 'order'? What 'justice'? And he got very angry indeed at the cant of 'liberty': 'Liberty for Ourselves,' Beaconsfield might have said, 'and empire for the rest of the world.' Gladstone's increasing irritability and contempt for the extravagances of empire signified a new turn in the politics of liberalism. There had always been, of course, an element among the Liberals, especially orthodox free traders like the MPs John Bright and Richard Cobden, who were suspicious of expensive imperialist adventurism. But it was only in the late 1870s that a more self-consciously crusading anti-jingoism found its most eloquent voice in Gladstone himself. With Disraeli in the Lords and a shadow of his former self, it was Gladstone who for a moment – though just an opposition MP and not even the leader of his party – had the moral theatre all to himself; between 1876 and the election of 1880 he used it to put on the greatest one-man show in the whole of Victorian political history.

Gladstone's political crusades drew their power not just from moral fervour, but from thorny self-interrogations and exhaustive reading and reflection. At the beginning of his premiership in 1869 he had read a weighty discussion of the Irish land problem by an Indian civil servant, George Campbell. As Fenian (republican) militancy was becoming more serious, Campbell had visited Ireland and been startled to discover how closely the problems of its peasant tenants resembled those seen in parts of India. There, too, peasants who could not produce hard, English-style legal contracts of ownership were written off as 'tenants-at-will,' subject to summary rent increases and eviction for default, without any compensation for the improvements they had made. Cultivators who had farmed the same plot for generations were turfed off and turned into pauperized, landless labourers. As the British had become more educated in Indian land customs they had come to recognize that, in much of India, occupation over the generations was equivalent to a kind of 'moral co-proprietorship' that protected the peasants from being treated as mere tenants-at-will. This, Campbell felt (along with John Stuart Mill, who had written in much the same vein), ought also to be the case in Ireland. Although Campbell had grown up very much in the hands-off school of Trevelyan, he none the less believed that there was a place for government to act as the guardian of the defenceless. True liberalism would be honoured, not violated, by such an engagement. The alternative would be yet more cycles of bitter violence.

As Gladstone read on in his temple of peace at Hawarden, something crucial for him and for the history of British liberalism began to make itself felt: that there were places in the empire – India, Ireland and probably the dark places of industrial

England, too, for that matter – where the old gospel of pure self-reliance had become a bankrupt platitude. Not that this new awareness made Gladstone a radical interventionist. The main thrust of the Irish reforms in his first administration was still the dismantling, not the building, of state institutions – especially the disestablishment of the Church of Ireland. But even as a pragmatist (not a radical) he was beginning to understand the force of the Birmingham Liberal activist Joseph Chamberlain's arguments that good local government in the industrial cities of Britain often meant the aggressive assertion of public power to provide for the basic social needs of citizens – adequate housing, transport and medical welfare. The test of righteous liberalism in modern Britain, then, could not just be freedom of trade and property. Or rather those freedoms, if they were to survive, would have to be complemented by attention to social justice. For it was, as Campbell had said, the sense of being robbed of that justice that drove men to fury and violence – whether in the relief-camp strikes on the Deccan, in the dockyards of Britain, or, especially, in the countryside of the west of Ireland. 'Ireland is at your doors,' Gladstone told the House of Commons in typically prophetic manner, introducing a land bill that took a modest step towards protecting tenants from eviction for reasons other than default of rent; 'Providence has placed it there. Law and legislature have made a compact between you and you must face these obligations.'

At every stage in his long career Gladstone (like Moses, to whom his faithful often compared him) had found the True Path from moments of revelation, especially of the adversary – 'the hosts of Pharaoh,' whom he was called on to smite hip and thigh. (Sometimes that adversary was himself and, after meetings with the many fallen women he felt he had to redeem, beginning in his days at Oxford, he would flog the impurity out of his flesh.) Political and theological enemies received merely the lashing of his verbal or written rhetoric. Those first foes had been 'rational Christians' – Unitarians and their like, allied with the iniquitous reformers of 1832 – whom the young, solemnly High Church Gladstone believed, along with Wordsworth and Coleridge, were leading Britain down the primrose path to godless egalitarianism. (His hostility to the Reform Act of 1832, an acute embarrassment to the franchise reformer of the 1860s, he later put down to excessive youthful zeal and 'delusion.') The second cohort of villains consisted of those wicked men – especially, of course, Disraeli, whom Gladstone from the beginning detested as a self-glamorizing opportunist – who had crucified his sainted Peel. For Gladstone, who himself came from a manufacturing background, Peel's no-nonsense plainness, his self-evident integrity and the tormented way he had put devotion to the truth before personal power or even party was the epitome of virtue in politics. Those who had destroyed him while purporting (in Disraeli's case, he thought, preposterously) to represent the 'traditional' interests of landed Britain were guilty of a masquerade that was not only stupid but wicked.

What especially stuck in Gladstone's craw was the pretence by the likes of Disraeli to represent an authentic Britain of rolling acres and the true Church. The true Church! Disraeli! Who never went down on bended knee (much less applied the penitent lash) except with a wink and a nod to pure form. And by what right did he apostrophize the working people of Britain as their true friend and protector while appealing, as had the generally disgraceful Palmerston, to the worst instincts of their belligerent vanity? It was he, Gladstone, along with the real soldiers of God like Cobden and Bright, who represented the genuinely moral Britain. In his own origins and apprenticeship were woven the fibre of the true Britain – Scotland, Lancashire, Oxford; the factory and the theological college, the university and the loom. Everything he had done he had done, he felt, responsibly: not deceiving the working class into expectations of imminent full democracy, but counselling patience; offering the reward of the franchise to those who, by dint of industry, education and hard-earned property, truly merited it and could be expected to use it with wisdom and temperance.

And now, in 1876, with his old adversary raised into the realms of Beaconsfieldism, but a prime minister still capable of mischief and iniquity, Gladstone felt summoned once again to undeceive a public who might have been bewitched by Disraeli's 'Judaic' manoeuvres into believing that a policy designed for an 'Asiatic empire' – supporting the Turk; buying an Egyptian canal; putting a notorious opium-addicted madman like Lytton in charge of the destinies of the Indian empire – that all this exoticism could actually be worthy of the greatness of Christian Britain! The brutality of the Ottoman onslaught on the civilian population after an uprising in eastern Roumelia (modern Bulgaria) – the burned villages, rapes and sodomies; the mutilation of women and children – hit the British press in the spring of 1876 and triggered an immediate outcry against Disraeli's pro-Turkish foreign policy. Hundreds of meetings were convened up and down the country. Far from leaping into the breach, Gladstone (who was formally supposed to do what he was told by the Whiggish leaders of the party, Lord Granville and the Marquis of Hartington) held back until late in the year. But the opportunity for a politics of impassioned virtue finally proved too much to resist. His 'Bulgarian Horrors' pamphlet, written in the temple of peace, was an immediate best-seller and a few days later Gladstone was on the stump, sermonizing the faithful in an electrifying address on London's Blackheath in a rainstorm. Whatever effect it may or may not

William Gladstone leaving West Calder station on his Midlothian campaign, engraving, 1879.

have had on the politics of the country, those who were there, like the radical journalist W. T. Stead, remembered it as a moment of conversion.

The charismatic re-emergence of the blazing prophet may have deceived Gladstone into thinking he could do no wrong (however much hurrumphing the Hartingtons and Granvilles did). He was wrong. His attack on Disraeli for taking the country to the edge of conflict when Russia went to war with Turkey badly misjudged the public mood, whipped up by Disraeli's campaign into a lather of belligerent jingoism. Returning from his peacemaking at the Congress of Berlin in 1878, having obtained concessions from both Russia and Turkey, Disraeli was crowned, not stoned. By the end of 1879, however, the public mood had changed again with the expensive disasters in Zululand and Afghanistan. Innocent blood – both British and native – had been spilled, Gladstone thundered, in the name of vain adventurism. 'The sanctity of life in the hill villages of Afghanistan' was 'as inviolable in the eye of Almighty God' as that of every Briton at home.

And at home, the Liberals were presented with the political gift of a severe and sudden depression. The Almighty, Gladstone implied, was punishing those who indulged in the fleshpots for the wickedness of their Conservative rulers. Modern plagues were upon the back of Britain: bankruptcies, soaring unemployment, collapsing agricultural prices, stoppages of trade – even a potato blight in southwest

Ireland. Basking in his popularity as the man who had brought 'peace with honour,' and enjoying the divisions in the Liberal party, Disraeli had written Gladstone off as a tedious crank. But he had not reckoned with the extraordinary bolt of electrifying, almost messianic energy that seemed to have struck his old adversary, setting his oratory on fire – nor with the strikingly contemporary means he used to broadcast his withering attacks on the bungling extravagance of Beaconsfieldism. On 24 November 1879, Gladstone, accompanied by his wife, Catherine, boarded a train from one of his political heartlands, Liverpool, and travelled to another, lowland Scotland. Travelling through Wigan, St Helen's and on to Carlisle, Galashiels and finally Edinburgh, the old boy became a political locomotive himself; the pistons of his magnificent self-righteousness pumping away, the orator roared from platforms, waved from train windows, was escorted to hotels by rapturous crowds where he made speeches from balconies. In Glasgow, Gladstone gave his inaugural address as rector of the university and was treated to the spectacle of a torchlight parade, as if he were the prophet of a great evangelical revival – which, indeed, Gladstone thought he was. Some 85,000 people at 15 venues heard him in two weeks. The Midlothian campaign was the most American campaign Britain had ever seen, and it was an undoubted triumph.

When he had called the general election in March 1880, Disraeli assumed he would have no trouble in getting another Conservative majority. It turned out to be a massive miscalculation. The Liberals were returned with more than 100 more MPs than the Tories. 'Beaconsfieldism,' Gladstone wrote jubilantly, 'vanished like some vast magnificent castle in an Italian Romance.' Italian romances were not the Grand Old Man's sort of thing.

Along with 351 Liberals and 239 Tories in the parliament of 1880, however, were 65 Irish Home Rule MPs. They did not, as yet, hold the balance of power; but, disciplined as a force by their new leader, Charles Stewart Parnell, who had replaced the Irish Tory Isaac Butt, they could not exactly be ignored either. Even if their presence had not been so numerous, it is unlikely that Gladstone could, in fact, have stayed aloof from the open sore that was 'The Irish Question.' For one thing the country, especially in the west, seemed to be disintegrating into lawlessness as a result of the anti-eviction campaign mobilized by the Land League. Its founder, the formidable Irish activist Michael Davitt, came from County Mayo, the heart of the pro-French uprising in 1798 and among the worst-hit of all the famine counties. He had gone to Lancashire to find work, had lost an arm in an industrial accident at age 11 and been imprisoned for gun-running before travelling to the United States to raise funds and consciousness about what needed to be done to change the lives of

Above: Bailiffs force an entry to evict tenants who have fallen behind with the rent, *c.* 1888.
Opposite top: *Charles Stewart Parnell* (detail) by Sydney Prior Hall, *c.* 1890.
Opposite below: An evicted family in Glenbeigh, Ireland, 1888.

the Irish poor and the destiny of the nation. By the late 1870s, he and militant comrades had set up the Mayo Land League in the west, which, as the expanded Land League of Ireland, spread rapidly through the country. Its enemy was billed as 'landlordism,' and its goals were rent reductions – by intimidation if necessary – and resisting eviction. In fact, the pace of evictions in Ireland had slowed markedly from the all-out dispossessions of the 1850s. Charles Trevelyan's vision of a modernized Irish agriculture dominated by commercially minded large farmers, whether graziers in the west or arable farmers in the east, was well on the way to materializing. But capitalist farming is seldom socially pretty. The more profitable Irish agriculture became, the more inequitable was the distribution of its profits. And when – as at the end of the 1870s – it hit a slump, those who had depended on it for wages were of course the first to go; and those who were hanging on to their smallholdings were the first to be pressed with higher rents.

There was ample recruiting ground, in other words, for an army of the indignant. The Land League's tactics, officially at any rate, were supposed to be aggressive but non-violent: the social ostracism of landlords who were known to impose summary evictions. The wretched Captain Charles Boycott, an English farmer who leased land from an Irish absentee aristocrat, Lord Ernle, but collected both his own and the landowner's rents, was selected for exemplary and shockingly successful ostracism. Ernle was actually murdered. And despite the League's protestations of innocence there were epidemics of livestock mutilation, rick-burning, shots fired into houses as 'a warning' and the occasional assassination. Faced with this chronic lawlessness, many of Gladstone's own colleagues in the cabinet, especially the new chief secretary of Ireland, William Edward Forster, were in favour of an equally fierce counter-campaign of 'order,' including, if necessary, the selective suspension of habeas corpus and detention without trial. They were also deeply suspicious of Parnell, who, they believed, condoned the violence even as he pretended to deplore it.

For Gladstone, matters weren't as simple as a choice between passivity and repression. Even though, as yet, he had nothing to do with Parnell personally, he understood that the Land League was no longer a mere movement of aggrieved tenant peasants. Parnell himself, the half-American, Cambridge-educated, ostensibly Protestant (but actually agnostic) gentleman-landowner from the rolling hills of conservative County Wicklow (all horse shows, cucumber sandwiches and fêtes), was evidence that Davitt had succeeded in attracting all kinds of Irish people – teachers, shopkeepers, publicans, doctors, lawyers – to its ranks as the voice of Irish national, as well as social, aspirations. 'We created Parnell and he created us,' said another Leaguer, Tim Healy, a little boastfully but not inaccurately.

Years before he was formally committed to Home Rule, Gladstone had already understood the gathering Irish crisis as a fork in the road for the history of Britain itself: a test to see whether the constitution of the Union, both in respect of the land reform that Ireland needed and the more independent local government that it deserved, could take the strain and still survive. Previous generations of liberals like Charles Trevelyan had assumed that, whatever the sorrows of past history, there could be no greater fortune than to be part of the greatest empire the world had ever seen. But Trevelyan's son, George Otto (historian as well as politician), was now in Gladstone's government and he, like the prime minister, could see that some measure of land reform was needed to make continued membership of the Union legitimate. As a taster, in 1870, Gladstone had presented to parliament a bill designed to compensate evicted tenants for improvements they had made to their plots (although, as Roy Foster has pointed out, the kind of peasants who were 'improvers' were those least likely to be evicted). In any case, although this modest proposal was passed by the Commons it was shot down in the Lords as an unconscionable interference with private property. Taken aback by the tactical failure, Gladstone began to listen more carefully to his cabinet colleagues who insisted (as the tempo of rural violence increased) that coercion had to precede land reforms. In January 1881 a Protection of Persons and Property Bill went before the Commons, authorizing preventive detention. Outraged, the Irish bloc went into obstructionist mode, filibustering through the night; they tied up the business of the House so completely that on 3 February a resolution was passed to 'set aside' ordinary procedure. Infuriated Irish MPs, including Parnell, had to be forcibly removed.

After the stick, the carrot. With the Coercion Act in place Gladstone felt free to introduce his land bill in April without worrying about accusations of making concessions under pressure. None of its 'three Fs' – fair rent, free sale and fixity of tenure – was without its problems, not least for Gladstone himself, who fretted about their compatibility with the sanctity of private property. But the paramount need was to provide some sense of equity for the tenant smallholders of Ireland, and so to de-fang the violent wing of the Land League. Under the act, tenants who paid their rent could not be evicted (for example to enable the consolidation of small lots into large estates). More radical still, a government-appointed land court and a Land Commission were to arbitrate the 'fairness' of those rents. Gladstone needed to speak at 58 sittings of parliament to see the bill made law.

But if he had thought the bill would satisfy the Land League he was made to think again. Parnell (who supported the bill) continued to go on the attack, demanding rent reductions and an amnesty for arrears. More ominously, he began to talk of the connections between Britain and Ireland as if they were up for severance. Picking up the gauntlet, Gladstone in his turn threatened that any attempt to dissolve them would be met by the full weight of government. In October he went still further and had Parnell and other members of the Land League arrested and incarcerated in Kilmainham gaol on the outskirts of Dublin.

Cheering broke out from the hard men in the cabinet and the party. At last the Old Man understood what it took to lay down the law in Ireland (altogether reminiscent of Lytton's 1878 Vernacular Press Act, which gagged the uppity and seditious Indian press). But, although Gladstone joked at a dinner party about becoming accustomed to coercion 'much as a man might say (in confidence) that he found himself under the painful necessity of slaying his mother,' he was in fact deeply uneasy about governing by force, and never thought it could possibly be anything but the shortest-term answer to Ireland's distress and anger. In Naples in the early 1850s his stomach had been turned by the despotic Bourbon monarchy's treatment of political prisoners, and he had written that such regimes were in violation of natural rights and God's ordinance. Truly legitimate governments, he believed, could survive only so long as they were grounded in the 'affections' of the people. Whatever else liberalism meant in the age of the gunboat and the Gatling gun, it surely had to mean at least that.

So the prime minister opened secret negotiations with the imprisoned Parnell through the intermediary of Katherine O'Shea, the wife of another Irish MP but also the mistress of Parnell and the mother of his children. The oddest of couples, the two men needed each other – or at least, in 1882, thought they did. Gladstone needed Parnell to master the champions of nationalist violence, to try to persuade the Irish MPs that their wish for greater self-government could be met within the Union. Parnell needed Gladstone to deliver a more radical dose of land reform (especially a restraint on the collection of arrears) and to repeal or at least moderate coercion. An agreement – the secret 'Kilmainham Treaty' – was struck. Parnell would be freed, the better to bridle the hotheads; Gladstone would deliver the arrears bill. But in Parnell's personal absence the hotheads, incensed by his imprisonment, had got fiercer, not cooler. In May 1882 the brand-new chief secretary of Ireland, Lord Frederick Cavendish, and his permanent under-secretary, Thomas Burke, were murdered, while walking in Phoenix Park in Dublin, by terrorists committed to assassination and calling themselves the Invincibles. For Gladstone, the atrocity was doubly horrifying. Long surgical knives had been used to cut the victims' throats from ear to ear, and Burke's head had been all but severed from his body. And Cavendish was not just another political appointee; he was Freddie, a nephew

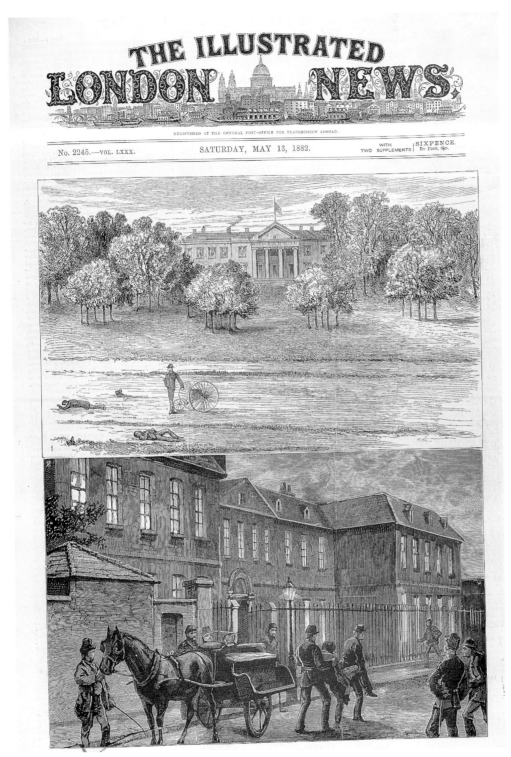

Front page of the *Illustrated London News*, 13 May 1882, showing the *Scene of the Murder of Lord Frederick. Cavendish and Mr T. H. Burke, in Phoenix Park, Dublin* (top), and *Conveying the Dead to Stevens's Hospital* (below).

of Gladstone's wife and a frequent guest at Hawarden. Horrified, Parnell, who had just been released under the terms agreed at Kilmainham, now offered to resign his leadership of the Irish party. But it was precisely in situations like this that Gladstone's instinct of Christian magnanimity served him well. He not only declined Parnell's gesture but promised closer collaboration and moved ahead with the arrears bill just a week after the murders. For some of his colleagues this was further proof that the Old Man had gone mad. Revolt was only pre-empted by the passage of another Coercion Act, in direct response to the Phoenix Park murders, extending powers of search, arrest and detention and creating special tribunals to act without the inconvenience of an Irish jury.

Despite the two measures cancelling each other out, Parnell and Gladstone did not yet break off their covert collaboration. Katherine O'Shea continued to bear messages and babies. (By this time Gladstone certainly knew, if he hadn't before, of her relationship with Parnell.) There was, the prime minister thought, a way out: through local government boards; these, the pet project of Joseph gas-and-water Chamberlain, could be directly elected by the Irish without affronting the constitutional principles of undivided sovereignty. Under the scheme, however, there was also to be a Central Board in Dublin for all-Irish business, appointed by the British government. The Central Board was a sop to those who thought local devolution was the thin end of the wedge. But it was taken by Conservatives and Unionists in precisely the opposite sense: as the embryo of a true Home Rule government. Red flags went up. The measure went down.

Parnell never quite believed that Gladstone had done everything in his power to promote it; or, if he had, that he no longer had the political muscle to make it happen – much less the substantial Home Rule measure he really wanted. The Old Man was frequently ill; at the height of a crisis he had fallen in the snow and cut his head badly, prompting him to say that he could feel the bleeding *inside* his skull. Who knew – perhaps there had been some serious damage? He seemed no longer master in the house of his cabinet: Whigs and Radicals were at each other's throats and both sides suspected the prime minister of bad faith. Chamberlain – whose allegiance to true devolution seemed, as the years passed, less and less solid – was waiting impatiently in the wings to seize the leadership. What was more, Gladstone, the scourge of imperialists, had, in South Africa and especially in Egypt, revealed himself to be just as partial to gunboat diplomacy and impetuous military expeditions as the vainglorious Beaconsfield. In 1881 there had been an uprising of military officers against the Khedive, whose profligate government – even after the sale of the Suez Canal shares to Britain – had amassed so huge a debt that it had put even a pretence of sovereignty into receivership. And the receivers were of course the Western powers, Britain and France, who assumed control over the revenues of Egypt to ensure proper service of the debt. (This was, in fact, an almost exact African replay of the beginnings of British rule in India in the 18th century, with European colonialists insisting on intervening to clean up the mess that they had been largely responsible for creating in the first place.)

The Egyptian revolt – a mix of military and Muslim unrest – put both powers in the position of either cutting their losses or going in for the kill, and for the long term. When the French rather shrank from the logic, not to mention the expense of the latter, Gladstone, to the amazement of many, dived in with guns blazing. The Royal Navy bombarded Alexandria. An army sent on a lightning 40-day expedition annihilated the Egyptian rebels. Gladstone the anti-imperialist ordered victory bonfires to be lit around the country. Many of his oldest friends were aghast at the apostasy, especially when Gladstone, like any colonial proconsul – or, indeed, like Disraeli – went on and on about how the expedition had been launched only in the interests of 'peace' and 'stability' and not to establish a British colony in Egypt, heavens no, merely the restoration of the 'legitimate' rule of the Khedive. He would, of course, need the odd British soldier or two for the foreseeable future to maintain that legitimacy, as well as to collect on funds owing to the likes of the Barings. No one was more distressed at Gladstone's foray into imperialism than his old comrade John Bright. At least Disraeli was candid about *his* imperialism. Gladstone, on the other hand, seemed pathetically deluded, wrote Bright: 'He seems to have the power of convincing himself that what to me seems glaringly wrong is evidently right and tho' he regrets that a crowd of men should be killed, he regards it almost as an occurrence which is not to be condemned as it is one of the incidents of a policy out of which he hopes for a better order of things.'

Instead of the 'better order' in Egypt, Gladstone got the General Gordon disaster at Khartoum. To be fair, this was not of his making, for Gordon, faced with the huge *jihadi* army of the Mahdi – the Chosen One – sweeping up from the southern Sudan, had been ordered to evacuate Khartoum smartly but had chosen instead to stay and court martyrdom. Furious with Gordon, Gladstone was personally prepared to grant him his wish; but it was politically unthinkable. Lord Wolseley was sent on a relief expedition up the Nile, which arrived at the end of January 1885 just a few days too late to save Gordon. Gladstone bore the odium for having 'sacrificed' the Hero, not least from Queen Victoria, reinforced in her aversion for everything about William Ewart Gladstone.

Above: *Joseph Chamberlain* by Frank Holl, 1886.
Opposite: The tomb effigies of William and Catherine Gladstone in Hawarden Church, Flintshire, Wales.

All these troubles persuaded Parnell that Gladstone's power was on the wane, and that he should look elsewhere for the furtherance of at least his short-term aims. Although in retrospect the tactical turn towards the Conservatives seems perverse, Parnell was in fact being heavily (and irresponsibly) wooed by the Tory magnate Lord Carnarvon, to the point where he believed that, if his Irish bloc defected from the Liberals, they could, together with dissidents in Gladstone's own party, bring down the government. His price to Lord Salisbury was the land bill and the dropping of a crimes bill that Gladstone had been unable to get through parliament. He got his wish. In June 1885, the Liberal government was defeated on a parliamentary vote through the abstention of a large number of their own number and the opposition of the Irish. But the Parnellite–Tory alliance was too unnatural a thing to last, especially since Parnell was plainly driving for full-scale Home Rule – an Irish parliament for everything except foreign policy.

This was a step too far, not just for Salisbury but for many among the Liberals, including the increasingly imperialist Joseph Chamberlain, for whom any talk of Home Rule was the same as secession and the end of the Union. But Gladstone had undergone another of those revelatory changes of heart. He had been deep amidst the stacks in the temple of peace again, and after intensive historical research had come to believe that, when the majority of the Irish people questioned the fruits of the Union, they had, in fact, a point: many iniquities and injustices had been inflicted on them. The choice – if not now, then at some inevitable stage in the future – was not between coercion and Home Rule, for coercion could not be perpetuated in a truly liberal Britain. It would be a choice between Home Rule and out-and-out separation. Conceding Home Rule was the best possible way to pre-empt a much more drastic break. Once convinced, he attempted to persuade the Queen (a hard case) that Irish self-government would be, in the truest sense, a conservative measure; agreed with Parnell (via Katherine O'Shea) that an Irish parliament was the way forward; and only then deigned to tell his own party what he might have in mind, informing Lord Derby at Hawarden that the Union was 'a mistake and that no adequate justification had been shown for taking away the national life of Ireland.'

Gladstone's tactics for bringing his party with him were at best peremptory. In mid-December 1885, with an election campaign under way, a kite was flown in the form of a newspaper story claiming to set out the Home Rule principles to which Gladstone was committed. He immediately repudiated it and insisted that what he had in mind was just a local-government scheme; but the shock waves inside the Liberal party were massively damaging. Both Whigs and imperialist radicals like

Chamberlain were appalled that they were being committed to a policy without consultation or consent, and began to pack their political bags. Most seriously, to his radical friends and colleagues, Chamberlain began to present the causes of domestic social reform and Irish Home Rule as mutually exclusive; the necessary improvements to the 'condition of England' held hostage to the obsessions of one old man, himself bewitched by an Irish quasi-traitor.

The election produced an Irish bloc of 86 MPs, which precisely and arithmetically held the balance between the two parties. Gladstone offered to support Home Rule if proposed by a Tory government. But the young stars of the Tories, Randolph Churchill and Arthur Balfour, led the charge against it, playing on the already militant paranoia of Ulster Protestants who were fearful that they were about to be swamped by a semi-independent 'ignorant' Catholic Ireland and that they would pay the price for generations of the Protestant ascendancy. Balfour, throwing scruples to the wind, told Unionists that Home Rule would mean they would be 'put under the heel of a majority which is greater than you in number [but which] is most undoubtedly inferior to you in political knowledge and experience – you the wealthy, the orderly, the industrious, the enterprising portion of Ireland, are to supply the money for that part of Ireland which is less orderly, less industrious and less ... law-abiding.' From the refined lips of the Oxford philosopher-scholar came the authentic strain of Ulster Red-hand Unionism.

When the Tories, unsurprisingly, opted for coercion Gladstone grasped the nettle himself. A bill providing for an Irish parliament within the empire was hastily prepared, much along the lines of what had been agreed between Parnell and Gladstone. Shortly afterwards another land bill was introduced to make good, in effect, on Mill and Campbell's argument that tenancy in Ireland brought with it virtual proprietorship. Landlords who sold to their tenants were now given the chance of compensation from a government fund. It was perhaps the most revolutionary thing Gladstone had ever put his name to.

On 27 May 1886 the Strangers' Gallery was packed early, and MPs crowded the chamber for the second reading of the Home Rule Bill. In a dramatic gesture of concession to dissidents in his own party Gladstone proposed that the vote be only on the *principle* of Home Rule; and that, if passed, a third reading would take place only after another election. Then followed, for 3½ hours, the speech of his life – the noblest thing he ever did, and the most doomed. This was, he told the House, 'one of the golden moments of our history – one of those opportunities which may come and may go, but which rarely return.' And with the grievous hindsight of everything that has happened since, who is to say he was wrong? His oratory rose to Ciceronian heights as if he could overcome the adverse lobby arithmetic that was staring him in the face by sheer force of eloquence, embodying Quintilian's definition of a true orator as a good man who speaks well. That day Gladstone spoke well, and perhaps all the sanctimoniousness, all the exasperating contradictions, all the acts of impulsiveness and intolerance that had marked his long, prodigious career faded away into nothing beside the deep truth and goodness of what he was saying, nowhere more urgently and more poignantly than when this most historically minded of all Britain's prime ministers (until Churchill) asked parliament to forget, this once, British history. Ireland was asking, he said, 'for what I call a blessed oblivion of the past. She asks also a boon for the future, and that boon … will be a boon to us in respect of her honour, no less than a boon to her in respect of happiness, prosperity, and peace. Such, Sir, is her prayer. Think, I beseech you,' he implored in his peroration, 'think well, think wisely, think, not for the moment, but for the years that are to come, before you reject this Bill.'

The prayer was not answered: 341 members voted against the second reading, 311 in favour. Voting against were 91 of Gladstone's own party: a greater number than had been anticipated, even on the prime minister's most pessimistic assessment, and including Chamberlain and the old warhorse of the liberal conscience, John Bright. Chamberlain was greeted by howls of 'Judas!' from the Liberal loyalists. The election that followed – the second in six months – was, as Gladstone honestly put it, 'a smash.' The Liberals mustered only 191 seats; the Conservatives gained 316 and the Parnellites got 85.

It would be six years before Gladstone was back in power for the last time, a very old man, now with a chance to bring Home Rule before the country again. But everything had changed, not least the fate of the Irish party and its leader. In 1889, Captain O'Shea brought a suit for divorce from his wife on the grounds of her adultery with Parnell. The Liberals, including Gladstone, professed to be shocked. The Catholic Church, which had been a crucial supporter of his Home Rule leadership, now excoriated him as a wicked fornicator. His mass support in Ireland, except in Dublin, crumbled away to a small group of die-hards. In Kilkenny they threw mud at him. Two years later, on 6 October 1891, he died, just 45 years old, at Brighton, in the arms of Katherine, now his wife. But in 1893 it was not only Chamberlain, now a Conservative, who was a gung-ho imperialist and as such unlikely to countenance the break-up of the empire, the reduction of Great Britain to a 'Little England.' 'All Europe is armed to the teeth,' Chamberlain said. 'Meanwhile our interests are universal – our honour is involved in almost every land under the sun. Under such conditions the weak invite attack, and it is necessary for

Britain to be strong.' Besides, why should the social and economic interests of the solidly loyal Welsh and Scots, or for that matter Londoners and Mancunians, not to mention Canadians and New Zealanders, be sacrificed to the compulsion to accede to Irish nationalist blackmail? The Home Rulers were nothing but terrorists in thin disguise – they didn't fool *him* – and, besides, he claimed, outrageously, it was now common knowledge that Parnell had been behind the Phoenix Park murders all the time. The lesson of the defeat of Home Rule, Chamberlain declared, was that 'the great majority of the British nation are proud of … the glorious and united British empire.' Many of the rising stars of Gladstone's own party, like the Foreign Secretary Lord Rosebery, were just as hot for imperialism – and they could cite the Gladstone of Majuba Hill and Egypt as their precedent. Tolerating a third reading of the Government of Ireland Bill was just a matter of humouring the Grand Old Man (since its defeat in the House of Lords was a certainty) before he was pushed out of the leadership and before long into his tomb. Not everyone was prepared to let him go in peace, however. In adamant opposition, now Tory–Unionist, Chamberlain made a personal attack on Gladstone of such malicious ferocity that to the Irish politician T. P. O'Connor it seemed like the voice of a '"lost soul" in hell: the Prime Minister calls "black" and they say, "it is good"; the Prime Minister calls "white" and they say "it is better." It is always the voice of a god. Never since the time of Herod has there been such slavish adulation.'

Not a god, perhaps, but a prophet who had, for that matter, been prophetic. The chance of satisfying Irish self-government *within* the Union would never again in British history come so close to peaceful realization; certainly not in 1911 or 1917, when there were further last-ditch efforts and Ireland was even more hopelessly crushed between hard-line Republican separatism on the one hand and equally hard-line Unionism on the other. Those who care about both Ireland and Britain may be allowed just a touch of wistfulness (doubtless sentimental) that we are still living with the consequences of that missed opportunity.

The failure of Home Rule was in fact more than a turning point in Irish or British history. It also marked the epitaph of the much older Liberal ideal of gradualist self-government, mooted in all seriousness and all sincerity by Macaulay a half century before. Although Joseph Chamberlain liked to believe that the empire would actually be stronger with the sacred cow of Home Rule slaughtered, frozen and locked away, he was, in the long term, staggeringly wrong. At the very moment when moderate Irish nationalism was attempting to find some sort of self-expression within the empire moderate Indian nationalists were doing exactly the same thing: 1885–6 was not just the moment of truth for Home Rule but the inaugural year of the Indian National Congress. It was founded, of course, by Allan Hume, the famine dissenter from Lytton's government, who had finally decided that the good intentions on which the empire had supposedly been founded, and which continued to be trotted out as the justification for its massive military power, would never actually be realized; not, at any rate, voluntarily.

Apparently in both India and Ireland the Liberals couldn't deliver on promises of self-government and economic and social justice, and the Conservatives wouldn't. Instead of bringing on the educated classes of the colonized to take responsibility for their own justice and government, British imperial power, especially as embodied in the Men on the Spot who claimed a superior, tougher wisdom than the remote idealists in London, was more than ever determined to keep them out. When Gladstone's genuinely liberal viceroy, Lord Ripon, perhaps the most decent India ever had, attempted to pass the Ilbert Bill, which would have allowed Europeans to be judged by Indian magistrates, cries of white outrage erupted from Calcutta to Madras. Inevitably the government was forced to beat a retreat; the presumptuous piece of legislation was withdrawn. In his sketch of the manners and mores of the post-Mutiny British, *The Competition Wallah* (1864), George Otto Trevelyan condemned 'That intense Anglo-Saxon spirit of self-approbation, which, though dormant at home, is unpleasantly perceptible among vulgar Englishmen on the Continents [and which] becomes rampant in India.' Nauseated by the snobbery, racism and hypocrisy of the sahibs, he saw only too clearly what had happened to the lofty ideals his father had hoped for in the 1830s. At the annual race meeting at Sunapur (originally an Indian festival of purification), where 'The wife of the Judge of Boglipore looks forward for months to meeting her sister, the Collectrix of Gya,' amidst the croquet and the betting, Trevelyan saw 'a tall raw-boned brute' rush at a gathering of well-dressed, well-to-do Indians and flog them with a double-thonged hunting whip until they had fled from the enclosure. 'One or two civilians said to each other it was "a shame," but no-one seemed astounded or horrified, no-one interposed, no-one prosecuted, no-one objected to meet the blackguard at dinner.' These were the kind of scenes that increasingly became commonplaces in the late-19th-century Raj, and in its literature, at exactly the time when lip service was being paid to the gradualism of self-government and sententious words were being uttered about the 'unreadiness' of the natives for the responsibilities of citizenship. Worse still, some of the most blatant race prejudice was articulated at home. The most shaming thing that can be said, perhaps, of British politics in the age of Victoria's Diamond Jubilee is that those radicals like Sir Charles Dilke and Chamberlain, who were most eloquent on behalf of the underclass in Britain, should also have been most ferocious in their conviction about the manifest superiority of the white race and the self-evident altruism of the British Empire.

At the turn of the century, then, there was an extraordinary gulf between the rhetoric of the Diamond Jubilee, Pax Britannica – pompously self-righteous, architecturally swaggering, militarily Maxim-gunned – and the embittered disillusionment of its subject peoples. Over the mass graves of the loyal fallen, Chamberlain after the Boer War and Curzon after the First World War might pretend (or even actually believe) that the empire had never been more united; but they were both deeply deluded. During the first two decades of the 20th century the failure to make good on Macaulay's, Disraeli's or Curzon's promises came home to roost, and in ways the makers of those promises could never have anticipated. Instead of the classical language of liberalism being used to advance an agenda drawn from English constitutional history, nationalists in India and Ireland repudiated the whole book and turned back to their own traditions (even when they had to reinvent them). Irish nationalism became coloured by the Gaelic movement, whose literary and political leaders such as Padraig Pearse developed a cult of peasant mysticism that was deliberately meant to move as far away as possible from the polite, reasonable 'my dear chappishness' of liberalism. Along with it, much less happily, went the development of a cult of violence and blood sacrifice that achieved its mythic consummation in the Easter Rising of 1916, with Pearse as one of its many victims.

Precisely the same chronology was followed in India. The more Westernized, constitutionalist-minded leaders of Congress – Surendranath Banerjee and the Poona brahmin Gopal Krishna Gokhale – lost ground to charismatic neo-traditionalists like Bal Gangadhar Tilak, also a Chitpavan brahmin but much more invested in the history of Maratha resistance to the Raj. In orchestrating the cult of Sivaji, the Maharashtra Maratha prince, Tilak may have been heavily embellishing his actual history, but he was liberating India from an equally preposterous British historical mythology that represented the continent as a place of darkness, poverty and anarchy before the advent of the peace-loving Clive and Wellesley. Instead of invoking John Stuart Mill, Tilak used precisely the elements of Hindu culture that British imperialists deemed to be politically infantile – the Ganpati festivals – to mobilize a mass following. Instead of using Oxbridge English he played the vernacular presses like a sitar. Instead of 'improving' Western art, Tilak revelled in the modern iconology of Ganesh and Kali. He even had Lord Bentinck turn in his grave by resisting a well-meaning attempt to raise the eligible age of marriage.

Most of all, Tilak knew exactly how to hit the Raj where it most hurt: in its pocket. Under *swaraj*, the demand for Indian Home Rule (for Tilak was, like the

Irish revolutionary Eamon de Valera, prepared to accept dominion status), the Hindi equivalent of Sinn Fein (Us Alone), was pressed most brilliantly through the means of *swadesh* or, as they said in Ireland, boycott. (In fact, some of the more sensitive souls in the pre-First World War Congress worried about using the term 'boycott' because of its overtones of Irish intimidation!) The closure of shops (which, for example, greeted the implementation of Curzon's partitioning of Bengal on 16 October 1906), the mass walk-outs and, above all, the ban on buying British goods, were a death-blow not just to the unequal commercial advantage of the home country but also to the transparently hypocritical cant of mutual prosperity that was still intoned by men such as Chamberlain. More aggravating still, three-quarters of a century of sneering at comically Westernized *bhadralok*, dressed up in their spats and starched collars, finally paid off in the campaign for homespun cloth. Jawaharlal Nehru's father, Motilal, who had started his political career very much as a Westernized liberal and sent his son to Harrow and Cambridge, traded in his jackets and ties for a traditional long coat and cap not because he felt comfortable with them, but because he knew they were a symbol of his legitimacy as a nationalist.

This embrace of neo-traditionalism as the form of resistance to British rule would have been surprising enough to the founders of the Raj. But they would have been even more unnerved and bewildered by the spectacle of British radicals – British *women* radicals – actually adopting the wisdom of the East, not the West, as the way forward for the national cause. Instead of deferential brown Englishmen the Raj now had to deal with troublesome white Hindus, Buddhists and other mystics. Annie Besant, co-defendant in 1877 with Charles Bradlaugh (another enthusiast of the Congress) in the 1875 obscenity trial for promoting contraception among the working classes, and organizer of the famous match girls' strike of 1888, had gone oriental with a vengance. When she went to India in 1893 Annie was still a devotee of Madame Helena Blavatsky's religion of Theosophy. But she went on to plunge much more fully into Hindu religion and politics, founding a Hindu College at Benares – thus closing the circle that had begun with Bentinck and Macaulay's decision to shut down the college of their day as a useless anachronism. And in 1916, as one of the most militant voices in favour of an accelerated drive for *swaraj*, Annie founded the Home Rule for India League and in 1917 became president of Congress.

There were some even more unexpected outcomes. Emily Lytton, daughter of the late earl-viceroy and sister of Constance, the militant suffragette, was proposed to in Kensington in 1896 by an ambitious 27-year-old architect, Edwin Lutyens. One of his impassioned love letters bears a drawing of himself as a knight-errant, out in the

Top: Front view of the Viceroy's House, New Delhi, India.
Above: Gandhi in London, *c.* 1913.

imperial style to conquer 'The World.' He briefly conquered Emily, but the union was a disaster. She was put off sex, and took up Theosophy instead under the guidance of the Indian teacher Krishnamurti. Edwin went on to build New Delhi just in time for it to be the epicentre of a dying empire.

The hecatombs of the First World War, not to mention millions more who died from the influenza pandemic of 1918, did nothing, for all the pieties of imperial cenotaphs and war graves, to make the ties of empire closer. The ANZAC soldiers who managed to survive the deathtraps at Gallipoli, the Canadians who crawled away from the carnage of Vimy Ridge, the Indians who were berated for surrendering to the Turks in Mesopotamia did not, by and large, treasure their military experience as a testimony to the wisdom and infallibility of the British officer-and-gentleman class. At least a million and a half Africans were conscripted during that war as labourers and porters of all kind, leaving to white men the adult task of actually tackling the Germans. George V, whose strong suit was not tact, thanked them for acting in these lowly but essential supporting roles and thus 'hurling their spears' at the Teutonic foe. In Ireland, 'England's disadvantage' was held to be the nationalists' opportunity. Although hundreds of thousands of Irishmen volunteered in 1914, the mass slaughter removed masses of Unionist patriots from the fray; whilst Sinn Fein recruited tens of thousands more for the cause of breaking, not preserving, the imperial connection. In India, the Ottoman Turkish sultan's declaration of the *Khalifa* (self-styled protectors of all Muslims) made huge inroads into the loyalty of the Muslim population, somewhat behind the Hindu community in their anti-imperialism (and alienated by its adoption of Hindu militancy). Both before and after the First World War the British government, with an eye to mobilizing the human, fiscal and military resources of the Raj, at last made some political concessions: forms of local government were created, elected by an Indian franchise and weighted to protect Muslims where necessary.

But it was very much a case of too little, too late. It is unclear whether British governments anticipated in return expressions of loyal gratitude. If so, they were to be badly disappointed. By 1918 *swaraj* had become a mass movement; and strikes, boycotts and the *hartal* action of non-cooperation – by which not just shop and factory workers, but the masses of clerks without whom everything in India, from the post offices to the heavily fortified railway stations, was incapable of running, walked out – had made the omnipotent Raj virtually ungovernable. Every so often frustration boiled over into bloody violence, the most murderous in 1919 at Amritsar in the Punjab when General Reginald Dyer, under directions from the provincial governor, Michael O'Dwyer (a hard-line Irish loyalist), ordered his troops to fire on an unruly but unarmed crowd, killing 379 of them. Afterwards Dyer regretted only that he had not been able to use heavier weapons.

It was the genius of the charismatic Indian Congress Party leader Gandhi to pity not just the victims but the perpetrators of Amritsar for their blind, animal brutality. In resistance he offered not counter-violence but *satyagraha*, the truth – or love – force. With the Mahatma, the 100-year illusion of self-improvement through Westernization reached its final moment of bathos. He was, after all, someone who had briefly become exactly what Macaulay had in mind, a 'brown Englishman,' a member of the Hindu Vaisya caste who had, through hard study, turned himself into a barrister of London's Inner Temple. But that was as far as the metamorphosis went. Instead, after early civil-rights activity in South Africa, Gandhi returned to India in 1914 and turned himself into something like the opposite; a holy man dressed only in a homespun dhoti, who advocated a return to village self-sufficiency and wanted Indian freedom to herald not just a political and social transformation but above all a moral one. Gandhi's hope was that this transformation could be extended from his own people to their benighted imperial masters, who seemed to know only profit and brute power. All his carefully calculated actions, therefore, were expressly meant as a refutation of Western styles of power. The ceremonial expression of imperial authority was the durbar procession, with its fanatical attention to the niceties of protocol, its glittering public bombast, its orgy of jewels and feasting. Gandhi's reply was the fast; the embrace of the Untouchables; the pilgrim's half-naked walk to the sea (to overthrow the government monopoly on salt), leading a slow march of millions indiscriminately jumbled together. The last message of the Raj was that it had brought 'Western civilization' to India. But when asked what he thought of that civilization, Gandhi's famously wry reply was, 'I think a good idea.'

But then, of course, Gandhi was assassinated by one of his own countrymen at the very moment of the realization of Indian freedom; and millions more would die then and since in sectarian bloodbaths that continue, both in India and in Ireland, to this day. Neo-traditionalism has found it easier to create and perpetuate differences than to dissolve them. Might the English language, or at least Ameringlish, liberated from its role as the language of imperial sovereignty, have a future, after all, as the solvent of sectarian conflict – an agency of modernization without mastery, whether in Bombay or Bradford? For the one thing we can be sure of in this history is that, when Macaulay chirpily told the electors of his constituency in Leeds that he would be happy to see the products of their industry again in the East, he would not have meant the appearance of saris in east Leeds. But that, again, is the fate of empire.

CHAPTER

7

It was in Bangalore that Winston Churchill began to gorge on history. 'In the long glistening hours' of the afternoon, while his fellow officers were snoring away the tedium between heavy lunches and light polo, he surveyed the gorgeous debris of the late Roman Empire with Gibbon, or, courtesy of Macaulay, sailed on the Protestant wind with Dutch William in 1688. He had come to India in 1896 as a junior officer of the 4th Queen's Own Hussars, thirsty for action. His head was full of the contemporary certainties, held especially by the young, that the British Empire was different; that it was, as Professor Seeley had promised in 1883, 'free of that weakness which has brought down most empires, the weakness of being a mere mechanical forced union of alien nationalities.' It never struck the slight, sandy-haired, rosy-faced 22-year-old that here he was, ready – impatient, in fact – to take the Maxim guns and the cavalry to the 'unruly Pathans' (or wherever he would be sent) on behalf of an empire whose entire existence turned on the success or failure of 'forced unions.'

Force? How one winced to hear of so un-British a thing. Power, now, was something else again. The power, the attraction of the empire, was not brute coercion but the self-evident, manifold blessings the empire had brought: peace, security, liberty, prosperity. (This was 1897. Bodies were being picked over by kites not so very far away from the fragrant rose gardens of Bangalore cantonment.) Take his own regiment, for example. Were they there to dictate to the nizam of Hyderabad how he should govern? Not a bit of it. They were there with his blessing, at his invitation indeed, to 'keep the peace' as agreed; just as other regiments had been assigned to the territories of independent princely states to keep them … independent. And if there were more troops on the northwest frontier, or for that matter in northern Nigeria or southern Egypt, well, that was to ensure that these places did not collapse into the kind of anarchy that would be taken advantage of by powers altogether less civilized, altogether less friendly, to the advance of progress – Russians; dervish mullahs; those Sorts of People. Churchill never doubted that the mission of the empire was

THE LAST OF BLADESOVER?

During the Boer War in South Africa, Winston acted as chief war correspondent on the *Morning Post*, 1899.

to 'give peace to warring tribes, to administer justice where all was violence, to strike the chains off the slave, to plant the seeds of commerce and learning … what more beautiful idea … can inspire human effort?'

And yet there was an awful lot of hanging around in the club, pending the accomplishment of these great goals. It was all very nice being waited on hand and foot in the pink and white bungalow he shared with two brother officers. Every month he rode back to the bungalow, tossed a bag of silver to the head manservant and then 'all you had to do was to hand over all your uniform and clothes to the dressing boy, your ponies to the syce [groom] and your money to the butler and you need never trouble any more … for a humble wage there was nothing they would not do. Their world became bounded by the commonplace articles of your wardrobe … no toil was too hard, no hours were too long. . . . Princes could live no better than we.' But for all the space of the subcontinent, how narrow this world of ponies and punchbowls was. The restive young Winston did things not quite *pukka* for an officer. He chased after gaudy butterflies, collected fleshy orchids and familiarized himself with all 150 specimens of the transplanted roses of Bangalore – passions that would stay with him for the rest of his life. And still it wasn't quite enough.

What then? He had always been impetuous, sometimes to his cost. Now he would buckle down to becoming wise – something his father believed was quite beyond him. Under the low-slung roof of the verandah, or inside with the punkah sailing to and fro, a glass of the weak whisky and soda that India had taught him to appreciate close by, Churchill read on and on in his self-devised remedial currriculum – Plato's *Republic*, Adam Smith and, more adventurously, the philosophy of Schopenhauer. But it was always history to which he returned again and again; not as romantic enter-tainment, and still less as monastic devotion to the documentary truth of the remote past, but in pursuit of a credo. For him it was something to live by that was greater and better than the complacencies of the barracks, the ignorant nostrums exchanged at tiffin about how the niggers should be so damned grateful they were all there.

So back, then, to Henry Hallam's relentlessly upright *Constitutional History of England* (1827); and back, especially, to Macaulay. The noble lord, his remains reposing in Westminster Abbey, had been dead for 30 years. Oxford scholars now dismissed his work as tendentious, Whiggish self-congratulation at its worst. Although Churchill himself would later berate Macaulay for traducing the memory of his ancestor, the Duke of Marlborough, in 1897 both his multi-volume *History of England* (1849–62) and the even more dazzling essays proclaimed Macaulay as the epitome of what a historian should be: an engaged citizen, a public teacher for the times, and, not least, an unapologetic best-seller. Macaulay wrote sentences as if they were speeches to be declaimed. Of the ex-Jacobin Bertrand Barère, who had had the impertinence to publish his memoirs, Macaulay declared: 'Whatsoever things are false, whatsoever things are dishonest, whatsoever things are unjust; whatsoever things are impure, whatsoever things are hateful, whatsoever things are of evil report, if there be any vice, if there be any infamy, all these things we knew were blended in Barère.' Churchill loved the rolling, gathering, accusatory force of the reiterations and made note of it. Macaulay's ghost, from the printed page, was in effect the first speech tutor of the lisping, stammering young aristocrat. But the *History of England* was far more than a tutorial in public style, literary and rhetorical. It gave Churchill the strongest sense he had yet had of his country's place in the great Scheme of Things, and thus of his own. As he read Macaulay, the claim that British history was unique became to him something other than loose, vainglorious hyperbole. His mentor was unarguably right that 19th-century Britain, uniquely among European countries, had not suffered from the twin evils of autocracy and revolutionary civil war; that 'while every part of the Continent, from Moscow to Lisbon, has been the theatre of bloody and devastating wars, no hostile standard has been seen here but as a trophy [that] the administration of justice has been pure ... every man has felt entire confidence that the state would protect him in the possession of what had been earned by his diligence and hoarded by his self-denial. Under the benignant influence of peace and liberty science has flourished.' And so on. Macaulay must, then, have also been right that the condition and cause of such a happy state of affairs had indeed been the preservation of Protestant England from a Catholic crown and its miraculous transformation into a constitutional monarchy. Everything that had followed, including the disinterested wish to extend the empire of liberty to remote parts of the world, was but the preservation and natural development of that original, momentous happening.

By giving Britons their modern history, it seemed, Macaulay had given them their nationality; a reason to pledge common allegiance; a reason to fight, if they had to, in Peshawar or Penang. In this sense, Macaulay had made history twice over. The writing had moved the soldiers and the administrators, the engineers, even the shipping clerks and the station-masters; and what they wrought in turn would make for more history-writing. You could write the empire, Churchill must have felt; and the empire would write you. Thucydides, after all, had been no cloistered archivist but an actor in the drama of his own work – a fighter, a thinker, a maker of speeches, a mover of men. His immersion in the world had made his work more enduring, not less so.

To be sure, Macaulay's opus was the history of England. But the Scots, Irish and Welsh who also peopled the barracks and the courthouses; who laid the railways and ordered the excavation of irrigation canals; whose flocks and herds grazed the

Australian outback and whose tea plantations prospered in Assam; who sat in parliament; who owned the banks, insurance and shipping companies – all these were surely evidence that Great Britain was indeed a true nation. Was not Macaulay (not to mention Carlyle) himself a Scot by origin? Seeley had even used the analogy of 'Celts' who spoke languages 'quite unintelligible' to the English, but yet felt themselves to be part of a common nation, as a promising precedent for the possibility of integrating even more apparently diverse peoples – Dutch Boers and 'Kaffirs,' the Xhosa people – into a true, lasting and 'unforced' imperial union.

Churchill, of course, like Macaulay, believed this parallel and mutually self-reinforcing coming together of nation and empire to be a natural process rather than a selfishly constructed one. And the notion that both were provisional unions, conditional on their continued prospering; that the process could, some day in the future, conceivably fold in on itself; that an imperial dissolution might be followed by a national dissolution, would have been utterly inconceivable. Perhaps there had been regrettable coercions such as Culloden *en route* to the Union, in defence of Protestant liberties and 1688. But once so united, the bond had been sealed by common ideals as well as common interests. After all, had not Flora MacDonald, the protectress of Bonnie Prince Charlie, turned into the most ardent Hanoverian loyalist in North Carolina during the American War of Independence?

Or perhaps, on the other hand, the flourishing of Great Britain *did* strike Churchill, in his later years at least, as conditional on the perpetuation of the empire. Perhaps that was why he remained so adamant in its defence, so obsessively deluded about its prospects of survival – barking even as late as 1942 that he had not become prime minister in order to preside over its dissolution (although, of course, the terms by which he accepted junior partnership in an American alliance would guarantee just that). By 1965, when he died, however adrift he had been from current events in the last decade of his life, Churchill must have known that Britain's imperial history was, if not at an end, well beyond the beginning of the end. The Anglo-French invasion of Egypt during the Suez Crisis of 1956, barely a year after Churchill had grudgingly and belatedly handed over power there to his foreign secretary, Anthony Eden, had been a fiasco: a bungled attack followed by a humiliating withdrawal at Suez. After Eden the two Harolds, Macmillan and Wilson, had committed themselves even more emphatically to the disappearing act. What had once been the Raj was now a friend and ally of the Soviet Union. The statues and busts that had memorialized the great and good all over Delhi had been removed from their pedestals and taken to a railed enclosure at the edge of what had been the durbar field – a ghostly open-air prison compound for the casualties of the modern

Top: *Thomas Babington Macaulay, Baron Macaulay* by Edward Matthew Ward, 1853.
Above: The dockers' cranes dip in homage as Churchill's coffin passes down the river Thames, 1965.

age. The empire was now Gibraltar and British Honduras, Anguilla and Hong Kong – a scatter of sundowner islands with the occasional isthmus. The Commonwealth was a fig leaf for capitulation, surviving more robustly in Test cricket than in anything resembling shared political community.

And yet in that freezing week of late January 1965, when hundreds of thousands filed past Churchill's coffin and many more lined the streets to watch it process from Westminster Hall to St Paul's, and then on to the Thames, British (not just English) history seemed to reconstitute itself in an immense assembly of mourning and memory. This was, for all concerned, an intensely felt demonstration of allegiance. But it also became commonplace, at the time and afterwards, to note that the valediction was being paid, not just to Churchill himself, but to the axiomatic sense of Britishness he had personified – a Britishness defined, above all, by history. Oddly enough the French president, Charles de Gaulle, looming over the congregation in St Paul's, had provided a back-handed compliment to the Churchillian definition of Britain two years earlier, when he had vetoed the Macmillan government's application to join the European Economic Community (as it was then called) on the grounds that Britain was, ultimately, an 'insular' maritime nation whose traditions and personality disqualified it from authentic European-ness. But many observers represented the funeral as the last hurrah of self-evident Britishness, just as this would be Richard Dimbleby's last broadcast. The failure of President Lyndon B. Johnson or any major member of his administration to show up at the funeral only sharpened the acute sense that the nation that had been born from imperial wars and sustained by imperial profits had now put itself into American receivership; that the Churchillian illusion of truly independent national self-assertion was being buried along with his Promethean old body.

Did that mean, too, that a particular kind of British history – written as well as enacted – was also no longer possible; that its sentimental longevity had far outrun anything resembling honest self-recognition; and that Churchill the historian-leader had been one of the main culprits in perpetuating its illusions? Now, with the patriarch finally gone, perhaps it was time for the country to grow up, face realities, kick away the crutch of sceptred-isle pageantry and take seriously Harold Wilson's challenge of 1963 to embark on the 'white heat' of a second industrial-scientific-technological revolution seriously. Was the condition of national maturity giving British history the boot, once and for all?

Or has there been, might there still be, something more? Might there yet be a Britain, Great or otherwise? And might it cherish, rather than own up to, its history?

Even if he had wanted to, there was no chance that Winston Churchill could have escaped the clutches of history. He had been born to it, at Blenheim Palace in Oxfordshire, the swaggering baroque pile designed by playwright-turned-architect Sir John Vanbrugh in the early years of the 18th century and intended as a gift of gratitude from Queen Anne and the nation to the victorious Duke of Marlborough. Since it cost a cool £300,000 (£24 million in today's value) the reserves of gratitude ran out along with the funds – much to the fury of the formidable duchess, who later complained that the place was grossly unfit for habitation. It was certainly as much an architectural proclamation as a dwelling place: a manifesto in limestone of Britain's intention of replacing absolutist France as the dominant imperial power. The language of this announcement at Blenheim is unsubtle. At the base of the exterior ceremonial steps of the façade lie stone cannon, balls, drums and flags. Atop the triumphal arch of the kitchen court a sharp-toothed British lion, carved by Grinling Gibbons, lunches on a French cockerel. The swaggering bust of Marlborough's arch-enemy Louis XIV, removed by the duke from the captured fort city of Tournai, protrudes from the roofline of the south front like the decapitated head of a common criminal stuck on a spike as warning and reproof. Inside, one-upmanship on the pretensions of Versailles continues with the parade of captured French flags in the Great Hall, and in the Saloon the illusionistically painted figures of Versailles's Ambassadors' Staircase are repeated in Louis Laguerre's personifications of the Four Continents looking down on Marlborough's splendour and spoils.

Winston's birth at Blenheim on 30 November 1874 was a double-shotgun affair. He was delivered, suddenly and prematurely, only seven and a half months after the marriage of his parents, Lord Randolph Churchill and his darkly beautiful 20-year-old American bride, Jeanette ('Jennie') Jerome. Heavily pregnant though she was, Jennie was not one to pass up a shoot at Blenheim. Following the guns, she took a spill. The jolting of the pony trap that took her back to the house brought on the contractions that, eight arduous hours later, produced Winston. As the grandson of the 7th Duke he would not be brought up in Blenheim, but time and again during his long life he would come back to the place in moods of melancholy, elation or despair. In the wintriest years of his career in the 1930s, isolated from power, Churchill would repair his own damaged reputation by vindicating Marlborough's in a huge four-volume biography.

History was always just a shout away from Winston Churchill. His first memories were of the 'Little Lodge' near Phoenix Park in Dublin, where his father lived for a while as secretary to the duke, who had been made Lord-Lieutenant of Ireland. Both parents were remote and tantalizingly glamorous. Randolph's glittering,

Top: The south front of Blenheim Palace, Oxfordshire, family seat of the dukes of Marlborough.
Above: The Clock Tower at Blenheim, decorated with stonework by Grinling Gibbons, depicting a British lion savaging a French cockerel, *c.* 1830s.
Opposite top left: *Lord Randolph Churchill* by Edwin Long, *c.* 1888.
Opposite top right: *Lady Randolph Churchill*, sketch by John Singer Sargent, *c.* 1880.
Opposite below: Winston Churchill, aged seven, 1881.

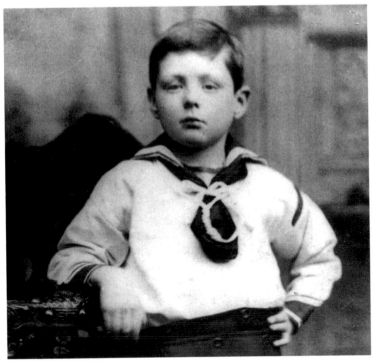

bulging eyes and oversize whiskers hiding a small, intense face caused him to resemble a tenacious miniature Schnauzer, while 'darling Mummy' was another spectacle altogether, remembered by her son as clad in a riding jacket, tight as a second skin, 'beautifully spattered with mud'; or with a diamond pin in her piled-up, raven hair. Filial longings – of any kind – failed to make any impression on their objects during the Churchills' dizzying ascent to power and fame. As usual with boys of his class Winston was consigned to a nanny, Elizabeth Everest, nicknamed without a trace of ironic self-consciousness 'Woom.' It was from Nanny Everest that Winston learned something, though not a lot, about an England sensed dimly beyond places like Blenheim or Banstead Manor, the house near Newmarket that Randolph bought during his pedigree horsey period. According to Woom, essential Britain was Kent, 'the garden of England,' a bursting cornucopia of strawberries, cherries and plums. At Ventnor on the Isle of Wight, Nanny Everest took the small boy to see her sister and brother-in-law, a retired prison warder who regaled him with lurid stories of gaol uprisings satisfyingly quashed in the name of the queen. He walked the pine-wood cliffs with Nanny and family not far from Victoria's house at Osborne, chased rabbits and scrambled over the cliffs.

The rituals of the upper class proceeded according to time-honoured plan and custom. At eight, Winston was taken from his 1000-strong and expanding army of toy soldiers, his play fort and his real steam engine, and dispatched to what, even by the standards of the day, seems to have been a particularly brutal prep school at Ascot, where he listened to the the screams of small boys being given 15 strokes of the birch by the headmaster. As a prison-reforming home secretary in 1910–11 during the Liberal government of Asquith, Churchill claimed that his sympathies for inmates owed much to his time spent 'in the private and public schools of England.' Jennie took pity on her terrified and often sickly little boy and transferred him to the tenderer mercies of a school at Brighton run by the Thompson sisters. In the spring of 1888 he entered Harrow, where he would have been just two years ahead of Macaulay's great-nephew and Charles Trevelyan's grandson, George Macaulay Trevelyan, one of the few historians in the 20th century whose popularity came near Churchill's own. The apocrypha of young Winston the Harrovian has him as a dunce, which he certainly was not; but he was clueless at classics, the predictor of statesmen. When told that Mr Gladstone read Homer for fun, Churchill 'thought it served him right.' But he learned history (as did Trevelyan) from a gifted teacher, George Townsend Warner, and was taught English by Robert Somervell, from whom Winston 'got into my bones the essential structure of the ordinary British sentence – which is a noble thing.'

Harrow was the Whig academy to the Tories' Eton, where Randolph himself had been (although he made sure Winston didn't know this). But by 1888 Lord Randolph Churchill, MP, and the Tory party were, in any case, no longer hand-in-glove. To the landed grandees Randolph's demagoguery, artfully vituperative despite the Churchill lisp, had always been suspect. It had taken the broadacres some time to become accustomed to Benjamin Disraeli, whose own doubtful populism had at least been balanced by expressions of gushy reverence for Church, throne and aristocracy. Randolph Churchill, on the other hand, seemed to have dreamed up something called 'Tory democracy,' which seemed altogether too oxymoronic for its own good, not to mention the good of the party; though they conceded it seemed to go down well in the industrial constituencies of the Midlands and the north. Although he had the Marlborough pocket constituency of Woodstock sewn up, Randolph was spoiling for the kind of fight that would make enough noise to bring him celebrity. At the 1885 general election, he chose – rather brilliantly – the octogenarian Liberal patriarch John Bright for his target and stood against him. In Birmingham, before he lost, he was able to make much of the redundancy of classical radical Liberalism and its promised supercession by Tory social welfare. The crowds loved him; even his lisp. The party elders hummed and hawed and pulled nervously on their beards. In a party of thoughtful worriers – Lord Salisbury, Sir Stafford Northcote, Sir Michael Hicks-Beach – Lord Randolph, still in his 30s, seemed to be a dangerously loose cannon. He was shameless about storming the organizational machinery of the Tories that the party's reformer John Gorst had put in place for Disraeli; and even more shameless about playing the Ulster card in Ireland. For every sharp play there was a smart epigram that landed like a grenade, none inflicting more long-term collateral damage than 'Ulster will fight and Ulster will be right.'

Miraculously, however – not least because he was soft on a coercive 'Crimes Bill' – Randolph managed to be on good terms with Parnell as well as with the Belfast Unionists, to the point of being instrumental in getting the Irish MPs to bring down Gladstone's government (the ultimate case of cutting off a nose to spite a face). When a Tory administration was established on the ruins of Home Rule in July 1886, Salisbury (perhaps through gritted teeth) felt he had no option but to share power with Randolph Churchill. At 37 years old he became leader of the House of Commons and chancellor of the exchequer. But his appetite grew with the eating. Churchill began to meddle egregiously with foreign policy, the acknowledged preserve of the prime minister. A fight was picked with Salisbury over the army and navy estimates. Failing to get his way, and fatally over-estimating his indispensability, Randolph threatened to resign. The bluff was called. He had been chancellor of the exchequer for just four months. One imagines Salisbury and Northcote lifting a private glass in huge relief.

Lord Randolph's time in power was over before most politicians had begun theirs. Worse than being kept at a distance from office was his accurate certainty that he would never recover it. He collapsed into a baleful, bitter, taciturn gloom that settled on the whole Churchill–Marlborough clan like a coating of ash. 'Darling Mummy' letters from Winston became more pathetically needy while Darling Mummy was taking lovers and failing to show up on parents' days. Summers at Blenheim presided over by the aged Duchess Fanny, around whom slippered foot-men obsequiously shuffled in the candlelight, were especially grim. Encounters between father and son were rare, which was just as well since Winston, physically unprepossessing, halting of speech and, so Randolph thought, irremediably dim, had become an intolerable irritant to his short, sharp temper: 'I am certain that if you cannot prevent yourself from leading the idle useless unprofitable life you have had during your schooldays & later months, you will become a mere social wastrel, one of the hundreds of public school failures, and you will degenerate into a shabby unhappy & futile existence.' Frightened of tongue-lashings, Winston invariably committed the small crimes and misdemeanours that guaranteed them. At Harrow he remained lonely, conscious of his clumsiness (he managed to fall from a tricycle and concuss himself) and carrying the distinction of his birth and rank like a sorry burden. 'I would far rather have been apprenticed as a bricklayer's mate,' he would later write, 'or run errands as a messenger boy, or helped my father dress the front windows of a grocer's shop. It would have been real; it would have been natural, it would have taught me more, and I would have done it much better. Also I should have got to know my father, which would have been a joy to me.'

Later, Winston wrote that he had had no more than three or four long con-versations with Randolph in his entire life. One of them, however, changed his life. Catching Winston marshalling his now massive army of lead soldiers with what seemed a surprisingly shrewd tactical eye, Randolph asked whether he might not like to go into the army? For the father, of course, the sub-text was that Winston was too dense to become something solid like a lawyer or a churchman, much less a politician. But the son heard the bugle call of history's vindication. He would pick up his father's broken sword and charge the enemy. That would show them what he was made of.

The 'Army Class' (not for the future Gladstones) at Harrow was followed by Sandhurst (after three tries at the entrance examination). There, Winston's un-coordinated energies were at last given some sort of outlet; he became more gregarious even while lamenting that the great age of generals and battles was over, dreaming dreams of dragoons. He hoped to get into a cavalry regiment, but Randolph balked at investing in the horses from which he assumed Winston would fall. Undaunted, with his mother's help he hired them from the local livery stables and dashed around a good deal after foxes. Inevitably, there were mishaps of the kind which brought down the wrath of Randolph, by now terminally ill with what seems to have been not syphilis, as traditionally accepted, but some sort of wasting neural disease. A gold watch given to Winston by his father had been damaged in a collision with another cadet and then secretly repaired. But two weeks later the doomed timepiece fell out of Winston's fob pocket into a stream that fed a large pond. Horrified at the disaster, Winston did what Churchills did best: he mobilized a small army of 23 infantrymen and a fire engine to pump the pond, where eventually the timepiece was found covered in mud and irreparably ruined. When his father caught wind of the accident, there was nothing for it now but to own up: 'I know I have been very foolish and clumsy with the watch and fully deserved to have it taken away. I am very sorry to have been so stupid and careless – but I hope that you will not be cross with me … Once more saying how sorry I am to have made you angry, I remain ever your loving son. . . . Please don't judge me entirely on the strength of the watch.' The appeals from the 19-year-old to his father were in vain. He received back a stinging denunciation of his irresponsibility and general worthlessness (unlike his brother Jack, so much more trustworthy and mature; why do I bother etc. etc.).

In November 1894, about to graduate quite creditably from Sandhurst, Winston appeared for the first time as a public tribune. But the target of his and his friends' demonstration was evidently chosen as much for its hilarity as for the high constitutional principles that Churchill pretended were at stake. Shocked by spotting tarts at the theatre bar, Mrs Laura Ormiston Chant of the Purity League had forced the owners of the Empire, Leicester Square, to put up a canvas screen in the promenade separating the vicious from the virtuous – a puritanical interference, Churchill claimed, with the liberties of free-born Englishmen. A speech invoking the shade of John Hampden (not famous for his penchant for prostitutes) was written but not delivered before the screen was torn down. Standing on the wreckage, Winston addressed his first crowd: 'I discarded the constitutional argument entirely and appealed directly to sentiment and even passion, finishing up by saying, "You have seen us tear down these barricades to-night; see that you pull down those who are responsible for them at the coming election." ' Much cheering followed. Winston, sailing uproariously into Leicester Square, was reminded of the demolition of the Bastille. The Purity League caper would have been just the kind of juvenile outing – more prank than politics, complete with young bloods dissolved in hilarity and

Taittinger, missing last trains back to Sandhurst, with much midnight giggling and hammering on doors ('Stout yeoman, pray lend us your trap') – to provoke one of Randolph's fulminations. But Randolph was beyond fulmination, well into the final stages of his illness. Ironically, the last months before he left with Jennie for a world tour were the friendliest he ever spent with his still deeply intimidated elder son. The boy seems to have smartened up a bit, was Randolph's thought, and he meant it as a compliment to more than Winston's inherited dandyism. He was smart enough, at any rate, to be introduced to the Tory statesman Arthur Balfour and the Liberal imperialist Lord Rosebery, and saw that political adversaries could be supper-club friends.

It was too late, however, to make up for lost opportunities. Rushed back to London in a state of near paralysis, Randolph died in January 1895 at the age of 45. 'Woom' Everest, whom Winston had enjoyed parading down the High Street at Harrow, died the following July. Now there were just his brother Jack, with whom he had an easy-going but never very close relationship; and of course Mummy, still only 40, still luscious, available and irresistible. The New York social tigress re-emerged, her fur and claws trimmed for the job at hand, which was to open doors for her boy. For Winston, his father was a lot easier to deal with as a memory. Liberated from that reproachful stare, he could devote himself to his father's vindication, whether on the battlefield or the hustings, and become the successor Randolph could never have imagined. Winston's journey to filial redemption culminated in 1905 in an almost hagiographic biography of the misunderstood, ill-treated genius father.

A conventional military-imperial career was possible. The commander of the 4th Hussars, the Irish peer Colonel John Brabazon, whom Winston remembered for his lordly inability to pronounce his 'r's ('Where is the London twain?' 'It has gone, Colonel.' 'Gone? Bwing another!'), had returned the compliment by noticing Winston at Sandhurst and Aldershot. But even at 21, before his Bangalore epiphany with Gibbon and Macaulay, Winston knew he needed to carve out a different kind of life from the mess room and the parade ground. He was not at all sure, he confessed to his mother, that the military *métier* was really right for him. But if he were to wield the pen along with the sword, making two kinds of imperial history simultaneously, now that would be something.

So Lady Randolph did her best anticipation of Evelyn Waugh's Lady Metroland and assignments were duly landed and introductions made, not least in New York, where Winston listened to the Irish-American politician William Bourke Cockran, the snap-brimmed Tammany Hall manipulator of money and men, and thought his oratory just fine. From Cuba, where the Spanish rulers were fighting a guerrilla war, he sent the *Daily Graphic* his first war reports. They confirmed a flair for the kind of campfire journalistic adventurism that sold newspapers, especially of the new kind, which thrived on Our Man Under Fire moments, the ancestor of the on-the-spot television correspondent: 'We are on our horses, in uniform; our revolvers are loaded. In the dusk and half-light, long files of armed and laden men are shuffling off towards the enemy. He may be very near; perhaps he is waiting for us a mile away. We cannot tell.'

For the first time, Winston was shot at. A horse behind him was ripped open and died. The bullet, he reflected, was only a few feet away from hitting him and he felt the adrenaline surge of survived peril. A parade of imperial adventures followed in which this early sense of physical fearlessness (never to be lost) made him an impetuous soldier and a brilliant war correspondent who intuited that history-making needed both writing and fighting. Instinctively, Winston went where the most imperial action was.

On the northwest frontier of India – where fighting would continue, on and off, for another century into our own time – he served under Sir Bindon Blood (noting, of course, that the general was directly descended from the Colonel Blood who had tried to steal Charles II's Crown Jewels from the Tower of London and as a reward for his temerity had been given an estate in Ireland rather than a beheading by the magnanimous king). This family history of noble larceny, Winston commented, gave Sir Bindon a healthy sympathy with his foes, the Pathans or Pashtoun tribes of the Afghan border.

Skirmishes became copy for articles. Articles turned into book manuscripts, which Jennie sent to Longmans, who had published Macaulay. The publicity opened some doors and closed others. His father's old nemesis, Lord Salisbury, actually sent for the young author of *The Story of the Malakand Field Force* (1898), gave him his blessing and pretended there had been no ill will. But Major-General Kitchener, conducting operations in the Sudan against the Islamic fundamentalist Mahdi Muhammad Ahmed, resisted almost to the last having Churchill foisted on him (a suspicion that would endure right through to their shared disaster at Gallipoli in 1915). None the less Winston was there at the battle of Omdurman in 1898 – and there, moreover, in the most epic persona he could contrive, as a dark-blue 21st Lancer in the thick of the last great, massively futile cavalry charge in British military history, colliding with the 'Dervish' army as 'two living walls crashed together.' The experience provided Churchill with the perfect subject for his word-painting, a skill that was getting better, even cinematically gripping, with every adventure: 'Riderless horses galloped across the plain. Men, clinging to their saddles, lurched helplessly about, covered with blood from perhaps a dozen wounds. Horses, streaming from tremendous gashes, limped and staggered with their riders. In 120 seconds five officers, 66 men, and 119 horses ... had been killed or wounded.'

Even by the time he published *The River War: An Historical Account of the Reconquest of the Sudan* – quickly in 1899 – Churchill knew that sympathy for the gallant, fallen, dusky foe was a crucial ingredient of the successful ripping yarn. But, following Gibbon's famously sympathetic, even heroic, portrait of Muhammad and the birth of Islam, Churchill too attacked the wicked cast of characters, the 'greedy trader, the inopportune missionary, the ambitious soldier and the lying speculator' who had perverted the ideals, especially of Anglo-Egyptian government in the Sudan. Muhammad Ahmed appears not as 'the mad Mullah' of imperial caricature, but as the austere and puritanical reformer he actually was, whose call to rebellion was entirely understandable. This leaves Churchill (again in ripely pseudo-Gibbonian form) to lament that 'the warm generous blood of a patriotic religious revolt congealed into the dark clot of a military empire.' But he still reserves some of his most powerful writing for the mutilated horsemen and foot soldiers of the 'Dervish' army; and was genuinely horrified to hear that Kitchener had allowed the Mahdi's tomb to be desecrated and that the skull of the holy warrior was being used as a conversation piece for the general's desk.

Whilst he had his doubts about the generals, he had none about the results of their battles. The creation of a euphemistically titled 'Anglo-Egyptian Sudan' in turn made possible a continuous belt of British Africa running Cape-to-Cairo along with the railway. Churchill accepted the defensive rationalization for the lion's share of the partition of Africa – that it had happened, pre-emptively, to contain what would otherwise have been unacceptable instability in Egypt, the lifeline to India, trebly threatened by the Khedive's profligacy, French military expansionism and Islamic fundamentalism. Never mind, of course, that this was precisely the wilful muddling of means and ends that had landed Britain with an immense territorial empire in India a century before. And never mind that the India syndrome was already repeating itself, with the military and governmental costs of the 'holding operation' pushing its custodians into yet more adventures in the hope of capturing the perfect bonanza (palm oil in West Africa, gold in South Africa), which would deny it to its European competitors, above all the French, and one day would surely balance the books. The redness of the British Empire was already a fiscal, as well as a carto-graphic, compulsion.

In South Africa fame and fortune went together. Randolph had invested in Rand mining shares, which had appreciated by at least 50 times their original face

Lieutenant Winston Churchill of the 4th Queen's Own Hussars, 1895.

Winston held captive with fellow prisoners in a South African gaol, 1899.

value – a small fortune that, unhappily for Jennie and Winston, was largely consumed by the late Lord's equally substantial debts. But Churchill also shared the indignation of the colonial secretary, Joseph Chamberlain, and the empire builder Cecil Rhodes that the might of the British Empire was being held to ransom by the obstinacy of a bunch of Dutch farmers who dictated what political rights British settlers might and might not enjoy in the Transvaal. Mostly, however, the Boer War was another opportunity for the kind of military-literary adventure that Winston had made his trademark. Through more of his mother's shameless finagling he resigned his commission in the Hussars and was made chief war correspondent for the *Morning Post*. He sailed with the commander-in-chief of the expedition, Sir Redvers Buller; managed to be taken prisoner while defending an armoured train against Boer attack; escaped from a military gaol at Pretoria (leaving behind two comrades who were supposed to escape with him), hid in a coal wagon and then walked hundreds of miles to freedom; and finally returned to active duty with the South African Light Horse in time to be at the relief of Ladysmith. The escapades were almost too fabulous to be true, and they turned Churchill from a purveyor of ripping yarns on the frontier into a genuine, nationally known war hero. Writing about his Boer War and lecturing about it with lantern slides in Britain, Canada and America (where in New York he was introduced, thrillingly, by Mark Twain) put £10,000 into his bank account. Just as important, it gave the patrician practical experience of what it meant to hold a crowd in the palm of his hand. And he was still in his mid-20s.

In 1900 Churchill translated all this busily, boldly earned fortune into political success, embarking on the career for which his father had assumed he was hopelessly disqualified by standing as Tory Unionist candidate at Oldham and winning the seat. It was his second attempt. In 1899 he had been handed a by-election opportunity in the same industrial constituency, which had two Tory MPs – a practical instance of what his father had meant by working-class conservatism – but had been defeated. During the campaign Winston discovered that his Churchillian lisp and even his occasional stammer, on which speech tutors had laboured to not much avail, was far from being a liability. It could actually be managed, theatrically, to brilliant effect – the pregnant pause followed by the mischievous witticism. He was all the better for earning his debating spurs, not in the mock-Commons chambers of the Oxbridge Unions but the hard way, on the tops of omnibuses, in theatres and town halls.

But did parading through Oldham in a landau during the post-war 'Khaki Election,' surrounded by mill girls, mean that Churchill really understood Britain any better than, say, Colonel Bwabazon or Sir Bindon Blood? During the Second World War, his wife Clementine was to say – kindly but accurately – that to understand Winston you had to know that he had never ridden on a bus in his life. It is possible, however, to overdo Churchill's patrician remoteness from the life of the British people. Curzon was an example of an aristocrat of temper as well as of birth – someone who had to brace himself for contact with the commonplace. Churchill, on the other hand, marched lustily towards it and revelled in its commotion. His father had invented 'Tory democracy' as a vote-getting conceit; the son more or less lived it.

Notwithstanding return trips to Blenheim, Churchill was actually ambivalent towards his own class and, once he was in the Commons as a predictably insubordinate back-bencher, towards his own party. Joseph Chamberlain's obsession with imperial tariffs and rejection of free trade left him cold and, increasingly, the political pragmatist in him scented a movement of power away from the landed dynasts of Victorian England and towards men who combined business, professional or industrial fortunes with maverick talent; men like the Liverpool lawyer F. E. Smith and the Welsh lawyer David Lloyd George.

Although, until the Liberals came to power in 1905, the majority of cabinet members were still drawn from the landed classes, their near monopoly of government was on its way out, shaken not so much by the advance of egalitarian democracy as by a long, steep agricultural depression. To all intents and purposes, between 1870 and 1910 Britain ceased to be a serious agricultural producer. Since it was unable to compete with colonial and American imports, 3 million acres were taken out of cultivation. By 1911 just 8 per cent of the 45 million people of Great Britain were earning their living from the land. Agricultural incomes in Britain over the same period fell by a full 25 per cent. Rents followed, to the point where they were often insufficient to service the mortgages taken out to provide for country-house weekends, the season in town, the well-stocked stable and cellar, the fashionable table and wardrobe, and the increasingly expensive daughters. When the pressure of death duties (inheritance tax), introduced in 1894 and then imposed in a much more punitive way in 1907, was added, sales were inevitable. And since – both before and after the First World War – there seemed to be no sign that land values would recover, the sales needed to be sooner rather than later, the process feeding on itself and turning into an avalanche. Almost a quarter of the privately owned land of Britain, David Cannadine has determined, went on the market between the 1870s and 1930. Many of the estates of those whom he calls 'coroneted casualties' were bought by the relatively recent rich whose fortunes had been made in industry, shipping, mining, insurance or publishing; often, as with the father of the newspaper baron Lord Beaverbrook, in the Dominions. There were Australian and Canadian accents now at the point-to-points and grouse shoots, and the relics of the old nobility tried not to flinch. Churchill's cousin, the 9th Duke of Marlborough (who never forgave Winston's rhetorical onslaught on the aristocracy in the campaign for the 'People's Budget' of 1909), lamented that 'the old order is doomed.'

This was unnecessarily apocalyptic, especially since Blenheim was not about to go on the rocks. But a certain way of life was indeed going under – subsiding rather than abruptly disappearing, but going under all the same. When the young socialist and active Fabian Society member H. G. 'Bert' Wells, the son of a professional cricketer, bowling coach and proprietor of a high-street glass and china shop in the small town of Bromley, published his masterpiece *Tono-Bungay* in 1909, he looked back not so very far to the time when 'Bladesover House,' located in Wells's Kent, was the apparently unchanging centre of the English social universe. Wells knew what he was talking about because his father's fall from grace, or rather from a grapevine he was trimming, had resulted in a broken leg that ruined his sporting career, and necessitated the boy's mother, Sarah, becoming a servant at Uppark,

Cartoon of Churchill as a persuasive speaker in the House of Commons, from *Vanity Fair, c.* 1900.

a 'great house' in Hampshire. Wells remembered, and felt keenly, the assumption of its infinitely graded hierarchies, and the web of subterranean tunnels beneath the house through which the servants, Morlock-like, scurried to do their masters' bidding. But the Eloi were still very much on top:

> ... the unavoidable suggestion of that wide park and that fair large house, dom-inating church, village and the countryside, was that they represented the thing that mattered supremely in the world and that all other things had significance only in relation to them. They represented the Gentry, the Quality, by and through and for whom the rest of the world, the farming folk and the labouring folk, the trades-peoples of Ashborough, and the upper servants and the lower servants and the servants of the estate, breathed and lived and were permitted.

But even by 1909, that certainty had gone. Although the look of the countryside was the same – 'The great houses stand in their parks still, the cottages cluster respect-fully on their borders, touching their eaves with their creepers. . . . It is like an early day in a fine October. The hand of change rests on it all, unfelt, unseen. ... One frost and the whole face of things will be bare, links snap, patience ends, our fine foliage of pretences lie glowing in the mire.'

Or so Wells hoped, a little prematurely. He, after all, was unequivocal about the dead weight of the past on the British future. And as a scientist – a student of the great Darwinist T. H. Huxley, no less – Wells made it clear many times that it was the future in which he and the rest of us ought to be interested. Nations and national histories were tribal anachronisms. True history was the history of the human species, not some absurdly arbitrary territorial and linguistic micro-division. To save that future needed a planetary view.

That view would come with his great *Outline of History* in 1919, a work about as far removed from Churchill's island epics as anyone could possibly get. But for the moment Wells's future, along with his future histories, was still science fiction. The masters of Uppark/Bladesover and their ilk continued to define Britishness, even if the cheque books that paid for the gardeners were now drawn on business accounts. (Predictably, Wells has 'Sir Reuben Lichtenstein' eventually buying Bladesover.) Social democracy was not just over the Fabian horizon. Those who did survive the shake-out of the estates belonged to an even more exclusive elite: by 1914, half the acreage of England and Wales belonged to just 4500 proprietors.

But not all the plutocracy chose to put their money into parks, stables and grouse moors, aping the old blood. Many of them, like Joseph Chamberlain, the screw manufacturer who had committed the unforgivable solecism of wearing his hat when being sworn in as an MP for Birmingham, were now barons of the new Britain and created their own version of estates in the suburbs. Chamberlain's mansion, called Highbury after the north London district where he had spent his youth, was originally surrounded by 18 acres rather than the thousands typical of the old aristocratic houses. It had been designed by another Chamberlain (John Henry, whose reputation had been formed as the architect of Birmingham's schools, civic buildings and municipal fountains) and was built in solid orange industrial brick with stone embellishments, the materials of choice for industrial-Italianate. Inside, everything was dark and very shiny. 'No books, no work, no music,' sneered the patrician socialist Beatrice Webb, 'to relieve the oppressive richness of the satin-covered furniture.' Outside, there was croquet, tennis and late Victorian picturesque complete with rushy bogs, dells, brooks and pre-weathered bridges. Chamberlain himself could often be seen on an inspection tour of his orchids, azaleas and cyclamen – each species, naturally, with its own glasshouse.

Not very far from Highbury, just 4 miles south of the then city limits, the Quaker cocoa-and-chocolate magnate George Cadbury built his house, Woodbrooke, also with the standard tennis, croquet and a newly obligatory feature – the seven-hole golf course. But Cadbury had a much more ambitious social vision for his estate than mere vulgar plutocratic self-celebration. As a response to social critics like John Ruskin and William Morris that factory industrialism represented, by definition, the destruction of community, Cadbury built at Bournville a new-old village in which workers would be housed in half-timbered cottages gathered round a green. The resurrected paternalism of Merrie England would be the antidote to the horrifying slum tenements that Cadbury remembered from the days before Chamberlain's social reforms in Birmingham, which still persisted in the worst sinks of destitution such as the East End of London, graphically documented in Charles Booth's *Life and Labour of the People in London* (1892–7). By 1900 there were 140 of Cadbury's mock-medieval workers' dwellings, and to complete the effect he had bought two authentically old houses, the 13th-century Minworth Greaves and the Tudor Selly Manor, which he had had moved to Bournville and lovingly restored. This attempt to re-create the imagined 'organic' community that Carlyle, Pugin and Ruskin claimed had existed in the medieval past was the precise opposite of the Hanoverian policy of obliteration, by which awkwardly placed villages were removed from the sight of the newly rich. At Bournville, Cadbury even reinvented the old traditions of manorial feasting, organizing fêtes and theatricals and day trips for other workers in the Birmingham area to see what life might be like under the new industrial baronies.

At Port Sunlight, on the banks of the Mersey near Liverpool, Bolton-born William Hesketh Lever, who had also made his fortune by processing a colonial raw product (in his case palm oil), did the same for his soap-factory workers. Some 30 architects were commissioned to create a complete 'garden' village in what was unapologetically called the 'old English' style – a lot of Jacobean-Flemish gables, much ornamental plaster pargetting and, of course, ubiquitous exposed timbering and leaded windows. To complete the effect of an old England reborn through the 'Spirit of Soap,' two cottages were built as 'exact' reproductions of Anne Hathaway's house. Rents for the Port Sunlight cottages – there was a basic 'kitchen' type and a fancier 'parlour' type, but both, as at Bournville, had their own running water and indoor bathroom – were benevolently pegged at around one fifth of the average weekly wage of 22 shillings. To help sustain the family life that critics of industrial Britain claimed had been destroyed by factory work, schools were built for the 500 children of Port Sunlight and, for girls and working wives and mothers, special classes were offered in cooking, dressmaking and shorthand. By 1909 there were 700 cottages, a concert hall and theatre, a library, a gymnasium and an open-air swimming pool.

Fortunate as the industrial villagers of Bournville and Port Sunlight undoubtedly were, they were hardly typical of the condition of the 40 per cent of Britons who, by the turn of the 20th century, lived in cities of more than 100,000 inhabitants. Surveys of late Victorian slums, like Booth's of the East End or Seebohm Rowntree's 1901 study of poverty in York, gave the impression to social critics then and since that life for working people in the larger cities must have been hell on earth. Of these notoriously and persistently squalid concentrations of overcrowded destitution there were perhaps none worse than those in turn-of-the-century Glasgow, where unskilled workers still lived in a single room or at most two in a tenement block. That small space would have to do for a family's sleeping, eating and such ablutions as were possible. Even by 1911, 85 per cent of Glasgow's accommodation consisted of three rooms or fewer.

But true slum-dwellers constituted perhaps no more than 10 per cent of the total urban working population. Insecure and unpredictable as employment might be in a trading world now less favourable to industries traditionally dominated by British exports such as coal, textiles and heavy engineering, for the vast majority of people the physical conditions of their lives – diet, health, housing, crime rates – had been transformed since the Great Exhibition of 1851 or even the queen's Golden Jubilee of 1887. Cities like Cardiff, with 128,000 inhabitants riding the crest of the south Wales coal export boom, had grown by seven times since the mid-19th century. In older cities like Manchester or Sheffield, the most noisome tenements

Top: The garden village at Port Sunlight, near Liverpool, commissioned by William Hesketh Lever in 1888.
Above: A family living in a one-room slum in London's East End, 1912.

had been taken down and replaced with two-up, two-down, four- or even five-room terraced houses (six in the Midlands and southeast), built in brick, sometimes faced with a little stone or stucco, of the kind that gave the industrial towns of England and Wales their classic look. To guard against overcrowding local by-laws, enlightened for their time, laid down regulations about the width of streets or the heights of ceilings. Today, of course, those streets look like some of the more depressing relics of the vanished industrial empire (although, arguably, they have weathered Britain's 20th-century history better than the post–Second World War tower blocks that replaced many of them).

Unlike the housing of virtually the rest of the industrial world in Europe and America, British terraced houses were based on the nuclear family unit, perhaps with extended family such as uncles, aunts and grannies, as well as neighbours, congregating in back gardens and sometimes on the street and in local shops, churches and pubs. Rooms were separated by function – kitchen, living room, bedrooms and, in the better-off or more socially ambitious houses, a parlour, seldom used except for special occasions and to display domestic treasures such as the piano and sideboard. Like gas for lighting and cooking, water was now supplied municipally and delivered through taps directly into sinks instead of through an outdoor pump. Water closets were fast replacing earth closets, and dungheaps and human waste were removed through town sewers, even if lavatories were almost invariably outdoors. In Exeter, beginning in 1896 the town council spent the enormous sum of £88,000 to construct a local sewage system, and rightly boasted of the transformation brought to the town, not least by reducing the risk and rate of infectious diseases like typhoid, typhus and cholera. Ruskin had a point when he declared that 'a good sewer is a far nobler and a far holier thing … than the most admired Madonna ever painted.'

Although plumbed-in bathtubs were still a middle- and upper-class luxury, a municipal bath-house revolution at the turn of the century meant that for the first time British working people, even those who didn't possess one of the prized tin slipper baths (a must for mining families), could now get their bodies clean on a regular basis. At Bow in the East End of London, 73,000 people used the baths in 1892–3, their first year of operation. By 1897 Lambeth in south London had a spectacular house with three swimming pools and 97 slipper baths. In London in 1912, as Anthony Wohl has chronicled, over 5 million visits were made to public bathhouses, many of them ornately, even exotically designed, their floors and walls dressed in gleaming tile. Together with the use of public laundries, the arrival of mass hygiene (making yet more money for the benevolent autocrat of Port Sunlight) was as great a change in the social body as the arrival of the vote was for the body politic.

Diet, too, was much changed, mostly for the better. A second industrial revolution in the late 19th century had brought processed and cheaply marketed foods like margarine, mustard and commercially produced jam into the diet of the working population. And the agricultural depression that was the countryside's misfortune was the urban consumer's opportunity, with prices for staples — tea, bacon, flour, bread, lard and sugar, most of them either colonial or Irish in origin — dropping by a quarter to a third between 1870 and 1914. With the import of refrigerated meat the market among the poor for 'slink' (prematurely born calves) or 'broxy' (diseased sheep) mercifully contracted, although few families could have forgone tripe (cow's stomach lining).

None of this meant that British social democracy was round the corner. Imperial wealth had done little to reduce the colossal inequalities of fortune. On the eve of the First World War, according to the social historian José Harris, 10 per cent of Britain's population owned 92 per cent of its wealth. As many as 90 per cent of the deceased, on the other hand, left no documented assets or property whatsoever. And, although unprecedented numbers of people in the Edwardian era might have thought of themselves as relatively well-off, the economic outlook for Britain in the new century was going to make holding on to those gains harder, not easier. It was exactly in the traditional labour-intensive, export-led industries — coal, metallurgy, textiles — that the pressure was already piling up. Countries that had once imported from Britain — especially the United States and Germany — were now competitors, in some cases protected by their own tariffs. Three-quarters of all Welsh tinplate, for example, had been exported to the United States. But after the imposition in 1890 of the McKinley tariff, designed to nurture the American domestic industry, the value of those exports collapsed by nearly two-thirds in just seven years. And what was true of tinplate would be equally true for coal, pig iron and locomotive rails.

Two not necessarily mutually exclusive options were available to counteract these ominous signs of the beginning of the end of British industrial supremacy. Britain could respond, as Joseph Chamberlain wanted, with its own imperial tariff system, creating an economic Fortress Britannia, behind whose customs walls colonies would be preserved as exclusive reservoirs of raw materials and markets for manufactures. (Quite what the colonies might get out of it in the long term was best left to future discussion.) Even before he had gone public, dragging a reluctant and divided Conservative party behind him, Chamberlain had been excited enough about this prospect to confide to Winston Churchill, whose constituency of Oldham was a town very much invested in the fate of textiles, that this would be the great political issue of the future. In the election of 1905 he would break the Tories by forcing the issue, just as he had broken the Liberals 20 years earlier over Ireland.

The second option, which industrialists themselves were taking without waiting for help in the form of legislated protection, was to reduce the unit costs of their products. This could be achieved by investing in labour-saving machinery, thus reducing the size of the workforce; by cutting the wage costs of the current work-force; by getting more hours and more product for their money; or indeed by all three combined. The result of their concerted attempts to press these changes resulted in some of the bitterest labour disputes, involving lock-outs as well as strikes, seen since the 1840s. For the rationalizing-economizing drive of management ran athwart the trade unions, who were disciplined enough to mobilize their labour and committed not just to a holding position but to fighting for a minimum wage, an eight-hour day (for miners in particular) and special rates of pay for 'abnormal' or particularly dangerous work (again in the mines). Although the biggest unions succeeded brilliantly in recruiting the overwhelming majority of workers into their ranks, the results of the confrontations of the 1890s and 1900s were mixed. When the Amalgamated Society of Engineers decided to resist the introduction of new 'self-acting' machines in 1897, which inevitably meant the downgrading of the skills and numbers of workers needed to man them and a resultant lowering of wages, they found themselves facing a determined lock-out. After seven months it culminated in a humiliating return to work on the industrialists' terms. Still worse was the 1901 court decision upholding the right of the Taff Vale Railway to sue the railwaymen's union for damages (in this case the enormous sum of £23,000) for lost revenues incurred during a strike.

Since it seemed unlikely, especially in the years of Tory supremacy, that parliament would ever undo decisions of that kind, the need for the unions to have their own representation became urgent. The veteran of the great London dock strike of 1889, ex-docker John Burns, became an MP, allied with the Liberals but with an agenda to look after workers' interests. But in the much more polarized climate of the 1890s and 1900s Burns was suspect as an example of the gold-watch-and-waist-coat, shiny shoed, bowler-hatted 'old' unionist, as much concerned with working-class respectability as with mobilizing industrial action. The miners in south Wales, for example, who had their own strike in 1893, looked rather for a politician who would not be beholden to either of the major parties. In the previous year the Scottish socialist James Keir Hardie had become the first Independent Labour MP, taking his seat at West Ham South; after losing it in 1895, he was elected MP for Merthyr Tydfil in 1900. 'Independent' announced Hardie's refusal to compromise the cause of union representation in this way. In 1900 a Labour Representation Committee was established, which six years later changed its name to the Labour party. Just 29 Labour MPs were elected to the parliament of 1906, the same year that at the other end of the empire, in Bombay and Calcutta, Indian nationalists repudiated both Liberal promises of self-government and Conservative promises of benevolently firm administration.

From the beginning there was a struggle for the soul (and in fact for the bodies) of the Labour party among three groups, all claiming to be the authentic voice of British socialism: revolutionary Marxists; trade unionists, who with some justification saw the party as their creation; and the non-revolutionary intellectuals of the Fabian Society. Inevitably, for the Marxists of H. M. Hyndman's Social Democratic Federation (SDF), the British component came second to the revolutionary solidarity of the international working class. And the SDF was, in fact, strongest in non-English industrial areas of Britain, on Clydeside and amongst the immigrants and political refugees from Europe, who flocked to London's East End. Trade unionists could, and did, see themselves as belonging to an old tradition of working-class self-help that went back to the Chartists and perhaps even to the radicals of the Civil War. (Strikers in Scotland would, more than once, rewrite the National Covenant of 1637 as a call to working-class solidarity.) But the Fabians, too, claimed pedigree from Milton, John Lilburne, Tom Paine, Cobbett and Carlyle. What all those patriarchs of the people had in common was their mastery of confrontational rhetoric, and from its foundation in 1883 the Fabian Society saw itself above all as a voice.

Its original charismatic founder, Thomas Davidson, the illegitimate son of a Scottish shepherd, was an itinerant lecturer, mystic and socialist who had taken radical London by storm in 1881 with lectures on the woes of industrial society. Two years later the starry-eyed and the socialists split (naturally), the latter forming a club named, obscurely but tellingly, after Quintus Fabius Maximus, the Roman General who 'waited patiently,' to the exasperation of the impetuous, before choosing his moment to strike hard at Hannibal. Fabianism committed itself to eschewing the half-baked, half-thought revolution in favour of a long campaign of re-educating both the political elite and the working class – the first to a new sense of their social responsibilities, the latter to a new sense of their legitimate social rights. Between them they were to make a modern, just and compassionate industrial society, without violence and without the sacrifice of freedom. There have been worse ideologies in the modern age.

But seldom have there been more dazzling propagandists. As early as 1884 the young Irish journalist George Bernard Shaw was writing regular, spectacularly vituperative Fabian essays denouncing the heedlessness of the landed and monied classes. Shaw was also an inexhaustible public speaker, giving 67 lectures in 1887 alone, talking, through the flame-red beard, almost always off-the-cuff in working men's clubs, parks, town halls, pubs and on street corners. The message was the same. Unless the politicos and the plutocrats woke up to the serfdom that their infamous system perpetuated, the serfs would one day come and get them and then only two alternatives would remain – a police state or a bloody uprising against the propertied classes. When Shaw finally tired of oratory, describing it as 'a vice,' his essay-writing for William Stead's *Pall Mall Gazette* left no sacred Victorian cow unslaughtered, including the biggest, most sacred cow of all. Of a hagiographic jubilee history of the queen's reign, Shaw wrote:

> We know that she has been of all wives the best, of all mothers the fondest, of all widows the most faithful. We have often seen her, despite her lofty station, moved by famines, colliery explosions, shipwrecks, and railway accidents. . . . We all remember how she repealed the corn laws, invented the steam locomotive ... devised the penny post ... and, in short, went through such a programme as no previous potentate ever dreamed of. What we need now is a book entitled 'Queen Victoria: by a Personal Acquaintance who dislikes her.'

It was when Shaw met Sidney Webb and his wife Beatrice that Fabian essay-writing really took fire. Beatrice had come from a family of businessmen and Liberal politicians. Her father, Richard Potter, had been director of the Great Western Railway and had made money from the development of the Barry docks, the principal outlet for the export of south Welsh coal. But her grandfather, also Richard Potter, had been a Benthamite reformer and campaigner for the Reform Act and Wigan's first MP. Beatrice had carried on the radical family tradition, finding work as a researcher for Charles Booth, disguising herself, somewhat improbably, as an East End Jewish girl looking for work so that she could report on the sweatshops. On the rebound from a heated but doomed passion for Joseph Chamberlain she met his diametric opposite, the short, rotund ex-tradesman and civil servant Sidney Webb, whose head was colossally out of proportion to his body. He wooed her with excitable talk of social justice, but when he made the mistake of sending Beatrice a full-length photo she recoiled in horror, reminding Sidney that it was his head alone that she had agreed to marry.

The Webbs' strategy (which both Shaw and H. G. Wells on occasions ridiculed) was 'permeation,' and those whom they meant to permeate were the great and the good of late Victorian and Edwardian society. *Fabian Essays*, which sold first by the tens and then by the hundreds of thousands, were the means of persuading the middle class, from clerks and librarians to solicitors and doctors, of the inequities and injustices of modern society and of the responsibility of the state to correct them. Sidney and Beatrice also conducted an intensive dinner-party campaign to permeate with Fabian doctrines the great and the good in political life. They brought together round the same table Shaw or Wells (though the two often quarrelled), sympathetic Liberals like Richard Haldane or Herbert Henry Asquith, and even those Tories who, for all their suspicion and condescension, seemed to be ready at least to listen – including the prime minister, 'Prince' Arthur Balfour.

Above all, they turned the daunting tomes of Booth and Rowntree into an impassioned argument for rethinking and, in fact, overturning the kind of nostrums about the poor that Beatrice would have heard from most of her rich social equals. There was unmistakable evidence that the problem of extreme destitution in towns and cities was seldom to do with issues of moral character, as the Victorian reformers had insisted. There might be a core of able-bodied persons who were incorrigibly dissolute, drunk or criminal (although the Webbs thought one of the most revolting aspects of hard-hearted Victorian philanthropy was to deny charity to aged alcoholics on the grounds of their dissipation). But the mass of the very poor were made up of men and women victimized by the fickleness of the business cycle: extreme fluctuations in seasonal employment; and the increasing ruthlessness (at the docks, for example) by which floating immigrant labour was exploited to drive down wages. It was subsistence or below-subsistence wages that reduced men and women to working outrageously long hours; sleeping in the overcrowded squalor of tenements; turning those places into breeding grounds of infection; or, if even those job opportunities deserted them, taking to the streets for a life of petty crime or prostitution or both. This kind of misery, argued the Webbs and other Fabians such as Sydney Olivier and Graham Wallas, was not going to go away. In fact, as competition in tailoring or boot-making or hosiery became more intense, dependence on insecure piece-work in unregulated conditions was likely to increase. Testimony given to a Commission on Physical Deterioration had also suggested that low pay rather than any defect of character was the major factor in condemning the poor to a life of squalor and disease and to producing the 'stunted' children who would be unfit to defend the empire.

It was time for the government to take responsibility for safeguarding the decent working class from this kind of pauperization; to see them through years of difficulty over which they had no control; to think of introducing unemployment insurance, labour exchanges and old-age pensions. This was not, the Fabians argued (to the irritation of Wells in particular, who thought the entire approach a mealy-mouthed version of socialism that dared not announce itself as such), the high road to revolution. On the contrary, it would be the best way to prevent one.

One of those listening to the Webbs – more carefully than Beatrice's judgement of him as a bumptious, egotistical reactionary suggested – was Winston Spencer Churchill. It is true that Churchill was no shrinking violet. He seemed to have taken seriously his own observation that life was just like a cavalry charge – 'So long as you are all right, firmly in your saddle, your horse in hand, and well-armed, lots of enemies will give you a wide berth.' When in doubt, Winston certainly charged. Violet Bonham Carter, Asquith's daughter, remembered 'the slightly hunched shoulders from which his head jutted forward like the muzzle of a gun about to fire.' But the enemies, around 1903, were more likely to be on his own side of the House of Commons than on the Liberal opposition benches. He had made no bones about his rejection of Chamberlain's policy of imperial protection, a line that did not go down well in his constituency of Oldham, where the beleaguered textile manufac-turers were all for it. He attacked his own front bench for inflated army and navy estimates. But more than anything, he sensed that the intellectual spirit, the energy of ideas, was all on the other side. H. G. Wells, then a Fabian socialist, would become a regular at Churchill's 'Other Club' dinners where the two became friends, notwith-standing the fact that Wells regarded with undisguised contempt the Macaulayite historical epic to which Winston was so attached. It was history, Wells insisted, that had dragged Britain down. Instead of being sedated by the past it badly needed to think about the future, in particular how Britain could become the techno-scientific society that alone would master what was to come. While Churchill was pottering around writing the vindicatory history of his father, Wells was writing *Anticipations of the Reaction of Mechanical and Scientific Progress upon Human Life and Thought* (1902).

But Wells's antiseptic utopia of a classless Britain, its memory wiped clean of the congested absurdities of the past, would never have changed Winston Churchill's party allegiance. When in May 1904 he finally, and unsurprisingly, crossed the floor of the House of Commons to join the Liberals, he aligned himself with the long tradition of pre-emptive progressive reform personified by the Whigs in 1832; by Disraeli sponsoring the Reform Act of 1867; and, as he imagined, by his father's rein-vention of 'Tory Democracy.' To make sure no one missed the filial significance of the gesture, he seated himself in Randolph's old place amidst the opposition benches. He was now, he told an audience during his first election campaign as a Liberal in Manchester, devoting himself to the 'popular cause.'

Top: H. G. Wells, *c.* 1904.
Above: David Lloyd George, 1904.

No one amongst the Liberals had any cause to suspect Churchill of mixed feelings or suspect loyalties, even if he did protest a bit too much and a bit too often about his current hatred of the Tories. They were, he told a Manchester audience in May 1904, 'a party of great vested interests, banded together in a formidable confederation, corruption at home, aggression to cover it up abroad … dear food for the millions, cheap labour for the millionaire.' After the 1906 election, which removed the Conservatives from power and reduced their number in the Commons to 137, Churchill revelled in their annihilation and gave the distinct impression to the more radical members of the new government, like David Lloyd George, that, if Balfour did carry out his threat to use the huge Tory majority in the House of Lords to frustrate legislation, then the child of Blenheim would be in the van of the counter-attack. As a new boy he was fortunate to get a government office, even if it was only colonial under-secretary, answerable to Lord Elgin, the ex-viceroy of India. The post enabled Churchill to combine a radical posture with imperial swagger and not see any contradiction. It also let him go with Elgin on a tour of Africa, where he revisited the battlefield of Omdurman, bagged a rhino, netted butterflies for his collection and wallowed for hours in his bath like a hippo, dictating memoranda and articles for *Strand Magazine*. 'Sofari sogoody' was his famous verdict. The same could be said for his initiation as a government minister.

But all this was a prelude to the real business at hand. When the prime minister, Sir Henry Campbell-Bannerman, died in the spring of 1908 he was succeeded by Asquith, with whom Churchill was on good personal terms – although, like everyone else, he never quite understood what really made him tick. Lloyd George took Asquith's post as chancellor of the exchequer and Churchill moved up into Lloyd George's place at the board of trade. He was in the cabinet at 33, even younger than his father when he had joined Salisbury's government.

Asquith's cabinet was rich with talent, but it was also a comprehensive portrait gallery of the history of liberalism, both old and new. It included Gladstone's biographer, the gaunt, high-minded John Morley, who was there to uphold Victorian canons of moral improvement, and John Burns, who despite his leadership of the strike of 1889 was the personification of 'respectable' labour. But as far as Churchill was concerned the entire cabinet, including Asquith himself, was overshadowed by the fiery light coming from David Lloyd George. It is unlikely that Churchill had ever encountered anyone quite like the former lawyer from the Welsh village of Llanystumdwy – a background that (while a lot less impoverished than Lloyd George made out) was not supposed to produce the razor-sharp intelligence, the political ferocity and the quicksilver oratory, peppered with dangerous, sly jokes, which the 'wizard' could turn on, seemingly, at the drop of a hat. The backgrounds of the two men could not have been more dissimilar, yet they quickly recognized each other as kindred spirits: both were possessed by burning personal ambition, both were driven to take the fight to the enemy. In parliamentary tactics as well as public speaking, Lloyd George was very much the teacher and Churchill the student. Winston had a tendency to rumble and bellow; Lloyd George charmed people to self-destruction. Churchill raised his voice in the Commons; Lloyd George made sure to soften it, giving his best impersonation of reasonableness. But as a political double act they were unbeatable: the hammer and the stiletto.

By 1908, both felt much the same about the needs of imperial defence. Lloyd George had been as ferocious a public enemy of the Boer War (alongside Campbell-Bannerman) as Churchill had been a supporter. But both now recognized that the war had burdened successive governments with a huge debt; compounded by the expensive necessity, as it was thought, of keeping the Royal Navy at a superior strength to its major rival, imperial Germany. But defending the empire was, by this time, not just a matter of military book-keeping. The Fabians had argued that imperial survival depended as much, if not more, on the social health of Britain as on dreadnoughts. Germany, after all, was hardly a socialist state, and yet the government there had accepted the need for labour exchanges and unemployment insurance. To the modern-minded chancellor and the president of the board of trade Germany seemed the model of an organized state, whereas Britain was a muddle of habits and prejudices. As far as they were concerned the introduction of comparable reforms, along with old-age pensions, was as much a matter of effective self-defence as it was of social justice. The question, however, was where the money would come from to fund both pensions and battleships. The Conservative answer had always been to impose indirect taxes, often on the staple commodities of daily life. But apart from the inherently regressive nature of those taxes, 1907–8 was a period of economic slump, especially in the most embattled industries such as coal mining. This was certainly not the time to be paying for pensions by taxing those who could least afford it.

Out of those deliberations came one of the epic confrontations of British political history, to rank alongside the debate over the Petition of Right in 1628–9 and that over the Reform Act of 1832. And, arguably, more was at stake between 1908 and 1911 than at either of those times: a double revolution that saw assumptions about the legitimate business of the British state transformed, and the power of the House of Lords emasculated.

The gauntlet was thrown down by Lloyd George in 1909 in a budget that proposed paying for old-age pensions, and raising the rest of the £16 million extra annual revenue needed to put the desired social reforms in place, by a stiff rise in death duties. He favoured the introduction of a surtax of sixpence in the pound on incomes over £5000 and, most explosively of all as far as the old aristocracy were concerned, a duty of 20 per cent on the unearned appreciation of land values, to be paid whenever estates were sold, inherited or transferred. There was also to be a charge of a halfpenny in the pound on undeveloped land and mineral sources, and fairly steep tax increases on alcohol. The slap in the face of the old governing class was so obvious that it left even the most ardent members of the cabinet slightly breathless; looking at the document, as John Burns said, 'like nineteen rag pickers round a heap o'muck.' Apart from anything else, its execution presupposed a complete survey of British land.

Marshalled by Balfour, up to this point the Lords had been obstructionist but not over money bills. This time it was different. They rose to Lloyd George's loaded bait like trout to the hook. Off on the stump went Lloyd George and Churchill, the latter now president of the Budget League (formed in opposition to the Budget Protest League), doing what they loved doing best: savaging the stuffy. In May 1909, Churchill had seen his Labour Exchange Act through the Commons, and now he felt entitled to present himself as the people's champion. What was more, who better than a baby of Blenheim to judge what history did, and did not, entitle their noble lordships to? At Norwich in July he sounded half like Edmund Burke, half like Tom Paine, declaring the upper house 'an institution absolutely foreign to the spirit of the age and to the whole movement of society.' It was absolutely natural for a country so attached to tradition to sustain a 'feudal assembly of titled persons,' but they had long outstayed their welcome. Had the Lords been content with their largely decorative status, they could have had a gentle twilight: 'Year by year it [the House] would have faded more completely into the place to which it belonged until, like Jack-in-the-Green and Punch and Judy, a unique and fitful lingering memory would have remained.' But no, they insisted on resisting the will of the people. *They* had launched a class war. Let the outcome be on their own heads. At the Victoria Opera House in Burnley in December, Churchill had a lot of fun with Curzon's claim in nearby Oldham that the 'superior class' by blood and tradition had inherited the right to 'rule over our children.' What did the noble lord say? That ' "all great civilisation has been the work of aristocracies." They liked that in Oldham (laughter). ... Why, it would be much more true to say the upkeep of the aristocracy has been the hard work of all civilisations" (loud cheers and cries, "Say it again").'

On the People's Budget road show, however, Winston was merely the warm-up act; it was Lloyd George who was the star. The great mesmerizer, by turns wicked comedian, saw-them-in-half illusionist-cum-juggler, and (to slay the audience at the end) master of tragic opera, was nowhere more on song than back home in Wales. At Swansea in October 1908 he apostrophized the well-to-do about the need for unemployment insurance:

> What is poverty? Have you felt it yourselves? If not, you ought to thank God for having been spared its sufferings and its temptations. . . . By poverty I mean real poverty, not the cutting down of your establishment, not the limitation of your luxuries. I mean the poverty of the man who does not know how long he can keep a roof over his head, and where he will turn to find a meal for the pinched and hungry little children who look to him for sustenance and protection. That is what unemployment means.

And he was yet more powerful in a speech made at Limehouse in London's dock-lands where, mockingly, he compared the costs of a duke and a dreadnought, but then took his audience to a place that Churchill could not: down the mines.

> We sank down into a pit half a mile deep. We then walked underneath the mountain. . . . The earth seemed to be straining – around us and above us – to crush us in. You could see the pit-props bent and twisted and sundered, their fibres split in resisting the pressure. Sometimes they give way, and then there is mutilation and death. Often a spark ignites, the whole pit is deluged in fire and the breath of life is scorched out of hundreds of breasts by the consuming flame. … and yet when the prime minister and I knock at the doors of these great landlords, and say to them: 'Here, you know, these poor fellows have been digging up royalties at the risk of their lives, some of them are old … they are broken, they can earn no more. Won't you give something towards keeping them out of the workhouse?' They retort, 'You thieves!' And they turn their dogs on to us. . . . If this is an indication of the view taken by these great landlords … then I say their day of reckoning is at hand.

Churchill's old friend Lord Hugh Cecil compared the Limehouse Lloyd George to a small boy deliberately getting his trousers dirty in a puddle. But that was to do the speech and its orator an injustice. However manipulative, it remains one of the greatest speeches in the whole of British political history: a complete one-act play. And it did exactly what the chancellor, Churchill and Asquith wanted it to do – it pushed the Lords to resist to the last ditch. They voted the budget down by 300 votes to 75. The government resigned and fought an election in January 1910, which, despite – or because of – the demagoguery, backfired badly, destroying their overall majority. The Liberals were now dependent on Irish Home Rulers and Labour members to help them see their programme of legislation through. The first order of the day was to make the Lords pay for their temerity. Asquith proposed a Parliament Bill threatening to abolish the Lords altogether and replace it with an elected upper house – but pending that doomsday would settle for a series of lesser resolutions: the Lords' veto on money bills was to be abolished, and legislation that had passed the Commons in three consecutive sessions could be no longer obstructed in the upper house. The Lords could either swallow this medicine or be deluged with an instant mass creation of peers, perhaps 600 – enough, at any rate, to swamp their opposition. Edward VII had been queasy about having the royal prerogative to create new peers used in this way, but after his death in 1910, and much agonizing, his successor, George V, felt he had no alternative but to agree. Still the fight went on. Asquith was shouted down by serried ranks of screaming Tory backbenchers while Balfour stretched out languidly on the front bench and stared at his nails. In the Lords debate the more moderate 'Hedgers' like the Marquis of Lansdowne spoke against the '[last] Ditchers' like Lord Willoughby de Broke and Lord Halsworth, who resolved to die with their armour on. On a division the Hedgers won, by a handful of votes; the Parliament Bill passed into law, and the Lords as an independent political power passed into British history.

This was the kind of battle that Winston Churchill, for one, really loved, and that he thought fitted well with the best traditions of British history: a war of principles, with the forces of progress triumphant and no blood spilled in the victory. But by the time the Parliament Act was going through the Lords, Churchill, as home secretary in the post-1910 election government, had two very different kinds of battle on his hands, both of them with the potential to turn not just ugly, but, as he thought, revolutionary. He had not, after all, become a Liberal to advance revolution, much less socialism, but on the contrary to pre-empt both of them with timely, humane, reasonable reform. And he believed the government had kept faith with the trade unions, steering through parliament the Trades Disputes Act that, in 1906, reversed the Taff Vale decision and removed financial liability for strikes from the unions. And had the unions, especially in the most militant regions like south Wales and Lancashire, repaid the government by calming their rank and file? Not a bit of it. By the summer of 1910 the Rhondda, where D. A. Thomas, a friend of the government, was the leading mine-owner, was boiling over with industrial action. The causes were the same as they had been and would be all the way to the final showdown between

On Budget Day, 1910, Winston Churchill and David Lloyd George, the new Chancellor of the Exchequer, head for parliament, accompanied by Lloyd George's wife, Margaret (far left), and his private secretary, Mr. Clarke (far right).

Arthur Scargill and Margaret Thatcher in the 1980s. The owners, faced with disappearing export demand, needed to retrench; the workers demanded a minimum wage and special pay for 'abnormal work.' The very fact that Lloyd George had used their case so insistently when pushing the People's Budget led the unions to believe that pressure would be put on the owners to yield, or, in default, that legislation would be passed. When neither happened, serious militants, and their publication *The Pleb*, began to make inroads on the more moderate unions. The situation became serious enough for the chief constable of Glamorgan to use police to guard some of the pits. When it threatened to tip over into rioting, he requested troops from Churchill. His cautious response was to send London policemen to Tonypandy. They were enough to cause further provocation, but not enough to restrain or repress it. On 8 November a serious riot broke out, in which a miner was killed and 60 shops looted.

It was only after the riot that Churchill decided to send troops to Tonypandy, thereby ensuring himself a place in the demonology of the labour movement. Although he got himself a reputation for being trigger-happy in tight situations, and although there is no doubt that patience was never his strong suit, the situation in

Above: Striking miners asleep in the power house at Glamorgan Colliery, Wales, during the Tonypandy coal strike, 1910.
Opposite top: The militant suffragette Emily Davison throwing herself under King George V's horse at the Epsom Derby in 1913.
Opposite below: Suffragette leader Emmeline Pankhurst arrested at a demonstration outside Buckingham Palace, 1914.

the autumn of 1910 and into 1911 in the coalfields was in fact highly incendiary. A strong anarchist and revolutionary core led by Noah Ablett made no secret of its contempt for traditional union strategies, even more so for parliamentary lobbying, and was quite open about capitalizing on grievances about pay and conditions to further a radical revolution. In the baking summer of 1911 there were more riots at Cardiff and at Tredegar by railway workers, both of which took an ugly, racist turn. At Cardiff striking seamen attacked the Chinese community of shopkeepers and at Tredegar there was a virtual pogrom against the small Jewish community. It was at Llanelli, not Tonypandy, that troops fired on strikers (in this case railwaymen), killing two of them and triggering another riot that destroyed 96 trucks and ended up causing an explosion and four more deaths.

Handling this was not an enviable job for a home secretary. And the turn of the suffragette movement, led by Emmeline Pankhurst and her daughter Christabel, towards militancy didn't make it any easier. As with the miners, Churchill had been, on principle, tepidly sympathetic to the cause of votes for women, not least because his wife Clementine was a warm supporter. But as Asquith squirmed and procrastinated to the point of yielding a 'Conciliation Bill' intended to enfranchise women property owners, but then got the legislation snarled in procedural delays, the patience of the Women's Social and Political Union (WSPU) not unreasonably ran out. Cabinet ministers who had been heavily lobbied in the House were now stalked and harassed. By July 1910, a year after he had been attacked by the suffragette Theresa Garnett wielding a whip, Churchill himself declared in parliament that he would not support the enfranchising of women.

Faced with mass demonstrations in Parliament Square, Churchill gave directives to the police not to arrest the demonstrators but, on the other hand, not to allow them access to parliament. Intended to be cautious, the guidelines for handling the crowds were in fact a guarantee of disaster. Thousands of women and their male sympathizers, extremely well marshalled, pushed hard against the police. Helmets were, of course, knocked off. Rude things were said. Crowds gathered to chuckle. This was not what policemen like. On 18 November 1910, 'Bloody Friday,' the pushing and shoving turned into six hours of fighting, with the police manhandling and beating up as many suffragettes as they could get their hands on – and discovering, in their turn, the power and the pain of the raking scratch and the well-aimed kick. Instead of zero arrests there were, in the end, 280.

This only added fuel to the flames. Inside Holloway prison, following the lead of Mrs Pankhurst and Mrs Emmeline Pethick-Lawrence, suffragette prisoners went on hunger strike and in response were brutally force-fed using metal clamps, rubber tubes and nauseous fluids that they usually vomited up again. Ice-cold water was hosed into some of their cells to a depth of 6 inches. Outside, the WSPU campaign was evidently targeting property especially associated with men's stereotypical images of womanly behaviour. The little women loved shopping, did they? Stores such as Marshall & Snelgrove, Swears & Wells and Liberty had their big windows smashed in. The fancier streets of London – government offices in Whitehall, clubland in Pall Mall – became carpets of broken glass. Other sanctuaries of the British way of life were shockingly violated. 'Votes for Women' was spelled out by acidburns on the greens of golf courses including the one at Balmoral.

One of the most militant of the suffragettes, Emily Wilding Davison was constantly coming up with new tactics to take the women's guerrilla war into the heartland of the respectable classes. First she was caught standing by the Parliament Square postbox holding a paraffin-soaked piece of linen, about to light it. After a spell in prison she then organized an attack on Lloyd George's new house at Walton-on-the-Hill in Surrey, which succeeded in destroying half of it, although she was not caught in the act. And, finally and most famously, Emily achieved her evident wish for martyrdom by throwing herself under the first horse to come into sight at the Epsom Derby in 1913. It just so happened that it was the king's horse that was in the lead when she launched herself from the rails.

By 1913 the Liberal programme for the renewal of Britain, along with its own power base, seemed to be unravelling fast – so much so that the classic narrative of the period, George Dangerfield's *The Strange Death of Liberal England* (1936), sees it as a prolonged exercise in obtuse self-destruction. In particular, Dangerfield saw the Liberals' willingness to hitch themselves to John Redmond's bloc of Irish Home Rulers as a guarantee of future grief. But if this was a tactical obligation to stay in power, it was also, for the Liberals, a matter of principle. Churchill, who vividly remembered his father's role in hardening Ulster resistance, somehow wanted to square it with his own equally impassioned desire to see an Irish parliament within the empire. If this goal proved ultimately impossible to realize, the gains of the great reforming administration were less ephemeral. Like many of Churchill's policies in his early career, they have been discounted as facile in concept, insincere in commitment and short-sighted in outcome. But all these judgements have been made from the perspective of a socialist Britain that itself has all but disappeared along with the 'Old' Labour party that was committed to public ownership of the means of production. Paradoxically, it is just the liberalism – capitalism with a social conscience – that George Dangerfield, writing brilliantly from the eminence of a *Vanity Fair* desk in New York, assumed to be moribund that has stood the test of time better than the welfare-state orthodoxies of the late 1940s. A century on, New Labour looks very much like the grandchild of New Liberalism.

If Lloyd George had been to Germany to look at unemployment insurance, Churchill had been a guest of the kaiser and had seen military manoeuvres at first hand. He understood the deterrence game well enough to know that a show of force on the German side was meant to prevent war rather than hasten it, specifically by discouraging a close Anglo-French alliance and a Triple Entente between those powers and Russia, as had been signed in 1907. But the strategy had the opposite effect of pulling that alliance closer, not breaking it apart, especially after the summer of 1911 when the German government decided on a display of naval muscle. A warship, the *Panther*, was sent to the Atlantic port of Agadir in Morocco to serve notice that, should the French presume to impose a protectorate, they would have to reckon with German naval power. The Agadir incident also had the effect of speeding up the British government's determination to maintain a healthy naval superiority over Germany. Churchill, in a characteristically tactless red-rag moment, had described the German fleet as a 'luxury' (meaning that, while Germany had a huge army as well, Britain had only its navy as an essential arm of imperial defence). This did nothing to slow down the rate of competitive armament.

So when Churchill became first lord of the admiralty in the autumn of 1911, he took a razor-scraper to the barnacles sticking to the organization of the Royal Navy. Theoretically, it could be seen as a demotion from the home office; but that was not the way either Asquith or Churchill himself thought of the job. The prime minister recognized that this was a perfect way for Churchill's piston-driven energy, sometimes in overdrive in the home office, to be constructively used. And for Churchill, despite his prejudice that the navy was all 'rum, sodomy and the lash,' it was the fulfilment of a strong sense of historical appointment. The new broom swept through the admiralty in short order. The dyspeptic visionary and former First Sea Lord, Sir John Jacky Fisher, though in his 70s, was recalled to advise the admiralty (somewhat to the amazement of the cabinet), and Churchill set about implementing some of Fisher's most serious changes. Heavy guns were to be mounted on fast ships; and, most momentous of all, those ships would now be fuelled more cost effectively by oil, not coal. In retrospect this one decision, a commitment to the Anglo-Persian Oil company – so apparently innocent, or at least so purely logistical (and so lightly glossed over in most Churchill biographies) – was to have more profound effects on the fate of the British Empire, not to mention the history of the world, than almost anything else Churchill did until the May days of 1940. It made the survival of the British Empire conditional on a Middle East presence, a halfway link between India and Egypt. That in turn would make Churchill, as colonial secretary in 1921, a strong supporter of a British mandate in Palestine and a protective role in Iraq (the former Mesopotamia) and Jordan. That would beget Suez. And Suez begat Islamic fundamentalism. The Anglo-Persian Oil Company, in which Churchill made sure to acquire a 51 per cent holding for the British government in 1914, would beget joint Anglo-American oil interests in Iran, which would beget the CIA overthrow of the Mossadeq democracy and the restoration of the Pahlavi dynasty, which would beget the Ayatollah Khomeini. And all the while the coal mines of Britain were relegated to terminal redundancy. But on the eve of the First World War, the battle fleet was well tanked and ready for action.

The cabinet, however, was divided over when and whether the fleet would be needed. Churchill got a great deal of stick, especially from Lloyd George, for his spectacular naval estimates. Was he, Lloyd George wondered out loud, still really a Liberal at all? But though in a minority, Churchill, like the foreign secretary Sir Edward Grey, was convinced that, if a war should break out in the Balkans, Germany, allied with Austria and Hungary, was more likely than not to respond by sending its armies to the west to attack France, and in equal likelihood through Belgium. The best chance of deterring this scenario, he also believed, lay in a real, rather than paper, commitment to stand shoulder to shoulder with France, and in never hesitating to regard an attack on Belgium as a direct threat to Britain. Certainly he thought back to the similar stance taken by William Pitt the Younger in 1793. But lest he be accused of idle and anachronistic historicism he also believed, in his marrow, that apart from any ideological anti-republicanism Pitt and his colleague Henry Dundas had been right about the uncontrollable expansionism of revolutionary France. So, indeed, he felt about imperial Germany – without any knowledge of the Schlieffen Plan, which called for simultaneous war on two fronts, west and east, or of the still more aggressive German policy (made formal in 1916) to convert large parts of eastern Europe into slave colonies and regions of western Europe (the Netherlands, for example) into satellites of the greater Reich.

For most of the summer of 1914, war seemed more likely to break out in Ireland than in Bosnia. Ulster Unionists and nationalists were each forming armed camps; Churchill, who had gone to Belfast in 1912 to make an appeal for moderation, hoped against hope, and against probability, that the third attempt at a Home Rule Bill would be successful. But faced with the threat of direct Protestant revolt against the plan in Ulster, it collapsed. The First World War itself would finish off the last possibility of Home Rule.

It was at these moments that history came to Winston Churchill. In early August

1914, it was giving the first lord mixed signals. On the very brink of hostilities he went to see the fleet steam past at Portland Bill. As the great steel towers emerged from the mist, Churchill's romantic imagination sailed all the way back to 'that far-off line of storm-beaten ships ... which in their day had stood between Napoleon and his domination of the world.' But Churchill was already a good enough historian, and had seen enough carnage, for his up-and-at-'em euphoria to be qualified by deep fore-boding. He was, after all, no longer the cavalier lancer. He had a wife and young children as well as a high office. On 28 July 1914 he had written to Clementine:

> My darling one & beautiful,
> Everything tends towards catastrophe & collapse. I am interested, geared-up & happy. Is it not horrible to be built like that? The preparations have a hideous fascination for me. I pray to God to forgive me for such fearful moods of levity. Yet I w[oul]d do my best for peace, & nothing w[oul]d induce me wrongfully to strike the blow. I cannot feel that we in this island are in any serious degree responsible for the wave of madness w[hic]h has swept the mind of Christendom. No-one can measure the consequences. I wondered whether those stupid Kings & Emperors c[oul]d not assemble together & revivify king-ship by saving the nations from hell but we all drift on in a kind of dull catalep-tic trance. As if it was someone else's operation!
>   The two black swans on St James's Park Lake have a darling cygnet – grey, fluffy, precious & unique. . . . Kiss those kittens [their children] & be loved for ever by me. Your own W

The war that materialized tortured Churchill's impatience, as well as his perfectly decent wish to spare prolonged slaughter. Along with many others in command, both political and military, he greeted the beginning of fighting with a strange euphoria, but at the same time felt sheepish about his reaction ('Is it not horrible'). And as the war developed into a hideous, man-devouring stalemate, Churchill became desperate for something other than the strategy of men 'eating barbed wire.' It was this compulsion to experience action that had prompted him to go to Antwerp in October 1914, after consulting with the foreign secretary, Grey, and the war minister, Lord Kitchener. There he took command of its defences, even offering, rather amazingly, to resign from the admiralty if the government felt he would be better used in a position of military rather than political command.

    Flanders made him understand the critical importance of the western front about which the generals and Kitchener kept on hammering away to the cabinet.

But Churchill's pessimism – entirely justified, as it turned out – about a breakthrough there encouraged him to push for an altogether different strategy. Why not attack the German alliance at what must be its weakest point – the Ottoman Empire of Turkey?

Churchill's plan, seconded by Fisher, was to 'force the Dardanelles,' the narrow strait separating the Mediterranean from the Black Sea, and take Constantinople. This would have the double advantage of securing Egypt, not to mention the oilfields in Persia and Mesopotamia, from German attack, and of persuading Balkan countries such as Romania, which was still sitting on the fence, to commit firmly to the side of the Allies.

It did not work according to plan. The optimal strategy was for a combined naval–military operation, with warships softening up Turkish forts before the army landed a large expeditionary force. But Kitchener balked at the commitment of troops, so on 19 February 1915 Churchill went ahead independently with a naval assault. None of its objectives was realized. Minesweepers failed to sweep adequately; battleship guns failed to take out the Turkish fort artillery. Three ships, including a French battleship, were sunk by mines. When Kitchener finally gave his authorization, an attempt was made to land a combined Australian–New Zealand–Franco-British force (including Winston's younger brother, Jack) of 70,000 on a rocky peninsula called Gallipoli, but thousands were mown down from entrenched Turkish artillery positions. A beach-head and a hilltop were taken, which afforded a good view of the bodies lying in the sand and shallows.

The butchery at Gallipoli in early 1915 came close to destroying Churchill's career. It didn't help that Jacky Fisher now resigned and denied ever having supported an assault on the Dardanelles in the first place. Someone was going to have to take the blame and, without a strong party base, that someone was inevitably going to be Churchill. When Asquith formed a coalition government with the Conservatives in May 1915, one of the items on their shopping list was the eviction of the man who had betrayed them in 1904 and who had taken so much pleasure in savaging them through the campaign for the People's Budget. Churchill was duly demoted to chancellor of the duchy of Lancaster, an all but meaningless job in wartime. This was bad enough for someone desperate to perform some active wartime service; but after another attempt to land troops in Turkey failed in August that year, the campaign was abandoned and the inner-circle military-operations committee wound up.

Out of favour, out of power, out of sorts, Churchill crashed into one of his 'black dog' depressions. For a while Clementine, with some reason, feared for his sanity. Wandering around his brother's garden, in a state of incoherent misery,

Overleaf: *The Menin Road* (detail) by Paul Nash, 1919.

he came across his sister-in-law 'Goonie' (Gwendeline) painting watercolours. She put a brush in his hand. It saved his mind, lifted him out of self-annihilating gloom and, more important, gave him a campaign he knew he could win: 'The sickly inhibitions rolled away. I seized the largest brush and fell upon my victim with Berserk fury.' But he seemed not to be able to paint his way out of a guilty conscience, nor to get rid of the consuming frustration that he had been denied a chance to harness his tireless energy to the all-important end of hastening victory.

This left only one route to redemption, active service, and Winston took it. He was now in his early 40s but continued to insist that he was, after all, a soldier. Not any old soldier, of course, but one who rather fancied he might, as a brigadier, lead a regiment. This was aiming a bit high – even, or especially, for an ex-cabinet minister. So Churchill, growling, had to make do (eventually) with the rank of colonel and the command of a battalion of Royal Scots Fusiliers. The service was not very long – six months in all – and punctuated by leaves home and periods at staff HQ. When he did get to Ploegsteert, the Fusiliers' assigned position, in January 1916, the orders were to hold it rather than embark on some frontal assault of the German lines. It was real service all the same. Winston made a point of experiencing the trenches, and he got a proper dose of them over the winter of 1915–16. He stomped around the rat-run duckboards and half-frozen mud; ducked with the rest when the 'whizz bombs' came over; looked mournfully at the half-buried bodies; even – by mistake – went walkabout in No Man's Land, to find when he returned that his usual post in the trench had taken a direct hit. Amidst all these discomforts and terrors, Churchill kept up his usual ebullience and slightly uncoordinated surges of zeal, together with frequent exhibitions of disregard for his own physical safety. It helped, of course, that he used Clemmie like Fortnum & Mason. In November 1915, at Bout-de-Ville, he wrote to his wife:

> My darling,
> We have finished our first 48 hours in the trenches. . . . I have spent the morning on my toilet & a hot bath – engineered with some difficulty. . . . The line of trenches ... built along the ruins of other older lines taken from the Germans. Filth & rubbish everywhere, graves built into the defences & scattered about promiscuously, feet & clothing breaking through the soil, water & muck on all sides; and about this scene in the dazzling moonlight troops of enormous bats creep & glide, to the unceasing accompaniment of rifle & machine guns & the venomous whining & whirring of the bullets w[hich] pass over head. . . . Will you send now regularly once a week, a small box of food to supplement the

Top: An Australian soldier carrying his comrade across the battlefield of Gallipoli during the Dardanelles Campaign, 1915.
Above: Major Winston Churchill, wearing a French shrapnel helmet, with French officers at HQ French XXXIII Corps, Camblain L'Abbé, 1915.

rations. Sardines, chocolate, potted meats. . . . Begin as soon as possible. . . . Do you realize what a v[er]y important person a Major is? 99 people out of any every hundred in this g[reat] army have to touch their hats to me. With this inspiring reflection let me sign myself. . . . Kiss Randolph, Diana & that golden Sarah for me.

When he did get his colonel's rank and his Scots Fusiliers, Churchill saw at once that they were badly mauled and demoralized from the traumatic experience of the battle of Loos. He had just two weeks to get them combat-ready again for their assigned place on the line at Ploegsteert in Flanders. Junior officers and especially NCOs not unnaturally resented having this middle-aged, paunchy, noisy VIP foisted on them and were aghast at his unorthodox approach to parade and drill, generally the kind of enthusiastic shambles that did not go down well with the regulars. But it soon became obvious that Winston was genuinely prepared to share the perils and hardships (though not the sardines); that he had real loyalty to his men and determination that they should not suffer needless casualties. And even though their orders were only to hold their position, so that they never had to face going over the top in one of Field Marshal Haig's lethal Big Pushes, the dead and wounded rate in Churchill's battalion was far lower than the norm. This did not, however, prevent Clementine from worrying herself sick over her husband's fate; an anxiety not helped, perhaps, by the fact that he had already made his will.

But if Clementine was anxious about his departure, she was even more aghast to see him back so soon, in March 1916. Try as he might to be a good, steadfast soldier, it was not in Churchill's blood to abandon politics altogether. Parading his service as though he had been in uniform since 1914, he made a sudden, exceptionally ill-advised appearance in the Commons, where he attacked the naval conduct of the war since his departure from office and – to general consternation and disbelief – called for the return of the ancient, extremely unstable Jacky Fisher. The speech went down like a lead balloon. It did not, however, prevent Churchill from fighting an election (pursued by cries of 'What about the Dardanelles?'), nor – in the teeth of Tory hatred – prevent the new prime minister Lloyd George from listening whole-heartedly to his advice, and eventually naming him in July 1917 the new minister of munitions. As it turned out, this was a brilliant choice. Much of what Churchill was to do in the Second World War was anticipated by his work in 1916–18: the ferocious push to solve the perennial 'shell shortage'; the frank acceptance of conscription before anyone else in the government was brave enough or realistic enough to see it as inevitable; and the advocacy of a radically new weapon that might break the stalemate – the Land Ironclad or tank, an idea taken, as Churchill admitted, from one of his friend H. G. Wells's prophetic visions. Kitchener, predictably, dismissed the tank as a 'mechanical toy' and, to Wells's and Churchill's disgust, made sure the new fighting machines were initially used only as a defensive novelty rather than as a reconceptualized cavalry. But when unleashed as assault vehicles, they proved their worth at the battle of Cambrai in November 1917, advancing the British lines 5 miles in some places.

Some 8 million dead combatants and 25 million additional deaths later, the war ground to an end. On 11 November 1918, Armistice Day, Wells described military trucks riding around London picking up anyone who wanted a ride to anywhere, and 'vast vacant crowds,' consisting mostly of students, schoolchildren, the middle-aged and the old, and home-front soldiers, choking the streets: 'Everyone felt aimless, with a kind of strained and aching relief.' A captured German gun carriage was thrown on to a bonfire of 'Hun' trophies in Trafalgar Square. But Wells, at least, thought exhaustion and sorrow overwhelmed the rejoicing: 'People wanted to laugh, and weep – and could do neither.' Vera Brittain, who had left Oxford University to be a nurse, noticed that 'the men and women who looked incredulously into each other's faces did not cry jubilantly: "We've won the War!" They only said: "The War is over." ' Even this relief gave way to a stunned, chilly gloom, for almost all her best male friends were dead: 'The War was over; a new age was beginning, but the dead were dead and would never return.'

Perenially ebullient as he was, Churchill nonetheless understood this strange mix of emotions. As the new minister of 'war and air' (and an eager trainee flyer, until a crash impelled Clemmie to forbid Winston the cockpit), he was responsible for handling demobilization, which, before he took office, had become a source of immense anger and distress for all those who had survived the inferno. They were supposed to be discharged according to industrial and economic priorities, which inevitably meant slowly. Judging this inhuman, Churchill speeded up the rate of discharge and made wounds, age and length of service the priorities instead.

It was the least that could be done. At least 700,000 British servicemen had perished in the Great War, and a million and a half had been wounded. Another 150,000 were lost to the influenza pandemic of 1918-19. Some 300,000 children had lost at least one parent. One in ten of an entire generation of young men had been wiped out. One of them was Rudyard Kipling's only son, and the grief turned the great imperial tragedian towards deeper melancholy. In his wonderful *Mr Britling Sees It Through*, published in 1916, Wells (though his own sons were too young to serve) imagined the 'little Brit' similarly bereaved, along with a German father in the same torment: 'Man has come, floundering and wounding and suffering, out of the breeding darknesses of Time, that will presently crush and consume him again.' A predictable, perfectly human response would be to 'flounder with the rest,' to indulge again in 'Chestertonian jolliness, the *Punch* side of things. Let mankind blunder out of the mud and blood as mankind had blundered in.' But for Wells, as for like-minded writers such as Shaw and Arnold Bennett, this had to be the moment, perhaps the last, when the conditions that had produced the general massacre were removed. Away with preposterous empires and monarchs and the tribal fantasies of churches and territories. Instead there would be created a League of Free Nations, advocated also by Shaw, Bennett and the philosopher and pacifist Bertrand Russell. This virtual international government, informed by science and motivated by disinterested guardianship of the fate of common humanity, must inaugurate a new history – otherwise the sacrifice of millions would have been perfectly futile, the bad joke of the grinning skull. All of these 'new Samurai,' as Wells called them in his book *The Modern Utopia* (1905), were to be bitterly disappointed by what they took to be the vindictiveness of the Treaty of Versailles, which imposed the blame and the cost of the war on Germany. Wells was also frustrated by the limited authority given to the League of Nations, made even weaker by the United States Congress's repudiation of the treaty.

At home there were misleading signs that this new era, when the fate of the common man and woman would truly be the concern of their rulers, might actually come about. The burial of the Unknown Soldier in the nave of Westminster Abbey on Armistice Day 1920 seemed, at least symbolically, to herald just such a chastened democracy. The idea had been floated by the Reverend David Railton, a vicar from Margate in Kent who had served as an army chaplain at Armentières and had written to the Dean of Westminster. The battlefields were, of course, strewn with unmarked, improvised graves and this would be the ordinary soldier's counterpart of the Cenotaph, the monument to the war dead designed by Lutyens and erected in Whitehall. The king was against it and the appointment of Lord Curzon, not noted for his sympathy with or knowledge of the common man, as chairman of the committee did not bode well. But Lloyd George, presiding over the coalition government (with a huge majority), saw its propaganda value and the scheme went ahead in the deliberate glare of publicity. Six parties were sent out to six cemeteries in Flanders to exhume a body from each, and the anonymity of the soldier selected was preserved by blindfolding the officer who made the final choice. A coffin of English oak was prepared and inscribed, as would be the plaque of black Belgian marble in the abbey, with the utmost simplicity and gravity: 'A British warrior who fell in the

Londoners celebrate Armistice Day, 1918.

Great War 1914–1918 for King and Country.' Six destroyers escorted the coffin across the Channel where it received a gun salute from Dover Castle, then it moved by train to Victoria Station in London, from where on 11 November it was carried through the streets of the capital, the king following on foot. The pall-bearers included the three chiefs-of-staff, Field Marshal Haig, Admiral Beatty and Air Marshal Trenchard. In the tomb, at the feet of statues of the famous and the mighty, were buried, along with the soldier, 100 sandbags of earth from each of the great battlefields of the war. Over 1 million people came to pay their respects in the first weeks of the interment, and 100,000 wreaths were laid at the newly built Cenotaph.

Would post-war Britain, then, as Lloyd George had promised, be a 'country fit for heroes'? It would at any rate be a democracy of 27 million, even if the vote at last given to women in 1918 began at the age of 30 whilst 21-year-old men were deemed adult enough to exercise it; there would be no flapper franchise. A short, strong, post-war economic boom funded some, at least, of the government's promises. Christopher Addison, the minister of reconstruction, oversaw the building of 200,000 homes – effectively the beginning of council-house construction in Britain. The liberal historian and president of the Board of Education H. A. L. Fisher raised the school-leaving age to 14, a small act with immense significance, and standardized wages and salaries throughout the country. Old-age pensions were doubled, and unemployment insurance extended to cover virtually the entire working population of Britain.

It is not quite the case, then, that 'reconstruction' was the fraud that some historians have claimed. But where it was most visible, in the economics of heavy industry, 'war socialism' did indeed disappear as Lloyd George always meant it to; and with it went the sense, in the labour movement at least, that an activist government would do something to moderate the inequities of the old industrial system. The men who ran the government were, after all, born Victorians, and they did not hesitate in their determination to dismantle as quickly and completely as possible the state control of raw material, manufactures, communications, wages and rents. And even though Lloyd George was the prime minister, the political complexion of the government was a strong shade of blue since his majority was completely dependent on the alliance with the dominant Tories and Ulster Unionists.

So any talk, strong amongst the unions, of nationalizing the coal industry, the docks or the railways was discouraged. And when the boom turned to slump in 1920–1, there was nothing to prevent the people whom Stanley Baldwin called 'the hard-faced men who looked as though they had done well out of the war' from resuming the tough tactics they had adopted in the first decades of the century: wage cuts and lock-outs.

In any event Lloyd George did not need persuading by the likes of Andrew Bonar Law, leader of the Conservative Party, or the other hard-right figures in his government such as F. E. Smith and Lord Curzon that the termination of 'war socialism' was an important goal and the restoration of monetary orthodoxy was the *sine qua non* of British 'reconstruction.' If anyone pointed out that he had ensured there would be two contradictory interpretations of what reconstruction meant — that of a social democracy and that of Tory traditionalism — the prime minister would merely beam disconcertingly back until the ingenuous dimly understood that divide-and-rule was the point. Either you got it or you didn't, and if you didn't you were outside Lloyd George's charmed circle. Now, more than ever, he was convinced that he could govern through sheer charisma reinforced by tough political muscle. Up on a pedestal of his own making as 'the man who won the war,' in his own mind (and in many others' too) he was no longer a mere politician leading a party so much as the indispensable 'statesman.' With the evaporation of the authority of the US president Woodrow Wilson, and the short-lived office of the French wartime prime minister Georges Clemenceau, his fellow post-war peacemakers, it was Lloyd George who filled the vacuum as the arbiter of Europe, which was to say the world. The more this became apparent, the better he liked it — strutting, flashing his cherubically wicked smile and treating the obliging press like the complaisant mistresses he so unapologetically enjoyed. The coalition faced virtually no threats in parliament, where the 59 Labour members provided the main opposition along with the withered rump of 'pure' Liberals ostensibly led by the frequently drunk, wispy-haired figure of H. H. Asquith, who had never got over his dethronement by Lloyd George in 1916. With not much to challenge him, the prime minister rarely deigned to put in an appearance in the Commons, presiding instead from Downing Street over a regime of flashy cronies. It was rule by dinner party; its weapons the artfully targeted rumour, the discreet business sweetener, the playfully or not so playfully threatening poke in the ribs. Honours were up for sale; insider commercial favours expected. And the more gangsterishly presidential Lloyd George became, the less love was lost between him and his only obvious rival – Winston Churchill.

When this all turned bad – strikes and riots in Scotland, a brutal war in Ireland, boycotts, walk-outs and massacres in India – the imperial nation, which Curzon boasted in 1918 had never been so omnipotent, threatened to fall apart. The seams tore open most raggedly at the periphery, where there were outright rebellions. In Ireland, Volunteers – called for not just by Unionists but by John Redmond's Home Rulers – self-destructed precisely by virtue of their loyal service in Flanders. As they turned into the ghosts of Passchendaele and the Menin road, their deadly rivals, the Irish Republican Army (IRA), who in 1914 had been an insignificant group of militants, swelled to the level of a real army. The abrasive – or expedient – gesture of bringing the most unscrupulous and belligerent of the Unionists, Sir Edward Carson, into the coalition government, triggered not just the Dublin Easter Rising of 1916, but, even more damagingly, the sense that the British government would never deliver Irish independence unless forced to do so. In the 1918 elections the remains of the Home Rulers were politically annihilated by Sinn Fein (the political wing of the IRA), committed to an immediate, free republic.

There was also, for the first time, a serious Scottish Home Rule movement, fuelled in part by astonishingly disproportionate Scots casualties in the war: 26.4 per cent of the 557,000 Scots who served lost their lives, against a rate of 11.8 per cent for the rest of the British army. Ironically, it was the long Scottish tradition of being the backbone of the imperial army – from the American Revolution to the Indian Mutiny – that resulted in them being put in particularly perilous positions, or made the vanguard of some insanely suicidal lurch 'over the top' ordained by the likes of Haig or Field Marshal Sir Henry Wilson. But in Glasgow an eighth of the population was still living in single-room accommodation and the region's economy was especially vulnerable to retrenchment in the shipyards. As men were demobilized, unemployment rose. The unions responded with demands for a shorter working week, to spread the money available as broadly as possible, and for the retention of wage and rent controls. When they got no joy a 40-hour general strike was called, culminating in a demonstration of 100,000 in George's Square. A red flag was waved and the baited bull of the police lines charged. The demonstration was declared first a riot and then a 'Bolshevist' uprising. Mindful of having been caught by surprise in Dublin at the time of the Easter Rising in 1916, the government sent 12,000 troops and six tanks to occupy Red Glasgow.

Elsewhere in the empire, despite Curzon's complacency, all was not especially well. Or, rather, there were two empires, just as there were coming to be two regionally disparate Britains, affected in very different ways and degrees by the ageing pains of the classical industrial economy. Nearly 150,000 white troops from the empire lost their lives in the war. The extraordinary sacrifices made by the white Anglo-dominions – Canadians at Vimy Ridge, ANZAC troops at Gallipoli, South Africans at Delville Wood – may have made the families who suffered personal losses proud of the sacrifice of their sons, but also perhaps not unmixed in their feelings towards the empire that had taken them. After the Gallipoli debacle in 1915 it was understandable that enthusiasm for volunteering in Australia petered out dramatically, and there was intense opposition to conscription. And if it is undeniably true that, collectively, those nations saw their service as a spurs-winning moment on the road to recognition as imperial equals with the mother country, it is equally true that the non-British populations of Canada, and especially of Boer South Africa, were much less ardent in their support. There were recruiting riots in Quebec. In 1915 elections in South Africa demonstrated that, despite General Jan Smuts's loyalist efforts, more than half the Boers were unreconciled to a war against Germany – a country that they associated with support for Afrikaner nationalism.

Macaulay's vision of a confederation of the educated and the self-governing had come true – but for white, English-speaking farmers, bankers and plantation owners. In the off-white empire, this reciprocity of gratitude and shared self-interest was a lot less apparent. Nearly 1 million Indian troops were in service, both in the 'barracks in the east' in Asia itself on the Western Front and, during the war, in the ultimately disastrous campaign in Mesopotamia, where General Sir Charles Townsend's besieged army had ended up surrendering to the Turks at Kut el Amara in 1916. Official estimates of Indian losses were put at 54,000 dead and another 60,000 wounded. At least 40,000 black Africans had served as bearers and labourers with the British armies in France, as well as a larger force fighting in the colonial African theatre; needless to say, their casualty rates are impossible to ascertain, though likely to have been very high.

At any rate, the African-Near Eastern empire was much shakier in its loyalty after the war than before. In 1918, partly driven by the accumulating momentum of post-*Khalifa* Muslim nationalism and the collapse of the Ottoman Empire, a delegation of Egyptian intellectuals and politicians – the *wafd* – asked the British authorities to set a timetable for the end of the protectorate that had been in force since 1914. The high commissioner in Egypt, Sir Reginald Wingate, did not dismiss them out of hand but was not optimistic. Even this degree of cooperation was laughed off in London by the likes of Curzon as deeply unwise. When the rejection became known, the Egyptian government resigned and there were strikes and riots – precisely the same kind of demonstrations that occurred in India at the same time, and with even more tragic results. Some 1500 Egyptians were killed over two months of fighting between the British army and the nationalists. As in Iraq, an anti-*wafd* monarchy of convenience was now established on the understanding that Egypt would be 'protected,' along with the Suez Canal, by British troops. From this moment of disenchantment and resentment countless evils sprang.

Before he became colonial secretary in February 1921 Churchill had attacked the spinelessness of anyone compromising with the *wafd*, whom he clearly thought of as the IRA in tarbooshes. And this Churchill – the jaw-jutting, table-pounding belligerent defender of empire; the warmonger who couldn't stop fighting; the defender of the Black and Tans' brutalities in Ireland; the delusional, obsessive anti-communist who spoke of bolshevism as an international infection – is often said to be the 'true' Churchill, the aristocratic reactionary, reverting to type after his brief, uncharacteristic fling with social reform. Unionism is said to have flowed in his veins along with his father's blood, his calls to strangle the Russian Revolution at birth springing from a deep well of sentimental class solidarity with the Russian aristocracy and the tsars.

But these truisms about the post–First World War Churchill seem to be confounded by the bitter, incontrovertible truths of the rest of the 20th century. Looked at from the viewpoint of 2002, almost all of Churchill's positions – on Russia, Ireland, the Middle East and even the issue of German reparations and the blockade put in place by Balfour to force assent – seem prophetic or optimistic. Often he would swerve from a hard to a soft line, but those changes were the result of replacing visceral belligerence first by reflection and then by magnanimous second thoughts. Having banged away in Lloyd Georgian vein about making Germany pay through the nose, he then made appeals for greater flexibility and leniency and opposed the blockade. In Ireland it was Churchill who negotiated a two-state solution with the Sinn Fein leaders Michael Collins and Arthur Griffith, with whom he struck up a surprisingly positive personal relationship. The outcome was a southern Irish state, with a Protestant-dominated Northern Ireland remaining part of the United Kingdom. If an Irish Free State with dominion status was not Home Rule inside Britain, it represented at least the continuity of some sort of connection. It was an inter-Catholic *Irish* civil war in 1922 that would break that connection, kill off hope and, for that matter, take the life of Michael Collins.

It may be that Churchill was reckless as well as tireless in calling for a commitment of men and money to try to reverse the communist revolution in Russia by supporting the pro-Tsarist White Army (certainly no force for democracy). But if he was deliberately goading British socialists by harping on about the Bolsheviks as a dictatorial conspiracy, it turns out that this diagnosis of what had happened in Russia in October 1917 was exactly right. There was ample reason to feel gloomy about the fate of liberty in the new Soviet Union. By 1919 anyone could see that what had been destroyed was not just the Constituent Assembly but any semblance of multi-party democracy in Russia, although of course the perpetuation of the war gave the revolution's leader, Vladimir Lenin, the perfect pretext to institutionalize his police state.

In March 1921, Churchill, now colonial secretary, went camel-riding in Egypt with T. E. Lawrence (Lawrence of Arabia) and the orientalist Gertrude Bell. At the Middle East conference in Cairo in March he was, perhaps, captivated by a mirage:

the parallel development of Arab and Jewish communities side by side. The mandate that the League of Nations had given Britain for Palestine would, he said, include the setting up of a 'Jewish national home' as promised by the Balfour Declaration in November 1917, made a month before General Edmund Allenby's army had taken Jerusalem from the Turks. But Churchill emphasized, perhaps naïvely, that this would not be an 'imposition' on the Arab population. (At Gaza in March 1921 he was delighted to see a crowd of Palestinians shouting support for Britain, but was spared the translation of equally enthusiastically shouted slogans such as 'Death to the Jews.') In time, Churchill fondly hoped the Arabs might come to see Jewish settlement as the germ of a modernizing transformation of the entire region. Churchill was unequivocally a Zionist, in that he believed the answer to the hatefulness of anti-semitism was (in time) a Jewish state and that the only legitimate place for it to be was the place that had given both people and religion their identity. His hope was that by establishing monarchies in Iraq and Transjordan he could reproduce something like the *de facto* partnership, or at least acquiescence, that prevailed in India between princely states and the directly governed British centres of modernity like Bengal and Bombay.

But that calculation, of course, was coming badly undone in India itself. When he and Fisher had converted the British fleet from coal to oil Churchill had opened the second great Pandora's box (the first had been Gladstone's decision to occupy Egypt in 1882). There were now all kinds of reasons to hang on tight in the Middle East – the investment in oil; the strategic protection of the Suez Canal, where a huge new military base had been constructed; the careful management of the post-Ottoman Arab monarchies, to ensure they didn't fall into the hands of nationalists who might break the lifeline to India or even give support to 'malcontents' there; and perhaps Lloyd George's crudely bullish insistence that, since Britain had won Palestine 'by right of conquest,' it had the right to stay. The mandate confirmed this, but 40 years of British control would turn out to be neither happy nor particularly glorious.

In 1922 the coalition, which had been fraying for a long time, finally fell apart. In the November election that year the Liberal party – and especially Lloyd George's wing of it – virtually disappeared. Churchill himself went down at Dundee by 10,000 votes. Putting a brave face on it, he took himself and Clemmie off to the Riviera. A £42,000 advance for his war memoirs let him take a villa near Cannes, called the Rêve d'Or, for six months. There he padded around, looking at the Mediterranean, painting and writing *The World Crisis* (1923). He had no political allies to speak of, no party base, no constituency really. But under the umbrella pines, amidst dreams of gold, life, even a life outside Westminster, was not, after all, so very dreadful.

'Bert' Wells was looking at a very different stretch of water, and writing very different history. In 1918 he was to be found, often, at the semi-detached house on Marine Parade in Leigh-on-Sea in Essex that he had found for his lover, the writer Rebecca West, and their baby Anthony. Wells too liked strolls beside the water, but this was the murky, iodine-aromatic Thames estuary where the winkles tangled with the bladderwort and the scummy tidewater ebbed to reveal rust-brown mud. Wells loved this water and the cool grey sea horizon into which it flowed. But his thoughts and his history swept out beyond the edge of Britannia towards a vast oceanic expanse of space and time, the only history now that he thought worth writing: the history of the human species on the planet. The *Outline of History*, which he began to publish in serial parts in 1919, was subsequently bound into a single volume and, translated into most of the world's languages, became not just by far the best-selling history of the 20th century but a book that was outsold only by the Bible and the Koran. By the end of 1921, 150,000 copies of the 1300-page, densely detailed book had been sold in Britain, and half a million in the United States. By the end of 1922, when Churchill was poring over his memoirs, Wells had already sold a million in many other languages including Slovene and Japanese.

The *Outline* made its author rich, but more importantly it made him a global figure. This must have been deeply satisfying to Wells, who always intended his *Outline* to be a missionary statement as much as a narrative of world history. By beginning, not with the mists parting over the Channel to reveal to Caesar's boats the outline of white cliffs, but with a small, apparently insignificant ball of matter spinning in deep space, Wells was trying to rewrite history as biology, geology and archaeology, but did not assume, like Macaulay and Churchill, the ever onwards and upwards progress of civilized humanity, diffusing its blessings to the rest of the world. On the contrary, those disciplines submerged that saga into a much bigger epic of the appearance and disappearance of species, cultures and, not least, empires. The tale that geology and archaeology told was one of illusions of immortality buried in the rock strata or beneath shifting wastes of sand. And for Wells the scientist – connected, as he liked to think, with Darwin directly through his teacher T. H. Huxley – survival, or at least the prolongation of the reign of *Homo sapiens* after the cataclysm of the war, depended critically on history supplying a chastening sense of limits. By stepping sharply back from the European-Atlantic scene, looking with equally measured gaze at Hittites and Mongols, Mayas and Ottomans, Wells hoped to deliver a sense of shared fate before it was indeed too late: 'There can be no common peace and prosperity without common historical ideas.' So in this global perspective Muhammad and his heirs are rewarded with 30 pages; the story of the

Glorious Revolution of 1688, which filled Macaulay's volumes and which, in the Whig tradition, defined the point and purpose of British identity, was limited to a single, not very interesting paragraph.

What was desperately needed now, Wells thought, was a new Enlightenment – a scientifically based, universally recognized common store of knowledge that would transcend the parochial, self-congratulatory mythic histories of kings, states and nations. With this new universal encyclopaedia would also go (since people seemed to need it) a generalized theistic religion: 'religion itself, undefiled … the Kingdom of Heaven, brotherhood, creative service and self-forgetfulness.' This true, universal religion would make redundant the cruelties and barbarities that faiths like Christianity and Islam, claiming the monopoly of truth, had inflicted on each other. 'Throughout the world men's thoughts and motives will be turned by education, example, and the circle of ideas about them, from the obsession of self to the cheerful service of human knowledge, human power and human unity.' On the basis of these agreed principles would come a new world government, imposed not by accumulators of power but by those who would be sworn to resist them: the disinterested, platonic, intellectual class (like him) whom Wells called, with deliberate inappropriateness, the 'new Samurai.' He ended his *Outline of History*:

> War is a horrible thing, and constantly more horrible and dreadful, so that unless it is ended it will certainly end human society. . . . There are people who seem to imagine that a world order and one universal law of justice would end human adventure. It would but begin it. . . . Hitherto man has been living in a slum, amidst quarrels, revenges, vanities, shames and taints, hot desires and urgent appetites. He has scarcely tasted sweet air yet and the great freedoms of the world that science has enlarged for him.

Could one be British and think these heady, internationalist thoughts? What would be left of his father's village cricket and the green on which it was played in Mr Wells's new world order? Perhaps the young, at least, didn't care. One of Wells's old Fabian comrades, Graham Wallas, paid him the compliment he most treasured, that if he were now a 'sixth form boy of fifteen as I was nearly sixty years ago it [the *Outline*] would change the whole world for me.'

And there was at least one Etonian sixth former, Eric Blair (the future George Orwell), who read everything by Wells that he possibly could and who didn't – for the moment – give a damn what happened to the village green.

CHAPTER

8

George Orwell's history could never have been the same as Winston Churchill's, but his history teacher might have been. In the last year of his five-year internment at St Cyprian's, a prep school in Eastbourne, he won the Classics Prize and was first runner-up for the Harrow History Prize. The man who invariably came to St Cyprian's to present it was Churchill's (and G. M. Trevelyan's) old teacher, George Townsend Warner. Warner died in 1916, the year that Eric Blair won the prize, but there is no doubt that Eric would have seen the old master many times before, handing out the books and making the usual noises about the fate of the empire depending on its boys knowing their history.

Eric didn't think much of this. History lessons, like all the other lessons at St Cyprian's, were, he wrote much later in 'Such, Such Were the Joys' (1947-8), his adult revenge on the ordeals of the school, just fact-cramming routines designed to drill the boys for the public school entrance examinations from which the prep school made its reputation and money. The island epics that even at St Cyprian's Blair thought 'not bad fun' were reduced to 'orgies of dates, with the keener boys leaping up and down in their places in their eagerness to shout out the right answers, and at the same time not feeling the faintest interest in the meaning of the mysterious events they were naming.' What stayed in Blair's mind was the arbitrary coupling of names and phrases, or names and dates – Disraeli 'brought peace with honour,' Clive, 'astonished at his moderation' – without the slightest attempt to explain their significance. History became pure mnemonics, the initial letters of 'A black Negress was my aunt, there's her house behind the barn' for instance, spelling out the names of the principal battles of the Wars of the Roses.

Eric's real history teacher at St Cyprian's was not a Warner-like figure of erudite benevolence and inspiration but Flip (nicknamed for the flip-flop of her pendulous breasts as she advanced towards some cowering snot-nose). In Orwell's scarred recollection Flip was the presiding sadist of the school, dispatching eight-year-old

ENDURANCE

The National Hunger March passing through the village of Croughton, Northamptonshire, on its way to London, 1932.

bed-wetters (miserably home-sick) to her husband Sambo, the headmaster, for a brutal bend-over. Beating the bed-wetters to the rhythmic chant of 'You dir-ty lit-tle boy' guaranteed the anxiety that would bring on another episode of the crime. In 'Such, Such Were the Joys,' Orwell describes the experience of one such terrorized micturator, 'Night after night I prayed, with a fervour never previously attained in my prayers, "Please God, do not let me wet my bed! Oh, please God, do not let me wet my bed!" but it made remarkably little difference.' To the small boy this helpless syndrome – pee, get beaten; pee, get beaten – was proof that he had landed in a nightmare world where it was 'impossible to be good.'

Orwell's memory and even his honesty in 'Such, Such Were the Joys' were indignantly contested by contemporary schoolmates who protested that the formidable but motherly Flip had been unjustly caricatured, and that the regime at St Cyprian's taught 'character.' Exaggerated or not, if that character were created from being forced to plunge into a slimy, freezing swimming bath every morning before picking one's way through porridge eaten from pewter bowls, the rims caked with yesterday's glop and today's glop concealing unidentifiable foreign bodies of a generally hairy, crusty kind, then it was a character Eric Blair was not much interested in acquiring. The bright spots amidst the gloom were always moments when, left to himself and the English countryside (at its most gorgeous on the Sussex Downs), he would collect orange-bellied newts or the butterflies that, just as with Churchill, remained a lifelong passion. To England, and in fact to English history, Orwell would always respond with a leap of the pulse. At 11 he was enough of a little patriot to write a wartime recruiting poem, 'Awake! Young Men of England' (1914), published in his local newspaper in Henley-on-Thames. But St Cyprian's was the other England; a place where children torn from home were incarcerated amidst 'irrational terrors and lunatic misunderstandings.' It was the gap between the self-righteousness of the governing-class ideals – Christianity, cricket and civilizing the natives – and the reality of coercion that most offended him, even in his short-trousered days. The best that could be said for such places was that they gave the rulers of empire an opportunity of existing as white natives, of sampling what it was like to be on the receiving end of a system where good and evil were hopelessly confused.

Eric Blair had in fact been born into the narco-empire in Motihari, Bengal, in 1903. His father, Richard, was a small cog in a big business: assistant sub-deputy agent of the Opium Department, third class, devoted to stocking the Chinese (and the world's) hard-drug habit. In the first decade of the 20th century profits from opium exports, averaging 4000 tons a year, amounted to £6.5 million, or one-sixth of the total revenues of the government of India. Without the drug business Curzon would have been unable to build the Victoria Memorial Monument. Richard Blair's job was to stalk the poppy fields seeing that crop yields were satisfactory and the quality pure; then to see the product properly transported to shipping depots. Since the future of the trade was under a cloud, increasingly criticized both at home and abroad, the pressure on Blair and the department to amass all they could in the way of profits was probably intense. He must have done his job conscientiously, as if he were supervising Assam tea or Patna rice.

Transferred to a remote up-country area, Blair decided in 1904 to send his wife Ida (half-French), together with their daughter Marjorie and tow-haired, chubby-cheeked baby Eric Arthur, back to England. He would serve out his time, like countless other drones of the empire, by himself, in some hill station, and then come home. The Blairs were not particularly well off. In *The Road to Wigan Pier* (1937) Orwell would describe the family, accurately, as 'shabby-genteel' or 'lower-upper-middle class,' with an income of hundreds, rather than thousands, of pounds a year. This gave them the taste for, and knowledge of, a genteel life – how to order a meal in a restaurant, which knives and forks to use – without the means to enjoy it. At St Cyprian's he was constantly being reminded by Flip and Sambo that, unlike more fortunate boys, he did not have the luxury to waste his 'precious opportunities.'

'Home' was Vicarage Road, Henley-on-Thames, sempiternal England, the 'Lower Binfield' of Orwell's wonderful novel *Coming Up for Air* (1939): willows hanging over the river, cow parsley in the lanes, paddling swans, brick-fronted breweries, regatta blazers, cream teas, punts and the 'great green juicy meadows round the town.' Ida's house in Vicarage Road was decorated with exotic items – ivory and oriental rugs – which spoke of her 'difference.' In an upmarket move to Rose Lawn, Station Road, Shiplake, the Blairs acquired a garden of about an acre and Eric and his sister got a tantalizingly brief taste of real country pleasures. But the expenses were too much even after Richard Blair had finally been promoted to (full) sub-deputy agent, third grade. Bowing to criticism, the opium business was being quietly wound down and in 1913 would stop altogether as a result of a treaty with China. In 1912, Richard accepted early retirement and a pension of £400 a year, never quite enough to support the family pretensions. During the later years of the First World War, while Ida was doing some public-service work, the Blairs first lived in west London at Cromwell Court, Earl's Court. The Churchills, on the other hand, were living in the Cromwell Road. The verbal difference was minute; the social difference immense.

But it was Eric, not Winston, who went to Randolph Churchill's old school Eton. He went, of course, on a scholarship and, despite the usual initiation rites of

Eric Blair on vacation in Athens, 1919.

beatings administered by older boys, seems to have enjoyed it a lot more than St
Cyprian's. At Eton he affected a style of laconic rebellion, which in post-war Britain
was all the rage and made him, he admitted, both a snob and a rebel. There was much
debating the socialism of Shaw and Wells; much jeering at the cadet corps. Of a class
of 17 boys asked to nominate their hero, 15 chose Lenin. When Blair left, he presented the school library with a book of plays, which included Shaw's *Misalliance*, the
preface to which, 'Parents and Children,' featured a fierce attack on British schools,
which it castigated as prison camps of the young – worse, in fact, since they tortured
mind as well as body.

It may have been Eric's studied pose of taciturn insolence that deceived his
teachers into assuming that silence was a sign of intellectual dimness. At any rate, his
father was told by his classics master, 'Granny' Gow, that there was not the slightest
chance that the boy would win a scholarship to an Oxford or Cambridge college,
the next step on the routine ascent to the governing classes. On Richard's pension
there was no question of being able to pay for an education among the dreaming

In 1923 Blair (tallest in the back row) was posted to the Indian Imperial Police training school at Mandalay, Burma.

spires, so the plum-stone game in which Etonians chanted 'Army, Navy, the Church, the Law' did not apply. The obvious alternative was to follow in his father's footsteps and seek a career in the colonies, though no one ever thought of designating one of those plum-stones 'Police.'

While broken-down tenors were still singing 'On the Road to Mandalay' in the London music halls, in November 1922, Eric found himself actually on it, destined for the Indian Imperial Police training school. The Burma police has a good claim to be the most thankless service in the most poorly regarded colony in the British Empire. Burma was a paradigm of plunder, its long-time plantation wealth in teak and tea, as well as rubies, now supplemented by the best of all 20th-century bonanzas: oil in the Irrawaddy delta. The resources were so precious, the resistance of Buddhist priests so troublesome, and the old Burmese royal family so unreliable a collaborator that in 1885 the usual solution had been applied: a military campaign ending in the annexation of the entire country. But there were 13 million Burmese and an even thinner ratio of British administrators to natives than elsewhere in the Asian empire, which made the police force the crucial weapon with which to enforce order. It is entirely possible that, when he arrived, Blair shared at least some of the official idealism that the police were there to do good: keep the peace, round up bandits preying on defenceless villages – that sort of thing. But five years in the 'stifling, stultifying world' of British Burma cured him of that.

As George Orwell, he looked back with ironic gratitude to his time in the police because in that service, at least, the coercion on which imperial power was based was nakedly exposed. At the beginning of 'Shooting an Elephant' (1936), the essay that distilled the essence of that experience, he sardonically remarks, 'In Moulmein, in Lower Burma, I was hated by large numbers of people – the only time in my life that I have been important enough for this to happen to me.' Initially, the young officer in pith helmet and khaki shorts tried to do his job respectably if not enthusiastically, rounding up petty criminals, looking the other way when they were beaten. But it did not take him long to understand that, for all the lofty talk of keeping the Pax Britannica (known in the Rangoon brothels more accurately as the Pox Britannica), he was little more than the hired muscle of big economic interests. In Syriam on the Irrawaddy he supervised the guarding of Burmah Oil's tanks. Up-country, at Katha, he was in the heart of teak-planter country. Instead of being exhilarated by power, caught between the racist ranting of the planters and the sullen hostility of the Burmese, he squirmed at its exercise.

The British types he was forced to encounter in the club bored and repelled him with their predictable endless moans, faithfully recorded in his early novel *Burmese Days* (1934): '"We seem to have no *authority* over the natives nowadays, with all these dreadful Reforms, and the insolence they learn from the newspapers. . . . And such a short time ago, even just before the War, they were so *nice* and respect-ful! The way they salaamed when you passed them on the road – it was really quite charming. I remember when we paid our butler only twelve rupees a month, and really that man loved us like a dog."' It was when he was sneered at for being an Old Etonian that Eric understood the paranoia of this generation of sunset imperialists – their terror at being demoted to the true shabby-genteel class from which most of them had, in fact, come. The whole point of empire for them was the opportunity to acquire the horses and the servants that were simply unaffordable in Britain. This was the real affront and the threat posed by men like Gandhi or the 'Bolshie' journalists and silently defiant Buddhist bonzes: that they would take away those low-rent butlers.

But if Eric despised what the novelist E.M. Forster called the 'pinko-grey' classes, he found himself almost equally alienated from the Burmese – even though, intellectually, he knew that many of those classed as criminals ought to have been more accurately thought of as the victims of foreign conquest and occupation. To his horror he sometimes found himself treating the natives like sub-humans, delivering kicks or blows with his stick. The nausea accumulated: 'The wretched prisoners squatting in the reeking cages of the lock-ups, the grey cowed faces of the long-term convicts, the scarred buttocks of the men who had been flogged with bamboos, the women and children howling when their menfolk were led away under arrest – things like these are beyond bearing when you are in any way directly responsible for them.' Attending a hanging, he was suddenly shocked into recognizing gallows fodder as fellow human beings when one prisoner, walking to the scaffold, instinctively stepped aside to avoid a puddle. 'It is curious, but till that moment I had never realized what it means to destroy a healthy, conscious man. . . . His eyes saw the yellow gravel and the grey walls, and his brain still remembered, foresaw, reasoned – reasoned even about puddles. He and we were a party of men walking together, seeing, hearing, feeling … and in two minutes, with a sudden snap, one of us would be gone.'

Eric dealt with his self-loathing by cultivating the air of an eccentric outsider, racing his Harley motorcycle around the country roads; in Katha, keeping chickens, goats and pigs both inside his house and out; making the occasional foray into the whorehouses on the Rangoon waterfront. But he burned with violent guilt. One minute he wanted to smash his fist into the blustering boiled-over faces of the sahibs; the next minute he wanted to do the same to the 'yellow,' brown or black men who insisted on making his job so unbearably difficult. Most of all he hated the loss of free will that went with his job as the guardian of British law and order. As a petty tyrant he had become, unexpectedly, the slave rather than the master of the system; as impotent as the lowliest coolie.

It was when he was called on to shoot a sick elephant, which had killed a black Dravidian coolie, that this imprisonment of expectations came home to him in the most painful way. It would have been easier (if more frightening) to have taken a shot at a rampaging animal. But this elephant just stood there, peacefully throwing grass and bamboo shoots in its mouth. It was acutely obvious to Blair that there was no reason to kill the beast except that the huge crowd that had gathered expected him to:

> … suddenly, I realised that I should have to shoot the elephant after all. The people expected it of me and I had got to do it; I could feel their two thousand wills pressing me forward, irresistibly. And it was at this moment, as I stood there with the rifle in my hands, that I first grasped the hollowness, the futility of the

white man's dominion in the East. Here was I, the white man with his gun, standing in front of the unarmed native crowd – seemingly the leading actor of the piece; but in reality I was only an absurd puppet pushed to and fro by the will of those yellow faces behind. I perceived in this moment that when the white man turns tyrant it is his own freedom that he destroys.

Blair took his shot.

When I pulled the trigger I did not hear the bang or feel the kick – one never does when a shot goes home – but I heard the devilish roar of glee that went up from the crowd. In that instant, in too short a time, one would have thought, even for the bullet to get there, a mysterious, terrible change had come over the elephant. He neither stirred nor fell, but every line of his body had altered.

Horrified by the animal's standing transformation, he fired again, and after it fell, emptied his rifle into the elephant's throat and heart, but 'In the end I could not stand it any longer and went away. I heard later that it took him half an hour to die. … I often wondered whether any of the others grasped that I had done it solely to avoid looking a fool.'

To hate imperialism, he wrote later, you have to be part of it. From the inside it was obvious, if one were honest, that no amount of good intentions, or the actual good work that he recognized was done by doctors, nurses and forest rangers, would ever compensate for the evil of foreign domination. He often suspected that all over the decrepit, embattled empire there were men who felt the same way, but were trapped in a conspiracy of silence. Travelling on a train, one night when it was too hot to sleep, he found himself sharing a carriage with a man from the Educational Service. Without so much as exchanging names they confessed their hatred of their respective jobs 'and then for hours, while the train slowly jolted through the pitch-black night, sitting up in our bunks with bottles of beer handy, we damned the British Empire – damned it from the inside, intelligently and intimately. It did us both good. But we had been speaking forbidden things, and in the haggard morning light when the train crawled into Mandalay, we parted as guiltily as any adulterous couple.'

After five years of service, in 1927, Blair went back to Britain on leave, where 'one sniff of English air' convinced him he could not be part of 'that evil despotism' a day longer. He had been on the side of the strong against the weak; the bullies against the helpless. Never again. In 1921, his parents had moved from Henley to

Southwold on the Suffolk coast – originally a fishing village, but by the 1920s so congested with retirement cottages, many of them owned by old India hands, that it was becoming known as 'Simla by the sea.' Eric's mother played bridge; his younger sister Avril ran a tea shop; his father stared at the sea. When, looking gaunt and sporting a moustache, Eric announced that he was leaving the police (and his annual £660 salary) to become, of all things, a writer, Richard Blair's horrified disbelief and dismay can be imagined. To make matters worse, Eric decided he would return to the police the pay owed him for the period between the start of his leave and the date of his effective resignation. It had become blood money.

In Burma he had somehow failed by default. Now he was bent on failing deliberately. Failing, by the lights of people like his father, now seemed to be the only possible success. The oppression with which he had collaborated in Burma was just a symptom of an entire world of social domination, as pernicious in Britain as in the empire. If he were going to write, then he wanted to write about the homeless and the unemployed. And in the mid-1920s, there were more of them than at any time in the century.

The depth of the structural problems that had beset the British economy before the First World War had been temporarily masked by the wartime boom, but in the 1920s the slump returned on a punishing scale. The problem, as ever, was shrinking demand. Domestic population had levelled off at around 40 million. The dominions, even with India being forced to swallow manufactured goods, were starting their own industries. Textile exports in the late 20s were at half their pre-war level. In 1913 Britain had exported 73 million tons of coal; by 1921, that figure had dropped to 25 million. The share of world markets just kept on shrinking, as it would for the rest of the 20th century. While British manufacturing output was falling, American and Japanese output was accelerating spectacularly. Instead of aiming for higher productivity in order to stay competitive, mine owners, shipbuilders and manufacturers wanted wage cuts or extended hours, and because of rapidly rising unemployment (never much below 10 per cent throughout the 1920s) believed they could get them. The lock-outs and strikes of the immediate pre-war and post-war period became more frequent and more bitter.

Into this hornets' nest in 1925 had stepped the Conservative chancellor of the exchequer, Winston Spencer Churchill, now 50 years old. The social distress of industrial England had not done much to mellow his hot-tempered anti-socialism. Nor had writing the volumes of *The World Crisis* (1923-27), in which he saw socialism, among other things, as initiating the career of an international communist conspiracy that, left unchecked, would devour democracy as well as empire. The obsession

led him into absurd positions. In Rome in 1927 he waxed fulsome about the magnificence of Mussolini's resistance to the Bolshevik menace. And at home he tried
to present himself as the 'Independent anti-Socialist' candidate. When what remained
of the Liberal party declared in January 1924 that they would support the formation
of what would be the first ever Labour government, under the leadership of Ramsay
Macdonald, Churchill decided that there was no future for them and certainly no
future for him in their ranks. There was precious little sign that the grave and sober
men (including Charles Trevelyan, the grandson of that pillar of liberalism, the first
Charles Trevelyan, and Sidney Webb, now Lord Passfield and president of the board
of trade) who got themselves up in court dress for their swearing in at the Palace
were about to launch a Bolshevik revolution in Britain. Nevertheless Churchill
warned, as he would again in 1945, that 'The enthronement in office of a Socialist
Government will be a serious national misfortune such as has usually befallen great
states only on the morrow of defeat in war.' After another abortive campaign as an
Independent (in which, despite the new Tory leader Stanley Baldwin's attempt to
protect him, he lost to the Conservative candidate by 43 votes), Churchill accepted
the offer of a safe seat at Epping. He campaigned furiously against Ramsay
Macdonald's loan to the Soviet Union as 'our bread for the Bolshevik serpent;
our aid for the foreigner of every country; our favours for the Socialists all over the
world who have no country; but for our own daughter States across the oceans on
whom the future of the British island and nation depends only the cold stones of
indifference, aversion and neglect.'

After a Conservative landslide in October 1924 – which, however, preserved
151 Labour seats – Churchill finally declared his return to the party he had left
20 years before. Baldwin rewarded him (before the official announcement, and rather
to the surprise of many loyalist Tories) with the chancellorship of the exchequer.
His father had held the office for four months; Churchill would hold it for four
years. It was, however, a poisoned chalice. Despite his rediscovered conservatism,
Churchill wanted to make some gestures to the socially responsible capitalism he had
always upheld. And his first budget did in fact propose lowering pensionable age to
65, introducing pensions for widows, and decreasing the income-tax rate by 10 per
cent for the lowest earners among the tax-paying population. But his decision to
return Britain to the gold standard, suspended in 1914, was, as the economist John
Maynard Keynes, author of *The Economic Consequences of Mr Churchill* (1925), would
argue, a monetary disaster with huge macro-economic implications, not least the
inevitable devaluation of real wages. Churchill protested that, by once again fixing
the value of the pound against other currencies on the basis of its gold value, he was

merely following the decision taken by the monetarily conservative Labour chancellor, Philip Snowden. And so he was (along with cutting military budgets in keeping with the orthodoxy of disarmament!). Churchill's initial inclination, in fact, had been to overturn Snowden's commitment to the gold standard, and he had even recruited Keynes to deliver ammunition for his arguments. Ultimately, however, the wise men of the Bank of England and the prime minister prevailed, the bank because the gold standard would restore its authority over the treasury and Baldwin because he listened to the bank. Despite being flatly warned by the Cambridge economist Hubert Henderson that 'a return to gold this year cannot be achieved without terrible risk of renewed trade depression and serious aggravation of unemployment,' Baldwin told Churchill that it was the government's decision. Winston's choices at this point were either a change of heart or to follow his father's example and disappear into the wilderness whence he had come. Perhaps it was precisely the sad memory of those defeated glittering eyes and the increasingly drooping moustache that prompted Churchill to go along with Baldwin and the bank.

There was much trumpeting of the return of the great, solid, pound sterling and of the 'shackling' of the British economy to reality. But beyond the imperial fetishizing of sterling, that reality, as predicted by Henderson and Keynes, was shocking. The effect of a pound over-valued at $4.86 was to make the goods and services of the most labour-intensive industries even less competitive in export markets. Prices, and the number out of work, shot up; wages fell. In the worst-affected industries, like shipbuilding, unemployment was already approaching 30 per cent; in Barrow-in-Furness, indeed, it was a massive 49 per cent. The mine-owners' response to the deepening crisis, made even worse by the fact that the German coalfields were back in production, was to demand wage cuts and extensions to working hours. The unions, on the other hand, asked for wage increases and discounted coal prices.

Worried about the real possibility of a general strike, Stanley Baldwin was cool to the owners, who were bribed with government subsidies to postpone any precipitous action at least until a royal commission could study the problems of the coal industry. A truce had been bought, but when the Samuel Commission reported in March 1926 its first recommendation was a cut in wages. The union response, voiced by the miners' leader A. J. Cook, was 'not a penny off the pay, not a minute on the day.' Positions hardened. Churchill's old friend F. E. Smith, now Lord Birkenhead, said, with his usual tact, that he thought the miners' leaders the stupidest men he had ever met until he met the mine owners. As if to vindicate him, the owners locked union members out on 1 May 1926 and the Trades Union Congress (TUC) called for a general strike for the 3rd. The Bishop of Durham first wrung his hands, then shook his

Above left: Stanley Baldwin, prime minister, 1923.
Above right: Strikers read the news during the General Strike, 1926.

fist, declaring that 'England has ceased to be a constitutional monarchy and is making its first advance towards the dictatorship of the proletariat.'

The strike lasted just nine days. Some 1.5 million workers (90 per cent miners) came out in response to the TUC. Whilst the popular image is of Oxbridge under-graduates driving buses, the reality was that most of the strike-breakers were as working class as the strikers. In the end the TUC agreed to a compromise, deserting the understandably embittered miners. During the 'nine days of May' Churchill mobilized resources as if he were fighting a war. Troops delivered food supplies; he set up the *British Gazette* and ran it as a government propaganda sheet, with more soldiers guarding the printing presses. Both food shipments and *Gazette* deliveries were sometimes escorted by tanks. Attempts to press Lord Reith's BBC, inaugurated in 1922, to broadcast government bulletins and opinions were, however, defiantly resisted – a turning point in the fight to make the corporation truly politically inde-pendent, but no thanks to Churchill.

The official strike might have been over by 12 May, but the bitter polarization of classes remained. The miners tried to fight on alone, but in the end were forced back to work on the owners' terms. Whilst the participants in round-table talks between the unions and management, convened by the chairman of Imperial Chemical Industries Sir Alfred Mond, pretended over tea and sandwiches that men of good will and common sense could come to an agreement, the substantive action was taken by hard-liners. In 1927 a Trade Disputes and Trade Union Act made any strike intended to coerce the government illegal. Union members who wanted to support the Labour party now had to 'contract in' rather than specifically contracting out. The party instantly lost a large chunk of its operational income, as was the idea. On the Thames Embankment, Eric Blair met a 'screever' (a pavement artist) called Bozo who specialized in mild political cartoons. One was of Churchill 'when the Budget was on. I had one of Winston trying to push an elephant marked "Debt," and underneath I wrote, "Will he budge it?" See?' Eric saw. Bozo went on to tell him that he couldn't do any pictures in favour of socialism because the police wouldn't stand for it. One of his earlier efforts was a cartoon of a boa constrictor marked 'Capital' swallowing a rabbit marked 'Labour.' 'You rub that out,' the screever was told by the copper, 'and look sharp about it.' Bozo did as he was told. To disobey would have risked being moved on or locked up as a loiterer.

That was the winter of 1927 when Eric Blair took a nose-dive into the underclass; an act of expiation, he later wrote in *The Road to Wigan Pier*, for his five years policing the empire. He had started his new life as a writer, renting a cheap, one-room flat next to a craft workshop in down-at-heel Notting Hill. It was so cold that Blair warmed his fingers over candles when they became too numb to write. But this was positively well-to-do beside the 30-shillings-a-month squalor he felt should really complete his change of identity. Others had been in the lower depths before him, of course. At Eton he had read Jack London's chronicle of London's East End, *People of the Abyss* (1905), and he may well have been moved by the more recent account given in the new edition of *In Darkest London* (1926) by G. K. Chesterton's sister-in-law, Ada Elizabeth Chesterton, a *Daily Express* journalist who sold matches in Piccadilly (to the horror of those friends who recognized her) or polished the same doorknob for three hours to earn the right to sleep in a 'spike' (a shelter for the homeless). Here she observed that women were only given the dregs of the men's tea, and even that an hour or more after it had been brewed. Because only one night's housing in a spike was allowed, and the spikes were deliberately set far apart, Mrs Chesterton had a fair walk, on her first night of roughing it, from Euston to Hackney: 'I think I went a little mad. I felt that London ought to be burned down.'

Orwell followed, almost literally, in the footsteps of Jack London and Ada Chesterton. In Lambeth he sold his clothes for a shilling and received in their place a tramp's kit, 'not merely dirty and shapeless' but covered with 'a patina of antique filth, quite different from mere shabbiness.' It was his Franciscan moment – the disrobing of the bourgeois imperialist, the embrace of redeeming poverty. Once he felt himself dirty enough to be unrecognizable as a gent, he knew he was on his way. On the street, 'My new clothes had put me instantly into a new world. Everyone's demeanour seemed to have changed abruptly. I helped a hawker pick up a barrow that he had upset. "Thanks, mate," he said with a grin. No one had called me mate before in my life. . . .'

He spent the same night in a doss-house on the Waterloo Road, in a room reeking of 'paregoric [opium] and foul linen' and shared with six others. The sheets smelled horribly of old sweat. Every 20 minutes an old man would be taken by a fit of coughing, 'a foul bubbling and retching, as though the man's bowels were being churned up within him.' The morning light was not kind to the scene. Blair could see that the sheets, three weeks away from a wash, were 'raw umber' in colour and the washbasins covered in 'solid, sticky filth as black as boot-blacking.' He moved from common lodging houses to spikes – which were, if anything, even more squalid. At no point did he revel in this. On the contrary, it is hard to think of another great English writer more fastidious about cleanliness, and whose nose was so doggy in its exact registration of a universe of horrible smells. But the more repulsive the experience, the more cleansed he became of imperial guilt, rather like St Catherine drinking a bowl of pus to show that nothing human was beneath her.

In one particularly diabolical place the St Francis of the spikes finally got down to basic truths:

It was a disgusting sight, that bathroom. All the indecent secrets of our under-wear were exposed; the grime, the rents and patches, the bits of string doing duty for buttons, the layers upon layers of fragmentary garments, some of them mere collections of holes held together by dirt. The room became a press of steaming nudity; the sweaty odours of the tramps competing with the sickly, sub-faecal stench native to the spike. Some of the men refused the bath and washed only their 'toe-rags,' horrid, greasy little clouts which tramps bind around their feet.

For two years Blair did the Cook's tour of destitution, including about three months in Paris as a *plongeur* or washer-up, as well as tramping in and around London. Occasionally he might come back for a night or two to friends' houses in London or even show up disconcertingly in Southwold, looking grimmer and gaunter than ever before. He went hop-picking with itinerant labourers, working until his hands

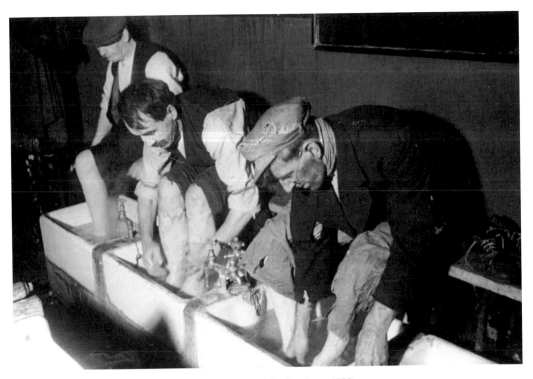

Homeless men bathing in a London 'spike,' funded by the Salvation Army, 1938.

were shredded; downed enough beer and whisky to get himself arrested, in the hope of accomplishing his heart's desire to spend a Christmas in prison; collected tramping slang; worked out the fine hierarchies of dossing, from the Embankment benches (get there by eight) through the 'Twopenny Hangovers' and the fourpenny wooden boxes called 'Coffins' to the high luxury of shilling Rowton houses and Salvation Army lodgings. One morning, he set off with an Irish tramp called — what else? — Paddy, going south on the Old Kent Road towards Cromley. In a meadow that, from the bits of sodden newspaper, rusty cans and worn grass, he could tell was 'a regular caravanserai of tramps' Blair sat down beside a patch of tansies, their pungent aroma competing with that of the tramps, watched the two carthorse colts trot around and listened to the men talk about their itineraries: Oxford was good for 'mooching' (begging); Kent very tight. The gossip went from stories of suicides to shreds of history, half-remembered, half-invented — 'The Great Rebellion,' the Corn Laws — carried around with them like the Oxo tins that held old cigarette ends.

Despite the clichés of the respectable, Orwell knew that not all, not even many, tramps were alcoholics, much less criminals. They wouldn't even be on the move were it not for that inflexible rule forbidding more than a single night's stay in any one spike. Tramps were the diametric opposite of the romantic cult of walking with which Britain's modern age had begun, and which was being resurrected in the rambling movement of the 1920s and 1930s. But for the pseudo-tramps like Orwell, or Frank Jennings, the 'Tramp's Parson,' and still more for truly destitute memoir-writers like Terence Horsley, wounded veteran of Passchendaele and electrician who trudged from Glasgow to London and back in desperate search of casual work, walking was not an ennobling experience, nor was hop-picking a merry country holiday of beer and flirting. The itinerant life was a merciless grind and those condemned to it were worn down in body and spirit.

When *Down and Out in Paris and London* appeared in 1933, the name on the book jacket was not Eric Blair but 'George Orwell.' Other names had been considered, such as 'H. Lewis Allways.' But since the Orwell is a river in Suffolk, not far from Southwold, it is likely that Blair, who in any case loved the countryside with a fierce passion, wanted to identify with the physical nature of England. Somewhere at the back of his mind, surely, was not just Jack London but William Wordsworth, who too sought communion with the authentic England through solitary walks and encounters with the broken and the poor. So Orwell's non-fiction books would almost all be journeys, for which there was, by the early 1930s, a huge publishing vogue. But no one was ever going to mistake his journeys for those of the writer who had driven the 'journeying' fashion: H. V. Morton.

Morton's *In Search of England* was published in 1927, the year Orwell changed his garments and his life. Its premise, announced in its very first sentence, was that it was the record of a 'motor car journey round England.' Since the distribution of cars between regions (27 per 1000 in Cambridgeshire, 5 per 1000 in County Durham) was extremely uneven, this meant, in effect, the motorized grandee inspecting the biking and Shanks's pony classes. Instead of the writer seeing the country on foot – bound in toe-rags and gaping boots – he would see it through the windscreen of his motor. He would drive about England (Britain, in fact, since volumes on Scotland (1929), Ireland (1930) and Wales (1932) followed), warning about the infestation of the countryside by the vulgarity of the town, in between filling up his tank with cheap petrol, courtesy of Anglo-Persian or Burmah.

His book is a threnody for the English Promised Land; Vaughan Williams in a Lagonda: 'I sped on into a green tunnel of a lane with England before me and the keen air was like wine to me and the green of the young leaves was like music.' There are moments when the unbearable perfection of the countryside sends Morton into a religious rapture when he tries, and fails, to be the Ruskin of the motoring classes: 'The low clouds were indigo blue and stormy, the high a soft apricot pink colour.

Wells in Smiling Somerset, railway poster (detail) by Michael Reilly, 1931.

The west was burning with gold light and the edges of the dark clouds were etched with thin lines of fire. The pageant moved, changed … the river against the sun was a sheet of dull silver on which a jet black duck moved noiselessly, a swan silhouetted as if cut in black paper, swam with his neck beneath the water, a wind came fretting the river blowing a handful of pale blossoms into the grass.' Pity, really, about that duck.

Although he is 'In Search of England' he makes sure to look for it (with one brief exception) only where there are no factories or polluted industrial canals, much less spikes and sevenpenny kips. The kind of places Morton favours are invariably cathedral towns (Canterbury, Lincoln, Norwich, York, Ely, Exeter) or market towns, best of all cathedral towns that are also market towns, like Wells ('How can I describe to you the whisper of the water that runs in gutters, musically tinkling past the steps of old houses?'). There his soul is eased by cosy pubs, where pewter 'glimmered like moonlight on still water' and the taps run with 'mahogany brew.' The best places of all are those that are mossy with memory; where ghosts drift through the ruins. At Beaulieu Abbey he meets a Miss Cheshire who actually lives above the ruined monks' dormitory 'alone with seven hundred years.' At Winchester he sees 'down a long tunnel of time, the Kings of Wessex riding through a country that was not yet England.' In fact he is constantly seeing and hearing things as if all England had been turned into an open-air Madame Tussaud's. Mile after mile, in between the moments of seraphic illumination in the fields, or rather on lay-bys near fields, Morton gives this nostalgia everything he has.

But of course there is a worm in the bud: the disagreeable 20th century. Two sets of barbarians are massing to despoil paradise: Yanks and yobbos. In Morton's pages, alternately quivering with bucolic ecstasy or wrinkle-nosed with distaste, Americans are constantly ruining the scenery with their vulgar, garish presence. In Clovelly in Devon, Morton wants to put his fingers in his ears lest he hear another Alabama college girl exclaim how everything is 'too cute for words.' Morton's parody Yanks speak a bizarre language, a sort of fractured, badly heard movie-speak overstuffed with 'gees' and 'sures.' He insists, unconvincingly, that 'no-one respects the average American traveller more than I do,' and says it just as ardently as his contemporaries protested that some of their best friends were Jews. But wait! There is hope for these loud, comical primitives, and that hope is called History. The ghosts of King Edgar and Henry VIII and the original Pilgrims (not yet American), summoned by the spirits of the place, stun the Americans into awestruck appreciation for All that Past and force them to confess that, although they affect to despise it, they are really in love with Tradition.

Not much hope, however, for the domestic enemies of the idyll, the 'charabanc parties from large manufacturing towns' – the Jacks and the Beryls, the Dougs and the Maureens. The countryside, alas, is in no condition to resist this coachborne invasion of the unwashed and the ill-mannered. 'An old order is being taxed out of existence,' an avalanche of sales, and 'the impossibility of growing corn because of the expense of labour and foreign competition.' (The Council for the Preservation of Rural England, founded in 1926, would make that lament its battle cry.) For someone so devoted to the countryside, Morton makes no mention of the pitiful plight of agricultural workers, their average wage, when they could find work, cut from 42 shillings a week to 30; or to the countless farms abandoned, the barns allowed to fall down; to the untended hedgerows bolting, thickening and turning into copses; to the fields shaggy with weeds. At least mass unemployment might have the inadvertent benefit of keeping These People in their own noisome little alleys and hovels, to stand around waiting for the dole. Morton can't quite escape the industrial enemy, though. His route takes him between Manchester and Liverpool – 'to the right there was an ominous grey haze in the sky which meant Manchester.' For a moment in the Black Country he is 'thrilled' by the smokestacks – but on closer inspection is not. In Lancashire he sees the only Englishmen he knows who squat like Arabs – coal miners with whippets. And then he sees 'a signpost marked "Wigan." Who could resist a glimpse of Wigan?'

Just a glimpse, of course. As a sampler Morton goes over the tired music-hall joke that is 'Wigan Pier,' 'sufficient to make an audience howl with laughter.' Its Roman name, Coccium, has him doubled up. But it turns out that Wigan is not quite the hell-hole he had been led to believe (and confesses he was eager to record). He sees half-timbered mock-Tudor buildings, which lead him to believe that in 20 years or so Wigan might be a perfectly fine-looking place (for a manufacturing town). The case for a kindly view is clinched when he discovers that the area had been staunchly royalist in the Civil War. Not just a coalfield, then, by God. To his own astonishment, Morton admits he 'would not mind spending a holiday in Wigan – a short one.'

Nine years later, in January 1936, George Orwell travelled to Wigan, stayed for two months and found it altogether less of a giggle. He recorded canal paths 'a mixture of cinders and frozen mud, criss-crossed by the imprints of innumerable clogs, and all round, as far as the slag-heaps in the distance, stretched the "flashes" – pools of stagnant water that had seeped into the hollows caused by the subsidence of ancient pits. . . . It seemed a world from which vegetation had been banished; nothing existed except smoke, shale, ice, mud, ashes and foul water.'

Orwell had had a modest success with *Down and Out in Paris and London* (perhaps 3000 copies sold in the UK), but he realized, paradoxically, that in writing about the outcasts of England he had documented a tiny population – tens of thousands – rather than the millions of the industrial working class in the Midlands and the north whom the depression had turned into the real *misérables* of Ramsay Macdonald's and Stanley Baldwin's Britain. Baldwin, who liked to present himself as a plain-as-a-pikestaff solid sort with (like Cobbett and Lord Emsworth) a passion for pigs, wrote his own sub-Housman lyric verse 'On England,' featuring the usual obligatory plough and team coming over the hill. But this was precisely the period when, if farmers (together with their labourers, now no more than 5 per cent of the working population) were going to survive, they would be riding tractors and combine harvesters. And the hill was going to be planted out, not with spears of golden English wheat, but with sugar-beet, one of the few surefire moneymakers of the 1930s.

Morton had expressed his horror that cornfields had become coalfields. Travelling through Northumberland, he liked to pretend it had never happened, that the industrial towns were 'mere black specks against the mighty background of history and the great green expanse of fine country which is the real North of England.'

On the other hand, socialist writers like J.B. Priestley, whose *English Journey* of 1933 was another antidote to Morton's rustic sentimentalism, and who himself came from the wool-manufacturing town of Bradford, were prepared to stare the disaster of industrial England in the face and certainly call it 'real.' In fact, for much of England industrial work had been the *only* reality and, for all the apparent grimness of the factory floors and terraced streets, not such a bad thing either. It was the white and shiny, tile and glass 'new' factories of London's Great West Road, from which Priestley set out on his journey by the miracle of coach comfort, that he couldn't quite see as places that could manufacture anything. It was 'bending iron and riveting steel to steel' that were 'the real thing,' man's work.

In the north of England it was the terrible quiet that got to Priestley: 'Grim and ugly as it might be, nevertheless if this riverside [the Tyne] had been black, and shattering with the smoke and din of tens of thousands of men hard at it, for the commonwealth and for their own decent comfort and self-respect, I think I would have found it wildly inspiring. . . .'

He wanted the guide-book description of Jarrow as a 'A busy town (35,590 inhabitants)' with ironworks and shipyards changed to 'an idle and ruined town (35,590 inhabitants, wondering what is to become of them).' Priestley remembered it had been Bede's abbey town; the cradle, then, of a self-conscious English history. Now it seemed to be its grave. 'The whole town looked as if it had entered a perpetual penniless bleak Sabbath,' he recorded, with thousands of men just standing around doing nothing. At nearby Hebburn he clambered through a derelict shipyard, the result of reckless speculation, now a 'fantastic wilderness of decaying sheds, strange mounds and pits, rusted iron, old concrete and new grass.' When Priestley got to the river bank he could see rows and rows of idle ships rotting into rusty hulks. As with the cotton mill in Blackburn he had seen put up for auction – with, of course, no takers – he felt he was present at the death-bed of the industrial empire. And when he heard the clatter of stones thrown at warehouses by boys in West Bromwich – 'I could not blame them if they threw stones and stones and smashed every pane of glass for miles' – it was the death rattle.

Orwell didn't think much of Priestley, whom he wrote off, not altogether fairly, as a sentimental accumulator of banal anecdotes and cosy homilies. He shared the socialist urge to stick the grim plight of industrial Britain in the face of the solid south and to shout: 'DO SOMETHING!' Unemployment overall had come down from a high of 2.5 million in 1932 to 1.5 million four years later. But its distribution was shockingly uneven; 4 per cent in Middlesex; 30–50 per cent in Barrow or Jarrow. As Priestley noted, there were actually three Englands (he could as easily have said Britains): the clapped-out wreckage of the old industrial heartland; then Morton-Albion, all limestone hamlets nestling (they always nestled) amidst velvety dales as larks soared into the sweet empyrean; but also a new England of lipstick and car assembly lines, Benny Goodman, sheer stockings and Friday-night cinema.

Symbolic recognition that everyone in Britain belonged, somehow, in the same boat seemed to Orwell not enough. The biggest symbolic gesture of all was made by the royal family, sending the Prince of Wales to the mining villages to express concern at the distress, a public relations move that worked like a charm. At the end of 1935 the silver jubilee of George V's reign was orchestrated in much the same spirit of democratic monarchism, with the genuinely popular king and queen touring London's East End in an open motor landau. Stunned at the public enthusiasm, George wondered why, since he was 'just an ordinary fellow' – which, as a courtier was quick to assure him, was precisely the point. The fatherly image of the king-emperor entered a new dimension altogether with the first royal radio broadcast, carried off with baritone aplomb. In another brilliantly conceived gesture, George V made a point of talking to the children of Britain – 'Now children, it is your KING who is talking to you,' something that is likely to have made them sit up and take notice. And with just a few more months to live the normally gruff and taciturn monarch happily talked and talked: most notably at Westminster Hall in a speech written for him by G. M. Trevelyan, which represented the empire as one great

King George V and Queen Mary on the Miniature Railway at the great Wembley
Exhibition, 1936.

'family,' the ultimate progeny of the great and glorious unwritten, immemorial
British constitution.

As far as Orwell was concerned, however, the ancient constitution had not done
a whole lot for Lancashire lately. So when his publisher, Victor Gollancz, suggested
that he go north and write about what he saw in Wigan, he leaped at the opportunity
to expose an England that was a long way from Jubilation and to write it as a
journey, stripped of all traces of folksiness. He may have succeeded all too well with
The Road to Wigan Pier, which was hated by much of both the right and the left.
Conservatives naturally dismissed it as Bolshevik propaganda; trade unionists and the
Hampstead socialists among whom Orwell had been living, working and running a
bookshop thought it too bleak, pessimistic and uncharitable a picture of working-
class heroes.

But, for Orwell, *Wigan Pier* was the first demonstration of the literature he was
meant to write: intensely and frankly political, but neither as arid as a Fabian essay
or a Labour party position paper, nor as mystically over-excited and fanciful as
D. H. Lawrence. Most of all, the writing was meant to deliver the reader, who might
be sitting in an armchair in Esher (or Southwold), into an alien world of sights,
like that of the 'scramblers' rooting around for pebble-sized lumps of coal on the

slag-heaps; the smells (especially, with Orwell, smells) hanging in the yellow fumes over the canal; and the sounds, like the clatter of clogs that awakened him before dawn in Wigan, every day as he lay in bed over the tripe shop where he lodged. What Dickens (a literary hero) did with fog at the beginning of *Bleak House*, Orwell did with the soot and grime of the mining town that covered everyone and everything: the fingers of his landlord who insisted on cutting the white breakfast bread, leaving black fingerprints on the soft white surface; the black beetles that he saw crawling over the whitish-yellow tripe (too commercially valuable to be served for tea); the second skin of thick soot that Orwell got when he went down the pit, and which would not wash off in the tepid water. (There was, of course, no hot water.)

As soon as he got down the pit, Orwell realized that if being unemployed in Wigan was hell, being employed was purgatory. Wake-up time for the day shift was 3.45 a.m. Along with the miners he stooped, or crawled, half-naked through 4-foot-high passages to the coalface, sometimes for miles – as far, he calculated one day, as from London Bridge to Oxford Circus – and this before the day's work had actually begun. The first day, the 6-foot-3-inch Orwell banged his head on a pit prop on his way to the face, and was so exhausted when he finally got there that, tough though he usually was, he fainted.

When the miners ended their shift, at 2.30 in the afternoon, they came back to terraced houses that Orwell thought should have been condemned many years before. There were always dirty dishes in the sink. A tea of heated-up tinned fish or stew, boiled potatoes, a bit of bread, jam and, Orwell's particular bugbear, margarine (nothing like the polyunsaturated diet-friendly spread of today), was served up on tables covered with a grimy oilcloth that itself rested on geologically encrusted strata of old Worcestershire-sauce-stained newspapers, crunchy with the crumbs of count-less greasy teas. Yet Orwell's horror for what the miners had to endure only increased his admiration for the way that working-class families managed to make real homes – assuming, that is, that 'Father' was in work. And he was touched by the genuine generosity and openness he found in Wigan, extended even to strange and snooping strangers like him: 'Curiously enough, it is *not* the triumphs of modern engineering, nor the radio, nor the cinematograph, nor the five thousand novels which are pub-lished yearly, nor the crowds at Ascot and the Eton and Harrow match, but the memory of working-class interiors … that reminds me that our age has not been altogether a bad one to live in.'

Orwell's mission in *The Road to Wigan Pier* was to force the different Englands to face each other squarely. Perhaps he didn't have much hope – especially since he was being published by Victor Gollancz's Left Book Club – of getting the Fair Isle

A mining family in the back streets of Wigan, Lancashire, 1939.

sweater–clad, Morton-reading motoring set to come with him into the soot-coated, bacon-greased kitchens of Wigan. But from the 'old England,' which had the power (the City, parliament, the law courts), not to mention the 'new England,' which had the money (the newspapers and the suburban commuters; the garage owners and the department-store salesmen), he wanted some recognition that they belonged to a common nation. Otherwise, what did all the cant about the blessings of the British constitution, of the imperishable empire of freedom, boil down to? The freedom to choose between accepting a reduced dole or booting out granny when the means-test inspectors told you the old girl was a 'lodger' and that, sorry as they were, they would have to cut your weekly allowance?

It was the smug cushioning of well-off Britain against the sting of grievance that most got to Orwell. Ramsay Macdonald's second Labour government, elected in 1929, with Snowden once more as chancellor of the exchequer and the trade-union leader J. H. Thomas as Lord Privy Seal, had been indecently eager to honour all the canons of Victorian economy – the gold standard, deflation, balanced budgets and public parsimony. When the inevitable run on the pound had happened and the government declared a deficit, Macdonald and Snowden had been so committed to the budget cuts that J. P. Morgan and others had demanded as the condition of a loan that in August 1931 they were prepared to end the Labour government and join Baldwin's Tories and the Liberals in a three-party 'national administration.' Only one Labour minister, Oswald Mosley, the chancellor of the duchy of Lancaster, had actually had the gumption to insist on a Keynesian solution, using substantial deficit financing to lower unemployment and invest in infrastructure. Failing to have his way, in May 1930 he resigned from the government, attacked it in the Commons, was expelled and formed his 'New Party.'

In March 1936, in the Yorkshire mining town of Barnsley, Orwell went to hear Mosley speak. By this time the 'New Party' had become the blackshirted British Union of Fascists. Mosley, surrounded by 100 blackshirts who beat the living daylights out of a heckler, was still committed to Keynesian public spending but full of praise for Mussolini and Hitler, who had done the same thing, and full of venom against the 'mysterious international gangs of Jews' who, not satisfied with having caused the slump in the first place, were now financing the Labour party, thus doubly betraying the workers. To Orwell's dismay the audience, which had begun by loudly booing Mosley, ended up applauding him.

Later that year Orwell, whose sense of history had been almost as insular as Churchill's, decided, after all, that there was an unavoidable battle coming between socialism and freedom on the one hand and fascism on the other, and that it needed to be faced sooner rather than later. This seemed all the more urgent since, just as Baldwin's government had its head in the sand about the miseries of the British poor, it was in even deeper denial about the coming crisis. When Orwell went off to the Spanish Civil War in December 1936, under the aegis of the Independent Labour party and as an officer in the POUM anarchist militia, he wanted it understood that it was as a fighter and not as a writer, since he was aggressively estranged from the coffee-house socialists in London who seemed, to him, all sanctimonious talk and precious little action. Finally, though, his own parade-ground history – the cadet corps at Eton and the Burma police college – stood him in good stead when he drilled raw Republican recruits. Eccentrically dressed in a modified balaclava and the longest woolly scarf anyone had seen, and unmissably conspicuous because of his great height, Orwell ended up taking a bullet through the neck outside Huesca. It miraculously missed both his carotid artery and his spine, but fatality rates for that kind of wound (given the rudimentary medical attention available) were nearly

80 per cent. Orwell, however, survived, although the damage to his vocal cords made it difficult if not impossible for him to shout. His faith in socialist solidarity, especially when masquerading as the 'Popular Front,' did not survive. In Barcelona he had witnessed first-hand the Republican cause being sabotaged by the bitter feuds of the left. The communists, driven by instructions from Moscow, seemed to be much more interested in hunting down heretics like the anarchists than in taking on General Franco's fascists.

Back home, his disgust with the official left's rhapsodies about the Soviet Union only deepened. When he tried to write the truth – that fascism and communism had more in common than most people realized, that in fact communism was 'furthest of all to the Right' – his work was inevitably rejected by pillars of the left like the *New Statesman and Nation*. Communist writers and critics like Harry Pollitt, general secretary of the Communist Party, resorted to name-calling, describing Orwell as a 'little middle-class boy' who had day-tripped through socialism but came out the other side the imperialist reactionary he had always been. *Homage to Catalonia*, when it appeared in 1938, suffered from being seen as a shot in the internecine wars of the left. And it might have been for that reason that Orwell had already begun to brood on how he might preach the same warning message but in a form that was unmistakably popular. 'On my return from Spain I thought of exposing the Soviet myth in a story that could be easily understood by almost anyone … However, the actual details of the story did not come to me for some time until one day I saw a little boy, perhaps ten years old, driving a huge cart-horse along a narrow path, whipping it whenever it tried to turn. It struck me that if only such animals became aware of their strength we should have no power over them, and that men exploit animals in much the same way as the rich exploit the proletariat.' The germ of *Animal Farm* (1945), then, was already there in Orwell's mind, even as he settled down with his wife Eileen in a freezing cottage in the village of Wallington, near Baldock in Hertfordshire. A cough that he couldn't shake off, the beginnings of tuberculosis, would rack him as he stalked around his small farm. Chain smoking probably didn't help. But he was still capable of beginning letters like this: 'Dear Geoffrey, Thanks so much for your letter. I am glad you are enjoying yourself in Denmark, though I must admit, it is one of the few countries I have never wanted to visit,' or, even better, in a review of some military memoirs in the *New Statesman and Nation*, August 1937, 'General Crozier is a professional soldier and by his own showing spent the years between 1899 and 1921 in almost ceaseless slaughter of his fellow-creatures; hence as a pacifist he makes an impressive figure, like the reformed burglar at a Salvation Army meeting.'

While Orwell was tending his goats and chickens and trying to make people see the futility of war, Winston Churchill was stalking around his ruinously expensive country house in Kent, compensating – only somewhat – for political impotence by empire-building in the grounds. Chartwell, near Westerham, had been snapped up for what seemed a bargain at a time when Churchill had been relatively flush with the advance for *The World Crisis*. He had summoned an architect, Philip Tilden, to give the house more neo-Jacobean presence (which meant bigger) and to exploit its stunning site so that the big dining room looked south over the rolling Kent country-side. By the time he was finished with it, Chartwell was grand enough to be the alternative political court that Churchill meant it to be – 9 reception rooms, 18 bed-rooms, 8 bathrooms; and then, in Winston's dig-for-conquest phase, a heated outdoor swimming pool where he could merrily wallow; a fine pond stocked with ornamental carp, ritually fed each day to strange noises by the man in the homburg himself; and not least a little pavilion at the corner of the garden terrace, which he had painted with winning, slightly child-like scenes of Marlborough's great battles.

That pavilion must have been an important place for Winston to sit and brood about the past and the future, and the difficult, important relationship between the two. The 30s he called his 'wilderness years,' when he was 'in exile.' Though in parliament, as MP for Epping, he was out of office for 10 years from 1929, when the Labour government came to power, until 3 September 1939, when, on the outbreak of war, he was summoned back to the admiralty by Neville Chamberlain. Throughout that admittedly long decade Churchill was neither idle nor especially solitary, although he was certainly isolated from power and direct influence in the Conservative party. Loyal friends and followers came to Chartwell all the time – Frederick Lindemann, the Oxford philosospher whom Churchill called 'the Prof' and on whom he relied for statistics about the terrible shape of things to come; his acolyte, the young journalist, lawyer and Tory MP Brendan Bracken; Lord Beaverbrook, the press baron; and Desmond Morton, the director of industrial intel-ligence for the department of defence, who very conveniently lived close by and who seems to have supplied Churchill with more ammunition for his rearmament campaign.

On these and many more Churchill lavished his hospitality – tanks of cham-pagne; vats of claret; vast lunches; roaring conversations; semi-hilarious tantrums. If the Chartwell years were indeed exile, they were a phenomenally gregarious and expensive one, as the long-suffering Clemmie learned to her cost. Supporting the nine indoor servants, the three gardeners, the two nannies and the chauffeur, not to mention the private secretaries and research assistants who helped Churchill with his

Top: Chartwell House near Westerham, Kent, bought by Winston Churchill in 1922.
Above: Churchill laying bricks to the wall around Chartwell House, 1930.
Opposite: Churchill, with his dog Rufus, in the grounds of Chartwell, photograph by C. Philippe Halsman, *c.* 1930.

writing, cost a small fortune. Nor was it always a delight to be in the service of this particular Man of Destiny. He could be abrasively rude and petulant, by turns needy or insulting or both simultaneously. His hours were, for those unaccustomed to them, a nightmare: long mornings in bed swathed in his green and gold Chinese dressing gown, papers mixed up with the marmalade and melon; the first of the nine daily Havanas; dictating between what was left of the hours between breakfast and lunch (another cigar; the first of the many weak whiskies and water); lunch itself, heavily lubricated; then the mandatory one- or two-hour nap; after which Churchill rose, pink and cherubic, took a stroll around the grounds, talked animatedly like Dr Doolittle to his many pets – the pigs, the two poodles, the black swans, the fish; frog-marched visitors to see the latest improvements; or made for the Marlborough pavilion overlooking the beeches, the cows and the hazy horizon, and brooded. Then there would be the second of the two daily baths (98 degrees or else); dressing for dinner; dinner, including more champagne and claret; after which, in a manner staggering to most human flesh and blood, Churchill would take himself off into the night for some *real* work, finishing at two or three in the morning. It would be like this throughout the 30s and right through the war.

And he was, almost all of the time, writing history: the dazzling and funny *My Early Life* (1930), books of essays on political leaders of the past; the four-volume biography of the Duke of Marlborough; then, by 1939, helped by research assistants from Oxford like Bill Deakin, half a million words of *The History of the English-Speaking Peoples*. And although he certainly needed the money to stave off ruin, to support the flamboyant life he refused to retrench and the entourage with which he travelled, history in the 30s meant something more to Churchill than just income. It was what gave him his moorings, his unshakeable sense of navigation. Both friends and enemies marvelled at Churchill's self-steering at a time when every day's news seemed to herald unwelcome surprises, rugs pulled out from under the feet. Anyone in their right mind, politically, ought to have trod very cautiously over this unstable ground and calculated very carefully the pros and cons of any given position before making a move. Now Churchill was just as prone as other politicians to weighing advantage and disadvantage, and was certainly not happy to be out of the centre of power. Time was not his friend. At his age there were only so many more ponds he could dig at Chartwell.

But his history-writing, sometimes misinterpreted as a panacea for political impotence, was something like the opposite: the humming engine of his ambition and his certainty. Looking back on the long history of the 'island nation' and the empire did not muddy Churchill's mind in romantic fantasies. On the contrary, it gave him the grip and clarity to see what needed to be done. What he wrote about Rosebery could more plausibly be applied to himself: 'The Past stood ever at his elbow and was the counsellor upon whom he most relied. He seemed to be attended by Learning and History and to carry into current events an air of ancient majesty.'

Passages of *Marlborough*, 'bronzed by African sunshine,' were the purest autobiography: 'Marlborough regarded the raising of his family to the first rank second only to the importance of raising England to the first place in Europe, and he saw no reason why these two processes should not be combined. His tireless industry and exertion, his profound sagacity and calculation, his constant readiness to stake, not only his life but all he had gathered in reputation and wealth, upon the hazards of war and of a well-chosen battle were faithfully offered to his country's service.'

However, standing back and looking at the great arc of Britain's history, especially in the age of Queen Anne when the history of the Union and of the empire had both begun in earnest, presented Churchill with a difficult paradox. The fate of the island empire and its involvement in Europe had often been presented, especially in the Victorian century into which he had been born, as mutually exclusive. But Churchill's history told him that this had virtually never been the case; just the opposite, in fact. It had been when England, and then Britain, had been *most* engaged in Europe that its empire had best prospered: in Marlborough's wars; in the Elder Pitt's global struggle with France; with his son's determination to resist the expansionism of the French Republic; even during Disraeli's plunge into treacherous eastern diplomacy in the 1870s. Little Englandism meant imperial self-effacement; shorn of the empire, Churchill staunchly believed, the 'Great' might as well be subtracted from Britain, and the united island kingdom itself would, in the end, perhaps be doomed to disintegrate.

It was this historically derived conviction that led Churchill to take positions in the 1930s that, on the face of it, were incompatible or at least impractical: both rearmament and imperial assertiveness in India. His reactionary truculence on the empire undermined his credibility as an authority on the future of Europe. But in Churchill's mind in the early 1930s, and then again during the Second World War itself, the two were inseparable. Whether he had been marinading his imagination rather too long in Macaulay's essays on Clive and Hastings, or dwelling on his own memories of Sir Bindon Blood and the Malakand War, Churchill's response to the rise of Congress nationalism was as anachronistic as it was intemperate. The Labour government's efforts to take the sting out of the Indian Congress militancy by hinting at eventual dominion status (meaning self-government within the empire) were attacked by Churchill as abject capitulation to sedition. A true commonwealth confederation of free nations, their allegiance commonly pledged to the monarch, he obviously believed could only work when there was a real bond of common ethnic ancestry and language as in Australia and for Canada – in other words, for the white sons of the empire.

The notion that British power (for which read 'force') could somehow evolve into affinity – strong enough to make for true common allegiance, especially in times of peril – struck Churchill, deep down, as contradicting everything he knew about human nature. But of course that was exactly the great promise that Macaulay had made in his speech in 1833: that language, law and literature would indeed achieve, in the fullness of time, precisely such a transformation. In fact Macaulay had gone even further, imagining that such ties would in the end prove stronger than the sword. It is a promise redeemed in this 21st century, although not quite in ways that Macaulay could have anticipated, on every page of great Indian Anglophone literature. But it was impossible for Churchill to imagine that a cultural bond could possibly take the place of paramount power. It would be the end not just of the empire but of Britain itself. 'The loss of India,' he said in 1930, 'would mark and con-summate the downfall of the British empire. That great organism would pass at a stroke out of life into history. From such a catastrophe there could be no recovery.' That Churchill, who believed so passionately in the power of the word, should be so much of a cultural defeatist is one of his saddest failings.

When in 1931 the viceroy, Baron Irwin, who, as Edward Wood, had once served under Churchill and who would later be Viscount Halifax, released Gandhi and 30 other Congress leaders from prison so that they could participate in talks about India's future, Churchill was apopleptic. Gandhi was famously dismissed in insulting terms that have never been forgotten or forgiven in India: 'It is alarming and nause-ating to see Mr Gandhi, a seditious Middle Temple lawyer, now posing as a fakir of a type well-known in the East, striding half-naked up the steps of the Vice-regal palace … to parley on equal terms with the representative of the King-Emperor.'

Although he had read Macaulay in Bangalore, Churchill evidently had not read, or had forgotten, the speech of 1833 in which the most glorious moment in the British Empire's history was supposed to be the day of its responsible self-liquidation. He seemed even to have lost track of his own remarks, made in 1920 after the Amritsar massacre in 1919, and the inquiry into General Dyer's conduct, that Britain neither could, nor should wish to, rule India by force alone: 'it would be fatal to the British Empire if we were to try to base ourselves only upon it. The British way of doing things … has always meant and implied close and effec-tual co-operation with the people of the country.' Churchill still believed, in fact,

Gandhi (centre) leading the Salt March in India, 1930.

in the late Victorian truism that the vast mass of the Indian people were content with British rule, and felt they were being disgracefully misled by an unrepresentative gang of 'agitators.' Put them out of action, by detention if necessary, and the rank and file would soon fall away. This, of course, had also been said about Irish nationalists, with whom, in the end, accepting the hollowness of the theory, Churchill ended up making peace.

Had he been to Blackburn, like Priestley, and listened to the mill hands lament the disappearance of their Indian market in 'dhootie cotton' (the coarse grey fabric used for Indian loincloths and loose trousers), Churchill might also have had more respect for Gandhi's powers of mass mobilization. And he might have understood why Gandhi's symbolic 'half-nakedness,' together with the campaigns to boycott imported cloth and favour the homespun alternative, were, alongside the unstoppable growth of other Indian manufactured foods, radically and unalterably changing what for so long had been the unequal terms of trade between Britain and India. This, too, was an old history lesson but one which somehow Churchill had missed: India had made printed cottons long before the British had ever come to the subcontinent.

Indeed, the very reason for their coming in the first place had been to buy those 'calicos.' Only the assertion of British power had prevented the restoration of what was economically inevitable.

Like many of those who had served briefly in the Raj, Churchill also probably overestimated the strength of British administration, police and military power, when faced with a genuine mass movement like Gandhi's. Although he had paid lip service to the British way of 'collaboration' he probably had in mind the 'responsible' native princes and magnates, rather than the millions of clerks, tax collectors and postal workers who walked out of their offices when Congress told them and were capable of shutting down the government of India almost overnight. By restricting any sort of suffrage in the 1930s to no more than 10 per cent of the population, British administration had actually forced the political nation to seek expression outside official channels. The economic discrimination built into imperial power still drove the engine of grievance. If Churchill had been in India in 1930–1 at the time of Gandhi's great march to the sea to break the enforced British monopoly on salt; had he even understood how the salt issue went to the very heart of the unequal imperial relationship; then perhaps he might have changed his mind about Gandhi as he had about Michael Collins. But salt, except on his lunchtime venison, was seldom on his mind. Instead, he attacked the national government at Westminster, and even more so Irwin in India, for weak-kneed buckling to agitators: 'The British lion, so fierce and valiant in bygone days, so dauntless and unconquerable through all the agony of Armageddon, can now be chased by rabbits from all the fields and forests of his former glory. It is not that our own strength is seriously impaired. We are suffering from a disease of the will. We are the victims of a nervous collapse.'

Churchill's reactionary determination to fight, tooth and nail, the promise of provincial self-government for India that was contained in the India Act of 1935 put him in the same company as men of the hard right who had always suspected the 'dear vicar,' Stanley Baldwin, of being a spineless compromiser, whether to the unions or to the Indian rebels. After the Act passed its second reading by a majority of 400 to 84, Churchill, showing his usual magnanimity, as well as a modicum of pragmatic self-preservation, had the sense to declare the matter closed. But his son Randolph still fought, and lost, an election as an anti–India Act candidate. And the effect of Winston's prolonged, furious and heavily publicized opposition had been to raise serious doubts in India itself about the sincerity of the British commitment to self-government. What, after all, if Churchill should return some day to power, perhaps even as foreign secretary?

Winston's bull terrier, teeth-in-the-thigh attack on the government did not, of course, do much to enhance his standing among the vast majority of Conservatives. He was now in his 60s and most saw him as a posturing has-been, too flash, too loud, too much in love with the Riviera good life and the country-house extravagance he could ill afford – and, worst of all, too enamoured with the sound of his own voice. Baldwin's not entirely ungenerous characterization summed up the way many of them felt: 'When Winston was born lots of fairies swooped down on his cradle [with] gifts – imagination, eloquence, industry, ability, and then came a fairy who said "No one person has a right to so many gifts," picked him up and gave him such a shake and twist that with all these gifts he was denied judgement and wisdom. . . . And that is why while we delight to listen to him in the House we do not take his advice.'

Churchill's shrill alarmism about the fate of the empire meant that, when he made similar noises about the German peril, most of the House of Commons simply turned the volume down. It was not that all its members were impervious to the brutal character of the Third Reich. As early as 1933, when Hitler came to power, at least some of them shared the startled repugnance felt by the British ambassador in Berlin, Sir Horace Rumbold, who recognized immediately that the new regime was not just another run-of-the-mill tinpot dictatorship. Rumbold had read Hitler's autobiography, *Mein Kampf* (1924). He believed it. He told the government that in all likelihood Hitler intended to expel the entire Jewish population from Germany. Before he retired (perhaps one of the invisible turning points in the rise of appeasement) Rumbold tried to tell Whitehall, as strongly as foreign-office form allowed, that Germany was being run by people who were not entirely 'normal': 'Many of us, indeed, have a feeling that we are living in a country where fantastic hooligans and eccentrics have got the upper hand.'

But for many in the governing class, including the editor of *The Times*, Geoffrey Dawson, Hitler, if a little strong meat, was absolutely normal – or rather would become so once his country was treated properly. Sir John Wheeler-Bennett, who had written authoritative histories of Europe, insisted that the chancellor was a reasonable man who was 'justly anxious to make Germany respectable again and is himself anxious to be respectable.' Compared with far more 'eccentric' types such as the propagandist Julius Streicher, perhaps, or the playboy Hermann Goering, Hitler was unquestionably 'the most moderate member of his party.' And if he did get steamed up occasionally, that was for public consumption at home – and, besides, was there not a great deal for Germany to be legitimately steamed up about? It had shouldered exclusive guilt for the Great War; had been punished by being stripped of territory in both Europe and Africa; had been saddled with massive reparations that had caused economic meltdown, with untold suffering for ordinary Germans, and had been denied the basic right of sovereign states to have armed forces. Yet all around it were countries bristling with military hardware. No wonder it felt 'encircled.' When in 1933, Germany walked out from both the Disarmament Conference and the League of Nations itself, the action was regarded merely as the understandable policy of a country that, after years of humiliation, wished to recover its proper sovereignty. When, in March 1936, Germany reoccupied the Rhineland, in direct violation of the Treaty of Versailles, that too was seen simply as the restoration to full sovereignty of territory that had been immemorially and incontrovertibly German. As for the Nazi hostility towards the Jews, reactions, with a few decent exceptions, ranged from shoulder-shrugging indifference to outright sympathy for the German policy. The Regius Professor of Greek at Oxford, Gilbert Murray, who would become an anti-appeaser, nonetheless let it be known that 'experience has taught me that they are in some peculiar and exceptional way a pernicious element in any country in the West. . . . I understand perfectly the German attitude towards these people and approve of it fully.'

Hitler himself was the object more of fascination, even infatuation, than repugnance. A constant stream of approving visitors to Berlin or Berchtesgaden came back glowing with enthusiasm for the miracles he had wrought in Germany – the autobahns, the Volkswagens, the cleaned-up cities. Most depressing of all, David Lloyd George declared him 'the greatest living German' and gushed to the readers of the *Daily Mail* that Hitler was 'a born leader … [a] magnetic, dynamic personality … a mixture of mystic and visionary … [who] likes to withdraw from the world for spiritual refreshment,' and an Anglophile to boot who wished nothing but the best for the British Empire. Lloyd George's only regret was that Britain had no leaders of his calibre. To the historian Arnold Toynbee, Hitler was indistinguishable from Mahatma Gandhi, both being teetotal, vegetarian men of peace. Lord Rothermere, the newspaper magnate, swore that he was a 'perfect gentleman.' When Joachim von Ribbentrop, the German ambassador in London, told the secretary to the cabinet, Thomas Jones, that the Führer was really just like Mr Baldwin – a shy and modest type, a gentle artist – Jones did not burst out laughing but felt that it indeed was so. Even Churchill, who throughout the 30s remained a warm admirer of Mussolini, praising the Duce's 'gentle and simple bearing, and his calm, detached poise,' allowed, in 1932, that since history had seen many strong men who had come to power using ruthless means, perhaps Hitler too would turn out, in the end, to be a fine specimen of a German patriot. On a research trip to Bavaria in 1932 for the Marlborough biography he came close to a meeting with Hitler in Munich.

It was Hitler, warned of Churchill's pro-Jewish stance, who decided it would be a bad idea.

This did not mean, however, that Hitler's admiration for the British Empire was at all qualified. He told Halifax that one of his favourite movies was *The Lives of a Bengal Lancer* (1935), since it portrayed a small group of white men holding hordes of dark men at bay and an entire subcontinent under its sword. The caravan of Savile Row–dressed gentlemen parading through his residences, awash with admiration, not unreasonably led Hitler to believe that an understanding could indeed be made between the British government and the Third Reich. Their fundamental interests, after all, were not in conflict. As von Ribbentrop told Halifax, Germany wished to have a 'free hand' in eastern Europe, while allowing Britain to protect and promote its empire in Asia and Africa. What could be neater or more harmonious? In London von Ribbentrop played this tune like a virtuoso, exploiting issues where he thought the British had a tender conscience. Well before the annexation of Austria in 1938, many in government circles and the party were deploring France's ill-judged alliances with small eastern European states, and saw the 'reorganization' of eastern Europe under German leadership as both inevitable and innocuous. After all, a strong German presence in the east would be a cost-free buffer against the Bolshevik menace that, as every right-minded fellow knew, was the real threat to freedom.

German strategic plans in the east, whatever they might be, were certainly not worth risking another pan-European war for. And here, Baldwin's and Chamberlain's governments were indeed in tune with the opinion of the vast majority of Britons right through the 1930s. Memories of the last war were still raw and traumatic. If scar tissue had formed over the physical wounds, mental wounds had proved much harder to heal. Many of those who had experienced the horrors of the trenches were now the most ardent for peace, at almost any cost. Some of these veterans, like Henry Williamson, the author of *Tarka the Otter* (1927) and *Salar the Salmon* (1935), were so determined, in fact, that they became fascists. But the passionate desire for peace was the monopoly of neither the right nor the left. Thoughtful men like Stafford Cripps and H.G. Wells believed deeply in general and if possible universal disarmament, with the policing of conflicts left to an international security force, run by the League of Nations.

Although he was tarred with the label, not least by Hitler, Churchill, of course, never thought of himself as a warmonger. He too had seen action in the last war; understood perfectly the scale and nature of its casualties; and wanted, as much as Halifax or Chamberlain, to prevent another. It grieved him deeply after the Second

World War to say, as he did over and again, not least in his memoirs, that of all wars in European history, this was the one that could have been most easily stopped. But he knew as early as 1933, when the true nature of the Nazi regime registered with him – perhaps as a result of the reports of his son-in-law Duncan Sandys, who had been an assistant of Sir Horace Rumbold – that it would certainly not be stopped by a policy of guilt-stricken ingratiation. If Britain were to be able to negotiate properly with Germany, it had better do so from a position of strength.

Hence the drumbeat, steady and unremitting, that Churchill kept up for the cause of rearmament. From the very early days of the Third Reich he was determined to make its exceptionally brutal nature apparent, especially to those who pretended that, however disagreeable, it was a regime that would obey the usual conventions of statecraft. Churchill's language in begging to differ was theatrical, to the point where his audiences were rolling their eyes at the performance and muttering behind their hands, 'There goes old Winston again!' But when Churchill spoke of 'a philosophy of blood lust ... being inculcated into their youth in a manner unparalleled since the days of barbarism' he was not exaggerating at all. He was echoing quite faithfully the cult language that the Nazis, especially in the youth movements and the elite militias, liked to use about themselves. Heinrich Himmler, the head of the Gestapo, after all fancied himself as a learned ethnographer-archaeologist. Churchill thought the view that under the Nazis the Germans were doing no more than learning national self-respect was pathetically naïve: 'All these bands of sturdy Teutonic youths marching through the streets and roads of Germany with the light of desire in their eyes to suffer for the Fatherland ... are not looking for status. They are looking for weapons.' On the Jews, another subject thought slightly impolite and altogether irrelevant in the House of Commons, Churchill was equally categorical, referring to the 'horrible, cold, scientific persecution' of the Jews, people 'reduced from affluence to ruin and then, even in that position, denied the opportunity of earning their daily bread, and cut out from relief by grants to tide the destitute through the winter, their little children pilloried in schools ... their blood and race declared defiling and accursed, every form of concentrated human wickedness cast upon these people by overwhelming power, by vile tyranny.'

There were certainly influential men in government, like the National Labour MP Harold Nicolson and, most significantly, the permanent under-secretary at the foreign office, Lord Vansittart, who shared Churchill's views and sometimes spoke their minds. But the closer they were to any sort of power the more tight-lipped they were forced to be, as long as appeasement was government policy. And none of Churchill's moral denunciations would have had the slightest effect had he not constantly invoked the national interest in taking rearmament seriously. That interest was, in the first instance, elementary self-defence. Influenced by his close friendship with Lindemann, 'the Prof,' Churchill had come to believe that the next war would begin with, and turn on, massive aerial bombardment of civilian populations. (The Luftwaffe's experiments in Spain during the Civil War, such as the saturation bombing of Guernica, would have done nothing to disabuse him of that impression.) The vision he had, guided by Lindemann, of what such a sustained air raid on London would be like was apocalyptic. A 60-day attack would produce at least 60,000 casualties (this would in the event be the entire total of civilian dead during the war) and render hundreds of thousands homeless. Millions might be left to flee chaotically into the overwhelmed countryside. Churchill's own flying experience, however brief, doubtless strengthened the drama of these beliefs. It would be the Allies at Dresden, Tokyo and Hiroshima who would produce fire-storms on this kind of scale.

The best way to avoid such an eventuality, however, Churchill believed, was to keep pace with German aircraft production, which he knew was already rapidly outstripping that of the RAF. His estimate that the Germans were producing approximately two and a half times as many planes as Britain was so close to the mark that he was probably fed some of this information by well-placed sources in the foreign office or central intelligence, perhaps Desmond Morton, who themselves were deeply opposed to appeasement. Baldwin always thought of himself as committed to rearmament as well, but wanted to do so in a quiet way without giving Hitler a pretext to accelerate his own militarization, which might lead to endless escalation. Churchill, on the other hand, actually wanted the potential enemy to pay attention to rearmament by an official recognition of a 'half-state' between ordinary peacetime and actual war. The mixture of procrastination and denial that was characteristic of government policy was, he believed, fatal. The government, he said in a Commons speech that perhaps overdid the paradoxes, had 'decided only to be undecided, resolved to be irresolute, adamant for drift, solid for fluidity, all powerful to be impotent. We go on preparing more months and years – precious, perhaps vital for the greatness of Britain – for the locusts to eat.' Supplied with damning material by his informants, including some from inside the RAF itself, like Squadron Leader C. F. Anderson, Churchill kept wrong-footing Baldwin, forcing him to back-track on earlier, more optimistic estimates of the plane-gap. The nadir of Baldwin's defensiveness came after the general election in November 1935, when the prime minister, speaking with what he described, with good reason, as 'appalling frankness,' told the House that, if he had gone to the country and told them that Germany was

Winston Churchill and Viscount Halifax on their way to parliament, from the *New York Times*, 1938.

rapidly rearming, 'this pacific democracy' would never have returned him to office, and then where would that leave everyone? Once the jaws had stopped dropping Churchill pointed out, fairly gently for him, that he had always supposed it was the leadership of the nation, rather than the timing of the election, that determined the prime minister's policy.

After the Germans reoccupied the Rhineland in 1936, unopposed, it seemed that Churchill's views were steadily gaining more momentum, even if (as Baldwin rightly surmised) the country was not yet ready to batten down the hatches and crank up the air-raid sirens. A great rearmament rally was planned in the Albert Hall that autumn. Chamberlain, Sir Samuel Hoare and Anthony Eden, respectively chancellor of the exchequer, home secretary and foreign secretary, were on the defensive. But on the point of this crusading moment Churchill inflicted an extraordinary, almost unforgivable act of sabotage. George V had died earlier that year, and Winston now threw his support flamboyantly behind Edward VIII's campaign to marry Mrs Simpson and still remain king. For Winston's anti-appeasement friends and allies this was more than a bizarre distraction from the main event – it was an excruciating embarrassment. But Churchill was all of a piece and his sense of romantic attachment to the monarchy, as well as a long acquaintance with Edward VIII, impelled him to ride to the rescue. He was, of course, half-American himself and, though mostly bemused by the philanderings of the rich and famous, he may also have had little time for the stuffiness that looked on a king married to a divorcee (who, however, had not been divorced at the beginning of their liaison) as a contradiction in terms. In the end Churchill was more ardent for the king's cause than Edward was himself. The crisis gave Baldwin a chance to recoup all his fortunes; he leaped at it with gratitude, appearing as the calm statesman in the midst of a constitutional crisis, carefully managing the painful passage of sovereignty from one king to another. In contrast, Churchill seemed all absurd and incoherent bluster. When he got up to criticize Baldwin's clear alternative to the king of, essentially, dropping Mrs Simpson or abdicating, he was howled down for the first time in decades.

In May 1937 Neville Chamberlain replaced the worn-out 'dear vicar' as prime minister; Churchill, sensing correctly that Chamberlain was a much more ardent, principled appeaser than Baldwin, got a second wind. Baldwin, Chamberlain and Halifax all personified, in different ways, a Toryism, or for that matter a Britishness, that Churchill knew very well and was even fond of (although with Chamberlain that would be stretching it a bit). Baldwin had been the embodiment of slightly sleepy village virtues: solid, intelligent, tolerant and generous, not just slow, but almost impossible, to anger. Like many in his generation, he continued to bleed inwardly for the sufferings inflicted by the war of 1914–18, and had promised himself and his country that those evils would never be repeated. 'Its memory,' he said, 'sickens us.' It was just because the soil of Britain was not fertile for the growth of extremes such as fascism and communism that it had to be protected from their onslaught, so that the British Difference, the national 'estate,' might be passed on to generations of children and grandchildren.

Halifax, tall, gaunt, Anglo-Catholic, intensely loyal to Yorkshire, the master of the Lyttelton hunt and a famous rider despite having a withered arm, was, both his friends and enemies readily acknowledged, very shrewd. He had spent a lifetime in public office of one sort or another, and prided himself on taking no nonsense; seeing behind the guff of rhetoric; knowing exactly when and how the wheels of power were to be oiled. In India he thought of himself, rightly, as a realist, determined not to have his head turned by the staggering splendour of Lutyens's Viceroy's House, which he was the first to occupy; and he was prepared, always, to do what it took to keep the imperial, or as modern men called it, the Commonwealth, connection. Chamberlain, on the other hand, represented the empire of middle-class business and municipal virtue, even though his father's mansion, Highbury, was a long way from both screw manufacturing and the gas and water municipal radicalism that had first brought the Chamberlains to power. It had been his more patrician step-brother, Austen, who seemed for many years the more likely of the two to lead the Conservatives, especially since foreign and imperial business had been his speciality. Neville, on the other hand, remained, as he thought, true to his roots: committed above all to the improvement of local government, especially education, possessed of a strong instinct for what the man in the high street, the solicitor or the bank manager, would wish from a properly Conservative prime minister. And that something for Chamberlain, as for Baldwin, was the preservation of peace.

Churchill did indeed understand, though not exactly from personal experience, this England, this Britain of the gymkhana, the village institute, the small town chapel, the brass band. But he differed from them by insisting that it would never survive by humouring a hegemony and hoping that it would leave Britain alone. That would be, as his disciple, the Conservative MP Duff Cooper, said, to depart from 250 years of British opposition to one-power dominance in Europe. Churchill himself put it even more vividly in a BBC broadcast in November 1934: 'There are those who say, "Let us ignore the continent of Europe. Let us leave it with its own hatreds and its armaments, to stew in its own juices, to fight out its own quarrels, and decree its own doom. . . ." There would be very much to this plan if only we could unfasten the British islands from their rock foundations, and could tow them three thousand miles across the Atlantic Ocean. . . .'

But then Chamberlain did not think of himself as an isolationist; rather as someone who would engage actively with Hitler and make him see reason by promoting the peaceful 'rearrangement' of Europe. Halifax had already been to Germany at the end of 1937, in his capacity as the government's fox-hunter, on the occasion of Goering's enormous game and hunting exhibition in Berlin. The fact that Britain won the prize for overseas trophies – all those kudu and eland – must have heartened Halifax in his belief, already indicated by von Ribbentrop, that a deal by which Germany was left to do what it wanted in Europe and Britain left alone in the empire could indeed be struck. After the annexation of Austria in March 1938, when German tanks rolled through Vienna to the delight of rapturous crowds, this engagement seemed to become more urgent, especially as Hitler was making noises about the plight of some 3 million ethnic Germans in the Sudetenland region of northern Czechoslovakia. When those noises turned into demands for the Sudetenland to be annexed to Germany, on pain of military action, Chamberlain launched a series of flying visits in an attempt to defuse the crisis. This meant, essentially, persuading the Czechs that, despite the violation of their sovereignty, they had no option but to yield up the territories; persuading the French, who had been co-guarantors of that sovereignty, which had been granted when Czechoslovakia became an independent republic after the First World War, to go along with this plan, and persuading Hitler himself that he could obtain what he wanted without recourse to military action – the last not exactly a hard sell.

At Berchtesgaden in September 1938, after a meaningless exchange of pleasantries, both Chamberlain and Hitler seemed to have got what they wanted. But at a second meeting, at Bad Godesberg in the Rhineland, Hitler suddenly started making further territorial demands, in particular that areas of Czechoslovakia with Hungarian and Polish populations should also be hived off from the republic. Distressed, quite cross in fact, Chamberlain was still prepared to humour Hitler, especially as the arch-appeasing new ambassador in Berlin, Sir Nevile Henderson, who dreaded getting the rough end of Hitler's tongue, cautioned against anything that might provoke, upset or enrage the hair-trigger Führer. But in a moment of incautious courage and common sense Halifax decided that enough was enough and led a cabinet revolt against Chamberlain, insisting that Hitler should be made to honour the substance of the Berchtesgaden agreement and that, in the event of a military attack, Britain and France would consider an attack on Czechoslovakia as an attack on themselves.

For a week at the end of September 1938, with Hitler's sabre-rattling undiminished, it looked very much as though there would indeed be a war. Provisional plans for mass evacuations were accelerated. On the 27th Chamberlain made a broadcast to the nation that did little to cheer the nervous. Nor did it exactly suggest a leader buckling on his broadsword for the commencement of hostilities: 'How horrible, fantastic, incredible,' he helpfully intoned, 'it is that we should be digging trenches and trying on gas masks here because of a quarrel in a far away country between people of whom we know nothing.' Colonel Josiah Wedgwood, a sometime Labour MP and militant anti-appeaser, commented that Chamberlain was just trying to terrify old ladies so that he could be greeted as the strong silent hero when he came back from doing business with the Devil. 'Will there be a war, dear?' Celia Johnson asks Noël Coward, the destroyer captain in the film *In Which We Serve* (1942). 'I rather think there will,' he replies. 'No point worrying about it until it comes, and no point worrying then, really.'

Sure enough, on the 28th, while delivering an account of the situation to the Commons, Chamberlain received a note from Samuel Hoare and interrupted his own speech (or purported to) to announce that he had accepted an invitation from Herr Hitler to go to Munich. Someone shouted, 'Thank God for the prime minister!' from the back-benches. There was much cheering and waving of order papers. The house, Labour as well as Conservative, got on its feet to give Chamberlain an ovation, with the conspicuous exceptions of Churchill, his friend Leo Amery and Anthony Eden, who, after months of sniping at his own colleagues, had resigned from the government. Churchill did, however, go over to Chamberlain later to wish him luck. Off went Chamberlain to Germany where, not surprisingly, he managed to persuade Hitler that he could have everything he wanted without the need to do anything unpleasant. Although greeted as an extraordinary dipomatic accomplishment, this was not like pulling teeth. On 1 October the Czechs would be told that they must bow to the inevitable and withdraw their border forces from the Sudetenland, at which point German armour would be free to move in. Of course, he added, should the Czechs be 'mad enough' to resist he understood perfectly that the Führer would have no option but to invade the rest of Czechoslovakia; but would he take care not to bomb Prague? Oh, said Hitler, I always do my best to spare civilians – and added that he just hated the thought of little babies being killed by gas bombs. Quite so, quite so. Chamberlain then produced a paper of unforgettable sanctimoniousness and futility, the holy scrip of appeasement, which declared Britain and Germany's desire never to go to war with each other again, and pledged to resolve any and all future difficulties by consultation. Hitler probably could not believe his eyes as he reached for the pen.

The prime minister Neville Chamberlain at Heston Airport on his return from Munich, 1938.

Chamberlain came home as the saviour of European peace, to a chorus of hosannas. He was cheered at Heston aerodrome, where he waved what the Labour politician Hugh Dalton was to call that 'scrap of paper torn from *Mein Kampf.*' On the balcony of Buckingham Palace, flanked by the king and queen, he faced a huge crowd singing 'For he's a jolly good fellow.' Outside Number 10 Downing Street it was just the same. Appearing at an opened upstairs window, and smiling his for once less than wintry smile, Chamberlain asked one of his staff what he should say to the cheering throng and got the advice to tell them what Disraeli had said when he came back from Berlin in 1878. 'My good friends, for the second time in our history,' Chamberlain declared, 'a British Prime Minister has returned from Germany bringing peace with honour. I believe it is peace for our time.' He then told the crowd to go home 'and get a nice quiet sleep.' In France, where the majority of public opinion was equally happy about the reprieve, the newspaper *Paris-Soir* offered him a stretch of French trout stream as a token of its gratitude for sparing the country the horrors of war. In the *Sunday Graphic*, Beverly Baxter wrote that 'because of Neville Chamberlain the world my son will live in will be a vastly different place. In our time we shall not see again the armed forces of Europe gathering to strike like savage bears.'

There were lonely exceptions to all this euphoria, especially outside London: C. P. Scott's *Manchester Guardian*, and *The Glasgow Herald*, which called Munich a 'diktat.' Duff Cooper resigned as first lord of the admiralty, where his demands for rearmament were being opposed, and wrote that, while Chamberlain believed Hitler should be spoken to in the language of sweet reason, he thought a mailed fist might be the better tactic. The historian A. J. P. Taylor wrote to thank Cooper for proving that 'in this hour of national humiliation there still has been found one Englishman not faithless to honour and principle and to the tradition of our once great name.' G. M. Trevelyan, on the other hand, who had been an admirer of Baldwin (especially Baldwin's rural passions), now threw his wholehearted support behind Chamberlain and Munich, deploring the 'war whoop' and believing it madness to sacrifice England for 'Bohemia.'

On the last day of the debate in the Commons, 5 October, with Czechoslovakia already reduced to a defenceless rump state, Churchill made a speech of enduring, tragic power; the most deeply felt, to date, of his career. Ridiculing the claim that Chamberlain had got Hitler to 'retract' claims made at Bad Godesberg, Churchill said sardonically, 'One pound was demanded at the pistol's point. When it was given, two pounds were demanded at the pistol's point. Finally the dictator consented to take one pound seventeen and sixpence and the rest in promises of goodwill for the future.' He quoted (of course) the *Anglo-Saxon Chronicle*'s lament for the attempts of Ethelred the Unready to buy off the Danes and then spelled out the unpalatable truth: 'We are in the presence of a disaster of the first magnitude.' The system of alliances in eastern Europe on which France relied had been swept away. Chamberlain wanted peace between the British and German peoples and no fault could be found with that aim,

> but there can never be peace between the British democracy and the Nazi Power … which vaunts the spirit of aggression and conquest, which derives strength and perverted pleasure from persecution, and uses, as we have seen, with pitiless brutality the threat of murderous force. . . . What I find unendurable is the sense of our country falling into the power, into the orbit and influence of Nazi Germany, and of our existence becoming dependent on their good will or pleasure.

It was to prevent that, he said, that he had tried to urge timely rearmament. But 'it has all been in vain.' Rejecting Chamberlain and Halifax's insistence that Germany was now 'satisfied' and would make no more territorial demands, Churchill prophesied that in a very few months the government would be asked to surrender some more territory, some more liberty. Then he became even more apocalyptic, predicting that conceding those would mean censorship in Britain, since no one could be allowed to oppose such decisions.

What solution could there be? The sole recourse was to 'regain our old island independence' by acquiring the air supremacy he had been asking for. Churchill noted that Lord Baldwin, as he now was, had said he would mobilize industry 'tomorrow.' He was not going to let the former prime minister off the hook. This was all very nice, 'But I think it would have been much better if Lord Baldwin had said that two and half years ago.' He did not begrudge Britain's 'brave people' their relief and rejoicing at what seemed to be a reprieve from disaster. But, Churchill said, in his closing words, they should know the truth:

> they should know that we have sustained a defeat without a war, the consequences of which will travel far with us along our road; they should know that we have passed an awful milestone in our history, when the whole equilibrium of Europe has been deranged, and that the terrible words have for the time being been pronounced against the western democracies: 'Thou art weighed in the balance and found wanting.' And do not suppose that this is the end. This is only the beginning of the reckoning. This is only the first sip, the first foretaste of a bitter cup which will be proffered to us year by year unless by a supreme recovery of moral health and martial vigour, we arise again and take our stand for freedom as in the olden time.

The Chamberlains' Christmas card in 1938 showed a photograph of the prime ministerial aircraft flying over a bank of clouds *en route* to Munich. Three months later, on 14 March 1939, as if determined to vindicate Churchill's dire prophecy, German tanks rolled into defenceless Prague. At first Chamberlain still spoke of peace, but when he sensed a sudden backlash amongst Tory backbenchers and read a sharp attack in the *Daily Telegraph* he decided, at last, to lead from the front. At a speech in Birmingham on 17 March, he spoke of his shock and dismay. On the 31st he announced to the House of Commons that the British and French governments were offering a guarantee to Poland, the latest item on Hitler's shopping list, his ostensible claim being to the port of Danzig, now known as Gdansk (otherwise landlocked Poland's access to the Baltic via the so-called Polish Corridor that separated the bulk of Germany from East Prussia and had been created after the First World War). Should Poland be attacked, Britain and France would come to her aid. The logistic impossibility of this aid being delivered to Lodz or Warsaw meant, of course, that there would be a war in the West. But Chamberlain's apparent conversion to a firm alliance policy concealed the fact that he believed the announcement of the guarantee would deter Hitler, and that it would never have to become operational.

The unprecedented Nazi-Soviet non-aggression pact, announced on 23 August, blew that assumption sky-high. Without the collaboration of the Soviet Union, the Franco-British guarantee seemed to be a paper threat. Hitler assumed it was a bluff and that, when it was called, neither state would actually go to war. At dawn on 1 September 1939, in response to an alleged attack on a German radio station in Gleiwitz, a brutal land and air attack was launched on Poland. A 'note' was duly handed by the British ambassador to the government in Berlin, stating that if German troops were not immediately withdrawn France and Britain would honour their obligations. The next day the House of Commons, in grim but resolute mood, expected to hear that war had been declared. What they got instead, to general consternation, was an exercise in procrastination from Chamberlain: he suggested that if, through Italian mediation, German troops would fall back, the *status quo ante* 1 September would still be in place and a conference of representatives from France, Poland, Italy, Britain and Germany could be convened. That, after an initial explosion of rage, was indeed Hitler's idea, too: he assumed that another Munich would give him what he wanted without the inconvenience of a war. Both Labour and some Tory members were appalled. The Conservative MP Leo Amery shouted to Arthur Greenwood, the Labour leader, three devastating words: 'Speak for England!' And Greenwood did, to tremendous and moving effect. When he had finished there were loud cheers. As usual, it was only a threatened revolt among his own ranks that finally overthrew Chamberlain's latest attempt at appeasement, and later that evening he agreed to turn the 'note' into an ultimatum that would expire at eleven o'clock on the morning of 3 September. His most intense reaction, however, was wounded egotism, stressing to the House that, whilst it was a 'sad day, to none is it sadder than to me.' When, in the mournful tones of someone announcing the passing of a maiden aunt, Chamberlain took to the airwaves a few minutes after 11 to inform the nation 'that no such undertaking has been received and that consequently this country is at war with Germany,' he could not help but add again, 'You can imagine what a bitter blow it is for me.' 'Well,' says Shortie Blake, the seaman in *In Which We Serve*, at this news, 'it ain't no bank holiday for me neither.'

Almost immediately the air-raid sirens went off: two minutes of the rising wail. But when the all-clear sounded, nothing seemed to have changed. No bombs had dropped from the sky. Nor was there any great surge of chest-beating, patriotic

Toddlers from Southampton await evacuation to the relative safety of the country, 1940.

rowdiness as there had been in 1914. 'There'll Always Be an England,' the Ross Parker hit of the autumn, seemed more resigned than ra-ra. Everything seemed merely muffled; shadowed. Blackouts were ordered; cinemas and theatres were shut (except, of course, the defiantly naughty Windmill, where girls waggled their tassels for Britain throughout the war). Barrage balloons – silver, gold, even a strange shade of lavender – rose lugubriously into the air as if advertising a party that no one really wanted to go to. And by their hundreds of thousands little boys and girls and not so little boys and girls – some in their best flannel short trousers; some, from the terraced streets of Stepney and Salford and Swansea, a bit snottier and scruffier and, as horrified evacuation hosts discovered, lousier – lined up at railway and bus stations on their way to the unthreatened countryside.

Over 3 million Britons – not just children, but anyone on the high priority list including some hospital patients; Important Civil Servants; BBC Variety (to Bristol); even, strangely, the Billingsgate Fish Market – were redistributed around the country. If the Second World War represented a great coming together of the three Britains

Priestley had identified – antique-rural, electro-modern and clapped-out industrial – then the evacuations of 1939 were the first act in this exercise in national reacquaintance. As with the stately home opened to the public, it was all, at first, a bit strained. A perfectly wonderful account of politesse under siege to the Cockneys is given by Evelyn Waugh in his brilliant comic novel of the phoney (or 'Bore') war, *Put Out More Flags* (1942). Oliver Lyttelton, President of the Board of Trade, confessed he had no idea that the working classes seemed to be so lacking in rudimentary hygiene. The story of the indignant Glasgow mother who barked at her little girl not to do it on the nice lady's sofa, but against the wall like she was told, became a favourite piece of apocrypha. And those children who were lucky enough to encounter the stricken conscience of the possessing classes found they quite liked it. A 14-year-old in Cambridge wrote home that 'we have very nice food here such as venison, pheasant and hare and other luxuries which we cannot afford.' When, however, 1939 turned to 1940 – a bitter winter in which the Thames froze – and there were still no air raids, no invasions, 316,000 at least were returned home, the government decreeing that evacuation would be put into operation again only when raids had actually started.

Although nothing much was actually happening in these unreal months of the phoney war, many Britons still wanted it to be stopped. In the five weeks after 3 September, Chamberlain received 1860 letters urging him to do so. He felt the same way himself: 'How I do hate and loathe this war. I never was meant to be a war minister.' Others were more pessimistic but also more steely in their resolve. One of them was George Orwell, who had rediscovered, somewhat to his surprise, that he was a patriot.

The night before the Stalin–Hitler non-aggression pact had been announced, George Orwell dreamed that war had already broken out (a dream, or a nightmare, shared probably by many less imaginative Britons). Since coming back from Spain he had spent years denouncing the coming of war, even though he knew it was more or less inevitable. His still largely unread novel, *Coming Up for Air*, published in June 1939, has its anti-hero, the insurance agent George Bowling, a tubby, balding Great War veteran, desperate to get out of his stale life and return to the country town of his childhood, 'Lower Binfield' (standing in for Henley), a place of fresh-baked pies and big, dark fish waiting in the river's weedy depths to be hooked. 'Fishing,' says Bowling, is 'the opposite of war.' Needless to say, he finds his Lower Binfield completely, almost literally, unrecognizable: a tawdry hell of cheap cafés, petrol stations, chain stores and plastic. The sentiment is Orwell at his most conventionally pastoral, lamenting the passing of an earlier England in much the same tone voiced by

Clough Williams-Ellis, founder of the Council for the Preservation of Rural England, in *Britain and the Beast* (1937), edited by Williams-Ellis and including G. M. Trevelyan, E. M. Forster and John Maynard Keynes, who all registered the same prim dismay at pylon modernity.

Then, suddenly, Orwell takes a different tack. At a Left Book Club meeting, set around the time of Munich, a young idealistic anti-appeaser gets up and makes a Churchillian speech of defiance. Bowling tells him, ' "Listen, son you've got it all wrong. In 1914 *we* thought it was going to be a glorious business. Well, it wasn't. It was just a bloody mess. If it comes again, you keep out of it. Why should you get your body plugged full of lead? Keep it for some girl. You think war's all heroism … but I tell you it isn't like that. . . . All you know is that you've had no sleep for three days, you stink like a polecat, you're pissing your bags with fright and your hands are so cold you can't hold your rifle." ' But later Bowling listens to a high-minded pacifist – ' "Hitler? This German person? My dear fellow, I *don't* think of him at all" ' – and explodes in silent nauseated rage: ' "It's a ghastly thing that nearly all the decent people, the people who *don't* want to go around smashing faces in with spanners … can't defend themselves against what's coming to them, because they can't see even when it's under their noses. They think that England will never change and that England's the whole world. Can't grasp that it's just a left-over, a tiny corner that the bombs happen to have missed." '

But that was before Munich, before the occupation of Prague, before the Nazi-Soviet pact that Orwell read about in his breakfast papers the morning after his dream. Now, as he confessed in his 1940 essay 'My Country Right or Left' (1940), he found himself, mysteriously, a patriot, although he hastened to say that patriotism had nothing to do with conservatism. 'To be loyal both to Chamberlain's England and to the England of tomorrow [his socialist England] might seem an impossibility, if one did not know it to be an everyday phenomenon.' To this day, he admitted, 'it gives me a faint feeling of sacrilege not to stand to attention during "God Save the King." That is childish, of course, but I would sooner have had that kind of upbringing than be like the left-wing intellectuals who are so enlightened that they cannot understand the most ordinary emotions.' So even though for many reasons – his lungs, his wound – it seemed that no one wanted him to do any fighting, when it came to it George Orwell was ready to do what he could, after all, to resist Hitler.

Churchill, of course, had none of these hesitations to overcome. After the German occupation of the rump of Czechoslovakia, and Chamberlain's change of heart, Churchill became as supportive as he could of the prime minister, on the assumption that military preparations would now begin in earnest. At Chartwell, later in the spring, the anti-appeaser Harold Macmillan found him already fully mobilized, knee-deep in maps, secretaries, urgent phone calls and scribbled strategies: 'He alone seemed to be in command when everyone else was hesitant.' He would get his wish for action. On the day war was declared, Chamberlain, bowing to public opinion and a campaign led by the non-appeasement newspapers, in particular the staunchly Tory *Daily Telegraph*, offered Churchill the post of first lord of the admiralty. Famously, the admiralty then signalled the fleet: 'Winston is back!'

It is just possible, of course, that those in the government who were still cool towards Churchill hoped he might burn his boats at the admiralty as he had done so spectacularly in the First World War. And they were not far wrong. For putting on his sailor's peaked cap again had brought back memories of the Dardanelles – not, moreover, as a chastening lesson but rather as the nagging instance of what might have been. 'If only' circulated in Churchill's mind, as in 'if only he had had proper military backing for the naval assault on the forts.' In fact, he had never abandoned the basic strategic principle of hitting an enemy at his weakest, not strongest, point. And he spent much of the Second World War trying to find the Achilles' heel of the Axis – North Africa, Greece, Sicily – with decidedly mixed results. His first instinct, formulated straight away, was to blockade Norwegian territorial waters and deprive the Germans of the Swedish magnetite iron ore that was critical to their munitions programme. Never mind, though, that this would mean violating Swedish and Norwegian neutrality.

Had the operation worked, that fact might have been overlooked. But in a chilling rerun of some of the blunders of 1915, nothing did work as planned. Instead of holding the Germans at bay, the expedition, launched in April 1940 after many delays, afforded an excuse for the pre-emptive strike already planned by Hitler. As the mining of Norwegian waters had been fatally held up by one of Churchill's flying trips to Paris to persuade the French to embrace the plan, a modest German force was enabled to establish itself by 7 April, and then, embarrassingly, to frustrate attempts at a British landing. Churchill had also grievously miscalculated, as it turned out, the exposure of battle cruisers to attack from the air. The whole thing was a wretched mess and by June the only substantial British bridgehead, at Narvik, was abandoned.

As first lord of the admiralty Churchill might have been expected to take the lion's share of the blame, yet somehow he escaped the whipping. This may have been, at least in part, because he had begun to broadcast on the radio, and had already established some of the persona – honest, resolute, intensely engaged – that was to boost public morale so powerfully during the rest of the war. He was still not at all popular with most of the Tory rank and file in the Commons, and even less popular with the Labour MPs, many of whom had memories that stretched back to the general strike and even Tonypandy. Some of his speeches in the House seemed, even to supporters like Harold Nicolson, stilted and bumbling, taking refuge in stale clouds of oratory when clear information was what was needed. In the country, however, the contrast between Churchill and Chamberlain was becoming clearer, not least because Chamberlain (beginning to suffer from what turned out to be stomach cancer) had backed into the war and somehow never seemed to manage to rouse himself from what had been a personal defeat. Churchill, on the other hand, having argued for armed resistance to the Third Reich, was flush with vindication.

By the time the Norway fiasco was due to be debated on 7 May, the Labour opposition was roiled by dissatisfaction. 'It is not just Norway,' Clement Attlee would say in the debate. 'Norway comes as the culmination of many discontents. People are asking why those mainly responsible for the conduct of affairs are men who have had an almost uninterrupted career of failure.' A growing number of Tories (though still a minority) took the point and made an approach to see if Labour would be receptive to the idea of a national coalition. Churchill himself remained steadfastly loyal to the government, allowing himself to be used, as Lloyd George wickedly said, 'as an air raid shelter to keep the splinters from hitting his colleagues.' But his old gang were ready to roar their heads off. Leo Amery, normally one of the quieter anti-appeasers, concluded a devastating indictment of Chamberlain's war leadership by invoking Oliver Cromwell's famous dismissal of the Rump Parliament: 'You have sat too long here for any good you have been doing. Depart, I say, and let us have done with you! In the name of God, go!' And there were other surprises at the debate, the most startling being the appearance in full dress uniform of Admiral of the Fleet Sir Roger Keyes, who seemed to be saying (the rigid upper lip made it hard to hear him) that the navy had been prevented from playing their part in Norway by being told that the army was doing such a splendid job.

Suddenly a slightly sticky parliamentary statement (which Chamberlain petulantly thought he hadn't needed to make anyway) turned into a court martial of the government for dereliction of duty. The Labour front bench decided to divide the House, simply on a motion to adjourn. When they filed into the opposition lobby they found themselves mixing, as one of them remembered, with young Conservatives in uniform; a further 41 Tories abstained. When the roll was called and it was discovered that the government's majority had dropped to 81, shouts of 'Go! Go! Go!' hounded Chamberlain as he left the House. One Tory MP started singing very loudly 'Rule Britannia.'

To Chamberlain's preliminary inquiry, Arthur Greenwood and the Labour leadership made it clear that a condition of their serving in a national war coalition was that it would not be under him. Only two serious candidates were possible, Halifax and Churchill, but Labour did not specify a preference. Churchill was still deeply suspect to them and most of them assumed, since many of the Tories disliked him too, that the job would go to Halifax. Nor did they mind. On 9 May Chamberlain then called a remarkable meeting that changed British history. Present were himself, Halifax and Winston. Explaining that it was beyond his power to form a coalition government, Chamberlain then asked the two men whom he should advise the king to send for after his own resignation had been accepted. There was a very long pause before Halifax, making by far the best decision of his life, said that his peerage made it impossible for him to take the post. He meant that it would be difficult for him to control his party from the Lords or to run the government as a peer. But that was disingenuous: it would have been easy to find him a seat in the Commons if that were really the objection. It was something inside Halifax's own make-up that stopped him. Perhaps he had no stomach to be the next in the firing line for discontented Labour and Tory barrackers. Perhaps he thought, with western Europe on the point of being over-run, that to accept would be tantamount to political suicide. Chamberlain's experience of taking the blame for Norway showed that he would in any case be an 'honorary PM' while Churchill ran the war without, it seemed, having to take real responsibility. Better that Churchill should actually carry the can for the disaster that was surely about to happen. Then, perhaps, Halifax could step in to clean up the mess and rally the sensible for a sensible peace.

So when Chamberlain went to the palace and George VI asked him whom he should send for, the king may have been surprised to hear that it was not the good egg, the sound Lord Halifax, whom both he and queen liked and who had been a shooting regular at Balmoral. It was Churchill who kissed the king's hands the next afternoon on 10 May. The premiership could not have come at a more testing time. Early the same day, the Germans had invaded Holland and Belgium. A lesser man, or at least one without Churchill's sense of historical appointment, might have flinched. But as he wrote in his memoirs, 'I was conscious of a profound sense of relief. At last with Destiny and that all my past life had been but a preparation for this hour and for this trial.' On Whit Monday, 13 May, when King George had been contacted personally by Queen Wilhelmina of Holland asking for help (and, if necessary, asylum for her government-in-exile), Churchill went to the Commons to deliver a short speech, shocking in its quiet, truthful sobriety, its absolute moral clarity and its defiant optimism:

I would say to the House, as I said to those who have joined the Government: 'I have nothing to offer but blood, toil, tears and sweat.' We have before us an ordeal of the most grievous kind. We have before us many, many long months of struggle and suffering. You ask, what is our policy? I can say: It is to wage war, by sea, land and air, with all our might and with all the strength that God can give us: to wage war against a monstrous tyranny, never surpassed in the dark, lamentable catalogue of human crime. That is our policy. You ask, what is our aim? I can answer in one word: It is victory, victory at all costs, victory in spite of all terror, victory, however long and hard the road may be; for without victory, there is no survival.

The cheers, however, came overwhelmingly from the Labour benches. There was now a sense – with Clement Attlee in the small war cabinet, and Greenwood, Herbert Morrison, the one-eyed policeman's son, and, above all, Ernest Bevin at the ministry of labour – that Churchill was *their* prime minister. Chamberlain had been damaged by his failure to win the trust of the unions, but that was no longer an issue since Bevin and Morrison had been given massive powers. It was, in fact, the realization of that most unideological trade unionist Bevin's passion for genuine management-union cooperation. War had brought those two Britains back together.

And however the Tories felt about Churchill, the speeches of May, the Commons speech repeated for radio, and the almost equally extraordinary prime ministerial broadcast of 19 May in which he had the unenviable task of announcing the German breakthrough into France three days earlier, steeling the public for a battle ahead 'for all that Britain is, and all that Britain means,' irreversibly changed the way the country felt about him. A primitive opinion poll conducted in 1941 found that 78 per cent of those asked approved of Churchill's leadership, and that measure of appreciation was never to diminish significantly throughout the war.

Many years later Clement Attlee wrote that, if someone asked him, 'What, exactly, Winston did to win the war, I would say, "talk about it."' Edward R. Murrow, the American news correspondent, said much the same when he wrote of Churchill's mobilization of words. The effect of his speeches on British morale is incalculable – meaning, literally, that despite most of those early opinion-soundings it can never be precisely measured. But anyone of my generation (born as the war ended) who talks to anyone of my parents' generation knows, at least anecdotally, that those speeches can be described, without hyperbole, as transforming. Some 70 per cent of the country listened whenever the prime minister spoke. And in stark

Churchill's small war cabinet in 1941. From left to right: seated, Sir John Anderson, Winston Churchill, Clement Attlee, Anthony Eden; standing, Arthur Greenwood, Ernest Bevin, Lord Beaverbrook and Sir Kingsley Wood.

contrast to what had been happening in the phoney war, his words bound parliament and the rank and file of the political parties firmly to the war government. They also gripped the attention – as they were meant to – of both politicians and people in the United States and anywhere else that an English-speaking population had radios. They seriously irritated the Nazis and arguably contributed to Hitler making ill-advised strategic decisions such as switching bombing raids from British airfields to civilian centres. But most of all they made Britain – not just England – a whole nation again. Even Orwell, who needless to say had deep misgivings about demagoguery, breathed a sigh of relief in May 1940 that at last the country had a leader who understood 'that wars are won by fighting.'

Of course, Churchill had been revelling in oratory for his entire life, ever since he had stood on top of Mrs Ormiston Chant's screen in the Empire, Leicester Square, in November 1894, and certainly since he had graduated with honours from the Lloyd George school of verbal manhandling. Occasionally, perhaps more than occasionally, he had been guilty of shameless grandstanding; sometimes the reach for Shakespearean diction and cadence had been a reach too far and the effect thudded into hollow bombast. But this all changed in May 1940. Churchill felt that he was, in some peculiar way, possessed by his nation's history. This gave him the strength and the sincerity to make millions of Britons feel, through listening to him, that they too, without ever seeking the moment, had become embodiments of the British will to endure in freedom. Blue-blooded or not, Churchill had an almost perfect ear for what the public needed to hear. This was no small achievement in a country where social divisions were marked, above all, by accent and mannerisms of speech. But Churchill's diction, however romantically high-flown, was never high-class in the sense of being the nasal twang of the point-to-point upper-crust, much less the thin refinement of philosophical Oxbridge. That his voice was so peculiar – by turns a growl, a rumble, a chuckle, a vocal swoop and, sometimes, a rising shout – detached it from any obvious class and made it instead a voice for, if not exactly of, the people; somehow both grandiose and familiar, both aristocratic and democratic. Everything Churchill did was calculated to have this same street-wise social cheekiness – not least the famous 'V' for victory sign, a reversed and therefore ostensibly cleaned-up version of a famously profane gesture, deliberately designed to retain something of the original's up-yours defiance.

Many of the great speeches followed a set structure, no less effective for being so often repeated: an opening motif of solemn, if not tragically weighted, confessional frankness ('Tonight I must speak to you'; 'The situation is very serious'); a slow movement in which the solemn theme gets elaborated into detail; a sparkling scherzo of sly jokes at the expense of Hitler and the 'Nahzees,' ('Some chicken, some neck'); and a great finale of ferocious resolution, comradely obstinacy and often poetic salvation, the coda delivered with a glorious, almost offhand dip of the voice ('But westward, LOOK [voice up]. The land is [voice down] bright!').

This extraordinary instrument of mobilizing allegiance did not work by itself. It took Churchill between six and eight hours to get each speech right, and he would rehearse them relentlessly until he felt he had each line perfectly weighed and timed. It was as important for him, as for any great thespian, to pace himself between reassuring gentleness (of which there is much more than meets the eye in reading the printed text) and heroic apostrophe. In the performance of 'we shall fight them on the beaches,' done for both parliament and the BBC, the reiterated mantra of defiance is actually spoken very softly, almost ecclesiastically, with the resignation of someone who knows he is merely stating the obvious. 'We shall fight them in the hills' thus becomes not a summons but simply a statement of confident fact.

This was, of course, to pay Britons – many of whom were undoubtedly not looking forward to fighting either on the hills or on the beaches – an enormous compliment. But then Churchill was full of compliments for the people whom in 1940, whether they were waving at him from the smouldering rubble of their cities, exiting from the cockpit of a Hurricane, or just standing around a village green with an ancient shotgun, he transparently loved with a rich passion that was decidedly un-British in its intensity and completely foreign to politics. This love was so powerful that it persuaded him to do something else unheard of in politics, and that was to tell the truth. Not the *whole* truth, of course (this was not fairyland), but an astonishing measure of it. Most of the five great speeches of 1940 had little good to report except the raw fact of survival, and when, as in the speech made after Dunkirk, there seemed to be something to feel relatively happy about, Churchill was quick to guard against premature self-congratulation. 'Wars are not won by evacuations,' he said on 4 June 1940, and took care to enumerate just how much equipment had been left behind in France along with the loss of 30,000 men. Another compliment was being paid to the British people by his not treating them like children in need of the consolations of lying propaganda. By not disguising the gravity of the situation, but without making any concession to defeatism, Churchill won credibility. When he eventually did have good news to report, he could be trusted not to be indulging in idle hopes.

Not least, Churchill and his government gave the British people something to do. In October 1939 he had suggested that a Home Guard of half a million men ought to be formed, to release the armed services from routine sentry and patrol work. The day after the 'blood, toil, tears and sweat' speech on 14 May, Anthony Eden announced the formation of a Local Defence Volunteer Force (later called the Home Guard) for men between the ages of 15 and 65 (although in practice the upper age limit was not very rigorously adhered to). Within 24 hours, a quarter of a million had come forward. By mid-1943 there were some 1.75 million men in the Home Guard, organized in 1100 battalions. In 1940 they had drilled in bowler hats and cheese-cutter cloth caps, carrying an old fowling gun or a Lee-Enfield left over from the Indian Mutiny; three years later they were more or less uniformed and equipped with usable if not bang up-to-date weapons.

Neither a Home Guard nor speeches were going to win the war by themselves, however. And by the third week of May 1940 it seemed to some of the war cabinet, in particular Chamberlain and Halifax, that *nothing* was going to win the war. The Maginot Line, the solid line of French defences on their eastern border, had held. The trouble was that the Germans had simply gone round it. The desperate French premier, Paul Reynaud, pleaded with Churchill for more RAF air support since the Germans seemed to be able to fly at will over France, but Churchill, torn between two instincts — to support his European ally, and to think ahead to the defence of his own island — was reluctant to risk Britain's own, still thin, air defences for a risky proposition on the other side of the Channel. The French, especially General de Gaulle, would always feel that by acting prudentially lest France fall, Churchill and Air Marshal Dowding guaranteed it. The declaration of a 'union' between Britain and France, ancestral enemies joined to fight the common foe, was an extraordinary symbolic gesture from Marlborough's descendant but in the end could be no more than that.

The news kept getting worse. Churchill had asked Franklin Roosevelt to allow a British aircraft carrier into an American port to load planes bought from the United States, but the president declined on the grounds that this would violate his country's neutrality. For Halifax the destruction of the French army, not so long ago routinely described, not least by Churchill himself, as 'invincible,' was a harsh education in the new reality. For one thing, it meant that the nearly 300,000 troops of the British Expeditionary Force who had been retreating towards one of the last open Channel ports, Dunkirk, looked certain of being cut off. The Netherlands had been over-run. Belgium was on the point of capitulating. The Luftwaffe was thought to have massive numerical superiority over the RAF and the Channel suddenly seemed very narrow. He cast his mind back to his talks with von Ribbentrop in 1937 and to the offer that had come from Berlin to leave Britain and its empire, both of them admired so much by Hitler, alone in return for a free hand in the east. Suppose now that offer, or something like it, was still on the table, this time in return for accepting the status quo in western Europe and whatever it was that the Germans wanted to do in those 'far away' countries? The key was Italy, until then not at war with Britain or France. Halifax believed it might be possible for a joint Anglo-French exploratory approach to be made through Mussolini, to see what terms might be available for the preservation of British independence. He fully expected Churchill to reject such an approach, but then Halifax knew that, even if his speeches sometimes pulled the wool over simple people's eyes, they didn't fool the people who mattered, who knew just how desperate the situation was: the military men, the civil servants, his reliables among the Conservatives who still sniggered when they heard Winston do yet another impersonation of Henry V before

Overleaf: *The Withdrawal from Dunkirk, June 1940* by Charles Cundall, 1940.

Charles Cundall 1940

Agincourt. Churchill, Halifax told a friend rather grandly, was talking 'the most frightful rot' and he didn't know how long he could continue working with him. But this was, perhaps, Britain's last chance of salvaging something from the disaster, of pre-empting a catastrophic invasion. In June, Halifax went home to the Vale of York, looked at the glory of the countryside and made up his mind that the 'Prussian jackboot' would not be allowed to desecrate it. If that meant an exit from the unwinnable war, so be it.

Halifax's epiphany in the Vale of York was part of the cult of the English countryside that had become something of a fetish in the 1930s. The legions of the right-minded and the wellington-booted had closed together to keep out chara-bancs and pylons, and now they would do the same to keep out the jackbooted Hun. It would stay perfect for ever. History would pass right by the sheep and the lowing herds and the thatched pubs and the millstreams. H. V. Morton's Miss Cheshire could sleep undisturbed above the ruined dormitory of Beaulieu Abbey. Everything would be all right.

But Churchill knew that if Britain threw in its lot with a defeated France and went cap in hand to Germany, whether through Mussolini or not, everything would not be all right. The truth was that he was not interested in saving the Vale of York, the Weald of Kent or Britain at all in the sense of a mere piece of scenic geography. He would rather see them go up in flames than go down without a fight. Scenery might recover in a year or two; a slave Britain would not. What he was committed to saving was the *idea* of Britain; an idea, moreover, that was not just airy theory, not just what scholars nowadays are pleased to call a 'cultural construction,' an invention, but a lived-in human community, and one that he believed had been the great gift of British history to its countless generations, even to the world: a free political society, governed by the rule of law. He may have been simple-minded to believe this. He may have been an incorrigible 'Whig' historian to believe this. But he was not mistaken to believe this. That was, indeed, the Britain that would not survive capitulation, however dressed up it might be as a 'peace.' What was the point of rambling through Yorkshire when British liberties existed by permission of the Nazi hegemony? What was the point of riding to hounds in a puppet kingdom?

Revisionist historians have wondered, given Britain's dependence on the United States after 1940 and the accelerated end of empire, whether, since Churchill had claimed so often and so militantly that he wanted to save the empire, he should not have taken whatever deal he could have got in May 1940? But co-existence with Hitler would not have saved the empire, which was falling apart for its own inde-pendent and internal reasons. And the subsequent experience of Vichy France hardly suggests that the limited autonomy granted to vassal states would have been respected, especially when it came to the matter of handing over Jews, the great point of it all for Adolf Hitler. This, too, Churchill felt in his marrow: as he said many times, there could be no co-existence with so iniquitous a tyranny.

On 27 May, under increasing pressure, Churchill did waver just a little, to the point of not ruling out any German offer on the basis of accepting the status quo in *eastern* Europe – presumably meaning a German withdrawal from occupied countries in the west. But this, he said, was unlikely to happen. The following day he had to report that the capitulation of Belgium had put the British force in France in an even more perilous predicament. But when he spoke that afternoon to the five members of his small, inner, war cabinet about Halifax's suggestion of at least exploring Italian mediation 'provided we can secure our independence,' Churchill hardened his position. This, he said, was the worst possible time to stop fighting. Nations that went down fighting rose again, but those that surrendered tamely were finished. The Labour members of the war cabinet, Attlee and Greenwood, added that, after everything the prime minister had said about fighting on, backsliding could have catastrophic effects on the morale of working people in the industrial towns who were giving their all for the patriotic cause. Chamberlain was, interestingly, silent.

It was at that moment, in the late afternoon of 28 May, that something momentous happened to change British history. Although it has been described as a Churchillian 'coup,' it was psychological rather than political. And it was merely the effect of committee protocol. At around five, seeing that the discussion was going neither for nor decisively against him, Churchill adjourned the war-cabinet meeting. The Important People left Number 10, and Churchill, exhausted as he was from arguing the case for defiance, brought as many members of the larger full cabinet as could be found – about 25 – into the room. Not many of the Labour members knew him very well. But the presence of this bigger group suddenly emboldened Churchill, broke the dam of tension, flooded him with a sense that this was a historical turning point and, not least, switched on the golden words. He began with sorrowful candour, as he did in his broadcasts. France would fall; Hitler would be in Paris; and the Italians would offer terms that must at all costs be rejected. Any thought of using the United States, as Halifax had also suggested, to make a 'grovelling appeal' was out of the question. According to the Labour politician Hugh Dalton, who had just become minister of economic warfare, Churchill then became 'magnificent' and proceeded to deliver a speech of absolutely intractable determination, saying that even if a hundred thousand could get away from

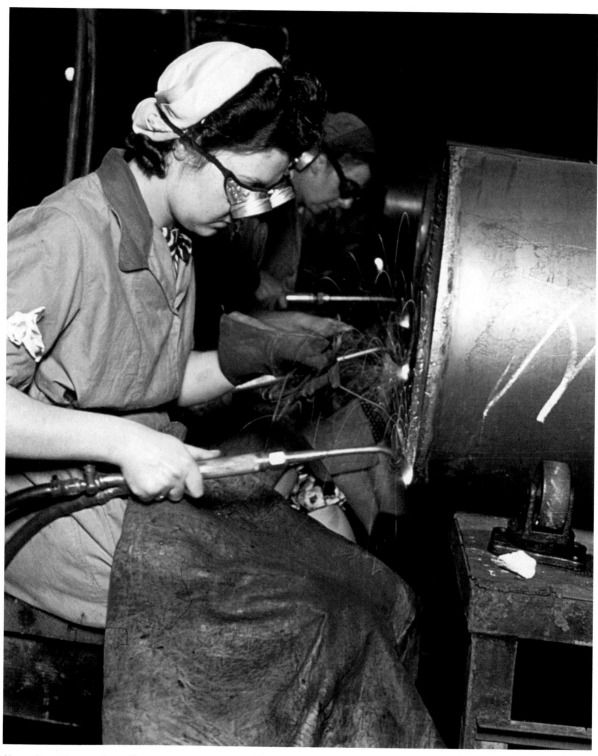

Above: A munitions worker milling parts at an armaments factory, 1940.
Opposite: *Ship Building on the Clyde: Welders* (detail) by Stanley Spencer, 1941.

Dunkirk it would be 'wonderful' and that no one should imagine for a moment that Britain was finished. There were reserves, there was the empire. Then he went on to say that:

> I have thought carefully in these last days whether it was part of my duty to consider entering into negotiations with That Man. But it was idle to think that, if we tried to make peace now, we should get better terms than if we fought it out ... The Germans would demand our fleet ... and much else. We should become a slave state, though a British Government which would be Hitler's puppet would be set up – under Mosley or some such person ... And I am convinced that every man of you would rise up and tear me down from my place if I were for one moment to contemplate parley or surrender. If this long island story of ours is to end at last, let it end only when each one of us lies choking in his own blood upon the ground.

With the cabinet doubtless moved by the certainty that the old boy really meant it, Dalton records: 'There were loud cries of approval all round the table.' Not much more was said. Before they left, Dalton went and patted Churchill on the back as he stood brooding darkly before the cabinet-room fireplace and said, ' "Well done, Prime Minister! You ought to get that cartoon of Low, showing us all rolling up our sleeves and falling in behind you, and frame it and stick it up there." He answered with a broad grin, "Yes, that was a good one, wasn't it?" '

It was better than good; it was itself the first great battle of the Second World War fought and won, not with Hurricanes and Spitfires but with words, passion, history. Churchill suddenly felt, and he was quite right, that the instinctive reaction of the 25 ministers was the reaction of the nation. When the small war cabinet reconvened at seven o'clock he was in a position to tell them that he had never in his life heard a body of men in high positions express themselves so emphatically. This time neither Chamberlain nor Halifax bothered to contradict him. For some reason, in his memoirs Churchill – perhaps out of generosity – preferred to conceal what had really happened in the war cabinet, preferring to write of a 'white glow, overpowering, sublime, which ran through our Island from end to end.' This was, to put it mildly, an optimistic view. But it is true that after 28 May 1940, a date that every school student ought to know as one of the great dates in the nation's history, and after the great 'we shall never surrender' speech to the nation, there was no longer any prospect of a British Vichy. British Jews would not be rounded up at Wembley and shipped to Auschwitz. To some of us, this is not a trivial thing.

Having behaved honourably and bravely, Churchill received a reward so miraculous he could hardly believe it himself. Instead of the 50,000 that the government thought might survive Dunkirk, 330,000 soldiers had been rescued, 200,000 of them British and a flotilla of over 800 boats, the likes of which, it is safe to say, had never been seen in a major war before: round-the-harbour pleasure boats, shrimpers and fishing smacks; ferries and tugs; anything that would float. Some, like the *Gracie Fields*, dive-bombed by Stukas, paid the price. But it was the clearest evidence imaginable that, in the worst possible circumstances, the country that Baldwin had described as a 'pacific democracy' (and in 1935 he had not been wrong) had what it took to become a true national community once more.

In the year that followed there would be overwhelming evidence of this new-found cohesiveness and mutual loyalty. The complete isolation of Britain, fighting on alone, which Hitler not unreasonably assumed would make it a soft target, had precisely the reverse effect. Churchill turned on the 'island nation' rhetoric and the British people across all classes, with very few exceptions, echoed him. This did not, of course, mean that there was not bitterness and alienation among the nearest and dearest of those who lost any one of the 60,000 civilians killed in the war, or the 300,000 combat troops (half the number killed in the First World War), or the millions who had been made homeless by the destruction of the Blitz or the V1 and V2 rockets at the end of the war. Nor did all social divisions dissolve into a brew of patriotic cheerfulness. The first time that the king and queen visited Stepney, according to Harold Nicolson, they were booed, which is precisely why, after Buckingham Palace had taken its first hit on 14 September, it meant so much for Queen Elizabeth to be able to 'look the East Enders in the face.'

With all these reservations it is still impossible not to be struck by the degree to which Britain, which had been such a divided society between the wars, managed to pull together when it mattered most. It was one thing for a people accustomed to doing what they were told to accept rationing as a matter of course; but it was another for the unions and employers, so bitterly at odds for so long, to work together for the nation in arms. It helped, of course, to have Bevin and Beaverbrook (the latter in charge of aircraft production) in the same government, a tandem that could hardly have worked at any other time, and that Herbert Morrison was in the critical role of minister of supply. But no undue pressure needed to be applied to have factories, many of them, of course, staffed by women, working 24 hours a day, seven days a week. The collaborative push made a critical difference to the production of munitions in general, but especially of war planes, which in turn made the difference between winning and losing the Battle of Britain in the summer of 1940.

Misled by overestimates of their numerical superiority, Goering's Luftwaffe kept on writing the RAF's obituary – only to have Spitfires and Hurricanes rise from the ashes to mock their mistaken confidence.

The 'few' weren't, in fact, all that few at all. In mid-August, when the Battle of Britain began to be intense, the RAF actually had 1032 fighter planes to the Luftwaffe's 1011. Even by the end of the first week of September, when the Germans thought they had disposed of all but a hundred or so fighters, the RAF had 736 available with another 256 waiting to be made operational. The Germans also suffered from other disadvantages. Plane for plane, there was nothing in the Luftwaffe that could beat the eight-gun British Spitfire for speed, manoeuvrability and concentrated firepower, at least at 20,000 feet and below. (Richard Overy argues that if the Battle of Britain had been fought at 30,000 feet the British would have lost it.) By having to protect bombers, German fighters lost the tactical flexibility they would have had if they had been allowed to roam freely, and their distance from base meant their operational time was severely limited. Although it was not always accurate, and not much use inland, radar – together with the 30,000 men and women who manned the Observer Corps – gave early warning of the raids. Wrecked or damaged aircraft that fell on British soil could be recovered and rebuilt. British pilots who bailed out could be back in the air the same day; German pilots and crew were quickly captured. The country responded in its own way to the exceptional sacrifices that the airmen were making: ground staff serviced planes round the clock, whilst civilians contributed to Spitfire Funds, voluntary donations that ran at about £1 million a month in 1940, to build more planes. By the autumn almost every town in Britain could claim its own sponsored Spitfire. When Lord Beaverbrook called for the donation of aluminium pots and pans to be melted down and reconstituted as aircraft parts, the kitchens of Britain emptied.

Between 12 August and 6 September there were 53 big raids on British airfields. On the 13th, 400 bombs fell on Lympne alone, chewing up the landing strips. On 15 August, the Luftwaffe committed its maximum strength to the battle but was bested by the RAF: 75 German planes were downed for the loss of 34 British aircraft. On the 18th there was a similar score. On the 20th, Churchill told the Commons that 'never in the field of human conflict has so much been owed by so many to so few,' to which, according to Angus Calder, one airman is said to have commented, 'That must refer to mess bills.'

The human price paid for this relentless engagement was severe. The casualty rate of pilots in August was a shocking 22 per cent and in early September no fewer than 133 pilots were killed, although this brought the British total of pilots down to

Top: RAF fighter pilots scramble to their planes during the Battle of Britain, 1940.
Above: Londoners shelter in the comparative safety of the London Underground, 1940.

around 600, rather than the 177 of which Goering boasted. When, on 8 September, Churchill asked Air Vice Marshal Park, 'What other reserves have we?,' he got an answer of unwelcome candour: 'There are none.'

On 7 September 'Cromwell,' the code word to be used when a German invasion was under way, was signalled. A concentration of barges and flat-bottomed boats had been reported on the Channel and at the Dutch port of Rotterdam. Field Marshal Alan Brooke, the Ulster puritan at the head of Home Defence (Southern Command), was deeply pessimistic about the British army's ability to defend the country when, as he believed, rather than if, invasion came. As many as 80 divisions had not been enough to hold the line in France. Britain had just 22, of which only half were capable of the mobile operations needed to defend a long coastline.

Fortunately, the German navy was just as pessimistic about its chances of landing invasion troops, outnumbered by the Royal Navy and with no guarantee of air supremacy. German admirals and generals were apparently put on a crash course of reading Caesar, Tacitus and accounts of the Norman Conquest.

German doubts about the viability of Operation Sealion did nothing, however, to soften the impact of the air war. If anything, they intensified what Hitler believed to be the necessary terrorizing of the population prior to the assault across the Channel, not by sea but from the air. Bombing attacks had already been made on civilian centres in the southwest of England well before the Battle of Britain, let alone before the RAF raids over Berlin at the end of August, the impertinence of which, admittedly, did not put Hitler in a terribly good mood. But Liverpool, Newcastle and Southampton had all been bombed in late June, and southwest England in late July. On 28–29 August the London suburbs – areas from St Pancras to Hendon (where there was an important airfield), Finchley and Wembley – were hit, and on 2 September it was the turn of Bristol, Liverpool and Birmingham. By the 7th the scale massively intensified, when the Luftwaffe sent 350 planes to destroy London's dockland. Woolwich Arsenal, together with the Royal Victoria and Albert docks and the East India and Surrey Commercial docks, were hit. A huge, rolling fire started, which swept through the streets and houses of Southwark and Rotherhithe. Sailing up the river the writer A. P. Herbert, now a petty officer in the Thames auxiliary patrol, saw, as he rounded the bend at Limehouse, 'a scene like a lake in Hell. Burning barges were drifting everywhere … we could hear the roar and hiss of the conflagration, a formidable noise, but we could not see it, so dense was the smoke.'

The next night the target area widened into the West End. Without a tin hat, and dodging the splinters from anti-aircraft fire that were still burning as they came down, General Brooke saw 60 bombs fall on the same small area in a single hour. Madame Tussaud's, the Natural History Museum, power stations and hospitals were all hit. On the first Sunday after this massive raid the prime minister went on a tour of the damage amidst the oil and glass and smashed timbers and haggard firemen. There he went into one of his astonishing routines, twirling his hat on the end of his cane and roaring, 'Are we downhearted?' Back came the equally amazing (although he would have said predictable) response: 'NO!' Londoners were adapting, sleeping under railway arches, crooned to sleep by the lullaby of the famous music-hall duo Flanagan and Allen. By 15 September, when 158 German fighters and bombers got through the Spitfire Hurricane shield to attack London, 150,000 were spending the night underground in tube stations. On 15 October a bomb fell on the treasury, killing three and missing the Downing Street staff only because Churchill had ordered them into a Pall Mall shelter. As a result the prime minister was himself implored to leave Number 10, where the shelter was thought neither deep enough nor strong enough, and move underground into the heavily reinforced Cabinet War Rooms, completed only a week before the German invasion of Poland. But until a special residential annexe was built for himself and Clementine he spent only three nights there, often returning to Number 10 to sleep and even going up on to the roof to look at the blaze.

George Orwell, too, had been drawn to the inferno. His bloody coughing fits (still undiagnosed as TB) were bad enough to exempt him from military service, something that he said most men would give their balls for but that was a curse to him. As always, he needed to be close to the action. So he left his Bedfordshire cottage and moved to an equally freezing, equally austere small flat in northwest London. From there he wrote for *The Observer*, broadcast propaganda to India for the BBC ('half whoreshop, half lunatic asylum' was his verdict two years later), and served as a sergeant in the Home Guard among the leafy streets and boarded-up mansions of St John's Wood.

Orwell's patriotism, especially in the 'Cromwell' weeks from early September to mid-October, after which, with winter weather coming on, Hitler effectively cancelled any last hope of an invasion, was now militant. For the pacifists of the left, with whom he had already had serious rows over the Spanish Civil War and the Nazi-Soviet non-aggression pact – the exiled poets and the conscientious objectors, the no-war-at-any price brigade who argued that they were the only true anti-fascists – Orwell reserved his most withering contempt when he wrote in the July issue of *Pacifism and the War: A Controversy* (1942), referring to the attitudes of such people, 'If [they] imagine that one can somehow overcome the German army by lying on one's

Above: Churchill inspects the damage in Battersea, south London, 1940.
Opposite top: During the war, George Orwell broadcast to India over the BBC Eastern Service.
Opposite below: Women made homeless in the London blitz, 1940.

back, let them go on imagining it, but let them also wonder occasionally whether this is not an illusion due to security, too much money and a simple ignorance of the way in which things actually happen.' England, he wrote, was the only great country he knew of where the intellectuals were ashamed of their own nationality.

Orwell certainly had not traded in his socialism for some sort of Colonel Blimpery. What stuck in his craw was the elitism of left-wingers who were simply too good, too fine, too precious for patriotism; who refused to understand that it was one of the most populist sentiments of all, wired into actual living human communities. What he rejected was any confusion between patriotism and conservatism. In his mind, the Home Guard was not a quaint bunch of superannuated geezers playing at soldiers while endlessly going on about Wipers and the Menin Road; it was, especially if Sergeant Blair had anything to do with it, the first line of defence of a People's Army, perhaps even the vanguard of a social revolution. Orwell's idea of how to drill Dad's Army was to train them intensively in street fighting.

He and Churchill drew on very different, though not entirely mutually exclusive, visions of British history and national community to explain to themselves and to the country why it was important that Britain fight on to the end. Churchill's *History of the English-Speaking Peoples*, which would be swiftly resumed after the war, was the unfolding pageant of liberty, by which he meant parliamentary government, consummated ultimately in a democratic Commonwealth. Orwell too was interested in the idea of a Commonwealth, but his version owed a lot more to Oliver Cromwell and the Levellers, to the great tradition of popular insurrections from the Peasants' Revolt to the Chartists. Churchill thought it was no accident that in 1942 the Luftwaffe deliberately set out on a 'Baedeker tour' to destroy the greatest buildings of medieval and Georgian England: Canterbury, Norwich, York, Exeter and Bath. They were out to bomb their worst enemy – British history. He set himself in the tradition of popular princes and heroes, always ready to defend the 'island race' against invading tyrants: the same drama Alexander Korda had produced in 1937, with Raymond Massey playing the satanic Philip II of Spain and Flora Robson the armoured Virgin Queen in *Fire over England*. When Churchill went stamping round the rubble, not just of Stepney but also of blitzed Plymouth and Manchester, he was, as Laurence Olivier would demonstrate in the 1944 film of Shakespeare's *Henry V*, 'a little touch of Harry in the night,' stalking through the camp, listening to the grumblings of the ordinary soldiers and trying to explain why they were fighting and why, even in misery and terror, they should fight.

Orwell recognized – generously, in fact – that this was Churchill's special genius; that he could somehow connect with people with whom socially he had nothing whatsoever in common. But Orwell looked round him and he saw multitudes of unrecognized, undecorated heroes – the quarter of a million Londoners who had been made homeless after just six weeks of the Blitz. (It would move on to other industrial centres like Coventry and Birmingham, returning to London in December to strike the City, and then again in the first two weeks of May when more high explosives were dropped than at any other time in the war, hitting the House of Commons, Westminster Abbey, the Tower of London and the Royal Mint. Some 76,000 people were made homeless.) Orwell looked at the air-raid wardens and the Women's Volunteer Service – not to mention the 6 million ordinary serving men and women in uniform – and thought that if this 'total' war was being fought by them, it should also be fought for them. 'Probably the battle of Waterloo *was* won on the playing-fields of Eton,' he wrote in 1941 in his essay 'England Your England,' 'but the opening battles of all subsequent wars have been lost there.' The working people of Bristol and Clydebank, where 80 per cent of the population had been bombed out, were not taking it on the chin from the Luftwaffe in order to make Britain safe for the likes of the boys of St Cyprian's, for the country-house set. All this heartbreak, destruction and misery was only worthwhile if a country could be created that would finally give the miners of Wigan, and the millions like them, the common decencies of life – houses that were not verminous slums; basic food that would nourish rather than sicken; schools for their children; proper medical care; help for the aged and infirm.

The Britain that had gone into the war, Orwell said in the same essay, resembled a stuffy Victorian family with 'rich relations who have to be kow-towed and poor relations who are horribly sat upon ... in which the young are generally thwarted and most of the power is in the hands of irresponsible uncles and bedridden aunts ... A family with the wrong members in control.' But as J. B. Priestley – another broadcaster with a radio audience almost as massive as Churchill's – had commented, the country had been bombed and burned into democracy. And there were now Labour ministers with their hands on the economy, including, by 1942, Stafford Cripps. Orwell thought it unlikely – and certainly undesirable – that they should relinquish it. As laid out in his 1941 essay, 'The English Revolution,' this blueprint of the new socialist Britain needed to include the nationalization of major industries – coal, railways, banks, utilities; the creation of a democratic, classless education system (away with St Cyprian's!), limitations on incomes, and the immediate grant of dominion status to India, with the right to full independence once the war was over. The House of Lords should be abolished as an absurd anachronism, but the monarchy should probably stay. For Orwell had no intention of wiping away

British history in the name of his new Jerusalem. On the contrary, he thought it would 'show a power of assimilating the past which will shock foreign observers and sometimes make them doubt whether any revolution has happened.'

Many of those in government shared some, at least, of Orwell's reformist fervour and were already looking towards a post-war Britain that would not, like the Britain of 1918, slide back to the raw inequalities of Victorian individualism. In December 1942 the Beveridge Report was published, ostensibly concerned with comprehensive social insurance and full employment but promising that post-war government would be committed to giving 'freedom from want by securing to each a minimum income sufficient for subsistence.' In other words, the British state would care for the citizen from cradle to grave. These things were not minority interests. The Beveridge Report sold 635,000 copies, surely a record for a government white paper. A number of Tories, the 'reform group' that included Anthony Eden, Harold Macmillan and R. A. Butler, sensing a big change in public opinion in the country and anxious not to lose post-war elections, promised 'a great programme of social reform.'

But before any of this could be realized, a war had still to be won. And it was exactly the circumstances of *how* it was eventually won that caused trouble for the vision of the new 20th-century Britain: one that attempted to reconcile the romance of back-to-the-wall island history with the obligations of a welfare state. Not everyone was enamoured by Beveridge. The Employers' Confederation felt it had to say that the war was being fought not to set up social insurance but to secure the country's freedom from German tyranny. And even Churchill wondered out loud just what the bill for the Beveridge reforms might be, especially since British foreign reserves had all but disappeared: 'The question steals across the mind whether we are not committing our forty-five million people to tasks beyond their compass and laying on them burdens beyond their capacity to bear.' As long as the issue was just endurance, all the contradictions could just be set aside. Once endurance was no longer in question, the difficulties in the way of reaching Albion-Jerusalem, especially the matter of who should shoulder the fiscal burden, were already apparent.

In this odd sense 1940 had been both the hardest and the easiest year of the war, because the reborn community of the nation was so incontrovertible. When the Japanese bombed Pearl Harbor on 7 December 1941, for all the sorrow and genuine sympathy Churchill showed Roosevelt he was secretly exultant, for he knew in his bones that victory was in sight. 'So we had won after all,' he wrote in his memoirs. 'We should not be wiped out. Our history would not come to an end.' But if he were right that 'England would live' – even right, as far as he could see, that 'Britain

Churchill watches a Boeing B-17 'Flying Fortress' manoeuvre over an RAF airfield, 1941.

would live' – Churchill's equally confident assumption that 'the Commonwealth of Nations and the Empire [for him interchangeable] would live' was misplaced. For whilst Churchill thought Britain's future depended on imperial revival, Roosevelt believed it depended on something like the opposite.

In the lead up to the Atlantic Alliance, of course, he was innocent of all this. When he and Franklin D. Roosevelt met in Placentia Bay on board HMS *Prince of Wales* in August 1941, as American and British sailors standing together sang hymns chosen by Churchill, the dream of a true Atlantic democratic partnership, the partnership Churchill carried in his own blood, seemed gloriously at hand. But it was indeed just a dream. There was a telling moment during his visit to Washington in June 1942 when Roosevelt asked Churchill to think of the relationship with India in the light of what had happened to the British 18th-century empire, meaning that Britain should grant India independence before that country was forced to fight for it. Churchill flared up into full imperialist fury. It was still on his mind at the Lord Mayor's Banquet that year, when he stated bulldoggedly that he had not been made His Majesty's prime minister only to preside over the demise of the British Empire. What Roosevelt had in mind was the granting of immediate dominion status to India to pre-empt the possibility of Subhas Chandra Bose's pro-Axis volunteer Bengal Tigers from triggering something like the great rebellion of 1857 but on an even larger scale. Needless to say, Churchill wouldn't hear of it.

But the demise of empire was happening anyway with the fall of first Hong Kong and then, more catastrophically in February 1942, of Singapore, where the commander-in-chief in southeast Asia, Archibald Wavell, had been ordered, rather bizarrely, by Churchill to instruct his troops to fight to the end over the ruins of the port city. Instead, the Japanese took into captivity 85,000 men, of whom 57,000 would die. HMS *Prince of Wales*, on which the two leaders had met, had been sent halfway round the world to cow the Japanese, only to end up ignominiously sunk in the China Sea. Whether Churchill imagined it or not, the Commonwealth that emerged from the Pacific war would emphatically not be the one that had existed in 1940.

Hitler's Operation Barbarossa, launched against the Soviet Union on 22 June 1941, was another double-edged sword for Churchill and Britain. The most famous anti-Bolshevik in the land found himself in alliance with a Soviet leader who really did embody all of Churchill's ferocious stereotypes about satanic communist monsters. But, as he said of Stalin, he would make friends with the devil himself if it helped win the war. Whilst Barbarossa would be the nemesis of the Third Reich, the chumminess between Stalin and Roosevelt at the conferences, in Teheran in

Top: General Montgomery watches his tanks advance toward German lines, North Africa, 1942.
Above: From left to right, Winston Churchill, Franklin Roosevelt and Joseph Stalin at the Yalta Conference in 1945, on the eve of Allied victory.

November 1943 and Yalta in 1944, made Churchill depressingly aware of Britain's suddenly shrivelled place in the scheme of things. Tying down German manpower on the Russian front had allowed the British Eighth Army to take north Africa, first from the Italians and then (after the initial disaster at Rommel's hands at Tobruk, where 30,000 Allied prisoners were taken) from the Germans as well. For a brief moment when Churchill ordered bells to be rung to celebrate the victory at El Alamein in November 1942, or when he sat beneath the palms with Brooke at Siwa Oasis in January 1943, *en route* from Cairo to Turkey, eating dates and sipping mint tea, listening to the local sheikhs complaining about the Italians eating their donkeys, it must have seemed that all was well with the empire of palm and pine.

But until El Alamein, 1942 had been a terrible year: Hong Kong, Singapore, Tobruk. In the House of Commons, Churchill no longer seemed quite so invulnerable. The socialist Aneurin Bevan spoke of the prime minister winning debate after debate and losing battle after battle: 'The country is saying that he fights debates like the war and the war like debates.' He had experienced the only serious threat to his leadership – the possibility (strange in retrospect) of being replaced by Stafford Cripps. And although he went conscientiously about his diplomatic travels and errands, travelling, for a man nearing 70, astonishing distances in rugged forms of transport from Washington to Moscow to Cairo to Persia, as the outlook for the war improved he paradoxically seemed to enjoy it less and less. As Roy Jenkins notes in his recent biography, Churchill was almost always the visitor. Suffering from the knowledge that, in the end, Britain would have to defer to American military leadership when the time came to launch an invasion of Europe, he regularly threw tantrums when it came to strategic arguments with the field marshals, Auchinleck, Montgomery and Brooke. Although Churchill was certainly right to argue that 1943 was too soon to launch Operation Overlord, the invasion of France, he became obsessed by the alternative Operation Torch in Italy (reverting to the Dardanelles syndrome) and by the notion that Roosevelt and his generals never thought it anything more than a sideshow.

By 1944 he was also, unquestionably, becoming a more difficult leader of the cabinet. Those closest to him felt he was drinking more and thinking less. The days when he would still look 'fresh as paint' to Brooke, after night flights of thousands of miles and a pre-breakfast potion of two whiskies, two cigars and a tumbler of white wine, were no more. He was suffering alarmingly regular bouts of pneumonia. In May that year he seemed to Brooke 'very old and tired. He said Roosevelt was not well and that he was no longer the man he had been, this he said also applied to himself. He said he could always sleep well, eat well and especially drink well but that he no longer jumped out of bed the way he used to and felt as if he would be quite content to spend the whole day in bed.' Increasingly he would bluff his way through cabinet meetings, muttering into his cigars, focussing bewilderingly on some small detail that had nothing to do with the main task at hand, making the meetings unconscionably long. Often he seemed incapable of making members shut up, so that there were times when everyone was talking at once. Decisions, especially military ones, had to be dragged from him. Alarmed by this loss of grip, Brooke, who had come to the conclusion that Churchill had no grasp whatsoever of basic strategy, was many times on the point of resigning. The quiet Attlee became so dismayed by Churchill's glaring lack of familiarity with the papers he was supposed to have read that in 1944 he wrote a stiff memorandum of rebuke, rather like a headmaster chastising the class idler. In the House of Commons, too, Churchill's oratory seemed in danger of degenerating into mere windy bombast. The coalition was already beginning to fray, with differences between Labour and Conservative ministers becoming more substantive. That it didn't fall apart altogether was probably due to the fact that Bevin and Morrison hated each other more heartily than either of them disliked Churchill. But strikes broke out once again in the old heartland of industrial grief: south Wales and Yorkshire.

Pride in D-Day, when it finally came on 6 June 1944, and the heroic Normandy campaigns that followed, along with the sudden return of terror as unmanned V1 flying bombs, then V2 rockets hit the south-east from the summer of 1944 until March 1945 (killing nearly 9000 people and injuring many more) closed the rifts for a while and made Churchill's standing as war leader suddenly important again. When on 8 May, VE Day, he stood on the balcony of Buckingham Palace, with the king and queen, he could take satisfaction in the realization that he had indeed accomplished a task given to very few – he had saved not only his own country but, arguably, the existence of European democracy, which had it not been for British resistance in 1940 would indeed have been overwhelmed by tyranny.

But the election campaign that followed in July taught Churchill not to confuse heartfelt applause with votes. Pugnaciously over-confident, despite hearing some boos in Walthamstow in northeast London, he ran a campaign of abrasive vilification against the welfare state plans of the Labour party. Executing the plans of a true socialist government, he said in a broadcast on 4 June (strangely anticipating some of the themes of Orwell's *Nineteen Eighty-Four*), would necessarily involve 'some form of Gestapo, no doubt very humanely directed in the first instance. And this would nip opinion in the bud ... it would gather all the power to the supreme party and the party leaders, rising like stately pinnacles above their vast bureaucracies

of civil servants, no longer servants and no longer civil … My friends, I must tell you that a Socialist policy is abhorrent to the British ideas of freedom. . . . a free Parliament – is odious to the Socialist doctrinaire.' The attempt to demonize social-ism as being somehow outside the mainstream of British history was an extraordinary reversion to the polemics of the 1920s, notwithstanding all the collaboration of wartime government and the acceptance by a section of the Conservatives of many of the social reforms outlined in the Beveridge Report. In a quietly devastating, sar-donic reply Clement Attlee, still a shadowy figure to most people, told the country that he realized what the aim of Churchill's travesty of Labour policy had been: 'He wanted the electors to understand how great was the difference between Winston Churchill, the great leader in war of a united nation, and Mr Churchill, the party leader of the Conservatives. He feared that those who had accepted his leadership in war might be tempted out of gratitude to follow him further. I thank him for having disillusioned them so thoroughly.'

Churchill was confident enough of the outcome to go to a summit meeting at Potsdam with Stalin and Roosevelt's successor, Truman, on 15 July while waiting for votes to be counted from servicemen scattered around the world. These, he felt sure, would make the difference, although an apocryphal story has him asking Air Vice Marshal Park how he thought the airmen would vote and getting the unwelcome answer that at least 80 per cent of them would vote Labour. Back home, just before dawn on 25 July, Churchill woke up with a 'sharp stab of almost physical pain,' convinced he had lost. How right he was. When all the votes were counted – and the turn-out had been a high 73 per cent – it was apparent that Labour had won a phenomenal and, even to its leaders, shockingly unexpected victory. They would return 393 members to the Conservatives' 213. Whole areas of traditional Tory strength like the Midlands Unionist constituencies – Chamberlain-land – had been wiped out. Churchill put the bravest face he could on the disaster, although when Clementine tried to say at lunch on results day that perhaps a defeat would be a blessing in disguise Winston growled back: 'If this is a blessing, it is certainly very well disguised.' When the time came to leave the prime ministerial country retreat, Chequers, the family all signed the visitors' book; Winston signed last of all, adding below his signature 'Finis.'

It was not, of course; neither for Churchill, nor for the country he recognized as his home. His disastrously ill-judged, ill-tempered election campaign had been fought on three assumptions: first, that the obligations of gratitude (although he was never complacent about this) might return him to power; secondly, that there could not be a socialist Britain that would still recognizably *be* Britain; and thirdly, that the

Opposite: Churchill cheered by the crowds on his way to the Commons on VE Day, 8 May 1945.

nation's continued existence was conditional on the survival, in some meaningful form, of the empire. He was wrong on all three counts. It had in fact been Churchill's own wartime government that had set out the blueprint for a welfare state, had led the public to expect one and that had given Labour ministers the confidence and experience (unlike the previous Labour administrations of 1924 and 1929) to make it happen. In the summer of 1945 the vast majority of the electors punished Churchill for walking away from the better life that they had assumed he had shared. Had not Eden talked about a programme of social reform?

Instead, what they heard were the kinds of noises about a Trojan horse for communism that some of them at least remembered from the 20s, and which, even in the nippiest days of the subsequent Cold War, did not seem to make much sense. However hard the Tories tried, they failed to make Clement Attlee look like a British Stalin. The Labour government was, in any case, at pains to make its collectivist economic programme look patriotically legitimate. Taking 20 per cent of the economy into public ownership was called 'nationalization.' The proposed new public enterprises were likewise to be given patriotic corporate identities: British Steel, the British Overseas Airways Corporation, British Railways. The effort was to recast the meaning of being British as membership of a community of shared ownership, shared obligations and shared benefits: co-op Britain. And because the Labour party had such huge majorities in Wales, Scotland and the most socially damaged areas of industrial England, it would at last be a Britain in which rich southern England did not lord it over the poor-relation regions. This time, in Orwell's terms, the *right* family members would be in control.

That, at least, was the idea inaugurated with such idealistic energy in 1945. Earlier generations had been taught that the British Empire would last for ever. My own generation, born with the welfare state, was taught that this new empire of British social benevolence would also last for ever. This conviction became even stronger when successive Conservative governments in the 1950s and 1960s, including Churchill's own from 1951 to 1955, and from 1957 to 1963 that of his old disciple Harold Macmillan (he who had spoken of British miners as 'the salt of the earth' and who in 1938 had published a little book, *The Middle Way* (1938), advocating, among other things, the abolition of the Stock Exchange), decided against reversing most of the essential institutions of this new Britain: the National Health Service created by Bevan in 1948; the public ownership of railways, steelworks and mines; and especially the commitment to building publicly owned, rented council housing. Seen from the perspective of 1970, it seemed a good bet that this reinvented Britain would see out the 20th century.

Top: Clement Attlee, leader of the Labour party, chats with workers on a tour of his constituency, 1945.
Above: Women and children on the new county council estate at Hemel Hempstead, Hertfordshire, 1954.

But the British welfare state turned out to be much more ephemeral – lasting perhaps two generations – than its founders and tutors, like Professor Harold Laski at the London School of Economics, could possibly have imagined, and the answer to why that was the case is not just Margaret Thatcher. From the very beginning, the Labour government was not insulated from the perennial headaches and imperatives of 20th-century British government – monetary viability, industrial over-capacity and, especially, imperial or post-imperial global defence. The odd thing was that it showed no signs of wanting to be liberated from those constraints. What choice, after all, did it have? The only option, other than shouldering these familiar burdens with a sigh and getting on with the new Jerusalem as best they could, was to plunge into a much more far-reaching programme of collectivization, Keynesian deficit financing, disarmament and global contraction, as indeed those like Laski heartily recommended. But that was never actually on the cards, for the reason that the members of this Labour government, like those of the Liberal administration of 1906, were not cold-blooded social revolutionaries; nor in the sense of a Lenin-like Brest-Litovsk (the treaty that took newly Bolshevik Russia out of the First World War), committed to a wiping of the slate. The slate was Britain; its memories, traditions, institutions, not least the monarchy. Attlee, Ernest Bevin and Herbert Morrison were emotionally and intellectually committed to preserving it, not effacing it. They were loyal supporters of what Orwell called *The Lion and the Unicorn* (1941).

Ernest Bevin, the Somerset farm labourer's boy risen to be foreign secretary, turned out to be almost as much of an imperialist as Churchill and at least as much devoted to the chimera of British military independence from the United States. The decision to keep an independent nuclear deterrent, and to sustain the projection of British power in Asia (through Hong Kong) and even more significantly in the Middle East, came at a huge price: $3.5 billion, to be exact – the amount of a US loan. Britain was estimated to have lost in the region of $10.5 billion or a quarter of the economy as a result of fighting the war. Now that defence costs had risen to fully 10 per cent of gross domestic product – incomparably higher than for any other European state – that American help was desperately needed. So Bevin's goal of keeping independent of the United States had the effect of actually deepening long-term dependence. But the capital infusion, it was thought by Cripps and others, would jump-start the economy as well as pay for investment in new infrastructure, after which surging economic growth would take care of the debt burden. The most idealistic assumption of all was that public ownership of key industries, the replacement of the private profit incentive by cooperative enterprise, would somehow lead to greater productivity. There were periods in 1948 and again in 1950 when, in export-led mini-surges, it looked as though those projections were not as unrealistic a diagnosis of human behaviour as they were, alas, to prove in the long term. Britain was benefiting from the same kind of immediate post-war demand that it had experienced after 1918; the eventual reckoning with the realities of shrinking exports was merely postponed rather than structurally reversed.

The American loan and backing for the stability of the pound – an indispensable condition for the preservation of London's continued dominance as a world centre of finance – came with strings of steel attached. Its condition was that Britain should continue to play a leading (that is, cripplingly expensive) part in the Atlantic Alliance but also bear its share of costs and responsibilities for resisting the communist threat, or nationalist threats that looked like communist threats, in the regions of its old imperial dominance. Hence the obligation to take part in the Korean War of 1950–3 and to combat communist insurgents in Malaya in the 1950s; and, above all, to remain active in the Middle East where Britain and the USA had become corporate partners in the exploitation of oil. That fateful switch that Churchill had made from coal to oil as the fuel of choice for the Royal Navy in 1914 was now bearing bitter fruit.

In any case, though, Bevin and Anthony Eden after him turned out to be eager partners for US secretaries of state Dean Acheson and John Foster Dulles in fighting the Cold War and resisting any attempt at contraction in the Middle East. It was almost uncanny how exactly the map of Middle Eastern oil reserves resembled the old Disraeli-ite map of strategic links between the Mediterranean and India; and how ardent Bevin was to keep that map British. Bases were built or consolidated along the Persian Gulf and round to the southwestern tip of the Arabian peninsula, from Iraq to Aden. Until 1948 Palestine was still under the British mandate set up after the First World War and, despite everything that had happened to the Jews of Europe and the terrible distress of the survivors in refugee camps, Bevin did his level best to reverse Churchill's commitment to a Jewish homeland as a way of strengthening the strategic ties with the oil states of the Arab world. He even proposed that former Italian colonies in Libya and Somalia be put under British trusteeship as a way of extending this zone of influence. And it was Attlee's government that created the 'Persia Committee' to consider the implications of the Iranian prime minister Muhammad Mossadeq's nationalization of the country's largely British-owned oil industry. The Americans were encouraged to think of some sort of defensive response – the kind that led, two years later in 1953, to a CIA-engineered overthrow and the reinstatement of the Pahlavi 'imperial' monarchy.

So even though the Labour government did live up to its obligation to see the Union Jack come down on the flagstaff of the Viceroy's House in New Delhi, and

A Hindu killed in communal riots between Muslims and Hindus in Calcutta, 1946.

to hand over, as if in a Macaulayite dream of redemption, Lutyens's and Sir Herbert Baker's great ensemble of parliament and secretariat buildings to Jawaharlal Nehru and his government in August 1947, welfare state Britain was deeply committed to replacing an old empire with a new one. The far-flung stations of Bevin's empire, to be sure, were called things like the Overseas Food Corporation and the Colonial Development Corporation, but it was designed to finance the British economy in ways that did not look all that different from its 19th-century predecessors. The flow of crucial raw materials, now including oils of all sorts – palm from West Africa, ground nut from East Africa, petroleum from the Gulf and Iran – would be guaranteed in return for the blessings of receiving Morris Minors; Sanderson's wallpaper; Liberty soft furnishings; sterling payment accounts; an aircraft fleet, humming with Rolls-Royce engines, on which the countries could paint their 'flagship' colours; for the sheikh a Bentley, also humming with a Rolls-Royce engine; a visit from Yehudi Menuhin, courtesy of the British Council; and good seats at the coronation in 1953. Charles Trevelyan would have had no difficulty recognizing this at all.

As the bill for maintaining pseudo-great power status *and* welfare-state benevolence mounted, so did doubts and misgivings about the premises on which it had been thought the armed new Jerusalem could be funded. Stafford Cripps, who had once been the most ardent of the collectivizers, became, after 1949, an equally determined advocate of the mixed economy. A hard pound, that other fixture of the inter-war period, likewise became orthodoxy after the decision had been taken not to float it in 1951. The decision of the next Labour party leader, Hugh Gaitskell, to oppose nationalization and Harold Wilson's pragmatic switch from Bevanite advocate of unilateral disarmament to determined opponent of it were bound to put a hold on any return to the socialist idealism of 1945-8. It also meant that the threshold of post-imperial panic, whenever 'vital interests' (the buffer between Britain and late 20th-century reality) were threatened, was much lower.

For the Conservatives, the temptation to invoke the great days of post-Munich defiance (conveniently forgetting the part they had played in Munich in the first place) became irresistible every time Britain was faced with an inconvenient nationalist who threatened to repatriate imperial assets like the Suez Canal. Egypt's president Colonel Gamal Abdel Nasser was thus absurdly portrayed as a Levantine Mussolini, whose violation of treaty agreements and 'grab' of the canal must at all costs be resisted if the torch of freedom were not to go out in the Middle East. The result, of course, was the pseudo-empire's most ignominious fiasco, a farcical replay of Gladstone's worst moment in 1882, when, in the name of preserving free trade and civilization from the threat of 'anarchy' unleashed by a nationalist revolt, a British military occupation was imposed on Egypt. In 1956 the fraud was even more egregious, for the pretence was that red-beret paratroops would be loftily 'separating' the belligerent armies of Israel and Egypt from a confrontation that the British and French had planned in the first place. So aghast was even the Republican administration of Eisenhower at this independently planned campaign that an exercise which had been planned to demonstrate how the British lion could still roar retreated in a mouse-like squeak in the face of a US-led United Nations ultimatum.

After Suez – with the two Harolds, Macmillan and Wilson, scrambling to dismantle what was left of the post-imperial presence, Hong Kong excepted – Britain was forced to come to terms with its loss of status, assets and, in an intangible way, national swagger. The occasional Happy Event, like England's World Cup victory in 1966, royal jubilees and weddings, even the 1982 Falklands War in the south Atlantic, which Margaret Thatcher represented as a triumph of 'freedom and democracy' over Argentinian dictatorship, was no real compensation. But the satire culture of the 1960s turned the mournful fatalism of retreat into a reason to celebrate, not grieve;

Queen Elizabeth II and the Duke of Edinburgh after the coronation, 1953.

the disconsolate arm round the shoulder became the gleeful punch in the ribs. The second-coming of mutton-chop sideboard whiskers, droopy moustaches, neo-Victorian steel-framed glasses and heavily embroidered, brilliantly coloured 'Nehru jackets,' half imperial military band, half Hindu *swami*, popularised by the Beatles, was exactly the moment at which the loss of empire turned from a massive case of denial into affectionate acceptance.

There was, in fact, still one empire left: Britain indisputably survived as a dominant centre of world finance. But even this advantage turned into a liability when the defence of sterling forced successive governments, especially Wilson's, into accepting humiliation conditions either from the United States or the International Monetary Fund, usually involving deep spending cuts. Yet again, a policy intended to arrest the shrinkage of sovereignty only ended up accelerating it. This would go on – with increasingly brutal battles over slices of an ever-diminishing economic pie, fought out between unions and management or between unions and government –

Top: British paratroopers on flight to Suez during the Suez Crisis, 1956.
Above: Anti-bomb protesters march from Trafalgar Square, London, to the Atomic Weapons Research Establishment at Aldermaston, Reading, 1958.

so long as the original post-1945 Labour party assumptions to keep Britain as a substantial military power and a fully funded welfare state remained in being.

All the alternatives mooted and attempted from the 1960s to the 1980s ran into trouble. Relying exclusively on the United States for nuclear defence was ruled out as anathema by both Labour and Conservatives: seen as an abdication, not just of great power but of any power status, equivalent to a transatlantic recolonization in the opposite direction. A European solution, through membership of the EEC, was vetoed by General (now President) de Gaulle twice, in 1963 and 1967, over what he described as Britain's incorrigible insularity and post-imperial mentality (rich, coming from him, embroiled as his country had been in its own colonial wars in Indo-China and Algeria). Particular irony was attached to his emphatic 'Non' on the second occasion, since this was precisely the moment when Harold Macmillan was determined to abandon both attitudes. In 1967 – a year before egg was to fly into his own face in the Paris riots – de Gaulle loftily instructed 'this great people' to embark on the economic and social transformation that would qualify them to be truly part of Europe rather than a satellite of the United States.

The third way in 1970, initiated by free-enterprise, anti-collectivist Tories like Anthony Barber, Edward du Cann and Keith Joseph at the Selsdon Park conference during Edward Heath's ascendancy (although Heath himself had mixed feelings about it), would prepare the way for Margaret Thatcher's attempt in the 1980s to liquidate what was left of the welfare state. Billed as a return to the values that had made Victorian Britain great, it was not in fact a revival of Gladstonian liberalism, nor even of the Palmerstonian anti-continental gunboat-sending and chest-thumping (or handbag-swinging) which at times it rhetorically resembled. Thatcher's government, elected in 1979, was a reversion, rather, to the empire of the hard-faced 1920s, when war socialism had been energetically dismantled, leaving industries that could survive and profit to do so and those which couldn't to go to the wall. As in the 1920s, resistance to brutal rationalization through closure or sell-off of uneconomic enterprises, or by wage or job reductions, was met by determined opposition, never tougher than in the confrontation in 1984-5 between Thatcher and the leader of the National Union of Mineworkers, Arthur Scargill – a battle, however, in which the Iron Lady comprehensively routed the King of Coal.

The trouble with this retro-capitalism masquerading as innovation was that, 60 years after the policy had first been implemented, the regions that were the weaker species in this Darwinian competition were not just poorly but prostrate. South Wales, Lancashire, the West Riding, Tyneside and Clydeside happened to be precisely those regions that had risen to extraordinary prosperity as part of the

British imperial enterprise. Now they were being told, in effect, to drop dead, written off as so many disposable assets in a fire sale. What interest did the Welsh and Scots, in particular, have for remaining part of the firm? (The same would have happened in the shipyards and defunct linen mills of Belfast, had not the Provisional IRA given the Unionists a very strong reason for waving their Union Jacks.) The understandable euphoria over Thatcher and her party winning three successive general elections disguised the fact that those majorities were built at the price of perpetuating a deep rift in Britain's social geography. Not since Edward I in the 13th century had a triumphant England effectively imposed its rule on the other nations of Britain.

Thatcher's constituency was, overwhelmingly, the well-off middle and professional classes in the south of England, whilst the distressed northern zones of derelict factories, pits, ports and decrepit terraced streets were left to rot and rust. The solution of her governments, in so far as they had one, was to let the employment market and good old Gladstonian principles of bootstrap self-help take care of the problem. People living in areas of massive redundancy amidst collapsing industries ought simply to 'retrain' for work in the up-and-coming industries of the future, and if need be move to places such as Milton Keynes, Basingstoke or Cambridge where those opportunities were clustered. But this vision of ex-welders lining up to learn how to use computers was conspicuously unassisted by much in the way of publicly subsidized retraining. And even if was available, there was no guarantee of a job at the end of it. The point of the computer revolution in industry was to save, not to expand, labour. Finally, the kick-up-the-rear-end effect of the Thatcher counter-revolution ran into something that was neither her responsibility nor her fault: the Coronation Street syndrome. Millions in the old British industrial economy had a deeply ingrained loyalty to the place where they had grown up, gone to school, got married and had their kids; to their pub, their park, their football team. In that sense, at least, the Beveridge-Labour social revolution – and behind it the Liberal–Lloyd George revolution – had indeed created cities that, for all their ups and downs, their poverty and pain, were real communities. Fewer people were willing to give up on Liverpool and Leeds, Nottingham and Derby than the pure laws of employment opportunity and the Iron Lady demanded.

But not everything the Thatcher government did was out of tune with social reality. The sale of council houses created an owner-occupier class which corresponded to the long passion of the British to be kings and queens of their own little castles. Nationalized industries had conspicuously failed to do well in an opportunity climate. Sales of those state industries, on the other hand, presupposed a hunger for stakeholdership that was much less deeply rooted in British habits, and the subsequently mixed fortunes of those stocks did nothing to help change those habits. Most misguided of all was the decision to call a poll tax imposed on house and flat owners (the bitter pill to be swallowed by the newly propertied class) a 'community charge.' Since the Thatcher government had specialized in liquidating metropolitan local governments, including London's, especially where those authorities were Labour-dominated, few people were fooled by a regressive tax disguised as civic enthusiasm. In the end, Thatcher's became just the latest in a succession of post-war British governments that had seen their assumptions rebound on them disastrously. Governments run by middle-class, aggressively anti-patrician Tory leaders like the grocer's daughter from Grantham and the garden-gnome salesman's son John Major (in both cases rightly proud of their origins), committed to 'family values,' in Major's notorious formula, as well as to economic self-sufficiency, ended up being overwhelmed by an avalanche of sexual and financial scandals and blunders (sometimes perpetrated by the same people).

By the late 1990s another indispensable marker of British identity, the monarchy, was looking shaky, perhaps even mortal. The strain of being simultaneously a ceremonial and a familial institution, a job description that, since the abdication of Edward VIII, was thought to require standards of personal behaviour well above the norm of late-20th-century expectations, was proving a bit much. Just as the monarchy had gained from its marriages, especially the filmed-for-television romance of the Prince of Wales and Lady Diana Spencer, whose wedding in 1981 had a world audience of at least 800 million, so it lost commensurately from the failure of those unions. The year 1992, referred to by a hoarse-voiced queen as her 'annus horribilis,' saw not just the separation of Charles and Diana but a major fire at Windsor Castle in November. When the secretary for Scotland (for some reason) announced that the crown would pay only for the replacement and repair of items in the royal private collection, and that repairs to the fabric of the building would come from the taxpaying public, a serious debate was triggered about the monarchy's finances. When polled, eight out of ten people asked thought the queen should pay tax on her private income, hitherto exempt. A year later, Buckingham Palace was opened to public tours and the crown did indeed agree to pay taxes. In 1994 the royal yacht *Britannia*, the floating emblem of the Queen's global presence, was decommissioned.

The most difficult moment was yet to come. After Princess Diana's death in a car accident in Paris in 1997, the royal family were criticized for following protocol (which prohibited the flying of flags at the palace when the queen was not in residence) rather than fulfilling the deep need of a grief-stricken public to see the

Union Jack fly there at half-mast. The crown lives and dies by such symbolic moments. And the immense outpouring of public emotion in the weeks that followed seemed both to overwhelm, and in some distinctive way be different from, the more conventional devotion to the queen herself and to her immediate family. The crisis was rescued by a speech made by the queen, striking for its informality and obviously sincere expression of personal sorrow. The tidal wave of feeling that swept over the country testified to the sustained need of the public to come together in a recognizable community of sentiment, and to do so as the people of a democratic monarchy.

But was that country Britain or England? The relative indifference of the Tory ascendancy to the plight of industrial Scotland and Wales had transformed the prospects of the nationalist parties in both countries. Formerly just middle-class, rural and intellectual constituencies, Scottish and Welsh nationalists now made huge inroads into Conservative areas (where the Tories were wiped out in the 1997 general election) and even into the Labour heartland, and this despite three successive Labour leaders being Welsh, Scots and Scots again. In a 1992 poll in Scotland, 50 per cent of those asked said they were in favour of independence within the European Union. The devolution promised and instituted by Tony Blair's new landslide Labour government in the late 1990s did seem to take some of the momentum out of the nationalist fervour, but apparently at the price of stoking the fires of *English* nationalism, resentful at having Scottish and Welsh MPs represented in their own parliament as well as in Westminster. The final logic of devolution would be to have an expressly English parliament as well. Where? York? Bath? Right in the heart of the country at Milton Keynes?

Histories of modern Britain these days invariably come not to praise it but to bury it, celebrating the denationalization of Britain, urging on the dissolution of 'Ukania' into the constituent European nationalities of Scotland, Wales and England (which would presumably tell the Ulster Irish either to absorb themselves into a single European Ireland or to find a home somewhere else – say the Isle of Man). If the colossal asset of the empire allowed Britain, in the 19th and early 20th century, to exist as a genuine national community ruled by Welsh, Irish and (astonishingly often) Scots, both in Downing Street and in remote corners of the empire, the end of that imperial enterprise, the theory goes, ought also to mean the decent, orderly liquidation of Britannia Inc. The old thing never meant anything anyway, it is argued; it was just a spurious invention designed to seduce the Celts into swallowing English domination where once they had been coerced into it, and to persuade the English themselves that they would be as deeply adored on the grouse moors of the Trossachs as in the apple orchards of the Weald. The virtue of Britain's fall from imperial grace, the necessity of its European membership if only to avoid servility to the United States, is that it forces 'the isles' to face the truth: that they are many nations, not one.

But how many, actually? Why, in such a reduction of false British national consciousness to the 'true' entities of Scotland, Wales and England, stop with those acts of self-determination? Each of the sub-nations is, after all, just as much an invention as Britain, except that the inventions happened both earlier and, in terms of the 'rediscovery' of Celtic and Gaelic identities, also later. What possible grounds would there be in an independent Scotland for resisting the right of the Orcadians of Orkney, none of whom thinks they are Scots, to return to their Nordic roots and apply for reunion with Norway? Why should the still primarily Anglophone urbanized south Welsh feel they necessarily have more in common with the Welsh-speakers of mountainous Gwynedd than the English people of Gloucester or Bristol? Why should the Cornish be satisfied to remain the only Celtic culture obliged to co-exist within a country from which all other Celts have retreated to their ethno-linguistic heartland? Why should post-imperial Britain not resemble the happy patchwork of nations that is post-communist Yugoslavia?

Because, of course, of the unhappy patchwork quilt of nations that is post-communist Yugoslavia. Or, rather, that what post-imperial Britain has going for it is precisely its *resistance* to the chilly white purism of Euro-nationalism. Just suppose that, instead of the cruel but just fate of empire being the punishing disintegration of the nation that engineered it in the first place, its reward for surviving that process was actually to make something positive, a fresh Britain, out of its memories; out of the peoples who had been touched, for good or ill, by it? Suppose, instead of listening to the paranoid rant of an Enoch Powell prophesying that a multi-racial Britain would end like Rome with the 'River Tiber foaming with blood,' a multi racial Britain actually took pride in what Colin MacInnes, the 'rebel' writer of the 1950s, called even then its 'mongrel glory'?

The story of the colouring of post-war Britain was not, of course, without its painful, even tragic, moments. It began as a hopeful arrival by the West Indian immigrants of the 1950s, spurred by the 1948 act of parliament that recognized Commonwealth citizenship as British citizenship and gave them the right of free entry. This was generous, but it was also self-interested. Both Labour and Conservative governments saw in those immigrants a population that would make up the shortage of unskilled, low-paid labour. Their presence when I was growing up in the 1950s, even in one of the most precociously multi-cultural areas of London, Golders

Green, was still somehow furtively exotic. What were Jamaicans and Trinidadians doing in Salford playing professional cricket in something called 'The Lancashire League'? When their number started to increase and move into Irish Kilburn and Notting Hill, as well as Brixton south of the river and Tottenham in the northeast, the result was explosive friction. In 1962 the Commonwealth Immigrants Act would be passed, severely restricting the categories of Commonwealth citizens allowed into Britain on grounds of both skills and degrees of blood relationship with native-born Britons. The same reason that immigrant labour was welcomed in the 1950s was now the reason for keeping it out.

The effect of the announcement of these forthcoming restrictions was to accelerate the wave of immigration, so that by 1961 around 100,000 a year were arriving, both West Indian and, increasingly, Asian. Racist politics warmed up, despite the Labour government's passage of race relations bills designed to stamp on crimes of hate and incitements to violence. There had already been riots in Notting Hill in 1958. There would be rioting again in Brixton in 1981. But there was also the annual Notting Hill carnival from 1959; and 41 years later, under the ill-fated but momentarily festive Millennium Dome, dancers from that carnival would sashay their stuff before the queen on New Year's Eve 1999, one of the few moments from that memorably chaotic night that said something genuine about the future of 21st-century Britain.

It is, of course, true that even though half of today's British-Caribbean population and a third of the British-Asian population were born in Britain, they still constitute only a small proportion of the total population. It is also true that any honest reckoning of the post-imperial account needs to face up to racist calamities like the murder in London in 1993 of the black teenager Stephen Lawrence, and the appeal of separatist fundamentalism in Muslim communities, alongside the fact that in 2002 the captain of the England cricket team is of Anglo-Indian descent and there are black players in an England football team managed by a Viking. More important for a multi-coloured British future, a 1997 opinion poll found that 50 per cent of British-born Caribbean men and 20 per cent of British-born Asian men had, or once had, white partners. In 2000 Yasmin Alibhai-Brown found that, when polled, 88 per cent of white Britons between the ages of 18 and 30 had no objection to inter-racial marriage; 84 per cent of West Indians and East Asians and 50 per cent of those from Indian, Pakistani or Bangladeshi background felt the same way.

The colouring of Britain exposes the disintegrationist argument for the pallid, defensive thing that it is. British history has not just been some sort of brutal mistake or conspiracy that has meant the steamrollering of Englishness over subject nations. It has been the shaking loose of peoples from their roots. A Jewish intellectual

Above: A playful reveller apprehends a policeman at the Notting Hill Carnival, *c.* 1985.
Opposite: An inspector bloodied by flying bricks during the Brixton riots, 1981.

expressing impatience with the harping on 'roots' once told me that 'trees have roots;
Jews have legs.' The same could be said of Britons who have shared the fate of
empire, whether in Bombay or Bolton, who have encountered each other in streets,
front rooms, kitchens and bedrooms. Scots, like James Boswell, Thomas Carlyle or
Charles Kennedy, have found their way in London; Welsh, like David Lloyd George,
have done not half badly; as have Irish, like the Protestant George Bernard Shaw,
who revelled in the fact that, like many Irishmen, he came from Yorkshire; and for
that matter Jews from remote places such as Izmir in Turkey and Botosany in
Romania, like my father, who donned a boater and blazer to cruise down the
Thames with his nine-year-old son and recited passages from *The Wind in the Willows*
(1908) and *Three Men in a Boat* (1889) while the putt-putt got stuck in the over-
hanging branches near Datchet.

Born and bred in him (for he himself was born in Whitechapel, not Botosany)
was the sense that being British meant being a European, but also being something
else too. Whether that something else extended Britain's sense of place out west into
the Atlantic or much further across the world, it was not something, even with the
vanishing act of empire, to feel defensive about. Nor should it now. It is true that I

Top: Royal Marines march towards Port Stanley during the Falklands War, June 1982.
Above: A sea of flowers laid in tribute to Diana, Princess of Wales, outside Kensington Palace, London, 1997.

argue this as a transatlantic Briton myself, but the increasing compulsion to make the choice that General de Gaulle imposed on us between Britain's European and our extra-European identity seems to order an impoverishment of its culture. It is precisely the roving, unstable, complicated, migratory character of its history that ought to be seen as a gift for Europe. It is a past, after all, that uniquely in European history combines a passion for social justice with a tenacious attachment to bloody-minded liberty, a past designed to subvert, not reinforce, the streamlined authority of global bureaucracies and corporations. Britain's place at the European table ought to make room for that peculiarity or they should not bother showing up for dinner. What, after all, is the alternative? To surrender that ungainly, eccentric thing, British history, with all its warts and disfigurements, to the economic beauty parlour that is Brussels will mean a loss. But, properly smartened up, Britain will of course be fully entitled to the gold-card benefits of the inward-looking club of white restaurant-goers and villa-renters, bonded together by some imagined notion of cultural sophistication, whilst pretending not to notice that the washers-up in the kitchen just happen to come from Somalia, Algeria, Turkey and Sri Lanka. Nor should Britain rush towards a rebranded future that presupposes the shame-faced repudiation of the past. For its history is not the captivity of its future; it is, in fact, the condition of its maturity.

Two writers, busy scribbling away about the past in their own respective ways in the mid- and late 1940s, knew as much. Winston Churchill, risen from his post-election depression and his Riviera deckchair, had got back to his *History of the English-Speaking Peoples*. Even with all the research assistance at his disposal, Churchill couldn't quite face taking the story beyond the beginning of his own life at the end of the 19th century. So the colossus of his last volume (written in the 1950s) was Abraham Lincoln, whom Churchill rightly regarded as the sublime common hero of the transatlantic community. At the same time, and although his last government notoriously resembled a reunion from the war, Churchill's final crusade – against a nuclear arms race that would result in the annihilation of human civilization – was very much directed towards the future. But, as it had been throughout his life – in the imperial 1890s, in the anti-appeasement 1930s and now – Churchill's history-writing, in this case the epic, as he understood it, of modern democracy, made his pleas to turn back from thermonuclear destruction the more urgent, the valediction more poignant: 'The day may dawn,' he told the House of Commons in his last speech, in March 1955, introducing the defence white paper, 'when fair play, love for one's fellow-men, respect for justice and freedom, will enable tormented generations to march forth serene and triumphant from the hideous epoch in which we have to dwell. Meanwhile, never flinch, never weary, never despair.'

Five years earlier, on 21 January 1950, George Orwell had died in University College Hospital in London. His last published piece was a review of Churchill's memoir *Their Finest Hour* (1949). One might have supposed that Orwell, so eagle-eyed when it came to exercises in self-justification, so suspicious of sentimental reminiscence, might have been wary of the book and its author. But not a bit of it. He paid Churchill the highest compliment he was capable of by writing that, although parts of the book seemed to be taken from an election address, his memoirs read 'more like those of a human being than of a public figure.' There was, he thought, 'a certain largeness and geniality,' which made him rightly cherished by ordinary people, and the stories circulating about Churchill – like his adding to 'we shall fight them on the beaches' the words 'we'll throw bottles at the b—s, it's about all we've got left' – testified to that affection.

There is no doubt, too, that part of Orwell's appreciation of Churchill the warrior derived from the naturalness with which the old man had assimilated British history almost involuntarily into his bones and blood. It may not have been Orwell's kind of past, but it still made room for Wat Tyler and Cromwell and Cobbett as well as Elizabeth I and Disraeli. And Orwell was the one who thought that, in any future Britain, the past should be unapologetically woven through its society; that the lion and the unicorn should still, as he wrote, appear on uniform buttons.

Orwell's sense that for all his aristocratic Toryism (and for many years Orwell had described himself as 'a Tory anarchist') Churchill was part of the world of the ordinary man was embodied in his decision to call his 'Last Man in Europe' Winston Smith. *Nineteen Eighty-Four*, his imperishable masterpiece, published in 1949, is usually remembered as a nightmare vision of the doublespeak future, in which the tyranny of Big Brother presides over a grimly homogenized state in which War is Peace and Lies are Truth. Most of it was written when the widowed Orwell was staying in a cottage lent to him by the newspaper proprietor David Astor on the island of Jura, on the very rim of the Hebrides: population about 300; post once a week, maybe; no telephones, no electricity. The TB that would kill him was getting much worse but he typed away, sometimes with the machine on his knees, and had his adopted son, Richard, with him as well as his sister Avril, who after the nanny had left, looked after them both. Although Barnhill Cottage is impossibly remote, Orwell was not lonely. Friends came and went if they could brave the odyssey of getting there. Orwell had just wanted to get away from the static, everyday hum of politics and the London literary life to concentrate his mind on what was most important to him: the fate of freedom in the age of the super-power and the super-corporation, which are hybridized in the brutal monstrosity of Big Brother's regime, the Party.

Top: Barnhill Cottage, George Orwell's last home, on the island of Jura.
Above: Orwell at work on a manuscript during the winter of 1945.

Until one reads the book as the English novel it is, rather than as an extended lecture on the abuses of power, it is easy to overlook that up there in Jura, among the eagles and the red deer and the sea otters, Orwell was also penning one of the most impassioned arguments for the indispensability of history. History and memory are not the antithesis to free will, but the condition of it. When O'Brien, the arch-deceiver who has persuaded Winston Smith that he is running a resistance group, suggests sealing his recruitment with a toast to the future, Winston lifts his glass and drinks instead ' "To the past." "The past is more important," agreed O'Brien gravely.' And, of course, for the reason that history is the enemy of tyranny, oblivion its greatest accomplice. By encouraging forgetfulness, the Party became free to impose on its hapless subjects its own version of whatever past it chose. Winston's lover, Julia, had 'no memories of anything before the early sixties.' But, somehow, memory was not quite obliterated from Winston's consciousness. How else to explain his strong sense of revulsion, unless through a sense that things had not always been as they were in the present? And then the past starts to come back. An old prole remembers, illicitly, that the beer used to be better. In a junk shop he buys a glass paperweight, at least a century old, with a piece of coral encased inside it; kept in his pocket, this becomes the trigger of memory, the talisman of imaginative freedom. Euphoric at the recovery of time, he is reckless enough to denounce the revolution and the Party for destroying all archives: 'History has stopped. Nothing exists except an endless present in which the Party is always right.'

Nothing could be more British – all right, more English – than for George Orwell to insist that to have a future, a free future at any rate, presupposes keeping faith with the past. Only one thing mattered more to him, and that was nature. Winston Smith does not have time for, nor access to, the archives that would allow him to imagine the alternative outcomes embedded in past time. But he does dream, not unlike those earlier sometime radicals Wordsworth and Coleridge, of a 'Golden Country.' In his dream, 'It was an old, rabbit-bitten pasture, with a foot-track wandering across it and a molehill here and there. In the ragged hedge on the oppo-site side the boughs of the elm trees were swaying very faintly in the breeze, their leaves stirring in dense masses like women's hair. Somewhere near at hand, though out of sight, there was a clear, slow-moving stream where dace were swimming in the pools under the willow trees.' And of course there is, because in Orwell's fugi-tive Golden Country nature, love, freedom and history are all ravelled up together. Some before him called such a place of hopes and blessings 'Jerusalem.' And some of us, obstinately, think we can still call it Britain.

SELECT BIBLIOGRAPHY

Abbreviations BM Press – British Museum Press; CUP – Cambridge University Press;
OUP – Oxford University Press; UCL – University College, London; UP – University Press

PRINTED PRIMARY SOURCES

Bagehot, Walter, *The English Constitution* (Chapman & Hall 1867, OUP 2001)

Bamford, Samuel, *Passages in the Life of a Radical*, 2 vols (Simpkin, Marshall & Co. 1844)

Bartrum, Katherine, *A Widow's Reminiscences of the Siege of Lucknow* (J. Nisbet 1858)

Beeton, Mrs Isabella, *Book of Household Management* (S. O. Beeton 1861)

Bewick, Thomas, *A Memoir of Thomas Bewick, Written by Himself* (Jane Bewick and Longman & Co. 1862)

Booth, Charles, *Life and Labour of the People in London*, 10 vols (Macmillan & Co. 1892–7)

Brittain, Vera, *Testament of Youth: An Autobiographical Study of the Years 1900–1925* (Gollancz 1933)

Burke, Edmund, *Reflections on the Revolution in France, and on the Proceedings in Certain Societies in London Relative to That Event* (J. Dodsley 1790)

Campbell, George, *The Irish Land* (Trubner & Co. 1869)

Carlyle, Thomas, *Past and Present* (Chapman & Hall 1843)

Carlyle, Thomas, *Signs of the Times* (William Paterson 1882)

Churchill, Winston S., *Great Contemporaries* (Thornton Butterworth 1938)

Churchill, Winston S., *My Early Life: A Roving Commission* (Thornton Butterworth 1930)

Churchill, Winston S., *The Second World War*, 6 vols (Cassell 1948–54)

Churchill, Winston S., *The World Crisis, 1911–18*, 2 vols (Thornton Butterworth 1923, 1927)

Cobbett, William, *Rural Rides in the Counties of Surrey, Kent, Sussex – with Economical and Political Observations Relative to Matters Applicable to, and Illustrated by, the State of those Counties Respectively* (William Cobbett 1830)

Coleridge, Samuel Taylor and Wordsworth, William, *Lyrical Ballads, With a Few Other Poems* (Biggs & Cottle and T. N. Longman 1798)

Eden, Emily, '*Up the Country*': Letters Written to Her Sister from the Upper Provinces of India, 2 vols (1866)

Elphinstone, Mountstuart, *The History of India*, 2 vols (Murray 1841)

Gaskell, Elizabeth, *Mary Barton: A Tale of Manchester Life*, 2 vols (Chapman & Hall 1848)

Gubbins, Martin Richard, *An Account of the Mutinies in Oudh, and of the Siege of the Lucknow Residency* (Richard Bentley 1858)

Keith, A. B. (ed.), *Speeches and Documents on Indian Policy, 1750–1921*, 2 vols (OUP 1922)

Kay-Shuttleworth, Sir James Phillips, *The Moral and Physical Conditions of the Working Classes Employed in the Cotton Manufacture in Manchester* (James Ridgway 1832)

Macaulay, Thomas Babbington, *Macaulay's Essays on Lord Clive and Warren Hastings* (Ginn 1931)

Mill, James, *The History of British India*, 3 vols (1817)

Mill, John Stuart, *Autobiography* (Longmans, Green, Reader & Dyer 1873)

Mill, John Stuart, *On Liberty* (Longmans, Green, Reader & Dyer 1859)

Mill, John Stuart, *Principles of Political Economy*, 2 vols (John W. Parker 1848)

Mill, John Stuart, *The Subjection of Women* (Longmans, Green, Reader & Dyer 1869)

More, Hannah, *Village Politics. Addressed to All the Mechanics, Journeymen, and Day Labourers, in Great Britain. By Will Chip, a Country Carpenter* (Simmons, Kirkby & Jones 1793)

Moritz, Carl Philipp, *Travels, Chiefly on Foot, Through Several Parts of England …* (G. G. and J. Robinson 1795)

Morton, H.V., *In Search of England* (Methuen 1927)

Orwell, George, *The Complete Works of George Orwell*, 20 vols (Secker & Warburg 1998)

Paine, Thomas, *Rights of Man: Being an Answer to Mr Burke's Attack on the French Revolution* (J. Johnson 1791)

Paine, Thomas, *Rights of Man. Part the Second. Combining Principle and Practice* (J. S. Jordan 1792)

Pennant, Thomas, *A Tour in Scotland, and Voyage to the Hebrides* (B. White 1772)

Pennant, Thomas, *A Tour in Wales, 1773* (1773, H. Hughes 1778–9)

Price, Richard, *A Discourse on the Love of Our Country, Delivered on Nov. 4 1789, at the Meeting-House in Old Jewry, to the Society for Commemorating the Revolution in Great Britain* (T. Cadell 1789)

Priestley, J. B., *English Journey … During the Autumn of the Year 1933* (1933, Gollancz 1934)

Pugin, Augustus Welby Northmore, *Contrasts …* (1836)

Pugin, Augustus Welby Northmore, *The True Principles of Pointed or Christian Architecture* (John Weale 1841)

Rees, L. E., *A Personal Narrative of the Siege of Lucknow, from Its Commencement to Its Relief by Sir Colin Campbell* (Longman, Brown, Green, Longmans & Roberts 1858)

Rousseau, Jean-Jacques, *The Confessions of J. J. Rousseau; with the Reveries of the Solitary Walker*, 2 vols (1782, J. Bews 1783)

Ruskin, John, *Sesame and Lilies* (Smith Elder 1865)

Smiles, Samuel, *Self-Help: With Illustrations of Character and Conduct* (Murray 1859)

Smith, Barbara Leigh, *A Brief Summary in Plain Language of the Most Important Laws Concerning Women* (1854, Trubner & Co. 1869)

Strachey, Lytton, *Eminent Victorians* (Chatto & Windus 1918)

Strachey, Lytton, *Queen Victoria* (Chatto & Windus 1921)

Thale, Mary (ed.), *Selections from the Papers of the London Corresponding Society, 1792–9* (CUP 1983)

Thelwall, John, *The Peripatetic; or, Sketches of the Heart, of Nature and Society, in a Series of Politico-Sentimental Journals, in Verse and Prose, of the Eccentric Excursions of Sylvanus Theophrastus*, 3 vols (1793)

Trevelyan, Charles Edward, *The Irish Crisis; being a Narrative of the Measures for the Relief of the Distress Caused by the Great Irish Famine of 1846–7 …* (Macmillan & Co. 1880)

Tytler, Harriet, *An Englishwoman in India: The Memoirs of Harriet Tytler, 1828–58,* edited by Anthony Sattin (OUP 1986)

Wells, H. G., *The Outline of History: Being a Plain History of Life and Mankind* (George Newnes 1919)

West, Thomas, *A Guide to the Lakes, in Cumberland, Westmorland, and Lancashire,* (Richardson & Urquhart 1780)

Wollstonecraft, Mary, *A Vindication of the Rights of Men, in a Letter to the Right Honourable Edmund Burke Occasioned by His Reflections on the Revolution in France* (J. Johnson 1790)

Wollstonecraft, Mary, *A Vindication of the Rights of Woman: With Strictures on Political and Moral Subjects* (J. Johnson 1792)

Wordsworth, William, *The Prelude, or, Growth of a Poet's Mind: An Autobiographical Poem* (1798–9, Edward Moxon 1850)

Young, Arthur, *A Six Months Tour Through the North of England: Containing an Account of the Present State of Agriculture, Manufactures and Population, in Several Counties of this Kingdom* (W. Strahan 1770)

OVERVIEW AND GENERAL SOURCES

Bayly, C. A., *Imperial Meridian: The British Empire and the World, 1780–1830* (Longman 1989)

Brewer, John, *The Pleasures of the Imagination: English Culture in the Eighteenth Century* (HarperCollins 1997)

Brown, Judith and Louis, Wm. Roger (eds), *The Oxford History of the British Empire, Vol. 4: The Twentieth Century* (OUP 1999)

Cain, P. J. and Hopkins, A. G., *British Imperialism: Innovation and Expansion 1688–1914*, 2 vols (Longman 1993)

Cain, P. J., *Economic Foundations of British Overseas Expansion* (Palgrave Macmillan 1980)

Cannadine, David, *Class in Britain* (Yale UP 1998)

Cannadine, David, *Ornamentalism: How the British Saw Their Empire* (Allen Lane/Penguin Press 2001)

Corbett, David Peters *et al.* (eds), *The Geographies of Englishness: Landscape and the National Past, 1880–1940* (Yale UP 2002)

Fieldhouse, D. K., *Economics and Empire, 1880–1914* (Weidenfeld & Nicolson 1973)

Foster, R. F., *Modern Ireland, 1600–1971* (Allen Lane/Penguin Press 1988)

Groenewegen, Peter (ed.), *Feminism and Political Economy in England* (Elgar Publishing 1994)

Hobsbawm, Eric and Ranger, Terence (eds), *The Invention of Tradition* (CUP 1983)

Hyam, Ronald, *Britain's Imperial Century: 1815–1914* (Palgrave Macmillan 1993)

James, Lawrence, *The Rise and Fall of the British Empire* (Little, Brown & Co. 1994)

Kiernan, V. G., *The Lords of Human Kind: European Attitudes Towards the Outside World in the Imperial Age* (Weidenfeld & Nicolson 1969)

Lee, J., *The Modernization of Irish Society* (Gill & Macmillan 1973)

Mansergh, Nicholas, *The Irish Question* (Allen & Unwin 1975)

Porter, Andrew and Low, Alaine (eds), *The Oxford History of the British Empire, Vol. III: The Nineteenth Century* (OUP 1999)

Porter, Roy, *English Society in the Eighteenth Century* (Penguin 1982)

Prochaska, F. K., *The Republic of Britain, 1760–2000* (Allen Lane 2000)

Purvis, June and Holton, Sandra Stanley (eds), *Votes for Women* (Routledge 2000)

Schama, Simon, 'The Domestication of Majesty: Royal Family Portraiture 1500–1850' in *Art and History*, pp. 155–85, edited by Robert I. Rotberg and Theodore K. Rabb (CUP 1988)

Thompson, E. P., *The Making of the English Working Class* (Gollancz 1963, Penguin 1968)

Wright, Patrick, *On Living in an Old Country: The National Past in Contemporary Britain* (Verso 1985)

SECONDARY SOURCES
CHAPTERS ONE and TWO

Andrews, Malcolm, *The Search for the Picturesque: Landscape Aesthetics and Tourism in Britain, 1760–1800* (Stanford 1989)

Ayling, Stanley, *Edmund Burke* (Murray 1988)

Bannet, Eve Tavor, *The Domestic Revolution: Enlightenment Feminisms and the Novel* (Johns Hopkins UP 2000)

Barker-Benfield, G. J., *The Culture of Sensibility: Sex and Society in Eighteenth-century Britain* (University of Chicago Press 1992)

Barrell, John, *Imagining the King's Death: Figurative Treason, Fantasies of Regicide* (OUP 2000)

Bate, Jonathan, *Romantic Ecology: Wordsworth and the Tradition* (Routledge 1991)

Bate, Jonathan, *The Song of the Earth* (Picador 2000)

Behrendt, Stephen C., *Romanticism, Radicalism and the Press* (Wayne State UP 1997)

Blakemore, Steven, *Burke and the Fall of Language* (Brown UP 1988)

Briggs, Asa, *William Cobbett* (OUP 1967)

Bromwich, David, *Hazlitt: The Mind of a Critic* (OUP 1983)

Chard, Chloe and Langdon, Helen (eds), *Transports: Travel, Pleasure and Imaginative Geography, 1600–1830* (Yale UP 1996)

Claeys, Gregory (ed.), *The Politics of English Jacobinism: Writings of John Thelwall* (Pennsylvania State UP 1995)

Clark, J. C. D., *English Society 1688–1832* (CUP 1985)

Cookson, J. E., *The British Armed Nation, 1793–1815* (Clarendon Press 1997)

Cookson, J. E., *The Friends of Peace: Anti-War Liberalism in England, 1793–1815* (CUP 1982)

Crossley, Ceri, and Small, Ian (eds), *The French Revolution and British Culture* (OUP 1989)

Davis, Michael T., *Radicalism and Revolution in Britain, 1775–1848: Essays in Honour of Malcolm I. Thomis* (St Martin's Press 2000)

Deane, Seamus, *The French Revolution and the Enlightenment in England, 1789–1832* (Harvard UP 1988)

Duff, Gerald, *William Cobbett and the Politics of the Earth* (Edwin Mellen Press 1972)

Dyck, Ian, *William Cobbett and Rural Popular Culture* (CUP 1992)

Elliott, Marianne, *Partners in Revolution: The United Irishmen and France* (Yale UP 1982)

Elliott, Marianne, *Wolfe Tone: Prophet of Irish Independence* (Yale UP 1989)

Emsley, Clive, *British Society and the French Wars, 1793–1815* (Macmillan 1979)

Everett, Nigel, *The Tory View of Landscape* (Yale UP 1994)

Gaull, Marilyn, *English Romanticism: The Human Context* (W. W. Norton 1988)

Grayling, A. C., *The Quarrel of the Age: The Life and Times of William Hazlitt* (Phoenix 2001)

Hobsbawm, E. J. and Rudé, George, *Captain Swing* (Lawrence & Wishart 1969)

Holmes, Richard, *Coleridge: Early Visions* (Hodder & Stoughton 1989)

Holmes, Richard, *Coleridge: Darker Reflections* (HarperCollins 1998)

Jacobs, Diane, *Her Own Woman: The Life of Mary Wollstonecraft* (Abacus 2001)

Jarrett, Derek, *The Begetters of Revolution: England's Involvement with France, 1759–89* (Longman 1973)

Jarvis, Robin, *Romantic Writing and Pedestrian Travel* (Macmillan 1997)

Keane, John, *Tom Paine* (Little, Brown & Co. 1995)

Knight, Frida, *University Rebel: The Life of William Frend, 1757–1841* (Gollancz 1971)

Kramnick, Isaac, *The Rage of Edmund Burke: Portrait of an Ambivalent Conservative* (Basic Books 1977)

Kritz, Kay Dian, *The Idea of the English Landscape Painter: Genius as Alibi in the Early Nineteenth Century* (Yale UP 1997)

Newman, Gerald, *The Rise of English Nationalism: A Cultural History 1740–1830* (St Martin's Press 1997)

O'Brien, Conor Cruise, *The Great Melody: A Thematic Biography and Commented Anthology of Edmund Burke* (Sinclair Stevenson 1992)

O'Brien, P., *Debate Aborted: Burke, Priestley, Paine and the Revolution in France, 1789–91* (Scotforth 1996)

Paulin, Tom, *The Day Star of Liberty: William Hazlitt and Radical Style* (Faber 1998)

Porter, Roy, *The Enlightenment: Britain and the Creation of the Modern World* (Penguin 2000)

Robinson, Jeffrey C., *The Walk: Notes on a Romantic Image* (University of Oklahoma Press 1989)

Royle, Edward, *Revolutionary Britannia? Reflections on the Threat of Revolution in Britain, 1789–1848* (Manchester UP 2000)

Schweizer, Karl W. and Osborne, John (eds), *Cobbett in His Times* (Leicester UP 1990)

Solnit, Rebecca, *Wanderlust: A History of Walking* (Viking 2000)

Thomis, Malcolm I., and Holt, Peter, *Threats of Revolution in Britain, 1789–1848* (Macmillan 1977)

Tillyard, Stella, *Citizen Lord: Edward Fitzgerald, 1763–98* (Chatto & Windus 1997)

Todd, Janet, *Mary Wollstonecraft: A Revolutionary Life* (Weidenfeld & Nicolson 2000)

Tomalin, Claire, *The Life and Death of Mary Wollstonecraft* (Weidenfeld & Nicolson 1974, Penguin 1985)

Tyson, Gerald. P., *Joseph Johnson: A Liberal Publisher* (University of Iowa Press 1979)

Wallace, Anne D., *Walking, Literature and English Culture: The Origins and Uses of Peripatetic in the Nineteenth Century* (OUP 1993)

Wells, Roger, *Wretched Faces: Famine in Wartime England* (Sutton 1988)

Williams, Raymond, *The Country and the City* (Penguin 1973)

Worthen, John, *The Gang: Coleridge, the Hutchinsons and the Wordsworths in 1802* (Yale UP 2001)

CHAPTERS THREE and FOUR

Altick, Richard D., *Victorian People and Ideas* (W. W. Norton 1973)

Ashton, O., Fyson, R. and Roberts, S. (eds), *The Chartist Legacy* (Merlin Press 1999)

Auerbach, Jeffrey A., *The Great Exhibition of 1851: A Nation on Display* (Yale UP 1999)

Bolster, Evelyn, *Sisters of Mercy in the Crimea* (Cork 1964)

Briggs, Asa, *Victorian Cities* (Odhams 1963)

Briggs, Asa, *Victorian People* (Penguin 1965)

Briggs, Asa, *Victorian Things* (Batsford 1988)

Cannadine, David *et al.*, *The Houses of Parliament: History, Art and Architecture* (Merrell 2000)

Cecil, David, *Melbourne* (Constable 1965)

Curl, James Stevens, *The Victorian Celebration of Death* (Sutton 2000)

Davis, John R., *The Great Exhibition* (Sutton 1999)

Davidoff, Leonore and Hall, Catherine, *Family Fortunes: Men and Women of the English Middle Class, 1780–1850* (Hutchinson 1987)

Edsall, N. C., *The Anti-Poor Law Movement, 1834–44* (Manchester UP 1971)

Epstein, James, *The Lion of Freedom: Feargus O'Connor and the Chartist Movement, 1832–42* (Croom Helm 1982)

Freeman, Michael, *Railways and the Victorian Imagination* (Yale UP 1999)

Gernsheim, Helmut and Alison, *Queen Victoria: A Biography in Word and Picture* (Longman 1959)

Goldie, Sue M. (ed.), *Florence Nightingale, Letters from the Crimea* (Mandolin 1996)

Greenall, R. L., *The Making of Victorian Salford* (Carnegie Publishing 2000)

Hardie, Frank, *The Political Influence of Queen Victoria, 1861–1901* (Frank Cass 1963)

Harrison, J. F. C., *Early Victorian England, 1832–51* (Fontana 1988)

Hawarden, Lady Clementina, *Studies in Life, 1859–64* (V&A Publications 1999)

Hibbert, Christopher, *Queen Victoria: A Personal History* (Da Capo Press 2001)

Hibbert, Christopher, *Queen Victoria in Her Letters and Journals* (John Murray 1984)

Homans, Margaret, *Royal Representations: Queen Victoria and British Culture, 1837–76* (University of Chicago Press 1998)

Jones, David J.V., *The Last Rising: The Newport Insurrection of 1839* (Clarendon Press 1985)

Kaplan, Fred, *Thomas Carlyle* (Cornell UP 1983)

Kohlmaier, Georg and Sartory, Barna von, *Houses of Glass: A Nineteenth-century Building Type* (MIT Press 1986)

Langland, Elizabeth, *Nobody's Angels: Middle-Class Women and Domestic Ideology in Victorian Culture* (Cornell UP 1995)

Levine, Philippa, *Victorian Feminism, 1850–1900* (Hutchinson Education 1987)

Longford, Elizabeth, *Victoria, RI* (Weidenfeld & Nicolson 1964)

Munich, Adrienne, *Queen Victoria's Secrets* (Columbia UP 1996)

Nevill, Barry St-John (ed.), *Life at the Court of Queen Victoria* (Webb & Bower 1984)

Perkin, Joan, *Victorian Women* (John Murray 1993)

Pevsner, Nikolaus, *Studies in Art, Architecture and Design, Vol II: Victorian and After* (Princeton 1968, Thames & Hudson 1982)

Port, M. H. (ed.), *The Houses of Parliament* (Yale UP 1976)

Rose, Phyllis, *Parallel Lives: Five Victorian Marriages* (Chatto & Windus 1984)

Schwarzkopf, Jutta, *Women in the Chartist Movement* (Palgrave Macmillan 1991)

Seacole, Mary, *The Wonderful Adventures of Mrs Seacole in Many Lands* (Falling Walls Press 1984, OUP 1990)

Smith, F. B., *Florence Nightingale: Reputation and Power* (Croom Helm 1982)

Stone, Lawrence, *Road to Divorce: England, 1530–1987* (OUP 1990)

Thompson, Dorothy, *Queen Victoria: Gender and Power* (Virago 1990)

Thompson, F. M. L., *The Rise of Respectable Society: A Social History of Victorian Britain, 1830–1900* (Fontana 1988, Harvard UP 1989)

Vallone, Lynn, *Becoming Victoria* (Yale UP 2001)

Vicinus, Martha, *Independent Women: Work and Community for Single Women, 1850–1920* (Virago 1985)

Vicinus, Martha, *A Widening Sphere: Changing Roles of Victorian Women* (Indiana UP 1977, Methuen 1980)

Weaver, Mike (ed.), *British Photography in the Nineteenth Century: The Fine Art Tradition* (CUP 1989)

Weaver, Mike, *Julia Margaret Cameron, 1815–79* (Herbert 1984)

Weintraub, Stanley, *Victoria: Biography of a Queen* (Allen & Unwin 1987)

Young, G. M., *Victorian England: Portrait of an Age* (OUP 1936)

Ziegler, Philip, *Melbourne: A Biography of William Lamb, 2nd Viscount Melbourne* (Collins 1976)

CHAPTERS FIVE and SIX

Arnold, David, *Colonizing the Body: State Medicine and Epidemic Disease in Nineteenth-century India* (University of California Press 1993)

Arnold, David and Hardiman, David (eds), *Subaltern Studies, Vol. VIII: Essays in Honour of Ranajit Guha* (OUP 1993)

Bayly, C. A., *Empire and Information: Intelligence Gathering and Social Communication in India, 1780–1870* (CUP 1996)

Bayly, C. A., *Indian Society and the Making of the British* (CUP 1988)

Bayly, C. A., *Rulers, Townsmen and Bazaars: North Indian Society in the Age of British Expansion, 1770–1870* (CUP 1983)

Bayly, C. A., *The Raj: India and the British, 1600–1947* (National Portrait Gallery 1990)

Bayly, Susan, *Caste, Society and Politics in India from the 18th Century to the Modern Age* (CUP 1999)

Blake, Robert, *Disraeli* (Eyre & Spottiswoode 1966)

Clive, John, *Macaulay: The Shaping of the Historian* (Random House 1973)

Codell, Julie F. and Macleod, Dianne Sachko (eds), *Orientalism Transposed: The Impact of the Colonies on British Culture* (Ashgate Publishing 1998)

Cohn, Bernard S., *Colonialism and Its Forms of Knowledge: The British in India* (Princeton UP 1996)

Crosby, Travis L., *The Two Mr Gladstones: A Study in Psychology and History* (Yale UP 1997)

Davis, Mike, *Late Victorian Holocausts: El Niño Famines and the Making of the Third World* (Verso 2001)

Davis, Richard, *Disraeli* (Little, Brown & Co. 1976)

Donnelly, James S. Jr., *The Great Irish Potato Famine* (Sutton 2001)

Edney, Matthew H., *Mapping an Empire: The Geographical Construction of British India, 1765–1843* (University of Chicago Press 1997)

Edwardes, Michael, *A Season in Hell: The Defence of the Lucknow Residency* (Taplinger Publishing 1973)

Foster, R. F., *Charles Stewart Parnell: The Man and His Family* (Harvester Press 1976)

Gribben, Arthur (ed.), *The Great Famine and the Irish Diaspora in America* (Massachusetts UP 1999)

Guha, Ranajit and Spivak, Gayatry (eds), *Selected Subaltern Studies* (OUP 1988)

Hamer, D. A., *Liberal Politics in the Age of Gladstone and Rosebery: A Study in Leadership and Policy* (OUP 1972)

Hibbert, Christopher, *The Great Mutiny: India 1857* (Allen Lane/Penguin Press 1978)

Hoppen, K. Theodore, *Elections, Politics and Society in Ireland 1832–85* (Clarendon Press 1984)

Jenkins, Roy, *Gladstone* (Macmillan 1995)

Jordan, Donald, *Land and Popular Politics in Ireland* (CUP 1994)

Kinealy, Christine, *The Great Irish Famine: Impact, Ideology, Rebellion* (Palgrave Macmillan 2002)

Kissane, Noel, *The Irish Famine: A Documentary History* (National Library of Ireland 1995, Syracuse UP 1996)

Lyons, F. S. L., *Ireland Since the Famine* (Weidenfeld & Nicolson 1971)

Marsh, Peter, *Joseph Chamberlain: Entrepreneur in Politics* (Yale UP 1994)

Matthew, H. C. G., *Gladstone, 1809–74* (Clarendon Press 1986)

Matthew, H. C. G., *Gladstone, 1875–98* (Clarendon Press 1995)

Matthew, H. C. G., *The Gladstone Diaries*, vols 5–14 (Clarendon Press 1978–94)

Matthew, H. C. G., *The Liberal Imperialists* (Clarendon Press 1972)

McLaren, Martha, *British India and British Scotland, 1780–1830: Career-Building, Empire-Building and a Scottish School of Thought on Indian Government* (University of Akron Press 2001)

Metcalf, T. R., *Ideologies of the Raj* (CUP 1995)

Metcalf, T. R., *Land, Landlords and the British Raj* (University of California Press 1979)

Morash, Chris and Hayes, Richard (eds), *'Fearful Realities': New Perspectives on the Famine* (Irish Academic Press 1996)

Morris, James, *Farewell the Trumpets: An Imperial Retreat* (Faber 1978)

Morris, James, *Heaven's Command: An Imperial Progress* (Faber 1973)

Morris, James, *Pax Britannica: The Climax of an Empire* (Faber 1968)

Mukherjee, Rudrangshu, *Awadh in Revolt, 1857–8: A Study in Popular Resistance* (OUP 1985)

O'Cathoir, Brendan (ed.), *Famine Diary* (Irish Academic Press 1997)

O'Gráda, Cormac, *Black '47 and Beyond: The Great Irish Famine in History, Economy and Memory* (Princeton UP 1999)

Oldenburg, Veena Talwa, *The Making of Colonial Lucknow, 1856–77* (Princeton UP 1984)

Parry, J. P., *Democracy and Religion: Gladstone and the Liberal Party, 1867–75* (CUP 1986)

Roberts, Andrew, *Salisbury: Victorian Titan* (Weidenfeld & Nicholson 1999)

Sen, Amartya, *Poverty and Famines: An Essay on Entitlement and Deprivation* (OUP 1981)

Shannon, Richard T., *The Age of Disraeli and the Rise of Tory Democracy* (Longman 1992)

Shannon, Richard T., *Gladstone*, 2 vols (Penguin 1999–2000)

Shannon, Richard T., *Gladstone and the Bulgarian Agitation*, 1876 (Nelson 1963)

Stokes, E. T., *The English Utilitarians and India* (OUP 1963)

Stokes, E. T., *The Peasant and the Raj: Studies in Agrarian Society and Peasant Rebellion in Colonial India* (CUP 1978)

Stokes, E. T. and Bayly, C. A. (eds), *The Peasant Armed: The Indian Rebellion of 1857* (OUP 1986)

Townshend, Charles, *Political Violence in Ireland: Government and Resistance since 1848* (Clarendon Press 1983)

Veer, Peter van der, *Imperial Encounters: Religion and Modernity in India and Britain* (Princeton UP 2001)

CHAPTERS SEVEN and EIGHT

Addison, Paul, *Churchill on the Home Front, 1900–55* (Cape 1992)

Addison, Paul, *The Road to 1945: British Politics and the Second World War* (Cape 1975)

Alibhai-Brown, Yasmin, *Who Do We Think We Are? Imagining the New Britain* (Allen Lane 2000)

Barnett, Corelli, *The Audit of War: The Illusion and the Reality of Britain as a Great Power* (Macmillan 1986)

Beckett, Francis, *Clem Attlee* (Richard Cohen 1997)

Benson, John (ed.), *The Working Class in England, 1875–1914* (Croom Helm 1985)

Best, Geoffrey, *Churchill: A Study in Greatness* (Hambledon & London Ltd 2001)

Blake, Robert, *The Conservative Party from Peel to Thatcher* (Methuen 1985)

Blake, Robert and Louis, Wm. Roger (eds), *Churchill* (OUP 1993)

Blythe, Ronald, *The Age of Illusion: England in the Twenties and Thirties* (OUP 1983)

Bogdanor, Vernon, *Devolution in the United Kingdom* (OUP 1999)

Cairncross, Alec, *The British Economy Since 1945* (Blackwell Publishers 1992)

Calder, Angus, *The People's War: Britain 1939–45* (Cape 1969, Pimlico 1992)

Cannadine, David, *Aspects of Aristocracy* (Yale UP 1994)

Cannadine, David (ed.), *Blood, Tears, Toil and Sweat: The Speeches of Winston Churchill* (Weidenfeld & Nicolson 1989)

Cannadine, David, *The Decline and Fall of the British Aristocracy* (Yale UP 1990)

Chamberlin, Russell, *The Idea of England* (Thames & Hudson 1986)

Charmley, John, *Chamberlain and the Lost Peace* (Hodder & Stoughton 1989)

Charmley, John, *Churchill: An End of Glory: A Political Biography* (Hodder & Stoughton 1993)

Churchill, Randolph S. and Gilbert, Martin S., *Winston S. Churchill*, 21 vols (Heinemann, 1966–88)

Clark, Alan, *The Tories: Conservatism and the Nation State, 1922–97* (Weidenfeld & Nicolson 1998)

Clarke, Peter, *Hope and Glory: Britain, 1900–1990* (Allen Lane 1996)

Clarke, Peter, *The Keynesian Revolution and Its Economic Consequences* (Edward Elgar 1998)

Clarke, Peter, *Lancashire and the New Liberalism* (CUP 1971)

Collini, Stefan, *English Pasts: Essays in History and Culture* (OUP 1999)

Crick, Bernard, *George Orwell: A Life* (Secker & Warburg 1980)

Danchev, Alex and Todman, Daniel (eds), *Field Marshal Lord Alanbrooke: War Diaries, 1939–45* (University of California Press 2001)

Dangerfield, George, *The Strange Death of Liberal England* (Constable 1936; Serif 1997)

Darby, Wendy Joy, *Landscape and Identity: Geographies of Nation and Class in England* (Berg 2000)

Dell, Edmund, *A Strange Eventful History: Democratic Socialism in Britain* (HarperCollins 2000)

Devine, T. M. and Finlay, R. J. (eds), *Scotland in the Twentieth Century* (Edinburgh UP 1996)

Ferguson, Niall, *The Pity of War* (Allen Lane/Penguin Press 1998)

Gilbert, Martin, *Churchill: A Life* (Heinemann 1991)

Gilbert, Martin and Gott, Richard, *The Appeasers* (Weidenfeld & Nicolson 1967)

Grigg, John, *Lloyd George: From Peace to War, 1912–16* (Methuen 1985)

Grigg, John, *Lloyd George: The People's Champion, 1902–11* (Eyre Methuen 1978)

Harris, José, *Private Lives, Public Spirit: Britain, 1870–1914* (OUP 1993)

Harris, José, *William Beveridge: A Biography* (Clarendon Press 1997)

Harrisson, Tom, *Living Through the Blitz* (Penguin 1990)

Hennessy, Peter, *Never Again: Britain, 1945–51* (Cape 1992)

Hiro, Dilip, *Black British, White British* (Eyre & Spottiswoode 1971)

Hitchens, Christopher, *Orwell's Victory* (Allen Lane/Penguin Press 2002)

Holton, Sandra, *Feminism and Democracy: Women's Suffrage and Reform Politics in Britain, 1900–1918* (CUP 1986)

Howkins, Alun, *Reshaping Rural England, 1850–1925: A Social History* (HarperCollins 1991)

James, Robert Rhodes, *The British Revolution, 1880–1939* (Hamish Hamilton 1976)

James, Robert Rhodes, *Churchill: A Study in Failure* (Weidenfeld & Nicholson 1970)

James, Robert Rhodes (ed.), *Winston S. Churchill: His Complete Speeches, 1897–1963*, 8 vols (Chelsea House Publishers 1974)

Jenkins, Roy, *Asquith* (HarperCollins 1986)

Jenkins, Roy, *Churchill: A Biography* (Macmillan 2001)

Jones, Gareth Stedman, *Outcast London: A Study in the Relationship Between Classes in Victorian Society* (Clarendon Press 1971)

Joyce, Patrick, *Visions of the People: Industrial England and the Question of Class, 1848–1914* (CUP 1991)

Lukacs, John, *The Duel: Hitler v. Churchill, 10 May–31 July 1940* (Bodley Head 1990)

Lukacs, John, *Five Days in London, May 1940* (Yale UP 1999)

Mandler, Peter, *The Fall and Rise of the Stately Home* (Yale UP 1997)

Mandler, Peter, *History and National Life* (Profile Books 2002)

Marsh, Peter J., *Joseph Chamberlain: Entrepreneur in Politics* (Yale UP 1994)

Marwick, Arthur, *Britain in the Century of Total War* (Bodley Head 1968)

Marwick, Arthur, *The Home Front: The British and the Second World War* (Thames & Hudson 1976)

McKibbin, Ross, *Classes and Cultures: England, 1918–51* (OUP 1998)

Meyers, Jeffrey, *Orwell: Wintry Conscience of a Generation* (W. W. Norton 2000)

Morgan, Kenneth O., *Britain Since 1945: The People's Peace* (OUP 1990)

Morgan, Kenneth O., *Labour in Power, 1945–51* (Clarendon Press 1984)

Morgan, Kenneth O., *Rebirth of a Nation: Wales 1880–1980* (Clarendon Press 1981)

Parker, R. A. C., *Chamberlain and Appeasement: British Policy and the Coming of the Second World War* (Macmillan 1993)

Parker, R. A. C., *Churchill and Appeasement* (Macmillan 2000)

Paxman, Jeremy, *The English: A Portrait of a People* (Michael Joseph 1998)

Pedersen, Susan and Mandler, Peter (eds), *After the Victorians: Private Conscience and Public Duty in Modern Britain* (Routledge 1994)

Pugh, Martin, *The Making of Modern British Politics, 1867–1939* (Basil Blackwell 1982)

Pugh, Martin, *The Tories and the People, 1880–1935* (Basil Blackwell 1985)

Ramadin, Ron, *Re-imagining Britain: 500 Years of Black and Asian History* (Pluto Press 1999)

Roberts, Andrew, *Eminent Churchillians* (Simon & Schuster 1994)

Roberts, Andrew, *The 'Holy Fox': A Biography of Lord Halifax* (Weidenfeld & Nicholson 1991)

Roberts, Andrew, *Salisbury: Victorian Titan* (Weidenfeld & Nicholson 1999)

Rose, Norman, *Churchill: An Unruly Life* (Simon & Schuster 1994)

Samuel, Raphael, *Theatres of Memory, Vol. II: Island Stories: Unravelling Britain* (Verso 1998)

Shelden, Michael, *Orwell: The Authorised Biography* (Heinemann 1991)

Skidelsky, Robert, *The Politicians and the Slump: The Labour Government of 1929–31* (Macmillan 1967)

Spencer, Ian R. G., *British Immigration Policy Since 1939: The Making of Multi-Racial Britain* (Routledge 1997)

Stansky, Peter and Abrahams, William, *The Unknown Orwell* (Constable 1972)

Stewart, Graham, *Burying Caesar: Churchill, Chamberlain and the Battle for the Tory Party* (Weidenfeld & Nicolson 1999)

Taylor, A. J. P. et al., *Churchill: Four Faces and the Man* (Allen Lane/Penguin Press 1969)

Taylor, A. J. P., *English History 1914–1945* (OUP 1965)

Thompson, F. M. L., *The Rise of Respectable Society: A Social History of Victorian Britain, 1830–1900* (Fontana Press 1988)

Tiratsoo, Nick (ed.), *From Blitz to Blair: A New History of Britain since 1939* (Weidenfeld & Nicholson 1997)

Waller, P. J., *Town, City and Nation: England 1850–1914* (OUP 1983)

Weight, Richard, *Patriots: National Identity in Britain, 1940–2000* (Macmillan 2002)

Young, Hugo, *This Blessed Plot: Britain and Europe from Churchill to Blair* (Overlook Press 1998)

ACKNOWLEDGEMENTS

"Epic" is a word that suffers from over-use these days but the history of *A History in Britain* certainly has a long roll-call of heroes – other than its author – without whose unflagging labours neither television programmes nor book could possibly have been made.

I will always be deeply grateful to Tina Brown for her constant encouragement and enthusiasm from the moment she heard about this project. Tina and Jonathan Burnham at Miramax have given *A History of Britain* every imaginable support, even when they saw what was anticipated as one volume turned into three. Hilary Bass and Kristin Powers have, in their respective ways done sterling work in getting the book into the hands of American readers.

In every sense this work has been a collaboration between myself and an exceptionally gifted and devoted group of colleagues at BBC Television, in particular Ian Bremner, Martin Davidson, Liz Hartford, and Mike Ibeji. Melisa Akdogan, Ben Ledden, Ashley Gethin were exceptionally resourceful both in the libraries and on location. Had I not had the tireless and invariably considerate help of Sara Fletcher, I would have come unglued in locations throughout the British isles. Tanya Hethorn, Tim Sutton and Mark Walden-Mills have, in crucial ways helped the presenter present. Susan Harvey in Factual Publicity has been the gentlest and friendliest of promoters. It's been a source of great happiness to work closely with John Harle on the music for the series. Laurence Rees, Glenwyn Benson and Janice Hadlow have all cast a benevolently critical eye on our work when it most mattered and have both given us the sense of how much *A History of Britain* matters to the BBC. At the History Channel in the United States I'm grateful to Jim Dowd for his heroic promotion of our series and to Charlie Maday for his belief in its potential.

I'm deeply grateful to a number of colleagues who were kind enough to read both scripts and chapters for errors, in particular John Brewer, Ann Hughes; Holger Hoock, Peter Marshall and Steven Pincus. Any that remain are of course my own responsibility.

In a much larger and deeper sense though, I owe an enormous debt of gratitude to the wisdom and erudition of teachers, (including schoolteachers) from whom I first learned the great contentions of British and colonial history in the seventeenth and eighteenth centuries and from friends and colleagues whose scholarship and critical analysis is still a source of exhilaration illumination. Though they may well take exception to some (or many) of the views expressed in this book I hope that the overdue thanks offered in particular, to David Armitage, Roy Avery, Robert Baynes, mark Kishlansky, sir John Plumb, Roy Porter, Kevin Sharpe and Quentin Skinner will not go amiss.

My agents at PFD – Michael Sissons and Rosemary Scoular, have been, as ever towers of strength on whom I lean, and occasionally collapse. My thanks too to James Gill, Sophie Laurimore and Carol Macarthur. Provst Jonathan Cole at Columbia University has been exceptionally kind in allowing me the necessary leave to work on the series and I'm delighted to have played a part in pioneering the on-line seminar produced jointly by BBC Education and Columbia in partnership with Fathom.Com about the 18th century British Empire. Jennifer Scott was an extraordinary colleague in the production of that innovative departure in popular historical education.

Shifting back and forth between book and script-writing is likely to make the head spin and certain to make the writer-presenter generally impossible to be around. So I'm, as always more grateful than I can say to my friends for submitting to recitations from the Schama book of lamentations – thank you, again – Clare Beavan, Lily Brett, John Brewer, Tina Brown, Jan Dalley, Alison Dominitz, Harry Evans, Amanda Foreman, Eliot Friedman, Mindy Engel Friedman, Andrew Silverstone, Beverly Silverstone, Jill Slotover, Stella Tillyard and Leon Wieseltier. To my nearest and dearest – Ginny, Chloe and Gabe, I give my heartfelt thanks for riding the storms of their unreasonably cranky Dad and husband, and for the calm waters and always-open harbour of their love.

INDEX

Page numbers in italics refer to illustrations